THE JUDGES OF IRELAND, 1866–1921

Frontispiece The Four Courts, from the east (Lawrence Photograph Collection). Image courtesy of the National Library of Ireland.

The Judges of Ireland, 1866–1921

DAIRE HOGAN

FOUR COURTS PRESS
in association with
THE IRISH LEGAL HISTORY SOCIETY

Typeset in 10.5pt on 12.5pt EhrhardtMtPro by
Carrigboy Typesetting Services for
FOUR COURTS PRESS LTD
7 Malpas Street, Dublin 8, Ireland
www.fourcourtspress.ie
and in North America for
FOUR COURTS PRESS
c/o IPG, 814 N Franklin Street, Chicago, IL 60610.

References to this publication should cite the publisher as Four Courts Press
in association with the Irish Legal History Society.

A catalogue record for this title is available
from the British Library.

ISBN 978–1–80151–204–6

Printed in England,
by Antony Rowe Ltd, Chippenham, Wilts.

To Doreen

Contents

LIST OF ILLUSTRATIONS ix

LIST OF ABBREVIATIONS x

ACKNOWLEDGMENTS xii

INTRODUCTION 1

1 The road to 1877 5

2 Reforms and their implementation 32

3 Judicial lives – careers, incomes, honours 74

4 The judiciary in 1866 (1) 128

Maziere Brady, Thomas Berry Cusack Smith, Francis Blackburne, Thomas Lefroy, James O'Brien, Edmund Hayes, John David Fitzgerald, James Henry Monahan, William Keogh, Jonathan Christian, Thomas O'Hagan

5 The judiciary in 1866 (2) 167

David R. Pigot, Francis A. FitzGerald, Henry George Hughes, Rickard Deasy, Richard Keatinge, Mountifort Longfield, Charles James Hargreave, William Carey Dobbs, Walter Berwick, David Lynch, Thomas Kelly

6 Appointments between 1866 and 1868 191

Abraham Brewster and Joseph Napier, James Whiteside, John Edward Walsh, John George, Michael Morris, Hedges Eyre Chatterton, John Fitzhenry Townsend, Stearne Ball Miller, Michael Harrison, R.R. Warren

7 Gladstone's first government, 1868–74 229

James Anthony Lawson, Stephen Woulfe Flanagan, Edward Sullivan, Charles Barry, Richard Dowse, Christopher Palles

8 Disraeli's government, 1874–80 264

John Thomas Ball, Henry Ormsby, George Augustus Chichester May, Gerald FitzGibbon, Frederick Walsh

9 Gladstone's second government, 1880–5 286

Hugh Law, John O'Hagan, William O'Brien, William Drennan Andrews, William Moore Johnson, James Murphy, Andrew Marshall Porter, John Naish

10 The years of Unionist monopoly (1), 1885–92 313
Lord Ashbourne, Walter Boyd, John Monroe, Hugh Holmes, John George Gibson, Peter O'Brien, Edward Falconer Litton, Edmund Bewley, Dodgson Hamilton Madden, Samuel Walker

11 The years of Unionist monopoly (2), 1892–1905 363
John Ross, Richard E. Meredith, William Kenny, Dunbar Plunket Barton, George Wright, Gerald Fitzgerald, John Atkinson

12 Appointments between 1906 and 1914 383
James O. Wylie, William Huston Dodd, Richard Robert Cherry, Redmond Barry, Charles Andrew O'Connor, Ignatius O'Brien, Thomas Molony, John Francis Moriarty

13 Appointments between 1915 and 1921 411
Stephen Ronan, Jonathan Pim, John Gordon, James H.M. Campbell, William Moore, James O'Connor, John Blake Powell, Arthur W. Samuels, William E. Wylie

14 The first Irish Lords of Appeal in Ordinary 439

15 Change and continuity in the early 1920s 475

BIBLIOGRAPHY 493

INDEX 508

IRISH LEGAL HISTORY SOCIETY SERIES 517

IRISH LEGAL HISTORY SOCIETY 519

Illustrations

Frontispiece The Four Courts, from the east

Images appear between pp 244 and 245.

1 Maziere Brady
2 The Four Courts, from the west
3 James Monahan
4 Jonathan Christian
5 Thomas O'Hagan, 1st Lord O'Hagan
6 James Whiteside
7 'Her Majesty's judges in Ireland 1891' (*The Graphic*, 4 April 1891)
8 Lord O'Hagan, statue in Round Hall, Four Courts
9 James Whiteside, statue in Round Hall, Four Courts
10 David R. Pigot
11 Michael Morris
12 Edward Sullivan
13 Charles Barry
14 Richard Dowse
15 Christopher Palles
16 J.T. Ball
17 G.A.C. May
18 Gerald FitzGibbon
19 James Murphy
20 A.M. Porter
21 Edward Gibson, 1st Lord Ashbourne
22 'Some well-known Irish judges' (*The Graphic*, 10 June 1899)
23 Hugh Holmes
24 'Distinguished sons of Clongowes' (Christopher Palles, John Naish and Peter O'Brien)
25 Peter O'Brien
26 Dunbar Plunket Barton
27 John Atkinson
28 Richard Robert Cherry
29 Arthur Warren Samuels

Abbreviations

Ball — F. Elrington Ball, *The judges in Ireland, 1221–1921* (London, 1926), vol. 2
BL — British Library
DIB — *Dictionary of Irish biography*
HC Deb — House of Commons Debates
Healy, *OldMC*
Maurice Healy, *The old Munster circuit* (Dublin/London, 1939)
HL Deb — House of Lords Debates
Hogan, 'Vacancies'
Daire Hogan, '"Vacancies for their friends": judicial appointments in Ireland, 1866–1867' in D. Hogan and W.N. Osborough (eds), *Brehons, serjeants and attorneys: studies in the history of the Irish legal profession* (Dublin, 1990), pp 211–30
Holmes Memoir
Memoirs of Hugh Holmes (2 vols, PRONI, MIC197/1), p. 155. Extracts, edited by A.B. Cooke and J.R. Vincent, were published as 'Ireland and party politics 1885–7, an unpublished Conservative memoir', *IHS*, vol. 16, nos. 62–4 (September 1968–September 1969), pp 154–72, 321–38 and 446–71
IHS — *Irish Historical Studies*
ILT&SJ — *Irish Law Times and Solicitors' Journal*
King's Inns Admission Papers
E. Keane, P.H. Phair, T.U. Sadleir, *King's Inns admission papers 1607–1867* (Dublin, 1982)
Letters and leaders
T.M. Healy, *Letters and leaders of my day* (London, 1928)
NAI — National Archives of Ireland
New Irish Jurist
The New Irish Jurist and Local Government Review
NILQ — *Northern Ireland Legal Quarterly*
NLI — National Library of Ireland
ODNB — *Oxford dictionary of national biography*
Oxford history of laws, vol. 11
William Cornish, Stuart Anderson, Raymond Cocks, Michael Lobban, Patrick Polden and Keith Smith, *The Oxford history of the laws of England*, vol. XI, *1820–1914: English legal system* (Oxford, 2010)
Parl Arch — Parliamentary Archives, London
P.P. — Parliamentary Papers
PRONI — Public Record Office of Northern Ireland

Ramm 1868–71
Agatha Ramm (ed.), *The political correspondence of Mr Gladstone and Lord Granville, 1868–1876*, vol. 1, *1868–1871* (London, 1952)

Salisbury–Balfour correspondence
Robin Harcourt Williams (ed.), *Letters exchanged between the third marquess of Salisbury and his nephew Arthur James Balfour, 1869–1892* (Hertfordshire Record Society, 1988)

SCJNI 1922 Memorandum
Memorandum on the setting up of the Supreme Court of Judicature of Northern Ireland and other matters incidental thereto, 1 October 1921–31 July 1922 (PRONI, CAB6/57/T311)

TNAUK The National Archives (United Kingdom)

UCDA University College Dublin Archives

WSHC Wiltshire and Swindon History Centre, Chippenham, Wiltshire

1877 Act Supreme Court of Judicature (Ireland) Act 1877

1897 Act Supreme Court of Judicature (Amendment) (Ireland) (No. 2) Act 1897

Acknowledgments

I ACKNOWLEDGE WITH GRATITUDE the assistance and access to and/or permission to quote from collections that have been afforded by the following libraries and archives: the Bodleian Libraries, Oxford; the British Library; the Cadbury Research Library – special collections, University of Birmingham; the Cambridge University Library; the Dublin Diocesan Archives; the Gloucestershire Record Office; the Grand Lodge of Freemasons of Ireland, Dublin; the archives at Hatfield House, Hertfordshire; the Library of King's College, London; the Honorable Society of King's Inns, Dublin; the Law Society of Ireland; the Linenhall Library, Belfast; the Liverpool Record Office; the Library of the Middle Temple, London; the National Archives, Kew; the National Archives of Ireland; the National Gallery of Ireland; the National Library of Ireland; the National Portrait Gallery, London; the Parliamentary Archives, London; the Public Record Office of Northern Ireland, Belfast; the Registry of Deeds, Dublin; the Library of Queen's University, Belfast and the Naughton Gallery at that university; the Library of Trinity College Dublin; the Library of University College Dublin; and the Wiltshire and Swindon History Centre, Chippenham.

For their permission to quote from papers and other material in which they hold the copyright I thank the Earl of Antrim, Earl Balfour, Diarmuid Bourke, Earl Cadogan, Earl Cairns, the Earl of Derby, the Dufferin Foundation, Alex Horsburgh-Porter, the Blenheim Palace Heritage Foundation, Sir Charles Napier, the Deputy Keeper of the Records, the Public Record Office of Northern Ireland, the Marquess of Salisbury, Earl Selborne and Earl Spencer. Every effort has been made to establish contact with all copyright holders, but if any have been inadvertently overlooked I apologise, and hope that this general acknowledgment will be taken as sufficient.

I have been fortunate to receive assistance, advice, ideas, support and encouragement in many ways from, among others, Michelle Bracken, Sorcha Clarke, Ben Crothers, Pat Crowley, Martin Fanning and Anthony Tierney of Four Courts Press, Roy Foster, John G. Gordon, Robin Harcourt Williams, Michael Laffan, the late John Temple Lang, Lord Lexden, Robert D. Marshall, Joseph McBrinn, Des McCabe, Renate Ní Uigín, Mari Takayanagi and Sarah Whale and I thank each of them most warmly.

My deepest debt is to Doreen, whose love, support and infinite good humour sustained me on this long journey of exploration.

Introduction

THE LATE 1860S AND THE 1870s are important years in the history of the Irish judiciary. In a few months in 1866 five new judges were appointed, the beginning of what transpired to be a period of rapid turnover or replacement in the personnel of the superior courts. In 1877 a fundamental reorganisation and consolidation of those courts and of the court system generally was enacted, to take effect on New Year's Day 1878.

Judges exercise the judicial power of the state, in the administration of justice and the interpretation of law in civil and criminal matters. Their function is one of great responsibility, as constituting one of the three classical branches of government – legislative, executive and judicial. They hold a position of respect and honour in civic society, and by virtue of their office and character may occupy other places of social importance and prominence. This book is a biographical study, individual and collective, of the men who formed the senior judiciary of Ireland in the last third of the nineteenth century and the initial years of the twentieth century up to the political settlements of the early 1920s, years which were of significance for the structure and culture of the courts. How the courts and judges worked in that era and the nature of their connection to wider civic and political society has not been an extensively explored aspect of social and political history.

The Supreme Court of Judicature (Ireland) Act 1877 established a new High Court and Court of Appeal, in succession to a number of historic indeed ancient courts, and made numerous ancillary reforms. Reconstituting legislation was similarly enacted for the County Courts. The 1877 Act followed, with some local variations, the general scheme of the corresponding reforming statute for England that had been enacted in 1873, and thus continued a pattern over the years and centuries of adaptation for Ireland of English judicial legislation. Reform proposals, including reductions in the numbers of judges, encountered resistance and objections from the Bar and, before 1877, also from leading members of the judiciary, and a number of reforms took longer to implement in Ireland than in England.

Initial chapters trace the road to 1877, describing the preparation of the Act, the scope of the reforms that it introduced and their subsequent implementation. This analysis of the framework within which the judges of Ireland worked in this era introduces and provides the context for a comprehensive set of detailed biographical studies of the members of the judiciary of the superior courts in this era. A final chapter addresses the further constitutional re-organisations of the courts that took place, north and south of the new border on the island, in the 1920s.

In 1866–7 two-thirds of the nineteenth century had passed, and those years might thus in any event be a good standpoint from which to take stock of the judicial system in Ireland. However they are of particular significance for the senior judiciary because within the space of 30 months between 1866 and 1868 there was considerable change in its membership, in which half of the sitting judges of the superior courts ceased to hold office, through either death or retirement. Many of the men who were appointed to replace them were to be prominent figures in the reform era.

About 80 men held high judicial office in Ireland between 1866 and 1921, three-quarters of whom were appointed in or after 1866. In many years there were no vacancies to be filled, whereas in others – such as in 1866–8, 1885–9 and 1916–18 – there was a flurry of appointments. On 1 January 1866 there were 22 senior judicial offices, comprising (1) the court of Chancery (lord chancellor, master of the rolls and lord justice of appeal, soon to be joined by a vice-chancellor), (2) the three historic common law courts of Queen's Bench, Common Pleas and the Exchequer (each of which had four judges), (3) the Landed Estates Court (three judges, soon to be two) and (4) the courts of Probate (one judge), Bankruptcy (two) and Admiralty (one). These last mentioned courts had a lesser status (and salaries) than what were literally the historic four courts, but the appointments to them were valued as full-time judicial offices (unlike those to the County Courts before 1877) and raised similar patronage issues to those in the higher courts. Their separate jurisdictions were over time amalgamated into the new High Court. The total number of senior judges, including some new judicial positions in the Land Commission, had been reduced to 15 by 1921.

The lives and career paths of these judges had many features in common, in such aspects as where they were educated, the manner of their progress at the Bar and often in politics, and thereafter in the place they held in society and their style of living. Unsurprisingly the great majority were educated at Trinity College Dublin, Dublin University, which some of them subsequently represented in Parliament prior to appointment to the judicial bench. There were many reasons why a member of the Bar might aspire to hold a position on the judicial bench, including of course a concept of rendering a public service, but one consideration was that (unlike the case in England) judicial salaries were regarded as attractive in comparison to levels of income at the Bar. Judges were not then subject to retirement at a set age, and the capacity of judges of mature years or in ill health to perform their duties was at times a subject of controversy. A number died in office.

This general overview of the judiciary between 1866 and 1921 leads to a series of individual biographical profiles of its members. These are generally in a more detailed and annotated format than appears in any contemporary obituaries or in entries in the *Dictionary of Irish biography* or the *Oxford dictionary of national biography*. (There are such dictionary entries for about half of the judges in this period.) Taken together they amount to an overall narrative for that era of appointments, retirements and judicial issues. The set of profiles begins with the judges holding office in 1866, and then addresses those subsequently appointed, in the order in which they first held any judicial office. The Conservative party held office between July 1866 and December 1868, and in those thirty months more judicial appointments and promotions fell to be made than were available to any other government in any comparable period. The reflection of party politics in the making of subsequent appointments can best be considered in three broad periods, namely (a) the period from the end of 1868 to the first half of 1885, essentially the era of Gladstone and Disraeli, alternating in office as prime minister, (b) the years between 1885 and 1905 when there was in effect a Unionist monopoly on such appointments, and (c) the period 1906–21.

As touched upon above, political connections and the recognition of services rendered to a party were understood, and at times explicitly (if privately) acknowledged, to be a major consideration when judicial appointments were being made. Irish legal patronage was closely connected with party politics at Westminster, and throughout this period members of the Bar put themselves forward as candidates for Parliament and associated themselves with the Conservative (Unionist) or Liberal parties. Decisions on judicial promotions and appointments, and on what were almost invariably preliminary appointments to a position as a law officer (attorney general or solicitor general), were generally made at the highest political level, by the prime minister of the day. The lord chancellor of Ireland had a role in advising on these appointments, but did not have authority (unlike the lord chancellor in England, after having consulted the prime minister) to determine upon most such judicial appointments himself.

The prime ministers of the era, from Lord Derby (1866–8) to Lloyd George (1916–22), had a potentially delicate task in weighing and addressing the claims and hopes and representations of ambitious lawyers and political supporters. The obvious public interest in the appointment of lawyers of ability and character to the bench, and to the law officer posts, had to be balanced with the more prosaic reality of maintaining political support and goodwill and with the utility for the government of retaining the services of efficient law officers, whose services (if they were MPs) would extend to taking part in debates and arguments in the House of Commons. Many prospective judges were adept at making and using their connections, some took it easy, or indeed had it easy, others made something of a nuisance of themselves to their political friends by forceful or persistent canvassing and self-promotion, and a number (generally but not only law officers) exhibited at times a sense of entitlement to a judicial place. A subsequent patronage concern of some judges was the seeking of an honour (a peerage, baronetcy or knighthood), frequently in connection with retirement from office.

A particular study has been made of the three Irish lawyers who were appointed to be lords of appeal in ordinary before 1921, namely Lords Fitzgerald (1882–9), Morris (1889–1900) and Atkinson (1905–28), and of the controversy that arose in 1900 when the prime minister decided not to appoint an Irish lawyer in succession to Lord Morris. Prior to their respective appointments Fitzgerald and Morris had each held judicial office in Ireland for over 20 years and Atkinson had been attorney general for over ten years. The judicial record of the Irish Law Lords (up to and including Lord MacDermott) was the subject of a commentary by Lord Lowry, himself a lord of appeal in ordinary (between 1988 and 1994), in an address given in 1996 to a meeting of the Irish Legal History Society in Dublin. He remarked that he was in a position to give only the most superficial account, and that perhaps some of his audience might feel 'the impulse to dig a little deeper and perhaps take the investigation further in relation to particular individuals'. In that spirit of invited review of what Lord Lowry had to say on three of the Irish Law Lords, a close examination has been made of the circumstances of their appointments and of their contributions to the judicial (and parliamentary) work of the House of Lords.

This study of the judiciary over slightly more than half a century, addressing their individual careers and putting them in a broader context, will I hope contribute to a greater understanding both of the judiciary itself and of its role in wider civic and political society, and will render the history of the courts and their connection with that wider society more accessible outside the field of legal history itself.

CHAPTER ONE

The road to 1877

ON 1 JANUARY 1878 THE SINGLE MOST significant reform of the Irish court and judicial system in the nineteenth and early twentieth centuries took effect, when the Supreme Court of Judicature (Ireland) Act 1877[1] came into operation. This restructured the judiciary by establishing the High Court and Court of Appeal in succession to a number of historic courts and appeal procedures. In parallel to this fusion of the courts the Act also effected a fusion of the historically different systems of the common law and equity (the latter as administered by the court of Chancery). Section 28(11) of the Act provided that 'generally in all matters not hereinbefore particularly mentioned, in which there is any conflict or variance between the rules of equity and the rules of the common law with reference to the same matter the rules of equity shall prevail'.[2]

The Act followed the general format of the Supreme Court of Judicature Acts 1873 and 1875,[3] which had brought about dramatic reforms in the court system of England and Wales, although the translation of the English reforms into a corresponding Irish statute was not a straightforward exercise. Legislation for Ireland was delayed by a recasting of the English reforms themselves, most notably in a reappraisal of whether (as originally provided) the House of Lords should cease to be the final court of appeal. Three years would pass between the publication in May 1874 of the initial proposals for Ireland and the enactment of the reforms, amended in various respects, in Parliament in August 1877.

This pattern of adopting English reforms, with modifications, was followed again a century later when the courts in Northern Ireland were reconstituted by the Judicature (Northern Ireland) Act 1978 in broadly the same manner as the courts in England and Wales had been modified by the Courts Act 1971. Earlier in the 1970s three committees headed respectively by Lord MacDermott, Sir Robert Lowry (as he then was) and lord justice Edward Jones had made comprehensive recommendations for reform of the court system. When introducing the second reading of the legislation in the House of Commons in 1978 the solicitor general, Peter Archer QC, MP, said that,

> every legal system requires a shake-up from time to time. Indeed, if it has been responsive to public need, each new situation will have led to a further

1 40&41 Vict., c.57 (1877). It was repealed for Northern Ireland by the Judicature (Northern Ireland) Act 1978 (26 Eliz. 2, c.23), and such parts of it as had not previously been repealed were preserved and maintained in force in Ireland by the Statute Law Revision Act 2007 (no. 28 of 2007).

2 This corresponded to section 25(11) of the Supreme Court of Judicature Act 1873, applicable to England.

3 36&37 Vict., c.66 (1873) and 38&39 Vict., c.77 (1875).

> addition or amendment to the existing structure, until it becomes difficult to follow the original simple pattern. Occasionally, therefore, there is a need to redesign the system and to adapt it to the needs of another age. The legal system of England and Wales met with such an experience in 1873 and again in 1971. In Northern Ireland there was last a fundamental review of the system in 1877.[4]

Hugh McCalmont Cairns, the first Lord Cairns (1819–85), was lord chancellor of Great Britain when the amending legislation for Ireland was introduced and passed. He was born in Belfast and was one of the members of Parliament for the city between 1852 and 1866. He made his career at the Bar in England and had been attorney general and a lord justice of appeal before being appointed lord chancellor (1868 and 1874–80). He was chancellor of Dublin University from 1866 up to his death in 1885 and was the first graduate of Trinity College to be a member of the British Cabinet.[5] The significance of the Judicature Acts was described by him in the House of Lords in 1875:

> It would be impossible to overstate the magnitude of the Act of 1873. Beyond all question it is the largest measure of law reform which I have ever known to be passed in this country. It covers the whole field of the judicature of the country and it pervades every nook and cranny of our judicial arrangements. I might add that, the system of law and judicature in Ireland being almost the same as the system in England, it is proposed to introduce for Ireland a change similar to that which the Judicature Act will effect in this country.[6]

The principle that the structure and practice and procedure of the Irish courts should follow and be based upon the corresponding arrangements, as reformed, in England was not generally contested, and Irish lawyers were supportive of 'the abstract proposal' to adopt the English reforms in Ireland.[7] However the implementation of that principle of adopting such reforms gave rise to very considerable difficulties and delay. The reform process received little public support from members of the Irish judiciary and legal profession, indeed was to be the subject of sustained resistance and criticism. Although specific discontent focused on about half a dozen particular proposals this was accompanied by many expressions of generalized alarm and unhappiness. A narrative that developed in Ireland between 1874 and 1877, and that would be articulated again in later years, was of modifications being unreasonably demanded to a court system that was broadly fit for purpose, if admittedly in need of some updating and modest improvement. The reform policy was held out as being driven by the Treasury, 'English prejudices' and critics in London who were uninformed and heedless or

4 HC Deb, vol. 948, col. 181 (17 April 1978).
5 Entry in *ODNB* (by David Steele). See also entry in *DIB* (by Richard Hawkins).
6 HL Deb, 3rd series, vol. 223, col. 581 (9 April 1875); *ILT&SJ*, vol. 9, p. 190 (17 April 1875).
7 *ILT&SJ*, vol. 10, p. 322 (3 June 1876).

uncaring of considerations applicable to the Irish system, and supposedly intent on an unlikely course of 'destruction of existing institutions for mere destruction's sake'.[8]

The sense of the Irish legal establishment keeping its distance from the developing proposals was evidenced by a report in 1876 that the Irish law officers had not been consulted on them: 'we may add that if rumour speaks correctly he [Cairns] has up to the present but little availed himself of the assistance which the law officers in Ireland are so eminently qualified to supply'.[9] That was not the case, but such talk was in itself indicative of the lack of commitment of the judiciary and Bar to reform. Proposals for these originated in England and were carefully reviewed by the Irish legal officers. The attorney general, J.T. Ball, had been involved in the preparation of the initial Bill in 1874, which in the time available was not pushed forward, and it was withdrawn at the end of that Parliamentary session that year.[10] Some months later, shortly after being appointed as the lord chancellor of Ireland in the New Year 1875, Ball reviewed the Bill again and, having taken 'the opinion of some of the ablest judges at a private meeting',[11] forwarded a printed amended draft to Cairns in February 1875 'with all the improvements … and the only matter remaining is to [read] it all over so as to make it consistent with itself all through … The Bill is much improved'.[12] In April 1876 the common law judges prepared a detailed memorandum of suggested amendments to a revised version of the Bill recently reintroduced in Parliament (which was soon made public, and is referred to in more detail below (see p. 26).[13] Whiteside, the chief justice of Queen's Bench, described this to Cairns shortly beforehand as constituting 'a few but important amendments', which he said would remove 'all judicial opposition'.[14] In fact, as appears below, judicial reservations continued to be expressed up to February 1877, in the week before the final Bill was introduced in the House of Commons.

Some changes in the structure of the judiciary that had formed part of the initial reform proposals were not pressed at the time, although they were simply postponed, not abandoned. When they were put forward again in the spring of 1885 they met with strong objections from the judiciary although they were ultimately adopted, most notably by an amending statute in 1897.[15] The reforms were to be subject to a further legislative amendment in 1907 which reduced the number of superior court judges.[16]

8 *ILT&SJ*, vol. 10, p. 179 (25 March 1876).
9 *ILT&SJ*, vol. 10, p. 238 (22 April 1876).
10 History of Judicature (Ireland) Bills, 1874 and 1876 (P.P. 1877 (181) lxviii.145).
11 Ball to Cairns, 13 January 1875 (Cairns Papers (TNAUK), PRO 30/15/17).
12 Ball to Cairns, 4 February 1875 (Cairns Papers, PRO 30/15/19).
13 Paper on the subject of the Supreme Court of Judicature (Ireland) Bill signed by the common law judges of Ireland (P.P. 1876 (278) lxi. 357); vol. 10, pp 309–11 (27 May 1876).
14 Whiteside to Cairns, 5 April 1876 (Cairns Papers, PRO 30/51/113).
15 Supreme Court of Judicature (Ireland) (No. 2) Act 1897 (60&61 Vict., c.66).
16 Supreme Court of Judicature (Ireland) Act 1907 (7 Edw. VI, c.44).

The Irish courts had been established in the first place, centuries before, with a view to replicating English models and authority. Irish courts were frequently presided over by judges appointed from England, a practice that was extensively followed until the 1820s, coming to an end only in the 1840s. The attorney general of England, John Campbell (then raised to the peerage as Baron Campbell of St Andrews – he was a Scotsman), was controversially appointed in June 1841 to replace Lord Plunket as lord chancellor of Ireland. Campbell undertook not to claim a pension, and his term in office transpired to last only a few weeks. He was succeeded, on a change of government, by an Englishman, Edward Sugden (later Lord St Leonards),[17] and the last member of the English Bar to be appointed to a senior judicial position in Ireland in the nineteenth century was Charles Hargreave of the Encumbered Estates Commission. Until 1885 it was a requirement for every intending member of the Irish Bar to have kept terms at one of the London Inns of Court, and in that year the obligation was converted by statute into an option, on the initiative of the Irish Parliamentary Party.[18]

English barristers would have been eligible for appointment as a resident magistrate, but the position of any such persons would have been quite different and not comparable to that of a member of the judiciary, in terms of functions, tenure, status, and salary. Such appointments were made pursuant to statutes passed in 1814[19] and 1836.[20] Under the 1836 statute (s31) the lord lieutenant might appoint 'during his or her pleasure one or more persons [for a county, town, etc.] to be magistrates [for that area] and may dismiss or remove any such magistrate at his will or pleasure'. Redmond Barry, the attorney general, acknowledged in 1911 in response to a Parliamentary question that 'no qualifications are prescribed by statute for the position of resident magistrate in Ireland. A resident magistrate ought to possess a knowledge of the law to the extent of being competent to hear and determine cases in a court of summary jurisdiction'.[21] The maximum salary was set at £675 in 1874 and was not varied until 1920.[22]

The adoption of statutory reforms of the court system in Ireland in the middle of the nineteenth century that would pick up earlier English reforms was a natural consequence of this long-standing cultural, political and professional connection and relationship. At the start of the century the office of master of the rolls had been reconstituted by a statute in 1801 in line with English precedent from the

17 See David Plunket, *The life, letters and speeches of Lord Plunket* (London, 1867), vol. II, pp 333–46; O.J. Burke, *History of the lord chancellors of Ireland from 1186 to 1874* (Dublin, 1879), pp 265–7. Sugden continued in office up to 1846, and had previously briefly held that appointment, in 1835. The fact that after his death his will could not be found gave rise to a leading case on the law as to lost wills (*Sugden v Lord St Leonards* (1876) 1 PD 155).

18 Barristers' Admission (Ireland) Act 1885 (48 & 49 Vict., c.20).

19 An Act to provide for the better execution of the laws in Ireland, by appointing superintending magistrates and additional constables in counties, in certain cases 1814 (54 Geo. III, c.131).

20 The Constabulary (Ireland) Act 1836 (6 Will. 4, c.13).

21 HC Deb, 5th series, vol. 21, col. 1668 (20 February 1911).

22 HC Deb, 5th series, vol. 130, col. 2557 (25 June 1920).

sixteenth century, if not earlier. The statute recited that it was expedient that this 'should be made a judicial office and assistant to the Lord High Chancellor of Ireland', and that he should have 'full power and authority to make orders and decrees on all matters and causes now depending in the court of Chancery, and that all such orders and decrees shall be deemed and taken to be valid orders, decrees of the said court of Chancery, but subject nevertheless, in each such case, to be discharged, reversed or altered by the Lord High Chancellor'.[23]

An Act to improve the administration of justice in Ireland in 1831[24] harmonised the law terms in Ireland with those in England, as was to be done again in 1877. Bankruptcy procedures had been rationalised in the court of Chancery in England in 1831, and in Ireland these were transferred in 1836 to a permanent commissioner and then in 1857 to the supervision of a new office of a chief judge in bankruptcy, subject in each case to a continuing general supervision in Chancery.[25] In criminal law the 1836 'Act for enabling Persons indicted of Felony to make their Defence by Counsel or Attorney'[26] was applicable in Ireland as well as in England, in granting all persons on trial for serious crime the right to be represented by defence counsel and 'after the close of the Case for the Prosecution to make full Answer and Defence thereto'. The tradition of prisoners making a 'speech from the dock' had derived from the previous historic limitations on how defence counsel could address the jury, although such counsel – most notably Daniel O'Connell – were adept at blending points of law with issues of fact. Legislation in 1865 extending these provisions, an 'Act for amending the Law of Evidence and Practice on Criminal Trials',[27] was applicable in Ireland as well as in England.

The Crown Cases Act 1848[28] recited that it was expedient to provide a better mode than that now in use of deciding any difficult question of law which may arise in criminal trials in any Court of Oyer and Terminer and Gaol Delivery (i.e., assizes) or court of quarter sessions. The Act established both in Ireland and in England a Court for Crown Cases Reserved, consisting of all of the common law judges in the relevant jurisdiction, who would consider any question of law so referred to them and had power to 'reserve, affirm or amend' any judgment,[29] which would not have been put into effect pending such consideration. This gave statutory effect to what had been a practice of long standing.[30]

23 Master of the Rolls (Ireland) Act 1801 (41 Geo. 3, c.25 (Ir.)).
24 1&2 Will. IV, c.31, s1.
25 An Act to amend the laws relating to Bankrupts in Ireland 1836 (6 Will. IV, c.14); Irish Bankrupt and Insolvent Act 1857 (20&21 Vict., c.60).
26 6&7 Will. IV, c.114 (1836). The statute is sometimes known as the Trials for Felony Act or the Prisoners' Counsel Act.
27 28&29 Vict., c.18 (1865).
28 An Act for the further amendment of the administration of the criminal law 1848 (11&12 Vict., c.78).
29 S2 of the Act.
30 Desmond Greer, 'A security against illegality? The reservation of Crown cases in nineteenth-century Ireland' in N.M. Dawson (ed.), *Reflections on law and history* (Dublin, 2006), pp 163–202.

The abolition in England in 1841 of the equity side of the Exchequer, with a transfer of its business to the court of Chancery, was followed in Ireland in 1850.[31] The Process and Practice (Ireland) Act 1850[32] followed the format of the Uniformity of Process Act 1832 applicable in England. It consolidated each separate common law court's Nisi Prius business[33] into a single court in Dublin for the trial with a jury of issues of fact,[34] having recited that 'the Process now in use for the Commencement of Personal actions in Her Majesty's Superior Courts of Common Law in Ireland is, by reason of its Variety, Multiplicity, and Fiction, inconvenient and objectionable, and it is expedient for the better Administration of Justice to establish Uniformity of Process and Practice in the Said Courts'. The Act acknowledged that by reason of the 'unequal distribution of business' among these courts' one is often insufficiently employed, while the others are unduly pressed.[35] In 1839 'the Common Pleas had so little business it rarely sat above one hour or two … A change in the distribution of business soon came and equalized, to a great extent, the working of the three law courts'.[36]

The Common Law Procedure (Ireland) Acts 1853 and 1856[37] were modeled on English legislation of 1852 and 1854, and (among other reforms) gave common law courts the jurisdiction to grant injunctions, a remedy previously available only in the court of Chancery. It also made provision for defendants to a common law action to plead equitable defences. A corresponding extension of the powers of the court of Chancery, enabling it to award damages in addition to or in substitution for an injunction, was made by the Chancery Amendment Act 1858.[38] That Act, which came to be generally known as Lord Cairns's Act (although he was not a peer at the time of its passing), was applicable to Ireland as well as England. The Court of Chancery Appeal in Ireland was established in 1856,[39] following English precedent from 1851.[40] The lengthy Chancery (Ireland) Act 1867[41] recited that 'it is expedient to alter the constitution and amend the practice and course of proceeding of the High Court of Chancery in Ireland with a view of establishing uniformity of practice and procedure in the courts of Chancery in England and Ireland'. It created the office of vice-chancellor (an office which had been created in England in 1813, under the Administration of Justice Act of that year), abolished

31 An Act for the transfer of the equitable jurisdiction of the court of Exchequer to the court of Chancery in Ireland, 13&14 Vict., c.51 (1850).
32 13 Vict., c.18 (1850).
33 The concept of Nisi Prius originated in the Statute of Westminster (Nisi Prius) in 1285. See W. Holdsworth, *A history of English law*, vol. I (London, 1903), pp 278–85.
34 S28 of the Process and Practice Act.
35 S31 of the Act.
36 J.R. O'Flanagan, *The Irish Bar* (London, 1879), p. 318.
37 16&17 Vict., c.113 (1853), 19&20 Vict., c.102 (1856).
38 21&22 Vict., c.27 (1858).
39 Chancery Appeal Court (Ireland) Act 1856 (19&20 Vict., c.92).
40 An Act to improve the administration of justice in the court of Chancery and in the Judicial Committee of the Privy Council, 1851 (14&15 Vict., c.83).
41 30&31 Vict., c.44 (1867). The Act had 195 sections.

the historic offices of the masters in Chancery, and also made provision for declaratory relief – the basis of much subsequent public law, such as judicial review – 15 years after the Chancery Procedure Act of 1852 had introduced this in England.[42]

In England the jurisdiction of the ecclesiastical (prerogative and consistorial) courts in probate and matrimonial matters was terminated in 1857 and 'the old ecclesiastical law was in practice brought within the scope of the common law'.[43] A corresponding change was made simultaneously to Irish law on probate,[44] and 13 years later the matrimonial jurisdiction was likewise transferred to a court for matrimonial causes and matters, with provision for the judge of the court of Probate also to be the judge of the new court.[45] The court of Admiralty was reconstituted and reformed in 1867 by the Court of Admiralty (Ireland) Act.[46]

The appeal (or 'error') process for civil cases in the common law courts, in Ireland as in England, was inconvenient and untidy before the judicial restructuring in the 1870s. In that context, the operation of the Irish Court of Exchequer Chamber, which dealt with that appeal process, is a rare instance of some reforms in Ireland preceding rather than following reforms in England.[47] An 'Act for the more speedy correction of erroneous judgments given in the courts of law in this kingdom',[48] which was passed by the Irish parliament immediately before the adoption of the Act of Union reconstituted the court, as an assembly of all the common law judges. A corresponding reform was made in England in 1830, one element of which (that the judges or barons of the court from which the appeal arose would not sit to consider the writ of error) was adopted in Ireland in 1857.[49] The Exchequer Chamber had 'power and authority to examine [relevant] judgments and to reverse or affirm the same', and the 1877 Act provided that all jurisdiction and powers of the court would be transferred to and vested in the new Court of Appeal.[50]

The legislation to address the problem of insolvency of many landed estates after the Famine has been generally regarded as one category of substantive Irish legislation applicable to the court system that did not have an English model, although its mechanism for settling claims on estates did have such a precedent. This chain of legislation began in 1848 with the Act to facilitate the sale of

42 Ronan Keane, *Equity and the law of trusts in the Republic of Ireland* (London, 1988), p. 273.
43 Brian Abel-Smith and Robert Stevens, *Lawyers and the courts: a sociological study of the English legal system, 1750–1965* (London, 1967), p. 43.
44 The Probate and Letters of Administration Act (Ireland) 1857 (20&21 Vict., c.79); An Act to amend the Law relating to Probates and Letters of Administration in England 1857 (20&21 Vict., c.7).
45 Matrimonial Causes and Marriage Law (Ireland) Amendment Act 1870 (33&34 Vict., c.110).
46 30&31 Vict., c.114 (1867).
47 Andrew Lyall, *The Irish House of Lords: a court of law in the eighteenth century* (Dublin, 2013), p. 139.
48 40 Geo. 3, c.39 (Ir.) (1800).
49 Administration of Justice Act 1830 (11 Geo. 4 and 1 Will. 4, c.70), s8; Court of Exchequer Chamber (Ireland) Act 1857 (20&21 Vict., c.6), s1.
50 1800 Act, s2; 1877 Act, s23(2).

Incumbered Estates in Ireland.[51] Originally petitions for the sale of estates under the Act were required to be filed in the court of Chancery, but this original procedure transpired to be quite ineffective, and 'only four petitions appear to have been presented and none of the four was actually prosecuted to a sale'.[52] The function was soon transferred (in 1849) to new Commissioners for the sale of such estates, who had the standing of a court of record.[53] What had initially been envisaged as a short-term sale procedure that would be available for a period of three years was extended by amending legislation in 1852, 1853, 1855 and 1856 for further short periods. Eventually in 1858 the recital to the Sale and Transfer of Land Act (Ireland)[54] acknowledged that 'it is expedient to create a permanent court for the sale and transfer of land in Ireland, whether the same be incumbered or unincumbered', and the Commissioners were folded into a new Landed Estates Court, which initially had three judges. (In considering subsequent controversies, particularly in the 1870s, over whether the number of judges was excessive the expansion of the judiciary in the 1850s and 1860s, in the Landed Estates Court, the bankruptcy court and the office of vice-chancellor should be borne in mind.)

The attorney general of England at the time, Sir John Romilly (later master of the rolls, and a peer), was primarily responsible for the drafting of the encumbered estates legislation, and said so in a letter to the *Times* a couple of decades later.[55] He introduced the amending Bill in the House of Commons in 1849, saying that the Commission would carry out its functions unfettered by the rules and clogs and the fees and antiquated systems of the court of Chancery, and that a sound precedent was the work of the West India Commission, established in 1833 on the abolition of slavery in the British colonies,[56] which had

> duties analogous to those contemplated now. It had to inquire into the ownership of estates, and into the claims of incumbrancers according to priority; and that commission had performed its functions not only without blame, but with great rapidity, little expense, few appeals, and general satisfaction, both on the part of the persons on whose rights it had adjudicated and on the part of the public at large.[57]

Before the passing of Judicature Act for England in 1873 raised the question of whether similar changes should be introduced for Ireland there was thus a well-trodden path of English statutory precedent for the organisation and procedure of

51 11&12 Vict., c.48 (1848).

52 R. Denny Urlin, 'The Landed Estates Court (Ireland) as it affects the profession and the public' (*Law Times*, vol. 38, p. 193 (7 February 1863)).

53 An Act further to facilitate the sale and transfer of incumbered estates in Ireland 1849 (12&13 Vict., c.77).

54 21&22 Vict., c.72 (1858).

55 The letter was reproduced in *ILT&SJ*, vol. 3, p. 213 (20 March 1869).

56 Slavery Abolition Act 1833 (3&4 Will IV, c.73).

57 HC Deb, 3rd series, vol. 104, col. 894 (26 April 1849). See also HC Deb, 3rd series, vol. 150, col. 38 (4 May 1858).

the courts being adopted in Ireland. In the governance of Ireland, more generally, approaches adopted by the government over time fluctuated along a spectrum between emphasizing the desirability of assimilating the laws of Ireland to those of England, and of eliminating distinctions in the cause of greater coherence and integration within the United Kingdom, and on the other hand focusing on special measures as appropriate for special Irish circumstances. The assimilation camp's most persistent efforts were made in the area of law reform and legal affairs in general, particularly in what might be termed the infrastructure of the courts.[58]

There was a general view at the time however that this process of transposition of English laws had not necessarily worked well, as was brought out by the first report (in 1863) of a Royal Commission that had been established with a view to 'assimilate, so far as may be practicable, the administration of justice in England and Ireland'.[59] Its members included an equal number of senior English and Irish judges and lawyers, including from the Irish bench and Bar Blackburne (lord justice of appeal and subsequently to be lord chancellor), Monahan (chief justice of Common Pleas), Brewster (previously attorney general and subsequently to be lord chancellor), Napier (former lord chancellor), Hughes (baron of the Exchequer), O'Hagan (then attorney general and subsequently to be lord chancellor) and Lawson (then solicitor general and subsequently to be a judge of the Common Pleas). It reported that up to recent decades, so far as the course and practice of the common law courts was concerned, there had been 'substantial uniformity in both countries from the reign of King John [1199–1216] to that of King William the Fourth [1830–37], [and that] up to the year 1828 the differences were inconsiderable'. For the court of Chancery, 'in Ireland we found that the practice and procedure of the two countries, originally similar, had by the effect of modern legislation become almost entirely different. It thus appears that the differences in Equity are of recent origin and have been caused by separate attempts at carrying out Chancery reform in each of the two countries'.[60] W. Neilson Hancock, a leading economist, statistician and lawyer, who had been a secretary to the Commission, referred subsequently to the 'very unequal application of modern legal reforms to the courts of the two countries' and to the laws of practice and procedure of the two countries having had 'an identity which to a large extent prevailed from the reign of King Henry II to the commencement of the law reforms in the reign of King William IV'.[61] (Henry II reigned from 1154 to 1189, and may have been thought a more respectable monarch than John from whom to trace anything.)

58 K. Theodore Hoppen, *Governing Hibernia: British politicians and Ireland, 1800–1921* (Oxford, 2016), pp 2 and 95.

59 First Report of the Royal Commission into the Superior Courts of Law and Courts of Chancery of England and Ireland, with statements of differences in practice and procedure between England and Ireland (P.P. 1863 (3238) xv.463).

60 Ibid., pp vii and xxiii.

61 *ILT&SJ*, vol. 10, p. 605 (25 November 1876). See also John F. McEldowney, 'William Neilson Hancock' in *Irish Jurist*, vol. 20 (1985), pp 378–402.

The 1873 Act had been drafted and passed into law in order to implement the recommendations of the first report of a Royal Commission, on the Judicature in England ('to make inquiry into the operation and effect of the present constitution of the courts'), that had been established in 1867.[62] A consensus then existed, in words later used to describe the Irish reforms, that the 'patching up of the existing system for the first three quarters of the century',[63] the most significant elements of which have been outlined above, had proved unsatisfactory. 'More was required than piecemeal reform. The courts had evolved without any rational plan. As society had recognised new needs, new courts had been created to meet them, or existing courts had been required to exercise functions for which they had not been designed. There had never been a review of the judicial system as a whole. Such a review was made the task of the Royal Commission on the Judicature'.[64] Its first report was issued in 1869.[65] When the prime minister, Benjamin Disraeli, was asked by an Irish MP in July 1874 whether a corresponding Royal Commission would be set up for Ireland in connection with judicial reform he replied that this would not be necessary, since the information was already in the possession of the government.[66]

The intention to extend court reform to Ireland had been indicated in the Queen's Speech on the opening of Parliament in March 1874 – the speech was actually read by Lord Cairns – in the following terms:

> You will probably be of opinion that the rearrangement of the judicature and the blending of the administration of law and equity, which were effected for England by the enactment of the last session, ought, on the same principles, to be extended to Ireland, and you will be asked to devote some part of your time to the accomplishment of this object.[67]

A couple of months later the first proposal for Irish legislation on the subject was introduced in the House of Lords by Cairns,[68] and after being passed by that house it was then introduced in the House of Commons by the attorney general, Dr John Thomas Ball.[69] As lord chancellor Cairns was the head of the judiciary in Great Britain and the senior legal (and presiding) member of the House of Lords. The lord chancellor of Ireland was not necessarily – indeed, at this time was not usually – a member of the House of Lords. He was – as in England – a member of the government, 'not only a judicial but a political officer. He is a confidential adviser of the lord lieutenant and the chief secretary. He may be considered himself a minister'.[70] The position had been left vacant in March that year when Disraeli,

62 P.P. 1868–9 (4130) xxv.l. See *ILT&SJ*, vol. 3, p. 638 (16 October 1869).
63 F.H. Newark, *Notes on Irish legal history* (Belfast, 1960), p. 22.
64 Abel-Smith and Stevens, op. cit., p. 48.
65 Other reports of the Royal Commission were subsequently issued in 1872 and 1874.
66 HC Deb, 3rd series, vol. 221, cols. 966–7, 30 July 1874; *ILT&SJ*, vol. 8, p. 416 (1 August 1874).
67 HL Deb, 3rd series, vol. 218, col. 24 (19 March 1874).
68 HL Deb, 3rd series, vol. 218, col. 1808 (7 May 1874); *ILT&SJ*, vol. 8, p. 235 (9 May 1874).
69 HC Deb, 3rd series, vol. 220, col. 1265 (7 July 1874).
70 Thomas MacKnight, *Ulster as it is* (London, 1896), vol. 1, p. 198. MacKnight was a confidante

the Conservative leader, succeeded Gladstone as prime minister, the seal of office instead being entrusted temporarily to commissioners ('lords justices'). Ball, one of the members of Parliament for Dublin University, was the person envisaged as ultimately holding the office, but was initially appointed as attorney general for Ireland with a view to continuing for a time his membership of the House of Commons, to give assistance there in connection with the impending judicial reforms. When it became clear that the reforms would be delayed, and in light of criticism of the continuing vacancy, he resigned his seat in Parliament and became lord chancellor at the start of 1875.

For a proposal of major law reform to be introduced in the House of Lords by the lord chancellor of Great Britain may have been appropriate anyway, as reflecting the high office and personal standing of Cairns and his connection with Ireland, but it also evidenced a view that opposition to reform could be expected in the House of Commons. The general election of 1874 had resulted in the Irish membership of that house including '18 barristers and four solicitors, exclusive of several country gentlemen who are members of the Irish Bar but who do not practise'.[71] Ball's apprehension of how any reform proposals might be dealt with in the commons, is evident in his advice in February 1875 that it was 'in the highest degree advisable' that, as before, the Bill should be introduced by Cairns in the first place in the House of Lords and that 'having done the best to make it what it ought to be, the rule in the commons should be, no change. If this is not laid down we shall never know where we are'.[72] As it transpired, the focus of opposition to reform was not to be found in the House of Commons.

The 1874 bill followed very closely the text of the 1873 Act. An initial reference to this was made by Serjeant Armstrong, at a meeting of the Bar called to consider the Bill, that 'it appeared to him that the measure must have been drafted by some person unacquainted with the practice of the courts in Ireland and the difference between the legislation of the two countries. The result was that many provisions imported by the scissors from the English Act were put into this Irish Bill – provisions totally unsuited to Ireland'.[73] The *Times* said that

> the English Act was copied with the minute exactness of a tailor following the pattern set before him, and the result was that it proved to be an awkward and uncomfortable misfit. One judicial arm was too long, another too short, and the skirts of official patronage to which so many like to cling were too stinted to satisfy expectants. Whether the new Bill will please them better remains to be seen, but it will be, at all events, made to measure.[74]

of Lord O'Hagan, who was lord chancellor of Ireland, 1868–74 and 1880–1, O'Hagan thus both preceded and succeeded Ball in that office.

71 *ILT&SJ*, vol. 8, p. 145 (21 March 1874), quoting *The Times*.

72 Ball to Cairns, 4 February 1875 (Cairns Papers, PRO 30/15/19).

73 *ILT&SJ*, vol. 8, p. 301 (6 June 1874).

74 *ILT&SJ*, vol. 8, p. 576 (7 November 1874).

As mentioned, three years elapsed before the draft legislation, amended in a variety of respects, became law. The most fundamental reason was that the English reforms had been found almost immediately to need modification, resulting in amending legislation being passed in 1874, 1875 and again in 1876. Lord Cairns said in the House of Lords in April 1875 that 'it is useless to bring in a Bill for Ireland – though one is prepared and ready for introduction – until the English Act comes into operation',[75] reflecting the view of the Irish administration.[76] The Irish proposals were put on hold for the greater part of two more years, until that dust had settled and the shape of the English reforms, the prototype or model for the Irish changes, had been clarified and confirmed.

One particularly controversial aspect of the initial English reforms, potentially directly affecting the Irish court structure, was whether appeals could be taken to the House of Lords from the new Court of Appeal established by the 1873 Act. For litigation in England and Wales the Act had prospectively abolished, with effect from November 1874, that historic procedure for appeal while preserving it for decisions of the highest courts in Ireland and Scotland. To have such an incoherent or fractured structure of appeal within the United Kingdom, taken as a whole, was plainly undesirable, but how it all was to be addressed was not resolved until 1876.

Whether the House of Lords should retain a judicial function for England had not been particularly controversial in 1873, but it became a much more highly charged political question after Gladstone's government, which was responsible for the 1873 Act, was replaced by a Conservative government under Disraeli in February 1874. Before the issue acquired that political dimension, however, there had been widespread concern and opposition within the Irish (and Scottish) judiciary and legal profession at the impending separation of the ultimate court of appeal for those jurisdictions from that of England. The first comment of the Irish judges on reform had been made in the summer of 1873, in relation to the English proposals, when resolving (and so informing the chief secretary for Ireland) 'that it is of essential importance to the administration of law that there should be preserved a right of final appeal from the decisions of the courts in Ireland to the same tribunal as that to which the right of final appeal shall lie from the like decisions of the courts in England'.[77] The Bar of Ireland at a meeting in 1873 passed a resolution in similar terms, recording their collective opinion that 'to preserve uniformity of decision in the courts of law and equity in England and Ireland, as well as to ensure an efficient tribunal, it is essential that there be the same final court of appeal for English and Irish cases'.[78] A year later, after the initial Bill for Ireland had been published, the Bar called for the retention of the House

75 HL Deb, 3rd series, vol. 223, col. 582 (9 April 1875): *ILT&SJ*, vol. 9, p. 190 (17 April 1875).

76 Sir Michael Hicks Beach (chief secretary) to the duke of Abercorn (lord lieutenant), 11 April 1875 (Abercorn Papers (PRONI), D623/A/316/12).

77 Baron Dowse to Lord Hartington, 7 June 1873 (Resolution of Irish Judges on Judicature Bill (P.P. 1873 (273) liv.335)). See also *ILT&SJ*, vol. 9, p. 236 (9 May 1874), citing remarks by Lord Cairns in the House of Lords on 7 May 1874 with reference to that correspondence.

78 *ILT&SJ*, vol. 7, p. 310 (14 June 1873).

of Lords as the ultimate court of appeal for the United Kingdom as a whole,[79] as did the Incorporated Law Society of Ireland, representing solicitors.[80]

An early individual voice on the subject was lord justice Christian. The acerbic tone of his comments on some of his judicial colleagues in judgments, in letters to the newspapers and in a pamphlet published anonymously (although the identity of the author was quite clear), had given rise to controversy and created considerable offence in recent years and would continue to do so for some years yet.[81] A better reception was given to a pamphlet on 'The coming court of final appeal for Ireland' that he published in March 1874, in which he warned of difficulties that would ensue if the House of Lords was not retained as the ultimate court of appeal for both England and Ireland.

Lord Selborne had been the lord chancellor responsible for the initial English judicature legislation. He wrote in his memoirs that the Bill had 'narrowly escaped shipwreck upon the question of the appellate jurisdiction', since in June 1873, at an advanced stage of the parliamentary debate,

> there was a sudden expression of opinion among members of the legal profession in Scotland and Ireland against any change in which Scotch and Irish appeals should not be included; the form which it took being rather that of a demand that Scotch and Irish appeals, as well as English, should go before the new tribunal, than of opposition to the constitution of the new tribunal for English appeals. [However] it was not safe or expedient, in a constitutional point of view, to remove [such appeals] from the House of Lords without a deliberate expression of Scotch and Irish opinion in favour of that course [and] the government wisely determined to defer any legislation as to Scotch and Irish appeals until a future session.[82]

By 1875, when the matter returned to Parliament 'the opinion of the legal profession in Scotland and Ireland was declared to be in favour of restoring the jurisdiction of the House of Lords for English appeals rather than taking it away as to Scotch and Irish'.[83] A meeting of the Irish Bar at the end of January 1875 passed a resolution confirming its view of this, which was communicated to a 'Committee for Preserving the Jurisdiction of the House of Lords as a Court of Final Appeal for the United Kingdom' that had been established in London.[84]

79 *ILT&SJ*, vol. 8, p. 248 (16 May 1874) and p. 272 (23 May 1874).
80 *ILT&SJ*, vol. 8, p. 302 (6 June 1874).
81 The anonymous pamphlet (published in 1872) was entitled *The court of Chancery under the Chancery (Ireland) Act 1867*. See Daire Hogan, 'Arrows too sharply pointed: the relations of Lord Justice Christian and Lord O'Hagan, 1868–1874' in John McEldowney and Paul O'Higgins (eds), *The common law tradition: essays in Irish legal history* (Dublin, 1990), pp 61–83.
82 Lord Selborne, *Memorials: Part 2 – personal and political, 1865–1895* (London, 1898), vol. 1, pp 304, 306, 310 and 312.
83 Selborne, ibid., p. 313.
84 *ILT&SJ*, vol. 9, pp 65–7 (6 February 1875).

The core issue for the appellate framework was whether the House of Lords would retain any judicial function. A proposal was made in May 1874 by Cairns, who had replaced Selborne as lord chancellor, to abolish the Irish and Scottish procedure for appeal to the Lords, on the basis that the new English Court of Appeal would be re-named as the Imperial Court of Appeal and its jurisdiction extended to Ireland and Scotland, with the addition of some judges from those countries.[85] That did not gain general acceptance, and Disraeli described the complicated situation when writing to the Queen in March 1875:

> There is a strong party, in both Houses, which desires the restoration to the House of Lords of their position as Court of Ultimate Appeal.
>
> An Act to abolish this function, so far as England is concerned, has already passed, but does not come into force until next November.
>
> The House of Lords is still the Court of Ultimate Appeal for Ireland and Scotland, and it is not probable that that the Bills introduced, to assimilate those countries to England, will pass.
>
> The anomaly, then, will be established of separate Courts of Final Appeal for different parts of your Majesty's dominions.
>
> To remove this anomaly, it is understood that Mr Walpole[86] will bring the matter before the House of Commons, with the view of practically rescinding the English Act that comes into play in November. The circumstances are rather critical.
>
> Mr Disraeli attended, yesterday, a meeting of the peers, at the Duke of Richmond's, and succeeded so far as to induce them to take a prudent and moderate course for the moment, but their spirit was high and somewhat unmanageable. Peers who, two years ago, showed the greatest apathy on the subject, have become quite headstrong.[87]

Amending legislation in 1874 and again in 1875[88] each postponed for a year at a time the setting aside of the House of Lords for English appeals, giving more time for attempting to resolve the conundrum. Eventually, after what has been described as a story of 'intrigue, legislation and counter-legislation that virtually defies unraveling',[89] the controversy was settled by the passing of the Appellate Jurisdiction Act 1876.[90] This set aside the scheme of removing the House of Lords

85 HL Deb, 3rd series, vol. 218, col. 1817 (7 May 1874).
86 Spencer Horatio Walpole QC (1806–98) was MP for Cambridge University.
87 Disraeli to the Queen, 5 March 1875 (G.E. Buckle, *The life of Benjamin Disraeli, earl of Beaconsfield, vol. 5, 1868–1876* (London, 1920), p. 375).
88 The Supreme Court of Judicature (Commencement) Act 1874 (37&38 Vict., c.83), The Supreme Court of Judicature (Amendment) Act 1875 (38&39 Vict., c.77, s2).
89 Robert Stevens, *Law and politics; the House of Lords as a judicial body, 1800–1976* (London, 1979), p. 57. See also David Steele, 'The judicial House of Lords: abolition and restoration, 1873–6' in Louis Blom-Cooper, Brice Dickson and Gavin Drewry (eds), *The judicial House of Lords, 1876–2009* (Oxford, 2009), p. 13.
90 39&40 Vict., c.42 (1876).

from the English appeal system and introduced various improvements in the good order and standing of the house's appeal procedures, including new provision for the appointment of lords of appeal in ordinary ('Law Lords'), on whom life peerages would be conferred.

The House of Lords issue, although it had an Irish aspect, was primarily debated and settled as a matter of law and policy applicable to the United Kingdom as a whole. The other parts of the Irish reform proposals had a more purely domestic character, and caution was the order of the day. In 1873 Selborne advised Lord Hartington, the chief secretary for Ireland, that care should be taken in drafting an Irish Bill so that it would 'provoke no serious opposition from Irish judges or members of Parliament'.[91] A similar and prescient observation on the prospects for reform had been made at a still earlier stage of the whole process, in October 1872, by Christopher Palles, the attorney general. His comment to Lord O'Hagan, the lord chancellor of Ireland, transpired to be an accurate indication of how the reform process would actually develop over the next few years:

> I am considering the Judicature Bill with a view to seeing how we can best apply it to Ireland. I think we will have little difficulty in doing so, even without a Commission [as mentioned, the 1873 Act had been prepared on foot of a report of a Royal Commission], provided we do not attempt to interfere with the number, status or salaries of the Irish Bench. I am strongly of opinion that this is the course which ought to be pursued. The English measure was one for the better administration of justice and not one for the reduction of the judicial establishment.[92]

A reduction in the number of superior court judges, by not filling some existing or future vacancies, was one of the reforms that was proposed in 1874. The memorandum of the common law judges in April 1876 had expressed concerns for the preservation of certain administrative privileges and rankings among themselves, which were assuaged by a provision in the Bill as ultimately enacted that 'every existing judge … shall as to tenure of office, rank between himself and the other existing judges,[93] title, patronage, and powers of appointment and dismissal, and all other privileges and disqualifications, and also as to salary and pension, save as is herein provided, remain in the same condition as if this Act had not passed'.[94] A more complicated question of status arose in relation to the positions of the heads of the three common law courts (the chief justices of Queen's Bench and Common Pleas, and the chief baron of the Exchequer).

91 Selborne to Hartington, 13 December 1873 (forwarded by him to O'Hagan on 16 December 1873) (O'Hagan Papers (PRONI), D2,777/7/8).

92 Palles to O'Hagan, 2 October 1872 (Teeling Papers (NLI), MS 17872; O'Hagan Papers, D2777/9/89/1).

93 This was a variation on the corresponding provision (s11) in the 1873 Act, which did not contain the words 'between himself and the other existing judges'.

94 Section 15 of the 1877 Act.

No reductions in salary for judges were proposed, but a planned reduction in salary for the next person to be appointed as master of the rolls, from £4,000 to £3,500, drew adverse comments, mixing issues of status and salary, from Edward Sullivan, the existing holder of that office. He told Lord O'Hagan that the judicial duties were substantial, that some extra-judicial duties had been imposed by statute, and that 'if the salary of the Master in future is only to be the same as that of the puisne judges (indeed, having regard to the Circuit allowances[95] it will be less) I feel that the office will be the least coveted among the judicial places in Ireland'.[96] No change was ultimately made.

Any reduction of the number of judges by removal from office or compulsory retirement of any sitting judge was out of the question. The 'Act for securing the independence of judges and the impartial administration of justice', which had been passed by the Irish Parliament in 1782,[97] provided that 'the present and all future commissions of judges for the time being shall continue and remain in force during their good behaviour' rather than, as previously, during the King's pleasure. The Irish judges had thus been obtained the security of tenure given to judges in England by the Act of Settlement of 1701 and a statute (Demise of the Crown) enacted in 1760.[98] A prelude to this had been the granting to the recorder[99] of Dublin in 1759 of such security of tenure during good behaviour.[100]

Removal of a judge for good cause would require resolutions of both houses of Parliament to that effect. Sir Jonah Barrington in 1830 was the subject of such resolutions approving an address to the King for his dismissal from the court of Admiralty to which he had been appointed in 1797.[101] A second removal of an admiralty judge that was effected by statute in 1867 was not regarded as any kind of precedent. The Court of Admiralty (Ireland) Act 1867[102] had provided that 'the present judge, registrar [and other officers] of the High Court of Admiralty shall cease to hold their respective offices'. This remarkable episode of an effective dismissal of a judge (Thomas Kelly), to permit his replacement by a more suitable person,[103] would have been facilitated by section 18 of the Act, which provided that if the incumbent was not appointed to be the judge of the new or reconstituted admiralty court 'he shall be entitled to receive by way of compensation during his

95 Section 18 of the 1877 Act would provide that new judges would be entitled to receive £150 for each circuit (assizes) on which they sat.

96 Sullivan to O'Hagan, 15 April 1876 (Teeling Papers, MS 17874 (10)).

97 21&22 Geo. III, c.50 (Ir.) (1782).

98 12&13 Will. III (1701), c.2; I Geo. III (1760), c.23.

99 See address by Lord MacDermott on 'law and practice in Northern Ireland' (*NILQ*, vol. 10, no. 2 (1953), p. 47 at 65), as to the status of recorders in Ireland differing from that in England.

100 An Act for better regulating the corporation of the city of Dublin, and for extending the power of the magistrates thereof and for other purposes relative to the said city (33 Geo. II (1759), c.16), s20.

101 Court of Admiralty Act 1783 (23&24 Geo. III, c.14, s2); Kevin Costello, *The court of Admiralty of Ireland, 1575–1893* (Dublin, 2011), pp 156–72.

102 30 & 31 Vict., c.114 (1867), s5.

103 Costello, op. cit., pp 208–14.

life an annuity equal to his salary at the commencement of this Act'. Such a full salary payment would necessarily have been larger than a pension computed as a proportion of salary.

Removal of judges from office not being an option, the only other means of bringing about the desired reduction in numbers was to determine not to fill some existing or future vacancies as they arose. The 1874 Bill (and, unchanged in that respect, eventually the 1877 Act) thus provided that two such vacancies, in the court of Common Pleas and in the Exchequer respectively, would not be filled and that the number of judges in those two courts (i.e., divisions of the High Court, under the new framework) would accordingly be permanently reduced, with similar provisions for the bankruptcy, admiralty and one of the land judges.[104]

There were a number of other elements of the proposed reforms that had significant, if less obvious, implications for the structure and operation of the courts. Some of these were settled for Ireland in the 1877 legislation in a rather different fashion than had been determined for the English judiciary. These ancillary issues, which will be commented on (in chapter 2) below, were:

(1) what would be the composition of the divisions of the new High Court,
(2) what procedure ought to be followed for any modifications of that composition and amalgamation of divisions,
(3) whether the judges of the common law divisions of the High Court would sit individually or together, in (or en) banc, the expression (in French, literally 'on the bench', and otherwise styled 'in banco')[105] that was used to denote the historic practice of the full complement of the members of each separate common law court sitting together (in a somewhat different form, this became known after 1877 as a divisional court), and
(4) whether common law appeals would go straight to the new Court of Appeal (as Chancery appeals did) or whether any appeal would first be heard in a divisional court, from which an appeal could be taken to the Court of Appeal.

The Irish legal profession adopted a very defensive attitude to the then current structure of the judiciary as soon as the first detailed proposals for change were published in 1874. Reform along the general lines of the English legislation of 1873 seemed inevitable, in light of the universally acknowledged desirability of maintaining a harmony between the judicial arrangements in the two countries, and the historical pattern of English legal reforms being adopted in Ireland. There were many professions of goodwill to the concept of reform, and many calls for assimilation of Irish practice and procedure to the reformed English procedure, to ensure as close a degree of harmony as possible between the codes of law and procedure governing the two respective jurisdictions. These concerns were evident

104 Sections 6, 8 and 9 of the 1877 Act.
105 The court 'sitting in Banco' was the expression used in the 1877 Act (s46), whereas the English Act of 1873 referred to 'sitting in Banc' (s41).

in the editorial observations of the *Irish Law Times*, the common law judges' comments in 1876 and in what was said at meetings of the Incorporated Law Society of Ireland as representing the views of the solicitors' profession and at meetings of the Bar. The merits of any individual proposal for reform, and whether it should be implemented at the time or at some future date, could certainly be debated and challenged, and many positive sentiments were coupled with vehement objections to particular proposals (such as reductions in the number of judges), as being unnecessary and unconsidered. Differences in circumstances between Ireland and England that might justify a divergence in approach to reform were highlighted. One particularly negative expression of objections drew an observation from the *Times* that the lawyers 'would do well to anticipate inevitable changes with reasonable suggestions of reform rather than to entrench themselves in an undiscriminating protest against all attempts to economise judicial power'.[106]

The desirability of reform had not been particularly controversial before specific proposals were published. The *Irish Law Times* had acknowledged in 1870 that 'what our Irish judicial system requires is reconstruction, not reduction'.[107] In 1868 it had said that up to 1784 three judges had formed the judicial staff of each of the three common law courts 'and we conceive that a return to that number would prove far more than sufficient for the requirements of the present time'. It queried the necessity for three separate courts of common law, 'each performing almost the same functions as its neighbour', also saying that it was not necessary that there should be two judges on each [assize] circuit.

> Of course, our judges, when reduced in number, would have more to do, and why not? Their duties at present are far too light; their English brethren work, and work hard, and at the same time discharge their duties with satisfaction to the public. The Irish judges are just as well able to work, only they are not used to doing so – we mean particularly the puisne judges,[108] for the 'chiefs' are not generally idle – but the sooner our puisne judges learn to work hard the better.[109]

It confirmed that view in 1870, stating 'our belief that we had too many judges for the requirements of this country'.[110]

It called in 1871 for the reconstruction of the court system, saying that in the present law term,

> the spectacle of four eminent judges without any business beyond the decision of a few trifling motions, while courts over which a single judge

106 As reported in *ILT&SJ*, vol. 10, p. 42 (22 January 1876).
107 *ILT&SJ*, vol. 4, p. 225 (26 March 1870).
108 All judges of a common law court except the chief justice or chief baron were known as puisne (or ordinary) judges or barons.
109 *ILT&SJ*, vol. 2, p. 314/15 (13 June 1868).
110 *ILT&SJ*, vol. 4, p. 332 (20 June 1870).

> presides [i.e., in Chancery] are fully occupied with the decision of important cases, is an anomaly which cannot much longer be permitted to exist. The necessity for reconstruction is urgent ... the common law business disposed of in the superior courts of common law is inferior in relative importance to that which is disposed of by the courts of equity, including in the latter the Landed Estates' Court, while the staff of the common law courts is very much greater.[111]

In 1872 it commented that reconstruction 'could easily be accommodated by reducing the number of judges'.[112]

That disposition of the *Irish Law Times* consistently to favour reforms had disappeared by 1873, when the tenor of the English reforms, with obvious potential applicability to Ireland, had become clear. It raised an alarm then about the prospect, on foot of a report of a select committee of the House of Commons (on civil service expenditure), of a reduction in the judicial establishment 'to a condition which will surely interfere with their efficiency', conceding that 'it may be that some anomalies exist which might well be set right', but warned against radical change: 'For if the law be thereby less satisfactorily administered than it might be, such a feeling of discontent and annoyance would be excited as would considerably counterbalance the advantage of saving a few thousand pounds per annum'.[113] It said later that financial savings 'would be dearly bought by creating delay in the administration of justice'.[114]

The Bar initiated and indeed maintained the resistance to reform. The father of the Bar, when taking the chair at a general meeting of the Bar to discuss the subject in 1875, expressed his opinion that 'it would have been as well if Ireland had been left alone'.[115] He had been called to the Bar over half a century before. Three decades later, in 1904, much the same spirit reigned, as the Bar Council expressed the view that the abolition of judgeships under the legislation of 1877, and subsequently in 1887 and 1897 and the consolidation of divisions in the High Court, 'so far from effecting beneficial results to the public, on the contrary, led to both delay and inconvenience to suitors and consequent useless expense'. It was then protesting at proposals in a bill introduced in 1904 for a reduction in the numbers of judges, which was withdrawn later in the year but ultimately re-introduced, and enacted, three years later.[116] The Council's view was that it would not 'offer any opposition to a well-considered scheme of reform ... but the present time is a most inopportune one to make the experiment of a further reduction in the Supreme Court judiciary ... they protest against hasty legislation brought forward for departmental purposes'.[117] It was in 1897 that they had first said that

111 *ILT&SJ*, vol. 5, p. 195 (22 April 1871).
112 *ILT&SJ*, vol. 6, p. 55 (3 February 1872).
113 *ILT&SJ*, vol. 7, pp 335 and 339 (28 June 1873).
114 *ILT&SJ*, vol. 8, p. 233 (9 May 1874).
115 *ILT&SJ*, vol. 9, p. 65 (6 February 1875).
116 Supreme Court of Judicature (Ireland) Act 1907 (7 Edw. VII, c.44).
117 *ILT&SJ*, vol. 38, p. 207 (25 June 1904).

the Bar would offer no opposition to 'a well-considered and necessary scheme of reform',[118] an expression itself echoing a phrase used by chief justice Whiteside in 1876 (see p. 27 below). This evoked also the spirit of a resolution passed at a meeting of the Bar in May 1850, that 'while we recognize the expediency of legal reform, we deprecate the introduction of legislative changes in the practice of the law in this country without due consideration and careful preliminary inquiry'.[119] The *Irish Jurist* contended in that connection that 'no body of men were ever more disposed to receive favourably rational law reform than the Bar of Ireland'.[120]

A general meeting of members of the Bar in 1874 appointed a committee to review the Bill shortly after its publication.[121] The committee's report, adopted at an 'important and numerously attended' general meeting a few weeks later in June 1874, contained extensive criticisms of the Bill, including its proposed reduction in the number of judges and its provision for re-arrangement of the assize circuits, as leading to 'great public and professional confusion'.[122] The *Times,* which had been to the fore in demanding reform in England, heavily criticized the report of the Bar committee and trusted that Lord Cairns 'will not be moved – except to indignation – by these complaints', subsequently asserting that 'a judicial staff disproportioned to the work is kept up in Ireland, of course at the public expense, and of it is no doubt so kept up for political reasons … retrenchment[123] is in the eyes of most Irishmen a crime against society'.[124]

This demonstrated the belief of English commentators that maintenance of a system of patronage and of incomes being provided by the taxpayer for a flotilla of court officers was a (non-party) concern of the Irish judges and legal profession and indeed of Irish society. Some proof of this was to be offered some two decades after the initial reforms following the passing of the 1877 Act had taken effect. In 1897 a calculation was made that annual expenditure on the superior courts had been reduced by about £17,000 by virtue of 'the reduction in the number of the judges … and the abolition of their staff and of the several offices connected with them'. The author of this calculation, Arthur W. Samuels QC, who would in due course (in 1919) himself be appointed a High Court judge, added that 'almost the whole of the money paid to the judges and their staffs was spent in Ireland, and found its way, in one direction or another, into the pockets of Irish traders, merchants and other members of the public'.[125] The Treasury did not accept the

118 *ILT&SJ*, vol. 31, p. 309 (3 July 1897).
119 *Irish Jurist*, vol. 2, p. 146 (8 June 1850).
120 Ibid., p. 145.
121 *ILT&SJ*, vol. 8, p. 248 (16 May 1874).
122 *ILT&SJ*, vol. 8, p. 299 (6 June 1874).
123 'Retrenchment' was a common expression then, defined in the *Oxford English dictionary* as the act of economizing or cutting down expenditure, or excising, deleting and omitting. 'Peace, retrenchment and reform' was a slogan associated with the Liberal party at the time, popularized by John Bright MP in 1859.
124 As reported in *ILT&SJ*, vol. 8, p. 318 (13 June 1874) and p. 402 (25 July 1874).
125 Arthur W. Samuels, *A suggestion for the removal of taxes on litigation as a condition of the reduction of the judicial establishment* (Dublin, 1896).

idea that public expenditure on the judiciary was being reduced, and in July 1897 the chancellor of the Exchequer in response to a parliamentary question on the subject said that 'concurrently with the abolition of the judgeships mentioned the judicial officers of the Land Commission have been created and the amount of their salaries has exceeded those of the abolished judges. There has thus been no saving'.[126]

When it became clear that the initial reorganisation Bill would not be passed into law in 1874 the *Times*, in the first of a number of sharp comments on an apparent lack of urgency in dealing with the subject, saw in this postponement a situation in which 'every opposing influence is encouraged to fresh exertions against economical reform, while the influences favourable to it are weakened and dispirited'.[127] It remarked almost two years later that the legislation 'has been too long delayed, and the difficulties of the problem are perplexed and multiplied by procrastination'.[128]

Another 'large and most influential' general meeting of the Bar was held in the Law Library in February 1875 at the start of the annual Parliamentary session. It adopted resolutions calling for the retention of the House of Lords as the court of final appeal, for the maintenance of the present number of common law judges and for the filling of a longstanding vacancy in the Landed Estates Court. Francis Macdonogh QC, a leading if controversial member of the Bar,[129] referred at the meeting to the 1874 Bill as 'wild, speculative and destructive'. The *Irish Law Times*, its previous reformist tone now thoroughly abandoned, observed that the meeting will 'show the English members of the government that the proposed changes in the legal system are not only not acceptable in their entirety in Ireland but also that a considerable modification of the Irish Judicature Bill of last Session is absolutely necessary'.[130]

Observers across the Irish Sea were unimpressed. The *Solicitor's Journal* in London observed of the sentiments expressed at the meeting that 'we can draw nothing from a simple protest against change, unaccompanied by a single practical suggestion, embellished indeed by much magnificent declamation', practical reforms being 'all but ignored by the meeting while we are met by a passionate outburst of indignation against any alteration whatever' in the number of judges.[131] That critical comment was made by a legal periodical, with a degree of knowledge about and interest in legal issues, and there were a number of even less sympathetic commentators that 'were unrelenting in their demand that the administration of justice should not be judged by lawyers but by the requirements of public utility'.[132] Early in 1876 the *Times* bemoaned the failure to date to address 'the

126 HC Deb, 4th series, vol. 50, cols. 726–7 (29 June 1897); *ILT&SJ*, vol. 31, p. 309 (3 July 1897).
127 As reported in *ILT&SJ*, vol. 8, p. 416 (1 August 1874).
128 As reported in *ILT&SJ*, vol. 10, p. 324 (3 June 1876).
129 See his obituary as published in *ILT&SJ*, vol. 16, p. 177 (22 April 1882), and pp 105–6 below.
130 As reported in *ILT&SJ*, vol. 9, p. 64 (6 February 1875).
131 As reported in *ILT&SJ*, vol. 9, p. 95 (20 February 1875).
132 Raymond Cock, 'Victorian barristers, judges and taxation; a study in the expansion of legal work'

overmanning of the Irish Bench' through retrenchment, and remarked subsequently of the 1876 Bill that it 'effects little saving of public money – at present, indeed, we suppose, none at all ... the objections of the Irish Bar seem to us purely fractious'.[133] The *Irish Law Times* discounted such commentary as the work of 'a powerful class on England, who, in their reckless desire for retrenchment, persuade themselves, and try to persuade others, that all moneys expended upon the public service, the application of which they have not taken the trouble to, and do not, understand, is wasted'.[134]

The most detailed commentary on the reform proposals during the three or four years when they were under consideration was a memorandum of the common law judges in 1876. This disclaimed any interest in considering 'on its abstract merits and independently of the recent legislation in England the policy or general conception of the proposed measure, as an alteration of the existing constitution or procedure of the superior courts of this country'. This, they said, was both because 'it has not hitherto been the custom of the judges to volunteer suggestions to the legislature on questions of policy, and secondly as it is our opinion that it is for paramount reasons expedient that there should be (as far as may be) identity of constitution, practice and procedure in the superior courts of England and Ireland'.[135] It set out their observations on 'matters of detail in which the proposed Irish measure differs from the law in England under the Acts of 1873 and 1875', for which, in their view no (or no adequate) justification had been provided. (This self-denying ordinance on commenting on matters of policy was comprehensively ignored by Whiteside and was set aside more collectively by the judges in 1882 and again in 1920, when strong and effective objections were made to government proposals that non-jury courts be established for the trial of serious offences – see appendix 1 to chapter 2.)

The *Irish Law Times* offered a threefold explanation at a more practical level of the necessity for assimilation of practice and procedure in the two countries, namely (i) that the public in the two countries would understand that the laws are similar and would not be afraid to trust their money and other property from one to the other; (ii) 'in order that the exhausting and most worrying of all forms of legal expenditure – i.e., that which is expended in settling points of procedure under a new and vague system of procedure, without any benefit to the unfortunate suitor who has to pay for it – may not have to be incurred twice over'; and (iii) in order that 'it may be possible to have English textbooks and English decisions to guide us in Ireland, and corresponding advantages from Irish textbooks for our English fellow subjects'. They cited in that context the opinion of Hugh Law MP,

in G.R. Rubin and David Sugarman (eds), *Law, economy and society; essays in the history of English law, 1750–1914* (Abingdon, 1984), pp 450–1.

133 As reported in *ILT&SJ*, vol. 10, p. 42 (22 January 1876) and p. 324 (3 June 1876).

134 *ILT&SJ*, vol. 10, p. 179 (25 March 1876).

135 Paper on the subject of the Supreme Court of Judicature (Ireland) Bill, signed by the common law judges of Ireland (P.P. 1876 (278) lxi.357). This was reported in *ILT&SJ*, vol. 10, pp 309–11 (27 May 1876).

a well-respected member of the Irish Bar (who would later be appointed attorney general (1880–1) and lord chancellor (1881–3)), that 'even if our system of procedure were in itself as good as the English, it must be less satisfactory and efficient by the mere fact of its being different'.[136] On the proposal of Mr Law, although then in opposition, the Bill was amended to provide that in the making of (procedural) rules of court under the Act regard would be had to the rules of court for the time being in force under the 1873 Act in England 'so that the pleading, practice and procedure in the High Court of Justice and Court of Appeal respectively constituted by this Act [i.e., in Ireland] shall, so far as may be practicable and convenient, having regard to the difference of the laws and circumstances of the two countries, be the same' as in the courts of England.[137]

Two of the most senior judges made a number of general comments on the draft legislation, and despite the assertion in the memorandum of April 1876 of judges supposedly not commenting on matters of policy it was clear that these were made in a spirit of generalized discontent and unease at the prospect of reform. Remarks that were sceptical of or indeed hostile to reform were made by Whiteside, the chief justice of Queen's Bench, initially in 1874 and then on three separate occasions in 1876 (in January, February and July), and subsequently, early in 1877, also by Morris, the chief justice of Common Pleas. Whiteside's various observations constituted a sustained rhetorical attack on the concept of reform itself and on the manner in which it was being put forward by the government. The expression of such reservations by the most senior judges, setting and confirming a negative tone, was an encouragement to the Bar in its resistance to reform.

Whiteside spoke in December 1874 at a banquet given by the lord mayor of Dublin. He said that he spoke for the twelve common law judges, the 'twelve sentinels of the land', and that he trusted 'that the ancient twelve would still continue to administer the justice which, he believed and hoped, they had conscientiously done'.[138] (Since the 1874 Bill had envisaged that the number of common law judges would be reduced to ten the judicial opposition to reduction was very clear.) He expressed further dissent, this time from the Bench, in January 1876, deprecating any suggestion that the courts were over-manned, citing pressure of business, waiting lists and the difficulties in constituting courts of appeal or divisional courts.

> It was a part of the wise and paternal government under which they lived to consider all these matters and, if they chose, to change these tribunals, and he begged it to be understood that that the judges never offered any opposition to any wise and well-considered scheme for the amendment of the law … It would be presumption to obtrude opinion upon those charged with the important duty of resettling the judicature of the country. The notion

136 *ILT&SJ*, vol. 11, p. 84 (24 February 1877).
137 *ILT&SJ*, vol. 11, p. 264 (2 June 1877) and p. 291 (16 June 1877); section 61 of the 1877 Act.
138 *ILT&SJ*, vol. 8, p. 621 (5 December 1874).

> that the judges at any time had opposed any measure that was really intended for the better administration of justice was a monstrous fiction. [It was painful to hear suggestions] that the judges were in a sort of collusion with a sycophantic, intriguing and corrupt profession to preserve places for them, of which they were unworthy. He was of opinion that the last blow that could be struck at this country would be one which should break up and scatter a learned and educated profession and shake the confidence of the people in the administration of justice.[139]

He returned to those themes three weeks later at an inaugural banquet given by the lord mayor in the Mansion House, speaking of an independent judiciary as being essential to the well-being of the state, of his 'conviction that it ought to be maintained in its ancient dignity, authority and efficiency', and of the three common law courts having existed in Ireland for at least five hundred years. He referred to the report of the Royal Commission in 1863 as having been established with an intent to rectify and improve the judicial system, as they would 'touch up an old machine, after a certain time, varnish it or clean it'. The Commission had recommended no reduction in the number of superior court judges, and after such a review 'they were once more, it was thought, at rest; for certainly it was not to be supposed that they were to arrange and disarrange, to organize and disorganize, to weave at night and to unweave in the morning'. In 1874 he had been startled at provisions in the Bill then published:

> among other things it proposed to enact that a council might be appointed, which council might recommend to the Government the reduction of the judges and, if they thought fit, efface the old titles of the law courts and of the judges – titles that had existed for centuries. It occurred to him and to his brother judges of the Queen's Bench that the best thing they could do would be to address a respectful remonstrance on a certain clause of the bill to his Grace, who sat near him [the lord lieutenant, the duke of Abercorn] … and he thought it right to say that he believed that the most obnoxious clause in that bill had since been omitted (see p. 40 below), and he should not be at all surprised if it had been omitted owing to the influence of his Grace and of the lord chancellor,[140] who, he rejoiced to say, was equally inclined to maintain the ancient reputation of the judicial bench in this country. He wished it to be distinctly understood that the first court of criminal jurisdiction in this country was not a department of the British Treasury (hear hear, and cheers) and that they had no more authority over it than over the winds of heaven.[141]

139 *ILT&SJ*, vol. 10, pp 41–2 (22 January 1876).
140 J.T. Ball, lord chancellor of Ireland, 1875–80.
141 *ILT&SJ*, vol. 10, pp 89–91 (12 February 1876); *Irish Times*, 11 February 1876.

Whiteside's last public comments were made in the summer of 1876, when some correspondence with the Treasury was published by order of the House of Commons.[142] The Treasury had complained to him at the recent appointment of a clerk in the court of Queen's Bench, in light of existing overstaffing, saying that in connection with the impending court restructuring it 'may be found necessary to make some extensive modifications in the offices of the superior courts of law', and that if the office held by the person recently appointed were to be abolished he would not be considered as entitled to any compensation.[143] Whiteside responded vigorously, complaining at 'I, the chief justice of this kingdom, [being] called to account by Treasury officials, for the appointment, under the statute, of a petty clerk … You must excuse me for informing you that the court of Queen's Bench is not a department of the Treasury, and that the chief justice, who happens to be the first magistrate in this kingdom, is unaccustomed to receive admonitions as to how he is to fulfill his duty'. He added that as to

> the future designs of the Treasury upon the department of this and the other (still existing) superior courts of law I do not presume to offer an opinion. I have not the remotest conception of what your 'extensive modifications' may be. They will, as I collect from the tone of your communication, be worked without appeal to judicial authority, and without the guidance of judicial experience.

He referred to the Treasury's 'plans of legislation or, perhaps I should say, departmental demolition'. He concluded by objecting to such a threat 'to strip a humble but thoroughly respectable person of the rights which the existing statute gives him, and to disregard the judicial authority by which he was duly appointed. This and more in the same line may be accomplished, but it will be done against the existing law of the land and will be no less unjust in practice than revolutionary in principle'.[144]

This correspondence was published on foot of a query raised by Hugh Law MP at the behest of Whiteside, who had liaised with Edward Gibson QC, one of the MPs for Dublin University, telling him of his amazement at the Treasury's attitude, that his brethren of the Queen's Bench were furious about what they saw as its interference with the business of the court and that they thought the exchange should be publicised. They welcomed the interest in the subject of one MP, F.J. Cogan, a member for Co. Kildare, but thought 'that the correspondence might be more judiciously moved for by another – would Law do it, or any other suitable person?'[145]

142 Correspondence on the appointment of Mr Blackham (P.P. 1876 (332) lxi.351); *ILT&SJ*, vol. 10, p. 411 (15 July 1876).
143 W.H. Smith (chief secretary to the Treasury) to Whiteside, 18 May 1876.
144 Whiteside to Smith, 22 May 1876.
145 Whiteside to Gibson, 27 and 30 May 1876 (Ashbourne Papers, B.159/6&7).

That series of comments by Whiteside indicated, to put it no more strongly, a lack of enthusiasm for reform, as did observations expressing a generalized judicial discontent that were delivered by Morris, the chief justice of Common Pleas, at the next lord mayor's banquet early in 1877. His disposition, ordinarily unpredictable and volcanic according to one of his daughters,[146] may have been particularly poor at the time since it had just become clear that he had been passed over for appointment to succeed the recently deceased Whiteside as chief justice of Queen's Bench. Morris said that he did not know, indeed was entirely ignorant,

> in this transition period what might become of the survivors of the Irish bench … he was not aware – nor he believed was any other member of the Irish bench aware – what exactly was impending upon them at the present moment. If they were to be regarded – one would consider they should be somewhat taken into counsel, but they did not know what was before them – he presumed that nothing would be done which would interfere with the proper administration of justice. He believed the words used by the late chief justice Whiteside in this assembly twelve months ago had some effect at least in staying, if not postponing, that which he believed would not be conducive to the interests of the people.[147]

A few days later the Irish Judicature Bill was reintroduced in the House of Commons,[148] following the settlement of the wider issues over the House of Lords. In April Baron Dowse, seconded by Mr Justice Keogh, invited the benchers of King's Inns to declare by resolution that the delay in progressing the Bill was prejudicial to the administration of justice and that the reforms should be proceeded with 'or be at once definitively and finally abandoned'.[149] The initiative was taken as indicating Dowse's support for reform.[150] Consideration was postponed until May, when the benchers declined to resolve that the continued hesitancy was prejudicial, and the subject was dropped.[151] The Bill became law in August, to take effect on New Year's Day 1878, with little further controversy. An observation made by the *Dublin Evening Mail* in 1876 reflected accurately the spirit of grudging acceptance with which the Irish judiciary and legal profession contemplated unavoidable but minimal change in the judicial structure: 'The lust for change that has successfully raged in certain quarters in England has, we suppose, made some semblance of change in Ireland necessary and, so far as we can judge, lord chancellor Ball has satisfied that necessity without doing more mischief than could well be avoided'.[152]

146 Maud Wynne, *An Irishman and his family: Lord Morris and Killanin* (London, 1937), p. 36.
147 *ILT&SJ*, vol. 11, p. 65 (10 February 1877).
148 HC Deb, 3rd series, vol. 232, col. 241 (12 February 1877); *ILT&SJ*, vol. 11, p. 74 (17 February 1877).
149 Minutes of meeting of the benchers, 16 April 1877.
150 *Irish Times*, 26 May 1877.
151 Minutes of meeting of the benchers, 23 May 1877.

Commentaries and treatises on the new Act, and on the rules of court that were promptly drawn up by the judges and issued pursuant to section 61, were soon published (with precedents or forms of procedure) for the legal professional market, and these were updated at times to reflect new amendments or new consolidated versions of the rules. The commentaries emphasised that the books included tables of the corresponding English sections and rules,[153] and one stated that 'most of these [Irish] rules relating to general procedure are taken verbatim from the Rules of the Supreme Court in England'.[154] This reflected the section 61 requirement that in making rules of court regard should be had to the corresponding English provision, so that practice and procedure in the two countries should be harmonized, so far as might be practicable and convenient. One such commentary that was published in 1881 marked one of the first appearances in print of J.O. Wylie, later (1906–20) a judge of the High Court (as a judicial member of the Land Commission), in a co-editorial role. By 1895 he was publishing a commentary on the statute under his own name,[155] which was

> a new edition of the former textbook, popularly known as *Eiffe's Judicature Acts*, but which was really the joint compilation of that gentleman along with Mr Houston and Mr Wylie. The name of Mr Eiffe appears to have been given the place of honour in that volume as having been the only one of the three authors who was concerned in the compilation from start to finish. Messrs. Thom having secured the copyright on the death of Mr Eiffe acted very wisely in proceeding to retain the valuable service of one of the original authors – Mr Wylie.

His 1906 edition – with reference to new consolidated rules of court issued in 1905 – was the last such edition published before 1921. For many years after 1921 it was regarded as an authoritative guide to procedure in the court systems then established, north and south.[156]

152 As reported in *ILT&SJ*, vol. 10, p. 185 (25 March 1876).

153 E.g., L.S. Eiffe (assisted by A. Houston and J.O. Wylie), *The Judicature Acts (Ireland) 1877 and 1878 and Orders, Rules and Forms thereunder, copiously annotated* (Dublin and London, 1881); William Dwyer Ferguson LL.D. and Geo. Napier Ferguson BL, *A treatise on the Supreme Court of Judicature Act (Ireland) 1877, with Schedule of Rules, Orders of Court and Forms of Procedure and notes of cases* (Dublin, 1878); J.O. Wylie, *The Judicature Acts (Ireland) and Orders, Rules and Forms thereunder, copiously annotated* (Dublin, 1895); J.O. Wylie (1906) op. cit.

154 J.O. Wylie, *The Judicature Acts (Ireland) and Rules of the Supreme Court (Ireland) 1905, copiously annotated* (Dublin, 1906), p. 180.

155 *ILT&SJ*, vol. 29, p. 60 (2 February 1895).

156 'It is indeed remarkable that up to about 15 years ago there was little or nothing published dealing with civil procedure in the Superior Courts in this country. One had to survive with a dog-eared copy of the Rules of the Superior Courts, an ancient copy of the White Book [an annual directory of civil practice and procedure in England, which had a white cover] and by times Wylie's 'Judicature Acts' in order to navigate a passage for a piece of litigation.' (Mr Justice Peter Kelly, foreword to Delany & McGrath, *Civil procedure in the superior courts* (third edition, Dublin, 2012)).

CHAPTER TWO

Reforms and their implementation

THE IMPLEMENTATION OF THE 1877 Act in terms of court re-organisation and the fusion of law and equity had a less dramatic effect, and fewer practical consequences for the legal profession in Ireland, than the corresponding legislation was to produce in England. In itself, however, R.B. McDowell's reference to 1877 as 'the most revolutionary year in Irish legal history'[1] is well founded. The legal system in England had reflected a quite rigorous distinction between law and equity, not only in the workings of the profession but also in the locations of the courts, the law courts sitting in or around Westminster Hall in the Palace of Westminster and the courts of Chancery sitting at Lincoln's Inn, over a mile away to the east in the direction of St Paul's Cathedral and the City of London. A few years after the reforms enacted in 1873 had taken effect a long-drawn out project for the construction of new law courts in London came to fruition with the opening by the Queen in December 1882 of the new building in the Strand ('the greatest secular monument of the Gothic Revival in London after the Houses of Parliament'[2]), symbolizing the fusion of law and equity. 'Before the completion of the Royal Courts of Justice the necessary limitations imposed on human endurance by the laws of time and space ceaselessly operated so as to almost wholly divide the members of the Chancery Bar in London from common law practitioners at Westminster'.[3]

By contrast, in Ireland since 1796 the home of all the superior courts – what had been then literally the Four Courts of Chancery, King's Bench, Common Pleas and the Exchequer – had been a single handsome edifice on the Liffey. The building had grandeur, more especially after a thorough cleaning a century later; 'the transformation effected under the dome by a thorough scrubbing, and the hiding of the daily incrustations of years on the stone, was very desirable. The five statues around the hall, which were formerly eyesores, now grace the building, having been thoroughly cleaned. The interior of the hall has been painted'.[4] In 1905 electric lighting was installed.[5] In the 1850s permission had been given for some amenities in the yards of the building, with the setting up of stands for the shining of shoes and the sale of oysters, and subsequently for the sale of fruit and cake.[6]

1 R.B. McDowell, *The Irish administration, 1801–1914* (London, 1964), p. 111.
2 Simon Bradley and Nikolaus Pevsner, *The buildings of England, London 6: Westminster* (London, 2003), p. 311. The opening is noted in each volume of the law reports for 1882.
3 *Law Times*, vol. 79, p. 227 (25 July 1885).
4 *ILT&SJ*, vol. 30, p. 482 (31 October 1896).
5 *ILT&SJ*, vol. 39, p. 382 (11 November 1905).
6 C.P. Curran, 'Figures in the Hall' in *Record of the centenary of the charter of the Incorporated Law Society of Ireland, 1852–1952* (Dublin, 1953), p. 77 (reprinted in Caroline Costello (ed.), *The Four Courts: 200 years* (Dublin, 1996)).

The surroundings of the courts were rather less agreeable. The common law judges made representations to the government in 1868 about 'the pestilential condition of the Liffey', describing 'the daily stench which emanates from the bed of the river as not only oppressive and nauseous but dangerous to life',[7] lending support to a protest to the same effect that a couple of years previously had been made to the Dublin Corporation by residents of Lower Ormond Quay. In June 1870 it was reported that 'the stench from the river became so offensive that chief justice Monahan had to leave the court [of Common Pleas] and sit during the remainder of the day in the court of Chancery'.[8] The judges' complaint had some effect, as the chancellor of the Exchequer acknowledged,[9] since a couple of months later the Public Works Loan Commissioners were authorized by an amending statute to advance money to the Dublin Corporation to finance works 'necessary for the purification of the river Liffey and the completion of the main drainage of the city of Dublin'.[10] This was still an issue for the judges in 1875.[11] The river was the main outlet for waste water, and 'concern with the Liffey smell was increased by the contemporary belief that many diseases such as cholera were caused by the noxious effluvia arising from the smelly river or refuse heaps'.[12] The problem of inadequate mains drainage was not finally substantively addressed until the construction of a new treatment plant at the Pigeon House early in the twentieth century, a project that resulted in litigation between the contractor and the Corporation.[13] In the 1860s behind the court building, despite some recent site clearances, 'there still stretches a dreary amplitude of un-odoriferous and semi-ruinous looking thoroughfares'.[14] In the 1890s lurid reports were published of what had become the unsanitary and dilapidated condition of the Green Street courthouse, lord chief justice O'Brien being quoted as saying that it had been 'impossible to move or breathe in the court', the condition of which was an 'outrage upon civilization'.[15] This led to substantial repairs and restoration work in the 1890s, during which the criminal trials of the Commission of Oyer and Terminer were held in the Four Courts.

The nature of legal business in Ireland,[16] the smaller numbers at the Bar in Dublin and the proximity of the courts to each other (with the exception, in the

7 *ILT&SJ*, vol. 2, p. 333 (20 June 1868).
8 *ILT&SJ*, vol. 4, p. 452 (25 June 1870).
9 HC Deb, 3rd series, vol. 203, col. 1568 (4 August 1870).
10 Sanitary Act (Dublin) Amendment Act 1870 (33&34 Vict., c.106), s1.
11 *ILT&SJ*, vol. 9, p. 365 (17 July 1875).
12 Mary E. Daly, *Dublin, the deposed capital: a social and economic history, 1860–1914* (Cork, 1984), p. 250.
13 *Pearson v Dublin Corporation*, [1907] 2 IR 27, 82, 537. See p. 56 below.
14 *ILT&SJ*, vol. 2, p. 383 (11 July 1868).
15 HC Deb, 4th series, vol. 1, col. 880 (2 February 1892), vol. 17, col. 130 (5 September 1893).
16 John Atkinson QC, MP, attorney general in 1892 and between 1895 and 1905, 'used to say that Irish legal work consisted on the common law side of actions by absentee landlords to eject their tenants and on the Chancery side of suits by mortgagees to compel the absentees to pay their debts' (T.M. Healy, *Letters and leaders*, vol. 1, p. 29).

1850s, of the Encumbered Estates Court in Henrietta Street) had not given rise to the same degree of specialization of work as in London. This was remarked upon, in the context of the impending changes, by the *Irish Law Times* in 1871:

> In England the Common Law and Equity Bars form to all intents and purposes separate professions. The young barrister puts down his name in the law list as a special pleader, or Equity draftsman and conveyancer, as the case may be. Under the existing system this sub-division has its advantages, but it presents a serious although a temporary difficulty in the way of the successful fusion of Law and Equity. In Ireland, on the other hand, barristers, during the early years of their career at least, prepare themselves for and accept employment of every kind. The fee-book of an Irish junior would astonish some of our English brethren – sessions, circuit, bankruptcy, chancery, conveyancing, common law pleading, landed estates – all is fish that comes to his net.[17]

The paper refreshed that comment 23 years later, when reporting a comment from the *Law Times* that

> in Ireland it is not customary, as in England, to elect to practise in any particular division or court. A man of good position will hold briefs in all divisions in one day – now examining a witness at Nisi Prius, now hurrying off to oppose an important motion in the Queen's Bench, now rushing breathless into court to open a case before the vice chancellor ... This ubiquity of practice is rendered inevitable by the fact that fees at the Irish Bar are not sufficiently large to admit of counsel devoting themselves exclusively to any special branch.[18]

Lord MacDermott LCJ noted this comparative lack of specialization as still applicable in the 1950s, while expressing doubt as to whether it was the case that the fusion of law and equity had on that account gone further and deeper in Ireland than in England.[19] The inconvenience caused by 'the absence, in many cases, of all the counsel engaged and paid, and the almost universal practice of counsel attending to but one part of any case, and running off to some other case in another of the courts'[20] was the subject of complaint by the Law Society, and at times by judges when no counsel appeared for business specially fixed.[21]

Immediately after the coming into force of the 1877 Act Baron Dowse made reference to 'what used to be called Nisi Prius cases, but which are now to be styled

17 *ILT&SJ*, vol. 5, p. 195 (22 April 1871).
18 *ILT&SJ*, vol. 28, p. 354 (21 June 1894).
19 Lord MacDermott, 'Law and practice in Northern Ireland', *NILQ*, vol. 10 (1953), pp 47–77, at 76.
20 *Irish Jurist*, vol. 9, p. 18 (15 January 1857).
21 *ILT&SJ*, vol. 33 p. 166 (22 April 1899).

jury cases',[22] although the old nomenclature lingered for many years. The nature of such work before a jury where facts would be established by examination and cross-examination of witnesses, appears from a reference made in the *Irish Law Times* to Thomas Lopdell O'Shaughnessy (1850–1925), who was appointed recorder of Dublin in 1905 (and a judge of the new High Court of the Irish Free State in 1924). He was 'probably the best example we can give of a prosperous Nisi Prius advocate. He is quite of the old school of lawyer. Knowing not much law beyond the rudiments, and forgetting that if the time requires it, he rings the old familiar changes on justice and right and common sense or Common Law as happens to be convenient'.[23] A reviewer of R.R. Cherry's book on the Land Act 1903 contrasted its 'legal erudition' with the 'mere glamour of Nisi Prius vapourings'.[24]

Judges would have appreciated and been influenced by traditional courtroom advocacy, at which many of them would have excelled while at the Bar, but such oratory would have been primarily directed at the hearts and minds of members of a jury. In criminal trials the jury had a central role, a potentially controversial one where the trial had a political aspect or was connected with land agitation. In civil litigation the function of the jury remained important throughout the nineteenth century, although as an institution it was in a long-term decline.[25] Judges were generally more respectful about its function as a determining body for matters of fact than a comment made by Christian J in 1866 might suggest. He reproved counsel in a civil trial for addressing the court with 'hollow and plausible platitudes of the sort which commonly find favour with juries'.[26] A decade later Lawson J, in ordering a new trial in a case where Dowse J had withdrawn an issue from the jury (see p. 247), had said that 'in matters of the ordinary affairs of life and the conduct of men it is the province of the jury and the jury alone to decide upon the facts', that the jury are to be 'at liberty to draw inferences and act upon their own convictions, founded upon a knowledge of men and things', and that this is better done by the scrutiny 'not of a single judge, who may have little experience in the ways of the world, but of twelve plain men accustomed to deal with the ordinary transactions of life and to scan the motives and actions of men'.[27]

The practical effects of joining of law and equity, as a matter of jurisprudence, took some time to emerge. Important aspects of procedure in litigation remained under the control of individual judges, whose enthusiasm for or interest in implementation of reforms might vary. It was noted in December 1881 that oral evidence, previously confined to the common law courts, was now frequently given

22 *ILT&SJ*, vol. 12, p. 19 (12 January 1878).
23 *ILT&SJ*, vol. 28, p. 3 (6 January 1894).
24 *ILT&SJ*, vol. 40, p. 49 (17 February 1906).
25 Patrick Polden, 'The Courts of Law – practice and procedure' in *Oxford history of laws*, vol. 11, p. 595.
26 *The Irish Society v Tyrrell*, ICLR, vol. 16 (1866), 249, at 286.
27 *Purdon v Earl of Longford*, IR CL, vol. 11 (1877–8), 267, at 275, 277 and 291.

in the court of the master of the rolls (Sullivan).[28] Six months earlier Chatterton VC had directed evidence in a case to be given on affidavit, declining to order that the evidence of three named witnesses should be given orally in open court.[29] Fifteen years later Chatterton said, on hearing an application to transfer a case concerning a right of way to one of the common law courts or to arrange for a jury to sit while he heard the case himself, said that he would not hear the case, or any other case, with a jury.[30] Five years later a decision of his to transfer a case from his court to the King's Bench was set aside by the Court of Appeal, which considered that the action could more conveniently be tried in the Chancery division.[31]

In 1904 an order made by Chatterton refusing to order a trial by jury was reversed by the Court of Appeal, the decision of which was upheld by the House of Lords on a further appeal. Lord Davey said that 'I am not prepared to advise your lordships to overrule the unanimous opinion of three learned judges so experienced in these matters as the lord chancellor [Ashbourne], lord justice Walker and lord justice Holmes. They know more than I do about Irish juries and the best mode of trying an action in Ireland. It is not a question of law but of judicial discretion'.[32] The case had a political aspect in that the plaintiff, a substantial landowner, was seeking to restrain members of the United Irish League from conspiring against him.[33]

The 1877 Act provided for the amalgamation of almost all existing superior courts into a single Supreme Court of Judicature, consisting of a High Court (with various specified divisions) and a Court of Appeal. The English and Irish Acts both provided for their new High Courts to consist initially of five divisions, being Chancery, the three historic common law jurisdictions of King's [Queen's] Bench, Common Pleas and Exchequer, and lastly (in Ireland) Probate and Matrimonial, which was envisaged ultimately (under s34 of the 1877 Act) as being named Probate, Matrimonial and Admiralty. The corresponding division in England was named Probate, Divorce and Admiralty ('PDA'). The seemingly random nature of the elements of the last-named division in fact had the logic of deriving from the common root of all such subject matter in the civil law rather than common law. Reform of the County Courts was undertaken simultaneously with that of the superior courts by separate legislation, the County Officers and Courts (Ireland) Act 1877.[34] This was introduced in the House of Commons on the same day as the Judicature Bill, in February 1877, and became law on the same day in August. One major reform in that court was the higher professional standing of its judges, since any newly appointed judge could no longer continue also to practise as a barrister.

28 *ILT&SJ*, vol. 15, p. 622 (10 December 1881).
29 *Oswald v Skipton*, 15 ILTR 51 (1881).
30 *Arnold v Jameson*, *ILT&SJ*, vol. 30, p. 117 (14 March 1896).
31 *Secretary of State for War v Studdert* [1901] 1 IR 346.
32 *Lord de Freyne v Johnston*, 38 ILTR (1904), at 143.
33 *ILT&SJ*, vol. 38, p. 98 (27 February 1904).
34 40&41 Vict., c. 56.

The 1874 Bill had contemplated that the new High Court would comprise every existing court, each to be a part of one or other of its divisions, the merged courts to include the Landed Estates Court, the Admiralty Court, and the Bankruptcy Court. The Landed Estates Court was amalgamated by the 1877 Act with the Chancery division, its judges being given the appellation of 'land judges', but the admiralty and bankruptcy jurisdictions remained separate and outside the High Court until 1893 and 1897 respectively,[35] reasons being found why it would be inconvenient to include them in the initial overall scheme. The Act provided that they would remain separate for the duration of the holding of office of the existing judges, although appeals could be taken from each of them to the new Court of Appeal. The exclusion of bankruptcy business from the new High Court was consistent with the English legislation. The London Bankruptcy Court had been joined to the new High Court as a division in the English 1873 Act, was restored to independence by the amending 1875 Act and was joined to the High Court again by the Bankruptcy Act 1883.[36] The exclusion of the admiralty jurisdiction was taken to derive from the probate judge at the time (Warren) either being considered unsuitable, or having refused, to exercise also that jurisdiction.[37] The 1877 Act provided (s9) that the intended joining of the admiralty jurisdiction with that of probate and matrimonial division would take place upon the filling of the vacancy next arising in the probate court.

Initially the divisions on the common law side in the High Court broadly corresponded to the respective jurisdictions of the various abolished courts, which over the years had preserved elements of their original functional separation. The Queen's Bench alone had a general criminal jurisdiction, and was the forum for all business in the name of the Crown or of a public nature (other than Revenue matters, for which the court of Exchequer had jurisdiction) and in which decisions of lower courts of criminal jurisdiction and of public officers and bodies could be challenged, through the prerogative writs.[38] Historically, in order to bring a matter before a court it was necessary to obtain a writ from the King, as issued by the Chancery, summoning the defendant to appear. The more important writs for public business, some of which would now be comprised in the more modern concept of judicial review, were Quo Warranto, Certiorari, Habeas Corpus, Prohibition and Mandamus. The Common Pleas had a general original jurisdiction in cases between subject and subject,[39] thus relating more to matters of private law, and had recently been given a new jurisdiction in hearing election petitions, under

35 Sections 7, 8 and 9 of the 1877 Act. 'The [bankruptcy and admiralty judges] have, for the time, what may be called their judicial individuality preserved.' (*The Times*, as reported in *ILT&SJ*, vol. 10, p. 324 (3 June 1876)).

36 Supreme Court of Judicature Act 1873 (36&37 Vict., c.66) s16; Supreme Court of Judicature (1873) Amendment Act 1875 (38&39 Vict., c.77) s9; Bankruptcy Act 1883 (46&47 Vict., c.52), ss92 and 93.

37 Costello, op. cit., p. 219.

38 William Dwyer Ferguson and Geo. Napier Ferguson, op. cit., p. 39.

39 F.H. Newark, op. cit., p. 13.

the Parliamentary Elections Act 1868.[40] However, as is suggested by the reference in the recital to the Process and Practice (Ireland) Act 1850 to fictions being employed in the pleading of cases, in practical terms intending litigants and their legal advisers had considerable flexibility as to which court they might commence any actions in, and plaintiffs in effect could choose their forum.[41]

The first report of the Judicature Commission in England had recommended the retention of the identities of the existing historic courts as distinct divisions of the new consolidated court, to facilitate the transition from the old to the new system. Lord Selborne noted that it was clear 'that reasons of principle and practical convenience would not permanently require more than three divisions [common law, Chancery and PDA] ... But at the outset policy and sentiment, which recommended the other course, could not be disregarded'.[42]

Judges were assigned to these various divisions, as they had previously been to the separate courts, but after 1877 the distinctions between the judges were more fluid than the simple fact of such assignment might suggest, in addition to the fact that, when on assize, they represented or constituted the High Court as such, not any division thereof. A judge might sit whenever required in any Divisional Court, or in a different division from his own, and might be transferred from one division to another. Lawson J was transferred from one common law division to another (Common Pleas to the Queen's Bench) in 1882, and Barton J from the King's Bench division to Chancery in 1904, when Chatterton retired.[43] Murphy J was initially a member of the Common Pleas division, which was merged with the Queen's Bench division in 1887, and then moved to the Exchequer division, which itself was merged with the Queen's Bench in 1897. The land judges were 'bound from time to time to assist in the general business of the Chancery division ... if the state of business in connection with their particular jurisdiction shall permit'.[44] More generally, the 1897 Act provided that 'whenever in the opinion of the lord chancellor the amount or state of business in any division of the High Court renders it desirable he may by order under his hand assign any judge of the High Court to discharge or assist in the discharge of such business'.[45] This happened sufficiently rarely for it to be noteworthy. In July 1913 'during the absence of the judges on Circuit the master of the rolls has taken pressing motions in the King's Bench division'.[46] Any judge of the Court of Appeal could sit as a judge of the High

40 31&32 Vict., c.125.

41 It was sometimes said that 'If you have the law on your side but no merits bring your action in the Exchequer. If you have the merits but little or no law go to the Common Pleas; but if you have neither law nor merits go to the Queen's Bench, because there is no knowing what they may not do there' (Maud Wynne, *An Irishman and his family: Lord Morris and Killanin* (London, 1937), p. 139). The saying is attributed to Morris himself in the authorized biography of Sir Edward Carson, and there are variations, including ones by Lord Shandon and A.M. Sullivan KC.

42 Selborne, *Memorials*, op. cit., p. 300.

43 1877 Act, s34; Ball, vol. II, pp 368 and 381.

44 1877 Act, s7.

45 1897 Act, s9.

46 *ILT&SJ*, vol. 47, p. 192 (12 July 1913).

Court if this was found expedient, through pressure of business in the Chancery division or by reason of absence of a judge through illness in other divisions,[47] and, as appears below, such judges sat frequently as assize judges of the High Court.

In the two decades after 1877 the ancient jurisdictions and divisions thus originally preserved were set aside by amending legislation. The original five divisions of the High Court in Ireland became four in 1887 and by the end of 1897 the High Court consisted simply of two divisions, Chancery and Queen's [or King's] Bench (which now also incorporated what had been the separate probate, bankruptcy and admiralty jurisdictions), a structure that was maintained up to 1921. Thereafter the small number of judges in the court system of Northern Ireland initially precluded any such formal division and although one High Court judge was assigned to deal with Queen's Bench business and the other with Chancery business there was necessarily a frequent interchange of function,[48] and the new courts in the Irish Free State organized themselves similarly.[49] The 1877 Act had made no reference to any procedure for merger of divisions, so the exercise of consolidation of divisions took longer in Ireland than in England, where by January 1881 the High Court consisted of only three divisions, namely Chancery, Queen's Bench, and PDA.

The benefit of retention of status as heads of a court came to be enjoyed by the men who held the positions of head of the three common law courts which became divisions of the High Court. The chief justice of Queen's Bench, G.A.C. May (born in 1817), had been appointed in February 1877, the chief justice of Common Pleas, Michael Morris (born in 1826), had been appointed to that position twelve months earlier, in February 1876, and the chief baron of the Exchequer, Christopher Palles (born in 1831), had been appointed in February 1874.[50] In England, in contrast, the heads were older, in two cases much older, than their Irish counterparts, so less personal difficulty would have been anticipated in effecting a merger of divisions. The chief justice of Queen's Bench, Sir Alexander Cockburn, had been born in 1802 and appointed in 1859, the chief justice of Common Pleas, Lord Coleridge, had been born in 1820 and appointed in 1873 and the chief baron of the Exchequer, Sir Fitzroy Kelly, had been born in 1796 and appointed in 1866. On the death of Kelly in September 1880 and of Cockburn two months later the opportunity was taken in December that year, on the initiative of Selborne as lord chancellor and with the consent of the judiciary, to merge the three divisions into the Queen's Bench, Coleridge being appointed lord chief justice.

47 Section 55 of the 1877 Act.

48 A.G. Donaldson, *Some comparative aspects of Irish law* (Durham, NC and London, 1957), p. 20; F.H. Newark, op. cit., p. 28; Lord MacDermott, op. cit., p. 70.

49 *Irish Times*, 12 June 1924 (assignment of Chancery business to Murnaghan J and Meredith J).

50 May's predecessor, Whiteside, had been born in 1806 and appointed in 1866, Morris's predecessor, James Monahan, had been born in 1803 and appointed in 1850, resigning owing to ill-health in 1876 and the predecessor of Palles, David Pigot, who had been born in 1796 and appointed in 1846, died at the end of 1873.

That expedited procedure was not possible in Ireland. The 1874 Bill for Ireland had contained a section (35) that would have permitted an order to be made reducing the number of divisions of the High Court, on the basis of any recommendation to that effect made by a council of judges to be established by the statute. This procedure for possible amalgamation of divisions corresponded to the provision in the English legislation of 1873 that was invoked in 1880. However (after representations by the judges of the Queen's Bench, as described by chief justice Whiteside in 1876) this provision was subsequently removed from the Bill. The vehemence of the objection is not easily explained by the intended procedure for consolidation, which (as in England) could not have proceeded without a recommendation to that effect from the new judges' council, set up under section 70 of the 1877 Act. It would have been highly unlikely that the procedure for any rearrangement of the divisions could have been initiated without the consent of the heads of each of them.[51]

On the appointment of Morris to be lord chief justice of Ireland and head of the Queen's Bench division in January 1887[52] the vacancy thus created in the office of chief justice of the Common Pleas was not filled. The office itself was abolished a few months later in the course of a statutory exercise to pick up amendments that had first been proposed in an abortive Bill in 1885, to which the judges had objected. The Act passed in the summer of 1887 amended the 1877 Act by providing for (1) the 'rank and title' of the chief justice of Common Pleas to be abolished with immediate effect, (2) the fusing or amalgamation of the Common Pleas division with the Queen's Bench, and (3) the future merger of the Exchequer division with the Queen's Bench, and the abolition of the office of chief baron of the Exchequer, to take effect on the occasion of the next vacancy in that office arising after the passing of the Act.[53] A decade later, there still being no sign of such a vacancy, a further comprehensive amending Act was passed that amalgamated the Exchequer division with the Queen's Bench and provided that Palles would retain his title of chief baron and would rank in precedence after the lord chief justice.[54] It transpired that he would continue in office until July 1916, when he retired at the age of 84. His long judicial career of over 40 years, distinguished bearded appearance and continuing designation as chief baron may have contributed to giving an air of antiquity in the first decade of the century to an otherwise modernised judiciary.

The amending Act of 1897 provided for a consolidation of all divisions, not only as stated (1) the merger of the Exchequer division with the Queen's Bench, but also (2) the court of Bankruptcy to be consolidated with the High Court with all bankruptcy matters thereafter being assigned to the Queen's Bench division

51 See P. Polden, 'The Judicature Acts' in 'The Courts of Law' in *Oxford history of laws*, vol. 11, p. 763.
52 *ILT&SJ*, vol. 21, p. 42 (22 January 1887).
53 Supreme Court of Judicature (Ireland) Act 1887 (50&51 Vict., c.6), ss1 and 2.
54 1897 Act, s1.

(s3), with the linked appointment of Walter Boyd, the sole surviving judge of the bankruptcy court, who had been appointed in 1885, to be a judge of the Queen's Bench division, filling an existing vacancy there (s2). It also provided for (3) all admiralty matters to be assigned to the Queen's Bench division (s6), formalizing a transitional arrangement that had been in force since 1893, when the last judge of the admiralty court had died,[55] and (4) the probate and matrimonial division to be amalgamated with the Queen's Bench on the occurrence of the vacancy next ensuing in the office of judge of that division. As it happened, that vacancy occurred almost immediately after the Act had been passed in August 1897 since Mr Justice Warren died in the following month. Thus, in stages, and the policy having been adopted of waiting until the judges of particular courts had retired or died or when (as with Palles and Boyd) it was thought that consolidation could no longer practically be postponed, the various courts that had been in existence in the mid-1870s finally came to be consolidated into two divisions, with a court of appeal.

The 1897 Act provided, in response to pressure from Irish MPs, that savings or reductions in government expenditure resulting from the abolition of judicial positions should be re-applied 'to such Irish purposes as Parliament may from time to time decide'. The next Act which reduced the number of judges, the Supreme Court of Judicature (Ireland) Act 1907,[56] provided that the next two vacancies in the High Court would not be filled and, to similar effect as in 1897, that an amount 'equal to the reduction of charge upon the Consolidated Fund of the United Kingdom effected by this Act shall be placed at the disposal of the Local Government Board for Ireland for the purposes of the Labourers (Ireland) Acts'.[57] Each thus provided that an amount equal to the salaries of abolished judgeships would remain a charge on public funds and continue to be spent in Ireland.

The last reduction in the number of Irish superior court judges before 1921, as thus prescribed by the 1907 Act, took effect at the end of 1909 on the retirement of Mr Justice Johnson and Mr Justice Andrews. Immediately prior to the passing of the 1877 Act there had been 22 judgeships, these being the six Chancery judges (the lord chancellor, the lord justice of appeal, the master of the rolls, the vice-chancellor and two judges of the Landed Estates Court), four each in the common law courts of Queen's Bench, Common Pleas and Exchequer, two bankruptcy judges, a probate and matrimonial judge and an admiralty judge. At the start of 1910, a third of a century later, there were four Chancery judges (the lord chancellor, the master of the rolls, Mr Justice Barton and Mr Justice Ross, the land judge), eight in the King's Bench division (the lord chief justice and seven puisne

55 This was John Fitzhenry Townsend, who died at the age of 82 in February 1893. See Costello, op. cit., p. 215 and *ILT&SJ*, vol. 27, p. 67 (4 February 1893) and p. 77 (11 February 1893).

56 This was first proposed in 1904, in a Bill which was not enacted, the Judicature and Development Grant (Ireland) Bill (*ILT&SJ*, vol. 38, p. 179 (28 May 1904)).

57 Supreme Court of Judicature (Ireland) (No. 2) Act 1897 (60&61 Vict., c.66), s13, Supreme Court of Judicature (Ireland) Act 1907 (7 Edw. VII c.44), s3. The Labourers Acts made provision for housing.

judges) and two lords justices of appeal. The 1877 Act had provided that a retired holder of the office of lord chancellor, lord chief justice or master of the rolls could be appointed, if willing, to sit as an additional lord justice of appeal,[58] and John Naish and Samuel Walker so acted after their respective terms of office as lord chancellor. Judges sat from time to time as members of committees of the Privy Council in Ireland which exercised functions of a judicial character (see appendix 2 to this chapter).

The Irish Land Commission was established in 1881[59] and consisted of three commissioners, one of whom was a judicial commissioner, who 'shall forthwith on his appointment become an additional judge of the Supreme Court of Judicature of Ireland with the same rank, salary and tenure of office and right to retiring pension as if he had been appointed a puisne judge of one of the common law divisions of the High Court of Justice'. The work and functions of the judicial commissioner were primarily administrative but obviously involved the determination of points of law. A curious case in 1897/8, in which, in their separate spheres, the judicial commissioner (Edmund Bewley) and the land judge (Mr Justice Ross) arrived at inconsistent conclusions gave rise to some controversy, and was resolved by the Court of Appeal, in favour of the view taken by Bewley.[60] The office was held by some distinguished lawyers, including Richard E. Meredith, who was appointed to succeed Bewley and subsequently became master of the rolls (in 1906) and two members of the Wylie family, and the successive commissioners are referred to and included in the chronological order in this study. (Ball's magisterial *The judges in Ireland 1221–1921* listed these commissioners, saying that 'since 1881 the members of the high court of justice have been increased by the head of the Land Commission, but limitations of space and inadequate knowledge have prevented reference to those who have held that office'.[61]) The Land Act 1903 provided that Gerald Fitzgerald, a member of the Bar and former county court judge who was one of the non-judicial commissioners, should have all the jurisdiction and powers of a judicial commissioner.[62]

The new High Court established in 1877 comprised also the courts created by the historic procedure of judges being nominated by 'commission of assize or by any other commission, either general or specific'.[63] The Act provided that sittings of the judges under Commissions [in the sense of the judges having been issued with a formal commission to perform certain duties] of Assize, Oyer and Terminer ('to hear and determine') and Gaol Delivery (to try all prisoners in jail or who had been released on bail) would have all the powers, authority and jurisdiction of a judge of the High Court, and would be 'deemed to constitute a court of the High

58 1877 Act, s10.
59 Land Law (Ireland) Act (44&45 Vict., c.49), s41.
60 *Re Harkness' Estate* 31 ILTR (1897) 176, 32 ILTR (1898) 16 and 58(CA).
61 Ball, p. 324.
62 Irish Land Act 1903 (3 Edw. VII, c.37), s86(3).
63 1877 Act, ss21(8) and 32.

Court of Justice'.[64] These regular assizes took place three times a year, the spring and summer assizes in March and July and a winter assize, usually in December, under the Winter Assizes Act 1876.[65] The winter assizes dealt only with criminal trials, except in Belfast, where civil cases were also heard.[66] Other courts known as Special Commissions were occasionally, and not as a matter of annual routine, specifically constituted for the purpose of trying and determining criminal cases within particular districts, or for events giving rise to multiple or complex criminal charges, principally outbreaks of agrarian disorder and murder.[67] Any such court thus established for the trial of certain charges, such as the Maamtrasna murders in 1882, is to be distinguished from the Special Commission, more in the nature of a tribunal of inquiry, that was established by statute in 1888 'to inquire into the charges and allegations made [by the *Times*, of complicity in murder and outrage] against certain members of Parliament', most notably Parnell.[68]

The number of days on which the courts sat was significantly increased by rules of court made in 1877, updated from time to time thereafter. A statute enacted in 1831,[69] following a statute passed for England the previous year,[70] had prescribed the duration of the law terms as being 11–31 January (Hilary), 15 April–8 May (Easter), 22 May–12 June (Trinity) and 2–25 November (Michaelmas). The 1877 Act had provided that 'the division of the legal year into terms shall be abolished so far as relates to the administration of justice' (although the expression 'law term' continued generally to be used rather than the new official expression of 'sittings'), and that the vacations to be observed by the courts would be prescribed by rules as advised by the judges.[71] The Hilary term after 1877 ran from 11 January to 1 April, and the other terms were likewise extended: the Easter term became 15 April to 18 May, the Trinity term now ran from 1 June to 8 August, and the Michaelmas term now became 2 November to 21 December. By 1905 the Trinity term ended on 31 July and the lost week was transferred to the Michaelmas term, which now commenced on 25 October.[72] The pre-1877 rules had not contemplated sittings at the Four Courts during the assizes, so the increase in total sitting days of the courts before and after 1877 was not as dramatic as the variation in dates alone would suggest, but it was still substantial.

One proposed reform was the subject of strong objections when first mooted in 1874. This was a provision for a rearrangement or amalgamation of one or more of the circuits, by order of the Privy Council in Ireland. The members of the Home circuit, which had been established in 1796 and comprised counties Meath,

64 1877 Act, ss32 and 41.
65 39&40 Vict., ch.57. This was applied to Ireland by s63 of the 1877 Act.
66 *New Irish Jurist*, vol. 3, no. 38, p. 301 (31 July 1903); *ILT&SJ*, vol. 38, p. 208 (25 June 1904).
67 W.E. Vaughan, *Murder trials in Ireland, 1836–1914* (Dublin, 2009), p. 87.
68 Special Commission Act 1888 (51&52 Vict., c.35).
69 An Act to improve the administration of justice in Ireland 1831 (1&2 Will. 4, c.31).
70 Law Terms Act 1830 (11 Geo. 4 and 1 Will. 4, c.70).
71 1877 Act, ss29 and 30.
72 Rules of the Supreme Court 1905, Order LXIII (63).

Westmeath, Kildare, Carlow, Queen's County (Laois) and King's County (Offaly), led the opposition. As the smallest, most central and least busy of the circuits, it was universally seen as the most likely candidate for abolition and absorption into neighbouring circuits. Its members protested that a reduction would 'not be attended with any advantages, economical or otherwise, but would occasion the disturbance of vested interests [a more neutral expression then than now], much inconvenience to the public by protracting the time of holding the assizes and pecuniary loss to the members of the discontinued circuit or circuits'.[73] Notwithstanding such protests the relevant provision in the Bill ((s62, as enacted) was not altered. Information given to Parliament in 1884 indicated that the civil business of the Home circuit had collapsed, with only six trials by jury on the circuit in 1882, as compared with 43 in 1873 (and 55 in 1875). In the ten years between 1873 and 1882 the total number of such trials was quite stable (651 in 1873, 658 in 1882), but the proportion heard on all circuits, taken together, as compared with those heard in Dublin, had diminished from over half to less than a third.[74] In 1885 the Home circuit was abolished, and its counties were redistributed among the five continuing circuits (the Connaught, Leinster, Munster, North East and North West circuits).[75] The circuits to which former members of the Home circuit transferred generally acknowledged or permitted them to retain their existing seniority or standing.[76] A further reorganization of the circuits was made in 1922 (see p. 480).

The assize courts were generally or ordinarily constituted by the judges of the common law division(s), but it was conventional (and expressly contemplated by the 1877 Act) for the relevant document (Letters Patent) constituting each separate assize commission also to nominate, and appropriately authorize, any ordinary judge of the Court of Appeal, any judge of the Chancery division appointed after 1 January 1875 and one or more serjeants or Queen's counsel.[77] For example, the Letters Patent dated 7 June 1899 that were addressed to the lord chief justice, all other judges of the King's Bench division, the members of the Court of Appeal and the three serjeants authorized and commanded them, on such days and places as they might appoint, to hold the assizes on the North East circuit (the counties of Meath, Louth, Monaghan, Armagh, Down and Antrim and the towns of Drogheda and Carrickfergus).[78] The summer assizes in the North East in 1899 were in fact conducted by chief baron Palles and Andrews J, and this (and the dates of assize in each county) had been determined before the commission was issued.[79]

73 *ILT&SJ*, vol. 8, p. 261 (16 May 1874). See also the comments on the subject of W. O'Connor Morris, a county court judge and former member of the circuit, in his autobiographical *Memories and thoughts of life* (London, 1895), pp 158, 165.

74 Return of Civil Cases in Ireland 1873–82 (P.P. 1884 (283) xv.389).

75 *ILT&SJ*, vol. 19, p. 109 (28 February 1885).

76 George Hill Smith, *The North East Bar* (Belfast, 1910), p. 39.

77 1877 Act, s41.

78 PRONI, D4287/1.

79 *ILT&SJ*, vol. 33, p. 231 (3 June 1899).

The judges were entitled to elect on the basis of seniority which circuits they would travel, and the maintenance of this privilege was one of the matters on which they expressed concern in their comments on the 1876 version of the Judicature Bill.[80]

Early in his judicial career Palles remarked to Lord O'Hagan that he liked the work on the North East circuit, for the 'heavy substantial character of the rights involved in these cases'.[81] Three decades later the *Irish Law Times* remarked that

> unless some change is made to relieve the pressure the North East circuit will become more and more unpopular with the judges. Although we are now well on in April and the Easter vacation is half over the assizes in Belfast are not yet concluded. Mr Justice Andrews and Mr Justice Wright have already put in three weeks of solid work there, sitting every day (even on Good Friday, but not on Easter Monday) at 10.30a.m. and rising at 6 or 6.30p.m. The business has been proceeding all that time at high pressure, and the three weeks' work represents as much work as would be done in six weeks by two judges in Dublin during term.[82]

FitzGibbon LJ had referred some fifteen years earlier to 'four weeks of very incessant work [on the Munster circuit assizes] – averaging more than nine hours a day of actual sitting on the bench. I've had everything, from two murders to nearly five hundred Civil Bill appeals'.[83]

The spring and summer assizes on each circuit were conducted by two judges, out of the multiplicity of persons nominated and authorised by each commission, so each series of assizes being held simultaneously around the country on six circuits required a total of twelve judges (ten after 1885) to be available. The going out of the assizes in effect brought the conventional common law business of the Four Courts to a standstill and, particularly after 1909, also affected the conduct of other judicial business there. There were then only ten High Court judges (the judicial commissioner having the status of a High Court judge, but not sitting as such), eight of whom sat in the King's Bench division, and there was a greater and eventually in effect a permanent reliance on the members of the Court of Appeal and/or a Chancery judge to go out on circuit.

In January 1912 and March 1914 Mr Justice Ross, the land judge and hence a member of the Chancery division, went on circuit, the first time owing to two of the King's Bench judges being unwell and unavailable, the second time owing to a vacancy in that division not having been filled.[84] If members of the Court of Appeal were required to go on circuit, to make up the numbers, that was also likely to suspend the business of that court. In 1896 FitzGibbon LJ had sat on the

80 *ILT&SJ*, vol. 10, pp 309–11 (27 May 1876).
81 Palles to O'Hagan, 28 October 1874 (Teeling Papers (NLI), MS 17872).
82 *ILT&SJ*, vol. 41, p. 93 (6 April 1907).
83 FitzGibbon to Lord Randolph Churchill, 3 April 1892 (LRC Papers, MS Add. 9248, 3897).
84 *Law Times*, vol. 132, p. 304 (27 January 1912) and vol. 136, p. 494 (7 March 1914).

summer assize in Belfast, one of eight occasions on which he attended the assizes in Belfast between 1880 and 1906,[85] and in March 1899 Walker LJ had been an assize judge on the Munster circuit.[86] In March 1898 the Court of Appeal was unable to sit. The lord chancellor was attending the cabinet in London, FitzGibbon was travelling in Egypt for the benefit of his health, lord chief justice O'Brien was recuperating from an injury on the hunting field, and the two other lords justices of appeal, Walker and Holmes, were sitting on the spring assizes.[87] Nor did the court sit in March 1901, since FitzGibbon and Holmes were out on circuit and Lord Ashbourne was at Westminster.[88] In 1905 'as usual, owing to the reduction in the number of King's Bench judges, two of the lords justices must do duty as assize judges'.[89]

The Bar Council opposed a proposal in 1904 – which did not proceed then but was in substance enacted in 1907 – for a further reduction in the number of judges.[90] It had a general view that the reforms of 1877, a quarter of a century before, had been misconceived and objectionable, but added that the Court of Appeal would be entirely closed during the twice yearly periods of the circuits (assizes), since if the retired lord chancellor (Samuel Walker, who as it happened would be reappointed to that office in 1906) ceased to give his services as an additional lord justice of appeal the two standing lords justices would have to go on circuit and a court of appeal could not be constituted. William Moore QC, MP made the same point in the Parliamentary debate on the 1907 legislation, asserting that due to the absence of appeal judges on circuit the work of the Court of Appeal was effectively paralysed at those times.[91]

In July 1911 the judiciary added its objections to this disruption of the work of the Court of Appeal. The *Law Times* noted that

> some strong comments were made by the master of the rolls and the chief baron in the Court of Appeal in the case of *Oswald v Farrell* with reference to the present state of business in that court. Owing to the way in which the number of judges in Ireland has been reduced it is necessary that the two lords justices of appeal should go on circuit. The practical result of that is that no appeal can be heard in the Court of Appeal during the months of March and July. With reference to the latter month the case of appellants is particularly hard as the Long Vacation intervenes before a full court can be formed.

85 George Hill Smith, *A sketch of the Supreme Court of Judicature of Northern Ireland* (Belfast, 1926), appendix.
86 *Leatham v Craig and others*, [1899] 2 I.R. 667; *ILT&SJ*, vol. 33, p. 80 (18 February 1899).
87 *Law Times*, vol. 104, p. 425 (12 March 1898).
88 *Law Times*, vol. 110, p. 443 (16 March 1901).
89 *Law Times*, vol.118, p. 360 (18 February 1905).
90 Judicature and Development Grant (Ireland) Bill 1904 (*ILT&SJ*, vol. 38, p. 179 (28 May 1904)).
91 HC Deb, 4th series, vol. 180, col. 481 (8 August 1907).

The appeal in question was ripe for hearing on 27 July but it was impossible to have it heard before lord justice Holmes and lord justice Cherry had gone out on circuit. The master of the rolls, with the chief baron, remarked that the actions of the authorities, in not providing adequate personnel for the court, had deprived a litigant of the opportunity of having his appeal heard in the month of July.[92]

The naming of the serjeants in the commissions of assize was not a mere formality. By reason of illness a number of judges were unable to travel to assizes for years in the 1850s, and 'the practice of sending barristers on circuit in place of the regular judges, which has of late years become the invariable rule, is regarded with a feeling the reverse of satisfactory'.[93] A serjeant sat as an assize judge on four occasions in the second decade of the twentieth century.[94] When Serjeant Moriarty sat on assize in 1912 it was noted that this was the first time for almost thirty years that a member of the Bar named in a commission of assize had so sat, and 'it is only the older generation of lawyers who remember the days when Serjeants Armstrong, Robinson and Sherlock frequently went Circuit as commissioners of assize'.[95] In 1876 a Parliamentary question was asked about the propriety of one of those men, Serjeant Richard Armstrong, being one of the commissioners of assize, in light of his having been found guilty (as was Francis Macdonogh QC) of corrupt practices (bribery of voters) at the general election in Sligo in 1865. This had led in 1870 to the disfranchisement of the borough, so that it could no longer return a member to serve in Parliament.[96] The government's response was in effect to say that the past was the past, that Mr Armstrong had been named in the commission for a number of years since that adverse finding and that he was not considered to be disqualified to discharge the duties of the office.[97] The other two serjeants at the time were members of Parliament and hence could not properly have performed any judicial function. Armstrong sat as an assize judge in Tullamore that summer,[98] and also in Kildare, where he dealt robustly with a litigant in person (a clergyman), telling him that 'I have given my decision. If you doubt it, there is the whole Bar to consult. This is the inconvenience of gentleman who do not understand the subject at all making themselves lawyers'.[99] Armstrong sat again on circuit in June 1877.[100] A Queen's Counsel, James Robinson was named to sit as an assize judge earlier that year, and in some subsequent years.[101] In 1918, when (unsuccessfully) canvassing the Unionist leader, Andrew Bonar Law, for appointment to a vacancy in the High Court, Charles L. Matheson KC referred

92 *Law Times*, vol. 131, p. 338 (12 August 1911).
93 *Law Times*, vol. 25, p. 93 (26 May 1855).
94 A.R. Hart, *A history of the King's Serjeants at law in Ireland* (Dublin, 2000), p. 121.
95 *ILT&SJ*, vol. 46, p. 66 (16 March 1912).
96 An Act to disfranchise the Boroughs of Sligo and Cashel 1870 (33&34 Vict., c.38).
97 HC Deb, 3rd series, vol. 230, col. 1176 (10 July 1876)]; *ILT&SJ*, vol. 10, pp 411–12 (15 July 1876).
98 Michael Byrne, *Legal Offaly* (Tullamore, 2008), p. 109.
99 *ILT&SJ*, vol. 10, p. 447 (5 August 1876).
100 *ILT&SJ*, vol. 11, p. 272 (2 June 1877).
101 *ILT&SJ*, vol. 11, p. 89 (24 February 1877); vol. 12, p. 364 (13 July 1878); vol. 13, p. 120 (1 March 1879).

to the fact that as a serjeant he had 'twice gone as judge of assize – the last time taking the place of chief justice Campbell, and I may refer to my colleague Mr Justice Ross as to the highly satisfactory manner in which I discharged the duties of that high position'.[102]

Much of the time of the High Court judges, certainly on the common law side, was thus occupied year by year in sitting not in their division(s) as such in the Four Courts but in courthouses in county towns throughout the country, hearing civil appeals and presiding over trials of serious criminal cases that were outside the jurisdiction either of the magistrates or of the Quarter Sessions sittings of the County Courts. In Dublin these Commissions of Oyer and Terminer and Gaol Delivery sat more frequently and had capacity to sit outside the usual law terms, pursuant to an early eighteenth century statute, the 'Act for speedy trial of criminals in the county of the city of Dublin and county of Dublin'.[103] The construction of the Green Street courthouse, where these sittings were held, was authorised by statute at the end of the 1790s.[104] The civil business of the assizes consisted primarily of appeals from decisions of the County Courts, under a historic jurisdiction dating back to 1796.[105] The judges of assize also had the function, prior to the establishment of county councils in 1898, of approving the expenditure proposals (known as presentments) of the grand jury of each county for public works, such as roads and bridges, and for certain local institutions, such as asylums and infirmaries.[106] The assizes in England did not hear civil litigation, and were regarded as 'ancient itinerant criminal tribunals'.[107]

These Royal Commissions had been issued for centuries past, term by term and year by year, authorizing the judges and others named in the commissions (in effect, those of them who went on a particular circuit) to try the prisoners presented for trial in each county in which the assize was to be held and, in Ireland, also to hear civil appeals. The model of a stately progress on set dates from one assize town or city to another co-existed with the frequent reality of inefficient procedures and a hurried and stretched conduct of business.[108] Their historical procedural basis was refreshed and maintained into the twentieth century, and it

102 Matheson to Bonar Law, 18 June 1918 (Bonar Law Papers (Parliamentary Archives), 83/4/14).
103 3 Geo. II, c.15 (1729).
104 An Act for establishing the New Courts of Justice and New Session House (35 Geo. III, c.25 (1797)). The Central Criminal Court for London and its suburbs – known by the street in which it was located, the Old Bailey – had likewise been established in the 1830s, under an Act for establishing a new court for the trial of offences committed in the Metropolis and Parts Adjoining (4&5 Wm. IV, c.36 (1834)).
105 An Act for the better and more convenient administration of justice, and for the recovery of small debts in a summary way, at the sessions of the peace of the several counties at large within this kingdom except the county of Dublin 1796 (36 Geo. III, c.25); An Act to consolidate and amend the laws relating to Civil Bills and the Courts of Quarter Sessions in Ireland 1851 (14&15 Vict., c.57, s126); County Officers and Courts (Ireland) Act 1877 (40&41 Vict., c.56, s55).
106 Ronan Keane, *The law of local government in the Republic of Ireland* (Dublin, 1982), p. 2.
107 C.S. Kenny, *Outlines of criminal law* (11th edition, Cambridge, 1922), p. 423.
108 *Law Times*, vol. 38, p. 190 (7 February 1863).

was continued in Northern Ireland after 1921. The ceremonial for assizes included a military escort and guard for the judges. This was not provided at the spring assizes in Cork in 1897, giving rise to a complaint in open court by the judges sitting on that assize (chief baron Palles and William O'Brien) and questions and a debate in both houses of Parliament, the debate in the House of Lords being initiated by Lord Morris. Palles said that,

> he thought it a very small matter indeed, but he was bound not to allow any privilege that belonged to the judge of assize to be lost by any omission on his part to call attention to any dereliction of that duty. To the judges personally the fact of there being a guard at their lodgings was a matter of no importance whatsoever; but it was a matter of some importance to the administration of justice and to her Majesty's Commission that everything that ancient usage had ordained in reference to their proceedings should be observed until altered by Act of Parliament.[109]

A considerable degree of ceremonial was observed for the opening of the Easter law term sittings at the Four Courts. A levee (reception) was held that morning by the lord chancellor at his residence, attended by the Bar, and traditionally the lord chief justice and the heads of the other courts or (after 1877) divisions of the High Court also held receptions at their respective residences. (The chief baron's levee at his residence, 28 Fitzwilliam Place, came to an end in 1897, when he ceased to be the head of a division of the High Court.)[110] The judges, if they were not already there, then assembled at the lord chancellor's residence and travelled in procession to the Four Courts.[111]

> The lord chancellor's carriage stopped at the front entrance and, preceded by the two tipstaves and his mace bearer and followed by his train bearer and purse bearer, the lord chancellor entered the [Round] Hall and passing upon a red carpet took his place opposite the entrance on a scarlet carpet under the clock, his tipstaves and attendants lining up at the side. The other judges then alighted from their carriages and in order of precedence passed before the lord chancellor and remained at either side until the lord chancellor turned and headed the procession in the same order to the Benchers' Chamber at the rear of the building.[112]

In later years the carriage procession was ended and the preliminary reception was held in the Benchers' Chamber, from which a procession to the Round Hall took

109 HC Deb, 4th series, vol. 47, cols. 1190–91 (23 March 1897); HL Deb, 4th series, vol. 47, cols. 1286–93 (25 March 1897); *ILT&SJ*, vol. 31, p. 137 (27 March 1897).

110 *Law Times*, vol. 115, p. 508 (10 October 1903).

111 *Law Times*, vol. 90, p. 444 (18 April 1891). See also *ILT&SJ*, vol. 28, p. 203 (21 April 1894) and vol. 33, p. 166 (22 April 1899).

112 C.P. Curran, op. cit., p. 77.

place. In 1919, as in earlier years, 'the lord chancellor and the other judges in their official robes made a goodly show, which attracted a large crowd of interested spectators'.[113]

The Chancery judges had train bearers for their robes, a position which was almost literally a sinecure and represented an opportunity for minor patronage, often within the family, paying £100 a year. One such functionary, Raymond F. Brooke, was appointed in 1904 by Dunbar Plunket Barton, a cousin of his mother, and he subsequently gave a cheerful account of his exiguous performance of even the nominal duties of the office for a dozen years from the age of 19.[114] He appreciated the income, however, since his salary at the time as a junior clerk in an insurance office was £45. A contemporary of Brooke, Richard E. Meredith, was the train bearer to his father, the master of the rolls.[115] During the Great War (1914–18) a Treasury official queried the need for appointing a new train bearer to fill a vacancy:

> I pointed out that during the war there were no ceremonial occasions ... To this the judge replied that he had already appointed his son, aged 16, to the post, that it was an understood thing that this should be done when a judge had a son of the right age, and that the money should be spent on his education at Trinity College. He regretted therefore that the appointment must stand. However, either he or his son thought better of it, and I received a letter in a round schoolboyish hand, offering to waive the salary for the duration of the war, on the distinct understanding that it should revive thereafter.[116]

A more substantive legal appointment that could be given by a judge to a young member of the Bar was that of being a circuit registrar for assizes. A description of the office in the middle of the twentieth century that was given by Lord MacDermott would have changed little since the previous century:

> each assize judge was (and still is) entitled to appoint a registrar who travels with him, draws orders, helps with hospitality and makes himself generally useful. These appointments are unrestricted in choice and constitute the final patronage of Her Majesty's judges ... Those appointed are paid a lump sum for their services which still remains the equivalent of £200 Irish per circuit. Nowadays the appointees are usually drawn from the [younger members] of the Junior Bar, and acting as a judge's registrar is still a valuable experience. The novice so appointed is not overworked but he can learn much.[117]

113 *ILT&SJ*, vol. 53, p. 100 (26 April 1919). See also vol. 55, p. 95 (9 April 1921).
114 Raymond F. Brooke, *The brimming river* (Dublin, 1961), pp 159, 162–4.
115 Thom's Directory 1908.
116 Maurice Headlam, *Irish reminiscences* (London, 1947), p. 68.
117 John Clarke MacDermott (Lord MacDermott), *An enriching life* (Belfast, 1979), pp 156–7.

O'Connor LJ in making his claim for compensation for loss of office in 1924 (see pp 429 and 491) said he would no longer have 'a position in his patronage which was of some family advantage – his circuit registrarship worth over £300 a year, this position was held by his son, who is a young barrister'.[118]

The protests in Ireland against any reduction in the number of judges in the 1870s had conceded or acknowledged some uneasiness at the levels of business in the courts. The first report in 1863 of the Royal Commission inquiring into the superior courts of common law, and the courts of Chancery of England and Ireland, had included a conclusion, often quoted between 1874 and 1877 by opponents of reform, 'that it is not expedient to reduce the number of judges in the courts of Queen's Bench, Common Pleas and Exchequer in Ireland'.[119] Less often cited was the Commissioners' observation that 'it is true that the common law courts would be able, without any increase in their staff, to dispose of a larger amount of business than at present devolves upon them'. The committee of the Bar appointed to consider the 1874 Bill reported that 'the disproportion of judicial strength to judicial business has hitherto been alleged to exist only in the court of Common Pleas, the probate and matrimonial court and the admiralty court. It has never been suggested that the judges of the Queen's Bench and Exchequer have not been fully occupied'.[120]

At the time of the controversy over chief justice Lefroy's capacity in the spring of 1866 it was observed that

> the common law business is so very limited that the illness or old age of even two or three judges would hardly inconvenience suitors to any appreciable extent, except perhaps the assizes, when an able-bodied judicial deputy has sometimes to be procured. It is no uncommon thing for the judges of a given court to sit at eleven o'clock in term time and to rise soon after one o'clock. The true conclusion to be drawn from the admitted facts is not that a retirement should be enforced so as to create a vacancy for one of the many expectant lawyers now in Parliament but that, on the contrary, the judicial staff should be reduced.[121]

In 1873 a number of the judges objected to a proposal to require them to assist in the work of the Landed Estates Court, to facilitate the intended abolition of a judgeship in that court which was currently vacant.[122] The judges potentially affected included the master of the rolls and the vice-chancellor, and they wrote to the chief secretary for Ireland to say that these provisions, on which they had not

118 Claim of Rt. Hon. James O'Connor for compensation for loss of office, 25 June 1924 (T 164/105/9 (TNAUK)).
119 *ILT&SJ*, vol. 8, p. 32 (17 January 1874).
120 *ILT&SJ*, vol. 8, p. 299 (6 June 1874).
121 *Law Times*, vol. 41, p. 407 (21 April 1866).
122 Landed Estates Court (Ireland) Bill 1873 (P.P. 1873 (182) ii.265); ILT&SJ, vol. 7, p. 83 (1 February 1873) and p. 279 (31 May 1873).

been previously consulted, were 'highly unreasonable … [and] they altogether object to be transferred to discharge the business of the Landed Estates Court'. This would 'seriously distract and interfere with their own duties', and require them to discharge business 'of a most peculiar and special character, which the judges are for the most part entirely unused to'. They expressed the hope, which was fulfilled by events, since the Bill did not become law, that no further steps would be taken in the matter.[123]

In the 1870s and afterwards the advocates of economy in the re-organisation of the superior courts in Ireland found much supportive material in replies given in the House of Commons to Parliamentary questions put down by a Scottish MP. In campaigning for 'Justice for Scotland', he asked regularly about the comparative total expenditure on the judicial systems in Scotland, England and Ireland. The replies to these brought out that the Scottish system had the lowest funding or that, put another way, it was the most economical, and that the Irish system in terms of numbers of judges (and, by extension, officials) by reference to population, was the most expensive. In 1873 and 1876 the aggregate of the salaries of the Irish superior court judges was almost twice the amount payable to a smaller number of Scottish judges.[124] The duke of Abercorn, lord lieutenant of Ireland, was informed early in 1876 that 'the Irish Bench and Bar are very much better off than the Scotch'.[125] In 1885 the chancellor of the Exchequer told the House of Commons that 'the salary list of the judicial bench in Ireland was now more than half that of the English bench, although the population was little over one sixth, and nearly twice that of the Scotch bench with less than a third more population'.[126] In 1890 a Scottish MP could again refer to the 'extravagant expenditure' on an 'overgrown' judiciary in Ireland.[127] By then the cost in Ireland had been reduced so as to exceed the Scottish cost by a smaller margin, less than 50 per cent. It was said that if a wider comparison were made, by taking the county court system in each country also into account, there would be virtually no difference at all,[128] as the Bar Council maintained in 1904.[129] In 1908 the public funding of all courts in Ireland, from the superior courts to those of the magistrates, amounted to £368,742, whereas the corresponding government expenditure in Scotland on law and justice was £202,608.[130] The higher expenditure reflected the aggregate salaries of a greater number of superior court judges, in turn pointing to a proportionately higher number of court officials. One element of the debate on reform up to 1877 (and subsequently) focused on

123 Sullivan M.R. to Lord Hartington, chief secretary for Ireland, 21 June 1873 (Correspondence re Landed Estates Court Bill (P.P. 1873 (277) liv.389)); *ILT&SJ*, vol. 7, p. 361 (12 July 1873).
124 *ILT&SJ*, vol. 8, p. 2 (3 January 1874), vol. 10, p. 311 (27 May 1876).
125 J.J. Hall to Abercorn, 8 March 1876 (Abercorn Papers (PRONI), D623/A/321/19).
126 HC Deb, 3rd series, vol. 295, col. 102 (5 March 1885). *ILT&SJ*, vol. 19, p. 125 (7 March 1885).
127 HC Deb, 3rd series, vol. 349, cols. 723–4 (8 December 1890).
128 *ILT&SJ*, vol. 34, p. 184 (5 April 1890).
129 *ILT&SJ*, vol. 38, pp 208–9 (25 June 1904).
130 HC Deb, 4th series, vol. 186, cols.1641–2 (26 March 1908).

protecting or respecting the position of existing such officials. Morris complained to Ashbourne in 1887 about the difficulties in amalgamating court offices and reforming the work of clerks.[131]

Alvin Jackson has noted that an element in Scots patriotism in the nineteenth century was the view that the union [United Kingdom] was skewed in the interests of the Irish.[132] The population of Scotland was much smaller than that of Ireland at the start of that century, but subsequently increased and had become the larger by the start of the twentieth century. There were 105 Irish MPs from 1832 onwards (103 after 1870), a greater representation at Westminster than Scotland had – 53 MPs from 1832, 60 after 1868 and 72 after 1885.

While most judicial vacancies were filled very promptly, and in some cases a resignation was arranged with a view to an immediate appointment being made, significant periods of time occasionally elapsed between a vacancy arising and it being filled, particularly in the 1880s and 1890s when reduction of the judiciary was in the air. Over two years passed from the death of Baron Dowse in the spring of 1890 until a new appointment was made, since the position was being held open for the attorney general, Madden, and a similar period elapsed after the death of Mr Justice Harrison in October 1895, in light of the intention, eventually implemented by the 1897 Act, to merge the probate division with the Queen's Bench.[133] The fact that the judicial system could cope with the absence of judges through illness, or with extended periods of time when a vacancy on the bench was left unfilled, was taken to indicate a level of slack in court business. In January 1876 the *Times* remarked that the resignation of chief justice Monahan of the Common Pleas 'raises once more, and in a very pointed way, the question of whether the overmanning of the Irish bench is to be a permanent form of dealing with Irish patronage', saying that if a new appointment was made it would be because 'the number of judicial places must be rigorously maintained [rather] than because the work could not be done with fewer judges. For a year and a half chief justice Monahan has altogether withdrawn from his judicial duties, and his resignation will practically make no change in the judicial force available for the dispatch of legal business'.[134] Lord chief justice O'Brien was in effect unable to sit as a judge for a year or more before his retirement in the autumn of 1913, and reports of sustained ill-health preceded the retirement of a number of judges (including Hughes in 1866, May in 1887, Monroe in 1896 and Palles in 1916). There was no retiring age applicable to judges at the time.[135] The prime minister, Asquith, told one applicant for appointment to the vacancy created by the retirement of Palles

131 Morris to Ashbourne, 21 January 1887 (Ashbourne Papers, B77/4 and 5).

132 Alvin Jackson, *The two unions: Ireland, Scotland and the survival of the United Kingdom, 1707–2007* (Oxford, 2012), p. 137.

133 HC Deb, 4th series, vol. 50, cols. 1108–9 (5 July 1897); 1897 Act, s2(1).

134 As reported in *ILT&SJ*, vol. 10, p. 42 (22 January 1876).

135 A retiring age of 72 for judges of the superior courts was introduced in the Irish Free State in 1924 (Courts of Justice Act 1924, s24), and a retiring age of 75 for such judges in Northern Ireland in 1959 (Judicial Pensions Act 1959, s2/first schedule).

that the state of judicial business in Ireland had for some time past rendered continued employment of the full number of puisne judges unjustifiable, and that the government did not intend to fill the vacancy.[136]

An impassioned criticism of the Irish judicial establishment was made by Gladstone in 1893, in defending the provisions of the Home Rule Bill for the future appointment of judges. In 1874, at the end of his first period in office, he had been very reluctant to fill a vacancy in the court of Exchequer, succumbing to pressure to approve the appointment of Palles only in the last days before he resigned. Now he spoke of the judiciary as an 'astonishing excrescence, this monstrous overgrowth, which is totally indefensible', and said also that

> the numbers of judges in Ireland are, perhaps, the greatest scandal in Europe. I do not believe that in any country we can find anything approaching to the profligate extravagance of the Irish judiciary. The Irish judicial establishments are entirely the outgrowth of the Union and stand among the judicial establishments of Europe very much as the old Irish Church stood among the churches of Europe. It was particularly distinguished from them for the same kind of disproportion between pay and work.[137]

A major constraint on the efficiency of use of judicial resources was the ancient practice of the business in the common law courts being heard by two or more judges sitting together. This long-established concept was preserved by the 1877 Act. In Chancery each case and its preliminary and procedural aspects was heard and determined by a single judge, with no provision for a jury. In contrast, historically each of the three common law courts had sat 'en banc', with all the four judges (three up to 1784) sitting together. The possibility or prospect of modifying that practice was raised by the attorney general, Dr Ball, who when introducing the 1874 Bill in the House of Commons said that 'perhaps the judicial strength might be economized by having motions heard by two instead of four judges'.[138] The *Irish Law Times* had said three years earlier that 'apart from usage, there is no reason why four judges should preside in a common law court and a single judge over a court of equity'.[139]

Section 45 of the 1877 Act provided that 'such causes and matters which are not proper to be heard by a single judge shall be heard by Divisional courts of the said High Court of Justice … A Divisional Court shall be constituted by two or more judges thereof'. Section 46 provided that subject to any rules of court[140] all business belonging to the common law division(s) of the High Court which

136 Asquith to James O'Connor, 22 June 1916 (Asquith Papers (Bodleian Library, Oxford), MS 45:9).
137 HC Deb, 4th series, vol. 12, col. 266 (5 June 1893).
138 HC Deb, 4th series, vol. 220, col. 1265 (7 July 1874).
139 *ILT&SJ*, vol. 5, p. 195 (22 April 1871).
140 No such rules had been made between 1877 and 1906 (see Wylie, *The Judicature Acts (Ireland) and Rules of the Supreme Court (Ireland) 1905, copiously annotated* (Dublin, 1906), pp 109–10).

'according to the practice now existing in the superior courts of common law in Ireland, would have been proper to be transacted or disposed of by the court sitting in banco if this Act had not been passed, may be transacted and disposed of by Divisional courts'.

The Irish judicial system preserved the en banc concept (under its new guise of a Divisional court) much longer than in England. Sections 45 and 46 of the 1877 Act were drawn from sections 40 and 41 of the corresponding English Act of 1873, but although those latter sections had been repealed or amended quite substantially in 1876 no such changes were made to the Irish Bill, as finally enacted the following year. The Appellate Jurisdiction Act 1876 provided for England that 'every action and proceeding in the High Court shall, so far as is practicable and convenient, be heard, determined and disposed of before a single judge', with provision for any Divisional court to be constituted of two judges and no more, unless the president of the relevant division of the High Court should direct otherwise.[141] Sections 40 and 41 and other relevant sections of the 1873 Act were repealed accordingly, to the extent that they were inconsistent with this new provision.

Lastly in this context, section 51 of the 1877 Act provided that in the common law division(s) of the High Court certain business, including every motion for a new trial of any cause or matter on which a verdict had been found by a jury or by a judge without a jury, or a motion to reduce damages, was to be heard before a Divisional court. A Divisional court thus served both as an initial court to which an appeal of some nature could be taken (under section 51) and as a substitute for, or a new form of, sitting en banc (under sections 45 and 46). There was no provision in the English Judicature Acts corresponding to section 51,[142] since the corresponding provision (from which section 51 had been drawn) originally contained in the 1873 legislation had been repealed in 1875.[143] Section 51 transpired to be something of a make-work scheme for the High Court in Ireland, although the judiciary in their comments in 1876 on the Judicature Bill had suggested that the section be omitted, for consistency with the English statute.[144] (Every such motion for a new trial in the Chancery division, both in England and in Ireland, would be brought before the Court of Appeal.) Notwithstanding the absence in England of an express provision corresponding to section 51, the conservatism of the courts and Bar there led to a continuation of the practice of such applications being made to a Divisional court,[145] leading eventually to the

141 Appellate Jurisdiction Act 1876 (39&40 Vict., c.59), s17.

142 Wylie, op. cit., p. 115, remarked that the Irish provision, as supplemented by Order 39.1 of the Rules of Court adopted in 1905, 'differs very materially' from the provision applicable in England.

143 Section 48 of 1873 Act, which was repealed by section 33 of 1875 Act (36&37 Vict., c.66, 38&39 Vict., c.77). Section 51 was repealed by the Government of Ireland Act 1920 (10&11 Geo. 5, c.67), s41(1).

144 P.P. 1876 (278) lxi.357; *ILT&SJ*, vol. 10, pp 309–11 (27 May 1876).

145 Patrick Polden, 'The Courts of Law: VI The Judicature Acts: 4. Teething troubles' in *Oxford history of laws*, vol. 11, p. 768.

enactment of the Supreme Court of Judicature Act 1890,[146] directing that all such common law motions were to be brought before the Court of Appeal.

In contrast, in Ireland any such motion seeking to set aside the decision of an initial hearing in the High Court would be heard by a Divisional court, before (if either party saw fit) the case might proceed to the Court of Appeal. This led to a number of cases being heard before a significant proportion of the members of the Irish judiciary at the time, before a further appeal was in turn heard before the House of Lords. Three cases in the first decade of the twentieth century illustrate this point. The important case ultimately reported as *Quinn v Leatham* ([1901] A.C. 495) began under the name of *Leatham v Craig* ([1899] 2 IR 667), which was tried before FitzGibbon LJ (sitting as a High Court judge) at the summer assizes in Belfast in 1896. It was then the subject of a motion by the defendant to set aside the verdict and judgment before a Divisional court (consisting of O'Brien LCJ, Palles CB, O'Brien and Andrews JJ) which by a majority refused this relief, but the judgment of which was reversed by the Court of Appeal (Ashbourne LC, Porter MR, Walker and Holmes LJJ), before that court was in turn reversed by the House of Lords (where six members sat on the appeal). A total of nine Irish judges thus heard the original case, the motion to set aside the verdict and the appeal.

The case of *Pearson v Dublin Corporation*,[147] a dispute that arose over the construction of the Pigeon House drainage treatment works at Ringsend, was heard at first instance by Palles CB, who directed a verdict for the defendant, which was reversed by a majority of the Divisional Court (Wright, Boyd and Gibson JJ, O'Brien LCJ dissenting), which was then itself reversed by the Court of Appeal (Walker LC, FitzGibbon and Holmes LJJ), which was in turn reversed by the House of Lords (an unusually large panel of eight members, including two Irish judges, Ashbourne and Atkinson), which unanimously directed a new trial. The law report records that a compromise was arrived at between the parties before such a second trial could take place. The *Irish Law Times* remarked that 'on a question of common law the lord chief baron, the lord chief justice, the lord chancellor, lord justice FitzGibbon and lord justice Holmes have been reversed by the House of Lords'.[148]

In *Cooke v Midland & Great Western Railway*[149] judgment for the plaintiff in a case first heard before O'Brien LCJ was upheld by a majority of the Divisional court (Palles CB, and Johnson J, with Kenny J dissenting) on a motion to set aside, which was reversed by the Court of Appeal (Walker LC, FitzGibbon and Holmes LJJ) which held that the case should have been withdrawn from the jury, in the absence of any evidence of negligence. The case, having been considered by seven Irish judges, was then taken to the House of Lords, which reversed the Court of Appeal.

146 53&54 Vict., c.44.

147 [1907] 2 IR 27, 82, 537; [1907] AC 351. See W.N. Osborough, *Law and the emergence of modern Dublin* (Dublin, 1996), pp 117–21, for an informative commentary on the circumstances and legal principles arising in the case.

148 *ILT&SJ*, vol. 41, p. 156 (15 June 1907).

149 [1909] AC 229.

The re-organisation of the judiciary in the decades after 1877 reflected a general acknowledgment that the level of legal and judicial business did not justify – or at least no longer justified – the level of judicial resources that had been left in place at the time of the initial reforms. The effective rhetorical opposition to more radical proposals for reorganization and reduction of the judiciary had tempered those initial proposals for reform, and judicial alarm and opposition was strong again in 1885 when further comprehensive re-organisation proposals were published.[150] The fact that the Bill on its formal first reading in February 1885 in the House of Commons (it did not receive a second reading) was introduced in the name of the chancellor of the Exchequer, as well as the chief secretary for Ireland, was an indication of the strong Treasury interest in the subject. Morris later told Ashbourne that after the lord chancellor [Sullivan] 'professed to be ignorant of many of its clauses' the judges had met, with the chief justice [May] in the chair, and had drafted a very strong commentary and protest but which never was finalised as the Bill had not been taken any further.[151] They unanimously resolved that the government should be called upon to set up a Royal Commission before any grave changes such as the Bill proposed were made; 'I have not the words but that is the substance and Naish [who had become lord chancellor after the death of Sullivan in April 1885] undertook to lay it before the government'.[152] Arthur Balfour referred to the 1885 Bill when speaking of the 1887 Bill as having been intended 'to remedy a state of things which has long been recognized as an evil in Ireland – namely the excess of strength in the Supreme Court of Judicature for the duties to be performed'.[153]

Complaints about Treasury interference with the administration of justice, and concern about the functioning of the Court of Appeal, continued to be a theme of opposition to judicial reform. From the end of the 1880s however all public reports and comments on the state of legal business indicated a considerable slackening in the volume of litigation. It was noted in 1894 that since 1859, a third of a century before, the numbers in the legal profession in England and Wales had increased by 38%, in Scotland by 44% and in Ireland by only 2%.[154] The judicial restructuring effected by statute in 1897 and 1907 was based largely upon the 1885 proposals, and the defence of the status quo put forward then lacked the passion that had animated the opposition to reform in the 1870s.

Unfavourable comparisons that were drawn between the apparent levels of productivity of the judges in Ireland and their counterparts in England were deflected with suggestions that the problem of mismatched resources lay not in Ireland but in England – where, it was said, there were insufficient judges to transact judicial work efficiently. A typical observation, made by the *Irish Law*

150 Supreme Court of Judicature (Ireland) Bill 1885 (P.P. 1884–5 (55) v.531).
151 Morris to Ashbourne, 9 July 1887 (Ashbourne Papers, B77/5).
152 Morris to Ashbourne, [undated] June 1885 (Ashbourne Papers, B77/3).
153 HC Deb, 3rd series, vol. 313, cols. 983–4 (14 April 1887).
154 *ILT&SJ*, vol. 28, p. 275 (2 June 1894).

Times in 1898, was that 'the question arises whether the English bench is not undermanned, with the result that trials are hurried over and wrong decisions often arrived at',[155] and it suggested that any imbalance in judicial numbers should be rectified by the appointment of more judges in England rather than by diminishing the number in Ireland. It was not contested that in general the Irish judges had easier working lives than their English counterparts, although in 1909 the master of the rolls Meredith, provoked by a renewal of unfavourable comparisons of the productivity of the Irish Courts with that of their English counterparts, expressed his opinion in court that 'individually, judge for judge, the Irish judges did more work than the English judges'.[156] In the late nineteenth century Britain was one of the leading economies, and London was the largest city and commercial and financial hub of the world, the centre of the largest empire that the world had ever seen. The nature and volume of the business brought before its superior courts were thus of an entirely different order to the litigation conducted in Dublin in those decades.

The necessity for a spacious or liberal view of judicial work was set out in a speech at a general meeting of the Bar in February 1875 by Serjeant Sherlock: 'It was of the utmost importance to suitors that judges should come to their business with calm heads, prepared to listen patiently to every minute detail of each case, and not hurried by excess of business, or worried by over-labour'. He said that a hostile press 'seemed to fancy that a judge should continue at his work, like a railway points man, for nineteen hours a day, and with the same fatal consequences that were so constantly seen to result from that practice'.[157] (Railway accidents in Britain in 1874 resulted in the deaths of more than a thousand people.)[158] Three decades later the same contention was made again by the *New Irish Jurist*: 'The public – even the educated public – do not at all realise the amount of work that is gone through by the judges in a single sittings. From early morning till late at night they are at work, for there is as much work to be done in the evenings and at night as when the courts are actually sitting. Of course, the vacations are fairly lengthy and frequent; but without the vacations it would be impossible for any ordinary intellect to stand the strain and stress of the work'.[159]

One further expansive view of the nature of judicial work and standing was expressed in 1923 by a sitting judge, James O'Connor of the Court of Appeal, in the course of a critical commentary (in a letter published on 8 October in the *Irish Independent* and *the Irish Times*) on the Courts of Justice Bill 1923.[160] He protested at

155 *ILT&SJ*, vol. 32, p. 279 (18 June 1898).
156 *ILT&SJ*, vol. 43, p. 265 (30 October 1909).
157 *ILT&SJ*, vol. 9, p. 67 (6 February 1875).
158 Annual Register 1875, p. 236, annual return (for 1874) of persons killed (1,424) and injured (5,041) on railways.
159 *New Irish Jurist*, vol. 4, no. 29, p. 189 (27 May 1904).
160 Enacted as the Courts of Justice Act 1924.

> the cutting down of the salaries of the High Court bench. The argument that the bench is too highly paid is a fallacy. The emoluments ought to be such as to attract the best brains in Ireland. If you want to keep a young, brilliant and ambitious lawyer from trying his chances in London you must give to the plums of the profession a flavour comparable with that on the other side of the Channel. That is not all: a supreme judge must have prestige. His prestige will, of course, partly depend upon himself, upon his legal acumen, his general erudition and, above all, on his character. But it will partly depend upon something else, to wit, his social station. This ought to be of the best. He should have the little elegancies which refine the mind and lift him up in the estimation of his neighbours. He is necessarily more or less aloof from the community; that aloofness should not be that of a hermit in a cottage but of a personage who lives a life of repose, contemplation and dignity. And it is because Great Britain has furnished its judges with these things that its judges have a prestige and a reputation which is found nowhere else.[161]

The *Irish Law Times* said in 1870, on a theme that would become familiar in subsequent decades, that the required level of the judicial establishment could not be properly assessed in a 'period of unusual depression in those classes of trade and commerce which necessarily produce a certain proportion of litigation'.[162] By 1875 a slightly different argument was advanced that no reduction should be made 'in view of the steadily increasing legal practice of the country … as it recovers from the horrid drain in money and population induced by the famine of twenty years ago'.[163] The concept of 'unripe time', that temporarily depressed or (as the case may be) currently improving business conditions should not be a basis for reduction in the number of judges, was a constant element of arguments against reform. A good example of this, incorporating a protest against Treasury interference, is found in the paper read by Arthur W. Samuels QC before the Statistical and Social Inquiry Society of Ireland in February 1896.[164] Referring to an intimation that 'Treasury officials have determined to promote a Bill for the reduction of the judicial staff in Ireland', he said that questions arose as to 'whether it is an opportune time for statesmen, as opposed to Treasury officials, to choose for the purpose of further curtailing the numbers of the judiciary which was established, after prolonged debate and consideration in Parliament in the year 1877, and whether after Ireland having experienced in the eighteen years since then 'a social revolution, a deep commercial depression, and an agrarian war, time ought to be given for confidence to revive and business to recover, before her legal establishment is further docked'. He had previously acknowledged that there had

161 Office of the attorney general, file ref. 2002/14/1396 (NAI).
162 *ILT&SJ*, vol. 4, p. 225 (26 March 1870).
163 *ILT&SJ*, vol. 9, p. 64 (6 February 1875).
164 Arthur W. Samuels, op. cit.; *ILT&SJ*, vol. 30, p. 77 (15 February 1896).

been some falling off in legal business but argued that 'with the return of commercial confidence and a revival of industrial effort there undoubtedly would be a considerable increase of legal work'.[165]

In 1887 the *Law Times* remarked, on the occasion of Morris being appointed lord chief justice and the merger of the King's Bench and Common Pleas divisions of the High Court, that

> the Irish common law bench is altogether overmanned in proportion to the work it has to do. The courts in Dublin sit for less time in the day, and for fewer days in the year than those at Temple Bar [i.e., at the Strand in London, not the district of that name in Dublin], and yet divisional courts of two or three learned judges have to eke out their time and to demonstrate their *raison d'etre* by solemnly adjudicating as tribunals of first instance upon the right of a plaintiff to sign judgment upon a specially endorsed writ etc.

Matters of that nature, it said, were expeditiously dealt with by masters in chambers in London, and reached a divisional court only as a second appeal after having been heard in chambers by a master and by a judge.[166] In the 1894 defamation case of *Pike v Beamish* panels of three judges in the Queen's Bench division sat to determine preliminary procedural applications (motions) for further and better particulars and for further discovery.[167] In 1891 the Dublin correspondent of the *Times* remarked, after new comprehensive rules of court procedure had been promulgated, that 'the judges appear to have faith in the future, and think the time opportune for framing a comprehensive code of regulations when there is no business to be embarrassed by them, and solicitors and barristers have abundant leisure to study them'.[168]

The *Times* returned to the subject of divisional courts in 1894, this time saying that

> from lack of more arduous work, and to save the appearance of absolute idleness, the common law judges in Ireland are in the habit of constituting themselves into imposing tribunals of three or four members, and with all the pomp of the court *in banco,* hearing summons and trivial applications of a kind that in England is disposed of by a master in chambers. It happens commonly, even in the middle of the sittings, that every court has risen for the day before three o'clock, and rarely that all the courts are still at work after one o'clock. It is no wonder that the life of an Irish judge has come to be regarded as the ideal of ease and leisure.[169]

165 Letter to *Irish Times*, as reported in *ILT&SJ*, vol. 29, p. 541 (9 November 1895).
166 As reported in *ILT&SJ*, vol. 21, p. 68 (5 February 1887).
167 *Irish Times*, 23 February 1894 and 21 April 1894.
168 As reported in *Law Times*, vol. 90, p. 279 (14 February 1891). See also p. 275.
169 As reported in *ILT&SJ*, vol. 28, p. 353 (21 July 1894).

In 1908 a King's Bench divisional court of six judges sat to hear a motion for certiorari to quash the convictions (with fines of £1 each) in the magistrates' court of two publicans in Clontarf for selling alcohol on a Sunday afternoon. The point at issue was whether (as the publicans maintained) their premises were subject to the same regulations under the licensing Acts as the city of Dublin or not. The case was heard in the High Court, and then ordered to be re-argued before a divisional court, whose members gave four separate judgments, Palles CB dissenting at some length from the decision to uphold the convictions.[170]

An obituary of Baron Dowse in 1890 referred to 'the departed days when the Hall [of the Four Courts] was thronged with busy life'.[171] In 1892 the *Irish Law Times* reported that business in the Chancery division was 'a trifle slack, to say the least of it', citing recent official statistics that the number of court orders made in that division in the last couple of years had fallen by over 10%.[172] A year later, on the opening of the Michaelmas law term (on 25 October), 'much speculation was indulged in as to the prospects of the sittings from a business point of view. It is generally understood that the members of the Bar will not have a very lucrative sittings'.[173] In December 1896, shortly before the 1897 legislation was introduced, it declared in an editorial column that more recent official statistical information 'proves conclusively that there has been a steady and almost universal decline of business in the High Court'. 'In almost all cases this decrease has followed on similar decreases in the previous years. It would appear that ere long, if this process goes on, legal business in Ireland will have totally ceased to exist'.[174] This decline in business extended also to the county court system, which had been modernised by separate legislation in 1877. Observers initially considered that, after a decade, the extension of its jurisdiction had 'effected a revolution' in legal business, civil and criminal, with 'a vast amount of the entire legal work of the country [being] performed in these local courts, a fact which accounts in some measure for the general slackness of business at the Four Courts'.[175]

A few weeks earlier the *Law Times* had remarked 'that Irish judges are not overburdened with work may be inferred from the fact that Sir Peter O'Brien, LCJ, was enabled on Tuesday last week, which was the second day of the Michaelmas Sittings, to have a "day off" which he spent at the opening meet of the Kildare Hunt'.[176] Some years later O'Brien was unable to sit for a time, being 'laid up from injuries sustained in the hunting field'.[177] In 1899 O'Brien had complained about business being paralysed one day because counsel were not in court, saying that 'it was wholly unbecoming to the dignity of the court that [it] should be occupied, as

170 *The King (Powell) v Mahony*, *The King (McCormack) v Mahony* (*Irish Times*, 8 and 15 May 1908).
171 *ILT&SJ*, vol. 34, p. 163 (22 March 1890).
172 *ILT&SJ*, vol. 26, p. 594 (12 November 1892).
173 *ILT&SJ*, vol. 27, p. 538 (28 October 1893).
174 *ILT&SJ*, vol. 30, p. 562 (26 December 1896).
175 *ILT&SJ*, vol. 23, p. 12 (9 March 1889) and vol. 26, p. 678 (24 December 1892).
176 *ILT&SJ*, vol. 30, p. 502 (14 November 1896), quoting the *Law Times*.
177 *Law Times*, vol. 104, p. 425 (12 March 1898).

it had been for over half an hour, sending the officers of the court and solicitors engaged in the cases to try to get counsel to come to court', and threatening to strike out such cases if they were not argued.[178]

Mr Justice Grantham of the English High Court visited Dublin in 1896, when a week committed to circuit work in Liverpool transpired to finish within three days and

> I took advantage of the spare time to run over to Ireland to learn something of its legal and judicial work and of the way in which that work was performed. I need hardly say that, accustomed as we are to our daily crowded cause lists at the Royal Courts in London, I was much struck by the poverty in character of most of the work that our judicial brethren in Ireland, equally as able as ourselves, were called upon to perform, and by the wasted strength that was employed to try the few causes appearing in their daily lists. The work was, in fact, mostly of the character now performed by our County Court judges.[179]

In 1899 the *Law Times* noted of the Michaelmas sittings earlier in the winter that they

> were not remarkable for any great amount of business. On the Chancery side the vice-chancellor was never very busy and on many days he did not sit at all. The Ulster Plantation case occupied a good deal of the time of the master of the rolls, and judge Ross was kept fairly busy in selling off bankrupt estates in his court under the compulsory powers given by section 40 of the Land Act 1896 … In the Queen's Bench division however, the work was very much less. There were one or two cases of importance, but as a rule the Divisional court had nothing better to occupy its attention than remitting motions, applications for leave to mark formal judgment or to issue executions and such like. It seems a pitiable waste of talent and energy for a bench of three or four eminent judges to sit listening to such applications.[180]

Some five years later it observed that 'it is of course true that legal business in Ireland has declined very much in recent years. That declination was the natural outcome of the decrease in the population'.[181] In August 1904 an *Irish Law Times* editorial described an hour spent in the King's Bench court, where Palles CB and Boyd J were sitting together.[182] While this may have been a day on which procedural rather than substantive business was listed to be transacted the overriding impression of the proceedings as reported is of judicial ability and court

178 *ILT&SJ*, vol. 33, p. 166 (22 April 1899).
179 A letter to the *Times*, as reported in *ILT&SJ*, vol. 30, p. 543 (12 December 1896).
180 *Law Times*, vol. 106, p. 213 (7 January 1899).
181 *Law Times*, vol. 117, p. 193 (2 July 1904).
182 *ILT&SJ*, vol. 38, p. 251 (13 August 1904).

time being applied for work of little legal substance. In June 1905 the *Irish Law Times* noted that 'the prospects of business are by no means bright'.[183] A memoir of a Victorian barrister, William Bennett Campion, who had been called to the Bar in 1840 and died in 1907, that was published in 1911, referred to 'law business of every class, but especially Chancery and Landed Estates Court work, [being] far greater then [in the 1870s and 1880s] than it has been for the last twenty years'.[184] On 21 December 1909 two High Court judges retired, Johnson and Andrews JJ. Neither was replaced, as decreed in 1907,[185] and 'it will now be necessary to assign two of the judges of the King's Bench division to perform the probate and matrimonial and admiralty business respectively of that division'.[186]

A careful analysis of declining court business was given in May 1897 by Thomas Kennedy, a young barrister. He noted that the number of writs issued in Ireland, a rough proxy for the level of litigation, had been 20,150 in 1875, 22,504 in 1885 and 16,493 in 1895, and that appearances to writs [i.e., notices of intention to defend] averaged about 20%, less than half the level in England. 'The high ratio which exists in England between appearances and writs shows the substantial character of the actions, and that defendants had strong inducements to defend either their characters, rights or property. On the other hand, the low proportion of appearances to writs in Ireland shows that the majority of defendants are either indifferent to the consequences, or have nothing to lose, and that the large bulk of litigation commenced in Ireland is of an insubstantial character'. He cited the gloomy forecast in December 1896 of the *Irish Law Times*, and then referred to an article written for an American legal publication in 1893 by Denis Douthwaite, previously an assistant librarian in the King's Inns and then the librarian of Gray's Inn: 'It has been said by an Irish jurist that the business of the American courts is not much disturbed by formality. Nowadays the formality of the Irish courts is not much disturbed by business'.[187] An analysis of official statistics of criminal trials at the assizes and quarter sessions (County Courts) showed that in the five years 1906–10 2,152 cases were brought to trial annually, whereas in the comparable period forty years before, 1866–70, the figure had been 4,400 cases.[188]

Kennedy's article, which had drawn conclusions about the future prospects of the Bar from his analysis of litigation trends, concluded with a pointed reference to the General Council of the English Bar (which had been established in 1894) as advancing and protecting the interests of the Bar, and being 'watchful and active. One vainly seeks in Ireland for an organisation similar in scope, tendency and achievements'. An anonymous member of the Bar had written to the *Irish Law Times* in February 1896 along similar lines, also drawing attention to the English precedent, and remarking that it would be as well 'if, before being extinguished or

183 *ILT&SJ*, vol. 39, p. 160 (3 June 1905).
184 William Bennett Campion, *Memoir* (Dublin, 1911), p. 58.
185 Supreme Court of Judicature (Ireland) Act 1907 (7 Edw. VII, c.44), s1.
186 *ILT&SJ*, vol. 44, p. 2 (1 January 1910).
187 *ILT&SJ*, vol. 31, pp 212–14 (8 May 1897). See also *Law Times*, vol. 103, p. 135 (5 June 1897).
188 W.E. Vaughan, *Murder trials in Ireland, 1836–1914* (Dublin, 2009), p. 100.

starved out of existence, the Bar of Ireland, in the present depressed condition of business, and its still more gloomy prospects, would, like any other body of men with a common cause to serve, look after their own interests in a practical, proper way by combination and organisation'.[189]

The members of the Bar up to that time had organised their collective interests, such as they were, through a library committee known as the Law Library Society,[190] and occasional general meetings. 'Meetings of the Bar are not summoned frequently, and wisely so; if they were called for every petty occasion they would lose the weight that has always hitherto, and we trust always will, attend them'.[191] A Bar Benevolent Society had been set up in 1894.[192] In June 1897, a month after Kennedy's article was published, a general meeting of the Bar in the Law Library passed a resolution that 'it is expedient that a General Council of the Bar be constituted', and the proposer in the course of his remarks strongly deprecated the proposed reduction of the Irish judicial bench. Later that month the Council was formally constituted, and at its first meeting adopted a statement protesting at the imminent reductions in the number of judges and 'what appears a hasty interference with the long-existing constitution of the Irish courts'.[193] Shortly afterwards, on 22 July, the Supreme Court of Judicature (Ireland) Bill was introduced, suppressing a number of judicial positions, as described above (see p. 41). Edward Carson QC, MP spoke in favour of the Bill, not ingratiating himself with his colleagues at the Irish Bar – which, as they might have reflected, he had largely left for practice in England.[194] In 1909 he proposed a resolution at a general meeting of the English Bar, which was adopted unanimously, that there was an imperative necessity for the immediate appointment of additional judges.[195]

In 1898 the *Law Times* returned to the subject of overmanning of the Irish bench, drawing invidious comparisons with the English bench: 'it would be difficult to exaggerate the wasteful character of the Irish judicial expenditure when thus poignantly contrasted with the expenditure on similar institutions in this country'. The *Irish Law Times* in a riposte referred instead to the 'alleged overmanning', and took issue on various grounds with the statistical basis of the charge – that the 'peculiarities of the Irish land system and land laws' require the dedication of two judges, so that the costs of that part of the judicial system should be left out of account for comparison, and that the Irish courts had functions in bankruptcy that the English courts did not.[196]

189 *ILT&SJ*, vol. 30, p. 102 (29 February 1896).
190 See for instance the reference to the Library Committee submitting an annual report, in *ILT&SJ*, vol. 33, p. 257 (18 May 1889). See also Tomas Clancy, 'The Four Courts building and the development of an independent Bar of Ireland' in Caroline Costello (ed.), *The Four Courts: 200 years* (Dublin, 1996), pp 80–104, in particular pp 89–93.
191 *Irish Jurist*, vol. 2, p. 146 (8 June 1850).
192 *ILT&SJ*, vol. 31, p. 598 (25 December 1897).
193 *ILT&SJ*, vol. 31, p. 274 (12 June 1897) and p. 308 (3 July 1897).
194 *ILT&SJ*, vol. 31, p. 352 (31 July 1897).
195 *Law Times*, vol. 127, p. 2 (1 May 1909).
196 *ILT&SJ*, vol. 32, p. 247 (28 May 1898), citing *Law Times*, and p. 279 (18 June 1898).

In February 1900 'the lack of business this term at the Four Courts is almost unprecedented. Probably this is one of the results of the war [in South Africa]'.[197] Two years later the *Daily Telegraph* (London) remarked that 'to those with a memory of even moderate duration – say extending over twenty years – the most pathetic spot in Dublin is the Round Hall of the Four Courts during term. The empty floor of the famous Round Hall, its lonely atmosphere, are the best commentaries on the state of the legal profession in Ireland at the present moment'.[198] Such gloom about the future of the Bar made the prospect of judicial office all the more attractive. Excess judicial capacity had been acknowledged by the 1907 Act providing for the next two judicial vacancies not to be filled (see p. 41). Seventeen months elapsed after Palles retired in 1916 before William Moore KC, MP was appointed. In 1919 Sir John Ross advised Austen Chamberlain, the chancellor of the Exchequer, that 'the next two vacancies in the King's Bench should not be filled up. There is no work to justify the retention of 8 KBD judges, there is hardly work for 6',[199] and had previously remarked that 'the KBD judges were working barely half time'.[200] James O'Connor similarly observed, four years later, that even in the pre-war days it was only the Chancery judges who had been regularly engaged for much more than half of their time.[201]

APPENDIX 1: THE JUDGES AND NON-JURY COURTS

Government policy on the maintenance of law and order, and its responses at different times to political campaigns involving protests and potentially giving rise to civil disorder, necessarily had implications for the administration of justice in the courts. Statutes were frequently passed or amended to create additional crimes and give additional powers to the authorities, including the magistrates and the constabulary.[202] The attorney general could apply to court for a direction that the venue of a trial for crimes allegedly committed in a district 'proclaimed' by official order as one where disorder prevailed would be changed to another specified county.[203] Critical comments by judges about the acquittals of accused persons by

197 *ILT&SJ*, vol. 34, p. 71 (10 February 1900).
198 As reported in *ILT&SJ*, vol. 36, p. 85 (8 March 1902).
199 Ross to Chamberlain, 21 January 1919 (Cadbury Research Library: special collections – University of Birmingham, Austen Chamberlain Papers, AC 24/1/38).
200 Ross to Edward Shortt, chief secretary for Ireland, undated (Autumn 1918), as forwarded by Ross to Chamberlain, 21 January 1919 (Austin Chamberlain Papers, AC 24/1/39).
201 Lord justice O'Connor, submission to the Judiciary Committee, memorandum on changes in Irish judicial system, undated [April] 1923 (Hugh Kennedy Papers (UCDA), P. 4/1092 (95)).
202 See generally Virginia Crossman, *Politics, law and order in nineteenth-century Ireland* (Dublin, 1996), and Niamh Howlin, 'The prehistory of the Offences against the State Act' in Mark Coen (ed.), *The Offences against the State Act 1939 at 80: a model counter-terrorism act?* (Oxford, Dublin, 2020).
203 Peace Preservation (Ireland) Act 1870 (33 Vict., c.9), s29; Criminal Law and Procedure (Ireland) Act 1887 (50&51 Vict., c.20), s4.

juries were held out as demonstrating that the ordinary criminal law was inadequate to the challenges it faced. In general, however, the function of the judiciary was to administer the law as it stood, or was amended, from time to time, and with two notable exceptions, in 1882 and 1920, they had no input or standing or function in deciding how trials of persons accused of very serious crimes allegedly committed in the course of civil disorder would be conducted. In those two years the judges drew the line at government proposals that they would sit without juries in such trials.

The Prevention of Crime (Ireland) Bill,[204] which was introduced in May 1882, was intended to facilitate and enhance the enforcement of criminal law. It had been in preparation for some time,[205] but was given added urgency by the Phoenix Park murders on 6 May. On 8 May the lord chancellor said in court that the judges had met to consider 'whether we should all adjourn today in token of respect for those who have been foully murdered, and to mark our detestation of so atrocious a crime. It has however been thought that we shall best do this by steadily holding on in our course for the due administration of justice'.[206] The Bill recited that 'by reason of secret societies and combinations for illegal purposes in Ireland the operation of the ordinary law has become insufficient for the repression and prevention of crime'. It made provision for trial without a jury of the most serious criminal cases of a political or agrarian character if the government considered in relation to any particular offence that 'a just and impartial trial cannot be had according to the ordinary course of the law' (s1(1)). Panels of three judges would form a special commission for charges of murder and treason (for which a death sentence would follow conviction) and other serious crimes.

On 11 May Sir William Harcourt, the home secretary, outlined its principal features, starting with the intention to provide for non-jury courts. He said that 'the first and greatest of all evils in society is insecurity in the punishment of crime … The ordinary juryman – we can hardly wonder, we can, perhaps hardly blame him – wants [i.e., lacks] the firmness to meet the pistol which is levelled at his back, the dagger which is levelled at his breast, the rifle which is fired into his house by night'. A special tribunal was needed, 'some body that shall have the firmness and authority to assert the law and lead to its just execution … The judges of the land, as a body, are the only persons who have the knowledge, who possess the authority, to bear such a responsibility … If it is necessary to secure the safety of the state we have a right to appeal with confidence to the patriotism of the judges of Ireland'.[207]

Lord Spencer, the lord lieutenant, foresaw difficulty with the Bill, telling Harcourt that 'the judges will be very troublesome, but I will try what I can to work them up to their duty. I dare say we shall find those who will act. Lawson, J.D.

204 Enacted as 45&46 Vict., c.25.

205 Gladstone to Forster, 5 April 1882 (Gladstone Papers, Add. MS 44160.89); Virginia Crossman, op. cit., p. 143.

206 *ILT&SJ*, vol. 16, p. 210 (13 May 1882).

207 HC Deb, 3rd series, vol. 269, cols. 465–6 (11 May 1882).

Fitzgerald and some others'.[208] The lord chancellor, Hugh Law, convened an urgent meeting of the judges to consider the provisions of the Bill as relating to their position. Harcourt thought 'in very decided terms' that what Parliament might decide upon was no business of the judges, but Gladstone shared Spencer's view that to seek a postponement of such a meeting would make a bad situation worse.[209] All the judges were present at their meeting on 18 May except Lawson and Morris (who were in England) and Dowse (who was unwell). They passed a resolution 'that in the opinion of the judges of the Supreme Court the imposition upon them of the duties proposed by [the Bill] would seriously impair public confidence in the judicial office and thereby permanently injure the administration of justice in Ireland'.[210]

This was forwarded to Law by the lord chief justice, G.A.C. May, and in advance of the formal communication Law told Spencer that all of the judges objected in the strongest language against being forced to try criminal cases without a jury. A number of them had said that they would retire rather than undertake such work, and others that they would refuse to co-operate and would in effect dare the government to impeach them and seek to remove them from office by a vote in Parliament. 'They all unite in expressing their clear opinion that to have criminals now tried by judges without juries will be a fatal mistake with reference to the future administration of justice'.[211] Confusion later reigned as to how the government had dealt with the judges' memorandum. Gladstone initially said that it 'was not forwarded to us in any way',[212] although it transpired that it had been received and handed around on the front bench in the House of Commons between him, Harcourt and Trevelyan, the new chief secretary for Ireland.[213] He later said that it had not been communicated in a manner that seemed to require any formal response, and (following Harcourt) that it was for Parliament to decide upon what the government had proposed.[214] Law soon confirmed Spencer's impression about Lawson's attitude, although adding his view that the chief baron [Palles], though he appeared to have joined in the resolution, would not refuse to act if the duty was laid upon him.[215] Gladstone's view, from an early date, was that the judges must be faced down, and their reluctance and

208 Spencer to Harcourt, 11 May 1882 (Harcourt Papers (Bodleian Library, Oxford), MS 39); Peter Gordon (ed.), *The red earl, the papers of the fifth earl Spencer (1835–1910)* (Northampton, 1981–6), p. 196.

209 Spencer to Gladstone, undated [May] 1882, Gladstone to Spencer, 13 May 1882 (Althorp Papers, Add. MS 76854.7 and 76854.13).

210 May to Law, 18 May 1882 (Althorp Papers, Add. MS 76982); *ILT&SJ*, vol. 16, p. 232 (20 May 1882). The text of the resolution, as reported in the *Irish Law Times*, differed slightly from the text as forwarded to Law by May.

211 Law to Spencer, [undated, May 1882] (Althorp Papers, Add. MS 76982).

212 HC Deb, 3rd series, vol. 270, cols. 77–8 (5 June 1882).

213 Spencer to Trevelyan, 6 June 1882; Trevelyan to Spencer, 9 June 1882 (Althorp Papers, Add. MS 76944.29).

214 HC Deb, 3rd series, vol. 270, col. 838 (12 June 1882).

215 Law to Spencer, 18 May 1882 (Althorp Papers, Add. MS 76982).

reservations be overridden, unless indeed they were to produce reasons stronger than those so far advanced.[216]

It was thus clear that, for all the complaints which judges were wont to make (both before and after 1882) about the unsatisfactory nature of many jury trials, and the propensity of juries to disagree or to arrive at seemingly perverse verdicts of acquittal, they did not care for the prospect of taking over the jury's function of arriving at findings of fact in such cases. They were being provided after the murders in the Phoenix Park with police guards at the courts and at their homes against the danger of more assassinations,[217] and it would have been human nature also to consider whether what the government had proposed might expose them to additional personal risks. Harcourt had admitted that the proposal 'is an arduous and invidious – it may be, a dangerous – duty',[218] and Spencer told Trevelyan that some of the judges 'are afraid of acting and consider that their lives will be in danger if they sentence without a jury'.[219]

The Bill became the subject of extended opposition in the House of Commons from the Irish Parliamentary Party. John David Fitzgerald, recently nominated as a new Law Lord, suggested to the government that for the judges not to have a power to impose a sentence of death would make the Bill less objectionable and would have relieved many of the judges and lessened their unwillingness to accept the new duties to be cast on them.[220] He drew attention to a statute of 1833[221] (also mentioned in Parliament by Harcourt) setting up special courts in which a proviso to that effect was set out, but his advice to omit murder and treason from the category of crimes with which the new court might deal was not accepted. An amendment was made to the Bill so that the judges to sit in a non-jury court would be drawn by ballot from a set rota rather than be selected by the government, Spencer acknowledging that such a power of direct selection 'implies that we shall select for a particular object'.[222]

The Bill did not become law until 12 July 1882. The actual establishment of such a special commission court would have required a government decision, under s1 of the Act, and as it transpired no such direction was ever made. The opposition of the judges to the concept of a non-jury court, and the resignation of baron Francis FitzGerald (see pp 171–2), may thus have had its effect since although provision had been made for such a court (and also for a court of criminal appeal)[223]

216 Gladstone to Spencer, 13 May 1882 (Althorp Papers, Add. MS 76854.12).
217 *ILT&SJ*, vol. 16, p. 232 (20 May 1882).
218 HC Deb, 3rd series, vol. 269, col. 466 (11 May 1882).
219 Spencer to Trevelyan, 6 June 1882 (Althorp Papers, Add. MS 76944.28).
220 FitzGerald to Spencer, 6 June 1882 (Althorp Papers, Add. MS 77077).
221 An Act for the more effectual suppression of local disturbances and dangerous associations in Ireland 1833 (3&4 Will. IV, c.4).
222 Spencer to Trevelyan, 6 June 1882 (Althorp Papers, Add. MS 76944.28)
223 Section 2 of the Act; Desmond Greer, 'A security against illegality? The reservation of crown cases in nineteenth-century Ireland' in N.M. Dawson (ed.), *Reflections on law and history* (Dublin, 2006), pp 163–202, at 198.

this was never put into operation. It lapsed when the period of three years for which the Act was in force expired in the summer of 1885.

In 1920 in the course of the War of Independence the government set about creating special courts and unsuccessfully sought the co-operation of the judiciary for this. At a meeting on 31 May between members of the cabinet and the lord lieutenant, chief secretary and attorney general of Ireland, Winston Churchill, then at the War Office as secretary of state for War and for Air, spoke forcefully about the necessity for

> a special tribunal for trying murderers. It is monstrous that we have some 200 murders and no one hung. What strikes me is the feebleness of the local machinery. After a person is caught he should pay the penalty within a week. Look at the tribunals which the Russian government have devised. You should get three or four judges whose scope should be universal, and they should move quickly over the country and do summary justice.

Denis Henry, the attorney general, then said (as was confirmed by Lord French) that the judges had indicated some months ago that 'they did not want to touch it', to which Churchill responded that this 'shows all the more need for extraordinary action. Get three generals if you cannot get three judges'.[224] Two months later Sir Hamar Greenwood, the chief secretary, said at a cabinet meeting that a special tribunal should be set up with powers to inflict the death penalty, presided over by a judge; 'he had consulted several Irish judges, but none of them thought that they should be called in for this work', and Henry again confirmed that no judge would serve in that way.[225]

The Restoration of Order in Ireland Act,[226] enacted in August 1920, made provision, by reference to the Defence of the Realm Consolidation Act 1914,[227] for trial of offences by courts martial or courts of summary jurisdiction. It required (s1(2) (b)) that a court martial when trying a person charged with a crime punishable by death would include one person (not necessarily an army officer) nominated by the lord lieutenant, 'being a person certified by the lord chancellor of Ireland or the lord chief justice of England to be a person of legal knowledge and experience'. The latter reference reflects the possibility that members of the English Bar might be nominated in this way ('it was thought right to make provision for the contingency that a sufficient number might not be available from the Irish bar'),[228] but also brings out that the Irish judges, with the possible exception of the lord chancellor, would not have been prepared to do so. The lord chancellor had a dual position or responsibilities, as not only the head of the

224 Thomas Jones, *Whitehall diary: vol. 3, Ireland 1918–1925* (London, 1971), p. 19 (31 May 1920).
225 Thomas Jones, op. cit., p. 33 (26 July 1920).
226 10&11 Geo. 5, c.31.
227 5&6 Geo. 5, c.8.
228 Lord Birkenhead (lord chancellor), HL Deb, 5th series, vol. 41, col. 1025 (9 August 1920).

judiciary but also a member of the government, but the incumbent, James Campbell, made his view of the matter clear in saying shortly afterwards that he had not been for many months past associated with His Majesty's executive.[229]

It was thus absolutely clear that the judiciary would take no part in the working of courts martial and military tribunals, but they were soon required to consider and determine issues as to whether, and if so the extent to which, the civil courts had any jurisdiction to oversee or restrain the operations of such bodies. Applications that were made to prevent the carrying out of capital sentences imposed by courts martial in areas where martial law had been proclaimed (counties Cork, Kerry, Limerick, Tipperary, Clare, Kilkenny, Waterford and Wexford)[230] and by military tribunals not so constituted in other areas were refused by the courts.[231] In July 1921, however, O'Connor MR ordered the release of men on whom a sentence of death had been passed, taking a view of the basis of martial law that has generally been regarded as mistaken, although its correctness was not the subject of appeal or further review at the time[232] (see pp 397–8).

APPENDIX 2: THE JUDGES AND THE PRIVY COUNCIL OF IRELAND

The Privy Council of Ireland was for centuries the primary executive and advisory organ of government, consisting of a broad range of office holders and dignitaries.[233] Every attorney general (but not solicitor general),[234] was sworn in as a member when appointed. In the twentieth century – unlike in England[235] – what had been a common practice[236] for superior court judges who had not held that office also to be thus sworn in became a standard practice. These judicial members (both sitting and retired, since membership was held for life) constituted, in practice and sometimes formally, a committee which would consider and advise on matters which by statute were required to be determined by 'the lord lieutenant in Council'. The Government of Ireland Act 1920 provided that the ministers of Northern Ireland for the time being would constitute an executive committee of the Privy Council of Ireland (to be called the Executive Committee of Northern Ireland) to aid and advise the lord lieutenant in the exercise of his executive powers

229 *Law Times*, vol. 150, p. 149 (4 September 1920); *ILT&SJ*, vol. 54, p. 223 (11 September 1920).
230 Charles Townsend, *The British campaign in Ireland, 1919–1921* (Oxford, 1975), pp 86, 135, 141.
231 *R v Allen*, [1921] 2 IR 241. See also pp 88 and 405.
232 *Egan v Macready*, [1921] 1 IR 265.
233 The Act of Union 1800 (40 Geo. 3 (Ir.), c.38) provided, in Article X, that 'His Majesty may, so long as he shall think fit, continue the privy council of Ireland, to be his privy council for that part of the United Kingdom called Ireland.'
234 *ILT&SJ*, vol. 43, p. 318 (25 December 1909).
235 *ILT&SJ*, vol. 30, p. 114 (7 March 1896); *Law Times*, vol. 103, p. 217 (3 July 1897).
236 Those so sworn in in the nineteenth century included Mountifort Longfield (1867), Stephen Woulfe Flanagan (1876), Gerald FitzGibbon (1879), James Murphy and William O'Brien (1890) and W.D. Andrews (1897).

in relation to Irish services [as defined] in Northern Ireland, and a Privy Council of Northern Ireland was established in 1922.[237]

The encumbered estates legislation of 1849 had provided for a formal judicial committee of the Privy Council (similar to one constituted a half century later by the local government legislation of 1898), for the purpose of hearing appeals from decisions of the Commissioners under the Act.[238] The quasi-judicial functions of the Council were increased by other legislation towards the end of the nineteenth century. Powers for tramway and light railway companies and local authorities to acquire land compulsorily for various public purposes, including housing, were contained in the Tramways and Public Companies (Ireland) Act 1883,[239] the Labourers (Ireland) Act 1885,[240] the Irish Education Acts 1892 and 1893[241] and the Local Government (Ireland) Act 1898.[242] Provisions were made for tramway companies to raise money with publicly funded guarantees of dividends. What would otherwise have been a necessity for the exercise of such powers to have a specific statutory authority in each case was avoided by providing, as an alternative procedure for public oversight, the ratification thereof by the lord lieutenant in Council. Affected parties could petition the lord lieutenant not to approve the intended compulsory acquisition or other proposed statutory action, and the lodging of a petition stayed or suspended the approval process until it had been considered by a committee of the Council, potentially after a public hearing.

Lord Ashbourne observed in a Parliamentary debate that 'Parliament should watch most carefully any proposals for the compulsory acquisition of land'. The Labourers' Dwellings Act of 1885 had made provision for appeals to the Privy Council 'where he had himself presided for six years with the valuable assistance of several of the judges. That procedure in the Privy Council had worked well and efficiently. Without its interference injustice would have been done in many cases and many orders open to the most serious objection would have been passed'.[243]

Other functions of the Council arose under the Educational Endowments (Ireland) Act 1885[244] (as to the ratification of decisions taken by the two judicial commissioners under that Act – see p. 278), and the consideration of fishery bye-laws made by the Department of Agriculture and Technical Instruction to regulate nets and trawling.[245] The university legislation of 1908 established a committee of the Council, to be styled the Irish Universities Commission, to consist of not less

237 Government of Ireland Act 1920, c.67, s8(5); Irish Free State (Consequential Provisions) Act 1922 (13 Geo. 5, c.2), first schedule, para. 2.
238 12&13 Vict., c.77, ss51 and 52; 61&62 Vict., c.37, s10.
239 46&47 Vict., c.43.
240 48&49 Vict., c.77.
241 55&56 Vict., c.42; 56&57 Vict., c.41.
242 61&62 Vict., c.37.
243 HL Deb, 4th series, vol. 15, col. 868 (31 July 1893).
244 48&49 Vict., c.78.
245 *Irish Times*, 17 January 1914 and 2 June 1915; *ILT&SJ*, vol. 49, p. 138 (5 June 1915).

than five members, at least two of whom were to be sitting or retired judges, for the purpose of considering petitions as to the lawfulness of actions of a university or constituent college.[246] Petitions were filed on which hearings took place (a) as to whether the internal statutes governing Queen's University Belfast could lawfully permit the teaching of scholastic philosophy – the objecting petition was dismissed (1909)[247] – and (b) seeking to set aside a statute of University College Cork providing for a lectureship in Russian language and literature as not having been properly adopted, in which the objection was sustained (1917).[248]

Hearings of a committee, of which an annual average of about ten took place,[249] were held in public in Dublin Castle, and counsel might attend on behalf of interested parties that were seeking or as the case might be objecting to an order proposed to be made pursuant to statutory powers. A hearing took place in 1873, for instance, to consider objections to a bye-law proposed to be made by Dublin Corporation regulating the hay and straw market at Smithfield.[250] Hearings were typically attended by a good number of judges, perhaps five or six.[251] Ten judges (including Lord Morris) and half a dozen other members of the Privy Council attended a hearing in 1893 which considered objections to schemes drafted under the Educational Endowments legislation and applications under the labourers' dwellings provisions.[252]

The full Council would ratify and give effect to the reports of committees, whose proceedings took the form of reports or recommendations to the lord lieutenant on their subject matter. In addition to various ceremonial duties the Council would also have a function in the issuing of orders or proclamations to give effect to decisions of the executive branch of government. Any judicial involvement in this latter class of business of the Council, where the underlying decision might have a political character, was potentially more controversial, and more open to misunderstanding, than the discharge of functions of a broadly judicial nature outlined above. The attendance of judges at meetings of the Council gave rise to a perception of an involvement on their part (separate from their ordinary function of the conduct of trials) with the implementation of government policy on crime.

In August 1887, for instance, the lord lieutenant, 'by and with the advice of the Privy Council in Ireland', proclaimed the Irish National League to be a 'dangerous association', and hence unlawful, pursuant to s6 of the Criminal Law and

246 Irish Universities Act 1908 (8 Edw. 7, c.38), s18.
247 *ILT&SJ*, vol. 43, p. 254 (16 October 1909); *The value of scholastic philosophy* (Catholic Truth Society, Dublin, 1909).
248 *ILT&SJ*, vol. 51, p. 290 (1 December 1917).
249 T.P. Le Fanu, Memorandum on the Privy Council and Committees, 28 January 1909 (NLI, MS 26061(9)). Mr Le Fanu was a senior official in the chief secretary's office.
250 *Irish Times*, 11 April 1873. This was attended by the lord chancellor (Lord O'Hagan), Sir Joseph Napier, Baron FitzGerald, Justice Fitzgerald and Baron Dowse.
251 *ILT&SJ*, vol. 48, p. 17 (17 January 1914) and p. 138 (16 May 1914); vol. 49, p. 138 (5 June 1915).
252 *Irish Times*, 25 October 1893.

Procedure (Ireland) Act 1887.[253] The proclamation was signed on behalf of the Council by the lord chancellor, Ashbourne, and the vice-chancellor, Chatterton, two Chancery judges who would have no involvement in any criminal trial. Earlier that year Sir Michael Morris, the lord chief justice, had made a statement in court disclaiming any involvement of the judges with criminal prosecutions:

> It having been publicly asserted in Parliament and elsewhere that the institution of criminal prosecutions and the action of the government in connection with the administration of criminal law are discussed and advised on at the Privy Council of Ireland, we, the judges of the Supreme Court of Justice in Ireland, who are members of the Privy Council, give to all such statements the most explicit and positive denial. The Privy Council in Ireland is never, under any circumstances, consulted in criminal prosecutions at any stage, nor within the memory of any of us, have such matters been brought before the Privy Council in any shape or form.[254]

The practice of not involving common law judges in any consideration of matters arising from criminal statutes had been adopted for many decades. However public criticism or misunderstanding of any judicial involvement at all did have an effect, and by the early years of the twentieth century 'it has been considered more expedient only to summon members of the government to attend the Councils at which such documents are to be submitted for signature'.[255]

253 50&51 Vict., c.20; HL Deb, 3rd series, vol. 319, cols. 1063–4 (19 August 1887).
254 *Law Times*, vol. 103, p. 217 (3 July 1897). The statement had been made on 25 February 1887.
255 Memorandum on the Privy Council and Committees, 28 January 1909, op. cit.

CHAPTER THREE

Judicial lives – careers, incomes and honours

ALL JUDGES IN IRELAND UP TO 1921, as for decades afterwards, were selected by politicians. To express that more formally, all judicial appointments in the United Kingdom of Great Britain and Ireland after the Act of Union in 1800 were made by the Crown (in Ireland by the lord lieutenant, the viceroy) on the advice of the government, or in effect by the prime minister of the day. Subsequent chapters review the appointments made to the superior courts in Ireland between 1866 and 1921 in light of the more general considerations outlined here. That political considerations would or might influence judicial appointments in any country at any time is hardly surprising. Lord Salisbury, the prime minister for a total of more than 13 years between 1885 and 1902, took a very keen interest in the nomination of Irish judges, and in particular in the Parliamentary implications of any promotions. W.E. Gladstone on the other hand remarked in 1869 when seeking an alternative to appointing the attorney general to be master of the rolls that 'want of knowledge of the Irish Bench and Bar very much disables me', adding that 'I am confident something could be arranged if public spirit prevails'.[1]

Edward Stanley, the 14th earl of Derby, was prime minister in 1852, 1858–9 and 1866–8. He professed a willingness to delegate decisions on judicial positions, this playing down of his role a result perhaps of being plagued by direct canvassing by candidates for promotion. He told the chief secretary for Ireland in 1866 that although he was happy to be consulted and advise (and he was in fact very well informed on the subject, and alert to party considerations) the selection of judges 'really rests' with the Irish government, namely the lord lieutenant and the chief secretary.[2] Stanley has been a neglected prime minister – indeed, a 'forgotten' one, in the title of his most recent biography.[3] He had a considerable personal knowledge and familiarity with Irish affairs, owning a substantial estate at Ballykisteen, Co. Tipperary, which he visited regularly. As Edward Stanley MP he was chief secretary for Ireland (formally, chief secretary to the lord lieutenant) between 1830 and 1833 and introduced the system of national schools, decades before a similar system of primary education was set up in England. In 1843, when he was colonial secretary, a settlement in the Falkland Islands was named Port Stanley in his honour.

1 Gladstone to Granville, 16 December 1869 (Granville Papers, GD 29/57); *Ramm 1868–71*, p. 78.
2 Derby to Naas, 6 September 1866 (Derby Papers (Liverpool Record Office), 192/1, p. 2).
3 Angus Hawkins, *The forgotten prime minster: the 14th earl of Derby* (Oxford, 2007 (vol. 1) and 2008 (vol. 2)). Better perhaps to be forgotten than unknown – see Robert Blake, *The unknown prime minister: the life and times of Andrew Bonar Law, 1858–1923* (London, 1953)?

Between 1866 and 1868 Derby made a significant number of judicial appointments in Ireland (see chapter 6). In 1832 he had made some observations on the operation of judicial patronage, which can be seen to have still informed his approach to this a third of a century later. He wrote to Francis Blackburne, then the attorney general,

> upon the subject of the vacant assistant-barristership[4] of the county Cavan. I am quite satisfied of the necessity of filling up these situations with reference to personal qualifications for office. At the same time, looking to the current in which government patronage has run for so many years, and the numerous complaints that are made against us, it is essential that we should give the preference to those whose political opinions accord with those of the government, and who perhaps on that ground have been hitherto kept in the background. We owe also something to our supporters in Parliament; but I am sure you will give me credit for sincerity when I say that no parliamentary considerations should induce me to nominate a man whom I thought unfit for the office. I have therefore, in conjunction with Lord Anglesey [the lord lieutenant], agreed to submit to you, in confidence, three names for your opinion of their legal merits; and while I do so, I will add also that, if you think they are any or all of them incompetent, you will at once say so, and suggest any others whom you may think to have superior claims ... Let me have an immediate answer on this subject, as the early settlement of it will prevent a multitude of applications which are continually pouring in.[5]

The political framework within which judicial appointments were made, in Ireland as much as in England, and which was well understood by the Bar, was articulated by Salisbury in 1897. He was perplexed at the time about difficulties in filling a vacancy in the office of master of the rolls in England, and the claims of a leading Conservative lawyer, Sir Edward Clarke QC, to that position or to the office of attorney general.

> There remains the third course – to throw Clarke over altogether and tell him that the highest point of his career has been reached. I confess that the more I consider this alternative the more I dislike it. It is at variance with the unwritten law of our party system; and there is no clearer statute in that

4 In 1787 the lord lieutenant was given power to appoint a barrister to act as 'a constant assistant to the justices' at quarter sessions, and in 1796 this officer in each county was given power to determine, on foot of proceedings initiated by civil bill, suits involving less than £20. In 1858 the title of the office was changed to chairman of quarter sessions, and it was changed again in 1877 to county court judge (27 Geo. 3, c.40; 36 Geo. 3, c.25; 21&22 Vict., c.88; 40&41 Vict., c.56); R.B. McDowell, *The Irish administration, 1801–1914* (London, 1964), pp 113–14.

5 Stanley to Blackburne, 14 April 1832 (Edward Blackburne, *Life of the right hon. Francis Blackburne* (London, 1874), p. 132).

> unwritten law than the rule that party claims should always weigh very heavily in the disposal of the highest legal appointments ... Perhaps it is not an ideal system – some day no doubt the MR [master of the rolls] will be appointed by competitive examination in Law Reports, but it is our system for the present; and we should give our party arrangements a wrench if we throw it aside.[6]

A couple of months later he remarked that 'the judicial salad requires both legal oil and political vinegar; but disastrous effects will follow if due proportion is not observed'.[7]

Party considerations had been set out in more public fashion in Parliament by two Irish MPs at intervals of a decade, in 1864 and 1874. They were on different sides of the House of Commons, and each of them was at the time the attorney general and would shortly be appointed as lord chancellor of Ireland. In 1864 Thomas O'Hagan, who was to be chancellor between 1868 and 1874, and again between 1880 and 1881, disputed the idea – something of a straw man – that 'the mere ground of political connection' could mean that the ignorant would be preferred to the able. 'But if it be only meant that, full competency and integrity being secured, the chancellor, for ordinary appointments, would prefer his political friend to his political adversary, it is no charge at all and requires no refutation. So long as we have constitutional government and conflicting parties, regard must be usually had, on the one side or the other, to political claims'.[8] A few years earlier the attorney general at the time, Rickard Deasy, had told the House that 'services honourably rendered to a party in opposition should not be forgotten when the party was in power'.[9] Political 'friends' or supporters who had been elected as members of Parliament would expect and receive particularly favourable consideration, as appears also below, and as was deplored by the *Irish Law Times* in an editorial in 1868.[10]

In 1874 Dr J.T. Ball QC, MP, then the attorney general but who would shortly be appointed lord chancellor in the Conservative government led by Disraeli, replied to a debate on a motion proposed by Isaac Butt QC, MP that 'it would be to the advantage of the administration of justice if the Irish judges were appointed to the same extent as they are in England, upon the recommendation of the lord chancellor and without reference to political claims'. (That was a rhetorical and quite unrealistic view of the process of appointment in England.) Ball remarked that the lord chancellor himself was a political appointee and was better placed to act as an adviser on appointments than to be 'an arbitrary selector. It was a mistake to suppose that the appointment of a judge rested with the lord lieutenant. All he

6 Salisbury to Halsbury, 19 September 1897 (Halsbury Papers, Add. MS 56371.74); R.F.V. Heuston, *Lives of the lord chancellors, 1885–1940* (Oxford, 1964), pp 52–3.
7 Salisbury to Halsbury, 23 November 1897, cited in R.F.V. Heuston, op. cit., p. 57.
8 HC Deb, 3rd series, vol. 173, col. 200 (5 February 1864).
9 HC Deb, 3rd series, vol. 159, col. 1534 (8 July 1860).
10 *ILT&SJ*, vol. 2, pp 631–2 (21 November 1868).

did was to recommend. The appointment was with the Cabinet, and he had known an instance in which an appointment was wished for in Ireland but was not given by them'.[11]

It is human nature to favour one person over another, while professing or making a comfortable assumption of all other things being equal. There is a handful of documented instances where it is clear that the government considered that some person should not be appointed to a judicial position because of doubts (to use O'Hagan's expression) about his 'full competency'. In 1866 the government of Lord Derby showed some firmness on questions of competence, and courted unpopularity and trouble, in declining to appoint James Whiteside to be lord chancellor and in not giving any appointment to another controversial figure, Francis Macdonogh QC. A more conventional or relaxed view of suitability for appointment was taken in 1888 when the appointment of the attorney general, John G. Gibson, to a vacancy in the High Court was made on foot of frustration at how he was performing his existing functions and the government's wish to remove him from that office without seeming to dismiss him.

Members of the Bar who had Home Rule sympathies, and certainly any who were Nationalist members of Parliament[12] (the great preponderance of Irish MPs for decades following the general election in 1874) who had taken a pledge 'to accept no post of any kind under government',[13] could not look for or have any expectation of appointment. As will be seen, early in the twentieth century some barristers with these sympathies adopted a Liberal colouring. The appointments of Thomas Molony (in 1913 and again, as a promotion, in 1918), J.F. Moriarty (in 1914) and James O'Connor (in 1918) were made with a view to courting favour with nationalist interests. When R.R. Cherry QC, who had stood unsuccessfully as a Liberal candidate in a Liverpool constituency in the 1900 general election,[14] inquired of John Redmond in 1904 whether he could stand in a Irish constituency without nationalist opposition he was told that so far as Redmond was concerned 'I will not publicly support any member of the Irish Bar unless on the understanding that he is not to look for [a] place [on the Bench]'.[15] The affiliations of candidates for judicial appointments thus continued up to the first decade of the century to be the traditional Conservative (or Unionist) and Liberal parties.

Political support or interest was helpful at all stages of a barrister's career, before the heights of being considered for appointment to be a law officer (attorney general or solicitor general) or a judge were reached. The early careers of men who

11 HC Deb, 3rd series, vol. 220, col. 436 (25 June 1874).

12 The numbers of MPs elected as members of the Irish Parliamentary Party who had been called to the Bar varied between 14 and 17 at the general elections held between 1892 and 1910 (F.S.L. Lyons, *The Irish Parliamentary Party, 1890–1910* (London 1951), p. 169).

13 Fergus Campbell, *The Irish establishment, 1879–1914* (Oxford, 2009), p. 317; Conor Cruise O'Brien, *Parnell and his Party* (Oxford, 1957), pp 141 and 143.

14 Daire Hogan, 'R.R. Cherry, lord chief justice of Ireland, 1914–1916' in D.S. Greer and N.M. Dawson (eds), *Mysteries and solutions in Irish legal history* (Dublin, 2001), pp 164–75.

15 Redmond to Cherry, 22 February 1904 (Cherry Papers (PRONI), D.2166/3/2/2).

later were appointed to be members of the judiciary show signs of early promise and/or government patronage in appointments as prosecuting counsel in particular counties, for instance. Taking a few examples from the end of the nineteenth century, Peter O'Brien QC, later to be attorney general (1888) and lord chief justice of Ireland (1889), was appointed junior Crown prosecutor for the city and county of Dublin (at the Green Street courthouse) in 1882 and then the senior such prosecutor (a financially valuable position, said to be worth about £1,500 or £2,000 annually)[16] in 1883. His protégé Edward Carson was appointed counsel to the attorney general in 1887, senior Crown prosecutor for Co. Wicklow in 1889 and senior Crown prosecutor in Green Street at the end of 1891. Carson was replaced there the following year (on his promotion to be solicitor general) by George Wright, who in 1887 had been appointed Crown counsel for Co. Kerry, a position previously held by John Atkinson. James Campbell was successively appointed senior Crown prosecutor for Co. Armagh and for Belfast in 1891, and senior Crown prosecutor in Green Street in 1900. Arthur W. Samuels QC was successively senior Crown prosecutor for Co. Tipperary and (in 1897) Co. Kildare.

The position of law adviser was a first step upon the ladder of official patronage at Dublin Castle itself, frequently leading to appointment as solicitor general. The position had been established in the 1830s 'in order to promote a uniform and homogenous administration of the law at petty sessions',[17] and its primary function was the furnishing of succinct advice as might be requested by magistrates at petty sessions upon the law applicable to cases pending before them. 'The duties were by no means heavy. They consisted chiefly of setting the Irish magistrates right upon questions arising from often confused and sometimes obscure Acts of Parliament; the powers of police in the execution of their duty; legality of convictions; how far the justices of the peace could act under peculiar circumstances, and such like matters, which unprofessional gentlemen, however intelligent, could scarcely decide correctly'.[18] Other undefined duties, generally assisting the law officers, arose from time to time.[19] The concept of any advisory link between the executive at Dublin Castle and the magistracy came to be seen as increasingly undesirable, and the post was abolished in 1883[20] (its title, although not its original function, was revived briefly in 1919 for the appointment of W.E. Wylie). Those who held it in the later decades of the nineteenth century included

16 Ashbourne to Cadogan, 10 December 1899 (Cadogan Papers, CAD 1685/1); Cadogan to Salisbury, 18 January 1900 (Papers of the 3rd marquess of Salisbury, Hatfield House, Hatfield, Herfordshire (henceforth Salisbury Papers)).

17 HL Deb, 3rd series, vol. 279, col. 378 (10 May 1883) (Lord Fitzgerald).

18 J.R. O'Flanagan, *The Irish Bar* (London, 1879), p. 340; see *ILT&SJ*, vol. 10, p. 556 (21 October 1876), for an example of a terse response to a procedural query made by magistrates at Killorglin, Co. Kerry.

19 R.B. McDowell, *The Irish administration, 1801–1914* (London, 1964), pp 120–1; J.P. Casey, *The office of the attorney general in Ireland* (Dublin, 1980), p. 37.

20 HL Deb, 3rd series, vol. 279, col. 378: *ILT&SJ*, vol.17, p. 233 (28 April 1883) and vol. 22, p. 285 (9 June 1888).

Edward Sullivan (1861), Charles Robert Barry (1865), David Plunket (1868), William Moore Johnson (1869), G.A.C. May (1874), Gerald FitzGibbon (1876), Hugh Holmes (1877) and John Naish (1881).

Candidates for office might be taken at their own estimation, and Ignatius O'Brien observed that 'if one hoped for a high preferment at the Irish Bar it was a mistake to place a county court judgeship as the ultimate goal'.[21] The appointment of Jonathan Pim to the High Court in 1915 resulted from an inquiry he made as to whether he could become a county court judge (see p. 414). Over half a century earlier, Hedges Eyre Chatterton had similarly asked for such an appointment, and the lord chancellor, Napier, 'wrote me back a very kind letter … … strongly advising me not to [press this request] as he considered that I was entitled to look for something better. I took his advice and here I am [vice-chancellor]'.[22]

Barristers could demonstrate support and loyalty to their chosen party by standing for election to Parliament and, even better, by winning such an election and taking a seat in the House of Commons and attending there. Participation in electoral politics involved trouble and expense, not only at election time but also in monitoring the annual revision of the electoral register, in the era before universal franchise when a right to vote was derived from meeting a property-owning qualification of considerable potential complexity (see issues on electoral register in Derry, p. 365). W.E.H. Lecky noted to a friend in 1869 that 'pushing, eloquent and logical people should become lawyers'[23] and, while such qualities were obviously important for professional advancement, an ability to push oneself forward had particular significance for political success. (A different and honoured tradition at the Bar was noted in 1879 – 'men who sought convivial society in preference to professional toil, yet who earned reputations worth preserving; the wits and humorists of the Irish Parliament and the Bar; men who possessed more wit than wisdom, more *bon-mots* than books, more brilliancy than briefs'.)[24]

A law enacted in 1868, the Parliamentary Elections Act,[25] contained a sanction against electoral misconduct or corruption that was of particular relevance to members of the Bar. Section 43 provided that if bribery was found to have been committed by or with the knowledge and consent of a candidate he would not only be debarred from being elected, and from being a magistrate, for seven years but would not be capable for the same period of holding any judicial office. The *Irish Law Times* thought that the prospect of ineligibility for any judicial appointment

21 Daire Hogan and Patrick Maume (eds), *The reminiscences of Ignatius O'Brien, lord chancellor of Ireland 1913–18* (Dublin, 2021), p. 242.

22 Hedges Eyre Chatterton, biographical sketch (Trinity College Dublin Library), IE TCD MS 640/1, p. 18.

23 Lecky to Wilmot Chetwode, [undated] March 1869 (H. Montgomery Hyde (ed.), *A Victorian historian: private letters of W.E.H. Lecky, 1859–1878* (London, 1947), pp 77–8); Donal McCartney, *W.E.H. Lecky: historian and politician, 1838–1903* (Dublin, 1994), p. 26.

24 O'Flanagan, *The Irish Bar*, p. vii.

25 31&32 Vict., c.125.

would have, and perhaps had already had in the general election taking place later that year, a salutary effect upon the conduct of candidates from the Bar.[26]

The parliamentary constituency that was most closely associated with members of the Bar was that of Dublin University. Lawyers – more precisely, Conservative or Unionist barristers – virtually monopolized the representation of the university.[27] In the nineteenth century 16 of the 20 elected university MPs were members of the Bar, 14 of whom were appointed to be law officers and all except one of whom (David Plunket – see p. 87) were subsequently appointed to be judges.[28] Between 1903 and 1916 the two university MPs were Sir Edward Carson KC and James H.M. Campbell KC (who became attorney general in April 1916, and lord chief justice at the end of the year), and between 1903 and 1905 both held office as solicitor general, Carson in England and Campbell in Ireland. When Campbell stepped down as an MP his seat was won by Arthur Samuels KC, who himself was appointed attorney general in 1917 and as a judge in 1919. The election of a member of the Bar as one of the university's MPs was thus a virtual guarantee of appointment as a law officer and hence in due course to be a judge. Derby's lament, in the particular circumstances of 1866, that 'it is not desirable to make the representation of the University a regular stepping-stone to legal office'[29] was borne out by a contemporary observation that the independence of the university's representatives was comprised by so many of them having been lawyers, presumed to be ambitious for advancement.[30]

The university constituencies in Britain and Ireland were exempted from the introduction of the secret ballot in 1872,[31] and their parliamentary elections continued to be held by means of a poll, extending over a few days. In elections in Dublin University there were daily disclosures of the running totals of the votes cast for each candidate, and at nomination meetings and after the declaration of the result an atmosphere of high spirits, at times somewhat disorderly, prevailed in and around the college.

The corresponding parliamentary seats for the universities of Oxford and Cambridge were contested on party lines, and were held by many lawyers, but those universities also had some tradition of electing members with a connection to the underlying educational and research functions of the university. Between the 1880s and 1920 the MPs for Oxford University included the warden of All Souls College, who was the author of a classic work on the law of contract (William Anson), and for Cambridge they included a professor of Greek (Richard

26 *ILT&SJ*, vol. 2, p. 632 (21 November 1868).
27 One member from 1801 to 1832 (Act of Union), two members thereafter (Representation of the People (Ireland) Act 1832 (2&3 Will. IV, c.88), s11).
28 *ILT&SJ*, vol. 27, p. 331 (8 July 1893); *Law Times*, vol. 113, p. 409 (6 September 1902).
29 Derby to Naas, 6 September 1866 (Derby Papers, 192/1, p. 2).
30 *Law Times*, vol. 43, p. 301 (31 August 1867).
31 'Nothing in this Act [except Part III thereof – personation] shall apply to any election for a university' (An Act to amend the law relating to procedure at parliamentary and municipal elections [the Ballot Act], 1872 (35&36 Vict., c.33), s31).

Claverhouse Jebb), another classicist and president of the British Academy (Samuel Butcher) and a professor of mathematics (Joseph Larmor).[32]

Lecky, one of Dublin University's MPs between 1895 and 1903, was the only representative of the university who, although he did not hold any academic position, had a scholarly (as contrasted with a primarily legal) reputation. He was the author of an authoritative history of Ireland (and of England) in the eighteenth century. The other candidate in the bye-election in 1895 (caused by the elevation of David Plunket to the House of Lords, as Lord Rathmore of Loughlinstown) was George Wright QC, a leader of the Munster Bar. 'A strong feeling has prevailed for several years past among the fellows and professors that the university should have a representative in whom the academic spirit would be pre-eminently reflected, and on this ground Mr Lecky was induced to come forward as a candidate'.[33] In 1892 an unsuccessful candidate, J.C.J. Lowry, a Tyrone landowner, observed that nine successive MPs for the university had been appointed as judges, and said that 'the university returned two members, they asked only for one of these to be a representative of landlords, and not restricted to legal gentlemen who want to make it a ladder to get to the bench'.[34]

A constituency that was created and first contested in 1885[35] which also had something of a legal character, although nothing like the university, was the Stephen's Green division of Dublin. A significant number of its voters (over 600)[36] were members of the legal profession. It was represented by lawyers between 1892 and 1900, up to 1898 by William Kenny QC (a Liberal Unionist) and then (following Kenny's appointment to be a High Court judge) by James H.M. Campbell (a straightforward Unionist), who lost his seat in the 1900 election. He lived in the constituency, at Upper Pembroke Street, and as mentioned subsequently represented the university from 1903 to 1916.

The city and county of Londonderry were represented in Parliament in the late nineteenth and early twentieth century by a total of eight men who attained judicial office. The city seat was held by Richard Dowse (1868–72) and John Ross (1892–5) and was contested by Christopher Palles (1872). The county seat was held successively by Hugh Law (1874–81), Andrew Marshall Porter (1881–3) and Samuel Walker (1884–5), all Liberals. After the division of the county into two constituencies in 1885 North Londonderry was held by John Atkinson (1895–1905) and the South division successively by John Gordon (1900–16) and Denis Henry (1917–21), who as mentioned was appointed in 1921 to be the first lord chief justice of Northern Ireland. The neighbouring seat of Tyrone North was contested without success by J.O. Wylie in 1886 and was won by W.H. Dodd (1906–7) and Redmond J. Barry (1907–11).

32 See a letter on the subject from J.G. Swift MacNeill MP, *Irish Times*, 28 December 1916.
33 *ILT&SJ*, vol. 29, p. 603 (14 December 1895).
34 *Irish Times*, 5 August 1892.
35 Redistribution of Seats Act 1885 (48&49 Vict., c.23), s8 and 6th Schedule, Part III.
36 *Law Times*, vol. 104, p. 265 (22 January 1898), vol. 109, p. 490 (6 October 1900).

Any regular attention by MPs to their Parliamentary functions in London during the sittings of the House of Commons (generally between February and August in each year) would have cut across their legal careers (and incomes) in Dublin. MPs were not paid until 1911, when an initial salary of £400 (not in any event a material amount to a senior member of the Bar) was resolved upon,[37] and indeed would typically have been expected to contribute to their own election expenses. MPs developed a sense of entitlement to promotion or judicial preferment over other colleagues at the Bar who had not made such sacrifices nor been elected. That was particularly the case for MPs who did not have the almost guaranteed promotion prospects associated with appointment as a law officer (see below). Such expectations were forcefully expressed to Derby by two different men, Stearne Ball Miller and Francis Macdonogh, in 1866–7.

Joseph Napier, one of the MPs for Dublin University between 1848 and 1858, was said to be 'the first Irish lawyer in the imperial parliament who was willing to sacrifice professional emolument for political reputation'.[38] R. Denny Urlin, a court official, wrote of Napier that 'he would have had a large equity and other business but for (1) frequent absences on parliamentary duties and (2) deafness; consequently he was, to my knowledge, poor until he obtained office'.[39] Hugh Holmes, who was solicitor general between 1878 and 1880 and attorney general for two periods amounting to about 16 months in 1885–7, was frustrated by expectations that he would remain active in politics and 'do something for the cause', writing that 'an Irish barrister cannot retain his practice and at the same time acquire a parliamentary reputation. If he tries to keep in touch with the law courts and the House of Commons he will fail in both, and I preferred following a career for which I knew I was well fitted to engaging in a new and doubtful enterprise'.[40]

John Ross, an MP between 1892 and 1895, wrote in a memoir that he had been obliged to abandon his practice for a while, and after failing to be re-elected 'I went over my accounts and reviewed the situation. My savings were all spent, my little investments were all sold, and I was literally down and out'. Happily it transpired that solicitors were loyal to him, work returned, and the following year he was appointed as a judge.[41] James Campbell asserted in the course of the general election campaign of 1900 that his political commitment and interests so far from being in furtherance of his professional career had in reality been a hindrance,[42]

37 HC Deb, 5th series, vol. 29, cols. 1579–1682 (14 August 1911).

38 Ball, pp 295–6.

39 R. Denny Urlin, *Journal and reminiscences* (Letchworth, 1909), p. 134.

40 Memoirs of Hugh Holmes (2 vols, PRONI, MIC197/1), p. 155. This memoir, written after 1901 for his family, is hereafter referred to as 'Holmes Memoir'. Extracts, edited by A.B. Cooke and J.R. Vincent, were published as (and citation page numbers herein are, unless otherwise specified, taken from) 'Ireland and party politics 1885–7, an unpublished Conservative memoir', *IHS*, vol. 16, nos. 62–4 (September 1968–September 1969), pp 154–72, 321–38 and 446–71. (The third article is an analysis of the extracts published in the two preceding editions.)

41 John Ross, *The years of my pilgrimage* (London, 1924), pp 102 and 118.

42 *Law Times*, vol. 109, p. 490 (6 October 1900).

and John Atkinson, then the attorney general, said this privately to the chief secretary (see p. 379). In Campbell's later persistent correspondence over his own sense of entitlement to a judicial position, he told the prime minister, Asquith, of the hardship and difficulty of trying to maintain links in Ireland while also attending Parliament, often involving in the same week the journey twice between Dublin and London.[43]

Work as the attorney general, the government's principal legal adviser, or as solicitor general, his deputy and 'colleague or understudy',[44] imposed greater strains in travel and attendance in London than those applicable to MPs generally. From the government's point of view these offices were most usefully held by an MP, who would be able to participate in debates and answer questions in the House of Commons, and whether a prospective appointee was an MP influenced some appointments. Gladstone appointed Charles Barry as solicitor general in December 1868 and, while regretting that he had lost his seat at the recent general election, hoped and trusted that before long he would obtain another, 'as, in the struggles that must come, we shall need to have all our champions in the field'.[45] About forty years later Augustine Birrell, then chief secretary, outlining what Parliamentary support might be given by a law officer, took the view that doing without would be preferable to unsuitable assistance. He was canvassing names for nomination as a candidate at a bye-election in North Tyrone caused by the appointment of the sitting MP, Redmond Barry QC, to be lord chancellor. He told the bishop of Raphoe that

> there is nobody now on our side at the Irish Bar likely to be of any use to me next year in the House of Commons when the great tussle – and a great tussle it will be [he was referring to Home Rule] – comes on. Neither Ignatius O'Brien nor [Thomas] Molony have either parliamentary experience or aptitude. A mere lawyer is not of much use. I want experience, knowledge, courage and a man who will be listened to … neither of the two legal gentlemen would be anything but a hindrance to me at Westminster – they or whichever of them is selected can stay and do the legal work in Dublin and draw the salary.[46]

He told T.M. Healy a couple of years later in that context that he was 'tired of duffers'.[47] At times in the 1870s and 1880s the attorney general had been an unsuccessful Parliamentary candidate (Christopher Palles, G.A.C. May and Peter

43 Campbell to Asquith, 3 October 1915 (Asquith Papers (Bodleian Library, Oxford), 28:15).
44 Campbell to Bonar Law, undated [July] 1919 (Bonar Law Papers, 87/3/4).
45 Gladstone to Barry, 11 December 1868 (Gladstone Papers, Add. MS 44417.76).
46 Birrell to Dr O'Donnell, 21 August 1911 (Leon Ó Broin, *The chief secretary: Augustine Birrell in Ireland* (London, 1969), pp 44–5; J.P. Casey, *The office of the attorney general in Ireland* (Dublin, 1980), p. 31; J.P. Casey, *The Irish law officers* (Dublin, 1996), p. 41; *Ignatius O'Brien reminiscences*, p. 245.
47 T.M. Healy, *Letters and leaders*, vol. 2, p. 525.

O'Brien). When Denis Henry QC, MP, was appointed as attorney general early in 1919 'it is generally recognized that promotion has come rather slowly. Mr Henry has been one of the undisputed leaders of the Bar for over a dozen years, but he did not succeed until a couple of years ago in obtaining a seat in Parliament, and the fact was unquestionably against him, having regard to the course of promotion in this country'.[48]

The *Law Times* described the general stress on an Irish barrister,

> if he attempts to carry on simultaneously, or as nearly simultaneously as possible, the regular work of the Bar and Parliament. The journey from Dublin to London occupies some twelve hours. [He] is obliged either to be constantly crossing and recrossing the Channel, or to be absent from one or the other of the spheres of his labours for considerable intervals at a stretch. If he desires to be in London in good time for a debate on a particular day he must leave Dublin the day before, at the latest, and travel all night to reach his seat at Westminster. A law officer accordingly, if he be fortunate enough to find a constituency willing to return him, generally lives almost entirely in London during the period of his Parliamentary labours.[49]

There was a general understanding or 'accepted practice'[50] that the attorney general had an entitlement, at times referred to as a prescriptive right, to be invited to fill any vacancy that might arise in the superior courts while he held office, subject to the two exceptions noted in the second next following paragraph. The solicitor general had a similar or ancillary expectation of being offered any judicial position not taken up by the attorney general, and of in turn filling the attorney's shoes if he did take one up. One attorney general, Edward Sullivan, expressed this entitlement in strong terms to the prime minister in 1869 when he was encountering resistance to his wish to be appointed as master of the rolls. Sullivan pitched his argument primarily on the grounds of ill health that had been, as he believed, caused by the strain of his existing office, while adding that although he believed that he could express his claim to be master of the rolls in Ireland as a question of actual entitlement he had not done so.[51] A resolution made by the government in 1873 no longer to recognize formally any claim as of right of the law officers in England to judicial appointments (see p. 249), following the enactment of the Judicature Act for that jurisdiction, had little practical effect, and no sustained effort was made to adopt any similar principle for Ireland.

It was openly acknowledged, for instance, for one of the first judicial vacancies that arose after the coming into force of the 1877 Act, a place in the Court of

48 *ILT&SJ*, vol. 53, p. 53 (1 March 1919).
49 *Law Times*, vol. 79, p. 227 (25 July 1885).
50 Lord Carswell, 'Founding a legal system: the early judiciary of Northern Ireland' in Felix M. Larkin and N.M. Dawson (eds), *Lawyers, the law and history* (Dublin, 2013), p. 17.
51 Sullivan to Gladstone, 15 December 1869 (Gladstone Papers, Add. MS 44423.313).

Appeal, that the choice lay anyway on grounds of merit between the two law officers, Edward Gibson and Gerald FitzGibbon.[52] When Gibson declined appointment to that vacancy in November 1878 he asked that the lord lieutenant would formally acknowledge that his right as attorney general to this had been supplanted by his acceptance of a government request that he would pass it up.[53] He was told in reply that the offer had been made by the prime minister, 'I presume in accordance with the custom which has prevailed with attorney generals in Ireland, in the absence of any other consideration'.[54] In debating the proper salary for the attorney general in 1886 the Treasury made reference to 'the right enjoyed by the attorney general to promotion to the judicial bench, if any vacancy should occur during his tenure of office'.[55] R.R. Cherry complained in 1906 at not being officially informed or consulted about some impending judicial promotions, saying that while he had no wish to go to the Bench at present and was conscious of the contribution expected of him in the House of Commons at the time, it was most unusual for an attorney general to be treated in that way. When accepting the chief secretary's assurance that he had not been aware of the usual practice in Ireland and that no discourtesy had been intended he noted that 'the lord chancellor [Walker] cannot plead the same ignorance'.[56]

Nomination to the office of lord chancellor, with its governmental as well as judicial functions, was always made as a political calculation in light of the circumstances of the day. As often as not, that day occurred when a new government was being formed after an election. Of the 13 men who held the office between 1866 and 1921 five were appointed in that way (some more than once – O'Hagan, Ashbourne and Walker) and the others were appointed when casual vacancies arose or were engineered. The office of lord chief justice was also an exception to any claim of an attorney general, as was noted by the two law officers in 1878.[57] Three sitting attorneys general (May, Peter O'Brien and Campbell) were appointed to that office in the same period, 1866–1921, and each of the other four appointees was either a former holder of the office (Whiteside) or was a sitting judge (Morris, Cherry, Molony) who had previously so served.

In 1888 Arthur Balfour, the chief secretary, was at pains to indicate to Peter O'Brien, the incoming attorney general, that intended reductions in judicial numbers would place him

52 Ball to duke of Marlborough, 28 October 1878 (Political Papers of the 7th duke of Marlborough (Cambridge University Library), MS Add. 9271/4/10); James Lowther (chief secretary for Ireland) to Marlborough, 5 November 1878 (Marlborough Papers, MS Add. 9271/4/157).

53 Gibson to Marlborough, 5 November 1878 (Marlborough Papers, MS Add. 9271/4/116).

54 Marlborough to Gibson, 6 November 1878 (Ashbourne Papers, B.102/2; Marlborough Papers, MS Add. 9271/4/117).

55 Treasury correspondence, 22 May 1886 (Correspondence between the Treasury and the Irish Government as to the remuneration of the attorney general and solicitor general for Ireland, PP (1887), lxvii, 379-94); J.P. Casey, *The office of the attorney general in Ireland* (Dublin, 1980), pp 32–5; J.P. Casey, *The Irish law officers* (Dublin, 1996), p. 43.

56 Cherry to Bryce, 10 and 13 October 1906 (Bryce Papers, MS 11,014(2)).

57 FitzGibbon to Gibson, 22 October 1878 (Ashbourne Papers, B.50/9).

> in a somewhat different position as regard the terms of your office from many of your predecessors, [as] it has hitherto been customary to fill up vacancies in the judicial bench from among the law officers, unless indeed they happen to have held office for an exceptionally brief period, and one effect of [such reductions] will be to retard somewhat the course of promotion among the law officers.[58]

O'Brien acknowledged and accepted the situation, as did the incoming solicitor general, Dodgson Hamilton Madden.[59] In fact, neither of them, nor subsequent law officers, did experience any such delay in promotion, although an element in the consistent opposition of the wider Bar to judicial reform was the loss of promotion opportunities resulting from the reductions in the numbers of superior court judges effected by statute between 1877 and 1907.

The attorney general for the time being was the leader of the Bar and hence, as ordinarily in any event a barrister of high standing, was potentially suitable to receive a judicial appointment, altogether apart from any sense of a political favour being owed and any disposition on the part of the government to appoint to the bench a person familiar with the conduct of government business. But, more than that, to be attorney general or solicitor general was to be virtually guaranteed a subsequent appointment as a judge. In the nineteenth century 50 men held office as attorney general (some more than once), only three of whom were not appointed to senior judicial office, either as a direct promotion from that office or subsequently. Between 1900 and 1921 13 men were appointed (not including John Atkinson, who was attorney general between 1895 and 1905, and accounting for him only in the nineteenth-century column), all of whom became judges. (The last two holders of the office, Denis Henry (in office 1919–21) and Thomas Watters Brown (1921) were appointed to the High Court of Northern Ireland, Henry as lord chief justice.) The three men not so appointed were John Stewart (in office 1800–3), John Hatchell (1850–2) and Hugh Hyacinth O'Rorke MacDermot (1892–5). Stewart (*c.*1758–1825) was MP for Co. Tyrone and was made a baronet in 1803. Hatchell (1788–1870) was MP for Windsor between 1850 and 1852, when he did not seek re-election, and was appointed a commissioner of the Insolvent Debtors Court in 1854.[60] MacDermot (1835–1904), who had also been solicitor general briefly in 1885 and 1886, could be regarded as unlucky in that while he held office no vacancies arose for superior court appointments, other than that of lord chancellor, which was given to an established and more senior colleague, Samuel Walker. He died before his party, the Liberals, returned to government in 1905. In 1893 Gerald FitzGibbon noted to Lord Randolph Churchill that having served as a judge for over 15 years he was now eligible for a pension but had no

58 Balfour to O'Brien, 12 January 1888 (Balfour Papers, Add. MS 49814.1).
59 Madden to Balfour, 13 January 1888 (Balfour Papers, Add. MS 49814.81).
60 *Law Times*, vol. 49, p. 316 (20 August 1870).

intention of creating a vacancy that would be filled by 'Morley's[61] attorney general'.[62]

The great majority of persons appointed to be attorney general between 1800 and 1921 had previously served as solicitor general (including Stewart, Hatchell and MacDermot), and all except four of the men who held the position of solicitor general either were promoted to that higher office or were appointed directly to the judicial bench (the latter category numbered 15 in total).[63] The four exceptions were David Plunket (in office 1875–7), Edward Carson (1892), Charles Hemphill (1892–5) and James Chambers (1917). Plunket was one of the MPs for Dublin University between 1870 and 1895, when a peerage (as Lord Rathmore) was conferred on him and he joined the House of Lords. He was the grandson of two men (Lord Plunket and Charles Kendal Bushe) who had been lord chancellor and chief justice of King's Bench respectively, and he might have seemed suitable hereditary material to be a judge, but he preferred a parliamentary and political career to a judicial one. His appointment as solicitor general early in 1875 was proposed with a view to ensuring that one of the law officers would have a seat in the House of Commons, and be in a position to join in debates and respond to questions, and he was assured that the substantive legal responsibilities of the position would be dealt with by the attorney general and the law adviser.[64] 'Promotion is a matter neither of consequence nor of ambition to him' it was said in 1877,[65] and more than a decade later, in 1891, Arthur Balfour described him as 'both idle and unambitious'.[66] Edward Carson (1854–1935) was very briefly solicitor general in 1892 but subsequently made his career in England, where he became both solicitor general (1900) and attorney general (1915), and subsequently a Law Lord (in 1921). Hemphill (1822–1908) shared the experience of MacDermot of no judicial vacancy arising while he held office between 1892 and 1895, and a decade later would not at his advanced age have expected that he would be re-appointed or receive any promotion. He was however given the honour of a peerage in 1906. James Chambers QC (1861–1917), the MP for South Belfast, died only a couple of months after he had been appointed solicitor general in April 1917.

The smooth path between the office of attorney or solicitor general and the judicial bench had some potential implications for the administration of justice

61 John Morley was the chief secretary for Ireland in the Liberal government, 1892–5.

62 FitzGibbon to Churchill, 12 December 1893 (LRC Papers, MS Add. 9248.4411).

63 William Cusack Smith (1801); James McClelland (1803), Charles Kendal Bushe (1822), John Doherty (1830), Philip Cecil Crampton (1834), Joseph Devonsher Jackson (1842), John George (1866), Michael Harrison (1868), Gerald FitzGibbon (1878), John Monroe (1885), William Kenny (1898), Dunbar Plunket Barton (1900), George Wright (1903), John Blake Powell (1918) and Daniel Martin Wilson (1921). Mr Wilson was soon appointed a judge of the High Court of Northern Ireland.

64 Hicks Beach to Plunket, 11 January 1875, Plunket to Hicks Beach, 12 January 1875 (Hicks Beach Papers (Gloucestershire Archives, Gloucester, D2455/X4/1/1/3 (6), (7), (8)).

65 *Irish Times*, 3 February 1877.

66 Balfour to Salisbury, 27–9 August 1891 (HH 6/48, *Salisbury–Balfour Correspondence*, p. 348).

and perceptions of good order at criminal trials. Law officers would personally have conducted prosecutions in major trials, if that seemed appropriate 'owing to their great importance and sometimes to their great difficulty' as stated in the House of Commons in 1911.[67] Although they were necessarily familiar with approaches likely to be taken by defence counsel and would previously have had their own experiences of criminal defence work at the Bar, work in government would have provided their most recent pre-judicial perspective on crime. Judges who had been law officers, in addition to engagement in individual prosecutions, would more generally have been involved in prosecution policy, and with government legal strategy on political agitation, agrarian crime and 'outrages'. The now familiar concept of prosecutions being the responsibility of an independent public prosecutor's office was not introduced in Northern Ireland until 1972 and in Dublin until 1974.

Judges for centuries had taken oaths upon appointment to execute their office faithfully, to 'do right to all manner of people after the laws and usages of the realm, without fear or favour, affection or ill will', in the formulation then most recently prescribed in 1868,[68] and the substance of that oath, with some verbal re-ordering and editing, continues to be applicable, in both jurisdictions in Ireland.[69] Such oaths of independence can be assumed to have been taken by judges in good faith, and as a French observer noted 'their rectitude, uprightness and personal honour are not in question'.[70] However, defendants in any case with some political aspect might not have been unreasonable if they had wondered about the fairness of a trial presided over by such a judge (or by more than one, in a divisional court). Four of the five judges in the divisional court which determined (and refused) a very significant habeas corpus application in February 1921, *R v Allen*,[71] had previously held office as attorney general, three of whom had been Unionist MPs, and the judge who had not been a law officer had also been a Unionist MP. (Only four of the judges of the superior courts at that time had not been law officers – Ross, Ronan, Dodd and Moore.) Arthur Balfour saw a danger of too plain a connection being made between service as attorney general and service as a judge when he resisted, for a time anyway, pressure from Peter O'Brien, a former attorney general who had been lord chief justice for less than 18 months, to be made a baronet: 'a baronetcy conferred on a chief justice immediately on his retirement from a stormy attorney generalship would look more like a reward to the law officer than a mark of honour to the judge'.[72]

67 HC Deb, 5th series, vol. 22, col. 2601 (17 March 1911). It was customary in England for the attorney general to lead for the prosecution in trials for murder by poisoning (*ODNB* entry on Lord Reading (Rufus Isaacs, attorney general 1910–13)).

68 Promissory Oaths Act 1868 (31&32 Vict., c.72), s4.

69 Constitution of Ireland, article 34.5.1, and Justice (Northern Ireland) Act 2002, c.26, s19.

70 L. Paul-Dubois, *Contemporary Ireland* (Dublin, 1908), p. 207.

71 [1921] 2 IR 241.

72 Balfour to O'Brien, 5 March 1891 (Balfour Papers, Add. MS 49814.322).

The manner in which T.M. Healy QC, MP expressed such concerns in the House of Commons in 1893 led to a rowdy scene:

> T.M. Healy. You have in Ireland a set of political judges. I go to the Queen's Bench in Dublin and whom do I find confronting me? Mr Justice Holmes, who sat upon that [the front government bench] and proposed the Coercion Act;[73] Mr Justice Gibson, who was second in command; and Mr Justice Madden, who also acted under the right hon. gentleman [A.J. Balfour]; and the chief justice of the Queen's Bench in Ireland [Sir Peter O'Brien] … [Cries of 'Order!']
>
> Mr Speaker. Order, order! The hon. and learned member is now perilously near the infringement of the rule which says that you must not comment, except upon motion in due course, upon the conduct of the judges of the land, or impute to them, arising out of political circumstances, any bias in their conduct.
>
> T.M. Healy. I shall carefully abstain from any infringement of the rule. All I say is this, that here you have four gentlemen who have been attorney generals under this Coercion Act. And when they go down through the length and breadth of Ireland to declare [at the assizes] that a particular state of things exists in the country, of course I cannot forget that I have seen these gentlemen at that table. [Cries of 'Order!']
>
> Mr Speaker. The hon. and learned gentleman is going very near an infringement of the rule, and I must ask him to faithfully observe the spirit of it.
>
> T.M. Healy. I shall simply say that I admire the character of the English judges, who never do anything of the kind. [Cries of 'Order!'][74]

The first Home Rule Bill in 1886 contained an acknowledgment of the difficulty that a devolution of some government powers to an Irish legislature might create for a number of the judges in Ireland (not all necessarily former law officers), as referred to by Gladstone when introducing the Bill:

> Under the particular circumstances of Ireland we cannot forget that some of these [existing] judges, by no fault of their own, have been placed in relations more or less uneasy with popular influences, and with what, under the new constitution, will in all probability be the dominating influence in that country. We cannot overlook the peculiarities of Irish history in framing the provisions of the Bill; and we therefore propose, both with regard to the judges now holding office and with regard to other persons who, in what they deemed loyal service to the Empire, have been concerned in the administration and conduct of the criminal law in Ireland, that Her Majesty

73 Criminal Law and Procedure (Ireland) Act 1887 (50&51 Vict., c.20).
74 HC Deb, 4th series, vol. 12, cols. 1806–7 (1 June 1893).

> may, not lightly or wholesale, but if she should see cause on any particular occasion, by Order in Council, antedate the pensions of these particular persons.[75]

This provision for potential early retirement of a judge before completion of the period of service entitling him to a pension was made also in the subsequent Home Rule Bills, and in the Government of Ireland Act 1920.[76] Gerald FitzGibbon facetiously speculated as to whether any existing judges who had not yet got into 'uneasy relations with popular influences' might think of setting about doing so, in order to become eligible for accelerated pensions.[77]

The lord chancellor was the head of the judiciary, and the powers, prestige and large salary of the office meant that it was the most highly prized appointment. For 25 years, between 1886 and 1911, it was held and exchanged (on a change of government after a general election) between only two men, Lord Ashbourne and Samuel Walker. The chancellor's historic functions included being the general guardian of infants and lunatics and having responsibility for the appointment of magistrates. He presided over the Court of Appeal. His authority extended over the legal profession, not only as chairman of the benchers of King's Inns but also as having regulatory functions under the Solicitors' Acts.[78] He was responsible for the calls to the Inner Bar, considering applications from barristers of standing to be appointed as Queen's [King's] Counsel. The lord chancellor was a member of both the executive and the judicial branches of government, having an office in Dublin Castle (adjoining that of the law officers[79]) as well as chambers in the Four Courts. The fact that Ignatius O'Brien was excluded from involvement in conventional functions of his office after May 1915[80] contributed to the subsequent dysfunction in the government of Ireland. The chancellor was the only judge not to be appointed for life, and thus in any event ceased to hold office on a change of government. Some chancellors retired due to ill health, and others did so after being heavily pressured to resign, as in the cases of Lord Plunket in 1841 and Francis Blackburne in 1867. O'Brien was in effect summarily removed from office in 1918.

The chancellor was one of the most influential voices in government in Ireland on judicial appointments and promotions, his legal perspective contributing to what were ultimately political decisions. The judicial appointments made in England during the periods, extending in aggregate over 17 years between 1885 and 1905, in which Lord Halsbury was lord chancellor of Great Britain, while Lord Salisbury and then Arthur Balfour was prime minister, have been the subject

75 HC Deb, 3rd series, vol. 304, col. 1070 (8 April 1886); s26 of Bill.
76 Government of Ireland Act 1920 (10&11 Geo. 5, c.67), seventh schedule, Part III, para. 1(b).
77 FitzGibbon to Churchill, 11 April 1886 (LRC Papers, MS Add. 9248.1470).
78 The Attorneys and Solicitors (Ireland) Act 1866 (29&30 Vict., c.84).
79 R. Barry O'Brien, *Dublin Castle and the Irish people* (London, 1909), p. 21.
80 O'Brien to Asquith, 8 May 1916 (Asquith Papers (Bodleian Library, Oxford), 36:160).

of a detailed study by Professor R.F.V. Heuston.[81] The appointments made in Ireland in that period, while Lord Ashbourne was lord chancellor of Ireland, received similar close political attention.

In 1872, 1894 and 1918[82] proposals were made for converting the status of lord chancellor into a purely judicial office that would not be subject to retirement from office upon a change of government. This was provided for in the Government of Ireland Act 1920, a change that took effect in June 1921 on the resignation of Campbell,[83] and it was in turn overtaken by the abolition of the office in 1922.[84] In Northern Ireland the home secretary (and, from 1949, the lord chancellor of Great Britain), ordinarily acting on the recommendations of the government in Belfast, exercised a function in relation to judicial appointments (see pp 478–9). The proposal made in 1872 came from lord justice Christian in the course of his remarkable public campaign of resentment, denigration and disrespect of lord chancellor O'Hagan. In an editorial in 1894 the *Irish Law Times* remarked that there was nothing inherent in the chancellorship that rendered it a party office any more than the office of lord chief justice, that its emancipation from the shackles of party would render it more practically useful in the administration of the law, and that greater independence of the holder would enable him to serve the public far more efficiently.[85] It had observed to rather different effect almost 20 years before that 'the lord chancellor, apart from his judicial eminence, must, in the nature of things, largely influence, by his advice and otherwise, the bestowal of patronage and the tendency of Government measures'.[86] It made no reference to the fact that between 1886 and 1892 a lord chancellor of Ireland had sat, for the first time, as a member of the cabinet.

The chancellor received a very large salary. John FitzGibbon, earl of Clare, who held office between 1789 and 1802 earned £9,000p.a.,[87] a sum that was increased to £10,000 (sterling, equivalent to £10,833 Irish currency) on the appointment of his successor, Lord Redesdale, by an 'Act for providing a proper salary for the office of the Chancellor or Keeper of the Great Seal of Ireland'.[88] The salary was reduced to £8,000 in 1832, which amount prevailed from then up to 1907, when another reduction, to £6,000, was made, with the consent of the incumbent, Sir Samuel Walker.[89] Such a reduction had been a long time coming, having been first

81 R.F.V. Heuston, *Lives of the lord chancellors, 1885–1940* (Oxford, 1964), chapter 2 (Lord Halsbury).
82 Anonymous [J. Christian], *The court of Chancery under the Chancery (Ireland) Act 1867* (Dublin, 1872), p. 52; *ILT&SJ*, vol. 18, pp 229–30 (5 May 1894); Report of the proceedings of the Irish Convention (P.P. 1918, Cd. 9019, x 697, p. 28 (para 18)).
83 Government of Ireland (lord chancellor of Ireland) Order 1921 (SR&O 1921, no. 1130 (27 June 1921)).
84 Government of Ireland Act 1920 (10&11 Geo. 5, c.67), s44(1); Irish Free State (Consequential Provisions) Act 1922 (13 Geo. 5, c.2, s3 and second schedule).
85 *ILT&SJ*, vol. 28, p. 229 (5 May 1894).
86 *ILT&SJ*, vol. 9, p. 17 (9 January 1875).
87 D.A. Fleming and A.P.W. Malcomson (eds), *'A volley of execrations': the letters and papers of John FitzGibbon, earl of Clare, 1772–1802* (Dublin, 2005), pp xxii and xxiii.
88 42 Geo. 3, c.105 (1802); E.B. Mitford, *Life of Lord Redesdale* (London, 1939), p. 213.

recommended in a report of a Select Committee of the House of Commons on Official Salaries in 1850.[90] In 1874 J.T. Ball, then the attorney general and soon to be the lord chancellor, had some uneasiness about whether £8,000 was excessive and had a reduction in mind.[91] No change was made however in the Judicature Act in 1877, and the amending Judicature Bill introduced in February 1885 which did provide for a reduction made no progress and was never enacted. It was suggested, 30 years after the event, that this envisaged reduction was one reason why Lord Fitzgerald declined a proposal that he be appointed as lord chancellor in 1885 (although a reduced salary of £6,000 would have been the same as his salary as a Law Lord).[92] In the view of Christian LJ the salary had initially been 'set up as prize rich enough to tempt the Mitfords, the Harts and the Sugdens of the English Bar, and when, consequently, English, not Irish, professional income was the regulating standard'.[93] Sir John Mitford (Lord Redesdale) was lord chancellor of Ireland between 1802 and 1806, Sir Anthony Hart was chancellor between 1827 and 1830, and Edward Sugden (Lord St Leonards), later lord chancellor of Great Britain (in 1852), was chancellor for a few months in 1835 and again between 1841 and 1846. John Campbell (first baron Campbell, 1779–1861), who was briefly lord chancellor of Ireland in 1841 and subsequently chief justice of Queen's Bench in England (from 1850) and lord chancellor of Great Britian (from 1859), expressed concern that the salary of the chancellor would be 'sufficient for him to keep a carriage, and to exercise becoming hospitality, [and] to make provision for his family'.[94]

Upon retiring from office a lord chancellor became entitled, without any qualifying period of service, to a pension of £4,000, as prescribed by a statute of the Irish Parliament.[95] This pension was thus originally payable in Irish currency, which had a value of 12/13ths of the pound sterling in Great Britain – thirteen Irish pence (one shilling and one penny) was worth one shilling in British currency. The Act that amalgamated the currencies with effect from January 1826 provided that a debt or obligation denominated or expressed in Irish currency would be satisfied by a payment of 12/13ths of that amount in the amalgamated currency.[96]

89 An Act to provide for the salaries of certain High and Judicial Officers out of payments heretofore made out of the Civil List Revenues 1832 (2&3 Will. 4, c.116), s1; Higgs (at Downing Street) to Bryce (chief secretary for Ireland), 3 January 1906 (Bryce Papers, MS 11, 012(1)); Supreme Court of Judicature (Ireland) Act 1907 (7 Edw. 7, c.44), s2.

90 P.P., 1850 (611) xv.179.

91 Ball to Cairns, 20 February 1874 (Cairns Papers, PRO 30/51/12).

92 *ILT&SJ*, vol. 29, p. 212 (28 April 1915).

93 Christian LJ, op. cit., p. 17.

94 Campbell, *Lives of the lord chancellors from earliest times* (4th ed., London, 1856), p. 26; *Irish Jurist*, vol. 9, p. 41 (1 March 1857).

95 An Act to enable his Majesty to grant Annuities to the Lord High Chancellor, etc. 1800 (40 Geo. 3, c.69), s1.

96 An Act to provide for the Assimilation of the Currencies and Monies of Account throughout the United Kingdom of Great Britain and Ireland 1825 (6 Geo. 4, c.79); F.G. Hall, *The Bank of Ireland, 1783–1946* (Dublin/Oxford, 1949), pp 108–9.

Consequently the pension payable thereafter was £3,692 6*s.*1*d.* sterling.[97] A former lord chancellor was eligible, if willing, to serve as an additional member of the Court of Appeal, being styled as an additional lord justice of appeal,[98] without any further payment for such services. John Naish served in that capacity between 1886 and 1890, as did Samuel Walker between 1895 and 1906.

Judges received a large and secure income, and in commenting on a proposal in 1850 to reduce salaries of puisne judges to £3,000 the *Irish Jurist* offered an explanation of why some such public employments 'require liberal endowments to invite men of ability, so that they may be filled satisfactorily'. An income of that level might be of interest to 'a brewer of small beer, a soap boiler, or a manufacturer of brown paper or any other respectable tradesman'. To be a judge 'necessitates the liberal expenditure of a gentleman', and salaries should not be measured on the scale of

> a Manchester trader nor by those continental precedents where the purity of the judgment seat is never above suspicion. It is by no means clear to us whether the position of a leading advocate, making between £4,000 and £5,000 per annum would not be preferable to that of a puisne judge with but £3,000. The former no doubt has harder work, but then he has more to interest and excite, with less of responsibility, and if he does not always gain his cause he does not inflict injury upon society by bad decisions; he can indulge in the play of the imagination, and the charm of eloquence; he can become a member of the House of Commons, and attain a higher social position than the puisne judge, who is trying persons for larceny in Green Street, or sentencing them to be hanged for murder at Nenagh.[99]

Criticism of the level of judges' salaries was accentuated by the fact that, as mentioned, in practice senior judicial appointments were not open to nationalist lawyers in the closing decades of the nineteenth century, and for some years afterwards. Nationalists had a settled view that the salaries of judges were unduly and unnecessarily attractive to members of the Bar, as being greater than their likely professional incomes, and that this was one aspect of an unhealthy dynamic of party patronage, affecting the independence of the Bar. The general level of superior court judicial salaries, existing and proposed, at the time of the reforming judicature legislation in 1877 was of the order of £3,500/4,000. The 1877 Act harmonised some small historical differences in salaries of judges in the various courts, now joined into a single court, that had most recently been prescribed by statute in 1832.[100] Salaries under the 1877 legislation were £5,000 for the lord chief

97 Treasury memorandum, 20 January 1923 (T 164/32/8 (20) (TNAUK)).

98 1877 Act, s10.

99 *Irish Jurist*, vol. 2, no. 99 (21 September 1850), pp 217–19.

100 An Act to provide for the salaries of certain High and Judicial Officers and of payments heretofore made out of the Civil List Revenues 1832, s1 (2&3 Will. IV, c.116). The Act introduced a major reform, in requiring that fees for any court proceedings customarily received personally by judges were now to be accounted for and paid to the Exchequer.

justice, £4,600 for the heads of the Common Pleas and Exchequer divisions of the High Court, £4,000 for the master of the rolls and each lord justice of appeal and £3,500 for the other judges, with a payment of £150 for each assize circuit. Judges were entitled to a pension of two thirds of salary after 15 years' service, or upon retirement due to ill health (upon a judge being 'disabled by permanent infirmity from the performance of the duties of his office').[101]

The salaries of the judges of the courts of bankruptcy and admiralty were lower, at £2,000 and £1,200 respectively,[102] reflecting a lesser status, but promotion to such a court was an object of ambition if no higher position was in prospect. In September 1868 Brewster, the lord chancellor, expressed a very dismissive view of the bankruptcy court. He had heard from Warren, the attorney general, that neither he nor Harrison, the solicitor general, envisaged seeking appointment to a bankruptcy vacancy. He had been glad to hear this, since he thought it would have reflected badly on the government if its law officers had not considered themselves to be above seeking appointment to a place in bankruptcy.[103] As it transpired Harrison did seek (and receive) the appointment a few weeks later, and in 1889 a bankruptcy judge, Walter Boyd, grumbled about his status. (For ease of reference, the expression 'superior court judges' will hereafter, unless otherwise expressly stated to the contrary, be taken to include the admiralty and bankruptcy judges. The jurisdictions of their respective courts were amalgamated with the High Court in 1893 and 1897.)

In the debates on the Bill in 1877 Charles Stewart Parnell referred to the general (and uncontroversial) view that 'in England a barrister of good standing deliberately forfeited a certain amount of his income when he accepted a seat on the judicial bench'. He contrasted this with the position in Ireland where 'with but a few exceptions, a barrister who was raised to the bench received a higher salary than he could possibly earn at his profession'. It was his opinion that very few Irish barristers earned more than £1,500 or £2,000 a year, that there were not more than five men at the Bar receiving £3,000 a year, and that 'the salary of a judge seemed to be twice, or in some cases three times, the amount he would earn by practising in his profession'.[104] John Dillon MP spoke to the same effect twenty years later in the debates on the supplemental 1897 judicial legislation, maintaining that the 'leaders of the Bar thought themselves well off if they were making £2,000 a year, [and that] the salaries of the Irish judges had been maintained at double the figure which would easily command the best intellect of the Bar of Ireland'.[105]

MPs who were barristers were better placed than Parnell or Dillon to know about the level of incomes at the Bar and did not accept, at least in public, that

101 1877 Act, ss17–19.
102 An Act to consolidate and amend the laws relating to Bankruptcy and Insolvency in Ireland 1857 (20&21 Vict., c.60), s15; Admiralty Court (Ireland) Act 1867 (30&31 Vict., c.114), s16.
103 Brewster to Naas, 23 September 1868 (Mayo Papers (NLI), MS 43,857/5).
104 HC Deb, 3rd series, vol. 235, col. 858 (5 July 1877), col. 278 (26 June 1877) and col. 161 (22 June 1877).
105 HC Deb, 4th series, vol. 52, col. 29 (31 July 1897).

there was any such substantial difference between these and the salaries of judges of the superior courts. In 1850 William Keogh MP, later to be a controversial judge, told a Parliamentary Select Committee that, having discussed the subject with other barristers, their view was that the average income of leaders of the Bar did not exceed £4,000 p.a., that not more than six men would earn that and that about eight men would earn between £2,000 and £4,000 annually.[106] In the 1877 debate Butt said that there were several eminent men at the Bar who had not come into Parliament who would lose considerably if they were to accept £4,000 a year, and that it was not correct to say that anyone at the Bar would jump at the offer of a place on the Bench at £2,500.[107] In 1872 lord justice Christian had given his opinion that £4,000 was an amount 'for which the elite and flower of the Irish Bar can always be commanded'.[108] In 1873 G.A.C. May, shortly to be appointed as attorney general and later as chief justice of Queen's Bench, estimated that two barristers were currently earning more than £4,000 a year, four or six were earning £3,000, twenty earned £2,000 and many were earning £1,500.[109] W. O'Connor Morris, a county court judge, wrote in 1895 that 'the incomes made at the Irish Bar are very much less than at the English; from £3,000 to £5,000 a year are the highest sums, I should say, in private practice'.[110] The *Law Times* (London) had remarked in 1894 that

> it is doubtful whether at present any Irish counsel (excepting the attorney general, whose salary is £5,000 a year) derives so much as £3,000 from his profession. A Queen's Counsel in Ireland making £2,000 a year is esteemed unusually fortunate ... Fees of five hundred or a thousand guineas, common in England, are entirely unknown in Ireland. Contrasted with this moderate remuneration of the Bar the salaries of the judicial bench must be considered large.[111]

It was the view of R.P. Carton QC, who was called to the Bar in 1863 and appointed county court judge of Co. Clare in 1899, that in the 1860s and 1870s 'the incomes of seniors in the first rank ranged from £4,000 to £6,000 a year', but that the reforms of the 1877 Act had led to 'a lamentable falling off of business', and that such incomes had been reduced by at least 50%.[112]

Edward Carson QC, MP, who again like Butt (and May) would have had some direct information on the subject, disagreed with Dillon in the Parliamentary debate in 1897, while acknowledging the possibility of reduced incomes

106 Report of select committee on official salaries 1850 (P.P. 1850 (611) xv.179), minutes of evidence Q2634, Q2641.
107 HC Deb, 3rd series, vol. 235, cols. 859 and 862 (5 July 1877).
108 Anonymous [Christian LJ], *The court of Chancery under the Chancery (Ireland) Act 1867* (Dublin, 1872), p. 53.
109 Report of the Commissioners on the local government board and general register office and minutes of evidence (P.P. 1873 (c.789) xxi.440).
110 W. O'Connor Morris, *Memories and thoughts of life* (London, 1895), p. 156.
111 *ILT&SJ*, vol. 28, p. 380 (4 August 1894), reproduced from *Law Times*.
112 R.P. Carton, 'The Irish Bar as a profession', *Clongownian*, vol. 1, no. 2 (June 1896), p. 12.

> within the last three or four years, because when he was more intimately acquainted with the Irish Bar [having in effect moved to London in 1892] there certainly were a very large number of men who were making sums equal to the salaries that were given to the Irish judges in the superior courts – £3,500 a year – and he believed at the present time there were several men who were making incomes in advance of the salaries given to the judges.[113]

Carson earned very high fees at the Bar in London, and the first volume of his biography, written with his guidance, contains an account of his first fee there of 500 guineas.[114] He left an estate of £150,000. R. Barry O'Brien's view in 1909 was that the few top barristers could earn as much as £5,000 a year,[115] a more liberal estimate than a curiously precise contention in 1914 by A.M. Sullivan QC that only six barristers earned over £2,000 a year and twelve earned more than £1,000, and that in any event none earned the salary of a puisne judge of the High Court.[116] It was Maurice Healy's view that 'no man became really rich at the Bar in Ireland, unless he was appointed a law officer … I do not think that any leader, other than a law officer, ever made £5,000 a year at the Irish Bar; I am certain that there were not more than ten earning £3,000 … it was generally believed that doctors in Dublin made much larger sums'.[117]

The salary of the attorney general was set at £5,000 in 1887, over a protest by the Treasury, which had proposed a salary of £4,000.[118] The actual income would have been greater than that, taking account of brief fees that would have been paid for contentious State business (for which, as mentioned, the attorney general would typically have personally led the prosecution in the trials of serious or sensational crimes) or from any private practice. Average annual earnings between 1881 and 1885 had been £9,265.[119] The salary of the solicitor general was then set at £2,000. Restrictions on the private practice of the law officers had been formally adopted in England in 1892,[120] but these were not made applicable to the Irish law officers.[121] In 1902 the chief secretary, George Wyndham, said that it was not intended to assimilate Irish practice in such matters to English practice when a question was asked about the solicitor general, James Campbell QC, not having attended to a Crown case in Ireland because he had been in London in the course

113 HC Deb, 4th series, vol. 52, col. 32 (31 July 1897).
114 Edward Marjoribanks, *The life of Lord Carson*, vol. 1 (London, 1932), chap. 15.
115 R. Barry O'Brien, *Dublin Castle and the Irish people* (London, 1909), p. 387.
116 *The Belvederian* (Dublin), vol. iii (1914), p. 246.
117 Healy, *OldMC*, p. 286.
118 *Law Times*, vol. 82, p. 324 (5 March 1887); *ILT&SJ*, vol. 21, p. 555 (15 October 1887).
119 J.P. Casey, *The office of the attorney general in Ireland* (Dublin, 1980), p. 35; J.P. Casey, *The Irish law officers* (Dublin, 1996), p. 43; Correspondence between the Treasury and the Irish government as to the remuneration of the attorney general and solicitor general for Ireland, P.P. 1887, lxvii, 379–94.
120 HC Deb, 4th series, vol. 22, col. 941 (29 March 1894).
121 HC Deb, 4th series, vol. 35, col. 574 (22 August 1895). This was stated in reply to a parliamentary question that had been asked by Edward Carson QC.

of representing a private client. Wyndham declined a Nationalist proposal that he would direct that the primary attention of law officers should be devoted to their public duties, while acknowledging that there had been an 'unforeseen clashing of dates', and expected that in accepting any private work Campbell would 'in future avoid even the appearance of conflict between his private practice and public duties'.[122]

The broad picture is thus that, even before taking into account pension rights, a judicial salary would ordinarily have been very attractive, if not to the extent suggested by Home Rule politicians. Appointment as a judge, with its associated prestige, security and standing, offered an opportunity for public service and also for what, perhaps not entirely facetiously, the *Irish Times* referred to as 'judicial repose'.[123] Gladstone, a famously industrious man, remarked in 1881 that the life of a judge was 'not on the whole [one] of excessive labour' (see p. 290). Judicial salaries were also significantly higher than the incomes of other people holding senior official or public positions. Top-ranking civil servants, who were in receipt of lesser salaries than the £2,000 paid to the highest ranking permanent public servant, the under-secretary at Dublin Castle, have been described as being 'extremely well-off. Most of them lived in prosperous and comfortable parts of Dublin'.[124] In the 1890s a recipient of a salary of £1,000 would be 'comfortable' and one of £1,500 'well-off', and a Georgian house of five storeys might cost between £2,000 and £3,000.[125] In the middle of the nineteenth century, prior to reforms in 1858, the total annual income of the provost of Trinity College, including a proportion of rents from college properties, was about £3,000,[126] and half a century later was £1,751,[127] half of a standard judicial salary.

Judges thus were well remunerated, and (as appears below with reference to some individuals in particular) enjoyed a comfortable lifestyle. The view of lord justice James O'Connor in 1923 of the appropriate social position of a judge has been mentioned above (see p. 59). He had previously expressed similar sentiments more privately in a submission made to the Judiciary Committee which had been set up to make recommendations for the judicial framework of the Irish Free State, emphasising the importance, in upholding the principle of their independence, of judges being well paid.[128] Sir John Ross made reference, vaguely if comprehensibly,

122 HC Deb, 4th series, vol. 108, cols. 381–3 (15 May 1902); *ILT&SJ*, vol. 36, p. 206 (31 May 1902).
123 *Irish Times*, 5 July 1887 (quoting the *Morning Post*). The comment, as to an entitlement to such 'repose', was made at the time of the appointment of the attorney general, Hugh Holmes, to the bench.
124 Fergus Campbell, *The Irish establishment, 1879–1914* (Oxford, 2009), pp 64 and 69.
125 R.B. McDowell and D.A. Webb, *Trinity College Dublin 1592–1952: an academic history* (Cambridge, 1982), p. 544.
126 W.E. Vaughan, 'Paying for the Christmas dinner: the College's income and expenditure' in Charles H. Holland (ed.), *Trinity College Dublin and the idea of a university* (Dublin, 1991), p. 73.
127 Tony Farmar, *Ordinary lives* (Dublin, 1991), p. 20.
128 Lord justice O'Connor, submission to the Judiciary Committee, memorandum on suggested changes in Ireland's judicial system, undated [April] 1923 (Hugh Kennedy Papers, UCDA, P. 4/1092 (84)).

to judges having always been 'obliged, pursuant to the traditions of the office, to live in a style supposed to be suitable to their rank. They had expensive establishments and house held on leases' which he said, in the straitened times of the Great War, 'they could not easily get rid of; the consequence was that they were obliged to live, to a great extent, on their capital laid by in better days'.[129]

Judges generally lived in a smart central area of Dublin, a few on the north side (O'Hagan in Rutland [now Parnell] Square, Whiteside, Harrison and Naish in Mountjoy Square) but increasingly on the south side. The *Law Times* noted in March 1900 that the route of a state entrance that Queen Victoria would make into Dublin from Kingstown [now Dun Laoghaire] the following month 'ought to give great satisfaction to the legal profession. It extends through Upper Leeson Street, Fitzwilliam Place [having crossed Leeson Street bridge], Fitzwilliam Square, Fitzwilliam Street and Merrion Square, a series of streets which are inhabited almost exclusively by members of the profession'.[130] That procession would have passed the residences of over half of the judges, and many more lived within a couple of minutes' walk of the route. Gibson, Holmes, Kenny and Palles lived in Fitzwilliam Place, Meredith and Ross (and the two law officers, Atkinson and Wright) in Fitzwilliam Square, Ashbourne, Boyd, FitzGibbon and Marshall Porter in Merrion Square, Andrews and Johnson in Lower Leeson Street, Walker in Upper Mount Street and Barton in Clyde Road. Chatterton lived in Blackrock, Madden at Booterstown, and Murphy in Glencairn (Sandyford). The home of lord chief justice O'Brien, at Newlands, Clondalkin (although he had previously lived in Merrion Square), was the farthest from the route.[131] The position was little changed 15 years later, when the only judge who lived outside the south central part of the city was William Kenny at Marlfield House, Cabinteely. Such a clustering of the residences of judges would have facilitated police protection operations for them, as were thought necessary from time to time, for instance after the Phoenix Park murders in May 1882.[132] In 1884, as reported a few years later, the Dublin Metropolitan Police provided three inspectors, six sergeants and 99 constables as personal protection for 17 senior persons (senior government officials as well as judges).[133]

Many judges who held office between 1866 and 1921 had substantial assets, as indicated by the values of their estates as declared for probate purposes. At least a dozen such estates were valued for probate at over £50,000, and a similar number were valued at over £25,000. The total values of their estates would generally have been greater, since such declared amounts related to assets characterised as personal property or chattel real property, and did not include interests in real

129 Sir John Ross, *The years of my pilgrimage* (London, 1924), p. 286.
130 *Law Times*, vol. 108, p. 505 (31 March 1900).
131 Addresses as stated in Thom's Directory, 1900 and 1915.
132 *ILT&SJ*, vol. 16, p. 232 (20 May 1882).
133 Donal P. McCracken, *You will dye at midnight; threatening letters in Victorian Ireland* (Dublin, 2021), p. 187; Return of numbers of persons specially protected by Royal Irish Constabulary, July 1887 and January 1888, P.P. 1888 [c.5809] lxxxiii.305.

property. Such property under the common law of devolution and inheritance at the time would have vested in or passed directly to the heir-at-law or devisee, not devolving upon an executor or administrator.[134] Since 1955 (Northern Ireland) and 1959 (Ireland) all property, real and personal, of a deceased person vests in the personal representative, who is responsible for vesting real property in the person entitled, in the course of administration of the estate.[135] Three of the largest estates were those of Sir Michael Morris (Lord Killanin), valued at £127,766, Sir James Campbell (Lord Glenavy) (£99,490) and Lord Ashbourne (£92,325), each of whom had expressed concern about his financial circumstances prior to appointment to the bench. Other large estates were those of Abraham Brewster, Edward Sullivan, Jonathan Christian, Hugh Law, Mountifort Longfield, Stephen Ronan, Christopher Palles, G.A.C. May, R.R. Cherry and Hugh Holmes.

In the last third of the nineteenth century, between 1866 and 1900, 66 men held office as superior court judges (including, as mentioned, for present purposes, Admiralty or bankruptcy judges), of whom 22 had been appointed prior to 1866 and the balance (44) were appointed in those years. In the first decades of the twentieth century, between 1901 and 1921, 19 new judges were appointed. The number of judicial appointments in those periods was greater in aggregate than the number of new judges, since an existing judge might be promoted to fill a vacancy, creating a new and different vacancy. For instance, when R.R. Cherry succeeded Lord O'Brien of Kilfenora as lord chief justice in 1914, his place as lord justice of appeal was taken by the attorney general, John F. Moriarty, a single vacancy thus leading to two appointments. Five of the 22 judges sitting in 1866 subsequently held higher offices (Blackburne, John D. Fitzgerald, Christian, Thomas O'Hagan and Lynch), and 14 of the 63 appointed from then up to 1921 (Morris, Harrison, Woulfe Flanagan, Sullivan, Charles Barry, Ormsby, Boyd, Holmes, Ross, Meredith, Cherry, Molony, Campbell and James O'Connor).

In 1866 the superior court judiciary consisted of the lord chancellor,[136] the master of the rolls,[137] a lord justice of appeal,[138] four judges each of the courts of Queen's Bench,[139] Common Pleas[140] and the Exchequer[141] (the head of the first two of each of which being styled a 'chief justice', the head of the Exchequer being a 'chief baron'), a judge of the court of Probate[142] and two judges of the Landed Estates Court.[143] Two other judges were members of the court of Bankruptcy,[144]

134 J.C.W. Wylie, *Irish land law* (Dublin, 4th ed., 2010), para. 15.05.
135 Administration of Estates Act (Northern Ireland) 1955 (c24); Administration of Estates Act 1959 (no. 8).
136 At the start of 1866, Maziere Brady.
137 Thomas Berry Cusack Smith.
138 Francis Blackburne.
139 Thomas Lefroy CJ, James O'Brien, Edmund Hayes and John David Fitzgerald.
140 James Henry Monahan CJ, William Keogh, Jonathan Christian and Thomas O'Hagan.
141 David Richard Pigot CB, Francis FitzGerald, Henry George Hughes and Rickard Deasy.
142 Richard Keatinge.
143 Mountifort Longfield and William Carey Dobbs. A third judge, Charles Hargreave, died in April 1866, and was not replaced.

with a lesser status (and salary) than the other judges, and there was one judge in the almost defunct court of Admiralty,[145] a backwater with little business. The number of judges was increased by the creation (a) in 1867 of the position of vice-chancellor,[146] (b) in 1877 of a second lord justiceship of appeal,[147] (c) in 1881 of the position, with the standing of an additional judge of the High Court, of judicial member of the new Irish Land Commission and (d) again in 1903 of a second such commissioner.[148] However with those exceptions the emphasis after 1866 was on a rationalisation and simplification of the court structure and diminution of judicial numbers, most notably by statute at, as it happened, intervals of a decade, in 1877, 1887, 1897 and 1907.

A remarkable number of judges were appointed during the twenty months or so between July 1866 and February 1868 during which, for the third time, Lord Derby was prime minister. In the two decades since the Conservative party had split in 1846 over the repeal of the Corn Laws it had been in office only for short broken periods (1852 and 1858–9). Now suddenly through resignations (Lefroy and Hayes), the creation of a new position of vice-chancellor (Chatterton), the statutory removal of a judge (Kelly) and the deaths of number of judges (including the master of the rolls) a number of vacancies arose. New men appointed in those years were Whiteside, Brewster, Walsh, George, Morris, Chatterton, Townsend and Miller and (later in 1868, after Disraeli had succeeded Derby) Harrison and Warren. Walsh and George died within a few years (their places, and also that of lord chancellor Brewster, being filled by appointments by the new Liberal government elected in 1868), but the others held office for decades, Whiteside for ten years up to 1876, Morris in various offices up to 1900, Chatterton up to 1904, Townsend to 1893, Harrison to 1895 and Miller and Warren to 1897.

The judges thus holding office or appointed subsequently had many things in common. The great majority had attended university, more specifically Trinity College (the only college of Dublin University), and a number of them retained a connection with the university, three (Brady, Longfield and Ross) being members of Royal Commissions which were set up to investigate and report upon its affairs (in 1851 and 1920 respectively)[149] and others being Visitors of the university, with regulatory functions. Of the 44 men who were appointed as superior court judges between 1866 and 1900, only six had not attended that university, those being G.A.C. May (appointed in 1877, Cambridge), William O'Brien (1882, no university), Andrew Marshall Porter (1883, Queen's College, Belfast), James Monroe (1885, Queen's College, Galway), R.E. Meredith (1898, also Queen's College, Galway) and Dunbar Plunket Barton (1900, Oxford). Dublin University

144 Walter Berwick and David Lynch.

145 Thomas Kelly.

146 Chancery (Ireland) Act 1867 (30&31 Vict., c.44), s4.

147 Supreme Court of Judicature (Ireland) Act 1877 (40&41 Vict., c.57), s10.

148 The Land Law (Ireland) Act 1881 (44&45 Vict., c.49), s41; the Irish Land Act 1903 (3 Edw. 7, c.37), s86.

149 McDowell and Webb, op. cit., pp 204–5 and 426.

was still by far the university attended by the greatest number (10) of the judges appointed between 1901 and 1921, although a similar number were educated elsewhere – John Atkinson (appointed a lord of appeal in ordinary in 1905, Queen's College, Galway), W.H. Dodd (1907, Queen's College, Belfast), Redmond J. Barry (1911, Queen's College, Cork), Ignatius O'Brien (1913, Catholic University in Dublin), Stephen Ronan (1915, Queen's College, Cork), John Gordon (1916, Queen's College, Belfast), and James O'Connor and John Blake Powell (both 1918, and initially solicitors, before being called to the Bar).

The judicial appointments in 1866–8 included successively four men who represented Dublin University in the House of Commons, the latter three having been elected unopposed in a series of bye-elections which followed the appointment of a university MP to be a judge, beginning with the nomination of James Whiteside as chief justice of Queen's Bench in July 1866. He was succeeded as MP by John Edward Walsh, who when he was appointed as master of the rolls a few weeks later was followed by Hedges Eyre Chatterton, who on his appointment as vice-chancellor in the summer of 1867 was succeeded by R.R. Warren, who was appointed as judge of the court of Probate in the autumn of 1868. That last vacancy in the constituency was quickly filled at a general election by J.T. Ball, who was appointed lord chancellor in 1875. Walsh, Chatterton and Warren (and also Morris, MP for Galway, appointed a judge in 1867) each briefly held office as attorney general in that period before being appointed to the Bench.

A promotion of a law officer required of course that a suitable judicial vacancy would have arisen during his term of office and, even then, that the government would not have pressed him, by assurances of eventual subsequent promotion, to retain his present office and pass up the opportunity of filling a vacancy. John David Fitzgerald more than once in the 1850s, Edward Gibson in 1878, Dodgson Hamilton Madden in 1890 and John Atkinson in 1897 each agreed to requests from the government that they would remain in office as attorney general and not seek to take up a vacancy that had arisen. No vacancy in the superior courts arose during the Liberal government of 1892–5, in contrast to the four judicial vacancies that had arisen during the previous government's term of office (1886–92), each of which was filled by the promotion of the attorney general (Holmes 1887, Gibson 1888, O'Brien 1889 and Madden 1892).

A number of judges were related to each other. John George Gibson (appointed in 1888)[150] was a brother of the lord chancellor at the time, Lord Ashbourne, who was also a brother-in-law of Edmund Bewley, the judicial commissioner of the Land Commission (1890). They had married sisters (named Colles). James Whiteside was married to a sister of Sir Joseph Napier (lord chancellor, 1858). Charles Barry (1872) was married to a sister of John David Fitzgerald (1860). John Monroe (1885) and Hugh Holmes (1887) were married to sisters, daughters of John Watkins Moule of Worcestershire. Gerald Fitzgerald, the additional judicial

150 The year first mentioned in brackets after each subsequent judge's name in this and in the following paragraphs is the year of (first) appointment to the Bench.

commissioner of the Land Commission appointed by the Irish Land Act 1903, was a son of Lord (John David) Fitzgerald. Four judges were married to daughters of judges, Michael Morris (1867) married a daughter of Baron Hughes (1859),[151] Gerald FitzGibbon (1878) married a daughter of Francis FitzGerald (1859), John O'Hagan (judicial commissioner, 1881) married a daughter of Thomas O'Hagan (1865), and James Murphy (1883) was the son-in-law of William Nicholas Keogh (1856). (Keogh inquired of the attorney general in 1878 whether Murphy could be appointed in his place if he were to resign.) Denis Henry married a daughter of Holmes (1887). Three judges were otherwise related or connected to other judges, Stephen Woulfe Flanagan (1869) was a nephew of Baron Woulfe (1838), Peter O'Brien (1889) was a nephew of James O'Brien (1858), and Samuel Walker (1892) married a niece of Baron Greene. Dunbar Plunket Barton (1900) was a cousin of David Plunket.

Some judges held office for decades, there being no fixed statutory retiring age at the time. Ronan Keane has remarked that 'mental infirmity, deafness, remoteness from ordinary life and increasing rigidity of views' marred some lengthy judicial careers.[152] An unremarkable but somewhat misleading average or median age of the judiciary (or average length of tenure of office) at any one time might be computed by putting together some who served into old age, with others who were appointed quite young, in a number of cases when they were in their 40s (or in a couple of cases younger still, Keogh being 39 when appointed in 1856 and W.E. Wylie the same age when appointed in 1920). Michael Morris (born in 1826) was appointed in 1867 and sat in one capacity or another as a judge for the rest of the century, retiring in 1900. Others who had not attained the age of 50, and in a few cases were in their early 40s, when first appointed were Edward Sullivan (1870), Richard Dowse (1872), Gerald FitzGibbon (1878), Andrew Marshall Porter (1883), John Naish (as lord chancellor in 1885, when aged 42), Edward Gibson (Lord Ashbourne) (also 1885), James Monroe (1885), Hugh Holmes (1887), John G. Gibson (1888), John Ross (1896), R.E. Meredith (1898), Dunbar Plunket Barton (1900), and James O'Connor (1918).

The longest period of judicial office, combining appointment at an early age with an extended career into old age, was that of Christopher Palles, who was appointed chief baron of the Exchequer in February 1874, at the age of 42 and sat as a judge until the summer of 1916. His retirement followed a couple of months after that of Walter Boyd, who had been born in 1833, and appointed a bankruptcy judge in 1885 and to the High Court in 1897. Two judges, Johnson and Andrews, who retired at the end of 1909 and were not replaced (by virtue of the provisions of the 1907 Judicature Act), had been born in 1825 and 1832 respectively, and each had sat for over 25 years. Other judges who had extended periods in office included

151 This relationship was noted by Naas to Disraeli in 1866 when it was contemplated that Hughes might be appointed as master of the rolls and Morris as attorney general (Naas to Disraeli, 17 August 1866 (Disraeli Papers, B/XX/BO/21)). Only Morris was eventually promoted.

152 Ronan Keane, entry on Christopher Palles in *ODNB*, although it is to be noted that he specifically exempted Palles himself from any such criticism.

Hedges Eyre Chatterton (1867–1904, when he retired at the age of 84), Michael Harrison (1868–95), R.R. Warren (1868–97), Charles Robert Barry (1872–97), Gerald FitzGibbon (1878–1909), Andrew Marshall Porter (1883–1906), John G. Gibson (1888–1921), Hugh Holmes (1887–1915), Peter O'Brien (1889–1913), Dodgson Hamilton Madden (1892–1919), and John Ross (1896–1922). The ages of some judges retiring (or dying in office) in or after 1909 were 71 (FitzGibbon), 84 (Johnson), 77 (Andrews), 81 (Walker), 46 (Redmond John Barry), 66 (Wright), 71 (O'Brien), 74 (Holmes), 60 (Moriarty), 83 (Boyd), 84 (Palles), 75 (Gibson), 64 (Barton), and 78 (Madden). The judicial career of Lord Ashbourne, encompassing sitting in the House of Lords in addition to being lord chancellor of Ireland for periods amounting to some 17 years, covered the years 1885 to 1913, and that of Lord Fitzgerald extended from 1860 to 1889.

A number of judges died while still holding office, including Cusack Smith in 1866, Walsh (1869), Law (1883), Sullivan (1885), Dowse and Naish (1890), Harrison (1895), Charles Barry and Warren (1897), FitzGibbon (1909), Walker (1911) and Moriarty (1915). Others resigned in ill health and died very shortly afterwards, including Meredith (1912), Redmond Barry (1913), Peter O'Brien (1913) and Holmes (1915). The retirements of some others took place, as just mentioned, at advanced ages, although none so elderly as Thomas Lefroy, who was aged 90 (having been appointed to that office fourteen years before) when retiring in 1866 as chief justice of Queen's Bench. Some endeavoured to manage their retirements so as to secure appointment by the government of a particular successor, or to negotiate a similar favour for a family member (Keatinge in 1868), and Lefroy plainly was waiting for a change of government before resigning. This was said also, unfairly, of Monroe.

Reflections on judicial retirement were sometimes melancholy. Philip Crampton (1783–1862), when retiring from the King's Bench in 1859, spoke of his regret at quitting

> the scenes, the pursuits and the associations which have, for so many years, occupied a large portion of my mind and my affections. But there is a time for all things. My advanced age invites retirement. It is becoming that, after holding my high office for five and twenty years I should retire and make room for younger and abler men. And a still higher call tells me that there should be an interval of serious rest before my departure from the bustle and excitement of forensic occupation and that final departure that opens to a rest that never ends.[153]

A legal historian, O.J. Burke BL (1826–89), noted melodramatically in the 1880s that 'judges as a rule, retiring from the bench, are short-lived. In the absence of

153 Philip Cecil Crampton, *Addresses and replies on Judge Crampton's retirement from the bench, with some of his charges to grand juries* (Dublin, 1859), p. iv; O.J. Burke, *Anecdotes of the Connaught circuit* (Dublin, 1885), p. 302.

the excitement to which they had been long used the hours heavily roll along – without business, without pleasure, they accuse the tedious progress of the sun, and in this comfortless state their repose hastens their decay'.[154] Lord Atkinson, then aged 86, foresaw 'lonely idleness' on his retirement as a Law Lord in 1928.[155]

Within a party there would be personal tensions and rivalry for appointment, what Derby described to the Queen in 1866 as 'mutual personal jealousies'.[156] After Napier had been compelled to stand down as a lord justice of appeal in 1866 he complained to his friend Cairns about 'a clique here who have always assailed me – often more falsely and unscrupulously', remarking that 'why any of our own men should join in the attempt to shelve me except in order to make more room for themselves or their friends I cannot understand'.[157] In another letter he spoke of 'many who joined in the petty intrigues against me whom I cannot respect and not a few whom I cannot but despise'.[158] In 1890 William Kenny QC wrote to the lord lieutenant, Lord Londonderry, about the possibility of being appointed solicitor general, remarking that he had heard that the position (for which, in the event, no vacancy then arose) might be given to Edward Carson. He said that this would be unfair since he was superior to Carson both in rank and, as he believed, in position at the Bar.[159] Occasionally – so rarely as to invite comment each time – a person without an open party political affiliation would be appointed, of whom James Murphy, appointed in 1883, was an example.

The connected issues of the claims of party loyalty, recognition of political service and competence arose in a particularly stark form when Lord Derby was prime minister between 1866 and 1868. The fact that his judicial appointments included a succession of MPs representing Dublin University led him to grumble that some of the persons appointed had had little Parliamentary or official service to justify such rapid promotion: 'I really think that, considering that neither our attorney nor solicitor general [Walsh and Morris] have even done us a day's work, we may fairly expect them to hold on for some little time at least'.[160] His initial frustration on the subject had cooled a few weeks later to a more resigned assessment of their prospects: 'Though I wish the AG [Walsh] had forborne to press his claims [to the position of master of the rolls] yet as he does press them so strongly I hardly see how they are to be overlooked, and the advantage of retaining him and Morris where they are would be in great measure countermanded by having them both dissatisfied'.[161]

Part of Derby's difficulty in filling judicial positions and turning down claims to office arose because the leading Conservative lawyers in the House of Commons

154 Burke, op. cit., p. 312.
155 Atkinson to Buckmaster, unstated date [February] 1928 (R.F.V. Heuston, *Lives of the lord chancellors, 1885–1940* (Oxford, 1964), p. 303.
156 Derby to the Queen, 12 July 1866 (Derby Papers, 191/1, p. 85).
157 Napier to Cairns, undated [but in 1866] (Cairns Papers, PRO 30/51/11, 8).
158 Napier to Cairns, undated [but in 1866] (Cairns Papers, PRO 30/51/11, 9).
159 Kenny to Londonderry, 13 March 1890 (Balfour Papers, Add. MS 49802.86).
160 Derby to Abercorn, 10 August 1866 (Derby Papers, 191/2).
161 Derby to Naas, 6 September 1866 (Derby Papers, 191/1, p. 2).

were not highly regarded by their own party. In the autumn of 1866 Derby observed to Lord Naas, the chief secretary for Ireland, that 'I am sorry that you cannot give a more favourable report of the Conservative Bar in Ireland'.[162] In those unusual circumstances he had thought in July, upon taking office, of appointing as lord chancellor Abraham Brewster, an elderly figure not associated with the Conservative party but whose ability was well respected. He was dissuaded from doing so by advice from Naas that this 'would alienate a considerable number of our Irish friends', and that 'political ties must be respected and an appointment distasteful to the majority of our supporters would be a bad thing to start with'.[163] Twelve years later the lord lieutenant, the duke of Marlborough, advised Disraeli to give no further thought to a proposal to appoint a Liberal MP, Hugh Law, as a judge, the duke considering it 'most desirable that in these judicial appointments our friends should not be disappointed'.[164]

In March 1867 in the immediate aftermath of the Fenian Rising Derby decided to replace the lord chancellor and appoint Brewster anyway. This gave rise to a bitter complaint to the lord lieutenant, Lord Abercorn, by Francis Macdonogh QC, a flamboyant and controversial member of the Bar. He had stood unsuccessfully as a Liberal in Carrickfergus in the 1857 general election and then was elected as a Conservative in Sligo in a bye-election in 1860, losing his seat in 1865. An obituarist remarked that 'in politics Mr Macdonogh was neither consistent nor successful. Beginning as a Liberal he became a Palmerstonian and finally a Conservative … his sincerity and the steadfastness of his convictions were more than doubted', but added that it was not so much his politics as 'his early yet still remembered faults of personal character that barred the way to promotion'.[165] Brewster believed that this ultimate association with the Conservatives had inadvisedly been fostered by Whiteside.[166]

He had been pressing unsuccessfully for preferment since Derby was appointed,[167] writing that he had travelled specially to London for the purpose of submitting his claims, the foundation of which was his professional position at the Bar and the financial loss and sacrifice which he had incurred in political life. Whiteside, he said, was the only member of the Bar who had been briefed more often specially [i.e., entailing an extra fee] outside his own circuit. He had fought the Sligo election with little support and had been put to great expense for five years, principally in minding the registration of voters. His income at the Bar declined by some £2,000 a year and he was now seemingly to be forgotten and discarded because he was no longer an MP.[168] Derby thus had grounds for remarking that Macdonogh was 'very hungry and very indignant at being

162 Derby to Naas, 6 October 1866 (Mayo Papers, MS 11,144).
163 Naas to Derby, 8 July 1866 (Derby Papers, 155/2).
164 Marlborough to Disraeli, 7 November 1878 (Disraeli Papers, C/V/20c).
165 *ILT&SJ*, vol. 16, pp 178–9 (22 April 1882).
166 Brewster to Mayo, 7 September 1868 (Mayo Papers, MS 43,857/5).
167 Derby to Macdonogh, 7 July 1866 (Derby Papers, 191/1, p. 48).
168 Macdonogh to Derby, 10 July 1866 (Mayo Papers, MS 43,825/1).

overlooked'.[169] A few months later, in October 1866, he was disappointed again after offering – if he was appointed as attorney general – to contest a bye-election in Belfast that would result from the impending appointment of Cairns, one of the two MPs for the city, as a lord justice of appeal in England. He had a strong connection and a wide acquaintance in the city, he told Naas and what he described as his liberal Conservatism would be well received there.[170]

A subsequent complaint that he made to the lord lieutenant, Abercorn, in 1867 about the injustice of having been overlooked drew together themes applicable to many aspirants for judicial office. It was suggestive of how articulate an advocate he may have been in court, in referring to his position at the Bar, his fidelity to the Conservative party, and assurances from Derby in August 1866 that Naas or Abercorn would be well disposed to give full weight to his professional and political claims. His experience in criminal and civil law was unrivalled, he said, he had fought two general elections at his own expense, had endured the frustrations of sitting in opposition in the House of Commons, only now to see judicial offices distributed among men who had not given any comparable services to the party or had previously actively opposed it.[171]

Once again Macdonogh's representations did not move the government. The impossibility of promoting him, although he continued to press his case for advancement, was explained to Derby by Lord Mayo (as Naas had become in 1867 on the death of his father, the 5th earl) a year later:

> I do not know what we can do for Macdonogh – anyone whose opinion in his own profession is good tells us that we could not make him a law officer or a judge. He is a good common lawyer but he does not hold at all a high position among his brethren. He would make an excellent Indian judge. He knows a great deal more law than most men on the Eastern bench and his habits and expressions are so gorgeous that he is well suited to administer justice on a white elephant or from an ivory throne. I think besides that the Irish Bar is entitled to an Indian judgeship as they have not had one for a long time.[172]

Outright personal unsuitability might prevent the advancement of a member of the Bar, but whether a person would have an actual fitness, by reference to his knowledge and legal experience, for appointment to any particular judicial vacancy would be very much a secondary consideration in filling it. The appointment of Thomas O'Hagan, a judge of the Common Pleas, as lord chancellor in 1868 drew an editorial protest from the *Irish Law Times*, which regretted a system of making appointments such as that thus made of 'an eminent common law judge to the highest place on the equity bench'. (His inexperience in equity matters was later

169 Derby to Abercorn, 10 August 1866 (Derby Papers, 191/2).
170 Macdonogh to Naas, 16 October 1866 (Mayo Papers, MS 43,826/2).
171 Macdonogh to Abercorn, 22 March 1867 (Abercorn Papers, D623/A/308/35 pt. 1).
172 Mayo to Derby, 10 January 1868 (Derby Papers, 155/5).

to be the subject of sustained abusive criticism by lord justice Christian.) Its editorial continued that

> learned judges and barons may be seen presiding at nisi prius, whose reputations have been made entirely as Chancery lawyers, and who are totally incapable of presiding at a trial before a jury, deciding between relevant and irrelevant evidence, and clearly unfolding a complicated state of facts, but who would make admirable chancellors, masters of the rolls or lords justices of appeal. On the other hand, the spectacle will soon be seen – not, indeed, for the first time – of an eminent advocate at nisi prius and leader of an important circuit, sitting in the high court of Chancery to interpret and regulate the practice of a branch of the law with which the occupation of his lifetime must necessarily render him unacquainted. The public will lose Mr Justice O'Hagan's services in a position for which he is eminently qualified. The round man will be put into the square hole and the square into the round.[173]

Such criticism may have been overstated. Most members of the Bar would have picked up some acquaintance with the principal areas of legal practice over the years and, if not, they could learn on the job. Obituaries frequently observed that judges without much if any experience in Chancery or common law work, as the case might be, had subsequently developed substantial reputations for their work in it. Joseph Napier, appointed as lord chancellor in 1858, soon told his friend Cairns that, although he had had 'great misgivings about taking my seat in Chancery, and my only comfort was that I had not sought it, by simplicity and diligence I soon found that all difficulty began to disappear, I got into the course of the court without effort and before I rose I found equity quite enjoyable – I now see how much it ranks above the quirks and vulgarities of the law courts', and he had been able 'without strain or weariness' to clear all arrears of business.[174]

A decade later, at the end of 1868, Napier wrote to O'Hagan, offering 'some of the experiences of one who had passed somewhat unexpectedly from the common law into the high domains of equity'. He recommended various books to him, said that 'you will find it useful to study the decisions of the House of Lords in which principles are well expounded'. He advised him to 'hear the Bar patiently, avoiding as much as you can any interruption that is not required reasonably. In every case of importance it is the wise and judicious course to put the judgments in writing. It contributes to exactness both of thought and expression. In motions it is always wise to attend to any suggestions from an experienced officer who knows the routine'.[175] All of which was sensible, if perhaps elementary, advice.

173 *ILT&SJ*, vol. 2, p. 681 (12 December 1868).
174 Napier to Cairns, 19 August 1858 (Cairns Papers, PRO 30/51/11/6).
175 Napier to O'Hagan, undated [December 1868] (O'Hagan Papers, D2777/7/M/92).

John Ross wrote that while on circuit in Omagh in 1896 he was astonished to be offered (on St Patrick's Day, not a bank holiday until 1903)[176] appointment as the Land Judge. 'If I had been called on to take command of the Channel Fleet I could not have been more astounded. A judgeship in the Chancery division offered to me, a common law man!! I had hardly ever been in this court, and I was aware that the work was most technical and special'. Lord justice Barry, one of the assize judges sitting in Omagh, steadied his nerve: 'don't you know that there only about ten principles of law and equity. You know them already and you have only to apply them. Wire an acceptance at once'.[177] Ross did so, and he came to be well-regarded over the next two decades for expertise in land law. On the appointment in 1918 of John Blake Powell to be a judge of the Chancery division of the High Court it was said that the fact that his practice was 'mainly in the common law courts was true also of Chatterton VC and Porter MR, two of our greatest Chancery judges'.[178]

Judges were drawn from the senior members of the Bar. Those who could plausibly be considered as eligible for any judicial appointment constituted a fraction of the total numbers at the Bar, being men who would generally (and with no more than a handful of exceptions) have been in practice at the Bar for at least 20 years and who had been called to the Inner Bar, thus having a nominal status of Queen's [King's] Counsel (QC/KC). The total number of members of the Bar fluctuated but was generally around 400. It was 399 in 1900, including 56 Queen's Counsel.[179] Barristers who were members of a circuit and hence did not practise only in Dublin amounted to 379 in 1860, 314 in 1881 and 320 in 1909.[180]

Barristers belonging to one Protestant denomination or another made up a majority of the Bar throughout the nineteenth and early twentieth centuries, in 1900 for instance being accounted for as 250 out of the 399 members and, more to the point in terms of eligibility for a judicial appointment, then making up almost three quarters of Queen's Counsel.[181] A number of the Catholic QCs would in any event have been unable or reluctant to accept judicial office, even if offered, having regard to their Home Rule principles. There was a virtual monopoly of judicial appointments by Unionist governments between 1885 and 1905. The office of lord chancellor was the only judicial position that was available to be filled by Liberal governments in those years (with Naish in 1886 and Walker in 1892).

The great majority of judges in the later part of the nineteenth century were members of the Church of Ireland, although they had become a minority by 1921. The first Protestant judge who was not a member was Andrew Marshall Porter (appointed in 1883), a Unitarian or non-subscribing Presbyterian. John Ross (1896), J.O. Wylie (1907), his nephew W.E. Wylie (1920) and John Gordon (1916)

176 Bank Holiday (Ireland) Act 1903 (3 Edw. 7, c.1).
177 Sir John Ross, *The years of my pilgrimage* (London, 1924), p. 120.
178 *ILT&SJ*, vol. 52, p. 290 (30 November 1918).
179 G. Hill Smith, *The North East Bar* (Belfast, 1910), p. 126.
180 Ibid. Twelve additional QCs were appointed in 1900.
181 *ILT&SJ*, vol. 34, p. 60 (3 February 1900).

were Presbyterians. W.D. Andrews (1882) was a Unitarian. Jonathan Pim (1915) was a member of the Society of Friends. Walter Boyd (1885) gave his religion as 'Protestant, no denomination' in the census return form in 1911.

Religious belief was seen, as so often, to be something of a proxy for political opinion. In the short biographical notes of judges in Ball's *The judges in Ireland, 1221–1921* the phrase 'was in religion a Roman Catholic' is employed with reference to 24 men appointed in the half century before 1921 and in 19 cases is followed by a further phrase 'and in politics a liberal'. The five judges out of the 24 not so characterised as liberals were Morris (appointed in 1867), Peter O'Brien (1889) and William Kenny (1898) (although both of them considered themselves as liberal unionists), Stephen Ronan (1915, but see below) and John Blake Powell (1918).

The religion of candidates, while it was noted, was rarely in itself and as such a factor when judicial appointments were being made. One example of it being a determining factor however was the appointment of Thomas O'Hagan as lord chancellor in December 1868, in Gladstone's first government. He was the first Catholic since the reign of James II (1685–9) to hold that office, an appointment made possible by the repeal in 1867[182] of the requirement that it should be held by a member of the established church. O'Hagan's selection was intended to 'inaugurate the beginning of a new era', symbolising a 'new spirit of religious equality'.[183] When an additional position as lord justice of appeal was created in 1877 Rickard Deasy, a judge since 1861, was promoted, and the lord lieutenant told Disraeli that apart from Deasy's inherent suitability 'he is moreover a Roman Catholic, and as the court will comprise two Protestants, the lord chancellor and the present lord justice, I am inclined to look upon this as an advantage in infusing confidence into its primary constitution'.[184] The appointment in June 1882 of William O'Brien to fill a vacancy in the High Court was directly linked to his religion. Lord Spencer, then the lord lieutenant, canvassed various names with Gladstone, remarking that 'I always dislike introducing religion into questions of qualification for offices of importance', before acknowledging how unsatisfactory it was that there was a small number of Catholics holding judicial positions. He then said that it 'would be impossible to ignore this in the present state of public opinion in Ireland' and that 'one of the vacancies therefore should be filled by a Roman Catholic'. Three days later he expressed his recommendation for O'Brien in more urgent terms, 'as I consider it essential to appoint a Roman Catholic'.[185]

The appointment in 1836 of Michael O'Loghlen to be a baron of the Exchequer (he later became master of the rolls) had been the first elevation of a Catholic to the bench for almost 150 years, and he was followed a couple of years later by Stephen Woulfe. Both men had short judicial careers, dying within a few

182 The Office and Oath Act 1867 (30&31 Vict., c.75), s1.
183 O.J. Burke, *History of the lord chancellors of Ireland, 1186–1874* (Dublin, 1879), p. 327.
184 Marlborough to Disraeli, 23 September 1877 (Disraeli Papers, C/V/15c).
185 Spencer to Gladstone, 7 and 10 June 1882 (Althorp Papers, Add. MS 76854.32 and 34).

years. In 1846 the next appointment of a Catholic (David Pigot, to be chief baron of the Exchequer) was made, and over the next twenty years the number of such appointments (and the longevity in office of those appointed) resulted in there being a virtual equality in the 1860s and 1870s in the number of Church of Ireland and Catholic judges. Between 1846 and 1865 eight Catholic judges were appointed, including each of the four men (apart from the lord chancellor) who were raised to the bench in the last period of office as prime minister of Lord Palmerston (1859–65). These eight judges and their periods of office were Pigot (1846–73), James Henry Monahan (chief justice of Common Pleas, 1850–76), William Nicholas Keogh (1856–78), James O'Brien (1858–82), Henry Hughes (1859–72), John David Fitzgerald (1860–82, when he was appointed a Law Lord), Rickard Deasy (1861–83) and Thomas O'Hagan (1865–74, and 1880–1). Napier complained to Derby that 'Lord Palmerston is turning our judicial bench into a monastic refuge – there are now seven Roman Catholics – and two more law officers. Of the five Protestant judges you appointed four – Lord Palmerston appointed four of the Roman Catholics'.[186]

In consequence of those appointments, in 1865 8 of the 15 judicial positions in the historic courts of Chancery, Queen's Bench, Common Pleas and the Exchequer were held by Catholics and since none of the 3 Chancery judges were Catholics the proportion in the common law courts was 8 out of 12.[187] The position was much the same in 1874, when Catholic judges were 9 out of 16.[188] (The overall ratio would not have constituted a majority of Catholics if the (less significant or remunerative) positions in the courts of probate, bankruptcy and Admiralty, and the Landed Estates Court, were also taken into account.) The appointments made by Disraeli's government between 1874 and 1880 commenced a swing in the pendulum away from that ratio. By 1885 12 out of 18 were Protestants, and in 1905 12 of 15.[189] In the years between then and 1921 however half of the men appointed were Catholics.[190] Such appointments, and those of Ronan, Pim and Gordon during the Great War, resulted in no more than one third of the judges in 1921 being members of the Church of Ireland.

The background of members of the judiciary might be compared with the religious composition of the holders of senior governmental and civil service positions in the period 1881–1911. Such posts (defined for the relevant analysis as the lord lieutenant, the chief secretary, the under-secretary, the heads of government departments and their immediate subordinates) were held by

186 Napier to Derby, 15 February 1860 (Derby Papers, 112).

187 *Law Times*, vol. 37, p. 602 (11 October 1862).

188 Ball, pp 297, 305. The 16th judge was the vice-chancellor, an office created in 1867. Lord Naas commented to Lord Derby in 1866 that if Morris [solicitor general] were to be appointed as master of the rolls 'that would involve the addition of another R. Catholic to the Bench, there being already 9 judges out of 12 of that religion' (Naas to Derby, 15 August 1866 (Derby Papers, 155/2)).

189 These variations in the total numbers of judges reflect statutory changes.

190 Ball, pp 314, 320 and 323.

165 people, the religious affiliation of 80% of whom could be determined. Of these 58% were members of the Church of Ireland, 34% Catholics, 5% Presbyterians and 3% other non-conformist. The corresponding proportions in the total population were approximately 13% Church of Ireland, 75% Catholic, 10% Presbyterian and 1% other non-conformist.[191]

A couple of Catholic judges were noted for their personal piety. Christopher Palles obtained ecclesiastical permission to have an oratory at each of his homes, at 28 Fitzwilliam Place and Mountanville House (later known as Knockrabo), near Dundrum in south county Dublin.[192] William O'Brien, who died in 1899, attended Mass daily and bequeathed to the Jesuit Order a valuable library of rare early printed books and medieval manuscripts.[193] Others took any religious connection lightly, as to which Maurice Healy's memoir, *The old Munster circuit*, makes reference to two judges of the Court of Appeal, John Francis Moriarty who was appointed in 1914 and Stephen Ronan who was appointed to succeed him after his early death in 1915.[194] Moriarty was 'devoid of religious principles' but prone to play-acting professions or affectations of religiosity if the situation called for it. Ronan 'professed the most complete atheism during his life', referring to himself in the 1911 census return form as having 'no denomination', and for him to have been classified by Ball as a Catholic (or indeed perhaps even as a Christian) as mentioned above seems an error.

For Catholics the canon law of the church was largely seen as a subject for clerical expertise and authoritative interpretation and application, whereas the governance structure of the Church of Ireland engaged and provided a significant role for laymen in its legal and administrative aspect. Probate and the divorce law jurisdiction had rested with the ecclesiastical courts of the Church of Ireland up to 1857 and 1870 respectively, when the old church law on those subjects was in practice brought within the scope of the common law. Lawyers and judges in those courts had necessarily had a strong connection with the church, and a number of judges, as prominent laymen, were active in the Church of Ireland.

For some this connection will have dated back to childhood. Three sitting judges in 1866 (Berwick, Longfield and Dobbs) were the sons of Church of Ireland clergymen and six appointed thereafter (Whiteside, Walsh, Ormsby, May, Johnson and Madden). Five were married to daughters of clergymen (Ball, Ormsby, Johnson, Gibson and Samuels). A.M. Porter was the son of a Unitarian minister and John Ross and W.E. Wylie were sons of Presbyterian ministers. The constitution of the Church of Ireland, as laid down by the Irish Church Act 1869 and a General Convention in 1870, had established a new Representative Church Body, which operated in conjunction with the General Synod. The elected

191 See Fergus Campbell, *The Irish establishment, 1879–1914* (Oxford, 2009), pp 64–5.

192 V.T.H. Delany, *Christopher Palles; his life and times* (Dublin, 1960), p. 111.

193 *ILT&SJ*, vol. 33, p. 518 (9 December 1899) and vol. 34, p. 34 (20 January 1900). A sale of some of the library took place in 2017.

194 Healy, *OldMC*, pp 92, 132, and 215.

membership of the RCB typically included sitting or retired judges, and at different times Napier, Longfield, Ball, Warren, Harrison, FitzGibbon, Holmes, Bewley and Samuels were members. The first four named of those judges were significant participants in the General Convention. Ball published a history of the Church.[195] Warren spoke strongly against Home Rule at a special meeting of the General Synod held in March 1886 and wrote a treatise on the law of the Church.[196] FitzGibbon was 'incomparably the most influential layman in the Church of Ireland'.[197]

The constitution of the courts (ecclesiastical tribunals) of the Church included a chancellor who would act as a legal assessor, being a fit and proper person who was a barrister of at least ten years' standing, and in practice judges were typically appointed to that office. Ball was vicar general of the archdiocese of Armagh. The court of the General Synod, to which an appeal could be taken from a decision of a diocesan court, consisted of three ecclesiastical judges (bishops) and four elected lay judges, those eligible for election in that capacity including persons who were or had been judges of the superior courts or had been chancellors of a diocese. FitzGibbon was chancellor of the united dioceses of Dublin, Glendalough and Kildare for over ten years, and Warren, J.G. Gibson, Holmes, Madden and Samuels all served in that capacity in various dioceses. An example of the involvement of judicial members in ecclesiastical proceedings is given by the first of what transpired to be an extended series of controversies over liturgical practices and furnishings in St Bartholomew's, Clyde Road, Ballsbridge. The initial proceedings which continued between 1892 and 1895 commenced in the diocesan court, where Ball and FitzGibbon participated, and four judges – Holmes, Murphy, Monroe and J.G. Gibson – were the lay members of the court which heard an appeal.[198] There are statues of Whiteside and FitzGibbon in the nave of St Patrick's cathedral in Dublin, which were erected in each case by private subscriptions a few years after their deaths (which occurred in 1876 and 1909 respectively), and in the cathedral there are a number of other less prominent memorials to judges, including Maziere Brady. R.R. Cherry, who is commemorated in the baptistry, was a bell ringer at the cathedral, to which he donated two bells. Other churches hold memorials to judges, including St Stephen's at Mount Street Crescent, in which there is a memorial window commemorating Lord Ashbourne.

Some judges were appointed by the government, or ex officio by statute, to positions that had some quasi-judicial functions, but for which no payment was made for their services. These included membership of boards of Commissioners

195 J.T. Ball, *The Reformed Church of Ireland, 1537–1886* (Dublin, 1886).

196 *The Church of Ireland and the present crisis: report of a special meeting of the General Synod holden at Dublin, 23 March 1886* (Dublin 1886), p. 52; R.R. Warren, *The law of the Church of Ireland: an essay* (Dublin and London, 1895).

197 Henry E. Patton, *Fifty years of disestablishment: a sketch* (Dublin, 1922), p. 219.

198 Kenneth Milne, *St Bartholomew's; a history of the Dublin parish* (Dublin, 1963), pp 22–4. F.D. How, *Archbishop Plunket, a memoir* (London, 1900), p. 322.

for national and intermediate education and of the Commissioners of Charitable Donations and Bequests for Ireland, the statute establishing which specified that the master of the rolls and the chief baron of the Exchequer would be members, and it was conventional for a number of the ten other 'proper and discreet persons'[199] who from time to time comprised the Commissioners also to be judges. In 1872, for instance, the Commissioners included not only the two statutory judges but also Lord O'Hagan (the lord chancellor), Mr Justice Fitzgerald of the Queen's Bench, Judge Stephen Woulfe Flanagan of the Landed Estates Court and one of his predecessors, Mountifort Longfield. Two of the Commissioners appointed under the Educational Endowments (Ireland) Act 1885[200] were required to be sitting or former judges and they in effect were responsible for the transaction of business under the Act.

James Lawson, a judge of the court of Common Pleas, was appointed to be one of the members of the Church Temporalities Commission, a body set up under the Irish Church Act 1869[201] to manage the properties of the disestablished church and agree compensation for the disturbance of various vested interests. It was a successor to a body with more limited functions, the Irish Ecclesiastical Commission, that had been established by the Church Temporalities (Ireland) Act 1833,[202] which provided that its membership would include the lord chancellor, the chief justice [of King's Bench] and three other 'proper and discreet persons, being members of the United Church of England and Ireland' (who might be lawyers, such as J.T. Ball, appointed in 1868).

Many judges were involved in civic and educational or other charitable bodies, such as schools and hospitals, which would generally have had some religious association. A number of judges were members of the Masonic Order, including Longfield, Morris, Chatterton, Townsend, Harrison, Charles Barry, FitzGibbon, Law, Boyd, Edward Gibson, and Campbell.[203] Lawyers played a prominent part in the foundation in 1847 of the Statistical and Social Inquiry Society of Ireland and in its affairs for decades thereafter,[204] and a number of men who were (or became) judges served as the president of the society.[205] A paper published by the society in 1852 included a comforting economic analysis for lawyers:

199 An Act for the more effectual application of Charitable Donations and Bequests in Ireland, 1844 (7&8 Vict., c.97), s2.

200 48&49 Vict., c.78, s4.

201 32&33 Vict., c.42, ss3 and 6.

202 3&4 Will. 4, c.37, s2.

203 Grand Lodge of Freemasons of Ireland, Membership Registers 1733–1923; *ILT&SJ*, vol. 4, p. 88 (5 February 1870).

204 Details of papers read and other contributions made to the society by members of the Bar and judiciary are set out in *ILT&SJ*, vol. 53, p. 24 (25 January 1919) and vol. 54, pp 187–8 (31 July 1920).

205 Mountifort Longfield (president 1863–7), Thomas O'Hagan (1867–70), James A. Lawson (1870–2), John O'Hagan (1890–1), W.H. Dodd (1894–6), A.W. Samuels (1906–8), R.R. Cherry (1908–11), T.F. Molony (1920–4).

> the wages of any craft whatsoever have a constant tendency to regulate themselves by what political economists call the cost of production; that is to say, they will be high in proportion to the outlay, labour and delay necessary for its acquisition. So long therefore as the law remains as we have shown it must remain – a science of great difficulty – so long a successful lawyer must be in receipt of a large income.[206]

A separate honour held by judges was membership of the Privy Council of Ireland, the members of which were designated or styled as 'Right Honourable' ('Right Hon'.) as contrasted with the 'Honourable' ('Hon'.) designation of judges of the superior courts (as such). Some judges were appointed to be members, but more commonly membership would date (for lifetime) from the person concerned having been sworn in as a member at the time of appointment as attorney general. The Council had advisory functions and certain other limited functions of a judicial nature (see pp 70–3). A small number of Irish judges were also appointed to be members of the Privy Council in London, which had quite significant appellate judicial functions for the British Empire (see pp 441–2).

A number of judges had scholarly or literary interests, and some members of the Bar in the nineteenth century who subsequently became judges were elected as members of the Royal Irish Academy, a learned society established in 1785. These were Joseph Napier (elected in 1840), David R. Pigot (1845), Rickard Deasy (1846), John George and John E. Walsh (both 1855) and Thomas O'Hagan and James A. Lawson (both 1857). Three judges became members early in the twentieth century, namely Dodgson Hamilton Madden (1901), Dunbar Plunket Barton (1917) and Arthur W. Samuels (1922).

In private life judges had a high social standing, and many were members of gentlemen's clubs, and of golf clubs. The membership of the Dublin University Club, at 17 St Stephen's Green, included a significant number of members of the Bar and of judges, and many also were members of the Kildare Street Club. When legal proceedings were instituted by Edward Martyn in 1906 to declare void his expulsion from the latter club there was some light-hearted speculation as to whether a judge could be found to hear the case who was not a member of the club.[207] Over half of the 15 superior court judges were members, and only three members of the High Court were not. One of these was R.E. Meredith, the master of the rolls, who presided over a trial that lasted five days. The process of attempted expulsion had been overseen by a committee in the club which included two judges, Andrew Marshall Porter (whom Meredith had succeeded in office in the autumn of 1906, and who was the first witness called by the club at the trial the following year) and Dunbar Plunket Barton.[208] Martyn was a prominent nationalist

206 J. O'Hagan BL (subsequently president, 1890–1) and S.A. Jackson BL, *An inquiry into taxes on law proceedings in Ireland* (Dublin, 1852), pp 4–5.
207 *Law Times*, vol. 120, p. 445 (17 March 1906).
208 R.B. McDowell, *Land and learning: two Irish clubs* (Dublin, 1993), pp 79–81.

whose sharp criticisms of the armed services had become increasingly objectionable to many other members of the club. Meredith set aside his expulsion, holding that the club, despite following the committee's advice, had adopted an incorrect procedure for an expulsion under its rules by conducting a poll or ballot over the course of a day rather than holding a meeting to consider and if thought fit pass a resolution for expulsion.[209]

That club was widely regarded as the social centre in the city of the landed interest and consequently, certainly from the later part of the nineteenth century, as being associated with unionism and the Conservative party. An inquiry made on behalf of senior members of the club to James Bryce, a Scottish MP who was appointed chief secretary for Ireland at the end of 1905, as to whether he would wish to join it produced an immediate reaction from the under-secretary in Dublin Castle, Sir Antony MacDonnell, who told Bryce that for him to have any association with the club would create enormous difficulties for his relations with Liberals and Nationalists.[210] Some prominent legal Liberals were members of the Stephen's Green Club, six of whom (J.O. Wylie, W.H. Dodd, Redmond Barry, Charles O'Connor, T.F. Molony and Jonathan Pim) were appointed to the bench between 1906 and 1915. The club was circumspect when a proposal was made for a dinner to be given in honour of Barry and O'Connor upon their appointment as attorney general and solicitor general respectively in 1909. The club committee decided that in light of the social and non-political character of the club 'and the danger of a party interpretation being placed on the proposed dinner if given under official auspices' any entertainment in that connection should be left to individual members.[211]

Dunbar Plunket Barton had a great interest in golf (see p. 375). Sir John Ross was captain of Royal Dublin golf club (as was W.H. Dodd),[212] and used a convoluted golfing analogy when asking that a position be found for him in the judiciary in Britain in 1922 in light of the impending abolition of his office of lord chancellor, remarking that he had yet to reach the top of his swing in terms of his judicial contribution.[213] Sir James O'Connor was president of Milltown golf club, and J.O. Wylie, John Gordon and James H.M. Campbell were members of the club at Greystones.[214] Lord Glenavy was president between 1928 and 1931 of Fitzwilliam lawn tennis club, the premises of which at the time, extending to two acres at Wilton Place beside the Grand Canal, adjoined Fitzwilliam Square. The

209 *Irish Times*, 4 and 6 July 1907; Denis Gwynn, *Edward Martyn and the Irish Revival* (London, 1930), p. 316.
210 Sir John Ross of Bladenburg to Bryce, 2 February 1906, and MacDonnell to Bryce, 2 February 1906 (Bryce Papers, MS 11,012(2)).
211 Cornelius F. Smith and Bernard Share (eds), *Whigs on the Green* (Dublin, 1990), pp 66–73, 166–73.
212 *ILT&SJ*, vol. 64, p. 71 (22 March 1930).
213 Memorandum by Ross forwarded to the home secretary (Edward Shortt MP), 27 August 1922 (HO317/67 (TNAUK)); also forwarded to Winston Churchill (then secretary of state for the colonies), 15 October 1922 (CO739/16 (TNAUK)).
214 *Irish Times*, 22 September 1908.

championships of Ireland were played within the square up to 1903 – 'one of the leading events in the fashionable world each year is the great lawn tennis tournament which opens in Dublin this day in Fitzwilliam Square'.[215] Glenavy's son Cecil was the men's singles champion in 1919 and 1921.[216]

Eight judges had attended the Royal Belfast Academical Institution (Napier, Hayes, Thomas O'Hagan, Andrews, Atkinson, Dodd, J.O. Wylie and Gordon), three went to Portora Royal School, Enniskillen (Boyd, J.G. Gibson and Wright) and three to Clongowes Wood College, Co. Kildare (Palles, Naish, Peter O'Brien). Four judges were educated at public schools in England, namely G.A.C. May (Shrewsbury), Dunbar Plunket Barton (Harrow), John F. Moriarty (Stonyhurst) and William Moore (Marlborough). The sons of some judges were sent to such public schools, in what has been termed 'a form of educational migration'[217] – it was estimated in the 1880s that over 1,300 Irish Protestant pupils and perhaps one-third that number of Irish Catholics, were being educated in England.[218] John D. Fitzgerald's sons (including Gerald Fitzgerald) attended Oscott, near Birmingham,[219] as did a son of Stephen Woulfe Flanagan, Morris favoured the Oratory school also near Birmingham, sons of May attended Harrow (as did sons of Porter and a son of Monroe) and Rugby, sons of Ashbourne attended Harrow and Wellington, sons of Holmes and Murphy attended Charterhouse, Sir John Ross's only son went to Eton, Redmond Barry's son attended Downside and the sons of James H.M. Campbell went to Charterhouse and Shrewsbury. Gerald FitzGibbon sent his sons to Clifton college, Bristol, one of whom (also called Gerald FitzGibbon, a member of the post-1924 judiciary) referred in a judgment in 1934[220] to the potential benefits to young men in attending such well-resourced schools. Sons of 14 judges served, and in a number of instances died, in the army or navy during the First World War.[221]

Judges actively participated in the solicitation from the government of titles of honour – as a peer, baronet, or knight – that was a constant feature of political and official life at the time. A certain standing in terms of formal precedence or protocol or official dignity would be derived solely from judicial status as such but this could be supplemented or enhanced by a title of some description. In 1894 the *Law Times* was of the view that 'the position in society which an Irish judge occupies in Dublin is much higher than that which an English judge, as such, enjoys in London. When lately it was proposed to confer knighthood upon the judges *en masse* the dignity was scornfully rejected. They desired no other social

215 *Irish Times*, 23 May 1898.
216 Ulick O'Connor, *The Fitzwilliam story, 1877–1977* (Dublin, 1977), pp 25, 65, 77.
217 Ciaran O'Neill, *Power and powerlessness in Union Ireland* (Oxford, 2024), p. 172.
218 Ciaran O'Neill, *Catholics of consequence: transnational education, social mobility and the Irish Catholic elite* (Oxford, 2014), pp 10–11.
219 Oscott was one of the most prestigious and socially exclusive of the Catholic schools of the time (O'Neill, op. cit., p. 75).
220 *In re Westby Minors (no. 2)*, [1934] IR 311, at 325.
221 *ILT&SJ*, vol. 49, pp 192–3 (7 August 1915).

pre-eminence than that which their office carries'.[222] That last observation was mistaken, as appears below, but in itself was a testament to the social position of judges. Honours were sought not only for their own sake, but also at times as part of a bargain for retirement from office. Men already holding the highest judicial offices, Lord Ashbourne as lord chancellor and Peter O'Brien as lord chief justice, each sought to enhance their status, in O'Brien's case in a very determined fashion.

Approaches for a baronetcy that were made by the lord chief justice, George Augustus Chichester May, in 1885 and 1886 bring out some of these issues and the underlying concerns of (comparative) social standing and potential retirement. Michael Morris, the chief justice of Common Pleas, had been created a baronet in September 1885, which led May to complain to Ashbourne, the lord chancellor, that he had been placed in an invidious position since the holder of his office – formally superior to that of Morris – had not been so honoured. He expressed a willingness to accept a similar honour 'gratefully and dutifully, as an honour conferred on the administration of the Law, which I represent, not upon any merits of my own'.[223] A few months later a family friend told Ashbourne fairly directly that May's family, being very concerned about a recent illness of his, were anxious for him to retire and considered that this might be expedited if a baronetcy were to be conferred on him.[224] Neither of these approaches, direct and indirect, nor a further approach at the end of 1886, succeeded, and May retained office until his retirement on grounds of ill-health in the New Year of 1887.

The last approach was the subject of an unflattering analysis by Sir Michael Hicks Beach, then the chief secretary for Ireland, and who had held the same position in 1877 when May had been appointed as chief justice (see p. 271). He told the lord lieutenant, Lord Londonderry, that a comparison could not be drawn with the conferring of an honour on Morris, who had been a judge for almost 20 years and had always been ready to help the government with advice if approached. He thought May to be an upright and honourable, man and a good lawyer, but having no remarkable ability nor claim upon the goodwill of the government. Although his political career had not been a success, he had been given the offices of law adviser and attorney general, after which he was quite soon elevated to be chief justice, where his service had not been regarded as being of any particular distinction. For some time past his deafness had given rise to difficulty in hearing witnesses and counsel in court, and – in the view of Hicks Beach – he was likely soon to retire from office in any event, otherwise risking a scandal if he sought to continue. In short, there was no good reason for making May a baronet, and if this was to be done in his case it could hardly be refused to anyone else who had been chief justice, which Hicks Beach considered would be absurd.[225]

222 *ILT&SJ*, vol. 28, 4 August 1894, p. 381 (reproduced from *Law Times*).
223 May to Ashbourne, 26 September 1885 (Ashbourne Papers, B107/1).
224 Lady Iddesleigh to Ashbourne, 14 December 1885 (Ashbourne Papers, B71/38).
225 Hicks Beach to Londonderry, 19 December 1886 (Salisbury Papers).

The conferring of an honour would potentially have had a particular social significance in the case of a married judge.[226] A judge of the superior courts would have a formal or protocol precedence over a knight, and wives when (but only if) accompanying their husbands would share in that standing. A judicial position was regarded as one of official dignity rather than of more general social status, however; 'the wives and children of great Officers of State, and of all who derive their places on the Scale from Official rank, have no consequent precedence. This rule applies to the wives and children of Archbishops and Bishops, the Chancellor, the Judges, etc'.[227] When in 1891 a proposal was made for knighthoods to be conferred on all judges of the superior courts one of their number when writing to Ashbourne on the subject said that 'I understand that there is an agitation concerning knighthood originating I presume with the ladies'.[228]

The Appellate Jurisdiction Act 1876 made provision for the appointment of lords of appeal in ordinary ('Law Lords') as life peers without there being any hereditary right of succession to the title. Every other peerage was a hereditary honour, with some expectation of a suitably elevated lifestyle being maintained. In calling for the institution of legal life peers in 1870 the *Irish Law Times* referred to men's reluctance to 'burden their posterity with the support of a peerage', noting that 'fortunes sufficient to support a hereditary dignity cannot now be made at the Irish Bar'.[229] The previous year, on the same lines, the paper had said that the conferring of a peerage on a person without adequate resources had the consequence of 'the infliction of an injury on their families, and the lowering of the status of the peerage'.[230] Within the hereditary peerage there were different levels of rank or precedence, these being, in ascending order, a baron (the rank of every Irish legal peerage referred to below), a viscount, an earl, a marquess and a duke.[231] Dukes were invariably referred to as the 'duke of [Wellington, or wherever]', but other peers might be described generically as 'Lord X' or alternatively by their particular style of titles. For instance, Lord Salisbury, prime minister for broken periods amounting to over 13 years between July 1885 and July 1902, was variously or interchangeably referred to under that name or as the [third] marquess of Salisbury. Baronetcies and knighthoods were each designated by the prefix 'Sir', but only a baronetcy was a hereditary honour,[232] also denoted by the

226 *ILT&SJ*, vol. 40, p. 146 (28 April 1906).

227 'The Roll of Ladies' Precedence in Ireland, note by J. Bernard Burke, Ulster King of Arms, Dublin Castle' in *Thom's Irish Almanac and Official Directory for 1872* (Dublin, 1872), p. 887.

228 Warren to Ashbourne, 14 July 1891 (Ashbourne Papers, B.153/1.) See also Marshall Porter to Ashbourne, 17 July 1891 (Ashbourne Papers, B.115/2), and Monroe to Ashbourne, 17 July 1891 (Ashbourne Papers, B.104/3).

229 *ILT&SJ*, vol. 4, p. 415 (11 June 1870).

230 *ILT&SJ*, vol. 3, p. 277 (24 August 1869).

231 Hugh Cairns, lord chancellor of Great Britain 1868 and 1874–80, was raised to the peerage in 1867 as Baron Cairns of Garmoyle in the county of Antrim. 'In 1878 he received the additional honour of two steps in the peerage, being created Viscount Garmoyle, in the county of Antrim, and Earl Cairns' (*ILT&SJ*, vol. 18, p. 327 (28 June 1884)).

232 See the first paragraph of *Persuasion* (Jane Austen, 1818), as to the satisfaction of Sir Walter

addition of the suffix 'Bt'. to the name of the relevant person. A baronet or a knight remained a commoner, not becoming a peer.

The lord chancellor of Great Britain, as presiding over the legislative proceedings of the House of Lords, was always a peer[233] (as had been the case for the lord chancellor of Ireland up to the Act of Union in 1800), and peerages had occasionally been conferred on senior judges, in Ireland as well as in England. For judicial services in Ireland these included two lord chancellors, both Englishmen, John Mitford (1802–6) who became Lord Redesdale and Thomas Manners Sutton (1807–27) who became Lord Manners. John Toler, the chief justice of common pleas between 1800 and 1827, became Lord Norbury. Prior to 1870 the most recent such peerages for holders of judicial office in Ireland had been those conferred (in 1827) on William Conyngham Plunket, who had been appointed attorney general in 1822, chief justice of Common Pleas in 1827 and lord chancellor in 1830, which last position he held, with a brief interval in 1834–5, until 1841 and (in 1841) on John Campbell, later chief justice of the Queen's Bench in England (1850) and lord chancellor of Great Britain (1859), who succeeded Plunket in very controversial circumstances in 1841.[234] Sir Robert Peel became prime minister for the second time in August 1841, and his aversion to creating hereditary honours was shown in his discouraging of expectations and refusal to accept claims for these based upon supposed precedents.[235] He turned down an explicit request from Charles Kendal Bushe, chief justice of Queen's Bench since 1822, although Bushe resigned anyway a few weeks later, and also was solicited by John Doherty, the chief justice of Common Pleas, and by Edward Sugden, who was re-appointed as lord chancellor.[236]

Between 1867 and 1921 honours were conferred on 15 Irish judges of the superior courts,[237] sitting or retired. These were Napier, Brady, Thomas O'Hagan, Sullivan, Edward Gibson, Morris, Peter O'Brien, Bewley, Porter, Johnson, Boyd, Barton, Ignatius O'Brien, Campbell and Ross. Six of the judges – Lawson, Flanagan, Ashbourne, Morris, Palles and FitzGibbon – were made members of the Privy Council in England. Four judges received honours more than once, namely Michael Morris (baronetcy, life peerage and peerage), and Peter O'Brien, Ignatius O'Brien and James Campbell (in each case, successively a baronetcy and

Elliott Bt. at his status. He was a man 'who, for his own amusement, never took up any book but the Baronetage'.

233 This may not have been technically or formally strictly necessary, but in practice it was essential (see R.F.V. Heuston, *Lives of the Lord Chancellors, 1885–1940* (Oxford, 1964), p. xvi).

234 Ball, pp 285–6; David Plunket, *The life, letters and speeches of Lord Plunket* (London, 1867), vol. 2, pp 330–46.

235 Ball, p. 287.

236 Bushe to Peel, 5 September 1841, Peel to Bushe, 17 September 1841 (Charles Kendal Bushe Papers (Library of Trinity College Dublin) IE MS 4002/4); E. OE. Somerville and Martin Ross, *An incorruptible Irishman* [a biography of Bushe] (London, 1932), p. 251.

237 Knighthoods were occasionally conferred on presidents of the Incorporated Law Society of Ireland, seven of whom were so honoured between 1868 and 1921, as were a number of senior legal officials, such as Sir Patrick Coll, chief Crown solicitor 1888–1905, who was knighted in 1896 (*ILT&SJ*, vol. 51, p. 68 (17 March 1917)).

a peerage). The life peerages conferred on John David Fitzgerald (1882), Morris (1889) and John Atkinson (1905) were necessarily connected with their respective appointments to be a lord of appeal in ordinary rather than honours or favours in themselves. In contrast the baronetcy conferred in 1869 on Maziere Brady (1796–1871),[238] who had been chief baron of the Exchequer (1840–6) and lord chancellor of Ireland three times, for a total of almost 20 years (between 1846–52, 1852–8 and 1859–66) was a straightforward honour conferred by the newly elected Liberal government, as an acknowledgment of a distinguished career.

In other cases, as appears below, the honours were conferred (or announced, the conferring taking place somewhat later) on sitting judges, or on judges who had recently retired or would shortly do so, at times or in circumstances that indicated that the honour had induced their retirement. In at least two cases a solicited honour was refused by the government (as mentioned, May in 1885, and (for a time) Peter O'Brien in 1890–1) and two judges declined an unsolicited honour that was offered as an inducement to retire (Chatterton in 1890 and Cherry in 1915).[239] Blackburne declined a baronetcy, and it appears that Lefroy also did so. When fresh pressure arose in the 1890s to reorganize the judiciary and reduce the number of judges it was reported in 1895 that 'Judge Miller will receive a baronetcy and retire from the court of Bankruptcy on a full pension'.[240] This did not happen, and he continued to sit as a judge until his death in May 1897.[241]

The sequence of honours for members of the judiciary in office from the 1860s onwards began with a baronetcy being offered in July 1866 (the actual conferment taking place in April 1867) to Joseph Napier, a former lord chancellor of Ireland (1858–9), in unusual circumstances. Napier had been nominated to be a lord justice of appeal by the incoming government of Lord Derby. This had given rise to an immediate controversy as to his capacity to discharge the duties of office on account of what was later described as 'an infirmity of deafness which rendered it out of his power to follow with accuracy the arguments of counsel'.[242] The lord chancellor in London, Lord Chelmsford, quickly interceded and induced Napier to resign, but to Derby's regret had 'undertaken that he [Napier] shall have a baronetcy, which he was scarcely entitled to promise'.[243] Derby showed no urgency in honouring this pledge to Napier, responding some six months later to an inquiry from him by saying quite directly that 'in the expectation which the chancellor held out to you he somewhat exceeded any authority I had given him', and that it was currently politically impossible for the government to proceed with it in light of numerous other claims for honours. If, however, Napier was 'disposed to accept in lieu of a baronetcy the immediate honour of an English Privy Councillorship I should have no hesitation in submitting your name for the Queen's approval'.[244]

238 *ILT&SJ*, vol. 3, p. 38 (16 January 1869).
239 Balfour to Chatterton, 23 May 1890 (Ashbourne Papers, B.9/11); R.F.V. Heuston, op. cit., p. 271.
240 *ILT&SJ*, vol. 29, p. 514 (19 October 1895).
241 *ILT&SJ*, vol. 31, p. 216 (8 May 1897).
242 *ILT&SJ*, vol. 32, p. 101 (26 February 1898).
243 Derby to Disraeli, 28 July 1866 (Disraeli Papers, B/XX/5/358); see Hogan, 'Vacancies', p. 222.
244 Derby to Napier, 11 February 1867 (Derby Papers, 192/2, p. 19).

Napier did not withdraw his claim, and the baronetcy was conferred in the spring of 1867, and in the following year he was made a member of the judicial committee of the Privy Council in London. As with the appointments of Law Lords, such an appointment as a member of the Council was usually considered to be a 'working' appointment, not simply a matter of honour. He told Cairns that he and his family would be willing to arrange his residence so as to enable him to attend in London and work diligently.[245]

The judicial vacancy for which Napier had been very briefly nominated had been created by the appointment as lord chancellor of the existing lord justice of appeal, Francis Blackburne, who had been born in November 1782 and was then aged 83. Eight months later, in March 1867, Blackburne was encouraged to resign, and in May he was offered a baronetcy. This he declined, causing family division, and an attempt by his eldest son to have the offer reissued. His refusal was thought by Derby to be tactical, in the hope of being offered a peerage but (as in the contemporaneous and analogous case of Thomas Lefroy, who had retired as chief justice of Queen's Bench in July 1866 when Derby took office) no further offer was made by the prime minister.[246] F.E. Ball remarked that 'whether these great lawyers would have accepted baronetcies if offered at a time when honours would not have had the appearance of a solatium for loss of office, or whether they thought a peerage was their due, is open to doubt'.[247]

The functions and responsibilities of the lord chancellor of Ireland extended over two of the branches of government, the judiciary and the executive, where he would in the ordinary course of events advise the government and participate in the drafting of legislation. In the case of a chancellor who was a peer he would also have a role in the third branch of government, the legislature, as a member of the House of Lords. In June 1870 a peerage was conferred on Thomas O'Hagan, lord chancellor of Ireland, who took the title of Lord O'Hagan of Tullahogue, Co. Tyrone. His initial contribution to debate in the House of Lords was on the bill which became the Land Act 1870, and he was active subsequently in the house, including in its judicial business. His perspective on the prospect of becoming a peer was communicated to Gladstone, the prime minister, by Lord Granville, the colonial secretary, at the end of March 1870:

> O'Hagan called on me this morning. He began about his peerage. Several persons had spoken to him about it. When he was first made chancellor, he was strongly opposed to such an idea, but he would like it now, if you were willing to entertain the idea. It had been the constant practice almost till the appointment of Sir M. Brady.[248] Lord Mulgrave's Govt.[249] had been subject

245 Napier to Cairns, undated [but before February 1868] (Cairns Papers, PRO 30/51/11, 9).
246 Derby to Naas, 7 May 1867 (Mayo Papers, MS 11,150).
247 Ball, p. 303.
248 Brady had been first appointed as lord chancellor in 1846.
249 Lord Mulgrave was lord lieutenant of Ireland from April 1835 to March 1839, when Lord Melbourne was prime minister.

> to violent attacks in consequence of the liberality of his administration. His chancellor [Plunket] was of the greatest use in defending the policy in the House of Lords. H.M.'s Govt were now effecting a peaceful revolution in Ireland and the same sort of attack was being renewed. A peerage would strengthen his position in Ireland and give him the opportunity which he much desired, of defending himself against charges of Ultramontanism, partiality and weakness which were freely made. It was fair to Ireland that the judges should be represented in the House of Lords to at least the extent that Scotland was.[250]

Abraham Brewster, O'Hagan's predecessor as lord chancellor, was reported in 1874 to have asked for a peerage as a condition of accepting re-appointment, but in the event he was neither re-appointed not ennobled (see p. 198). In December 1881 another honour was conferred on a working Irish judge when Edward Sullivan (1822–85), the master of the rolls, was appointed a baronet. This was widely seen as something of a compensation for not having been appointed lord chancellor the previous month, on the retirement of O'Hagan. Robert Phillimore (1810–85), an English judge, was similarly honoured at the time, Gladstone remarking that 'it is rare to make legal baronets, but it seems a reasonable thing, in proper cases'.[251] When Hugh Law (1818–83), the attorney general, had been appointed to succeed O'Hagan it seemed that Sullivan's opportunity of becoming lord chancellor had passed. As it turned out however, Law died in the autumn of 1883, and after an interval of some months, as the claims of the then attorney general, Andrew Marshall Porter, were also considered, Sullivan was appointed as Law's successor and was himself succeeded by Porter as master of the rolls.

In June 1885 Gladstone's second government resigned after losing a vote in the House of Commons on the budget over proposed increases in duties on beer and spirits. A general election could not be held until November, since time was required for the preparation of a new register of the electorate, as greatly expanded by virtue of the Representation of the People Act 1884 (sometimes called the Third Reform Act), in constituencies that had been redrawn by the Redistribution of Seats Act 1885.[252] It was eventually agreed that Lord Salisbury would form a minority or caretaker Conservative government for a few months until an election could be held. Edward Gibson QC, MP was appointed as lord chancellor of Ireland, and the conferring on him of a peerage, as Lord Ashbourne, reflected a desire to retain his political services in Parliament, as a member of the House of Lords. He had been a very effective debater in the House of Commons since his

250 Granville to Gladstone, 31 March 1870 (Gladstone Papers, Add. MS 44167.31); *Ramm 1868–71*, p. 96.

251 Gladstone to Granville, 22 November 1881 (Granville Papers, PRO 30/29/214); Agatha Ramm (ed.), *The political correspondence of Mr Gladstone and Lord Granville, 1876–1886* (Oxford, 1962), p. 311.

252 48 Vict., c.3 (1884) and 48&49 Vict., c.23 (1885); Annual Register, 1885, part I, pp 108–9.

first election, as a member for Dublin University, in 1875. That he should be appointed to the Cabinet was an unexpected and unprecedented step for a lord chancellor of Ireland. His friend Michael Morris, the chief justice of Common Pleas, when writing earlier to congratulate him on his judicial appointment had made the reasonable assumption that Ashbourne had chosen to take judicial office in preference to a political one, not contemplating that they might be combined in such an open way.[253] That honour to Ashbourne – in a sense a utilitarian one – was followed in September by a straightforward honour as such to Morris, who was made a baronet.

The practice in England over the years had been for knighthoods to be conferred on the judges of the various superior courts. In May 1890 Peter O'Brien, who had been appointed as lord chief justice six months before, approached Arthur Balfour, then the chief secretary for Ireland, seeking a baronetcy ('my family are very keen about the matter').[254] The view of Balfour and Salisbury, the prime minister, was that it was premature to think of such an honour, Salisbury noting that Morris had not been made a baronet until he had been on the Bench for fifteen [in fact, eighteen] years. Balfour did 'not think that Peter has been inadequately rewarded for his service – quite the contrary; but he is perpetually bothering me'.[255] This bothering continued into 1891, at which point Balfour wrote fairly plainly to O'Brien, acknowledging that 'it might not be unfitting that, apart altogether from your individual claims on the government, the head of the Irish Bench should have some special mark of distinction'. Then followed the passage cited above about appearances being important, and avoiding any honouring of a judge for services as attorney general. He said that if O'Brien could be patient his name would be submitted for approval to the Queen before the tenure of office of the government (which would not go beyond the summer of 1893).[256] Quite soon afterwards however O'Brien's persistence paid off, and in June 1891 it was announced that a baronetcy was to be conferred upon him.[257]

Perhaps prompted by this news a collective approach was made a few weeks later by a number of judges to Ashbourne as the head of the judiciary, to be transmitted for consideration by Salisbury, seeking the grant of knighthoods to all superior court judges in Ireland. Their leader, or at least spokesman, was Mr Justice Monroe, who had been appointed a High Court judge in 1885. One reason given by him for the request was that the word 'Judge' no longer had the same significance after it had been extended to the County Courts.[258] The County Officers and Courts (Ireland) Act 1877 had provided that 'the chairmen, not being

253 Morris to Gibson, not dated but in June 1885 (Ashbourne Papers, B.77/3).
254 O'Brien to Balfour, 7 May 1890 (Salisbury Papers, HH 6/11); *Salisbury–Balfour correspondence*, p. 310.
255 Balfour to McDonnell, 23 July 1890 (Salisbury Papers, HH 6/17); *Salisbury–Balfour correspondence*, p. 313. McDonnell was private secretary to Salisbury.
256 Balfour to O'Brien, 5 March 1891 (Balfour Papers, Add. MS 49814.322).
257 *ILT&SJ*, vol. 35, p. 321 (6 June 1891).
258 Monroe to Ashbourne, 25 June 1891 (Balfour Papers, Add. MS 49802.76/134).

Recorders, shall from and after the commencement of this Act be styled 'County Court Judges and Chairmen of Quarter Sessions'.[259]

Balfour was minded, as he told the lord lieutenant, Lord Zetland, to accommodate 'the singular appetite for knighthood which has developed in the Irish Bench, but I am decidedly of opinion that all must take it if it is to be given to any', a view shared by Salisbury, who otherwise saw 'no reason why the Irish judges should not be raised to that social position enjoyed by their learned friends over here'.[260] Their view was that knighthoods would be an honour to a class of office holders, not a reflection of individual merit, a point made a decade later by Cadogan, the lord lieutenant between 1895 and 1902, in describing the English system as constituting an 'ex officio rank'.[261]

It transpired that there was no unanimity among the judges on the proposal. Monroe kept Ashbourne informed of their reactions, initially advising him that of those whose views were to date known only Palles had refused.[262] He had told Monroe that his objection was so strong that he could not be bound by the decision of a majority, also remarking that if the prime minister was minded to bestow honours which would otherwise be well deserved he would hardly fail to do so because one man had a personal objection.[263] But, although Ashbourne thought likewise,[264] this transpired not to be the case. A week later Ashbourne was told that the vice-chancellor (Chatterton) and lord justice FitzGibbon would join Palles in objecting. It thus appeared that most of the judges who had a distinctive title were not willing to accept the proposal, and that the condition of unanimity could not be satisfied.[265]

The judges' application for knighthoods stood over for about six months after it was first raised in July 1891. At the end of the year Ashbourne was asked to raise the subject again, in light of the fact that 12 of the 15 judges appeared willing to accept the honour, but there was no change in the government's attitude.[266] The objectors had been joined now by Mr Justice Warren, the head (and sole member) of the probate division of the High Court, who had originally been prepared to accept but had changed his mind.[267] Monroe was very frustrated, telling his colleague Mr Justice Bewley that he did not understand the difficulty and would now drop the whole subject.[268] Zetland doubted whether acceptance of an honour could be made a condition of future judicial appointments.[269] Any frustration that

259 40&41 Vict., c.56, s3.
260 Balfour to Zetland, 14 July 1891 (Balfour Papers, Add. MS 49802.134); Salisbury to Balfour, 15 July 1891 (Balfour Papers, Add. MS 49802.135).
261 Cadogan to Ashbourne, 13 April 1902 (Ashbourne Papers, B.22/38).
262 Monroe to Ashbourne, 17 July 1891 (Ashbourne Papers, B.104/3).
263 Palles to Monroe, 14 July 1891 (Ashbourne Papers, B.112/2).
264 Ashbourne to Zetland, 16 July 1891 (Balfour Papers, Add. MS 49802.138).
265 Monroe to Ashbourne, 24 July 1891 (Ashbourne Papers, B.104/4).
266 Bewley to Ashbourne, 30 December 1891 and 9 January 1892 (Ashbourne Papers, B.18/1 and B.18/2).
267 Warren to Ashbourne, 14 July 1891 and 13 January 1892. (Ashbourne Papers, B.153/1–3).
268 Monroe to Bewley, 15 January 1892 (Ashbourne Papers, B.104/6).
269 Zetland to Ashbourne, 4 February 1892 (Ashbourne Papers, B.164/4).

the majority of the judges may have felt at the failure of the initiative was unlikely to have been eased by the news a few months later that the Unionist government, as it left office, had arranged for membership of the Privy Council in London to be conferred on Palles, as mentioned an uncommon but not unique honour to be given to an Irish judge. The only other honour conferred in that decade upon a judge of the superior courts was a knighthood for Bewley in 1898 on his retirement as judicial commissioner of the Land Commission. The recorder (or chief magistrate) of Dublin, Frederick Falkiner, was knighted in 1896, as was customary.

Marshall Porter, it transpired, had plans of his own for seeking an honour. On the same day that he told Monroe that he would acquiesce in the omnibus proposal he wrote also to Ashbourne to point out that all except four of the persons who had held the office of master of the rolls since 1800 had been made baronets. (Only eight people had held that office in the period, so the four cases that he referred to and analysed were not in fact exceptional.) He was thus 'venturing to suggest that the same distinction might be conferred upon me', in accordance with precedent. He would make no personal claim, 'such things are in no sense matters of right at all but simply favours'. He acknowledged that 'the question of means is not unimportant' for a hereditary distinction and was 'sufficiently well off in that respect to render it not imprudent in the interests of my family to take the responsibility'. His eldest son was the heir presumptive (through his mother's family) to a substantial estate in Scotland. 'If I am unduly presumptuous, place this in the fire'. He received no encouragement from Ashbourne.[270] He persisted in later years in seeking such preferment, and was proposed twice for an honour by Cadogan, in 1897 and 1901.[271] In 1902 in the Coronation Honours he received a baronetcy.

In May 1900 a number of honours were announced, following the visit of Queen Victoria to Ireland the previous month. Sir Peter O'Brien Bt became a peer, with the title of Lord O'Brien of Kilfenora, Lord Morris was granted a hereditary peerage as Lord Morris and Killanin of Spiddal, upon and seemingly as an inducement for his retirement as a lord of appeal in ordinary. FitzGibbon became a member of the Privy Council in London but (unlike other such appointments of Irish lawyers to the judicial committee of the Council) there was no expectation that he would contribute to its work. O'Brien's peerage was the result of further canvassing by him, half a dozen years after he had pressed his case for a baronetcy. The lord lieutenant, Lord Cadogan, had told Salisbury some eighteen months earlier that

> the lord chief justice, Sir Peter O'Brien, the 'Peter the Packer' of old, has been pressing much upon me his claim for a peerage. I believe he has also appealed to you. I send in his name because it is difficult to refuse to do so.

270 Marshall Porter to Ashbourne, 17 July 1891 and 23 July 1891 (Ashbourne Papers, B/115/2 and /3).

271 Schomberg McDonnell, Honours Nomination Book (PRONI, D4091/A/3/4/1).

> His services are undoubtedly very great, but he has had a baronetcy and was made lord chief justice. He has no son. If you do see your way to recommending him it will, I think, give considerable satisfaction to many, if I may judge by the letters I continually receive.[272]

A peerage that was conferred in 1906 upon Charles Hemphill, who had been solicitor general between 1892 and 1895, represented a political rather than judicial honour (although he had for a time been a county court judge). In the same year Samuel Walker, recently re-appointed as the lord chancellor, was made a baronet.[273]

Baronetcies were conferred upon three retiring judges between 1909 and 1918, in at least one case as part of a clear bargain to secure a vacation of office, and in the other cases immediately preceding or following retirement. William Moore Johnson (1826–1918), who had been appointed to the High Court in 1883, was appointed a baronet in November 1909, and he retired as a judge at the end of the law term the following month. When congratulations were tendered to him in court following the announcement of the honour, he said that 'it comes very unexpectedly upon me'.[274] If that remark were taken at face value it would suggest that the conferring of the honour (first contemplated in 1906) was a hint that he might wish to consider retiring rather than the fruit of an arrangement that he would actually do so. Walter Boyd (1833–1918) retired as a High Court judge in April 1916, at the instigation of James Campbell, and was made a baronet, in fulfilment of an explicit offer to that effect that had been made by the prime minister, Asquith, a couple of months earlier and accepted by Boyd.[275] In 1918 Dunbar Plunket Barton (1853–1937) was appointed a baronet on his retirement.[276]

In the New Year Honours List in 1916, Ignatius O'Brien, the lord chancellor, was made a baronet, widely interpreted as a gesture of support for his position after the controversy that had surrounded the attempt to remove him from office the previous summer. In June 1918, he was offered a peerage, and took the title of Lord Shandon, upon his retirement (in effect, his dismissal).[277] At the start of 1917 James Campbell became a baronet, having requested this, upon appointment to the office of lord chief justice.[278] In 1921 he was made a peer, with the title of Lord Glenavy, upon his retirement. In 1919 John Ross was appointed a baronet, 'in recognition of his long service in the Chancery Division'.[279]

272 Cadogan to Salisbury, 28 November 1898 (Salisbury Papers).
273 *ILT&SJ*, vol. 40, p. 213 (30 June 1906).
274 *ILT&SJ*, vol. 43, p. 278 (13 November 1909).
275 Boyd to Asquith, 26 February 1916 (Asquith Papers, 28:43); *ILT&SJ*, vol. 50, p. 96 (15 April 1916).
276 *ILT&SJ*, vol. 52, p. 2 (5 January 1918).
277 Daire Hogan and Patrick Maume (eds), *The reminiscences of Lord Shandon, lord chancellor of Ireland, 1913–18* (Dublin, 2021), p. 275.
278 Campbell to Asquith, 7 November 1916 (Asquith Papers, 28:50/51).
279 Ball, op. cit., p. 323; *ILT&SJ*, vol. 53, p. 2 (4 January 1919); Ross, *The years of my pilgrimage* (London, 1924), p. 287.

Three honours granted after 1921 were a baronetcy for Thomas Molony and knighthoods for James O'Connor, and Thomas Lopdell O'Shaughnessy. Both Molony and O'Connor when they retired from the bench on the reconstruction of the judiciary in 1924 had taken up residence in England (although O'Connor subsequently returned to Ireland). Their honours were conferred in the New Year Honours List in 1925.[280] The honour to O'Shaughnessy, conferred in 1927, reflected the practice of knighting the holder of the office of recorder of Dublin (although this was not a position in the superior courts), the position which he held between 1905 and 1924 when it was abolished and he was appointed to be a judge of the new High Court.[281] He told Sir Edward Carson that he had declined this honour in 1911 when it was offered to him in rather hurried circumstances on the occasion of a visit of King George V to Ireland.[282]

280 *ILT&SJ*, vol. 59, p. 5 (3 January 1925).
281 *ILT&SJ*, vol. 61, p. 8 (8 January 1927); see entry on O'Shaughnessy in *DIB* (by Robert Marshall).
282 O'Shaughnessy to Carson, 26 October 1917 (Carson Papers (PRONI), D1507/A/24/22).

CHAPTER FOUR

The judiciary in 1866 (1)

INTRODUCTION

IN 1866 MAZIERE BRADY was the lord chancellor of Ireland, as he had been for most of the period since 1846 with the exception of two short intervals, amounting to less than three years in total, during which the Conservatives were in government. The second Chancery judge, the master of the rolls, was Thomas Berry Cusack Smith, who also had been appointed in 1846. He died in office in August 1866. The third, Francis Blackburne, had first been appointed to the bench in 1842, had become chief justice of the Queen's Bench in 1846, had been lord chancellor for less than 12 months in 1852 and then was appointed as the (sole) lord justice of appeal in the new Court of Chancery Appeal in 1856.

The chief justice of the Queen's Bench was Thomas Lefroy, who had been born in 1776, and appointed as a baron of the Exchequer in 1841, before being appointed to succeed Blackburne as chief justice in 1852. The other justices of that court were James O'Brien, who had been appointed in 1858 and continued in office until 1881, Edmund Hayes who had been appointed in 1859 and resigned in September 1866, dying the following year, and John David Fitzgerald, who had been appointed in 1860 and some twenty years later became a Lord of Appeal in Ordinary (Law Lord). O'Brien was an uncle of Peter O'Brien, who would be appointed lord chief justice in 1889.

The chief justice of Common Pleas was James Henry Monahan, who had been appointed in 1850 and continued in office until shortly before his death in 1876. The other justices in the Common Pleas were William Nicholas Keogh, Jonathan Christian and Thomas O'Hagan.

The chief baron of the Exchequer was David Pigot, who held office from 1846 until his death a few days before Christmas in 1873, the vacancy thus arising being filled by the appointment of Christopher Palles. The other members of the court of Exchequer were Francis FitzGerald, who resigned in 1882 while still in good health, on a point of judicial principle, Henry George Hughes, who was appointed in 1859 and died in 1872, and Rickard Deasy, who as attorney general in 1861 had introduced the statute on landlord and tenant law that came to be known as 'Deasy's Act', and was appointed a member of the new Court of Appeal in 1878.

Of those 15 men 11 had been MPs and 12 had been law officers.

There were seven other principal judges holding office at the start of 1866. In the course of the next three years, mostly in the period of Conservative party government between July 1866 and December 1868, two of these men (Charles Hargreave of the Landed Estates Court ('LEC') and Walter Berwick of the bankruptcy court) died, three retired, one (David Lynch) was moved to another court, and the seventh (William Cary Dobbs, of the LEC) died in 1869. The judge of the court of Probate in 1866 was Richard Keatinge, who would be replaced in the autumn of 1868 by Richard Warren. The judge in the court of Admiralty, Thomas Kelly, was replaced in 1867 by John Fitzhenry Townsend. The judges in the court of Bankruptcy were David Lynch, who was transferred to the LEC in 1867 on the retirement of Mountifort Longfield, and Walter Berwick, who died in 1868 in a railway accident in North Wales. A vacancy in the LEC that arose in the spring of 1866 on the death of Hargreave was not filled.

On 1 January 1878, when the 1877 Judicature Act came into force, less than half of the judges in the principal courts had been in place before 1866, the majority having been appointed in or after that year. On the death of Deasy in 1883 the only remaining judge who had been appointed before 1866 was John David Fitzgerald, who continued in office as a lord of appeal in ordinary until his death in 1889. The judges are noted below, and in the following chapter, in the order of members of the courts of Chancery, Queen's Bench and Common Pleas (in this chapter) and then the courts of Exchequer, Probate, Landed Estates, Bankruptcy and Admiralty. In subsequent chapters the order of date of first appointment to the bench is followed.

Maziere Brady

Chief Baron of the Exchequer 1840–6, Lord Chancellor of Ireland 1846–52, 1853–8, 1859–66

Maziere Brady (1796–1871) was called to the Bar in 1819, taking silk in 1835, and was successively appointed as solicitor general (1837), attorney general (1839) and chief baron of the Exchequer (1840) while Lord Melbourne was prime minister. Ball described him as a protestant liberal of an advanced type,[1] and his support for a system of non-denominational education was demonstrated by him arranging for his eldest son Francis to attend the relatively new University of London.[2]

When Lord John Russell formed his first government in 1846 a high judicial position was needed for a prominent Catholic lawyer, David Pigot (see p. 167). At the time he was subject to a statutory prohibition, by reason of his religion, from holding the office of lord chancellor, to which he might otherwise have been appointed. Brady accepted appointment as lord chancellor, thus vacating a place in the court of the Exchequer for Pigot. A general view of the Bar was that 'a good chief baron has been spoiled to make a bad chancellor'.[3] He then held office as chancellor for most of the next twenty years, with the exception of two short intervals, in 1852–3 and 1858–9, when his political friends lost office to the Conservatives.

1 Ball, p. 284.
2 *ILT&SJ*, vol. 43, p. 231 (18 September 1909).
3 Anonymous [J. Christian], *The court of Chancery under the Chancery (Ireland) Act 1867* (Dublin, 1872), p. 8.

He was involved in a curious episode in 1855–6 when he endeavoured (unsuccessfully) to bring about the resignation of Richard Pennefather (1773–1859), who had been a baron of the Exchequer since 1821, on account of his admitted loss of sight.[4] Friends and colleagues of Pennefather, including the chief baron, David Pigot, did not accept that this compromised his ability to discharge his judicial functions.

Contemporary descriptions of Brady's demeanour were unflattering. George Hill Smith, a journalist at the time (subsequently called to the Bar in 1874, after Brady's death), wrote that 'he seemed small in stature, but somewhat stout, with a rather heavy face, having the nose and lips pretty broad, and rather large eyes. He appeared to me to be dull and listless ... There was no geniality in his countenance'.[5] A court official described Brady as

> plain, thickset and broad-faced. He was a little dull. but very steady and fond of justice. He must have been surprised at his own rare good fortune, for he was not eminent at the Bar,[6] and nobody deemed him to be a man of more than mediocre abilities ... Brady had, I think, no influence on politics or legislation at any time of his chancellorship or before it. He was not even consulted. He simply minded his court, in which he was painstaking, and a model of uprightness and justice.[7]

He left office on the resignation of the Liberal government in the summer of 1866. He received the honour of a baronetcy in 1869, and died in 1871 at his city home in Upper Pembroke Street. He was one of the most active and prominent workers in the 1850s in the founding of the National Gallery of Ireland, and 'due undoubtedly to Brady's great interest in art, numerous portraits of him were painted by prominent artists of the day'.[8] Portraits were exhibited at the Royal Hibernian Academy in 1841, 1850, 1851, 1852 and 1856, and a bust and a portrait respectively were shown at the annual summer exhibition of the Royal Academy in London in 1846 and 1851. The portraits now in the King's Inns and in the National Gallery were painted posthumously, and there is a memorial to him in St Patrick's cathedral in Dublin.

The Great Seal of Ireland was held in the custody of the chancellor for the time being and was a substantial two-sided object, with a diameter of six inches, from which wax impressions for official documents were produced. It was made of silver, and weighed some 15lbs (about 6.75kg),[9] and was placed in a large crimson silk elaborately embroidered purse when not in use. 'Chancellor's purses are

4 HC Deb, 3rd series, vol. 140, cols. 760–806 (14 February 1856).
5 George Hill Smith, *The North East Bar* (Belfast, 1910), p. 69.
6 Ball (op. cit.) wrote that he 'had no reputation at the Bar'.
7 R. Denny Urlin, *Journal and reminiscences* (Letchworth, 1909), p. 141.
8 W.G. Strickland, *Dictionary of Irish artists* (vol. 2, Dublin and London, 1913), p. 647; Wanda Ryan-Smolin, *King's Inns portraits* (Dublin, 1992), p. 9.
9 *ILT&SJ*, vol. 26, p. 174 (26 March 1892).

generally regarded as ornaments of the household. A Chancellor's purse, which is now only ordered when the old one is worn out, was formerly an annual perquisite of a lord chancellor … The late Mr Justice Lawson, who was given a chancellor's purse as one of the Commissioners of the Great Seal in 1874, converted the purse into a drawing-room fire screen'.[10] The purses that Brady received as lord chancellor were used to provide ornamental coverings or hangings for the backs of his dining room chairs.[11]

The Brady family name remained familiar to Irish lawyers for decades after his retirement by virtue of the extended period (1861–1909) for which his son, Francis Brady (1824–1909), the second baronet, held office as a judge. He was called to the Bar in 1846, and subsequently appointed as a Crown prosecutor in Co. Cork. He stood as a Liberal candidate in Dublin in the general elections of 1857 and 1859, and became a QC in 1860. He was appointed in 1861 to the first of his part time judicial positions, as chairman of the quarter sessions of magistrates in King's County (Offaly), afterwards transferring to Co. Roscommon and then Tyrone, this last appointment following a request on his behalf made by his father.[12] In 1877 the position of chairman was redesignated as 'County Court judge and chairman of quarter sessions', and each serving chairman (but not a new appointee) was entitled to continue to practise at the Bar.[13] Brady elected to do so, continuing in office up to his death in 1909, and also retaining his official post of prosecutor.

Thomas Berry Cusack Smith

Master of the Rolls 1846–66

Thomas Berry Cusack Smith (1795–1866) was the second son of Sir William Cusack Smith Bt (1766–1836), a baron of the Exchequer from 1801 up to his death in 1836, and a grandson of Sir Michael Smith, Bt (1740–1809), master of the rolls between 1801 and 1806, whose judicial robes he wore when he in turn held that office.[14] Smith was educated at Trinity College, and was called to the Bar in 1817. In 1830 (with Espine Batty BL) he published a set of reports of cases heard in the court of King's Bench 1824–5, and was called to the Inner Bar. He stood as the Conservative candidate in Youghal in the 1835 general election, losing narrowly to John O'Connell, a son of Daniel O'Connell. He was elected (unopposed) in 1843 as member of Parliament for Ripon, in Yorkshire.

In 1842 he was appointed solicitor general, and very shortly afterwards attorney general, in place of Francis Blackburne, who had been appointed master of the rolls. In that capacity Smith conducted the major trial of O'Connell and others for seditious conspiracy in 1843–4. He was noted for an excitability of temper, which

10 *LT&SJ*, vol. 47, p. 201 (19 July 1913).
11 *ILT&SJ*, vol. 38, p. 222 (9 July 1904) and vol. 43, p. 217 (4 September 1909).
12 O'Hagan to Spencer, 21 March 1869 (O'Hagan Papers (PRONI), D2777/8/26).
13 County Officers and Courts (Ireland) Act 1877 (40&41 Vict., c56), ss3 and 92.
14 *ILT&SJ*, vol. 31, p. 555 (27 November 1897).

led to a strange scene in the course of the trial when he took offence at something said by another counsel, Gerald FitzGibbon (father of the later lord justice of appeal), and challenged him to a duel. The court urged reconciliation, and with mutual expressions of apology and goodwill the incident was closed.[15] O'Connell was found guilty by the jury, but this conviction was set aside by the House of Lords.[16]

Early in 1846 on the retirement of Edward Pennefather Blackburne reluctantly agreed to become chief justice of Queen's Bench, and Smith was once more appointed to succeed him. He served as master of the rolls (an office 'whose duties were of a laborious and harassing character'[17]) for twenty years, until his sudden death in August 1866 while away 'at his usual autumn residence'[18] in Blairgowrie, Perthshire, in Scotland. The 1846 transfer made by Blackburne was described at the time as effected on foot of

> an urgent request from Sir Robert Peel [the prime minster]. It is understood that Mr Blackburne was anxious to retain the Rolls, and that he only consented to change to the Queen's Bench in order to relieve the government from the embarrassing position they would have been placed in if there were no alternative but the appointment of Mr Smith to the chief seat in that court, the scene of his famous quarrel with Mr FitzGibbon during the State Trials.[19]

Smith's bellicose temperament was manifested again in the summer of 1856 when, from the bench in a crowded court, he criticised the attorney general, John D. Fitzgerald, for not having initiated a prosecution of James Sadleir MP in connection with the affairs of the failed Tipperary Bank. Sadleir was a brother of the guiding spirit of the bank, John Sadleir MP, who had committed suicide earlier in the year when the fraudulence and insolvency of the bank had been revealed. Smith as master of the rolls had functions in connection with its winding up and, as Fitzgerald told the House of Commons, said in court that

> I wish to express my unbounded astonishment that the Irish Government have not thought fit to take any notice of this case. If they choose to remain quiescent and shrink from the duty that devolves upon them of placing this case before the prosecutors for the Crown I think that they will be guilty of a gross dereliction of duty [and] they can have no right to complain if the public charge them with connivance at conspiracy.[20]

15 *ILT&SJ*, vol. 16, p. 494 (7 October 1882) and vol. 33, p. 89 (25 February 1899).
16 Ian Holloway, '*O'Connell v The Queen*: a sesquicentennial remembrance', *NILQ*, vol. 46 (1995), pp 63–71.
17 Edward Blackburne, *Life of the Right Hon Francis Blackburne* (London, 1874), p. 218.
18 *Irish Times*, 15 August 1866.
19 *Law Times*, vol. 6, p. 306 (17 January 1846). See also Blackburne, *Life of Francis Blackburne*, pp 220–1 ('He yielded to pressure and solicitation').
20 HC Deb, 3rd series, vol. 143, col. 661 (11 July 1856).

The cry of incompetence and connivance was taken up and amplified by James Whiteside QC and Joseph Napier QC, two Conservative MPs, who asserted that Fitzgerald's supposed inaction derived from Sadleir having been a supporter of the government, and that Fitzgerald's initial indignant response had improperly called into question Smith's character and his fitness to be a member of the Privy Council of Ireland. After a number of such sharp exchanges in the House of Commons[21] Fitzgerald made a detailed personal statement in the house, refuting quite comprehensively Smith's 'irregular' assertions of inaction,[22] after which criticism died away.

On his death a severity and sharpness in his manner in court was remarked upon. Occasionally when sitting in court 'the impetuosity of his nature, and his undisguised abhorrence of any course which seemed to be harsh or ungenerous, although legal, led him to express himself in strong terms towards the legal gentlemen whose professional duties necessitated their attendance at his court'.[23] If any point arose which seemed to him to call for animadversion he did not hold back, a practice which 'rendered him the terror of all such practitioners as were not precise in their conduct and truthful in their statements [although] the very sharpness of manner which many practitioners disliked had its good effect on the conduct of business'.[24]

Francis Blackburne

Master of the Rolls 1842–6, Chief Justice of Queen's Bench 1846–52, Lord Chancellor 1852 and 1866–7, and Lord Justice of Appeal 1856–66

Francis Blackburne (1782–1867) was educated at Trinity College and was called to the Bar in 1805. He joined the Home circuit, and was called to the Inner Bar in 1822. He was attorney general between 1831 and 1835, and in 1841–2. He was appointed master of the rolls in 1842, as chief justice of Queen's Bench in 1846 and then for about eleven months in 1852 he was lord chancellor of Ireland in Lord Derby's first government. In 1856 he was appointed to the office of lord justice of appeal in the new court of Chancery Appeal. In 1858 he declined an invitation to be re-appointed as chancellor, telling Derby that he doubted whether he would be 'able to rely on my strength and ability again to undertake the cares and labour of discharging so important a trust'.[25] He repented of his refusal but his indication of willingness to be re-appointed came too late, as the position had been offered to and accepted by Joseph Napier.[26]

In July 1866 Blackburne agreed to once more accept the cares and labour of office after Derby had appealed to him (as described more fully on p. 201) to

21 HC Deb, 3rd series, vol. 143, cols. 381–3 (4 July 1856), cols. 652–74 and 708–9 (11 July 1856).
22 HC Deb, 3rd series, vol. 143, cols. 886–903 (15 July 1856).
23 *Irish Times*, 15 August 1866.
24 *Law Times*, vol. 41, p. 742 (18 August 1866).
25 Blackburne to Derby, 26 February 1858 (Derby Papers, 122/7B).
26 A.C. Ewald, *The life and letters of the Rt. Hon. Sir Joseph Napier, Bt.* (London, 1892), p. 134.

'consent again to take (if only for a short time) the duties of lord chancellor'.[27] A question was soon asked in the House of Commons as to whether, eight years previously, he had declined to accept that same office by reason of his advanced age (he had then been aged 75). Disraeli gave an airy reply that 'it is very difficult to remember all the offers of office that were made in the year 1858', adding that Blackburne's unwillingness was understood to derive not from his age but from his preference at the time to have a judicial position of a 'permanent character'.[28]

Some eight months later the inherent ambiguity in Derby's appeal, as to whether it was he or Blackburne who would determine when 'a short time' had elapsed, led to upset and disappointment when Blackburne was in effect asked to resign. He initially resisted this request although eventually stepping down unwillingly at the end of March.[29] Abraham Brewster, his intended successor, was informed by Blackburne's family at the time that he 'lies in extremis and is not expected to survive this day'.[30] In fact he lived some months longer, dying on 17 September 1867. The circumstances in which he had resigned, in the view of Blackburne's second son, Edward, 'if they did not accelerate, saddened the close of his life;' the shock of being required to resign, on foot of what he saw as the intrigues of others, 'proved too much for him: he felt that it was a harsh and cruel return for the abnegation of self and for the sacrifices which he had so cheerfully made'.[31] His eldest son, William, sought a baronetcy or peerage for his father from Derby,[32] although when an offer of a baronetcy was made a few weeks later it was turned down, Blackburne telling Derby that such an honour was unsought and unexpected.[33] That led to some discord between William and Edward, who had communicated his father's refusal.[34]

The final phase of Blackburne's judicial career was not regarded as enhancing his reputation, since although 'his legal instinct was often perfect, senility appeared when he had to deal with facts; and though sparks of the ancient fire were seen they were but a glimmer among dying embers'.[35] A posthumous portrait, showing him in his robes as lord chancellor, was presented to King's Inns by members of his family and friends in 1875. This is believed to be a copy of an earlier portrait of him as chief justice.[36]

27 Derby to Blackburne, 12 July 1866 (Blackburne, *Life of Francis Blackburne*, p. 301).
28 HC Deb, 3rd series, vol. 184, col. 1072 (19 July 1866).
29 Blackburne to Derby, 12 March 1867 (Derby Papers, 122/8); Derby to Blackburne, 20 March 1867 (Derby Papers, 192/2, p. 56); Blackburne to Derby, 21 March 1867 (Mayo Papers, MS 11,150); Hogan, 'Vacancies', pp 224–9.
30 Brewster to Naas, 24 March 1867 (Mayo Papers, MS 11,147 (13)).
31 Edward Blackburne, op. cit., pp 307, 312.
32 William Blackburne to Derby, 11 April 1867 (Mayo Papers, MS 11,147 (14); see also W. Blackburne to Naas, 30 April 1867 (also Mayo Papers, MS 11,147 (14)).
33 Blackburne to Derby, 6 May 1867 (Derby Papers, 53/2).
34 Mrs William Blackburne to Naas, 11 May 1867 (Mayo Papers, MS 11,147 (14)); Naas to Derby, 11 May 1867 (Derby Papers, 53/2).
35 *The Times*, 4 March 1875.
36 Wanda Ryan-Smolin, *King's Inns portraits* (Dublin, 1992), p. 7.

Thomas Lefroy

Baron of the Exchequer 1841–52, Lord Chief Justice of Queen's Bench 1852–66

Thomas Lefroy (1776–1869) was a judge for 25 years. He was called to the Bar in 1797. 'He remembered lawyers who had seen Swift and Berkeley,[37] and had many traditions of those illustrious men; he witnessed some of the horrors of 1798; he had often listened to debates in the Irish parliament'.[38] In 1841, after sitting as MP for Dublin University since 1832, he was appointed as a baron of the Exchequer. In 1852, when Lord Derby became prime minister for the first time, he was appointed chief justice of Queen's Bench, in succession to Francis Blackburne, who had become lord chancellor.

He lived in Leeson Street, and in the 1840s built Carriglass[39] Manor, a substantial mansion near Longford.[40] He eventually found the air of Bray to be preferable to that of Longford, where he was occasionally subject to bronchial attacks, and after leasing a villa at Newcourt, near Bray, he 'spent little time at his country seat'.[41]

In April and May 1866, when he was aged 90, a debate was initiated in Parliament[42] as to whether, having regard to the advanced age of some of the judges, the constitution of the Irish bench 'was satisfactory and conducive to the due administration of justice in Ireland'. This seemingly general query in fact related to (and the debate was focussed on) Lefroy's capacity to discharge the duties of his office. This arose from a macabre incident the previous year when a sentence of death in a murder trial at Tullamore had been mispronounced by him, and in repeating it he followed a dictation by the attorney general, James Lawson QC, MP.[43]

In early July 1866, a couple of months after the controversy, Lefroy resigned, a few days after Derby had again become prime minister. A farewell address was adopted by the grand jury of King's County (Offaly), and Lefroy in his acknowledgment of this referred to the parliamentary controversy as 'a course of proceeding as mischievous as it is unconstitutional'. He noted that most of the jury had witnessed the trial at Tullamore, and that the good opinion of men 'of your intelligence, rank and independence' was some compensation for the 'unworthy and unjust attacks' to which he had been subjected.[44] He twice declined the honour

37 Jonathan Swift was born in 1667 and died in 1745. George Berkeley was born in 1685 and died in 1753.

38 W. O'Connor Morris, *Memories and thoughts of life* (London, 1895), p. 159.

39 That is the spelling now generally adopted. Lefroy himself referred to 'Carrig-glas' (see Thomas Lefroy, *Memoir of Chief Justice Lefroy* (Dublin, 1871), p. 371).

40 Christine Casey and Alistair Rowan, *The buildings of Ireland: North Leinster* (London, 1993), pp 179–82.

41 Lefroy, *Memoir*, p. 382.

42 HL Deb, 3rd series, vol. 182, cols. 1628–36 (19 April 1866) and vol. 183, col. 744 (11 May 1866); HC Deb, 3rd series, vol. 183, col. 358 (3 May 1866) and cols. 778–90 (11 May 1866).

43 Hogan, 'Vacancies', pp 211–14.

44 Lefroy to the grand jury of King's County, 28 July 1866 (Lefroy, Memoir, p. 333); *Law Times*, vol. 41, p. 676 (28 July 1866) and p. 710 (11 August 1866).

of a baronetcy,[45] once shortly after his retirement and again after Disraeli had become prime minister in 1868. On the first occasion Derby's view was that – as in the comparable case of Blackburne – the family 'most likely want a peerage', which was not offered.[46] A comment made the following year by the lord chancellor, Brewster, to the lord lieutenant may support that: 'I fear that the Lefroys will not come to terms, indeed had I been in London and known that Tom Lefroy was to negotiate I should have told you as much', having had experience of dealing with him.[47]

Lefroy died in May 1869 at the age of 93. Many other members of his family had long lives. His brother Benjamin died shortly after him aged 88.[48] His eldest son Anthony, an MP for Dublin University 1858–70, who had previously sat for some years as a member for Co. Longford, died in his 90th year in January 1890. This was followed within weeks by the deaths at Carriglass of Lefroy's youngest daughter, Mary, and his youngest son, George (who had been born in 1814 and called to the Bar in 1840).[49] A daughter, Jane Christmas Lefroy, subsequently died in her 96th year.[50]

Lefroy's second son, Thomas (1806–91), the negotiator above referred to, wrote a memoir of his father, after composition of which his letters were destroyed.[51] He was called to the Bar in 1831 and became a QC in 1852. He was elected a bencher of King's Inns in 1860, and was chairman of quarter sessions, later a county court judge, in various counties, including Kildare, Armagh, Louth and finally Down, from which he retired shortly before his death.[52]

Naas, the chief secretary, told Derby in 1867 that Thomas's 'position at the Bar does not entitle him to expect high judicial office'.[53] His father later solicited the lord lieutenant, without success, to appoint him as a bankruptcy judge, referring to his son as being well qualified to serve the public usefully in such a position. He noted that the vacancy was the only opportunity that the government was likely to have of recognising his son's position at the Bar, since the law officers had recently monopolised judicial appointments and members of the Bar who did not desire to go into Parliament were virtually excluded from opportunities for such offices.[54] The implication that a bankruptcy position might be available because it was insufficiently attractive to either of the law officers was not borne out, as Michael Harrison, the solicitor general did take it. The *Irish Law Times* commented at the end of 1868 that 'the command of a seat in parliament to start with, and political

45 Lefroy, *Memoir*, p. 330.
46 Derby to Naas, 7 May 1867 (Derby Papers 192/2, p. 96).
47 Brewster to Abercorn, 31 October 1868 (Abercorn Papers (PRONI), D623/A/313/31).
48 *Irish Times*, 3 September 1869.
49 *ILT&SJ*, vol. 24, p. 42 (18 January 1890), p. 76 (1 February 1890) and p. 165 (22 March 1890).
50 *ILT&SJ*, vol. 30, p. 380 (29 August 1896).
51 Report of private collections 451 (National Library of Ireland), statement by Langlois Lefroy (1881–1959).
52 *ILT&SJ*, vol. 25, p. 76 (24 January 1891).
53 Naas to Derby, 19 July 1867 (Derby Papers, 155/4).
54 Lefroy to Abercorn, 9 September 1868 (Abercorn Papers (PRONI), D623/A/313/1).

service rendered, and connexions formed there, will always prevail over considerations of mere professional claims. To this must be attributed the deplorable waste of judicial ability and learning, in the courts here and in London'.[55]

Lefroy's grandson, also named Thomas (1836–1902), was called to the Bar in 1863, and was appointed registrar to his grandfather. 'On the lord chief justice's retirement and the consequent loss of his position as registrar Mr Lefroy, who was a gentleman of independent means, did not resume his practice at the Bar, but adopted the life of a country gentleman'.[56]

James O'Brien

Justice of the Queen's Bench 1858–17, of the High Court (Queen's Bench division) 1878–81

James O'Brien (1806–81) had a judicial career of over twenty years, just shorter than that of a nephew, Peter O'Brien, the lord chief justice between 1889 and 1913. He was born in 1806 and educated at Trinity College, where he was awarded a gold medal in mathematics. He was called to the Bar in 1830, became a QC in 1841 and was appointed third serjeant in 1848 and second serjeant in 1851.[57] His brother John was MP for the city of Limerick between 1841 and 1852, and although O'Brien was narrowly defeated when he endeavoured to succeed him, as a Liberal, in the general election of 1852, he was subsequently elected unopposed at a bye-election in 1854, and at the general election in 1857.

The following year, when Lord Palmerston was prime minister, a vacancy arose in the Queen's Bench through the death of Richard Moore (1783–1857), who had been a puisne judge since 1847, and O'Brien was appointed to fill the vacancy. Peter O'Brien served him as a registrar for some time after his call to the Bar in 1865, before finding the position burdensome as interfering with his own practice.[58]

John Ross had a high opinion of O'Brien, writing that while Whiteside CJ had great abilities he was 'not strong in law, and depended very much on his colleague Mr Justice James O'Brien, a quiet unassuming man, deeply learned in jurisprudence'.[59] O'Brien was reputed to have a repugnance to passing a death sentence, a duty falling to common law judges in jury trials where an accused person had been convicted of murder, and to have done what he could to avoid presiding at such trials.[60] He died in December 1881, and when paying tribute in court to him the chief justice referred to a physical weakness of O'Brien which he thought had recently begun to extend to his mental faculties.[61]

55 *ILT&SJ*, vol. 2, p. 681 (12 December 1868).
56 *ILT&SJ*, vol. 36, p. 493 (20 December 1902).
57 *Irish Times*, 30 December 1881; *ILT&SJ*, vol. 15, p. 654 (31 December 1881).
58 Georgina O'Brien (ed.), *Reminiscences of Lord O'Brien of Kilfenora* (London, 1916), p. 20.
59 John Ross, *The years of my pilgrimage* (London, 1924), p. 192.
60 *Irish Times*, 8 September 1914.
61 *ILT&SJ*, vol. 16, p. 15 (14 January 1882).

Edmund Hayes

Justice of Queen's Bench 1859–66

Edmund Hayes (1804–67) was a native of Millmount, Banbridge, Co. Down, where his family were linen manufacturers. He was educated at Trinity College and after his call to the Bar in 1827 joined the Home circuit. He compiled and published law reports of cases heard in the court of Exchequer[62] in his early years at the Bar, and also published a couple of editions of a digest of criminal law 'alphabetically arranged, with ample notes in which are discussed the powers and authorities of the several courts of criminal jurisdiction in Ireland, the duties, responsibilities and privileges of magistrates, coroners, constables and other officers in bringing criminals to justice; and also the practice of the courts in punishing offences upon indictment'.[63] He was knowledgeable also in property and conveyancing law.[64]

He became a QC in 1852, and in 1858 was appointed solicitor general in the second government formed by Lord Derby, to whom Lord Naas, the chief secretary, had outlined relevant considerations:

> Eglinton, Napier, Whiteside and I[65] have had a very long conversation about the appointment of the solicitor general. We agree that it is most desirable to make as far as possible a purely professional appointment, there is no doubt that Napier's appointment is looked upon as purely a political one and it is therefore most important that the solicitor general appointment should not bear that character. [After discussion of John George QC] – the man who we think ought to be appointed is Hayes. He was our law adviser the last time we were in office. He is in excellent and daily increasing practice. His appointment would be popular with the Bar and be considered a tribute to professional merit. It is most likely that you would have to appoint another solicitor general very soon as a vacancy must shortly occur on the Bench. Hayes would make an excellent judge and George's claims might then be fairly considered ... Blackburne [lord justice of appeal] mentioned yesterday to me the strongest opinion in favour of Hayes – in short I cannot express too strongly the importance of appointing him at once.[66]

Early in 1859 he was appointed to succeed Philip Crampton (1783–1862), who had been a justice of the Queen's Bench since 1834. Hayes was a Conservative, who had 'fought the battles of his party long and successfully in the courts of [voters'] registry, and he has won his spurs fairly and honestly'.[67] In addition to the ordinary

62 *Reports of cases argued and determined in the court of Exchequer* [1830–32] (Dublin, 1837), and [1832–4] (Dublin, 1843).
63 *Crimes and punishments, or a digest of the criminal statute law of Ireland* (Dublin, 1842, 2nd edition).
64 *ILT&SJ*, vol. 1, p. 240 (4 May 1867).
65 The three other men were respectively the lord lieutenant, lord chancellor and attorney general.
66 Naas to Disraeli, 12 March 1858 (Disraeli Papers, B/XX/BD/18).
67 *Law Times*, vol. 32, p. 221 (29 January 1859).

duties of a judge, including going on assize, Hayes sat as a member of the court of Delegates, hearing appeals on matters of the law of the Church of Ireland and admiralty matters.[68] He was taken unwell in court early in 1865, and further ill health in the New Year of 1866 prevented him from sitting as a judge.[69] His retirement was thought to be imminent in April.[70] He resigned in September of that year, and died in April 1867 at his home, Crinken House, Bray, Co. Wicklow.[71]

John David Fitzgerald (Lord Fitzgerald of Kilmarnock)

Justice of Queen's Bench 1860–2, Lord of Appeal in Ordinary 1882–9

John David Fitzgerald (1816–89) was born in Fleet Street, Dublin. He was educated at Trinity College, although not taking a degree at the time (he was awarded an honorary doctorate of laws by the university in 1870), and was called to the Bar in 1838. He joined the Munster circuit, and became a QC in 1847. In the general election of 1852 he was elected, as a Liberal, as MP for Ennis, Co. Clare, a constituency which, like many others at the time, had a very small electorate. He received 59 votes to his opponent's 46, and was not opposed at any subsequent election up to his retirement as an MP in 1860. He was appointed solicitor general in 1855 and as attorney general (succeeding William Keogh) in 1856, and held that office up to 1860, except for a short interval of Conservative government in 1858–9. A number of opportunities for judicial promotion arose while he was attorney general which he passed up at the request of the government. These were filled by Blackburne, James O'Brien, Christian and Hughes.[72] In 1860 he was appointed a judge of the Queen's Bench. He succeeded Mr Justice Perrin, of whom 'for the 20th time within the last few years the report is revived that [he], now in his 76th year, is about to retire'.[73]

Fitzgerald conducted litigation in England, while a judge, on behalf of and as next friend for his eldest son David (a minor) arising out of his expulsion from St Mary's College, Oscott, Sutton Coldfield, Warwickshire, a Catholic school. The complaint made was of assault (a forcible taking of papers from the son) and imprisonment (detention in a room prior to being sent away) rather than of the expulsion itself. The bishop of Birmingham attributed the verdict of the jury (awarding damages of £5) to anti-clerical prejudice, and encouraged the school to publish a verbatim report of the court proceedings. Members of the jury were reprimanded by the chief justice, Cockburn, for saying several times – after the son had given evidence, and then again at the end of both the first and second days

68 *Irish Times*, 12 July 1859, 15 December 1860, 18 May 1864.
69 *Irish Times*, 17 February 1865, 27 January 1866, 26 March 1866, *Law Times*, vol. 41, p. 211 (3 February 1866).
70 *Law Times*, vol. 41, p. 397 (14 April 1866).
71 *Irish Times*, 2 May 1867.
72 *ILT&SJ*, vol. 16, pp 248–9 (3 June 1882).
73 *Law Times*, vol. 34, p. 218 (28 January 1860). See also p. 269 (25 February 1860).

of the trial – that they had heard enough, and had come to a decision, and that it would be a waste of time to continue.[74]

Among the trials over which Fitzgerald presided were those of leading Fenians charged with treason-felony in 1865–6 (sitting on a Special Commission with Mr Justice Keogh), and of others arrested in 1867. In a debate in the House of Lords in 1889 on corporal punishment for criminals he gave an account of how these latter trials were conducted:

> Some noble lords may still recollect that in 1867 there was an armed insurrection in Ireland. On that occasion many hundred prisoners were arrested in a state of insurrection. They were captured by the military and marched into Dublin and subsequently committed for trial. It was my lot to have to assist upon the Special Commission with my late friend lord [chief] justice Whiteside in the trial of those prisoners. The then viceroy (Lord Abercorn) wisely considered that it would be simply elevating the prisoners to the level of political martyrs to try them for treason or high treason, and accordingly the government determined that the trial was to take place under an Act of George II which gave power to imprison, and in certain cases corporal punishment could be inflicted. Now chief justice Whiteside and I consulted together, and we ultimately came to the conclusion that as no violence had been used, as there had been no house broken into and no life had been taken, these were cases in which we ought not to inflict corporal punishment. In passing a short sentence of imprisonment on the first man tried under the Act, we announced from the Bench that where no outrage had been actually committed corporal punishment would not be inflicted. Now, what was the result? The result was that hundreds of trials were compressed into a few days because the people, relieved from the fear of corporal punishment, came in and pleaded guilty and received very moderate sentences.[75]

He presided as senior puisne judge (May LCJ having recused himself – see p. 272) at the trial in January 1882 of Parnell and others for seditious conspiracy in the course of the Land War, and his exposition of various points of criminal law that arose in the course of the trial was seen as authoritative.[76] A few months later he was appointed as the first lord of appeal in ordinary ('Law Lord') from Ireland. The circumstances in which he was appointed and his career in the House of Lords, as a judge and as a contributor to parliamentary debates, are noted in chapter 14. He declined an offer of appointment as lord chancellor made by

74 *Report of the proceedings in the case of Fitzgerald v Northcote and another* (London, 1866), pp v, 14, 85, 103, 156.

75 HL Deb, 3rd series, vol. 334, cols. 1366–67 (2 April 1889).

76 Porter MR in *Leathem v Craig*, [1899] 2 IR 667 at 761, referred to the charge to the jury given by Fitzgerald and Barry JJ as a statement of the law on conspiracy 'of the very highest weight'; *Irish Times*, 19 October 1899.

Gladstone in 1885. He died in Dublin in 1889, and after a funeral Mass at University Church, St Stephen's Green, was buried at Glasnevin cemetery.

He was married twice, first to Rose O'Donohue in 1846 and subsequently to Jane Southwell in 1860. His family home was a substantial house, Kilmarnock, at Killiney, Co. Dublin. In London he lived in Portland Place. Other members of his family distinguished themselves in the legal profession, including an older and a younger brother, David and Thomas, both solicitors, whose firm of D&T Fitzgerald was among the most prominent of its time.[77] The three sons of his first marriage, whose mother died when they were very young, were called to the Bar. David Fitzgerald QC (1847–1920), who was educated at Cambridge University and was also called to the Bar in England, practised on the North East circuit, where he was a prosecutor in Co. Down until his appointment as a county court judge in 1892, in which capacity he served in Kilkenny, Waterford and Queen's County (Laois).[78] John Donohue Fitzgerald QC (1848–1918) left an estate of £121,000,[79] having practised in England at the Parliamentary Bar, where large fees were charged. (A London contemporary, Balfour Browne KC, left an estate of £655,000 'which is probably the largest fortune ever amassed by a leader of the Parliamentary Bar ... The bulk of his money came from the gigantic fees that he earned as counsel for railway companies and other wealthy corporations'.[80]) For Gerald Fitzgerald (1849–1925), see pp 377–8.

James Henry Monahan

Chief Justice of Common Pleas 1850–76

James Henry Monahan (1803–78) was one of the first Catholics to be appointed a judge in the nineteenth century, in 1850. He was a member of a Co. Galway family and after education at Trinity College was called to the Bar in 1828. He joined the Connaught circuit, and was called to the Inner Bar in 1840. He was a 'handsome, large burly man, with bushy black eyebrows and a Connaught brogue',[81] also being described as 'talkative, rollicking, rather "hail fellow well met", but the most good hearted and simple of men'.[82] As a speaker he was 'powerful, without a spark of eloquence'.[83]

Monahan was politically active, being appointed solicitor general in the government formed by Lord John Russell in July 1846, and then attorney general in December 1847. In February 1847 he was elected MP for the borough of Galway at a bye-election, defeating a Repeal candidate by a majority of four votes out of over a thousand cast, but did not stand in the general election later that year.

77 *ILT&SJ*, vol. 46, p. 74 (23 March 1912).
78 George Hill Smith, *The North East Bar* (Belfast, 1910), p. 112.
79 *ILT&SJ*, vol. 52, p. 193 (10 August 1918).
80 *ILT&SJ*, vol. 55, p. 314 (17 December 1921).
81 R. Denny Urlin, *Journal and reminiscences* (Letchworth, 1909), p. 140.
82 W. O'Connor Morris, *Memories and thoughts of life* (London, 1895), p. 160.
83 O.J. Burke, *Anecdotes of the Connaught circuit* (Dublin, 1885), p. 309.

As attorney general he conducted the prosecutions in 1848 of John Mitchel and Charles Gavan Duffy and other members of the Young Ireland party for treason felony, and of William Smith O'Brien and Thomas Meagher for treason. In 1850 he was appointed as chief justice of the court of Common Pleas following the death of John Doherty, who had held that office since 1830.

The ordinary business of the court of Common Pleas was civil law, not involving criminal law, although its judges presided over criminal trials when on assize, and heard appeals on issues of criminal law in the Court for Crown Cases Reserved. Monahan presided over the dramatic trial of *Thelwall v Yelverton* in 1861, 'a strange and thrilling story of passion, treachery and desertion'.[84]

His extensive experience of criminal law included presiding at the Commission of Oyer and Terminer for the city and county of Dublin, at Green Street, and sitting on a special commission for the trial of Fenian prisoners in Cork and Limerick in 1867. W.E. Vaughan has noted that in giving a charge to a jury in a trial 'judges could draw attention to unpleasant facts by telling juries to ignore them'. Monahan at Trim, Co. Meath, in 1871 told a jury that 'they were not in consequence of the miserable state of the county, the prevalence of crime, and the number of murders and outrages that had been committed, to find a verdict against the accused unless they were satisfied beyond all doubt of his guilt'.[85] He was the judge in the trial at Tullamore, King's County [Offaly], in 1870 of Laurence and Margaret Shiels, a brother and sister, for the murder of a neighbour, Patrick Dunne. The principal point of legal interest was the validity or sufficiency of a declaration made by the dying victim at the scene of the crime that identified his assailants.[86] Between 1852 and 1921 47 women were sentenced to death, of whom Margaret Shiels was one of only four actually to be executed.[87]

His bluff forthright manner of expression when fulfilling the duty of an assize judge to address a grand jury on the state of crime in a particular county led to (or was seized upon for) political controversy and Parliamentary debate more than once. In 1861 the earl of Leitrim complained that Monahan's address to the grand jury in Donegal had not acknowledged the extent of serious crime in the county.[88] In 1870 the government was asked to comment on the opposite scenario, when he had deprecated the number and magnitude of serious offences in Co. Meath, implicitly criticising local policing, although Gladstone urged caution as to whether the overall context of his remarks would have been properly caught by selective quotations from local newspapers.[89] In 1865 the magistrates of Co. Down took

84 Burke, op. cit., pp 29, 235; M. McDonnell Bodkin, *Famous Irish trials* (Dublin, 1918, edited, with an introduction, by Eamonn G. Hall (Dublin, 1997)), pp 29–52.

85 W.E. Vaughan, *Murder trials in Ireland, 1836–1914* (Dublin, 2009), pp 254–5.

86 John Adye Curran, *Reminiscences* (London, 1915), pp 26, 39–40; Michael Byrne, *Legal Offaly* (Tullamore, 2008), pp 105–6; *Irish Times*, 27 May 1870.

87 W.E. Vaughan, op. cit., p. 332.

88 HL Deb, 3rd series, vol. 163, cols. 823–4 (10 June 1861); cols. 984–91 (13 June 1861).

89 HC Deb, 3rd series, vol. 199, cols. 1147–50 (3 March 1870).

offence at a suggestion by Monahan that they had acted in a party or sectarian spirit in relation to a trial of rioters at a disturbance near Rathfriland, after which only Catholic participants had been prosecuted. Monahan was described in the House of Commons by the chief secretary for Ireland, Sir Robert Peel, as 'a little hasty and impetuous at times', and apologised and acknowledged that he had apparently been misinformed and had spoken out of turn.[90]

He was absent from court in the spring of 1873, on medical advice that he should seek relaxation and rest from the duties of his position.[91] He became unwell again early in 1875, and was unable to sit in court or to go on assize or perform any other judicial duties.[92] Reports were subsequently published of, variously, incapacity and a supposedly imminent retirement or of restored good health and imminent resumption of judicial work.[93] A lofty dismissal by the *Irish Law Times* in early January 1876 of the last unfavourable report as being 'without foundation, and we are glad to be able to state that the chief justice is at present in the enjoyment of excellent health'[94] transpired itself to be unfounded, since he did resign within a matter of days.

The *Times* (London) was highly critical at this time, in the context of the impending judicature reform legislation, of what it saw as the over-manning of the Irish judicial bench. It remarked that, while Monahan's resignation placed a vacant office at the disposal of the government, it would in itself make practically no change in the judicial resources available for the despatch of legal business.[95] The government acknowledged that there was some force in that argument when deciding to fill Monahan's place by the promotion of one of the existing (puisne) judges of the court of Common Pleas, Michael Morris, but not also to fill the place thus vacated by Morris.[96] Consequently for the next two years there were only three Common Pleas judges, and the Act for judicial reform passed in 1877 specified that the vacancy would not be filled up,[97] thus reducing to three what had since 1784 been a complement of four judges in the court (now a division of a single High Court).

Monahan died in December 1878 at his residence, 5 Fitzwilliam Square. It was reported that a severe snow storm prevented the attendance of many at his funeral. An auction sale of his estate included 12 dozen bottles of madeira and 12 dozen bottles of finest old vintage port.[98]

90 HC Deb, 3rd series, vol. 178, cols. 196–202 (24 March 1865).
91 *Irish Times*, 29 April 1873.
92 *ILT&SJ*, vol. 10, p. 51 (22 January 1876).
93 *Irish Times*, 17 March 1875, 20 May 1875, and 8 January 1876; *ILT&SJ*, vol. 9, p. 182 (10 April 1875), p. 208 (24 April 1875) and p. 460 (11 September 1875).
94 *ILT&SJ*, vol. 10, p. 16 (8 January 1876).
95 *ILT&SJ*, vol. 10, p. 42 (22 January 1876).
96 Disraeli to Abercorn, 26 January 1876 (Abercorn Papers (PRONI), D623/A/321/14).
97 Supreme Court of Judicature (Ireland) Act 1877 (40&41 Vict., c.57), s6; HC Deb, 3rd series, vol. 231, cols. 1231–3 (15 August 1876).
98 *Irish Times*, 1 February 1879.

A son, James Henry Monahan QC (a second son was named Henry James),[99] stood unsuccessfully as a Liberal at a bye-election in the Galway constituency in 1874 ('encouraged by my father's former connection with you [and] the regard I know you feel for him').[100] He presented a portrait of his father to the King's Inns some years after his death. It is one of the few portraits known to have been painted by Augustus Burke, who was a brother of T.H. Burke, under-secretary at Dublin Castle, a victim of the Phoenix Park murders in May 1882.[101]

William Keogh

Justice of the Common Pleas 1856–78

William Keogh (1817–78) was appointed a judge of the court of Common Pleas in 1856. A political and judicial career of considerable controversy was ended by his death abroad some two decades later. He was the son of a solicitor in Galway, and educated at Trinity College, where he debated in the College Historical Society, of which he later became a vice-president.[102] He was called to the Bar in 1840, and joined the Connaught circuit.[103] He published a couple of pamphlets on Chancery practice and precedents, and became a QC in 1849. He stood in Athlone in the general election of 1847, with the support of the Catholic bishop of Elphin, George Browne, and many priests,[104] and also receiving assistance and encouragement from an English supporter. This was apparently Thomas Attwood, a prominent economist and political reformer from Birmingham,[105] although the *Irish Times* in its obituary said, more mysteriously, that he was backed by a 'well-known wealthy Jew, who was at the time a dominating individuality in the financial world, [who had] met young Keogh in society in London, where he was eating his terms as a law student'.[106] Athlone was a constituency with a small electorate of no more than 250 voters,[107] and he won the seat narrowly (101 votes to 95). He was re-elected in 1852 with a greatly increased majority (87 to 10), when his platform was independent opposition, tenant rights and (as one of 'the Pope's Brass Band') a vindication of the position of the Catholic church in England, affected by the Ecclesiastical Titles Act 1851.[108]

99 *Irish Times*, 17 January 1879.
100 Election address, reported in *Irish Times*, 27 May 1874.
101 Wanda Ryan-Smolin, *King's Inns portraits* (Dublin, 1992), p. 49.
102 Patrick Geoghegan, *The College Historical Society: oratory and debate, 1770–2020* (Dublin, 2020), p. 163.
103 O.J. Burke, *Anecdotes of the Connaught circuit* (Dublin, 1885), p. 184.
104 Burke, op. cit., p. 256.
105 Entry on Keogh in the *DIB* (by Desmond McCabe); Richard Viner, *Second city: Birmingham and the forging of modern Britain* (London, 2022), pp 50–3.
106 *Irish Times*, 5 October 1878; *ILT&SJ*, vol. 12, p. 499 (5 October 1878); O.J. Burke, op. cit., pp 256–7.
107 B.M. Walker (ed.), *Parliamentary election results in Ireland, 1801–1922* (Dublin, 1978), p. 251.
108 14&15 Vict., c.60 (1851), an 'Act to prevent the assumption of certain ecclesiastical titles in respect of places in the United Kingdom.'

An indication of Keogh's interest in, and ability to advocate, tenant rights might be seen in what he said about absentee landlords when addressing, as a judge, the grand jury of Co. Galway in 1869:

> The Law Life Assurance Company is an absentee corporate body, who carry on their business in London, and who never come to this country. They are the owner of vast estates in this county and in the county of Mayo.[109] Yet they never disturb their repose by contributing to the comforts or looking to the interests of their tenants. The term 'absentee' is an odious one, a person who derives his income in one country but resides in another, where he expends that income. The common voice of mankind says that this is an evil and an injustice. It points to lands imperfectly cultivated, to labourers inadequately employed, to ruined cottages, to uneducated children; and it proclaims that these things would not be if the proprietor resided upon his estate.[110]

An electoral pledge not to take office or support a government that did not address tenant grievances was breached by his acceptance of office in 1852 as solicitor general in the new government headed by Lord Aberdeen. He and John Sadleir (1813–56), MP for Carlow, who also took a government position, were to be denounced for many years as archetypes of untrustworthy and self-serving public representatives, although it has also been said that their supposed defection or treachery 'in the process came to be seen out of all reasonable perspective'.[111] A sympathiser wrote that 'unfortunately in the excitement of the moment he made some indiscreet after-dinner speeches which were treasured up by his enemies; and after he had accepted office no opportunity was lost in flinging in his face words which would probably never have been uttered in calmer moments and which probably in the moment of utterance were not intended to bear the extreme meaning which was put upon them'.[112]

Parnell, for one, said, 25 years later, that 'Keogh was not able to resist the bribe of a solicitor generalship, offered as the price of a betrayal of his cause. An Irishman of distinguished talent, he talked one doctrine to the peasantry of the West; but when the inducement of office tempted him, he forgot himself and accepted what he declared he would never do'.[113] The law at the time required any MP accepting government office to resign his seat[114] and stand for re-election and the controversy did not affect his local support, which ensured that he was

109 In 1849 the company acquired the large estates of the Martin family in Connemara, extending to over 190,000 acres including over 60,000 acres of the Ballynahinch Castle estate (Tim Robinson, *Connemara: listening to the wind* (Dublin, 2006), p. 345).
110 *Irish Times*, 24 July 1869; O.J. Burke, op. cit., p. 332.
111 R.V. Comerford, 'Churchmen, tenants, and independent opposition, 1850–56' in W.E. Vaughan (ed.), *A new history of Ireland; V, Ireland under the Union, I: 1801–70* (Oxford, 1989), p. 406.
112 O.J. Burke, op. cit., p. 259.
113 HC Deb, 3rd series, vol. 234, col. 606 (9 May 1877).
114 Succession to the Crown Act 1707 (6 Anne, c.7), s26.

comfortably re-elected (79 votes to 40). He was unopposed for re-election in 1855 when, after Lord Palmerston became prime minister, he was promoted to be attorney general. In April 1856 he was appointed to fill a vacancy in the court of Common Pleas. Sadleir had come to a bad end just before this, in February 1856, and took his own life on Hampstead Heath as his Tipperary Bank collapsed and was exposed as a 'gigantic swindle'.[115] Many documents of title provided to the bank as security for loans, included purported conveyances from the Encumbered Estates Court, transpired to be forgeries.[116]

Keogh's appointment took place at the age of 38. He had been born in December 1817, and was less than half of the age of the man he succeeded, Robert Torrens (1775–1856), who had been appointed in 1823. A remarkable scene at the Four Courts ensued:

> The announcement that Mr Justice Keogh was for the first time to take his seat upon the bench attracted an immense, indeed an overflowing, audience, a great part of which was composed of the fair sex. Upon the right hon. gentleman making his appearance in the Hall he was favoured with a reception which must have afforded ample compensation for all the abuse that has been poured upon his head, and upon that of the government which appointed him. Mr Keogh, in his judicial robes, instead of being a mark for popular odium, was cheered to the very echo by the dense crowd whom curiosity had attracted to the Hall to witness his debut. But the manifestation did not end here; another ovation awaited him in the Court of Common Pleas, and the moment he entered and made his bow he was greeted with a fresh cheer, the heartiness of which atoned in a great measure for the absence of dignity and the singular novelty of the whole spectacle.[117]

A trial over which he presided at the assizes at Nenagh in 1858 led to a debate in Parliament and, half a century later, to the exhumation and re-burial at Loughmore, Co. Tipperary, of the bodies of two brothers who had been convicted of murder. Daniel and William Cormack protested their innocence on the scaffold, and the inscription on the mausoleum in the churchyard where they were re-buried refers to a 'judicial murder', and to the tragedy of their deaths having occurred 'through false testimony procured through gold and terror, the action in their trial of Judge Keogh, a man who considered personally, politically, religiously and officially was one of the monsters of mankind, and the verdict of a prejudiced, partisan, packed, perjured jury'. In June 1858 James Whiteside who was both the prosecuting counsel at the trial and the attorney general, replied to a debate in the House of Commons initiated by The O'Donoghue, one of the MPs for Tipperary. He said that the house could not become a court of appeal from such verdicts, and

115 F.G. Hall, *The Bank of Ireland, 1783–1946* (Dublin, 1949), p. 226.
116 Ibid., p. 228.
117 *Law Times*, vol. 27, p. 44 (19 April 1856).

denied a suggestion by The O'Donoghue that the judge had addressed the jury 'in the excited tones and language of an impassioned advocate' for a conviction. He did say that 'one judge might speak more decidedly than another, and if he stated the law and the facts fairly to the jury it would be unjust to censure him for what might be no more than his ordinary manner',[118] perhaps an acknowledgment that 'judicial heat was not rare',[119] and that Keogh's manner of address to the jury had been quite forceful.

With Mr Justice Fitzgerald he presided at the special commission established in 1865 for the trials of a number of Fenians accused of treason felony and related offences. The speech from the dock of O'Donovan Rossa included a reading out of extracts of newspaper articles in the Fenian newspaper, the *Irish People*, 'in which the political career of Mr Justice Keogh was made the subject of animadversion', to Keogh's discomfort, according to a classic and frequently re-issued collection of such speeches. To certain prisoners, Thomas Clarke Luby and Charles Kickham, he extended some complimentary remarks while imposing heavy sentences.[120]

The Parliamentary Elections Act 1868[121] had provided that petitions to set aside election results should be heard in the first instance by a judge, and Keogh heard some of the earliest petitions, after the general election held in November and December 1868. (His friend Joseph Sheridan Le Fanu had believed earlier that year that Keogh had an ambition to return to Parliament.)[122] Results in 14 constituencies were challenged, of which six petitions were successful, the elected MP being unseated. Keogh declared void the election in Drogheda on the grounds of intimidation and undue influence,[123] and presided over an argumentative hearing of a petition on the election at Youghal, when he sought to commit an attorney for contempt of court.[124] Isaac Butt QC when defending the attorney's conduct, and himself exasperated with Keogh's interjections and demeanour, cited Shakespeare – 'be Kent unmannerly when Lear is mad'.[125]

Keogh's handling of a petition arising out of a bye-election for Co. Galway in 1872 added fuel to an already inflammatory series of events. This was one of the last elections to be held before secret ballots were prescribed by the Ballot Act[126] which became law in July that year. The defeated candidate, Trench, complained of intimidation of voters by clerical influence, and violent crowds, in favour of

118 HC Deb, 3rd series, vol. 151, cols. 16–26 (18 June 1858).
119 W.E. Vaughan, *Murder trials in Ireland, 1836–1914* (Dublin, 2009), pp 256–7.
120 *'Guilty or not guilty?': Speeches from the dock, or protests of Irish patriotism, containing, with introductory sketches and biographical notices, speeches delivered after conviction* (Dublin, 1867), p. 152 (Luby), p. 156 (O'Donovan Rossa) and p. 160 (Kickham).
121 31&32 Vict., c.125.
122 W.J. McCormack, *Sheridan Le Fanu and Victorian Ireland* (Oxford, 1980), p. 216.
123 *ILT&SJ*, vol. 3, p. 76 (30 January 1869).
124 *ILT&SJ*, vol. 3, p. 295 (1 May 1869).
125 *King Lear*, 1.1.145–6; H.R.N. [John Joseph Dunne], *Here and there memories* (London, 1896), p. 27; *ILT&SJ*, vol. 31, p. 297 (26 June 1897).
126 35&36 Vict., c.33.

Nolan, the Home Rule candidate. The judge unseated Nolan and referred to the full court of Common Pleas the decision on whether Trench should be seated in his place. The majority of the court (Lawson, Morris JJ and Keogh himself, Monahan CJ dissenting) held that Trench should be deemed elected.[127] Keogh had sat in the courthouse in Galway to hear evidence on the petition over a number of weeks in April and May, and in his judgment referred to the actions of members of the Catholic clergy in very disparaging terms. Gladstone told the Queen that 'in denouncing the grave mischief of priestly intimidation in Ireland, Judge Keogh has by his language quitted altogether the character of a judge, and glided into that of a heated and angry partisan … New food has been ministered to the causes of distrust between classes in Ireland, and a fresh blow struck at the growing popular confidence in the administration of justice'.[128] MPs lined up to denounce Keogh, the two MPs for the city of Dublin, Pim and Corrigan, saying that his language (1) was intemperate, referred to irrelevant topics and was inconsistent with the dignity that ought to be maintained by a judge, and (2) was 'utterly indefensible'.[129] Other reactions were much more forcible. There were street demonstrations in cities and towns against Keogh, and Butt asked the House of Commons 'can any Roman Catholics in Ireland trust him?'[130]

Keogh's decision created embarrassment for the government, since it included a certificate that 36 named individuals, including three bishops, had been guilty of undue influence and intimidation. The attorney general, Richard Dowse, reviewed the evidence and announced that prosecutions would be commenced against the bishop of Clonfert (although not against the archbishop of Tuam nor the bishop of Galway) and 19 members of the clergy and some others, including Nolan, the candidate. He made a point of saying that he had taken this decision having conferred with the solicitor general (Palles) and with the attorney general and solicitor general of England. By the time the prosecutions commenced, in February 1873, Dowse had been appointed a judge. The bishop was acquitted after the jury had deliberated for six minutes, and any further prosecutions were then abandoned.

The abuse and criticism directed at Keogh over the Galway judgment might have affected the strongest of men. J.G. Swift MacNeill, a younger man, speculated that the 'increasing public obloquy and the personal hatred under which he lived at length undermined his health and affected his reason'.[131] It was said that after his death that his judicial colleagues had subsequently regarded him as 'everything but equal to the responsibilities of his judicial position', having 'lost his head' in the judgment.[132]

127 *Trench v Nolan*, 6 ILTR 109 (1872).
128 Gladstone to the Queen, 6 July 1872 (*Letters of Queen Victoria, second series 1862–78* (London, 1926), vol. 2 (1870–8), p. 222).
129 HC Deb, 3rd series (1) vol. 212, col. 1804 (25 July 1872) (Pim), and (2) vol. 213, col. 827 (8 August 1872) (Corrigan).
130 HC Deb, 3rd series, vol. 212, col. 1783 (25 July 1872).
131 J.G. Swift MacNeill, *What I have seen and heard* (London, 1925), p. 117.
132 *Irish Times*, 2 October 1878.

Keogh was a strong supporter of the union with Great Britain. In 1867 he spoke in the College Historical Society of 'the great and glorious empire to which our destinies are inseparably attached … that great country which presents the greatest career to the young men of this island that any country has yet presented'.[133] Remarks that he made to the grand jury of Londonderry in 1878, when opening the assizes on the North West circuit, had a more political character, however. He deprecated as 'the ruin of the country' party processions and counter demonstrations, 'no matter from what side of the compass they may come', and particularly addressed himself to those loyal to the Crown of England and British institutions, saying that 'I thoroughly sympathise with their great historic aspirations, and I believe that I myself would not be at this moment able to think or speak as I choose but for the deliverance which was witnessed [in 1689] from your walls'.[134]

Shortly afterwards he was taken unwell at a dinner on circuit, and did not sit as a judge at the Four Courts in subsequent months, in the Easter and Trinity law terms. In June 1878 he wrote to Edward Gibson, the attorney general, referring to being minded to retire on account of poor health and inquiring whether Gibson thought it possible that James Murphy would be accepted as his successor. He observed that of course he would not wish to cut across the succession rights of Gibson himself or of the solicitor general (FitzGibbon), but had the impression that neither was at present thinking of a judicial position.[135] Murphy was Keogh's son in law, married to his daughter Mary. Ashbourne in reply noted that he was not surprised to learn that long service as a judge might have impaired Keogh's health and induced him to think of some rest. He confirmed that neither he nor FitzGibbon were at present seeking any judicial appointment but, while acknowledging Murphy's great abilities, also said that great difficulty could be anticipated in thinking of appointing as Keogh's successor a person so closely connected with him.[136] Murphy was eventually to be appointed a judge five years later (see p. 305).

Keogh travelled to the Continent later that summer, subsequent events perhaps lending colour to an account of his demeanour on board the ship to Holyhead: 'He was pale, emaciated, embarrassed in manner, and indifferent to all that was passing around him; speak to him, bring before him the glowing and impassioned images of the past, he gazes listlessly and mechanically at you, makes no sign and, dropping his head, buried it in his bosom, and sinks into a moody and melancholy abstraction'.[137] In August, while in Brussels, he attacked his valet with a razor in the middle of the night, and dramatic reports were made of his behaviour in what

133 *Law Times*, vol. 42, p. 464 (13 April 1867).
134 *Derry Sentinel*, 19 March 1878; HC Deb, 3rd series, vol. 238 cols. 1948–54 (25 March 1878); Copies of the charge addressed by Mr Justice Keogh to the grand jury of Londonderry, etc. (P.P. 1878 (112) lxii.463).
135 Keogh to Gibson, 23 June 1878 (Ashbourne Papers, B.81/3).
136 Gibson to Keogh, 25 June 1878 (Ashbourne Papers, B.81/4).
137 O.J. Burke, op. cit., p. 260.

was described as an episode of temporary insanity. The *Irish Times,* whose reporter spoke to the valet, a Mr Curran (who was 'dressed and sitting up, apparently not suffering very much, but extremely reticent'), and to Curran's doctor (who 'seemed not to consider the injuries inflicted very serious'), thought that the incident may have been exaggerated.[138] Be that as it may, Keogh died at Bingen, on the Rhine, at the end of September. Murphy was present.[139] There were later reports of a variety of conditions and diseases, apart from any mental disorder, from which he suffered.[140]

Among those who knew him Keogh was a popular and pleasant man. The historian of the Connaught circuit referred to his 'inexhaustible fund of information, fun, wit and humour',[141] and Swift MacNeill wrote of his 'unrivalled wit and extraordinary brilliancy in conversation'.[142] A legal official wrote that

> Mr Justice Keogh was personally the most popular judge I ever knew with his friends. He possessed fluency unbounded. Many others had this, but he had as well an attractive and clever face, and a voice of singular and musical richness. He was a small man, say about 5ft 5 inches, and rather square set, the head Napoleonic and square … A man of great memory, resource and humour … A sharp, strong and decided judge, hard on criminals, not great as a lawyer but by no means deficient.[143]

A sense of humour is conveyed by his thanks to Gibson for speaking up for him when attacked in Parliament by Joseph Biggar MP in 1877: 'he has pronounced an unfavourable opinion of my judicial impartiality, but what would I have done if he had put upon me the odium of his confidence?'[144]

After his death he was honoured in the King's Inns with, unusually, both a portrait and a bust,[145] for the commissioning of which his friends among the judiciary, the Bar and the solicitors' profession quickly subscribed several hundred pounds.[146] Friends and admirers also erected a tall (18 ft.) Celtic cross of Kilkenny limestone over his grave in Bonn.[147] The portrait is inscribed 'Presenti tibi maturos largimur honores' (Horace, Epistles, 2(1) – 'to thee the world its homage pays'), and the cross at his grave also bears an inscription from Horace (Odes, 3.3.1 – 'Justum et tenacem propositi virum' – 'The man of firm and righteous purpose'). (That latter expression was also employed (in more complete form) by Lord Lowry

138 *Irish Times*, 24 August 1878.
139 *Law Times*, vol. 65, p. 405 (12 October 1878).
140 *Irish Times*, 5 October 1878.
141 Burke, *Connaught circuit*, p. 256.
142 Swift MacNeill, op. cit., p. 115; see also A.M. Sullivan, *Old Ireland: reminiscences of an Irish KC* (London, 1927), p. 19.
143 R. Denny Urlin, *Journal and reminiscences* (Letchworth, 1909), p. 137.
144 Keogh to Gibson, 12 May 1877 (Ashbourne Papers, B.81/1).
145 Wanda Ryan-Smolin, *King's Inns portraits* (Dublin, 1992), pp 39 and 81.
146 *ILT&SJ*, vol. 12, p. 604 (14 December 1878).
147 *Irish Builder*, vol. 24, p. 189 (1 July 1882); *ILT&SJ*, vol. 16, p. 328 (8 July 1882).

in concluding his observations on the Irish Law Lords,[148] and a motto thus inspired by Horace, 'Tenax propositi', forms part of the seal of the Inn of Court of Northern Ireland, established in 1926.)[149] In wider Nationalist society his reputation, already poor from the 1850s, did not recover from the extended Galway election episode, and the bitter criticism that was directed at him during his lifetime was occasionally subsequently revived. A series of articles from the *Nation* first published in the excitements of June 1872 was reprinted in 1888 as *A record of traitorism; the political life and adventures of Mr Justice Keogh*, and, as mentioned, in 1910 the committee responsible for the memorial to the Cormack brothers caused a strongly critical characterisation of him to be engraved in stone.

Jonathan Christian

Justice of the court of Common Pleas 1858–67, Lord Justice of Appeal 1867–78

Jonathan Christian (1808–87) was a judge for twenty years, and in the second part of his judicial career was one of the most controversial judges of the nineteenth century. He expressed political opinions in judgments and in observations from the bench, in substantial pamphlets and in letters to the *Times*. Many of his views were articulated with what that paper once referred to rather coyly as 'a style somewhat disdainful of professional and social amenities',[150] but his conduct was more generally regarded as being entirely outside the bounds of propriety and the decorum of judicial office. The *Irish Law Times* said that his opinions were frequently expressed 'in language too undisciplined and on occasions which, to say the least of it, were unsuitable. His prolonged feuds with the late Lord O'Hagan, Vice-Chancellor Chatterton and with the official law reporters led to extra-judicial harangues of an unusual and unseemly character'.[151]

The journal previously acknowledged his ability in glowing terms, saying that 'in our opinion [he] is unrivalled – certainly unsurpassed – by any English judge',[152] and later that year that 'we have every respect for the brilliant abilities and learning of the Lord Justice'.[153] Soon, however, in terms that it would later frequently return to, it warned that the 'valuable services rendered to the public by the lord justice of appeal are all but neutralised by the irrelevant matter introduced into his judgments and his still more reprehensible attacks upon colleagues'.[154] His criticism of colleagues who took different views of a case or of the workings of the court system often took the form of personal denigration. Ironically, the manner

148 Lord Lowry, 'The Irish Lords of Appeal in Ordinary' in D.S. Greer and N.M. Dawson (eds), *Mysteries and solutions in Irish legal history* (Dublin, 2001), p. 216.
149 J.A.L. McLean, 'The Honorable Society of the Inn of Court of Northern Ireland', *NILQ*, vol. 23 (1972), p. 92.
150 *The Times*, 18 March 1874.
151 *ILT&SJ*, vol. 21, p. 590 (5 November 1887).
152 *ILT&SJ*, vol. 4, p. 15 (8 January 1870).
153 *ILT&SJ*, vol. 4, p. 735 (10 December 1870).
154 *ILT&SJ*, vol. 6, p. 333 (22 June 1872).

of his criticism of them for allegedly not observing proper judicial procedures may itself have constituted a far greater departure from proper judicial conduct than anything which he believed to merit criticism.

His father was a solicitor in Carrick-on-Suir, Co. Tipperary. He was educated at Trinity College Dublin and was called to the Bar in 1834. He joined the Leinster circuit, but 'was unfitted by a nervous susceptibility for the rough and ready work of nisi prius, and practice at the common law Bar was not his delight, so he betook himself to the court of Chancery'.[155] Decades later he gave an account in incidental remarks in open court (in the course of an attack upon law reporters) of 'having sat for long years in court, and having given up in despair the hope of being able to attain the position of a practising barrister, through the inability I felt of keeping up intelligently with the arguments of counsel or the judges'.[156] Such apprehensions seem to have been overwrought or in any event overcome, since he took silk in 1846 after only twelve years at the Bar, a much more rapid advancement in the profession than would be common. He was appointed law adviser in Dublin Castle in October 1850, a position from which he resigned within three months, 'it being incompatible with his heavy duties in the Equity Courts',[157] and subsequently became third serjeant (1851), and a bencher of King's Inns (1852). He was solicitor general in 1856 in Lord Palmerston's government and, following the death of a judge of the court of Common Pleas, Joseph Devonsher Jackson, at the end of December 1857, was appointed to fill the vacancy in the New Year, shortly before the government went out of office. In March 1867 he was promoted to be lord justice of appeal, in the Court of Appeal in Chancery, in succession to Abraham Brewster.

He was the junior member of the court of Common Pleas until 1865 when Thomas O'Hagan, the MP for Tralee, was appointed to fill a vacancy. The other members of the court were chief justice Monahan and William Nicholas Keogh. In his first ten years as a judge his opinions and his manner of expressing them were unexceptional and uncontroversial, but all changed when O'Hagan was appointed lord chancellor in December 1868.[158] Thereafter he criticised a wide variety of colleagues in the judiciary, including O'Hagan, Chatterton and James Whiteside, the chief justice of Queen's Bench, of whom he said that he 'seldom stops to measure his phrases by his knowledge of whatever subject he may take a fancy to declaim about'.[159] Christian's hostility to Chatterton also comprised counsel whom he associated with him. On the death of Hewitt Poole Jellett (1825–1911), a leading member of the Bar, it was said that Christian had disliked

155 *Dublin University Magazine*, vol. 84 (1874), p. 407.

156 *ILT&SJ*, vol. 11, p. 593 (24 November 1877).

157 *Law Times*, vol. 16, p. 352 (18 January 1851); *Dublin University Magazine*, vol. 84 (1874), p. 406.

158 See Daire Hogan, 'Arrows too sharply pointed; the relations of Lord Justice Christian and Lord O'Hagan, 1868–1874' in John McEldowney and Paul O'Higgins (eds), *The common law tradition; essays in Irish legal history* (Dublin, 1990), pp 61–84, for a more detailed review of this troubled relationship.

159 *Mulholland v Killen*, *ILT&SJ*, vol. 8, p. 652 (26 December 1874).

him and 'conceived an unaccountable prejudice against him ... had sneered at his arguments and poured contempt on his analogies and distinctions. It was as counsel in sustaining the judgments of Chatterton V.C. that Jellett was most frequently attacked. His practice was hardly affected by Christian's attempts to ruin it'.[160] Other targets over time included the ministers responsible for the reforming Land Act of 1870 and for judicial promotions in 1876, a Law Lord, the attorney general[161] and law reporters. An obituary observed that 'while himself so aggressive the lord justice was peculiarly sensitive to the remarks of others'.[162]

A provisional system of court procedure (all the matters now addressed by rules of court) under the Chancery (Ireland) Act 1867 was regarded by Christian as entirely unsatisfactory, a view not shared by O'Hagan, Chatterton and the master of the rolls, Edward Sullivan.[163] He had some support within the legal profession for many of his criticisms,[164] although not for the scathing and belittling observations on procedures in Chatterton's court[165] and elsewhere that he frequently made. In November 1872 a pamphlet, of about 60 pages, was published anonymously under the title of *The court of Chancery under the Chancery (Ireland) Act 1867*. However its tone and contents critical of the procedures under the 1867 Act, and of the learning and abilities of other Chancery judges, were so unmistakably associated with Christian that within a week he was obliged to authorise the publishers to state that he was the author of the document 'privately circulated among members of the Bar'.[166] The London *Spectator* remarked that 'judicial pamphleteering was as incapable of defence or explanation as judicial pugilism'.[167]

The Landlord and Tenant (Ireland) Act 1870[168] was enacted in order to legalise and confirm the Ulster tenant-right custom (and any similar customs elsewhere in Ireland) whereby a tenant evicted from his holding without due cause was entitled to compensation for disturbance. Christian thought the policy of the Act to be wholly mistaken, and that as drafted it did not implement its purpose. In a judgment on an appeal in 1871 he said (contrary to the view of O'Hagan, and of the judges of the Landed Estates Court, from a decision of which the appeal was taken) that the Act had not in fact conferred any new rights on tenants, and that (if it had) any such rights not specified in conveyances made by the Landed Estates Court (LEC) would be extinguished. Christian continued, more contentiously still, that if the Act was defective this was the result of the 'heedless levity ... shocking

160 *ILT&SJ*, vol. 45, p. 88 (1 April 1911).
161 *ILT&SJ*, vol. 11, p. 636 (22 December 1877).
162 *ILT&SJ*, vol.21, p. 590 (5 November 1887).
163 Sullivan referred in a letter to O'Hagan to his feelings of 'astonishment and regret' on reading comments made privately by Christian to O'Hagan (Sullivan to O'Hagan, 14 January 1871, (O'Hagan Papers, D2777/9/23)).
164 For instance, *ILT&SJ*, vol. 5, p. 316 (17 June 1871).
165 Such as in *Re Baltinglass Junction Railway Company*, *ILT&SJ*, vol. 5, p. 225 (6 May 1871).
166 *Freeman's Journal*, 28 November 1872.
167 *The Spectator*, 8 February 1873.
168 33&34 Vict., c.46.

to all our ideas of property law' with which it had been drafted.[169] When questions were raised in Parliament about this, the short debate was hampered by uncertainty as to what he had actually said, particularly in light of his denial that newspaper reports were accurate. The prime minister, Gladstone, said that Parliament would not allow its plain intent to be frustrated.[170] An amending declaratory statute, of one section, was hurriedly drafted and enacted in August,[171] to confirm the basis of LEC conveyances, since uncertainty on a major point of conveyancing practice could not be allowed to subsist while a further appeal procedure (to the House of Lords) was followed. It was not necessarily an acknowledgment that Christian's view of the law was correct (as the *Irish Law Times* believed it to be).[172] No amendment was thought necessary to address any wider point on the underlying effect of the 1870 Act

Christian's view of the Act, in effect a political rather than a legal objection, was expressed again in the following year when he said that the law had been made 'exceptionally harsh and severe upon the owners of land in this country. That may be quite right. It may be thoroughly as it ought to be. Observe I am not presuming to criticise recent legislation. That legislation may be the very height of transcendental statesmanship or it may be what one of the first of living statesmen [Disraeli, the leader of the Conservative opposition] called it not long ago, plunder'.[173] He concluded, in his most pointed attack from the Bench on O'Hagan, that the chancellor was in no position to lecture him on the good order of the court; 'I have known the Court of Chancery longer than he has. My acquaintance with it does not date from the day I first sat upon its Bench. The best years of my professional life were passed at its bar. I had my training under a Sugden, a Blackburne, a Brewster'. Fitzgerald J, sitting as an additional member of the court (since the appeal was from a decree of the lord chancellor at first instance), said that many topics alluded to by Christian 'appeared to him to be entirely foreign to the case before the court', and that it would be 'quite beyond his province to express any opinion as to the policy of the recent Land Act, which was in no way connected with the present case'. In 1873 Christian noted that 'I have drawn upon myself the displeasure of my brother judges, or at least some of them. I deeply lament it, but I cannot help it'.[174] Lawson J when subsequently sitting with Christian similarly explicitly dissociated himself from and expressed no opinion about certain matters that his colleague had referred to.[175] The lord chancellor expressed the classical view of the responsibilities of judicial office in 1873 when he said, in a judgment in the Court of Land Cases Reserved, that 'it is not my

169 *Re the Marquess of Waterford's Estates*, 5 ILTR (1871) 125, at 129–31. *ILT&SJ*, vol. 6, pp 314–15 and 320 (17 June 1872) and p. 332 (24 June 1872).
170 HC Deb., 3rd series, vol. 206, col. 1980 (13 June 1871).
171 Landlord and Tenant (Amendment) (Ireland) Act 1871, 34&35 Vict., c.92.
172 *ILT&SJ*, vol. 5, p. 333 (24 June 1871).
173 *Johnston v Marquis of Hertford*, *ILT&SJ*, vol. 6, p. 276 (25 May 1872).
174 *ILT&SJ*, vol. 7, p. 211 (26 April 1873).
175 *ILT&SJ*, vol. 8, p. 653 (26 December 1874) (*Mulholland v Kinlen*).

function to … assert the sufficiency of the reasons which justified the passing of the Land Act. Our duty in this place is merely to discharge, as best we can, our judicial business and, without criticism or complaint, to accept loyally and administer faithfully the provisions of the statute'.[176]

In one of Christian's last judgments (a minority view in the Court of Appeal, in 1878) he made reference to the 1870 Act as leading to uncompensated confiscation, the abandonment of the sacredness of property and of the inviolability of contracts. 'Partiality, onesidedness and partisanship, as between classes, were not nice things in themselves, but they were the very life and essence of the statute which they were considering. Its avowed purpose and policy were to take large masses of the land value of Ireland away from the landlord class and hand it over to the tenant class'.[177]

He had a very negative view of another legal reform associated with O'Hagan, the Juries Act (Ireland) 1871,[178] which had broadened the basis of jury composition, but was widely acknowledged to be problematic in its initial operation.[179] (The qualifications for jury service provided by the Act were in fact higher than those proposed in Bills introduced by previous (Conservative) governments in 1858 and 1868.) He had extensive experience of presiding over jury trials in his years as a justice of Common Pleas. He remarked that he 'should be slow to send the verdict of a jury, such as juries were in 1865, to be reviewed by a jury such as juries can be in 1874'.[180]

He participated in the debates and controversy over schemes of judicial reform for Ireland that would be analogous to those introduced in England by the Judicature Act 1873. The prospect of the House of Lords ceasing to be the final court of appeal from Ireland as an element of such reforms greatly alarmed him, and he published a detailed pamphlet on the subject in 1874, and wrote a number of letters to the *Times* subsequently.[181] He considered that any such development would diminish Irish jurisprudence, increase the likelihood of unfitting judicial appointments being made and weaken the Union of Great Britain and Ireland. Many of his old complaints and insinuations against O'Hagan (who left office, in the change of government after the general election of 1874, just as the pamphlet was being published) were recycled in the pamphlet. He proposed that the office of lord chancellor ought to be abolished, or converted into a permanent and non-political judicial position.

176 *Stevenson v the earl of Leitrim*, 7 ILTR (1873) 34, at 45.

177 *Shearman v Kelly*, *ILT&SJ*, p. 99 (23 February 1878). See p. 348 below for comments, more temperately expressed, critical of the consequences (and hence, by extension, of the policy) of the Land Acts that were made in 1903 by the lord chief justice, Lord O'Brien of Kilfenora,

178 34&35 Vict., c.68.

179 Niamh Howlin, *Juries in Ireland; laypersons and the law in the long nineteenth century* (Dublin, 2017), pp 12 and 50.

180 *Mulholland v Killen*, *ILT&SJ*, vol. 8, p. 652 (26 December 1874).

181 The Right Hon. J. Christian, *The coming court of final appeal for Ireland* (Dublin, 1874).

He had a particular objection to the separation from the Chancery jurisdiction of judicial sales of land and distribution of the proceeds of sale, a field of law that (since 1858) had been remitted to the Landed Estates Court. He believed this to reflect adversely on the overall standing and quality of the courts of equity. In 1876 he wrote to the *Times* on that subject, and about a related proposal to increase the jurisdiction of the County Courts, saying of Chancery that 'divorced from the territory [of estates] it is shorn of its most honoured province'.[182] Those comments were not without support, and the judicial reforms of 1877 did bring about a closer connection of the land courts with Chancery.

Attention focussed at the time, however, on another part of the letter that made some observations about recent judicial appointments, which were soon raised in Parliament. He wrote that 'a second judgeship of the Landed Estates Court, which had been dropped in 1872 and which two successive governments had publicly announced their intention of suppressing, has been suddenly revived and filled with the attorney general … It is well known that the learned judge who, for three years, single-handed, administered the Landed Estates Court, made no secret of his opinion that no aid was needed there'. (The attorney general was Henry Ormsby, and the existing LEC judge was Stephen Woulfe Flanagan.) He continued by saying that

> careers have been marred here, as well as made, by sinister influences. For example, what would be thought at Westminster of such a possibility as this – one of the ablest of living judges, to whom the State might be indebted for judicial services among the largest that had been done in our time, ostracised from a promotion for which position and seniority designated him, simply because, by the vigour and fearlessness with which he had rendered those very services, he had earned the hatred of a priesthood which is a power in politics, and of classes which are the enemies of England.

He was referring – although, as Disraeli, the prime minister, said (see below) 'the mode of expression is extremely obscure' – to the fact that in the previous month Mr Justice Keogh had not been appointed to succeed James Monahan when he retired as chief justice of Common Pleas. The position had been given to Michael Morris, another of the justices of that court, who had been appointed in 1867, having been attorney general and an MP for a couple of years, and was politically very well connected. It was entirely fanciful to think that Keogh might have been appointed, since, among other objections to him, his judicial standing had been gravely affected by the widespread unease and criticism, not confined to the clergy or nationalist opinion, that followed his judgment in the Galway election petition in 1872. Disraeli when asked in the House of Commons to comment on Christian's letter a few days later said that a government 'should avoid as much as possible entering into a controversy with those who use certain expressions in high judicial

182 *The Times*, 6 March 1876.

positions. I would trust rather to their own sense of propriety on reflection, and to the dignity of the position which they occupy'.[183] (In one of the court scenes involving Christian in 1872 O'Hagan referred to having 'exercised that quality which has been described by Lord Kingsdown as the golden energy of silence'.)[184]

In what transpired to be the last years of his career as a judge Christian conducted a running argument with the Law Reporting Council of Ireland as to the nature of the judgments which were reported by it and more specifically as to the reporting of his own judgments, on each front asserting that the law reports were quite unsatisfactory. On the first point he thought that the Council's focus should be on the reporting of 'a broad terrain of special Irish subjects' where the law of Ireland was distinctive, and would have 'infinite interminglings with the doctrines of general law', and not on reports of judgments involving those general points of law themselves. He said, taking a remarkably limited view of the role (and abilities) of the Irish judiciary, that 'when one wants to know what is the law of Ireland on a point of general jurisprudence, there is always a previous question – what is the law of England; that is, by the constitution, and has been, at least since Poyning's law [1494], the relation to each other, in things legal, of the countries. But it is at Westminster and Lincoln's Inn that the ... workshops for the authoritative judge-made law are only to be found. At the Four Courts we import that article, we do not manufacture it'.[185]

His second point related to the reporting of his own judgments. After he complained in 1877 about the accuracy of the report of his judgment in *Lewis v Lewis*[186] the Council of Law Reporting placed a note in the official reports that 'as the lord justice of appeal has declined to revise his judgments [for the reports] they will in future be published on the basis of their reporter's notes'.[187] He protested at that notice, saying that for the Council to 'promulgate, as if they were judgments of mine, their reporters' notes, will be to practise deception upon their readers and defamation upon the court'.[188] The Council solicited and published testimonials from the vice-chancellor and Mr Justice Lawson as to the ability of Ernest G. Swifte, the reporter of whom Christian complained.[189] When the lord chancellor, Ball, expressed the hope that he would reconsider this determination not to revise his judgments Christian dismissed this 'with profound respect'.[190]

183 HC Deb., 3rd series, vol. 277, cc 1871–73 (13 March 1876).

184 *Lamprey v Lambert*, *ILT&SJ*, vol. 6, p. 335, at 339 (22 June 1872). Kingsdown (1793–1867) was an English barrister, who sat as a member of the Judicial Committee of the Privy Council.

185 *ILT&SJ*, vol. 11, pp 589–90 (24 November 1877).

186 IR 11 Eq. (1876), 110, 340.

187 *ILT&SJ*, vol. 11, p. 278 (9 June 1877).

188 Christian LJ to the chairman of the Council, 7 June 1877 (*ILT&SJ*, vol. 11, p. 371 (28 July 1877)). See, more generally, V.T.H. Delany, 'Lord Justice Christian and law reporting', *NILQ*, 12 (1956–8), pp 46–52, and Eamonn G. Hall, *The superior courts of law: 'official' law reporting in Ireland, 1866–2006* (Dublin, 2007), chapter 4, 'Tension between judge and reporter: the Lord Justice Christian saga', pp 74–116.

189 *ILT&SJ*, vol. 11, pp 374–5 (28 July 1877).

190 *Mackey v The Scottish Widows' Fund and Life Assurance Company*, *ILT&SJ*, vol. 11, pp 358–60 (21 July 1877).

Mr Swifte had been called to the Bar in 1863. He had been secretary to the master of the rolls, John Edward Walsh, for the three years (1866–9) that Walsh held that office, and in 1875 had served briefly as counsel to the attorney general, Henry Ormsby. In later years, when the reporting controversy was long over, he was again so appointed, by Dodgson Hamilton Madden, and six months later was appointed as one of the Dublin magistrates. He was knighted in 1921.[191] His son was private secretary to Lord O'Brien of Kilfenora, the lord chief justice, for a number of years prior to the judge's retirement in 1913.[192]

Christian did not acknowledge that the difficulties in reporting his own judgments arose from his refusal to furnish or revise copies of them, or more generally to co-operate in the process of reporting, and from his custom of making ad hoc remarks from the Bench even when a printed copy of what he intended to say in judgment was available. He had previously said in an exchange of correspondence with Mr Swifte that 'my "written" judgments are usually only partly written and the written parts are constantly departed from in the very act of delivery'. In that letter he also set out a remarkable perspective on his work, saying that 'it ought to be known that judges speak with a view to being understood, not by reporters or the readers of reports, but by the counsel in the case; and they constantly leave unmentioned facts because, by reason of their very importance, they are assumed to be present to the minds of those whom the judge is addressing'.[193]

In November 1877 he said that he 'must either refrain from communicating to the parties litigant in open court my reasons [in that case, for concurring with the lord chancellor in dismissing an appeal] or I must take the risk of seeing those reasons laid before them by and by in print in a guise misleading to them and discreditable to the court'. Having referred to the supposed misreporting of his judgment in *Lewis v Lewis* 'I think it better for the parties in this case not to expose my reasons to the danger of sharing a similar fate. I shall therefore withhold them for the present but … I shall be happy to furnish them on application from the leading counsel at either side'.[194] The *Irish Law Times* said that he had no right to withhold judgments or to deliver them 'in a secret, clandestine and unconstitutional manner'.[195] His request shortly afterwards that his own judgments would not be reported by the Council ('far better [to] have no report than one false and ridiculous'[196]) was dismissed out of hand at a meeting of the Bar in December 1877, on the basis that a judge had no right to demand that his judgments be kept back in such a manner. Hugh Law QC, later to be lord chancellor (1881–3), said

191 *ILT&SJ*, vol. 23, p. 640 (7 December 1889) and vol. 24, p. 347 (28 June 1890). *Burke's Irish family records*, p. 1083.
192 *ILT&SJ*, vol. 48, p. 328 (21 November 1914).
193 Christian LJ to E.G. Swifte, 2 February 1876 (*ILT&SJ*, vol. 11, p. 375 (28 July 1877)).
194 *Hone v Bianchi*, *ILT&SJ*, vol. 11, p. 586 (24 November 1877).
195 *ILT&SJ*, vol. 11, p. 585 (24 November 1877).
196 Christian LJ to the Council, 30 November 1877 (*ILT&SJ*, vol. 11, p. 625 (15 December 1877)).

at the meeting that 'a judgment when once delivered was not the property of the judge, of the suitor, or the Bar simply, but became the property of the public. The public whose officer the judge was – although a very exalted officer – expected from him an authoritative exposition of the law'.[197] In 1878 Christian gave a protest and warning 'that anything that might be attributed to him in the Irish Reports he now, by anticipation, disclaimed and repudiated ... he [expressed] a hope that, in future, courts of first instance would be so good as to pay no regard to anything which they should find attributed to him in those Irish Reports'.[198] In the New Year he resigned as a bencher of King's Inns, perhaps an indication of strained relations with his judicial colleagues and senior members of the Bar.[199] Other retirements of benchers, for instance that of J.T Ball (lord chancellor 1875–80) in 1894, generally took place in a context of the person concerned withdrawing from public life, having ceased to exercise judicial functions some years before.[200]

One of his last letters to the editor of the *Times* was written in August 1877, when he wrote that he could not 'suffer to pass unchallenged' certain remarks made in the House of Lords in the course of determining an appeal, reversing one of his judgments.[201] In his judgment, which was the subject of the appeal, he had used very strong expressions of disparagement of one of the parties, which seemed to Lord Hatherley 'to be altogether unsupported by the evidence'. Lord Blackburn said that Christian seemed to have forgotten that 'it was the essence of justice not to decide against anyone on grounds which were not charged against him and as to which he had not had an opportunity of offering explanations nor calling evidence'. Christian's letter began by saying that 'I am not going to hint the slightest question as to the correctness of that decision', but he then set out a number of criticisms of the Law Lords' judgments. He concluded, in a manner reminiscent of a comment in 1872 on not being prepared to accept a rebuke from O'Hagan, that 'I cannot admit that I need a lecture from Lord Blackburn as to what is "of the essence of justice"'.[202] O'Hagan had been one of the judicial members of the House that sat on the appeal, and had concurred in the outcome.

The awkwardness, to say no more, of Christian's professional relations with his brother judges had its counterpart in 'a peculiarity of disposition and taste [which] prevented him from participating in the ordinary sociabilities of society and life. He never dined out, except at the King's Inns, when his obligations as a bencher entailed this on him, and his evenings were all spent at home.'[203] He came to be remembered not for his undoubted command of the law but for the unjudicial manner in which he would conduct – and, more generally, for what was seen as his

197 *ILT&SJ*, vol. 11, p. 627 (15 December 1877).
198 *Shearman v Kelly*, *ILT&SJ*, vol. 12, pp 100–1 (23 February 1878).
199 Minutes of meeting of Benchers of the King's Inns on 11 January 1878, referring to a letter dated 2 January addressed by Christian LJ to the Inn; *ILT&SJ*, vol. 12, p. 60 (2 February 1878).
200 *ILT&SJ*, vol. 28, p. 16 (13 January 1894), and vol. 29, p. 593 (7 December 1895).
201 *O'Rorke v Bolingbroke*, 2 App. Cas. (1876–7), 814.
202 *The Times*, letter dated 1 August 1877; *ILT&SJ*, vol. 11, p. 401 (11 August 1877).
203 *Dublin University Magazine*, vol. 84 (1874), p. 407.

propensity to start – arguments. He retired in November 1878, on account of increasingly impaired hearing.[204] He died at his home in Merrion Square in 1887.

Thomas O'Hagan

Justice of the court of Common Pleas 1865–8, Lord Chancellor of Ireland 1868–74, 1880–1

Thomas O'Hagan, the first Lord O'Hagan (1812–85), was the first Catholic in over 150 years to be lord chancellor of Ireland. His appointment in December 1868 by W.E. Gladstone, when forming his first government, was intended to be a token of adoption of a policy of religious equality. Gladstone had said a few days before that 'my mission is to pacify Ireland'.[205] O'Hagan became a peer in 1870 (see p. 121) and thereafter contributed to the judicial and Parliamentary work of the House of Lords. His title was Lord O'Hagan of Tullahogue, a place in Co. Tyrone associated with his clan or family for centuries, although his use of the place name drew a protest from descendants of those to whom the lands had been granted in the Ulster Plantation in the early seventeenth century.[206] A history of the lord chancellors of Ireland that was published in 1879 (and which was read over by O'Hagan prior to its publication)[207] refers to the distinction of the clan, stating that 'when the O'Neills reigned sovereigns of Ulster the chief of the sept of O'Hagan was chief brehon, or chief judge of that kingly race'.[208]

O'Hagan's family was engaged in the spirit trade in Belfast, and he was educated at the Belfast Academical Institution.[209] He entered his name in the King's Inns in 1831, and studied as a pupil with a member of the noted Chitty family of legal authors in London. Daniel O'Connell signed his King's Inns admission papers, and he was called to the Bar in 1836. During the 1830s, including his early days at the Bar on the North East circuit, he worked also as a journalist, editing a newspaper in Newry and Dundalk. In 1847 he was appointed assistant barrister (i.e., chairman of the Quarter Sessions of magistrates) in Co. Longford by the lord chancellor, Maziere Brady, on foot of a solicitation that he had prepared at the end of 1846, expressing the hope that 'my qualifications for the office appear to you not inferior to those of others who may seek it'.[210] He was later transferred to hold the same office for Co. Dublin. He became a Queen's Counsel in 1849, and a bencher of King's Inns and second serjeant in 1859. His experience was primarily in the common law courts, acting for the defence in some

204 Duke of Marlborough to earl of Beaconsfield, 4 November 1878 (Disraeli Papers (Bodleian Library, Oxford), C/V/20a); *Irish Times*, 19 November 1878.
205 John Morley, *The life of William Ewart Gladstone* (London, 1903), vol. 2, p. 252; Roy Jenkins, *Gladstone* (London, 1995), p. 290.
206 *ILT&SJ*, vol. 19, p. 67 (7 February 1885).
207 Oliver J. Burke to O'Hagan, 29 December 1878 (O'Hagan Papers, D2777/3/A/48).
208 O.J. Burke, *History of the lord chancellors of Ireland, 1186–1874* (Dublin, 1879), pp 314–16.
209 The Institution received the Royal prefix in 1831.
210 O'Hagan to Brady, draft letter 17 December 1846 (O'Hagan Papers, D2777/5).

trials of a political nature in the 1840s, including representing Charles Gavan Duffy when charged with seditious libel. He acted in the defence of Fr Petcherine, a priest accused of burning a bible at a mission in Kingstown (Dun Laoghaire) in 1855, securing his acquittal,[211] and was defence counsel for O'Donovan Rossa and other Fenians (members of the Phoenix National and Literary Society) in 1859 at their trials for conspiracy.

The government of Lord Palmerston appointed him to be solicitor general in 1860, in which office remarkably he was nominated and sat as a judge of assize that year,[212] and to be attorney general in 1861, in which capacity he was responsible for prosecutions. In May 1863 he was elected at a bye-election as member of Parliament for Tralee. His speech to the electors, given in the courthouse after it had become clear that he would be elected unopposed, describes his philosophy at the time, obviously with an electoral character.[213] He said that he had declined invitations to stand in other constituencies,[214] not having had much desire for a political career, and had not sought promotion through the avenue of Parliament. He was a 'Catholic Liberal', and emphasised his strong defence of Catholic interests:

> I am before you now, as I was when I laboured to organise the Catholic Bar against the Ecclesiastical Titles Bill[215] and received the unanimous thanks of the Catholic Hierarchy, or when I drafted the declaration of the Catholics of Ireland against the assault upon our Conventual Institutions (see p. 200) and aided, to the best of my power, in the effort by which that assault was repelled; or when, on very numerous occasions, I strove, as best I could, professionally or otherwise, to secure justice and protection for the Catholic priesthood and the Catholic people.

He was appointed as a member of the court of Common Pleas when a vacancy arose in 1865 on the retirement of Nicholas Ball (1791–1865), who had been a

211 See O.J. Burke, op. cit., pp 318–20, for an extract for his address to the jury.

212 A.R. Hart, *A history of the King's serjeants at law in Ireland; honour rather than advantage?* (Dublin, 2000), p. 120.

213 'Address delivered on the Hustings at the close of the election for Tralee in 1863' in Thomas O'Hagan, *Occasional papers and addresses* (London, 1884), pp 319–39.

214 He was invited in 1859 to stand in the constituencies of Drogheda, Cashel and Dundalk (Teeling Papers (NLI), MS 17874 (2) and (3)). He had also explored the prospect of standing in the constituencies of Ennis, Kinsale and Co. Cork.

215 This Bill, enacted as the Ecclesiastical Titles Act 1851 (14&15 Vict., c.60), prohibited Catholic bishops in England from adopting territorial titles. It 'combined minimal effectiveness with a massive amount of offence to catholics' (R.V. Comerford, 'Churchmen, tenants and independent opposition, 1850–56' in W.E. Vaughan (ed.), *A new history of Ireland, V. Ireland under the Union: I, 1801–70* (Oxford, 1989), pp 396–414, at 401). It was repealed in 1871. 'When Lord John Russell [the prime minister] asserted that the Irish people were not opposed to the Ecclesiastical Titles Bill all the Roman Catholic members of the Irish Bar assembled and protested against the measure, lest their silence might be construed as assent. The same Catholic members of the Bar attended the first Rotunda meeting, held to protest against the Bill, lawyers were then the chief speakers' (*Irish Quarterly Review*, vol. 1, p. 520 (19 August 1851)).

judge since 1839 and who died shortly afterwards.[216] As a member of the Court for Crown Cases Reserved, in that capacity, he joined in a majority decision limiting the extent to which information provided by an accomplice to a crime (an 'approver') could be used against himself.[217]

His appointment as lord chancellor in 1868 was

> prompted by [his] representing more than any other Roman Catholic on the bench national ideals. He had never allowed his patriotism to exceed constitutional limits, but he had in his name a recommendation to popular favour, and he did not permit the recollection of an association with O'Connell , at a time when he combined journalism with the practice of his profession to be forgotten. In those early days ... he was noted for his oratorical gifts and urbane disposition, and these qualities, for which he became with advancing years increasingly distinguished, and his capacity as a statesman, did much to justify Gladstone's choice of him as chancellor.[218]

O'Hagan was selected by Gladstone in preference to a number of other prominent Catholic common law judges – Pigot, Monahan and Deasy – who were thought to have a greater familiarity with equity and Chancery law and procedure, at least at some point in their careers.[219] His (initially) limited knowledge of Chancery was the subject of a friendly and supportive letter from Joseph Napier, lord chancellor 1858–9 (see p. 107).[220] Less agreeably his supposed unsuitability to be the head of the court of Chancery was to be the subject of a series of insulting and offensive comments from lord justice Christian (see pp 154–7). The decorum that he maintained in court in the face of Christian's abuse was much admired, and he was a much better judge than Christian would allow, although there was little warmth in a comment in his obituary in the *Irish Law Times* that 'if not a brilliant, he unquestionably proved an eminently satisfactory, Chancellor, whose decisions well stood the test of appeal'.[221] Contemporaries noted his judgments in *Croker v. Croker*,[222] in which the Court of Chancery Appeal set aside deeds prepared by a solicitor who was supposedly advising a son but in fact was acting on the instructions of his father, and *In re Meade's Minors*,[223] in which Catholic relatives were restrained from interfering with the parental rights of a father, who was a Protestant, to determine his children's religious education.[224]

216 *Law Times*, vol. 40, p. 125 (14 January 1865) and p. 179 (11 February 1865).

217 *R v Gillis* (1866) 17 ICLR, 512 at 533–6; W.E. Vaughan, *Murder trials in Ireland, 1836–1914* (Dublin, 2009), pp 201–3.

218 Ball, p. 303.

219 *Dublin University Magazine*, vol. 84 (1874), p. 412.

220 Napier to O'Hagan, undated [December 1868], (O'Hagan Papers (PRONI), D2777/7/M/92); Daire Hogan, 'Arrows too sharply pointed: the relations of lord justice Christian and Lord O'Hagan, 1868-74' in J.F. McEldowney and Paul O'Higgins (eds), *The common law tradition: essays in Irish legal history* (Dublin, 1990), pp 61–84, at pp 65–6.

221 *ILT&SJ*, vol. 19, p. 69 (7 February 1885).

222 4 *ILT&SJ* (1870) 181.

223 5 IR Eq. (1870–1), 98.

224 *ILT&SJ*, vol. 42, p. 276 (31 October 1908), biographical article by E.J. Moore.

O'Hagan, at least for a time after 1868, was disappointed at ministers not involving him more closely, outside his judicial duties, in government affairs.[225] Legal reforms with which he was associated during his first term as lord chancellor included the Irish Church Act 1869 (providing for the disestablishment of the Church of Ireland), the landlord and tenant legislation of 1870,[226] and two statutes in 1871, the Lunacy Regulation (Ireland) Act[227] and the Juries (Ireland) Act.[228] The former Act reformed procedures for the protection of persons of unsound mind, and was to be the primary statute regulating the subject for more than a century.

Overhaul and reform of the jury system had been acknowledged as necessary for decades. In his judgment (speech) in the appeal of Daniel O'Connell to the House of Lords in 1844 Lord Denman had famously remarked that trial by jury in Ireland 'instead of being a security to persons who are accused [was] a delusion, a mockery and a snare'.[229] O'Hagan was much exercised about a particularly blatant case of improper selection of a jury panel in Co. Monaghan in 1869.[230] The three objectives of the 1871 Act were, 'to broaden jury participation by introducing a rateable valuation qualification for jurors, to introduce summoning by alphabetical rotation and to abolish the sheriff's discretion when it came to summoning jurors'.[231] The implementation of these reforms turned out to be problematic, and a select committee was set up by Parliament in 1873 to inquire into its operation.[232] Many of the judges gave evidence to the committee, their attendance, particularly of judges well-disposed to the reforms, being shepherded by Palles, the attorney general.[233] O'Hagan later acknowledged various failings in the Act, and supported amendments, but regarded much of the criticism as unfair – 'ridicule, abuse, exaggeration were employed without measure or mercy, and the real effort was to reverse the principle of the law ... if [the rateable valuation for qualification as a juror had initially been set too low] the fault was not with the action of this house [i.e., the House of Lords] or of the author of the measure'.[234] Lord Fitzgerald in a later debate on jury laws characterised the Act as a 'leap in the dark'.[235]

225 Spencer to O'Hagan, 1 April 1870 (O'Hagan Papers, D2777/8/105) and 3 April 1870 (D2777/8/106); John F. McEldowney, 'Lord O'Hagan (1812–85): a study of his life and period as lord chancellor of Ireland (1868–74)', *Irish Jurist*, vol. 14 (1979), p. 360, at 364–5; entry on O'Hagan in *DIB* (by Patrick M. Geoghegan).

226 His first speech in the House of Lords was on the second reading of that Bill (HL Deb, 3rd series, vol. 202, col. 750 (23 June 1870)).

227 34&35 Vict., c.22.

228 34&35 Vict., c.65.

229 *O'Connell v The Queen* (1844) 8 ER 1061, at 1135.

230 John F. McEldowney, 'The case of *The Queen v McKenna* (1869) and jury packing in Ireland', *Irish Jurist*, vol. 12 (1977), p. 339.

231 Niamh Howlin, *Juries in Ireland: laypersons and the law in the long nineteenth century* (Dublin, 2017), p. 12.

232 HC Deb, 3rd series, vol. 215, col. 315 (28 March 1873). Select committee on working of jury system, P.P. 1873 HC (283) xv.389.

233 Palles to O'Hagan, 7 June 1873 (O'Hagan Papers, D2777/9/89/6).

234 HL Deb, 3rd series, vol. 231, cols. 497–8 (4 August 1876).

235 HL Deb, 3rd series, vol. 311, col. 1236 (4 March 1887).

Gladstone proposed legislation in 1873 that attempted to address the vexed question of improving the provision of university education for Catholics. This envisaged the University of Dublin becoming a national umbrella institution that would incorporate Trinity College, the Queen's Colleges in Belfast and Cork (while potentially closing down the college in Galway) and the Catholic University. The scheme found little favour with any interested party or vested interests in Ireland. The rejection of the legislation in the House of Commons in March 1873 greatly damaged the government's authority, although it remained in office for almost another year. A comment made by Cardinal Cullen, a strong opponent of the initiative, in the immediate aftermath of its abandonment indicates a degree of personal animus and of diminution of O'Hagan's standing with the hierarchy. He told a fellow cleric that 'we asked for fish and they gave us a serpent. Our catholic friends in high places will be quite disconsolate. No wonder – Lord O'Hagan, if Gladstone resigns, loses £4,000 per annum … and the attorney general [Palles], an excellent catholic, loses a large salary and his chance of becoming a judge'.[236]

O'Hagan left office as lord chancellor in March 1874 after Gladstone's defeat in that year's general election, and was re-appointed in May 1880 when Gladstone was re-elected. His resignation in the autumn of 1881 followed a visit to Gladstone's home at Hawarden, near Chester,[237] and was due to ill health, although naturally there was some speculation that it arose from unease over government policy in Ireland at a dramatic time in the Land War. Gladstone acknowledged when accepting his resignation that there might be such speculation that it arose from differences of opinion over policy, but was content that if any such false opinion were to arise O'Hagan would set it right.[238] He continued to sit as a judicial member of the House of Lords for some time after he had stepped down as lord chancellor, and had indicated his intention to do so when sitting for the last time as a judge in the Four Courts.[239]

O'Hagan married twice, first in 1836 to Mary Teeling, a native of Belfast, who died in 1868, and with whom he had six children. Three of their daughters died young,[240] and all of them except their daughter Frances, who married John O'Hagan (see p. 289), pre-deceased him. His second wife was Alice Towneley (sometimes spelled Townley), whom he married in 1871, and with whom he had a further six children. She was a member of a Lancashire family that was described as 'one of the oldest and most honoured among the Catholics of England. Its great possessions have been largely preserved', and whose father was 'one of the wealthiest commoners in England'.[241] The value of O'Hagan's personal estate on

236 Cullen to Kirby, 12 March 1873 (Dublin Diocesan Archives, AB4/42/1/18); James H. Murphy, *Ireland's Czar: Gladstonian government and the lord lieutenancies of the Red Earl Spencer, 1868–86* (Dublin, 2014), p. 132. As it transpired, it was the imminent loss of office by Gladstone, eleven months later, that determined him to appoint Palles as a judge.

237 *Irish Times*, 22 and 28 October 1881 and 9 November 1881.

238 Gladstone to O'Hagan, 20 October 1881 (O'Hagan Papers, D2777/7/F/7).

239 *ILT&SJ*, vol. 15, p. 584 (12 November 1881).

240 *Law Times*, vol. 40, p. 125 (14 January 1865).

241 *ILT&SJ*, vol. 5, p. 317 (17 June 1871).

death (£53,013),[242] while very substantial, would not have reflected her family's wealth. Their family seat, Towneley Hall in Burnley, Lancashire, dating from the fourteenth century, was sold to the town council (corporation) in 1901. A horse owned by his wife's uncle, Charles Towneley, won the Epsom Derby in 1861. O'Hagan's home in Dublin was in Rutland [now Parnell] Square, and he had what was described as a 'country seat' at Raheny House, Co. Dublin.[243] With his second wife he made a home in London, in Belgravia and later in Mayfair, where he died in 1885. He is buried in Glasnevin cemetery. His son, the 2nd Lord O'Hagan, served in the Boer War and died young, aged 22, in 1900, and was succeeded by his brother, the 3rd Lord O'Hagan, who was an active member of the House of Lords until his death in 1961. The 4th Lord O'Hagan (1945–2025) was for some years a member of the European Parliament, initially (1973–5) as an independent and subsequently (1979–94) as a Conservative.

O'Hagan was a man of culture and public spirit. He was a Commissioner of both National Education and Intermediate Education, and spoke strongly in favour of legislative proposals to advance intermediate and university education in Ireland.[244] At the time of his appointment as lord chancellor he was the president of the Statistical and Social Inquiry Society of Ireland, and throughout his career he showed an active interest in social and economic questions. In the 1870s he took an active part in the establishment of the International Association for the Reform and Codification of the Law of Nations. He was a trustee of the British Museum and a member of the Royal Irish Academy, which he warmly defended in the House of Lords in 1876, articulating its objections to any government plan for it to be amalgamated with the Royal Dublin Society.[245] In 1884 a collection of his lectures was published, and after his death a nephew edited a volume of his speeches.[246]

His standing in public life was very high throughout his career. His appointment as lord chancellor was marked by the commissioning of a bust by a leading English sculptor, Shakespeare Wood, and a statue was placed in the Round Hall of the Four Courts a couple of years after his death. The bust was first placed in 1869 in the Bar room of the county court house on the Crumlin Road in Belfast, 'the place destined for its preservation until we have a Town Hall in Belfast in which such memorials of our local worthies can be suitably enshrined'.[247] It is now in a place of honour in the Inn of Court (the Old Bar Library) in the Royal Courts

242 *ODNB*.

243 *ILT&SJ*, vol. 4, p. 489 (9 July 1870).

244 HL Deb, 3rd series, vol. 241, col. 417 (28 June 1878) on intermediate education (excerpts in Burke, op. cit., pp 337–44); HL Deb, 3rd series, vol. 247, col. 1834 (8 July 1879) on university education; HL Deb, 3rd series, vol. 270, col. 1554 (19 June 1882), moving the second reading of an amending bill on intermediate education.

245 HL Deb, 3rd series, vol. 230, col. 489 (27 June 1876).

246 Thomas O'Hagan, *Occasional papers and addresses* (London, 1884); George Teeling (ed.), *Selected speeches and arguments of the Right Hon. Thomas, Baron O'Hagan* (London, 1885).

247 *ILT&SJ*, vol. 3, p. 214 (20 March 1869), citing the *Northern Whig*.

of Justice. The statue was the last to be erected of six[248] that stood on plinths in the Round Hall until they perished, with so much else, in the destruction of the building in the Civil War in 1922. C.P. Curran (1883–1972), a court registrar best known as a writer on art and architecture, thought that the statue, the work of a prominent sculptor, Thomas Farrell, RHA, was undistinguished. His view of O'Hagan himself was little better, in remarking that 'a few years later [i.e., after 1887] and it would not have occurred to anyone so to commemorate him'.[249] The commissioning of the statue was not purely, perhaps not even primarily, a legal initiative. The meeting to set about the project was held in Tyrone House in Marlborough Street in Dublin, the administrative centre (as it remains to this day) of the education system in Ireland, with the Church of Ireland archbishop of Dublin in the chair, and the executive committee of five eminent men included a single judge, Sir Michael Morris.[250] A portrait of O'Hagan in his robes of lord chancellor was presented to the King's Inns by Lady O'Hagan.[251]

Two volumes of histories of the lord chancellors of Ireland were published in the 1870s, both of which were dedicated to O'Hagan. One (in 1870) was written by J.R. O'Flanagan, who later gathered materials for a contemplated biography of O'Hagan, which was not completed. The author of the second was Oliver J. Burke, whose book, published in 1879, concluded with an account of O'Hagan's career to date. Much of this work had been published in instalments in the *Dublin University Magazine*, and when O'Hagan was informed by Burke that financial difficulties were preventing the issue of this history in a more permanent form he confidentially subsidised the publication of the book.[252] Burke published a history of the Connaught circuit in 1885 which had likewise also previously been serialised.

248 The subjects of the other five statues were Plunket (lord chancellor), O'Loghlen (master of the rolls), Joy (chief baron), Sheil (member of the Bar, MP, and author of *Sketches of the Irish Bar* (1822–9)) and Whiteside (chief justice).
249 C.P. Curran, 'Figures in the Hall' in *Record of the centenary of the charter of the Incorporated Law Society of Ireland, 1852–1952* (Dublin, 1953), reprinted in Caroline Costello (ed.), *The Four Courts: 200 years* (Dublin, 1996), p. 81 (1952), p. 176 (1996).
250 *ILT&SJ*, vol. 21, p. 36 (15 January 1887).
251 Wanda Ryan-Smolin, *King's Inns portraits* (Dublin, 1992), p. 55.
252 Oliver J. Burke to O'Hagan, 30 October 1877 (O'Hagan Papers, D2777/3/A/41).

CHAPTER FIVE

The judiciary in 1866 (2)

David R. Pigot

Chief Baron of the Exchequer 1846–73

DAVID RICHARD PIGOT (1796–1873) was born in Kilworth, Co. Cork, where his father was a doctor. He was educated at Trinity College and in Edinburgh, where he studied medicine for a time, and was called to the Bar in 1826. He became a KC in 1835, was appointed solicitor general in 1839 under the Whig government of Lord Melbourne, and subsequently attorney general, retiring on the fall of the government in 1841. In that office he queried how certain members of a jury panel had been excluded from a murder trial in Co. Armagh, and his remark that it did not appear that 'any particular excitement prevailed at Newtownhamilton on the subject of the trial' has been taken to indicate a 'Carthusian remoteness' from the reality on the ground.[1] He was MP for Clonmel between 1840 and 1846. In that year, when Lord John Russell formed a new government, Pigot was appointed as head (chief baron) of the court of Exchequer in succession to Maziere Brady, who was transferred to become lord chancellor. The fact that Pigot was a Catholic and enjoyed the confidence of Daniel O'Connell was a factor in this promotion.

He soon acquired a reputation for punctiliousness in the conduct of court business. Within a few months of appointment a barrister told J.R. O'Flanagan, a historian of the Irish Bar, that 'the courts here are proceeding very slowly. Pigot is, I hear, doing the nisi prius business very well – of course not quickly'.[2] Two decades later the view of the *Irish Times* was that this 'one original demerit' of the judge had come to outweigh his many good qualities, 'his extensive legal knowledge, his forensic abilities and his engaging personal qualities'.[3] O'Flanagan wrote that 'through conscientious feelings, and an anxiety to render full justice, he investigated every case so minutely that days rolled into weeks before trials were over, and while the legal practitioners reaped harvests clients were undone, and the patience of witnesses and jurors exhausted'.[4] Conversely, a brisk trial had historically been acknowledged as potentially giving rise to injustice, 'And wretches hang, that jurymen may dine.'[5]

At criminal trials judges would take notes or summaries of evidence, to facilitate their work in charging a jury and for reference if an appeal for clemency over a

1 W.E. Vaughan, *Murder trials in Ireland, 1836–1914* (Dublin, 2009), p. 141.
2 Henry Baldwin to J.R. O'Flanagan, 6 December 1846 (J.R. O'Flanagan, *The Irish Bar* (London, 1879), pp 336–7).
3 *Irish Times*, 3 March 1871.
4 O'Flanagan, op. cit., p. 385.
5 Alexander Pope (1688–1744), 'The Rape of the Lock', canto 3.

sentence was made to the lord lieutenant, or if the judge wished to bring a point of difficulty before the Court for Crown Cases Reserved. Pigot's practice was to record both question and answer, and counsel would pause in their questioning while this careful note-taking took place, the intended effect of vigorous cross-examination thus being largely destroyed.[6] A half century later nothing much had changed, and Campbell LCJ called for greater use of shorthand note-takers in cases.

> Where, as in a case of this kind, very much depended on the cross-examination, as well as the direct examination, of witnesses, it was impossible for the judge, while taking a longhand note, to give counsel a proper opportunity of conducting the cross-examination ... Many of the cases were tried at assizes [and] counsel often got a stay [after judgment] to serve notice of a new trial; then the long vacation intervened; the judge never heard of the case, perhaps, for three or four months; and then he was asked to give a record of his charge to the jury. Even the most accurate judge was then placed in a very unfair position. Very often the whole case depended more upon the exact words used by the judge than upon the substance of his charge, because very often the form of expression might itself be a misdirection.[7]

Pigot intervened in a Parliamentary controversy in 1856 over the capacity of a member of his court, Richard Pennefather, to continue in office. Pennefather (1773–1859) had been appointed a baron of the Exchequer in 1821, before Pigot had been called to the Bar, and his impaired vison over many years and loss of sight had become increasingly problematic, leading to the lord lieutenant and the lord chancellor inviting him to consider his position. Joseph Napier QC, MP defended him in a debate in the House of Commons,[8] and cited a letter he had received from Pigot[9] praising Pennefather's judicial efficiency, notwithstanding his infirmity. His other colleagues in the court of Exchequer, barons Greene and Richards, also provided testimonials as to his capacity and ability. It was said that Pennefather had trained his memory such that his inability to take notes or examine documents in the course of a trial was of no significance, and similarly that any issue relating to the demeanour or credibility or candour of a witness was a matter in any event for a jury, not the judge.[10] Pennefather was unmoved by the controversy, resisting the initiative to induce him to retire, and remained in office for three more years. His brother Edward (1775–1847) had been chief justice of Queen's Bench between 1841 and 1846.

6 Vaughan, op. cit., pp 250–1; John Adye Curran, *Reminiscences* (London, 1915), p. 45.
7 *ILT&SJ*, vol. 53, p. 90 (12 April 1919).
8 HC Deb, 3rd series, vol. 140, cols. 760–806 (14 February 1856). Letters from colleagues were cited at cols. 773–4. See also *Law Times*, vol. 25, p. 93 (26 May 1855) and vol. 34, p. 92 (12 November 1859); *ILT&SJ*, vol. 30, p. 502 (14 November 1896).
9 It had been reported the previous year that Pigot's own health had 'obliged him to reside for the last 6 months in Spain' (*Law Times*, vol. 25, p. 93 (26 May 1855)).
10 HC Deb, 3rd series, vol. 140, cols. 760–806 (14 February 1856).

The manner or style of work of a judge would not be the only reason for lengthy trials. One of the last trials for murder over which Pigot presided took place in 1873 at the assizes at Maryborough [Portlaoise], and lasted for seven weeks, opening on 18 July and concluding on 10 September.[11] There were 114 witnesses, defence counsel took two days opening the defence, and prosecuting counsel occupied seven days in replying for the Crown. The prisoner, James Moore, was found guilty and on his appeal for clemency a reprieve from the mandatory sentence of death (and commutation of sentence to penal servitude for life)[12] was granted by the lord lieutenant after Pigot, who was ill, 'sent for Lord Spencer, the lord lieutenant, and told him that he could not die in peace or happy if the man were hanged'.[13] Spencer had been anxious and frustrated as Pigot was slow in advising on whether a commutation of the sentence would be warranted, and wondered if he might be ill or incapacitated. 'I feel greatly for him, but it is getting serious as the execution is ordered for Thursday'.[14]

Pigot was averse to police questioning of suspects, and was regarded as protective of the rights of prisoners, at least up to the point when a jury had determined the guilt of an accused person.[15] He had reservations about proposals for special legislation that would have permitted the trying of certain criminal cases without juries because of the intimidation of jurors, and about statutes passed in 1870 and 1871 for the purpose of remedying difficulties in the trials of serious agrarian crime.[16]

In 1871 he had presided, with chief justice Whiteside, at the trial of Robert Kelly for murder of a policeman. The defence counsel successfully argued that the wound resulting from an admitted shooting was not a mortal one, but had become so because of the supposedly reckless manner in which the victim had been treated in hospital. That controversial aspersion on the skills of the attending surgeon, Sir William Stokes, was accepted by the jury, which acquitted Kelly,[17] who was however immediately afterwards separately tried and convicted of attempted murder.[18]

Pigot lived at Merrion Square, and died on 22 December 1873. The *Irish Law Times* reported that he had 'broken down through his exertions and indefatigable industry in the discharge of the duties of his high office; and the protracted trial

11 *Irish Times*, 11 September 1873.
12 *Irish Times*, 15 October 1873.
13 Curran, op. cit., pp 47–8; Michael Byrne, *Legal Offaly* (Tullamore, 2008), pp 106–7.
14 Spencer to O'Hagan (Monday) 6 October 1873 (O'Hagan Papers, D2777/8/229).
15 Vaughan, op. cit., pp 190, 194–5, 257.
16 Under the Peace Preservation (Ireland) Act 1870 (33&34 Vict., c.9) the attorney general could seek a change of venue of a trial to another county. The Protection of Life and Property in certain parts of Ireland Act 1871 (34&35 Vict., c.25) – the 'Westmeath Act' – recited that sympathy with the perpetrators of crime and the terror that they had created impeded the due administration of justice and the protection of life and property.
17 *ILT&SJ*, vol. 5, pp 563–4 (18 November 1871); *Irish Times*, 20 October 2015 (Irishman's Diary).
18 *ILT&SJ*, vol. 52, p. 146 (15 June 1918).

at which he presided at the late assizes in Queen's County [now Co. Laois], we believe, completely prostrated his constitution'.[19] His funeral took place on 26 December, attended by 'a vast concourse;' the cortege left his residence at 7.45a.m. and went via Nassau Street, Dame Street and the quays to Kingsbridge station, from where his remains were taken by train to Cork, the funeral service taking place near Kilworth.[20] He was succeeded in office by Christopher Palles. A posthumous portrait was presented in 1874 to the King's Inns by his sons,[21] one of whom, also named David Richard (1823–1906), and who had been called to the Bar in 1846, had been appointed master of the court of Exchequer on foot of representations made by his father,[22] in 1869.[23]

Francis A. FitzGerald

Baron of the Exchequer 1859–77, Justice of the High Court (Exchequer division) 1878–82

Francis A. FitzGerald (1807–97) was born in 1807 in Madras (now Chennai), India, where his father was a physician in the service of the East India Company.[24] The family moved back to Ireland while he was a child, and he was brought up in Co. Limerick. His brother William (1814–83), a scholarly cleric, became bishop of Killaloe. His son Charles Edward (1843–1916) was an eye surgeon and was elected President of the Royal College of Physicians of Ireland in 1912.

He was called to the Bar in 1834, after education at Trinity College. His start at the Bar was reputedly slow, and his practice was held back by a form of scruples, or perhaps pride, since 'when still a very struggling junior he frequently refused briefs which he imagined were sent to him through the influence of friends'.[25] He enjoyed considerable success in due course, including in Chancery, becoming a QC in 1849 and being elected a bencher of King's Inns in 1857. In 1859 he was appointed to fill a vacancy in the court of Exchequer and at the time this was seen as an acknowledgment of his ability, since 'although he was reputed to be a high Conservative he had never taken any active part in politics'.[26] J.G. Swift MacNeill's view was that he was one of the most gifted and high minded men of his generation, and that although he was 'a Tory of the most pronounced type' his promotion (made by a Conservative government) was not due to any political

19 *ILT&SJ*, vol. 7, p. 628 (27 December 1873).
20 *ILT&SJ*, vol. 8, p. 2 (3 January 1874).
21 Wanda Ryan-Smolin, *King's Inns portraits* (Dublin, 1992), p. 59.
22 O'Hagan to Spencer, 25 June 1869 (O'Hagan Papers, D2777/8/63); Spencer to O'Hagan, 26 June 1869 (O'Hagan Papers, D2777/8/56).
23 *ILT&SJ*, vol. 38, p. 453 (31 December 1904).
24 *ILT&SJ*, vol. 31, p. 70 (6 February 1897). He has been referred to as having been born in 1806, but 5 June 1807 was the date of birth advised by him to the King's Inns at the time of his admission.
25 *ILT&SJ*, vol. 31, p. 70 (6 February 1897).
26 *Law Times*, vol. 32, p. 221 (29 January 1859).

influence.[27] He declined two offers of higher judicial offices, those of master of the rolls in 1866,[28] and of chief justice of Queen's Bench in 1877 (see pp 209 and 271).

As a common law judge he dealt with a wide variety of cases, including criminal law. A sentence of death that he pronounced in 1866 resulted in the last execution to be carried out in public in Ireland, and he was among the majority of Irish judges who told an official inquiry in that year that they favoured the retention of capital punishment for murder and certain other serious crimes.[29] His advice to the lord lieutenant on possible commutation of a sentence in 1865 was compassionate, in saying that the general character of the case would have struck him, as the trial judge, as aggravated manslaughter rather than murder, and the sentence of death was commuted to penal servitude for life.[30] Two important cases in the court of Exchequer in the mid-1870s were *O'Byrne v Lord Hartington*,[31] arising out of the banning of a public meeting in the Phoenix Park in 1871, and *Attorney general v Delany*,[32] in which the court held that a bequest for Masses not to be said in public was not entitled to exemption from legacy duty, as not being a charitable gift. The leading judgment of Palles CB noted that the issue of whether 'the celebration of the Mass in a public church would be a charity as a religious service tending to the edification of the public' did not arise in the case, and this was determined by the courts decades later.[33] FitzGerald sat as a judge in the courts of the Church of Ireland, and in the court of Delegates before the divorce jurisdiction was transferred to the civil courts.[34]

He resigned as a judge in 1882, in what was a very uncommon instance of a judge retiring otherwise than on grounds of ill health or on foot of a political request to do so. Many judges died in office but otherwise, there being no age limit in those decades, it was not uncommon for a judge to remain in office until he was literally unable to discharge his duties and/or was offered some inducement to step down. FitzGerald was then aged 75, had served as a judge for over 20 years, and had qualified for his judicial pension after 15 years' service.

The Prevention of Crime (Ireland) Bill[35] was introduced by the government shortly after the Phoenix Park murders on 6 May 1882. This was intended to facilitate and enhance the enforcement of criminal law, and FitzGerald's retirement arose out of a provision for trial without a jury of certain crimes of a political or agrarian nature. It was proposed that panels of three judges would form

27 J.G. Swift MacNeill, *What I have seen and heard* (London, 1925), pp 154–5.
28 Derby to Naas, 30 August 1866 (Derby Papers, 190/2, p. 241); *Irish Times*, 15 and 29 August 1866.
29 W.E. Vaughan, *Murder trials in Ireland, 1836–1914* (Dublin, 2009), pp 309, 258; Report of the capital punishment commission, together with minutes of evidence and appendix (P.P. 1866 (3590) xxi, 1).
30 Vaughan, op. cit., pp 323–4.
31 6 IR CL (1872–73) 517.
32 10 ILTR 34 (1876).
33 *O'Hanlon v Logue*, [1906] 1 IR 247.
34 *Irish Times*, 19 December 1870.
35 Enacted as 45&46 Vict., c25.

a special commission for charges of murder and treason (for which a death sentence would follow conviction) and other serious crimes. The judges publicly objected to this, and although the Bill, as enacted in July, contained such a provision it was never put into effect.

The fact that, among the judges, FitzGerald had a particular objection to the principle of non-jury courts seems to have been common knowledge. T.M. Healy asked the prime minister on 5 June whether any judge, and in particular FitzGerald, had sent in his resignation, and was told that no resignation had been received.[36] Spencer told Gladstone on 7 June that 'there is sure to be a third vacancy[37] by the resignation of Baron FitzGerald [whenever] the Prevention of Crimes Bill receives the Queen's assent. He told this in the most positive terms to the master of the rolls [Sullivan]'.[38] Both men hoped that he would not step down, although Spencer thought, correctly, that there was little chance of him changing his mind.[39] Amendments were considered that might help to avert his resignation, including a suggestion from the law officers, Porter and Johnson, that an amendment might be 'slipped through' without anything being said about it beforehand to exempt judges of over twenty years' standing from any obligation to sit in the intended new courts.[40] The only judges to whom such an exemption would have been applicable were FitzGerald and lord justice Deasy (who had been appointed in 1861). No such amendment was made before the Bill was enacted in the middle of July.

FitzGerald continued to sit as a judge in June and July, tendering his resignation before the opening of the new legal term in the autumn. A general meeting of the Bar was held in the Law Library (at which 'several of the judges were present') to present an address of tribute to him 'on our reassembling at the close of the summer vacation',[41] and the Law Society, representing solicitors, also marked the occasion by holding a special meeting with him for that purpose.[42] When paying tribute in court following his death, more than a decade later, Palles CB said that FitzGerald had represented the model type of the judicial character, and spoke warmly of his acceptance and support of Palles as head (chief baron) of the court of Exchequer in 1874, FitzGerald being more than twenty years older and then having fifteen years' judicial experience.[43]

FitzGerald lived for fourteen years after his resignation. 'Considering his advanced years his physical health and vitality were most remarkable; indulging in

36 HC Deb, 3rd series, vol. 270, cols. 77–8 (5 June 1882).
37 The government was then considering two existing judicial vacancies in the Queen's Bench by reason of the death of James O'Brien in December 1881 and the appointment of J.D. FitzGerald as a lord of appeal in ordinary in May 1882.
38 Spencer to Gladstone, 7 June 1882 (Althorp Papers, Add. MS 76854.53).
39 Gladstone to Spencer, 9 June 1882; Spencer to Gladstone, 10 June 1882 (Althorp Papers, Add. MS 76854.77 and .83).
40 Trevelyan to Spencer, 12 June 1882 (Althorp Papers, Add. MS 76944).
41 O.J. Burke, *Anecdotes of the Connaught circuit* (Dublin, 1885), p. 334.
42 *Irish Times*, 7, 9, 21 and 23 November 1882; *ILT&SJ*, vol. 16, p. 575 (25 November 1882).
43 *ILT&SJ*, vol. 31, p. 71 (6 February 1897).

long walks on the bleakest winter days without an overcoat, [striding] along at a good four miles an hour or even more'.[44] He died at his home at 50 St Stephen's Green in 1897. His daughter Margaret had married Gerald FitzGibbon, later a lord justice of appeal, in 1864.

Henry George Hughes

Baron of the Exchequer 1859–72

Henry George Hughes (1810[45]–72) was the son of a solicitor in Dublin. He was educated at Trinity College and was called to the Bar in 1834, and to the Inner Bar in 1844. He had a particular knowledge of Chancery law and the practice in the court of the master of the rolls, and in his early years at the Bar wrote a treatise on the subject.[46]

He took an active part in politics, as a Catholic liberal, and was briefly MP for Co. Longford, where he was elected unopposed at a bye-election in 1856. He did not stand for re-election at the general election in 1857. He had earlier stood unsuccessfully in a bye-election for Co. Cavan in 1855. He spoke once in the House of Commons, in defence of the system of national education.[47] He twice held office as solicitor general, initially between 1850 and 1852 and again for a short time in 1858.

He lived at 20 Merrion Square, and had extensive landed property in Co. Longford.[48] He was the father in law of Michael Morris, who married his daughter Anna in 1860. A brother, James Stannus Hughes (1812–84), was a prominent physician and surgeon in Dublin.

In 1859, soon after Lord Palmerston again became prime minister, Hughes was appointed a baron of the Exchequer in succession to Baron Richards, who had resigned. He had recurrent periods of ill health 'and was compelled to reside abroad for a time',[49] with a consequent absence from the courts,[50] and died in July 1872.

Rickard Deasy

Baron of the Exchequer 1861–77, Lord Justice of Appeal 1878–83

Rickard Deasy (1812–83) was a judge for over twenty years. His name has remained familiar to generations of lawyers by reason of what is generally known as Deasy's Act, a landlord and tenant statute introduced in Parliament in 1860 by

44 Ibid.
45 On his coffin his date of birth was stated to be 10 August 1810. The admission records of the King's Inns show this as 23 August 1812. See *King's Inns admissions papers*, p. 238.
46 *Practice of the court of Chancery in Ireland* (Dublin, 1837).
47 HC Deb, 3rd series, vol. 142, cols. 1632–5 (17 June 1856).
48 *ILT&SJ*, vol. 6, p. 404 (27 July 1872).
49 *ILT&SJ*, op. cit.
50 *Irish Times*, 14 January 1868, 5 July and 23 July 1872.

him as attorney general. He claimed no particular credit for this himself, fully acknowledging the work of other men, his predecessors in that office.[51]

He was 'the son of a gentleman of some position at Clonakilty, Co. Cork',[52] where his family were prominent citizens. In 1807 his father was instrumental in developing a family brewery (Deasy and Company), which became the town's chief industry, and a commercial business as merchants and shipbuilders was also carried on at Deasy's Quay. A report of the funeral of Deasy's wife in 1883, shortly before his own death, referred to the funeral procession to Deansgrange cemetery being headed by over fifty men who were employed by him,[53] which may suggest that he had retained some form of connection with the family businesses.

After education at Trinity College he was called to the Bar in 1835, joining the Munster circuit. 'He possessed the sharp mental qualities of the southern race in high development'.[54] In his early years at the Bar he prepared law reports, to a standard which met with the approval of lord justice Christian, at least in retrospect decades later when the judge was criticising the law reporters.[55] Christian also referred to him as 'that practised lawyer, approved judge and true gentleman', as a supposed contrast to lord chancellor O'Hagan.[56] Deasy took silk in 1849. He was a Catholic Liberal, and a few years later was elected to Parliament for Co. Cork, a constituency which had a comparatively numerous electorate. Over 8,000 votes were cast in 1855 at the bye-election at which he was first elected, and almost twice that number (15,905) at the general election in 1857. A prominent Conservative lawyer, James Whiteside QC, who was attorney general between March 1858 and June 1859, said of him that 'there is not a more active partisan in the House [of Commons] against us than the same Deasy', when consideration was being given to offering him a place on the Landed Estates Court.[57] He was appointed solicitor general in 1859, and attorney general the following year, holding each of those offices for less than a year, and in 1861 was appointed a baron (judge) of the court of Exchequer.[58]

In May 1860, some three months after being appointed attorney general, he moved the second reading in the House of Commons of what was soon enacted as the Landlord and Tenant Law Amendment Act Ireland 1860.[59] He said that it was 'a measure of law reform which all sides of the House consented to ... for consolidating the existing law of landlord and tenant in Ireland, and was principally taken from the Bill of the late lord chancellor for Ireland (Mr Napier)'.[60] It had

51 A somewhat similar sequence of events occurred in 1885 in relation to the enactment of what became known as the 'Ashbourne Act', for government facilitation of tenant purchase. See p. 317.
52 *Law Times*, vol. 34, p. 269 (25 February 1860).
53 *Irish Times*, 28 March 1883.
54 *Irish Times*, 7 May 1883.
55 *Hone v Bianchi*, *ILT&SJ*, vol. 11, p. 586 (24 November 1877); *Irish Times*, 17 November 1877.
56 J. Christian, *The coming court of final appeal for Ireland* (Dublin, 1874), pp 25–6.
57 Whiteside to Disraeli, 16 May 1859 (Disraeli Papers, B/XXI/W/301).
58 *Law Times*, vol. 36, p. 179 (9 February 1861).
59 23&24 Vict., c.154.
60 HC Deb, 3rd series, vol. 158, col. 1346 (15 May 1860).

105 sections, and repealed partially or wholly fifty-five Acts of Parliament. He later extended the credit to Whiteside, remarking that 'he did not claim any merit for [the Bill], but was free to admit that the merit belonged to [Whiteside and Napier]'.[61] He said that the measure

> would be a material improvement on the existing law, and would be highly beneficial to the tenantry of Ireland. Its object was to make the law more clear and simple, so that both landlord and tenant might be perfectly apprised of their relative rights and liabilities. The law ought not be left in such a state as to afford the tenant a continual temptation, instead of paying his rent, to spend his money in litigation with his landlord, and to waste among the attorneys those funds which might be better employed in stocking a new farm.[62]

(He returned to this point two decades later, when remarking in a dissenting judgment in the Court of Appeal that 'the county of Kerry is to be congratulated when in times like these a tenant could expend £200 and a landlord £400 in contesting a right to a 31 years' lease of an acre of bog'.)[63]

Landlord and tenant relations in Ireland, in all their aspects – social, commercial, financial – have of course been transformed since 1860, but in legal terms Deasy's Act has remained the basic statute governing the subject.[64] It was aptly described soon after its enactment by a judge as not

> an Act of codification, but, which is a totally different thing, an Act of consolidation and amendment. Its functions are two-fold. First it collects into one Act provisions from various former Acts, which Acts it wholly or partially repeals; secondly it amends certain experienced evils in the Law, both Statute and Common. But, subject to these partial operations, it leaves the Common and Statute Law in full force.[65]

Deasy was well respected as a judge, presiding over many criminal trials. He was promoted to be a lord justice of appeal at the start of 1878, and the government received some credit for appointing a person who had not been associated with the Conservative party.[66] The 1877 judicature legislation provided that that the next vacancy in the court of Exchequer (i.e., in the Exchequer division of the new High Court) would not be filled,[67] and his vacation of office through this promotion

61 HC Deb, 3rd series, vol. 159, cols. 281–2 (11 June 1860). See, more generally, Alan Dowling, 'The genesis of Deasy's Act', *NILQ*, vol. 40 (1989), p. 53.

62 HC Deb, 3rd series, vol. 159, col. 2154 (19 July 1860).

63 *Congdon v Collis*, *Irish Times*, 26 April 1880.

64 J.C.W. Wylie, *Landlord and tenant law* (4th ed., Dublin, 2022), para 1.08.

65 *Bayley v Marquis of Conyngham* (1863) ICLR 406 at 417 (Christian J.). See Wylie, op. cit., para 2.08.

66 *ILT&SJ*, vol. 11, p. 511 (13 October 1877) and p. 539 (27 October 1877).

67 40&41 Vict., c.57, s6.

effected the reduction. He continued, as a member of the Court of Appeal, also to sit at first instance in the High Court on assize and at the Court of Oyer and Terminer for Dublin (at Green Street). At that court he proposed two reforms, one being a reduction in the number of jurors in civil cases from twelve to six, and the other being an amalgamation of the jury panels of the city and county of Dublin, to spread the burden of jury service more evenly and ease the duties of gentlemen residing in the city by calling on 'the services of gentlemen residing in Rathmines, Rathgar, Kingstown and Monkstown, who now entirely escape from serving as jurors'.[68]

In his last years on the bench he suffered from ill health, and Ignatius O'Brien said of him that 'when a case had been in progress for about a quarter of an hour he seemed to go to sleep and slumber until the rising of the court. Whether he really went to sleep or not was never very certain; for he used occasionally to wake up and put some very pertinent question'.[69]

He died in May 1883. He had two substantial homes, at 41 Merrion Square and at Carysfort House, Blackrock, Co. Dublin.[70] He left an estate of over £37,000. A son, Henry Hugh Peter Deasy (1866–1947), after service in the British army, achieved some contemporary renown as a traveller and author (*In Tibet and Chinese Turkestan* (London, 1901)), and as an early motorist and motor industrialist. H.H.P. Deasy's son, Rickard Deasy (1916–99), was president of the National [later the Irish] Farmers' Association in the 1960s, and led a militant campaign for higher farm produce prices.

Richard Keatinge

Judge of the Prerogative Court 1843–57, Judge of the court of Probate 1857–68

Richard Keatinge (1793–1876), the son of a barrister, was called to the Bar in 1814, and joined the Connaught circuit. He was called to the Inner Bar in 1835, and appointed as third serjeant in 1842. He was a forceful speaker, and in addressing juries he 'veiled in varied language the same reasoning and arguments; he thus in the end made the stupidest and most inexperienced of jurors understand, however complex, the case'.[71]

He was legal assessor to the sheriff of Co. Clare for the famous bye-election in the summer of 1828 at which Daniel O'Connell was first elected to Parliament. Keatinge's personal views, in religion and in politics, did not favour Catholic Emancipation, but no complaint arose on that score. He was consulted by the sheriff on disputed votes, and at the end advised that the election was valid, and that it was a matter for the House of Commons to determine whether to admit

68 *ILT&SJ*, vol. 9, p. 82 (13 February 1875).

69 Daire Hogan and Patrick Maume (eds), *The reminiscences of Ignatius O'Brien, lord chancellor of Ireland, 1913–1918* (Dublin, 2021), p. 158.

70 The property at Blackrock was subsequently significantly developed, to be a teacher training college, and later the business school of University College Dublin.

71 O.J. Burke, *Anecdotes of the Connaught circuit* (Dublin, 1885), p. 306.

O'Connell to sit and vote as a member.[72] The house declined to do so pending the passing of legislation, setting aside religious oaths, the following year.[73] He acted also as legal assessor to the visitors of Trinity College (the archbishops of Armagh and Dublin) some fifteen years later on an appeal by Denis Caulfield Heron against refusal of a college foundation scholarship to him, as not being a member of the established church.[74]

In 1843 he was appointed to be judge of the Prerogative Court, an ecclesiastical court with jurisdiction over wills and other testamentary matters.[75] This was replaced in 1857 by the probate court,[76] to which he was transferred. It was said of him upon his retirement that

> his merits and defects were those of an intellect at once powerful and acute and a strong will. He was not entirely exempt from a failing to which judges are peculiarly liable whose intellectual characteristics are such as we have described, more especially if they have attained to eminence as nisi prius advocates. They are in danger not only of forming an early and strong opinion on the merits of the case before them (their keen and practised eye at once detecting the weakness of a case and recognising the familiar arts of the advocate), but they are tempted to go further and – often unconsciously and from sheer force of habit – to endeavour to impress their view of the case upon the jury. In ninety nine cases out of a hundred, probably, the judge is right, and the jury are guided to a right decision.[77]

Two reports of cases in Keatinge's final weeks on the Bench would confirm that view of a strong judicial personality. One barrister commencing an anodyne remark with the phrase 'speaking personally' was told to 'speak for your client'.[78] He told Isaac Butt QC, in the absence of the jury, that 'I should like to know whether you consider that there is any use in going further with this case'. Butt consulted his client, an executor under a will being challenged, and said that the case would be withdrawn, in light of the expression of opinion and intimation from the judge that the will could not stand, to which Keatinge said 'most decidedly'.[79]

The possibility of his retirement was mooted by him to the lord chancellor, Brewster, in 1868, but he did this in a manner that posed some difficulty even for those such as Brewster who wished him well and thought that, as a strong Conservative for over 50 years, nobody in Ireland had greater claims on the party

72 Burke, op. cit., p. 308.
73 An Act for the relief of His Majesty's Roman Catholic subjects, 1829 (10 Geo. IV, c.7).
74 J.G. Swift MacNeill, *What I have seen and heard* (London, 1925), pp 159–60; A.R. Hart, *The King's serjeants at law in Ireland* (Dublin, 2000), pp 130–1.
75 F.H. Newark, *Notes on Irish legal history* (Belfast, 1960 (2nd edition)), p. 22.
76 Probate and Letters of Administration Act 1857, 20&21 Vict., c.79.
77 *ILT&SJ*, vol. 2, p. 665 (5 December 1868).
78 *Browne v Esmonde* (*Irish Times*, 10 November 1868); *ILT&SJ*, vol. 2, p. 669 (5 December 1868).
79 *Dunphy v Kelly* (*Irish Times*, 26 November 1868).

in power than him. He indicated a willingness to stand down – as Brewster put it, to 'place his office at the disposal of the government' – if his son Maurice, a member of the Bar who had served as his registrar for over ten years, could be appointed to fill the vacancy in the court of Bankruptcy that had arisen through the death of Walter Berwick.[80] The obvious beneficiary of Keatinge's resignation would have been R.R. Warren, the attorney general and MP for Dublin University. It did not appear that the son would have been formally qualified, not having a practising barrister for years, to hold the bankruptcy position, nor an alternative that was mooted of being appointed as chairman of quarter sessions in some county. The chief secretary, Lord Naas, was not prepared to countenance any such arrangement, and it was acknowledged as a practical objection that 'it would be justly considered a job to get Warren into harbour'[81] (or, as later expressed, 'to get into a place of safety').[82]

After it had become clear that the particular suggested provision for Keatinge's son would not be made he agreed with Warren at the end of September that he would resign in any event,[83] and Warren announced a few weeks later that he would not stand for re-election at the imminent general election. Keatinge continued in office until the first week of December when Warren succeeded him, in the last days of Conservative government after the election. It was announced that he had been granted an annual pension of £3,333, a very high proportion of his salary as a judge (£3,500).[84] His son was also then appointed to be marshal of the court of Admiralty, without giving up his position in the court of Probate, a pluralism that drew a protest from the other probate registrar[85] and more widespread public complaints, and he was not permitted to delegate the functions of his new office.[86] Another son became a general in the Indian Staff Corps.[87] Keatinge lived in Merrion Square, and died in 1876.

Mountifort Longfield

Member of the Encumbered Estates Commission 1849–58, of the Landed Estates Court 1858–66

Mountifort Longfield (1802–84) is better known as an economist and for his prominent position as a layman in the Church of Ireland than for the judicial position that he held for 18 years. His family was prominent in Co. Cork, being associated with Longueville House, near Mallow, and other estates. His

80 Brewster to Naas, 2 September 1868 (Mayo Papers, MS 43,875/5).
81 Brewster to Naas, 7 September 1868 (Mayo Papers, MS 43,875/5).
82 Brewster to Naas, 28 October 1868 (Mayo Papers, MS 43,875/5).
83 Brewster to Naas, 26 September 1868 (Mayo Papers, MS 43,875/5); *Law Times*, vol. 45, p. 413 (10 October 1868).
84 *Irish Times*, 1 December 1868.
85 *Law Times*, vol. 46, p. 138 (19 December 1868).
86 Kevin Costello, *The court of Admiralty of Ireland, 1575–1893* (Dublin, 2011), pp 224–5.
87 *ILT&SJ*, vol. 38, p. 198 (11 June 1904).

grandfather, John Longfield, had sat in the Irish Parliament. His brother Robert (1810–68), a QC, who was 'a consistent though moderate Conservative',[88] represented the constituency of Mallow at Westminster between 1859 and 1865, and was aggrieved at not being appointed as a judge in the court of Admiralty in 1867.[89] Later that year he was appointed as chairman of the quarter sessions of Co. Galway, a position worth £1,000 a year, but died shortly afterwards.[90] Other members of the Longfield family had represented, variously, the city and county of Cork, and Mallow, in the first half of the nineteenth century.[91] Longfield was called to the Bar in 1828 and to the Inner Bar in 1842. He was active in the 1830s in the Irish Metropolitan Conservative Society.[92] In 1849 he was appointed as one of the three 'Commissioners for the Sale of Encumbered Estates in Ireland',[93] an institution re-constituted in 1858 as the Landed Estates Court. He retired at the end of 1866.

He was associated with Trinity College throughout his adult life. He was educated there, becoming a fellow in 1825. In 1832 he received the degree of LL.D. and was appointed as the first holder of a new professorship of political economy.[94] He had some practical business knowledge, being for a time a director of the Great Southern and Western Railway company. He stepped down in 1836 from the economics chair to become the Regius professor of Feudal and English Law, a position that he then held for the rest of his life. He advised the College for many years on legal and Parliamentary matters,[95] and his funeral took place in the College Chapel, in November 1884.

His legal expertise lay primarily in property law and equity, and the College lectures on those subjects formed part of new educational arrangements for students for the Bar that were made in 1850 between the College and the King's Inns. Henry Brougham Leech, the Registrar of Deeds and from 1877 a colleague of Longfield as a professor of law, wrote after his death that 'he had succeeded in impressing his contemporaries with the idea that, as regards questions concerning land, he made as near an approach to infallibility as is permitted to finite intelligence'.[96] His dismissive attitude to another branch of law was clear from evidence that he gave in 1846 to the House of Commons select committee on legal

88 *ILT&SJ*, vol. 2, p. 216 (2 May 1868).

89 Costello, op. cit., p. 213.

90 *Law Times*, vol. 44, p. 127 (21 December 1867) and vol. 45, p. 51 (16 May 1868).

91 John Longfield was MP for Mallow 1801–2, Mountifort Longfield was MP for the City of Cork 1801–18 and Richard Longfield was MP for County Cork 1835–7 and stood unsuccessfully for Mallow in 1841.

92 W.J. McCormack, *Sheridan Le Fanu and Victorian Ireland* (Oxford, 1980), p. 81.

93 'Encumbered' was alternatively spelled 'Incumbered'.

94 This chair, which was initially to be held for fixed periods of five years, was founded by Richard Whately, the recently appointed archbishop of Dublin, and was thus known as the Whately professorship.

95 R.B. McDowell and D.A. Webb, *Trinity College Dublin 1592–1952: an academic history* (Dublin, 1982), p. 254.

96 H.B. Leech, *Registration of title v registration of assurances* (London and Dublin, 1891), p. 58; McDowell and Webb, op. cit., p. 536.

education: 'I have never lectured on criminal law, not considering it worth calling the attention of students to. There are no fixed principles in it, except that men must not commit certain crimes, and if they do, there are certain punishments'.[97]

There was a strong connection between economic science and law reform in the middle decades of the nineteenth century. Lawyers were prominent in the establishment in 1847 of the Statistical and Social Inquiry Society of Ireland, of which Longfield was the second president (1863–7). The first three Whately professors were lawyers (Longfield, Isaac Butt and James Anthony Lawson) and it has been said of them that they 'were happiest in deriving economic principles from current practical problems, of which Ireland furnished many in a particularly stark form'.[98]

Longfield's initial lectures 'entitle him to a prominent place in the history of nineteenth-century economic thought'.[99] His economic writings, of which a collection was published in 1971, have been the subject of detailed studies.[100] He was prominent among his contemporaries in a reconsideration of classical economic theories of *laissez faire*, and over time, having regard to the nature and causes of the different levels of economic development in Great Britain and in Ireland, he came to advocate some degree of state intervention in the economy and adjustment of property rights, to remedy market failures.[101] Following the catastrophic experiences of the famine, campaigns in the second half of the century for better security and rights for tenant farmers were driven by the continuing miserable circumstances of much of the population. Longfield was well placed, as an economist and a lawyer, to see that the difficulties of land tenure as between landlords (absentees in many cases) and tenants had their economic counterpart in problems of land use and agricultural productivity.

The famine derived from enormous social and economic difficulties and created others. One consequence was that the finances of already heavily indebted estates were overwhelmed. An initial financial resolution procedure for such 'encumbered' estates had something of a false start in 1848 within the court of Chancery,[102] and a more radical approach was adopted the following year. In a major reform of land and conveyancing law a separate Commission, generally known as the Encumbered Estates Commission (EEC), was established, 'which shall be a court of record, and shall have all the powers, authority and jurisdiction of a court of equity in Ireland for the investigation of title'.[103] The Acts 'were

97 Report of select committee on legal education in Ireland and England, 1846 (P.P. 1846 (686) x.1), minutes of evidence, Q2835.
98 McDowell and Webb, op. cit., p. 169.
99 Antoin E. Murphy, 'Mountifort Longfield's appointment to the chair of political economy in Trinity College, Dublin, 1832', *Hermathena*, No. 135 (Winter 1983), pp 13–24, at p. 13.
100 R.D.C. Black, *Economic thought and the Irish question, 1817–1870* (London, 1960); Lawrence S. Moss, *Mountifort Longfield: Ireland's first professor of political economy* (Ottawa, IL, 1976).
101 McDowell and Webb, op. cit., p. 169.
102 An Act to facilitate the sale and transfer of encumbered estates in Ireland (1848), 11&12 Vict., c.48.
103 An Act further to facilitate the sale and transfer of encumbered estates in Ireland (1849), 12&13 Vict., c.77, s15.

designed drastically to simplify the transfer of landed property, allowing debtors to sell their estates more easily, and investors in Ireland and England (who had supposedly been shy of entering the legal maze of Irish land purchase) to acquire Irish estates with secure title'.[104] The new court cut through complexities of title and accumulations of mortgages on land by providing a system that would create a new root of title to affected land, and provide a title that would be 'discharged from all encumbrances'.[105] The simple conveyances made by the Commission under its seal came to be known as 'Parliamentary titles'. Lawyers investigating titles may occasionally come across such deeds for which the seal of the Commission was countersigned by Longfield. 'The efficient court for bankrupt landowners to which the famine gave birth helped them or their creditors to reorganise or liquidate what remained of their assets'.[106]

Longfield was appointed a member of a Royal Commission set up in 1854 to inquire into the workings of the EEC, the report of which recommended and led to its replacement by the Landed Estates Court (LEC) a few years later.[107] In subsequent years he published proposals for reforms in property law,[108] and in 1870 contributed a survey of issues on the law of landlord and tenant in Ireland to a publication of the Cobden Club, a body associated with a leading advocate of free trade, Richard Cobden (1804–65).[109]

His career as a judge was uncontroversial, the business of the EEC and in turn of the LEC having something of an administrative nature in tandem with its underlying judicial character. In 1866 however he raised an objection to a proposed restructuring of the court. The LEC had (as the EEC had had) three members, and the government had decided in February 1866 that in the event of a vacancy occurring it would not be filled up. When quite soon afterwards the death of a member, Charles Hargreave, did give rise to a vacancy this policy was made known in reply to a Parliamentary question,[110] and was set out in a Bill published in June. Longfield was then reported as having said in open court that not to replace his late colleague was unjust and tantamount to depriving him of office, 'imposing on him more business than, at his time of life, he could undertake to discharge', that it was unlikely that he could hold much longer the position that he at present filled, and that parties should expedite all cases then before the court to avoid the

104 W.E. Vaughan, *Landlords and tenants in Ireland, 1848–1904* (Dublin, 1984), p. 3.

105 1848 Act, s28; 1849 Act, s27.

106 James S. Donnelly Jr, *The land and the people of nineteenth century Cork: the rural economy and the land question* (London, 1975), p. 72.

107 Report of Royal Commission into Encumbered Estates Court, P.P. 1854–5 xix.527; HC Deb, 3rd series, vol. 140, col. 187 (4 February 1856); an Act to facilitate the sale and transfer of land in Ireland 1858 (21&22 Vict., c.72).

108 'A proposal for an Act to authorise the issue of land debentures in connection with sales made by the Landed Estates Court, with a copy of the proposed Act' (Dublin, 1861); *Law Times*, vol. 36, p. 525 (7 September 1861); 'Plan of "Parliamentary tenant right", applicable equally to all parts of Ireland' (Dublin, 1870).

109 *Systems of land tenure in various countries* (London, 1870), chapter 1 (Ireland), pp 1–91.

110 HC Deb, 3rd series, vol. 182, col. 2076 (26 April 1866).

inconvenience of re-arguing them before a successor judge. In answering a Parliamentary question about those remarks the chief secretary for Ireland acknowledged that there had been correspondence with Longfield on the subject but that he had not intimated an intention of resigning.[111] A salary increase of £500 was proposed as a 'personal augmentation', to which Longfield said that he would not accept any such payment that would not be given to his successor.[112] He was eventually placated and the reduction in the number of judges was duly made, the Act reciting that a vacancy had arisen on the death of Hargreave and that 'it is not expedient, having regard to the state of the judicial business of the court, that such vacancy should be filled up'.[113] He stepped down in December, having 'secured a large retiring pension',[114] and being made a member of the Irish Privy Council. When a further vacancy arose in 1872 the then sole continuing judge, Stephen Woulfe Flanagan, took a different attitude to whether this should be filled.

Longfield lived in Fitzwilliam Square, and left a substantial estate on his death, of £68,492.[115] His recreations included sailing, and he instituted (unsuccessfully) litigation arising out of damage to a yacht owned by him in the course of the Royal Irish Yacht Club regatta at Kingstown [Dun Laoghaire] in 1857.[116] He took a leading part in the administration of the affairs of the Church of Ireland, being a member of the General Synod and of the Representative Church Body, and its finance and legal committees. He was a generous benefactor of Church charities and of the Divinity School in Trinity College, making gifts of some £33,000 in his lifetime.[117]

Charles James Hargreave

Commissioner of Encumbered Estates 1849–58, Judge of the Landed Estates Court 1858–66

Charles James Hargreave (1820–66) was born in Leeds and studied law at University College London, in which he was appointed professor of jurisprudence in 1843. The following year he was called to the Bar at the Inner Temple, of which he subsequently became a bencher, and he was called to the Inner Bar in 1852. He was not called to the Bar in Ireland. He wrote a number of mathematical papers, and was elected a fellow of the Royal Society. A paper on which he had been working before his death was subsequently published privately.[118]

111 HC Deb, 3rd series, vol. 184, cols. 465–7 (15 June 1866).
112 *Law Times*, vol. 41, p. 699 (4 August 1866).
113 Landed Estates Court (Ireland) Act 1866 (29&30 Vict., c.99).
114 *Law Times*, vol. 42, p. 159 (29 December 1866) and p. 222 (19 January 1867).
115 Calendar of Wills and Administrations 1884.
116 *The Cambria* (1858) Ir. Jur. 445; Costello, op. cit., p. 233.
117 *Irish Ecclesiastical Gazette*, 29 November 1884, p. 992; *Irish Times*, 3 January 1885.
118 Charles James Hargreave (edited by George Salmon, FTCD), *An essay on the resolution of algebraic equations* (Dublin, 1866).

After practising at the Bar in England he was appointed in 1849 to be one of the first three members of the Commission for the sale of encumbered estates.[119] The principal commissioner was John Richards (1790–1872), a baron of the Exchequer since 1837, of whom it was later said that any deficiencies in his knowledge of land law were made good by the expertise of Hargreave.[120] The appointment of a member of the English Bar to a judicial position in Ireland (the last such appointment in the nineteenth century) initially was 'considered a dangerous step',[121] but he was later acknowledged as 'an excellent and admirable public officer. He has been always most impartial, punctual, laborious, and eminently courteous, and as a conveyancer, I believe, profoundly learned in that department of his profession'.[122]

Richards (1790–1872) had been called to the Bar in 1811 and was appointed to be one of the judges of the supreme court of Madras, India. He was subsequently appointed successively as solicitor general (1835), attorney general (1836) and a baron of the Exchequer (1837), from which position he retired in 1859. In 1857 he had resigned (but was in effect removed from office) as a member of the Commission.[123] A son, John Henry Richards (1818–1901), was called to the Bar in 1839 and was in due course appointed as county court judge of Co. Waterford and later Co. Mayo.[124] Two of that man's sons also held judicial office, Henry George Richards (1861–1928), a member of the Irish Bar, as a judge of the High Court at Allahabad (now Prayagraj) in the North West Provinces (now Uttar Pradesh) in India, and Whitmore Lionel Richards (1869–1954) as a county court judge in Cheshire.[125]

The Commission initially occupied premises in Henrietta Street, not at the Four Courts. Its accommodation in a house there, and the small stature of Hargreave, drew a sarcastic comment from an improvident peer, Lord Mountcashell (1792–1883), whose extensive lands, including Galgorm Castle and over 48,000 acres in Co. Antrim, were one of the largest estates to be sold through the Commission. He was reported to have said that it was bad enough to have his estates 'confiscated', but that to be 'sold up by a dwarf in a garret' was not to be endured.[126]

119 An Act further to facilitate the sale and transfer of encumbered estates in Ireland, 1849 (12&13 Vict., c.77).
120 *ILT&SJ*, vol. 6, p. 538 (26 October 1872).
121 J.D. Fitzgerald MP (HC Deb, 3rd series, vol. 150, col. 39 (4 May 1858)).
122 James Whiteside (attorney general) (HC Deb, 3rd series, vol. 150, col. 32 (4 May 1858)).
123 Correspondence between lord chancellor of Ireland and Mr Baron Richards, on removal of latter from office as chief commissioner of Encumbered Estates Court, P.P. (1857) (sess.2) (90) xlii.421; *Irish Jurist*, vol. 9 (1856–7), pp 37–44; HC Deb, 3rd series, vol. 144, cols. 217–18 (5 February 1857) and cols. 802–4 (18 February 1857).
124 *ILT&SJ*, vol. 35, p. 259 (8 June 1901).
125 *ILT&SJ*, vol. 62, p. 66 (17 March 1928).
126 A.M. Sullivan, *New Ireland* (London, 1877), vol. 1, p. 297; James S. Donnelly, Jr, 'Landlords and tenants' in W.E. Vaughan (ed.), *A new history of Ireland: V. Ireland under the Union, I: 1801–70* (Oxford, 1989), p. 346.

In 1858 the Commission was reconstituted by statute as the Landed Estates Court,[127] with a wider jurisdiction, and Hargreave continued in office as one of the three judges of the new court. His health was seemingly not strong: it was said in 1858 that he had 'impaired his health by his close attention to his duties as a Commissioner',[128] and subsequent to his death, after a protracted illness, that he was 'a victim of intense study of mathematical problems'.[129] He lived in Fitzwilliam Square, and died (at Bray) in April 1866, and was buried in his home city. The vacancy thus arising in the court was not filled, and the number of its judges was reduced to two by a further amending statute that summer.[130]

Hargreave was responsible for another young Englishman, Richard Denny Urlin (or Urling), moving to Dublin to become an official (an examiner of title) in the Commission. Urlin (1830–1907) was reading for the Bar at the Middle Temple when, in 1850, he met Hargreave at a friend's house

> and found that he was in search of someone qualified to fill a post under him in the Commission ... I was given to understand that in the event of no obstacle being thrown in the way by an individual who had previously been consulted, and in whose hands the matter had to a great extent been placed, the appointment would be offered to me. On the evening of 3 May I was informed that the Commissioner had written to say that the gentleman before mentioned had no son or other person whom he wished to nominate in preference, and that consequently the Commissioner wished for my services at the office in Dublin as soon as I could conveniently go.[131]

He left for Dublin three days later.

Urlin was called to the Irish Bar in 1856, which was not mentioned in a patronising reference made by the *Irish Jurist* when reviewing a manual on the law of trustees that he published in 1857.[132] The author was described as 'a member of the English Bar who, we understand, came some time since over to this country as an attaché of Mr Commissioner Hargreave and holds some employment in connection with his court'.[133] Urlin became a prolific author on legal and church subjects and was elected a member of the Royal Irish Academy, and a posthumously published autobiographical memoir gives insights into the culture of the judiciary and the legal profession in Ireland in the middle of the nineteenth century.

127 An Act to facilitate the sale and transfer of land in Ireland, 1858 (21&22 Vict., c.72).
128 HC Deb, 3rd series, vol. 150, col. 33 (4 May 1858) (Whiteside).
129 R. Denny Urlin, *Journal and reminiscences* (Letchworth, 1909), p. 35.
130 HC Deb, 3rd series, vol. 182, cols. 2075–6 (26 April 1866): an Act to reduce the number of judges in the Landed Estates Court in Ireland 1866 (29&30 Vict., c.99).
131 Urlin, op. cit., p. 24.
132 R. Denny Urling, *A manual of the law relating to the office of Trustee* (Dublin and London, 1857).
133 *Irish Jurist*, vol. 9 (IX), p. 31 (15 February 1857).

William Carey Dobbs

Judge of the Landed Estates Court 1859–69

William Carey Dobbs (1806–69) was a member of a prominent family in Carrickfergus, Co. Antrim. Arthur Dobbs (1689–1765)[134] was responsible for the building a couple of miles north-east of the town between 1750 and 1754 of Castle Dobbs, a substantial Palladian mansion, described by Sir Charles Brett as 'one of the most important buildings in the county'.[135] Members of the family took a leading part in public office in the town and the county, and in local enterprises, over many decades.

Dobbs was educated at Cambridge University (Trinity College, which was also attended by his son Richard Conway Dobbs (1842–1915)), and was called to the Bar in 1833. He took silk in 1858. He stood as a Conservative and was elected MP for Carrickfergus at the general election of April 1857, defeating Francis Macdonogh, then standing as a Liberal, by 560 votes to 383. His contributions to Parliamentary debates were thoughtful, and he showed an independent frame of mind in being one of the few Irish members to speak in favour of a proposal to abolish the office of lord lieutenant of Ireland.[136] He spoke against a bill proposing compensation to be given to tenants for improvements, saying that it infringed the rights of property and that the phrase 'tenant right' was mischievous, because the existing practice in Ulster 'was not a right but a mere custom, and had arisen out of the goodwill that existed between landlord and tenant'.[137]

Shortly before the general election of May 1859 he was appointed a judge of the Landed Estates Court (LEC), succeeding the late Henry Martley, who had died in March. The *Irish Times* approved the appointment, describing him as 'a distinguished scholar and a man of bland and courteous manner', and on his death reference was made to his 'amiable character and his intelligent and cultivated mind'.[138] He had been elected a member of the Royal Irish Academy in 1845.

Conway Edward Dobbs, who had been called to the Bar in 1795, was under-treasurer of King's Inns for many years, into the 1840s. His son, of the same name, was a senior official in the LEC while Dobbs held office, and made presentations on tenant right and the facilitation of land transfer to the Dublin Statistical Society in 1849 and 1853.

Dobbs built a substantial mansion, Ashurst, in the Gothic style in Killiney, Co. Dublin, which a century later was the home of Archbishop McQuaid of Dublin. He died in London in April 1869.

134 See entry on him in the *DIB* (by Eoin Magennis).
135 C.E.B. Brett, *Buildings of County Antrim* (Belfast, 1996), p. 80.
136 HC Deb, 3rd series, vol. 149, cols. 752–3 (25 March 1858).
137 HC Deb, 3rd series, vol. 150, cols. 1806–7 (9 June 1858).
138 *Irish Times*, 5 April 1859; *ILT&SJ*, vol. 3, p. 283 (24 April 1869).

Walter Berwick

Judge of the court of Bankruptcy 1859–68

Walter Berwick (1800–68) exercised part-time judicial functions of one kind or another for over twenty years before his appointment as a judge of the court of Bankruptcy. His mother was a sister of Henry Grattan.[139] After education at Trinity College Dublin he was called to the Bar in 1826, and to the inner Bar in 1840. He was appointed assistant barrister, presiding over the quarter sessions of magistrates, for Co. Waterford in 1835, and was transferred in that capacity to the east Riding of Co. Cork in 1847. On relinquishing that position he commissioned for the city of Cork the handsome Berwick Fountain, the inscription of which records that it was erected by him in 1860 'in remembrance of the great kindness shown to me by all classes in Cork while presiding amongst them for twelve years as chairman of quarter sessions'. It stands in Grand Parade and was refurbished by the city in 2018.

On 12 July 1849 a riot took place at Dolly's Brae, near Castlewellan, Co. Down, and Berwick was appointed as one of commissioners to prepare a report on the affray,[140] one consequence of which was the dismissal of a local magistrate, Lord Roden. The report was tendentiously criticised by Lord Stanley (later the 14th earl of Derby) in opening a debate on the subject in the House of Lords in 1850,[141] and Berwick was warmly defended by Lord Clarendon, the lord lieutenant. He described him as an experienced QC, with an excellent record of conduct of business as assistant barrister, and that he was 'by no means a party man, but a man of thoroughly impartial mind, as well as the most mild and conciliatory disposition'. Five years later, although not then a serjeant, he was nominated in a commission of assize and sat as a judge on circuit.[142]

He was appointed third serjeant a few weeks later in 1855,[143] a bencher of King's Inns in 1856, and second serjeant in 1858. In July 1859 he was appointed as one of the two judges of the court of Bankruptcy, succeeding the late Judge Macan who had died in June.[144] A commentary on his work as bankruptcy judge noted that 'in the discharge of his judicial duties he was remarkable for his desire to give the fullest consideration to everything that could elucidate the case before him, and, even at the expense of time, and much personal trouble, to do justice to all the parties concerned. In truth, his anxiety to act with perfect fairness sometimes partook of an almost morbid character, and gave an air of hesitance to decisions, upon which, in reality, his mind experienced no feelings of doubt'.[145]

139 *Law Times*, vol. 45, p. 350 (5 September 1868).
140 Report into incident at Dolly's Brae, P.P. 1850 [1143], li.331.
141 HL Deb, 3rd series, vol. 108, cols. 886–968 (18 February 1850). Derby's principal critical comments are at cols. 895 and 908–9, and Clarendon's vindication of Berwick is at col. 934.
142 *Law Times*, vol. 24, p. 242 (10 March 1855); A.R. Hart, *A history of the king's serjeants at law in Ireland* (Dublin, 2000), pp 119–20.
143 *Law Times*, vol. 25, p. 50 (28 April 1855).
144 *Irish Times*, 16 June 1859 and 16 July 1859.
145 *ILT&SJ*, vol. 2, p. 478 (29 August 1868).

Berwick died in tragic circumstances in a major train collision on the Euston–Holyhead line at Abergele, near Rhyl, in North Wales in August 1868. This was at the time the worst railway accident yet in Britain, and the remains of the victims, who also included his sister, were buried in a mass grave nearby.

David Lynch

Judge of the court of Bankruptcy 1859–67, of the Landed Estates Court 1867–72

David Lynch (1810–72) was born in Dublin and educated at Trinity College. He was called to the Bar in 1833 and to the Inner Bar in 1849. He joined the Leinster circuit, developed an expertise in mercantile law, and was chairman of quarter sessions in Co. Louth between 1857 and 1859. In the spring of that year he showed some interest in being nominated as Conservative candidate for the Dungarvan constituency in the general election that took place in May,[146] but nothing came of that. The Conservatives, who lost office at the election, had hoped to be able to replace one of the judges of the court of Bankruptcy, Patrick Plunket, who was in poor health.[147] Plunket, the fifth son of the first Lord Plunket, had been called to the Bar in 1820. Lord Naas, the chief secretary, who had wished to 'get Plunket to resign',[148] told Disraeli that he appeared on the bench at the bankruptcy court on the first day of term 'looking like one who had been buried some years in an iceberg – Irish officials never resign'.[149] In the event, after Lord Palmerston had again become prime minister, Plunket died on 31 July,[150] and Lynch was promptly appointed as his successor.[151] He became a bencher of King's Inns in 1860.

At the start of 1867 he was appointed as one of the two judges of the Landed Estates Court,[152] succeeding Mountifort Longfield as part of a complicated scheme to find a judicial place for Stearne Ball Miller QC, MP. The *Irish Times* welcomed this, saying that 'his promotion to the bench of the Landed Estates Court was a step on the part of the government which it would be as well should be oftener followed. A judge in a minor court should have before him the hope of promotion to a higher position'.[153] He became the senior judge of the court on the retirement of W.C. Dobbs in 1869. He died at his home, 27 Merrion Square, after a long illness, in December 1872.

146 *Irish Times*, 28 April 1859.
147 *Irish Times*, 16 June 1859.
148 Naas to Disraeli, 17 May 1859 (Disraeli Papers, B/XX/BD/10).
149 Naas to Disraeli, undated [but late in May] 1859 (Disraeli Papers, B/XX/BD/12).
150 *Irish Times*, 2 August 1859.
151 *Irish Times*, 9 August 1859.
152 *Irish Times*, 12 and 28 January 1867; *Law Times*, vol. 42, p. 159 (29 December 1866) and p. 205 (12 January 1867).
153 *Irish Times*, 19 December 1872.

Thomas Kelly

Judge of the court of Admiralty 1855–67

Thomas Kelly (1798–1876)[154] has the melancholy distinction of being the second judge in the court of Admiralty to be removed from office, following in 1867 in the footsteps of the egregious Jonah Barrington, removed by Parliament in 1830. Kelly was educated at Trinity College,[155] and was called to the Bar in 1823. He came to have extensive experience as an advocate in Admiralty law and in probate, two specialised areas of civil law with their own courts. He was appointed as the Admiralty judge in 1855 following the death of the incumbent, Joseph Stock, having acted as a surrogate or temporary judge in Admiralty in 1850.[156] He had been appointed previously as a divisional (or professional) magistrate in Dublin, and hence was prohibited from practising as a 'barrister in any court',[157] but this was not regarded as applicable to practising as an advocate in the civil law courts.[158] He lived at Clonturk House, Drumcondra.[159]

In the early part of the 1850s the court of Admiralty was at a very low ebb of business, and it sat for only eight days in 1855. The salary of the judge was small (£500, since 1832),[160] reflecting a limited work load. Kelly revitalised the court and reformed its procedures, and generally was given credit for a new level of court and judicial efficiency, which made it a more attractive forum for issues of shipping law.[161] A number of trials, such as those dealing with collisions between vessels, were heard with the assistance of legal assessors who were experts upon the law of the sea. Other cases included applications for the arrest of ships, and disputes on salvage, ship repairs and supplies, freight charges and seamen's wages.

He revived for a short period a practice which had been in abeyance for decades of the Admiralty judge sitting on assize as holder of a commission for the trial of criminal offences that had taken place on the high seas.[162] In 1859 he presided over a trial at the assizes in Cork arising out of a fatal incident that had occurred on a ship that had been bound from London for Havana, following which it had put in at Queenstown [Cobh]. At the trial a charge of manslaughter was substituted for that of murder, and the accused man was found not guilty.[163] The following year he sat at the Co. Mayo assizes, with Christian J, on a case of piracy, telling the grand jury that the proceedings would be the same as if a robbery had taken place on land.[164] In 1861, at a time of general reform or re-statement of the criminal law in

154 Kelly died in 1876 (Kevin Costello, *The court of Admiralty of Ireland, 1575–1893* (Dublin, 2011), p. 212).
155 *Irish Times*, 18 November 1868.
156 Costello, op. cit., p. 206.
157 Dublin Justices' Act 1808 (48 Geo. III, c.140), s14.
158 Costello, op. cit., p. 207.
159 *Irish Law Calendar and Directory 1846*, p. 105.
160 Lord Lieutenant's Salary (Ireland) Act 1832 (2&3 Will. IV, c.116), s1.
161 Costello, op. cit., p. 208, pp 246–50.
162 Costello, pp 267–9.
163 *Irish Times*, 27 July 1859.
164 *Irish Times*, 21 July 1860.

relation to offences against the person, malicious injuries and larceny, offences committed on the high seas were deemed to have been committed upon land and hence became subject to prosecution in the ordinary criminal courts.[165]

Kelly's downfall began in 1864, with a case that he initiated to establish the validity of a will in which he had been left a substantial residuary legacy. Nieces of the deceased woman contested the will, on the grounds that Kelly had exercised undue influence over her to their detriment, and he withdrew his suit, but not before details of some unattractive conduct on his part had been brought out in open court and widely publicised.[166] James Whiteside QC, MP was counsel for the nieces. In 1866 a general admiralty law reform bill was introduced by the attorney general which, if it had become law, would have removed Kelly from office, on full salary.[167] In August 1867 the chief secretary for Ireland, Lord Mayo, told the prime minister, Lord Derby, that Kelly was 'utterly unfit for office – was a party to a case not long ago that was almost fraudulent, who owes money to every practitioner in his court who will trust him, and whose character is of the most questionable kind'.[168]

The Court of Admiralty (Ireland) Act 1867,[169] which became law in August that year, provided (in section 5) that 'the present judge, registrar [and other officers] of the High Court of Admiralty shall cease to hold their respective offices'. No reference was made in public to the (unspecific) grounds of complaint against Kelly referred to by Mayo, extending beyond the 'almost fraudulent' will case, which were the background for that remarkable provision. The justification offered in the House of Lords for his removal from office and for the expressed intention not to re-appoint him was that he would not be technically competent to have charge of the major reforms and extension of jurisdiction of the court that would be effected by the new legislation.[170] Kelly protested at this, and there was some unease at the setting aside of the classical constitutional concept of judges holding office during good behaviour, and of being subject to removal only with the safeguard of adoption of a charge of unfitness by a parliamentary vote. The fact that, whatever about his good name, Kelly would not suffer financial loss may have eased some consciences, however, since section 18 of the Act provided that if the incumbent was not appointed to be the judge of the new or reconstituted admiralty court 'he shall be entitled to receive by way of compensation during his life an annuity equal to his salary at the commencement of this Act'. The salary of the new admiralty judge was fixed at £1,200.

165 Larceny Act 1861 (24&25 Vict., c.96), s115; Offences against the Person Act 1861 (24&25 Vict., c.100), s10.
166 *Irish Times*, 12, 13 and 14 December 1864; *Kelly v Dunbar, Costello*, op. cit., p. 210.
167 HC Deb, 3rd series, vol. 183, col. 281 (1 May 1866). Court of Admiralty (Ireland) Bill, P.P. 1866 (133), i.7.
168 Mayo to Derby, 29 August 1867 (Derby Papers, 155/4).
169 30&31 Vict., c.114 (1867); see generally for this episode Costello, op. cit., pp 208–14.
170 Lord Chelmsford (lord chancellor of Great Britain), HL Deb, 3rd series, vol. 189, col. 1213 (9 August 1867).

Kelly's intended replacement by John F. Townsend was announced in September 1867, and he continued to sit as a judge up to the end of October. On the day before the new Act came into force, when he sat for the last time as a judge, he told the advocates who had assembled in court that he was gratified by the tributes then paid to his courtesy, kindness, ability and diligence but felt 'indignant at the mode in which my retirement has been effected and the almost merciless manner in which I have been treated'.[171]

171 *Irish Times*, 2 November 1867.

CHAPTER SIX

Appointments between 1866 and 1868

FIFTEEN MEN HELD OFFICE IN the superior courts on 1 January 1866, and seven in the other principal courts. At the end of June that year the Liberal government headed by Lord John Russell resigned and, without a general election being held, was replaced by a government of the Conservative party. Lord Derby was prime minister until February 1868, when he was succeeded by Benjamin Disraeli, who left office in December after defeat in a general election.

In July, August and September 1866 five (or one third) of the superior court judges were replaced. A new lord chancellor would have been expected to be appointed in any event, and this transpired to be a sitting judge, Francis Blackburne. The four other vacancies arose from a voluntary resignation (Lefroy), Blackburne's vacation of his existing office as lord justice of appeal, death (Cusack Smith) and resignation owing to ill health (Hayes). Those changes were the prelude to further extensive changes in the composition of the judiciary. In the 30 months of Conservative government more judicial vacancies arose than in any comparable period, and no other government would have such opportunities for the exercise of patronage. Ten members of the Bar were promoted to the judicial bench – the appointments that were made for the initial vacancies, of Whiteside, Brewster, Walsh and George respectively were followed by promotions of Morris, Chatterton, Miller, Harrison, Warren and Townsend, and a number of sitting judges (Blackburne, Christian and Lynch) were transferred to other positions.

All that was in the future however when Lord Derby resumed office as prime minister in the first week of July. The positions that immediately required to be filled were the principal offices of lord chancellor and chief justice of Queen's Bench. The process of appointment turned out in each case to be not at all straightforward.

Abraham Brewster, Joseph Napier

Brewster was Lord Justice of Appeal 1866–7 and Lord Chancellor 1867–8
Napier was Lord Chancellor 1858–9

The career of Abraham Brewster (1796–1874) intersected in July 1866 with the careers of Francis Blackburne (1782–1867) and Joseph Napier (1804–82). What transpired then is most easily understood if their respective situations at the time are considered together, particularly those of Brewster and Napier. The incoming prime minister, Lord Derby, wished to appoint Brewster as lord chancellor, but this plan had to be abandoned after it met very stiff internal party resistance. Blackburne then was offered and accepted the position, and his existing office of lord justice of appeal was intended for (and offered to) Napier. However there was in turn immediate strong opposition to Napier, so he stepped aside and the position was filled by Brewster, who then some eight months later, after another crisis, was appointed to replace Blackburne. Both Napier and Blackburne were angry and frustrated at the turn of events affecting them and how their services were dispensed with by the government.

Brewster, who had joined the Leinster circuit following his call to the Bar in 1819, and had become a QC in 1835, had never before held judicial office. For a short time in 1846 he had been solicitor general, and between 1853 and 1855 he had been attorney general, in each case as a follower of Sir Robert Peel (who had died in 1850) or his political heirs. The Conservative party had split in 1846 and, although as a younger man he had been a 'stout and uncompromising Tory',[1] in the 1850s any association with what remained of the Peelite group denoted that he was out of sympathy with what had become mainstream Conservative thinking. His refusal to continue in office when Lord Aberdeen, prime minister since 1852, was replaced as prime minister by Lord Palmerston, a Whig, in 1855 was later described as 'proof of self-denying fidelity to the Peel party',[2] and his vote for the Liberal candidate in the city of Dublin at a subsequent general election was noted and resented by Conservatives. Blackburne had previously held office as lord chancellor for a period of less than a year in 1852. He was appointed to a permanent judicial position as lord justice of appeal in 1856, or it might be said was re-appointed, since he had previously held two such positions, as master of the rolls and as chief justice of Queen's Bench. In 1858 he declined Lord Derby's invitation to be re-appointed as chancellor and the position was offered to and accepted by Napier.[3]

Napier had been born in Belfast and educated at the Academical Institution there and at Trinity College. He was called to the Bar in 1831, joined the North East circuit, and was called to the Inner Bar in 1844. He was elected as one of the MPs for Dublin University in 1848, and had been attorney general in Derby's first short-lived government in 1852. He was a prominent layman in the Church of Ireland,[4] being known, even to some of his political friends, as 'Holy Joe'.[5]

He published proposals on land law reform, although at heart he believed that it was moral reform that was needed, and that the misery of tenants was due not to the land laws or the greed of landlords but to peasants' fondness for sedition and unwillingness to adopt the working habits and moral outlook of the Ulster Protestant 'yeoman class'.[6]

1 *Dublin University Magazine*, vol. 83 (January–June 1874), p. 652.
2 *Daily Express*, 27 July 1874.
3 A.C. Ewald, *The life and letters of the Rt. Hon. Sir Joseph Napier, Bt* (London, 1892), p. 134.
4 Ewald, *Life*, pp 40, 118, 165–88, 208–39.
5 Thomas Bateson to Naas, 5 August 1866 (Mayo Papers, MS 11,143 (8)). Bateson had been Conservative MP for Co. Londonderry, 1844–57. J.G. Swift MacNeill (1849–1926), who was not a contemporary of Napier, gives a disobliging sketch of him in *What I have seen and heard* (London, 1925), p. 47.
6 Ewald, *Life*, pp 32–3.

He was 'a small man, dark, with a long narrow head, good eyes and a voice slow and solemn, as of one preaching. For some reason, though loved by the clergy, he was suspected, not ill-naturedly, and laughed at, by all contemporary lawyers of all political shades and grades'.[7] In 1858, notwithstanding Napier's unfamiliarity with equity, his appointment was urged on Disraeli by the attorney general, James Whiteside, who was his brother-in-law, once it seemed that Blackburne would prefer to retain his existing office rather than to return as lord chancellor. Whiteside said that a promotion of Napier would be well received by and would encourage important elements in the Conservative party in Ireland, in the university, the Church and the Bar. He thought that Blackburne's attitude was connected with the refusal of the Peelites in England to join the government and that the Conservatives ought to show them that they were not indispensable and that 'we have men who are capable of discharging the duties of this or any other office'.[8] Napier was duly appointed, and enjoyed his period of some sixteen months in office as lord chancellor (see p. 107).

In the spring of 1866, immediately before the events here described, the quotation in a Parliamentary controversy of an observation that Napier had made about the capacity of chief justice Lefroy gave rise to embarrassment. Lord Chelmsford, a former (and future) lord chancellor of Great Britain, quoted a description given by Napier in a letter of Lefroy as 'the best judge we have, although he is very old and not very vigorous for complicated cases. But he always finishes his nisi prius cases sooner than the other chiefs'.[9] That comment led an Irish MP to ask 'Are the parties litigant to abbreviate and simplify their cases before they can, according to Mr Napier, hope to have them properly tried before the chief justice of the Queen's Bench in Ireland?'[10] Three weeks later Chelmsford was obliged to return to the House of Lords to say that he understood that the terms of the letter had given great offence to the presiding judges of the other two courts of common law, the Common Pleas [James H. Monahan] and the Exchequer [David R. Pigot], 'as it was supposed that they conveyed a disparaging comparison with them. Mr Napier had given them the strongest assurance that he had no such intention; but they would not be satisfied unless that explanation were given to their Lordships' House. He (Lord Chelmsford) therefore desired to state that Mr Napier had merely wished to convey his strong sense of the efficiency of the lord chief justice'.[11]

In early July rumours of Derby's intention to appoint Brewster as lord chancellor were met by what Derby subsequently described to Grey, the Queen's private secretary, as 'the great hostility of the strong Protestant party'.[12] Whiteside, whose 'political friends raised a violent clamour against the nomination',[13] told

7 R. Denny Urlin, *Journal and reminiscences* (Letchworth, 1909), p. 134.
8 Whiteside to Disraeli, undated [late February] 1858 (Disraeli Papers, B/XXI/W/318).
9 HL Deb, 3rd series, vol. 182, col. 1634 (19 April 1866).
10 J.F. Maguire, Liberal MP for Cork City, HC Deb, 3rd series, vol. 183, col. 790 (11 May 1866).
11 HL Deb, 3rd series, vol. 183, cols. 744–5 (11 May 1866).
12 Derby to Grey, 25 March 1867 (Royal Archives, VIC RA A35/52, in Hogan, 'Vacancies', p. 227).
13 *Law Times*, vol. 41, p. 710 (11 August 1866).

Edward Taylor, the Conservative chief whip,[14] that the appointment of Brewster would be damaging to 'judicial tone and purity in Ireland',[15] and that he would not himself accept judicial office if it went through. He told Derby that 'the rumoured arrangement would be fatal to the Conservative party in Ireland'.[16] Napier expressed his views to Derby at greater length, saying that it would not be possible to make a selection 'more likely to cool our friends and heat our enemies than that of Mr Brewster. He has been our most insidious and consistent opponent from 1852 to the present time. His money, his influence, his votes have been freely given to our inveterate opponents' and party loyalty would be undermined. He added that when in 1859 he had proposed to Lord Eglinton [then the lord lieutenant] to make Mr Brewster a puisne judge he had been told that this could not be done without giving intolerable offence to party supporters.[17]

Lord Naas, Derby's principal Irish adviser, told him that he was

> surprised at the storm that the rumour of Brewster's appointment has raised among our Irish political friends … if Taylor ascertains that Brewster's appointment to the chancellorship would alienate a considerable number of our Irish friends I do not think that you could venture to offer it to him. For the good of the public service and for the transaction of business I am of opinion that no arrangement would be so desirable … but political ties must be respected and an appointment distasteful to the majority of our supporters would be a bad thing to start with.[18]

Derby then turned to Blackburne, explaining to the Queen that the plan was for him to 'temporarily fill that office (though an old man he is a consummate lawyer). Lord Derby was very desirous of introducing Mr Brewster but the tide of political feeling was so strongly against him that he dare not attempt it at present. The temporary possession of the Great Seal by lord justice Blackburne may give time for these feelings to subside and facilitate a future fusion of parties'.[19] The same day Derby wrote to Blackburne asking him to 'consent again to take (if only for a short time) the duties of lord chancellor'. In also asking Cairns, who was then passing through Dublin after his re-election as MP for Belfast, to use his good offices to finalise the arrangement, Derby referred to Blackburne accepting office temporarily: 'a delay of a few months would serve to cool down the present excitement, and according to his conduct in the meantime we could judge whether to risk Brewster's co-operation or not'.[20]

14 Col. T.E. Taylor (1811–83) was the Conservative MP for Co. Dublin between 1841 and 1883 and was chief whip of the Conservative party between 1860 and 1868.
15 Whiteside to Taylor, undated [early July 1866] (Mayo Papers, MS 11,143(3)).
16 Whiteside to Derby, 4 July 1866 (Derby Papers, 122/8).
17 Napier to Derby, undated but early July 1866 (Derby Papers, 112).
18 Naas to Derby, 8 July 1866 (Derby Papers, 155/2).
19 Derby to the Queen, 12 July 1866 (Derby Papers, 191/2, p. 82).
20 Derby to Cairns, 12 July 1866 (Derby Papers, 191/1, p. 85).

On 13 July Blackburne accepted the appointment as lord chancellor, and the next day Whiteside accepted appointment as chief justice of Queen's Bench, declaring the other judicial arrangements to be 'satisfactory and expedient'.[21] Lord Naas was a strong advocate for Brewster and had suggested him as Blackburne's successor,[22] but in extending the invitation to Blackburne Derby had indicated his intention to offer that position to Napier.[23] Napier was prepared to fill the now vacant position of lord justice of appeal and, as Derby told Disraeli, 'the whole arrangement is of his concoction'.[24]

A controversy immediately arose as to whether Napier's hearing was good enough to enable him to properly carry out judicial functions, and Derby, writing 'as a friend and anxious for your reputation', asked him to consider 'carefully and conscientiously whether you would be competent to fulfil its duties with satisfaction to yourself and the public'.[25] Napier told him that while his hearing might not always have picked up all that was said in court this would not be of significance in the Court of Chancery Appeal,[26] and gave a more expansive account to his friend Cairns:

> In 1858–59 I never felt the smallest difficulty in the court of appeal. Of all departments of duty it was that in which I had the greatest facility, the cases being printed beforehand, and the arguments seldom if ever colloquial. I like work. I have no desire to eat the bread of idleness.[27] The duties of the court are light and I should discharge them with the greatest diligence. My hearing is not worse than it has been for nearly thirty years and it never was suggested that any suitor suffered by my infirmity.[28]

He told another correspondent at the time that he was at least as competent then as he had been seven or eight years previously, and that the duties in the court 'do not occupy one month of any year'.[29]

Napier told Derby that he was being 'most malignantly and unscrupulously assailed' by a section of his own party, but relied upon 'the sound opinion of upright and intelligent men'[30] and, as Blackburne was to do eight months later,

21 Blackburne to Derby, 13 July 1866 (Derby Papers, 920 DER (14), 122/7B); Derby to Naas, 13 July 1866 (Mayo Papers, MS 11,144); Whiteside to Derby, 14 July 1866 (Derby Papers 920 DER (14), 154/6A).
22 Naas to Derby, [undated but in July] 1866 (Derby Papers, 155/2).
23 Derby to Naas, 13 July 1866 (Mayo Papers, MS 11,144).
24 Derby to Disraeli, undated [but most likely 12 July 1866] (Disraeli Papers, B/XX/5/395). See also Derby to Cairns, 12 July 1866 (Derby Papers, 191/5, p. 85).
25 Derby to Napier, 16 July 1866 (Derby Papers, 191/2).
26 Napier to Derby, 17 July 1866 (Derby Papers, 112).
27 Proverbs 31:27.
28 Napier to Cairns, 20 July 1866 (Cairns Papers (TNAUK), PRO 30/51/11/8).
29 Napier to George Hamilton, undated but mid-July 1866, forwarded by Hamilton to Naas, 25 July 1866 (Derby Papers, 155/2).
30 Napier to Derby, 20 July 1866 (Derby Papers, 112).

initially furnished Derby with a comforting medical report. Not until 28 July did he accept persuasion and advice from friends, which included the offer of a baronetcy, that he should not take up the position.[31] Blackburne initially, according to Napier, 'quite approved of my acceptance of your kind offer and expressed to others the pleasure he felt in having me for his judicial colleague', but soon thought that his stepping aside was necessary and did him credit.[32] Brewster was then appointed as the lord justice of appeal. In 1868 Napier was appointed as a member of the Judicial Committee of the Privy Council in London, and thereafter was attentive to his duties there until failing health rendered him unable to travel to London, and early in 1881 he acceded to a request to resign his position.[33] He died in 1882, and a portrait by Thomas Bridgford (exhibited at the Royal Hibernian Academy in 1846) was presented to the King's Inns in 1884.[34] A portrait in his robes as lord chancellor, by Stephen Catterson Smith the elder, was exhibited at the Royal Hibernian Academy in 1860 and is in the collection of Trinity College.[35]

In early March 1867 Derby took steps to replace Blackburne with Brewster. The lord chancellor had been indisposed for some days through an acute attack of gout, a complaint with which Derby would have had sympathy, since he suffered badly from that condition himself, and his own poor health led to his resignation as prime minister in February 1868.[36] Blackburne had been isolated at his home, Rathfarnham Castle, during the alarms and rumours and excitement of an incoherent and leaderless rising by Fenians on 5 and 6 March, in which some small-scale military manoeuvres took place in adjoining districts in Co. Dublin, at Stepaside, Glencullen and Tallaght. Naas worked to bring about Blackburne's resignation as a 'very difficult and delicate matter' with the assistance of an old friend of the chancellor, Judge Keatinge. He told Derby that whatever 'our ultra friends' might think Brewster 'is really the only man we could have on the Woolsack. His experience and sagacity will be of the greatest use to us on all matters of administration, especially with reference to the forthcoming trials'.[37]

Blackburne wrote to Derby on 12 March to say that he had accepted the office of lord chancellor of Ireland at his request 'under very peculiar circumstances, and that he was willing to resign that High Office into the hand from which I received it' if Derby considered that this would be conducive to the interests of the party

31 Napier to Derby, 28 July 1866 (Derby Papers, 155/2); HC Deb, 3rd series, vol. 184, col. 1658 (30 July 1866).
32 Napier to Derby, 20 July 1866 (Derby Papers, 112); Blackburne to Naas, 4 August 1866 (Mayo Papers, MS 11,143 (8)).
33 Spencer to Napier, 11 January 1881 (Ewald, op. cit., p. 324); Spencer to O'Hagan, undated [January 1881] (O'Hagan Papers, D2777/8/245).
34 Wanda Ryan-Smolin, *King's Inns portraits* (Dublin, 1992), p. 51.
35 Anne Crookshank and David Webb, *Paintings and sculptures in Trinity College* (Dublin, 1990), p. 101.
36 Robert Adams MD to Blackburne, 12 March 1867 (Derby Papers, 920 DER, 122/8); Angus Hawkins, op. cit., pp 363–5.
37 Naas to Derby, 12 March 1867 (Derby Papers, 155/3).

he led and calculated to promote the peace and prosperity of this country.[38] However the letter also said that his eldest son who was carrying the letter to London would be able to communicate more fully Blackburne's own views and wishes on the subject, and what Derby was told led him to pause, 'greatly embarrassed [by it being] quite clear that if Blackburne is removed he will consider himself, and his friends will consider him, as "turned out" to make way for Brewster, [an outcome] which will certainly add to the dissatisfaction of the Ultra party'.[39] A week later Derby proceeded to accept the resignation, expressing himself as being compelled to do so by the advice of Lord Naas, who 'has represented to me in such strong terms the painful position in which the lord lieutenant is placed in these most critical times by the absence of a confidential legal counsellor with whom he may at any moment communicate upon matters of pressing urgency – the attorney and solicitor general being both required in London, or if in Dublin, overwhelmed with business'.[40]

Brewster was then appointed. His career on the bench, which extended from July 1866 to December 1868, when he retired from office after the Conservatives had lost a general election, was not seen as distinguished. An obituary noted that 'like many other eminent advocates [his] judicial career was scarcely in keeping with his previous reputation, and there are not in print more than 3 or 4 judgments delivered by him, either in the appellate court or in the court of Chancery. In truth his busy forensic life had unfitted him for the cool and calm atmosphere of the judicial bench'.[41] His years as a leader of the Bar thus did not seem to have prepared him for the exercise in calmness of a judicial function. In 1867 the *Irish Law Times* had expressed some apprehension about his temperament, although still confident that 'there will be no ground to apprehend that the advantages to be derived by the public from ability of the highest order, vast experience and profound learning shall be marred by anything resembling an exhibition of impatience during the progress of a cause'.[42] A contemporary historian remarked however that 'the irritable temper of Brewster on the bench is not recorded by the reporters, [and] whether his judicial career was in keeping with his previous reputation it is for those who practised before him to say'.[43]

When the Conservatives won the next general election, in February 1874, it was initially reported that he had been offered and had accepted the lord chancellorship again[44] but no such appointment was made. On his death only a few months later it was said (perhaps in light of the peerage that had been conferred in 1870 on Lord O'Hagan, his successor in office as lord chancellor) that he had

38 Blackburne to Derby, 12 March 1867 (Derby Papers, 122/8).
39 Derby to Naas, 13 March 1867 (Mayo Papers, MS 11,150).
40 Derby to Blackburne, 20 March 1867 (Edward Blackburne, op. cit., p. 311).
41 *The Times*, 28 July 1874.
42 *ILT&SJ*, vol. 1, p. 150 (30 March 1867).
43 O.J. Burke, *The history of the lord chancellors of Ireland from 1186 to 1874* (Dublin, 1879), pp 311, 314.
44 *ILT&SJ*, vol. 8, p. 99 (28 February 1874).

'made it a condition that if he again accepted the office it should be accompanied by a peerage'.[45] Disraeli, the new prime minister, balked at such a condition, in the same way that Derby had not been prepared to meet post-retirement expectations for honours to be granted to Lefroy and Blackburne.

Brewster lived at 26 Merrion Square. He 'found time for a genial hospitality [and] his dinner parties were of exceptional agreeability'.[46] He was a very wealthy man, his personal estate being stated to amount to less than £140,000, carrying an implication that it was in excess of, say, £130,000. A portrait was commissioned by the benchers of King's Inns in the year of his death.[47]

James Whiteside

Chief Justice of Queen's Bench 1866–76

James Whiteside (1804–76) was chief justice of Queen's Bench for ten years, between July 1866 and November 1876. His father was the rector of Delgany, Co. Wicklow. He attended Trinity College 'where his career was respectable rather than brilliant'.[48] He entered King's Inns in 1821, and after law studies in London was called to the Bar in 1830, becoming a QC in 1841. He was ambitious, 'a man resolved to rise in the world', as he said in a letter that early in his career he wrote to a friend: 'I rise before 6 – work in my study till half past 10 then hurry to court. I work within the court and in the library till half past 4 then home, wash, take a little walk and at the desk at 7 or ½ past. Sundays also are my very busy days … No one but a professional man can feel and understand the anxiety, the toll, the sleepless nights and laborious days which inevitably attend upon early business at the bar'.[49] He told that friend also that having initially joined the Connaught circuit he now intended to move to the North East circuit, as he had made good connections in Belfast and his prospects there were good.[50]

He married Rosetta Napier, whose brother Joseph was a colleague at the Bar and later in Parliament. He acted as defence counsel for Charles Gavan Duffy on his trial (with Daniel O'Connell, the principal defendant, and others) for seditious conspiracy in 1844, and for William Smith O'Brien on his trial for high treason in 1848, defendants for whose political views he would have had no sympathy. He withdrew from professional life for a time in his early 40s (the late 1840s), during which he travelled to Rome. 'Business flowed in too rapidly upon Mr Whiteside. His health gave way and for two years he was obliged to seek the repose of a southern climate'.[51]

45 *ILT&SJ*, vol. 8, p. 423 (1 August 1874).
46 *Dublin University Magazine*, vol. 83 (January–June 1874), p. 654.
47 Wanda Ryan-Smolin, *King's Inns portraits* (Dublin, 1992), p. 10.
48 *ILT&SJ*, vol. 10, p. 617 (2 December 1876).
49 Whiteside to W. Loader, 28 June 1833 (Whiteside Papers (NLI), MS 15733).
50 See also George Hill Smith, *The North East Bar* (Belfast, 1909), p. 64.
51 Oliver J. Burke, *Anecdotes of the Connaught circuit* (Dublin, 1885), p. 232.

He entered Parliament in 1851 as the Conservative MP for Enniskillen. He was appointed solicitor general in a short-lived government (February to December 1852) led by Lord Derby. When introducing the Common Law Procedure (Ireland) Bill, which became law later that year, he described the system of 'costly and utterly abortive' pleading in the superior courts that it was intended to replace:

> we had the writ, which gives the defendant no information; and the appearance which gives as little to the plaintiff; then the plaintiff's declaration, which must be adapted to a particular form of action, told the defendant nothing; and, next, the plea of the general issue by the defendant told the plaintiff nothing; and other proceedings followed which left the parties as little acquainted with the case as if there had been no pleadings at all.[52]

He was attorney general in Derby's second government (from February 1858 to June 1859), and introduced the legislation converting the Encumbered Estates Commission into the Landed Estates Court.[53]

J.R. O'Flanagan, whose history of the Irish Bar was published in 1879, devoted the best part of five pages to an account of Whiteside's eloquence, saying that he 'was all effervescence, reminding one of a mountain torrent after rain, foaming, seething, boiling, fuming, overrunning with power and impetuosity ... His manner was perfectly dramatic, and every art and effort that his abilities enabled him to use were enlisted in the cause of his client'.[54] The *Irish Law Times* was similarly effusive; 'matchless his rhetoric, brilliant his dialectic power, impressive and impassioned his language; every variety of forensic eloquence was at his command – humour, pathos, passion, stern sarcasm, seething invective, wit in its raciest vein, fancy in its most graceful sallies'.[55]

Whiteside had a handsome appearance, with 'a tall sinewy frame, a large massive head, his eager earnest features working with energy, a satirical smile playing around his mouth'.[56] Rather less flatteringly, an official in the Landed Estates Court described him as 'tall, pasty-faced and arrogant, with much humour in manner as well as in facial expression ... He was certainly a fine and captivating speaker, that is as to oratorical power; he was not a lawyer, or a logician or a statesman. I never saw an opinion [on title] by Whiteside and probably he was never asked for one'.[57]

The very facility for oratory that contributed to his success at the Bar had its uses also at Westminster, but may have helped to create the impression that he was

52 HC Deb, 3rd series, vol. 123, col. 257 (19 November 1852).
53 An Act to facilitate the sale and transfer of land in Ireland 1858 (21&22 Vict., c.22).
54 J.R. O'Flanagan, *The Irish Bar; comprising anecdotes, bon-mots and biographical sketches of the Bench and Bar of Ireland* (London, 1879), pp 401–5.
55 *ILT&SJ*, vol. 10, p. 618 (2 December 1876).
56 O'Flanagan, op. cit., p. 401.
57 R. Denny Urlin, *Journal and reminiscences* (Letchworth, 1909), p. 134.

impetuous and volatile. Lord Derby remarked in 1852 that he carried 'more sail than ballast'.[58] A friend wrote of him that 'when there was battle expected in the House [of Commons] Lord Derby would say to him "Now, Whiteside, where's your shillelagh"'.[59] He had an arm's length relationship with Disraeli, the Conservative leader in the House of Commons, who was something of a moderniser within the party. In the 1850s and 1860s the Irish Conservatives achieved considerable electoral success, but since these decades were a time of Whig or Liberal dominance in the United Kingdom as a whole the Tories were seldom in office, and then as a minority government.

Whiteside was 'authentically reactionary' in the words of a leading scholar of the electoral history of the period,[60] being associated with the more sectarian or narrow evangelical elements in the Conservative party, little concerned with any broadening of its base of support. In the 1850s he sought to promote legislation for state inspection of monasteries and convents, asserting that it was necessary to regulate and prevent undue influence in the disposal of any substantial property by a monk or nun to such an institution.[61] He spoke of the blessings of the Reformation in a lecture to the Dublin Young Men's Christian Association, referring to

> the wonderful part it had in awakening the human mind from the slumber of ages. It quickened the faculties of men, stimulated inquiry, gave an impetus to science, called forth the exertions of genius, stirred up the powers of the human intellect. It has been the cause of our freedom; to it we must ascribe our happiness in this life; to it we must ascribe the knowledge of the Book which is the foundation of all our hopes in the life to come.[62]

The *Times* referred in the early 1870s to 'that peculiar spirit of illiberality and distrust of the Irish race which is the distinctive feature of Irish Toryism'.[63] Whiteside opposed one of the initial attempts to abolish the obligation for King's Inns students to keep terms at one of the inns of court in London (it was eventually abolished in 1885), saying that 'no complaint has been made of that law. It had the sanction of antiquity'.[64]

A third period of minority Conservative government began in July 1866. The chief justice of Queen's Bench, Thomas Lefroy (1776–1869), was aged 90, and had been waiting for the Conservatives to re-enter office before he would resign. In the parliamentary debate on 11 May 1866 on his capacity to continue in office two

58 Derby to Eglinton, 1 June 1852 (Eglinton Papers (National Archives of Scotland), GD/3/5/53); Andrew Shields, *The Irish Conservative party, 1852–1868* (Dublin, 2007), p. 18.
59 Percy FitzGerald, *Memories of an author* (London, 1895), p. 82.
60 K. Theodore Hoppen, *Elections, politics and society in Ireland, 1832–1885* (Oxford, 1984), p. 279.
61 Shields, *Irish Conservative party*, p. 165.
62 James Whiteside, *The city of Rome and its vicissitudes: a lecture* (Dublin, 1861), p. 32.
63 *The Times*, 4 March 1875.
64 HC Deb, 3rd series, vol. 155, col. 81 (19 July 1859).

Irish Liberal MPs made pointed references to Whiteside and as to whether and how he could plausibly 'explain or justify' the judge's continuance in office. One had no doubt but that he 'would rise and attempt to cast the veil of his eloquence over these receding shadows of a past generation … [but] he would remind the right hon. gentleman that not even his vigorous eloquence could alter facts, and his large experience must have taught him how difficult it was to convince a jury when a client had no case'.[65]

Lefroy's son Anthony shared the Parliamentary representation of Dublin University with Whiteside (who had changed to that constituency in 1859), and liaised with Derby over the timing of his father's resignation.[66] Ordinarily the position of lord chancellor was the only judicial position that would be available to be filled by an incoming government, but Lefroy's retirement created another vacancy. Whiteside's divisive political profile, coupled with a lack of any background in Chancery law, rendered him unsuitable for the position of chancellor, generally regarded as the greatest (certainly the most remunerative) judicial prize. Derby wished to appoint Abraham Brewster, of whose ability and judgment he had a high opinion, although he was not a party figure. The Conservative lawyers had a strong view that legal positions should be given to those who 'had been fighting the Conservative battle with untiring zeal and indomitable perseverance, when the cause was a losing one and was thought hopeless',[67] and not to an outsider such as Brewster.

Derby and Disraeli thought that if Brewster was appointed lord chancellor a party schism would develop, as Whiteside 'would not accept anything under Brewster'.[68] Derby told the Queen that he was 'very desirous of introducing Mr Brewster but the tide of political feeling was so strong against him that he dare not attempt it at present'.[69] He had been told by Lord Naas, his principal Irish adviser, that Whiteside regarded himself as having the first claim to the position if Napier (lord chancellor in the 1858–9 Conservative government) was not appointed.[70] A complicated scheme was devised under which the elderly Francis Blackburne (1782–1867), who had been chancellor in the 1852 government, would retire from his present position as lord justice of appeal and be re-appointed as chancellor; 'all parties will agree to serve under him. Napier would take his place as lord justice of appeal and would join in urging Whiteside to take the chief justiceship, which indeed he would have no pretext for refusing. A delay of a few months would serve to cool down the present excitement'.[71] This proposal soothed Whiteside, who told Derby when accepting the position offered that 'the other arrangements made by

65 HC Deb, 3rd series, vol. 183, cols. 778–812 (11 May 1866).
66 See generally Hogan, 'Vacancies', pp 211–30.
67 Napier to Derby, undated (early July 1866) (Derby Papers, 112).
68 Derby to Disraeli, 12 July 1866 (Disraeli Papers, B/XX/5/396).
69 Derby to the Queen, 12 July 1866 (Derby Papers, 191/1, p. 82).
70 Naas to Derby, 8 July 1866 (Derby Papers, 155/2).
71 Derby to Cairns, 12 July 1866 (Derby Papers, 12 July 1866, 191/1, p. 85). See also Derby to Disraeli, 12 July 1866 (Disraeli Papers, B/XX/5/395).

your Lordship are satisfactory and expedient. I regret that your Lordship should have had so much trouble about this appointment of mine. I feel relieved that all your trouble respecting my position has now ended'.[72]

The overall scheme fell apart a matter of days later (but after Whiteside's appointment) on the grounds of Napier's deafness (see p. 195), and it was Brewster who was appointed as the new lord justice of appeal at the end of July. In March 1867 Blackburne resigned, under some pressure from Derby (and to the indignation of his family) after the Fenian Rising, having been isolated at his home at Rathfarnham Castle, Co. Dublin, for a week during the crisis.[73] Brewster was then appointed as lord chancellor, leading to Whiteside falling into a 'tempestuous state of rage'.[74] Naas was sanguine about this, noting to Abercorn, the lord lieutenant, that 'Whiteside will be in a fury. I hope that it will not dispose him to let off the Fenian prisoners'.[75]

Whiteside's political friends thus elected on two occasions not to offer him the highest judicial office in the country, although he was appointed to the highest permanent such office, chief justice of Queen's Bench. It was observed on his death that 'the office which he filled and which if it had fallen fairly to him, in the lottery of party and had no disparagement in the claim, might have been accepted with gratitude as one of the highest distinction. The slight which this proceeding seemed to convey weighed upon his sensitive pride and he never appeared to be quite at ease in his position as chief justice'.[76] He made no secret of his opposition to many of the judicial reforms that were proposed in and after 1874 and enacted in 1877.

His health was the subject of 'alarming rumours' in the summer of 1876,[77] which the *Irish Law Times* was gratified to be able to report were 'greatly exaggerated', nothing more than a heavy cold.[78] However a couple of months later there were fresh rumours that he was 'likely soon to retire from the Bench of which he is such a distinguished ornament [and] that he will be elevated to the peerage',[79] and speculation began as to who might succeed him. He died in Brighton, where he had gone on medical advice, on 25 November that year. The funeral cortege from his home in Mountjoy Square proceeded down Sackville [now O'Connell] Street and was one of the longest seen for many years.[80] He is buried in Mount Jerome cemetery, an earlier plan for interment in St Patrick's cathedral having been abandoned since the statutes governing the cathedral prohibited burial within its precincts.[81]

72 Whiteside to Derby, 14 July 1866 (Derby Papers, 154/6A).
73 Edward Blackburne, *Life of Francis Blackburne* (London, 1874), pp 299–320.
74 FitzGerald, op. cit., p. 82.
75 Naas to Abercorn, 24 March 1867 (Abercorn Papers (PRONI), D623/A/304/11).
76 *The Times*, 27 November 1876.
77 *Irish Times*, 13 July 1876.
78 *ILT&SJ*, vol. 10, p. 410 (15 July 1876).
79 *ILT&SJ*, vol. 10, p. 506 (16 September 1876).
80 *ILT&SJ*, vol. 10, p. 631 (9 December 1876).
81 *Irish Times*, 1 December 1876.

Two statues of him were erected in 1880, one in the cathedral representing him in a seated position the plinth of which states that he was chief justice and 'a brilliant advocate and orator'. The second showing him in 'the stance of an orator [which] made a single impression of rigid authority'[82] was placed in the Round Hall of the Four Courts, after a committee chaired by the lord chancellor was established with judicial support soon after his death to solicit subscriptions for a suitable memorial.[83] This, along with so much else, was destroyed in the explosion and burning of the building in June 1922.

It is Whiteside's reputation for oratory rather than for jurisprudence that survives. The *Irish Law Times* in its obituary referred to the fact that it was as an orator above all that he would be remembered, remarking that he 'can hardly be said to have been a great judge or a profound lawyer', and while reaching sound conclusions 'his judgments on the whole are not such as to command a lofty legal estimate. That which will perhaps be found to display his powers at their best, however open to controversy may be the decision at which he arrived, appears to us to be his judgment in *O'Keeffe v Cardinal Cullen*'.[84] That was a minority judgment given by him as a member of the full court of Queen's Bench arising out of a suit for libel taken by the parish priest of Callan, Co. Kilkenny, against the cardinal. Whiteside had presided over the trial, in which (on his direction) the jury found for O'Keeffe, but had awarded him a farthing in damages. The majority in the court set aside the verdict and directed a new trial, Whiteside unsurprisingly dissenting. In 1872 a common law action for damages for assault and battery had been brought against the lord lieutenant and the police arising out of the ban on a 'monster meeting to advocate the release of the Irish political prisoners' to be held in the Phoenix Park. The Queen's Bench (Whiteside CJ, O'Brien and Fitzgerald JJ) held, following the decision in *Luby v Lord Wodehouse*,[85] that an action could not be maintained against the lord lieutenant for any act done by him in his official or political capacity.[86]

John Edward Walsh

Master of the Rolls 1866–9

John Edward Walsh (1816–69) was better known as a writer than as a lawyer both in the initial stages of his legal career and after a short judicial career which lasted only three years. He was called to the Bar in 1839, and took silk in 1857. His obituary in the *Irish Law Times*, having noted that 'he was for some years without practice', remarked that his career 'affords a striking illustration of the legitimate

82 C.P. Curran, 'Figures in the Hall' in Caroline Costello (ed.), *The Four Courts: 200 years* (Dublin, 1996), pp 174–5 (originally published in *Record of the centenary of the charter of the Incorporated Law Society of Ireland, 1852–1952* (Dublin, 1953)).
83 *ILT&SJ*, vol. 10, p. 652 (23 December 1876); *Irish Times*, 23 December 1876.
84 *ILT&SJ*, vol. 10, p. 618 (2 December 1876); 7 ILTR 100 (1873).
85 17 IR CL Rep. 618 (1865).
86 *Sullivan v Earl Spencer*, IR 6 CL 173 (1872).

success which, sooner or later, awaits ability, industry and probity'.[87] The *Dublin University Magazine* in 1833 had warned that it was 'the general and almost natural course of events for a man of fair talents and competent knowledge to remain seven or ten years without holding a brief. What more painful than the struggle to preserve a gentlemanly appearance on scanty means'.[88] He spent these early years in the classic pursuits of the under-employed members of the Bar at the time, of reporting cases and writing law books. In 1841 he edited a 1,200 page compendium, with Richard Nun BL, of the law relating to magistrates, which was re-issued in 1842 and 1844.[89] In 1850 he wrote a shorter (300 page) guide to new legislation on the subject.[90]

He contributed articles to the *Dublin University Magazine* on subjects of more general or literary interest, a collection of which was later issued under the title of *Sketches of Ireland sixty years ago*. These were a 'racy and amusing account of duellists, gamblers, highwaymen and characters from the Liberties in pre-union Ireland'.[91] The book had enduring popularity, 'new and revised' editions being published after the author's death as *Ireland ninety years ago* (1876) and then *120 years ago* (1911), and in 1979 as *Rakes and ruffians; the underworld of Georgian Dublin*. In the introductory pages, written in 1847, Walsh set out a vision of the benefits of the Anglicisation of Ireland:

> The character of Ireland sixty or seventy years ago was an anomaly in the moral world. Though united to England for seven centuries, and every effort made during that period to assimilate the people to its sober, prudent and thinking neighbours, little progress seems to have been made in ingrafting their habits, manners and modes of thinking on the wild Irish stock … No person who knows the state of Ireland at the present day, and compares it with Ireland sixty years ago, can fail to be struck with her great improvement. Years of peace have taught us to prefer quiet and industry to violence and scheming … as we mix with our neighbours the rough prominences which distinguished our national character are rubbing off; fights in our streets, gambling upon coffins, bucks, bullies, rapparees, duelling, drunkenness, bull-baiting, idleness, abduction clubs and a thousand other degrading peculiarities which marked the higher as well as the lower classes have disappeared; and the propriety and decency, peace and good order, which have long been the boast of our English neighbours, have begun to form a part of our character also. The contrast between what we are and what we

87 *ILT&SJ*, vol. 3, p. 652 (23 October 1869).
88 'The Irish Bar as it was and as it is', *Dublin University Magazine*, vol. 1 (January to June 1833), p. 48.
89 *The powers and duties of the justices of the peace in Ireland and of constables as connected therewith, with an appendix of statutes and forms* (Dublin, 1841).
90 'The statutes 12&13 Vict., c.69, .70 and .16, relating to the duties of justices of the peace, out of quarter sessions and the protection of justices of the peace' (Dublin, 1850).
91 As described in the entry on Walsh in the *DIB* (by Bridget Hourican).

> were – between our present state of social peace, advancing enterprise and regular habits, and the brutal violence, barbarism and recklessness, from which we have emerged ought to encourage a hope of corresponding improvement for the future. And improve we will; notwithstanding the gloom which at present overspreads us, the forebodings of alarmists, or the abuse with which, in some quarters, Ireland and the Irish of all classes are so abundantly assailed.[92]

In 1847, when widespread gloom and alarm at the devastation of the famine would hardly have been surprising, the author addressed subjects somewhat removed from that final optimistic or improving note, such as Abduction, Duelling, Drunkenness and Gambling, to list a few of the chapter headings. A few years later he said of the squirearchy that 'their pride was only equalled by their ignorance and uselessness'. This was in a book on one of the most outrageous and feckless members of that class, George Robert ('Fighting') FitzGerald (*c.*1748–86), who was convicted (and hanged) for conspiracy to murder his father's attorney.[93]

One way or another Walsh's legal career picked up in the 1850s, and he took silk in 1857. In 1859 he was appointed as a Crown prosecutor at Green Street by the attorney general, James Whiteside. On 26 June 1866 Lord John Russell, the Liberal leader, resigned as prime minister, and the next day Lord Derby was asked by the Queen to form a government. On that day Walsh took steps to circulate voters in Dublin University, saying that 'a vacancy in the representation of the University is shortly expected upon the promotion and consequent retirement of one of the present representatives', although the arrangements for Derby to make an appointment of that representative, Whiteside, to a judicial position transpired to be complicated. Walsh said that in offering himself as a candidate he would endeavour to 'maintain my character as a consistent Conservative and steady advocate of the Established Church. I trust I may hope for your support. When the time comes I will advise you in more detail'.[94] In the event he was the only candidate, and was declared elected on 30 July, a few days after he had been appointed attorney general.

His Parliamentary career was, as he acknowledged himself, 'so brief that it seems almost absurd to refer to it',[95] and he never spoke in the House of Commons. His prospects were changed suddenly by the death on 13 August of the master of the rolls, Sir Thomas Cusack Smith (1795–1866). His succession to that position was not assured, and Derby's view as expressed to Naas was that 'the recently appointed attorney general will hardly push forward his claim to the vacant office,

92 John Edward Walsh, *Sketches of Ireland sixty years ago* (Dublin, 1847), pp 1 and iv.

93 J.E. Walsh, *The life and times of George Robert FitzGerald* (Dublin, 1852), p. 3; A.R. Hart, 'Fighting FitzGerald: mad, bad and dangerous to know – an eighteenth century murder trial', *NILQ*, 49 (1998), p. 221.

94 J.E. Walsh, letter (circular?) to unidentified recipient(s), 27 June 1866 (National Library of Ireland, MS 49,491/2/1215).

95 Walsh to Derby, 30 October 1866 (Derby Papers, 920 DER (14), 114W).

and that if he does so you will not be inclined to admit it. He ought to do us at least *some* service in his present office before he seeks promotion'.[96] There was thus a query as to whether the traditional prerogative of the attorney general to take up any judicial vacancy should apply in the case of someone so recently appointed. Derby proposed, and Naas and the lord chancellor Blackburne independently suggested, that the position be offered to Francis FitzGerald, a baron of the Exchequer since 1859, Naas saying that they had little choice, 'FitzGerald being almost the only man among the judges whom we could appoint'.[97] As to Walsh, Naas told Derby that 'I see the attorney general every day and as he has said nothing about himself and fully concurs with the chancellor and me in thinking Francis FitzGerald the right person we should have no difficulty with him'.[98]

Second thoughts were needed when at the end of August FitzGerald declined the office. The lord lieutenant, the chief secretary, the lord chancellor and Walsh 'had a long consultation today about the mastership of the rolls, and we could not see our way at present to any course which is not open to the gravest objection … There is no great hurry in the matter as no business is going on in the Rolls at present'.[99] Queries from Naas as to whether Cairns, then an MP, and shortly to become a lord justice of appeal in England, or Abraham Brewster, recently appointed a lord justice of appeal in Ireland might be approached were dismissed by Derby.[100] Walsh annoyed Derby by writing directly to him early in September (and his eventual letter of thanks noted the awkwardness that he had created by doing so),[101] but the letter contained a cogent argument for his appointment:

> The general understanding of the profession in Ireland has been that an option of taking the office of master of the rolls, when vacant, is the right of the attorney general. I do not shrink from a personal sacrifice which would produce any adequate benefit to our party but I see no advantage to be gained by forgoing what is understood to be my right in the present instance. Departures from the usual routine have a bad appearance and provoke criticism. The accident that the vacancy has occurred so soon was not of my causing and, if I pass the opportunity, would be to my disadvantage. I may add that I have heard a rumour that the chancellorship is [designed] for Mr Brewster, should it become vacant, and this removes what might perhaps have been a legitimate temptation to me to risk the dangers inseparable from a longer attempt to gain distinction in Parliament.[102]

96 Derby to Naas, 16 August 1866 (Mayo Papers, MS 11,144).
97 Naas to Derby, 15 August 1866 (Derby Papers, 920 DER (14), 155/2); Derby to Naas, 16 August 1866 (Mayo Papers, MS 11,144).
98 Naas to Derby, 17 August 1866 (Derby Papers, 155/2).
99 Naas to Derby, 26 August 1866 (Derby Papers, 155/2).
100 Derby to Naas, 30 August 1866 (Derby Papers, 920 DER (14), 190/2, p. 241).
101 Derby to Walsh, 6 September 1866 (Derby Papers, 192/1, p. 5); Walsh to Derby, 30 October 1866 (Derby Papers, 920 DER (14) 114W).
102 Walsh to Derby, 4 September 1866 (Mayo Papers, MS 11,144).

Derby's approach was constrained by what he saw as the unimpressive quality of potential appointees – he later regretted that Naas 'cannot give a more favourable report of the Conservative Bar in Ireland'.[103] He wrote to Naas on the same day that he gave a reproach to Walsh for writing to him:

> Although it is no doubt a disadvantage to us to move any law officers and though I wish the attorney general had forborne to press his claims, yet as he *does* press them so strongly I hardly see how they are to be overlooked, and the advantage of retaining him and Morris [the solicitor general] where they are would be in great measure countermanded by having them both dissatisfied. My opinion therefore (though I am quite ready to assent to any course which you may recommend) would be in favour of adhering to the ordinary routine of promotion; allowing the claim of the attorney general and letting Morris succeed as of right.[104]

Walsh was appointed at the end of October. His three years on the Bench gave little scope to develop any judicial reputation, and the only judgment that was referred to in his obituary in the *Irish Law Times* was that relating to a challenge to a supplemental charter of the Queen's University in Ireland.[105] This had been established in 1850 to conduct examinations and award degrees to candidates attending its constituent Queen's Colleges in Belfast, Cork and Galway, and was incorporated by charter in 1864. A supplemental charter granted in June 1866 contemplated, as stated by Chichester Fortescue, the chief secretary, that it might confer degrees 'upon all who pass their examinations without regard to their place of education'.[106] This was intended to facilitate education in a Catholic college under denominational control. The 'university question' was a vexed issue which up to the passing of the Irish Universities Act 1908 remained not only a grievance of the Catholic hierarchy and the wider Catholic community but also a source of concern to Protestant opinion as to what implications any accommodation of Catholic views might have for the status of Trinity College.[107]

The supplemental charter gave rise to a heated debate in Parliament,[108] and opponents sought a declaration that it was inconsistent with the underlying charter and that any steps to implement it were void. Walsh, having reviewed the nature of any interest that private persons would have in the actions of public bodies, held that the suit was not properly constituted. The Queen's University was replaced by the Royal University of Ireland in 1882.

103 Derby to Naas, 6 October 1866 (Mayo Papers, MS 11,144).
104 Derby to Naas, 6 September 1866 (Derby Papers, 192/1, p. 2).
105 *MacCormac v Queen's University*, IR 1 Eq. (1867) 160.
106 HC Deb, 3rd series, vol. 184, col. 720 (5 July 1866).
107 See generally Susan M. Parkes, 'Higher education, 1793–1908' in W.E. Vaughan (ed.), *A new history of Ireland; VI, Ireland under the Union, 1870–1921* (Oxford, 1989), pp 539–70.
108 HC Deb, 3rd series, vol. 184, cols. 842–910 (16 July 1866).

Walsh died suddenly in Paris in October 1869, at the age of 52, when returning from a holiday with his family in Italy.[109]

John George

Justice of Queen's Bench 1866–71

John George (1804–71) represented Co. Wexford as a Conservative MP for a dozen years (1852–7, 1859–66) before in October 1866 he was appointed a judge of the Queen's Bench. He had been called to the Bar in 1827, joining the Leinster circuit, and became a QC in 1844. His contributions to debates in the House of Commons included on several occasions a defence of the City of Dublin Steam Packet Company, of which he was a director.[110] The company operated ships between Dublin and Holyhead and held a contract for carrying the Royal Mail on the route. He spoke up when complaints were raised about its service.

For a few months in 1859 he held office as solicitor general in Lord Derby's second government. Lord Naas, the chief secretary, had outlined considerations for this position in March the previous year, when the government was being formed (see p. 138), which resulted in the appointment of Edmund Hayes, and having emphasised to Disraeli that the nomination should not have a political character observed that 'George would be altogether political. He scarcely ever practises at the Bar except on circuit. He has doubtless made great sacrifices for us and demands consideration, but he is not now in Parliament nor is it at all certain that he will get in for Wexford at the next election'.[111] Naas added that if, as he anticipated, a judicial vacancy would soon arise to which Hayes might be appointed then George's claims could be re-considered. Early in 1859 Hayes was duly appointed to a vacancy in the Queen's Bench arising from the resignation of Philip Crampton, and George was then appointed to succeed him as solicitor general.

Two of his Parliamentary contributions related to judicial matters, the first in 1856[112] when he spoke up for baron Pennefather, and then ten years later in May 1866 in the debate on the competence of the aged chief justice Lefroy. One object of the MPs raising the subject of the age and capacity of elderly judges was to attempt to shame or embarrass them into offering their resignations. No question arose of a formal impeachment by means of motions to that effect being passed by both Houses of Parliament. In his intervention in support of Lefroy, in what transpired to be his last contribution to a debate in the House of Commons, George referred to his own experience as a Crown prosecutor (on circuit), and said that it was 'melancholy that the fame and character of two such men [Blackburne

109 *ILT&SJ*, vol. 3, p. 647 (23 October 1869).
110 HC Deb 3rd series, vol. 131, col. 1410 (28 March 1854); vol. 154, col. 810 (7 July 1859); vol. 173, col. 425 (9 February 1864).
111 Naas to Disraeli, 12 March 1858 (Disraeli Papers, B/XX/BD/18).
112 HC Deb, 3rd series, vol. 140, col. 797 (14 February 1856).

as well as Lefroy] should be made the sport and plaything of individuals in that house, whether for party or other purposes'.[113]

Three months later, in August 1866 when a vacancy in the office of master of the rolls arose unexpectedly the new government's initial intention was to fill this by appointing an existing judge, Francis FitzGerald, a baron of the Exchequer, and to appoint George in turn to fill his place.[114] The readiness to appoint George was a sharp contrast to the uneasiness that the party leaders felt about the canvassing for promotion by another Conservative MP, Stearne Ball Miller (see p. 221). Naas was 'anxious to get George out of Wexford. By great management we have succeeded in getting the Wexford Tories – who are stiff Prots – to take Ram, as I fear they may cool on this ... I had great difficulty with one of them today whom George brought to see me'.[115]

FitzGerald did not accept the offered appointment, so no vacancy for George did arise in that context, but almost simultaneously a fresh opportunity presented itself when it became known that the state of health of Edmund Hayes would lead to his resignation. In his letter recommending FitzGerald Naas also told Lord Derby that 'Blackburne tells me that Hayes (whom he saw yesterday) would not sit again as his speech is much affected from a paralytic attack – so we must look forward to this difficulty arising before November'.[116] Writing to Derby about his own expectation of appointment as master of the rolls, J.E. Walsh made reference to George's prospects: 'George's professional studies have not fitted him for the office and he would not, I understand, accept it'. He then put forward a scheme of promotion which transpired to be the one that was eventually followed. He himself should become the master of the rolls and George would 'fill the place which will be vacated by Judge Hayes in the common law Bench. If considered desirable I have no doubt Hayes's retirement could be arranged so as to promote George before the mastership of the rolls is filled'.[117] As soon as the actual resignation was furnished George was once more appointed to succeed Hayes, this time on the Bench.[118]

George lived at 45 Fitzwilliam Square and had a substantial estate at Cahore, Clonevan, near Gorey, Co. Wexford.[119] He died in December 1871, having been unwell for some months.[120]

113 HC Deb, 3rd series, vol. 183, cols. 778–812 (11 May 1866).
114 Naas to Derby, 15 August 1866 (Derby Papers, 920 DER (14), 155/2); Derby to Naas, 16 August 1866 (Mayo Papers, MS 11,144).
115 Naas to Disraeli, 17 August 1866 (Disraeli Papers, B/XX/BD/21).
116 Naas to Derby, 15 August 1866 (Derby Papers, 155/2). The next law term, for court sittings, was to begin in November.
117 Walsh to Derby, 4 September 1866 (Mayo Papers, MS 11,144).
118 Naas to Derby, 2 October 1866 (Derby Papers, 155/2). *ILT&SJ*, vol. 1, p. 240 (4 May 1867).
119 *ILT&SJ*, vol. 5, p. 628 (23 December 1871).
120 *ILT&SJ*, vol. 5, p. 619 (16 December 1871).

Michael Morris, Lord Morris & Killanin

Justice of Common Pleas 1867–76, Chief Justice of Common Pleas 1876–87, Lord Chief Justice of Ireland 1887–9, Lord of Appeal in Ordinary 1889–1900

Michael Morris (1826–1901) was a judge for a third of a century, from March 1867 to May 1900, and he occupied some of the highest positions open to an Irish judge. A Morris family ancestor had been among the first Normans to come to Ireland in the twelfth century.[121] They and his mother's people, the Blakes, were among the leading families (the historic fourteen 'tribes') in Galway. Morris had a brilliant career in Trinity College, joining the Connaught circuit after his call to the Bar in 1849, and became a QC in 1863. Between 1857 and 1865 he was recorder of Galway, a part-time judicial position.

He was elected to the House of Commons in the general election of 1865 to represent Galway City. He was a moderate Liberal, supporting the government of Lord Palmerston (who died in October 1865) and then Lord John Russell, but in June 1866 he was one of about fifty party members who opposed their leaders on an aspect of electoral reform, the major political issue of the day. Their votes for a motion proposed by a Conservative MP, Lord Dunkellin, one of the members for Co. Galway, led to the defeat of the government. This precipitated the resignation of Russell and the installation of Lord Derby, for the third time, as head of a minority Conservative government. He endeavoured to obtain formal support from various Liberals, but 'only the Catholic moderate Liberal Michael Morris was secured, as Irish solicitor general, as an appointment from outside the party'.[122]

Derby and Lord Naas, his principal adviser on Irish affairs, had reservations about offering the post to Morris, Naas writing that 'if he accepts he must ensure his seat at Galway[123] and promise to resign if he is beaten. I also have misgivings about the appointment but Disraeli and Taylor press it so strongly that I suppose it had better be done. If he refuses he should understand that the offer was made confidentially'.[124] Morris accepted and was returned with a large majority in a bye-election on 2 August. A fortnight later the master of the rolls died, and Derby remarked that 'considering that neither our attorney nor solicitor general have even done us a day's work we may fairly expect them to hold on for some little time at least'.[125] The attorney general, John Walsh, was however soon appointed to the vacancy and Morris was promoted to succeed him, 'notwithstanding that the immediate elevation of Morris to be attorney general will not be relished by a large

121 Charles Ffrench Blake Forster, *The Irish chieftains, or a struggle for the crown* (Dublin, 1872), pp 672–6; *ILT&SJ*, vol. 31, p. 202 (1 May 1897).

122 Angus Hawkins, '*The forgotten prime minister; the 14th earl of Derby; vol. II, Achievement: 1851–1869* (Oxford, 2008), p. 308.

123 MPs accepting government office were obliged then to resign their seats and stand in a bye-election.

124 Naas to Derby, 18 July 1866, replying to a letter from Derby to him, same day (Derby Papers, 155/2).

125 Derby to Abercorn, 16 August 1866 (Derby Papers, 191/2).

number of our political friends',[126] and that his 'elevation is rather more rapid than might have been desired'.[127]

Some five months later, in March 1867, another opening arose, this time in the court of Common Pleas, and at the age of 40 Morris was appointed to succeed a judge promoted from that court, Jonathan Christian. Naas had once more been unenthusiastic about this last promotion, mindful that Morris was not a Conservative, and concerned about the ensuing bye-election: 'I sincerely hope Morris will do all he can to secure the seat in Galway. It would be very hard if we lost a vote after all the trouble we have taken about getting him landed. Will you see him tomorrow and tell him that though I am sure he will do all he can he must feel that I will be in an awkward position with my friends if we lose a seat by his promotion'.[128] In the event a brother of Morris was returned unopposed at the bye-election a few days later. At a dinner held in his honour in Galway in 1873, when he first sat there in his capacity as a judge of assize,[129] he remarked that 'a favourable gale had blown him upon the Bench'.[130] In the period of nine months from July 1866 he had been given three successively higher positions.

Morris was promoted from being a puisne judge to be the chief justice of Common Pleas early in 1876, on the death of the incumbent, James Henry Monahan. John Adye Curran, later a county court judge, wrote that Morris approached him at a dinner and said 'Curran, I hear from Dames [a QC] that you think that as chief justice I am a great improvement on what I was as a simple judge … You need not be angry with Dames, because I quite agree with what you told him. I feel in much better humour with everyone since I became chief justice'.[131]

He had some expectation of another promotion to fill the vacancy that arose later that year on the death of the chief justice of Queen's Bench, James Whiteside, in November 1876. (There had been a curious report some years previously about a personalised and rather juvenile exchange of words in court between Whiteside and Morris as to whether an item of evidence was irrelevant and of no interest (the view taken by Whiteside) or was important and potentially conclusive (Morris).[132]) His daughter Maud, presumably reflecting family lore or tradition, wrote in a memoir of her father (which was published over 30 years after his death)[133] that he 'had been approached as the obvious judge to fill [the vacancy]. But the Northern members of Parliament, finding that he was a Roman Catholic, made a protest against the appointment, and after some hugger-mugger the Roman Catholic was passed over and another judge given the position, whose two qualifications were

126 Naas to Derby, 11 September 1866 (Derby Papers, 155/2).
127 Derby to Abercorn, 14 September 1866 (Derby Papers, 191/2, p. 107).
128 Naas to Abercorn, 25 March 1867 (Abercorn Papers (PRONI), D623/A/304/14).
129 *ILT&SJ*, vol. 7, p. 93 (22 February 1873).
130 *ILT&SJ*, vol. 7, p. 131 (15 March 1873).
131 John Adye Curran, *Reminiscences* (London, 1915), p. 38.
132 *Law Times*, vol. 49, p. 52 (21 May 1870).
133 'A chatty and pleasantly informative autobiographical fragment of the modern sort' (review by J.J. Auchmuty, *IHS*, vol. 2, no. 8 (September 1941), pp 466–7).

that he was a Northerner and a Protestant'.[134] The appointment, which was announced in the first week of February 1877, was not in fact of another judge but of the attorney general, G.A.C. May. Morris was appointed lord chief justice in 1887 after the death of May, but in his daughter's view 'the incident of thirteen [sic., ten] years before had embittered him [and] he took little further interest'.[135] He was given a baronetcy in 1885, to the discomfiture of May (see p. 117), and became a life peer as Lord Morris of Spiddal in 1889 when he successfully sought appointment as the second Irish lord of appeal in ordinary. His retirement in May 1900 gave rise to controversy and surprise in Ireland because an English judge was appointed in his place, and there was no opportunity for advocating that his successor should be drawn from the Irish Bench or Bar (see p. 450). He received a hereditary peerage at the time, which invited the drawing of a connection with his retirement, and was reported to have preserved his precedence among the peerage by retaining the Morris element of his title, being known as Lord Morris and Killanin.[136]

Morris, as with Peter O'Brien, his successor as lord chief justice, was regarded as having a sympathy with and an understanding of ordinary people, it being said that his judicial decisions 'were of a kind which often warmed the public, being concerned with the spirit rather than the letter of the law, scorning precedent and being without pretence to legal erudition'.[137] Justice was tempered with mercy, and John Redmond BL, MP praised him in the House of Commons for decency in the conduct of trials at assizes at which Redmond was present: 'I was greatly struck by what I saw and heard. If a prisoner was undefended the judge allowed him in statement and in cross-examination the most enormous latitude'.[138] Morris told Dunbar Plunket Barton QC, MP that no prisoner tried before him was ever executed.[139] However his long judicial career was not regarded at the time as distinguished, he had (in the words of Henry Hanna (1871–1946), a judge of the High Court between 1925 and 1942) 'a very meagre reputation as a lawyer',[140] and his contribution to the judicial work of the House of Lords was modest (see p. 462). When O'Brien was pressing to be made a baronet in 1891 he made reference to Morris in very unflattering terms, saying that the baronetcy that had been given to him could scarcely have been regarded as merited by any distinguished services as attorney general or as a judge.[141]

Morris was regarded as an entertaining and clubbable companion. Hanna made reference to his 'great reputation for his rude Irish wit and great personality …

134 Maud Wynne, *An Irishman and his family* (London, 1937), p. 139.
135 Wynne, op. cit., p. 140.
136 Henry W. Lucy, *A diary of the Unionist Parliament, 1895–1900* (Bristol/London, 1901), p. 369.
137 Entry on Morris in *ODNB* (by G.C. Woods, rev. Sinead Agnew).
138 HC Deb, 3rd series, vol. 339, col. 941 (9 August 1889).
139 HC Deb, 4th series, vol. 4, col. 310 (6 May 1892).
140 Henry Hanna, 'The Bench and Bar of Ireland in the nineteenth century', *American Bar Association Journal*, vol. 22, no. 11 (1936), pp 761–7, at 764.
141 O'Brien to Balfour, 7 March 1891 (Balfour Papers, Add. MS 49814.327).

with a strong Irish brogue he prided himself on being extravagantly Irish, as it was understood fifty years ago'.[142] In London, the family resided in Grosvenor Place, between Hyde Park Corner and Belgrave Square. One observer referred to 'his bright and genial disposition, his warm and sympathetic nature, his strong and pungent but never ungenerous speech, his great conversational powers, and his ready wit'.[143] In her memoir his daughter made some fairly direct or frank references to a rather less congenial aspect of his disposition, a 'volcanic temperament' as witnessed by his children. 'We were all afraid of Papa, especially when he was in one of his short-tempered, silent, nervy moods'. He was 'one of the most impatient men ever born', and 'a very busy man, full of nerves and temperament and bad digestion'. His daughter wondered whether 'bad nerves give a bad digestion or vice versa'. A wet day, which was presumably not uncommon, at their home in Spiddal, Co. Galway, would leave him with 'a black cloud of thunderous bad humour over his face'.[144]

In 1860 he married Anna Hughes, a daughter of Henry George Hughes (1810–72), a baron of the Exchequer between 1859 and 1872. He and his wife had a numerous family, of whom four sons and six daughters survived to adulthood, three of whom became nuns, his eldest daughter dying in his lifetime at the convent of the Sisters of Charity, St Stephen's Green.[145] He was a wealthy man, leaving personal estate on his death in 1901 that was valued at £127,766 for probate, not taking into account whatever value the real estate inherited by his eldest son and heir, Martin Henry Morris, may have had.[146] The house at Spiddal, originally a small Georgian house, was redesigned by the second Lord Killanin, and having been burned in 1923 during the Civil War was later rebuilt. A grandson, also named Michael Morris, the third Lord Killanin (1914–99), was president of the International Olympic Committee between 1972 and 1980.

Hedges Eyre Chatterton

Vice-Chancellor 1867–1904

Hedges Eyre Chatterton (1819–1910) was born in Cork in July 1819, 'and had to a large extent the suavity of the Southern manner'.[147] His father was a non-practising solicitor, and his distinctive first names were those of his godfather, Captain Robert Hedges Eyre of Macroom Castle, Co. Cork. He was the only person to hold the office of vice-chancellor, a position that was created by the Chancery (Ireland) Act 1867[148] as a 'judge assistant' to the lord chancellor. Its abolition by the Supreme Court of Judicature (Ireland) Act 1877 did not affect the

142 Hanna, op. cit., pp 764–5.
143 *ILT&SJ*, vol. 28, p. 209 (21 April 1894), citing *The World*.
144 Wynne, op. cit., pp 36, 71, 28, 151, 66 and 33.
145 *ILT&SJ*, vol. 23, p. 348 (29 June 1889).
146 *New Irish Jurist*, vol. 2, p. 55 (20 December 1901).
147 *Irish Times*, 31 August 1910.
148 30&31 Vict., c.44, s4.

position of the incumbent, as his rank, precedence, privileges and powers were expressly preserved.[149] His period of office as a judge, for over thirty-five years, was one of the longest in modern times.

He was called to the Bar in 1843 – his custom of referring to the Wills Act 1837 as 'the recent Wills Act', was perhaps something of an affectation since it was enacted years before that call. 'I joined the Munster circuit on being called to the Bar but I did not much care for Nisi Prius work, and laid myself out chiefly for Chancery business'.[150] He was admitted an advocate in the admiralty court. He lived at different times at Hatch Street, Fitzwilliam Place and later at New Park, a villa, since demolished, at the Stillorgan end of Newtownpark Avenue, Blackrock, Co. Dublin. His home in Co. Cork was at East View, Glandore, where he pursued an interest in yachting, and in an autobiographical paper he set out details of vessels that he owned and sailed, increasing over time from 4 tonnes to 35. He encountered a storm when sailing from Kingstown to Cork on one occasion and eventually found land at Falmouth in Cornwall, following which he commissioned a still larger yacht, a 60-tonner.[151]

He took silk in 1859. In the autumn of 1866 he was appointed solicitor general by the new Conservative government, and he was elected unopposed as one of the MPs for Dublin University in February 1867. His appointment as attorney general in March, to replace Michael Morris, led to compliments of a type conventional on such occasions, it being said that 'honest in heart and conduct, courteous and obliging to all, without being weak or too facile, he has gained an extraordinary popularity, not alone with the members of his own circuit but with the whole legal profession in Ireland. Of his great learning and ability there cannot be a second opinion'.[152] He held that office for about five months. In May he conducted the prosecution of a Fenian leader, Thomas F. Bourke, who was sentenced to death on his conviction for treason-felony but reprieved after a public campaign for clemency.[153]

In Parliament he was responsible for introducing and securing the enactment of the Chancery Bill which (among many other reforms) created the post of vice-chancellor, to which he was appointed in August as soon as the Bill had become law. A report of a Royal Commission in 1863 had recommended assimilating Irish court procedures to those of the English court of Chancery. Bills to give effect to that report had been introduced in 1864, 1865 and again in 1866, and each time had been strenuously opposed and obstructed by the Conservatives, who were then in opposition. The introduction of a similar bill following the change of government in July 1866 was inevitably the subject of comment as to how the

149 40&41 Vict., c.57, ss6 and 15.

150 Autobiographical sketch of Hedges Eyre Chatterton (Library of Trinity College Dublin, MS 6401/1), p. 13.

151 *Irish Times*, 3 September 1910.

152 *ILT&SJ*, vol. 1, p. 169 (6 April 1867).

153 R.V. Comerford, *The Fenians in context: Irish politics and society, 1848–82* (Dublin, 1985), pp 143–5.

prospect of the exercise of patronage had led the party to abandon its opposition to the reform proposals.

On Chatterton's appointment as vice-chancellor the *Irish Law Times* resumed its compliments, referring to him as one of the finest Chancery lawyers:

> as an advocate he was zealous and temperate, forcible and clear in argument and ready in reply, while in chambers practice his opinion was always that of a sound lawyer, perfectly simple and explicit and free from all those refinements of special pleading which so often lead the suitor into hopeless litigation. We shall be much surprised if he does not make an able and efficient judge, and prove a valuable acquisition to the already brilliant Chancery bench of Ireland.[154]

On his retirement, some 36 years later, the attorney general, John Atkinson QC, MP spoke of him in more restrained terms when paying tribute at a special meeting of the Bar. He noted his long service while acknowledging that 'there might have been on the Bench lawyers more profound, reasoners more acute, rhetoricians more eloquent. He might have had his prejudices, but if he had prejudices they were in favour of what was right and just. If he had antipathies they were antipathies to what was crooked and deceitful'.[155]

His court was 'a room of the most unenlivening environment',[156] having no gallery for the accommodation of the public, and 'the benches on the floor of the court are more than sufficient to seat what few members of the general public may occasionally be present'.[157] As was common at the time he appointed a family member, his brother Abraham, to a position in his court, that of chief clerk.[158] He had a solemn demeanour, and a 'fortitude of endurance and a fairness of mind that make him one of the best judges on the bench'.[159] His popularity or standing with the Bar would have been enhanced by the expression of his view that counsel were not sufficiently well paid; 'it was very easy to raise a cry against counsel for not remaining in court until the very end of any particular case in which they might happen to be retained, but the fact was that having regard to the amount of remuneration that they received it would be unreasonable to expect them to do so'.[160] T.M. Healy described him as a 'decent upright old Tory. I can't say that to know him is to love him, but at any rate it is to appreciate and respect him'.[161]

Although, as will appear below, it was the reversals of a number of his judgments on appeal that attracted most attention, a distinguished English lawyer,

154 *ILT&SJ*, vol. 1, p. 511 (24 August 1867).
155 *ILT&SJ*, vol. 38, p. 30 (16 January 1904); *New Irish Jurist*, vol. 4, p. 61 (15 February 1904).
156 *Irish Times*, 31 August 1910.
157 Rhadamanthus [W.B. Campbell], *Our judges* (Dublin, 1890), p. 51.
158 *ILT&SJ*, vol. 29, p. 95 (16 February 1895); King's Inns Admission Papers, p. 84.
159 Rhadamanthus, op. cit., pp 53–4.
160 *ILT&SJ*, vol. 14, p. 569 (20 November 1880), *Lysaght v McGrath*.
161 T.M. Healy, *Letters and leaders*, vol. 2, p. 468.

Charles Harpum, considered that Chatterton was 'a highly competent and sound judge … and some of his decisions might be thought to be more compelling than their better-known English counterparts'.[162] Mr Justice John Kenny, a judge of the High Court (1961–75) and then the Supreme Court (1975–82), wrote that '[m]ost Irish lawyers are not, I think, aware of their rich heritage of Irish case law on chancery and property matters. Decisions given before 1924 are rarely cited in court though the judgments of Chatterton, Holmes, FitzGibbon and Walker are as learned and well-written as those of their contemporaries in the judiciary in England'.[163]

His early years on the court were marked by an animosity or hostility towards him by lord justice Christian, whose judgments upholding appeals against decisions or orders of the vice-chancellor were frequently expressed in sarcastic and unpleasant terms. The *Irish Times* in 1870 published two articles critical of the number of his decisions which had been set aside, saying that it was 'the manner of reversal, not the bare fact itself, that again and again excites the attention of the public. The reversal is usually a scathing and humiliating exposure'.[164] It also put forward a damaging hypothesis:

> If a judge is lazy, and will not study law, or if he is incorrigibly stupid and cannot master it, or if he is the victim of a prejudice in favour of the highly-placed or the lowly-placed in the social scale, or if he is viciously conceited and of that narrow and dogmatic temperament which leads him to fancy he sees the whole of a case when he has only apprehended some insignificant portion of it; if he has any or all of these defects (and others equally fatal might be named) the public has left itself without any effectual remedy. It must grin and bear it.

Although this abuse was largely referable to the nature of criticisms made by Christian he complained to the lord chancellor, O'Hagan, not so much on Chatterton's behalf (the newspaper 'has lent itself to some personal enemy' of Chatterton), but that it was 'an affront almost libellous on the court of appeal and upon me especially and upon the vice-chancellor [which] transcends all bounds of fair comment and is rank with personal malice'.[165]

Christian considered that Chatterton was permitting administrative clerks of the court to perform functions in chambers that should only properly have been exercised by him as a judge.[166] One of his judgments to that effect, in the case of

162 Charles Harpum, 'The vice-chancellors – an Irish postscript', *Law Quarterly Review*, vol. 99 (1983), p. 32 at 35. Mr Harpum, among other distinctions, was a member of the Law Commission (England and Wales).

163 Preface to J.C.W. Wylie, *Irish land law* (1st edition, Dublin, 1975).

164 *Irish Times*, 7 and 8 March 1870; *ILT&SJ*, vol. 4, p. 193 (12 March 1870).

165 Christian to O'Hagan, 9 March 1870 (O'Hagan Papers, D2777/9/23/2).

166 *Costello v O'Rorke*, IR 3 Eq. (1868–9) 172; *Re Baltinglass Junction Railway Company* (*ILT&SJ*, vol. 5, p. 225 (6 May 1871)); *Lamprey v Lambert* (*ILT&SJ*, vol. 6, p. 337 (22 June 1872)).

Howlin v Sheppard,[167] led to Chatterton subsequently placing the case in his court list,

> not for the purpose of any proceedings in the cause, which is now at an end, but to make from this place a statement in reference to observations [made by Christian] … purporting to contain a statement of what had taken place therein at my chambers, so entirely at variance with the facts, and so calculated to throw discredit upon the practice of my chief clerk and myself, that I think any further silence on my part would be a dereliction of my duty to the suitors and practitioners of my court.[168]

Two months later Christian in turn also put the matter in for mention in the Court of Appeal list, saying that he wished to present some explanations 'rendered necessary by some remarks which the vice-chancellor made upon that judgment on 17th February'.[169] Whatever the rights or wrongs of the particular issue, as a matter of law, they may have been overshadowed by the spectacle of a public judicial skirmish taking place at all.

Christian's animosity to Chatterton surfaced again in 1877, when the Court of Appeal unanimously allowed an appeal from a decree he had given in a probate case, with Christian remarking that 'it would be amazing to note how the vice-chancellor had arrived at his present conclusion if they (their lordships) had not sometimes seen things similar to it before. A very moderate breadth of vision only was necessary to show that his Honour's way of treating the will was a narrow-minded fallacy'.[170] The *Irish Times* soon afterwards noted that five of six appeals from orders of the vice-chancellor had recently been upheld, and that he had been 'flayed alive by the sharp and polished scalpel of judge Christian, who really seems to take delight in vivisecting him'.[171]

Chatterton heard a number of cases relating to prominent Dublin properties. He held in 1885 that the Dublin Corporation had no legal authority to re-name Sackville Street as O'Connell Street (a change which was not to be formally adopted until 1924), which led to the Corporation renaming temporarily one of the streets in a red light district as Chatterton Street.[172] The Court of Appeal reversed an injunction granted by him restraining alterations being made to a former hotel building at Portobello Harbour on the Grand Canal,[173] and also one granted in favour of the owners of houses at St James's Terrace in Clonskeagh seeking to prevent the construction of an isolation hospital for smallpox patients

167 IR 6 Eq. (1872–3) 38 and 497 (appeal), at 518.
168 *ILT&SJ*, vol. 7, p. 97 (22 February 1873).
169 *ILT&SJ*, vol. 7, p. 211 (26 April 1873).
170 *Watson and another v Arundell and another* (*ILT&SJ*, vol. 11, pp 19–20 (13 January 1877)).
171 *ILT&SJ*, vol. 11, p. 104 (3 March 1877).
172 *Anderson v Corporation of Dublin*, [1885] LR Ir. 410; W.N. Osborough, *Law and the emergence of modern Dublin: a litigation topography for a capital city* (Dublin, 1996), pp 46–50, 181–4.
173 *Grand Canal Co. v McNamee*, [1892–3] 9 LR Ir. 131; Osborough, op. cit., pp 69–71.

at the end of the terrace, at Vergemount.[174] (This latter case was an example of a *quia timet* injunction, which may be sought when injury or damage to the plaintiff is apprehended or threatened but has not to date been sustained.)

The master of the rolls, in paying tribute to him following his death, said that 'he had no timorous fears. He did not believe that it was necessary on all occasions to show in the forefront mercy when the forefront should be occupied by justice', an aspect of his character referred to also by the *Irish Times* in saying that 'he believed in treating a criminal as a criminal and not as an interesting invalid. He believed that the truest mercy lay in carrying out the demands of justice'.[175] As a Chancery judge he would have little or nothing to do with criminal law, but when acting as one of the lords justices appointed to perform functions of the lord lieutenant when he was absent from Ireland he would have had occasion to consider applications for clemency, for the commutation of a sentence of death on conviction for murder. It would have been from such occasions that any reputation for letting the law take its course would have been derived.

In 1876 the *Irish Law Times* published a report that the chief justice of Queen's Bench, Whiteside, would shortly retire, and that he would be succeeded by Chatterton.[176] When the chief justice died a couple of months later, Chatterton was offered but refused the position, which was then accepted by the attorney general, G.A.C. May. In 1890 it was noted that 'there have long been rumours of his intended resignation',[177] and that year he received a proposal that he would stand down and be appointed as a member of the Judicial Committee of the Privy Council in London, subject to an understanding that this would be done at a time of the government's choosing so that the attorney general, Madden, whose services the government wished to retain for the time being, could be appointed to the resulting judicial vacancy. A letter was written to Chatterton by Balfour, in consultation with Ashbourne (who handed it over after entertaining Chatterton to dinner in his home), and in appropriately cautious terms from a minister to a judge. He told Chatterton that before he [Balfour] had left town he had hoped to see him but that this unfortunately had not been possible, and that he was

> therefore constrained to lay before you in writing matters which might have been more easily discussed by word of mouth. I have been led to suppose that the idea of giving up incessant judicial work in Ireland has crossed your mind; so that an English Privy Councillorship, which without involving the same labour as the v chancellorship would give you ample opportunity of rendering most valuable service to the Judicial Committee of the Privy Council, might not prove unacceptable.

174 *Attorney general (Boswell) v Rathmines and Pembroke Joint Hospital Board*, [1904] 1 IR 141; Osborough, op. cit., p. 67.
175 *Irish Times*, 3 September 1910 and 31 August 1910.
176 *ILT&SJ*, vol. 10, p. 506 (16 September 1876). See also *ILT&SJ*, vol. 38, p. 30 (16 January 1904).
177 Rhadamanthus, op. cit., p. 55.

If retirement was in fact on Chatterton's mind, perhaps this could 'take place at a period convenient to the government and be accompanied with the assumption of less onerous but more important duties in the English P. Council'.[178] Chatterton declined to co-operate with this scheme.[179]

He had not pursued a suggestion made by a cousin, Sir James Charles Chatterton Bt, on whose death in 1874 a baronetcy originally granted to his grandfather (a brother of Chatterton's grandfather) in 1801 became extinct. 'He was very fond of me and lived to see me on the bench, much to his gratification. He begged of me not long before his death to apply to the Crown to extend the baronetcy to me but as I had no child and did not care much for a title which would not confer on me as high a rank as that of Privy Councillor which I possessed I did not take any step for the purpose'.[180]

In 1901 the *Irish Law Times* was 'glad to say that the vice-chancellor is looking in excellent health, and that there is absolutely no foundation for the rumour circulated by the daily newspapers as to his possible retirement'.[181] He stepped down two years later, in January 1904. A few months later he came to mind for Leopold Bloom:

> Ned Lambert is taking a day off I see. Rather upsets a man's day a funeral does. Old Chatterton, the vice-chancellor, is his granduncle or his greatgranduncle. Close on ninety they say. Subleader for his death written this long time perhaps. Living to spite them ... The right honourable Hedges Eyre Chatterton. Daresay he writes him an odd shaky cheque or two on gale days. Windfall when he kicks out. Alleluia.[182]

Chatterton left an estate of over £39,000 on his death in 1910.

John Fitzhenry Townsend

Judge of the court of Admiralty 1867–93

John Fitzhenry Townsend (1810–93) was appointed as the (sole) judge of the court of Admiralty following its reconstitution by the Admiralty Court (Ireland) Act 1867.[183] He had been called to the Bar in 1834, and admitted as an advocate to that court in 1847. He was requested by a Royal Commission inquiring into the differences between the practice and procedure in the judicial systems in England and in Ireland[184] to provide a detailed report on the differences in admiralty

178 Balfour to Chatterton, 23 May 1890 (Ashbourne Papers, B.9/11).
179 Ashbourne to Balfour, 29 May 1890 (Balfour Papers, Add. MS 49815.61); Balfour to Ashbourne, 30 May 1890 (Ashbourne Papers, B.9/12).
180 Autobiographical sketch, p. 4.
181 *ILT&SJ*, vol. 35, p. 505 (2 November 1901).
182 James Joyce, *Ulysses*, 'Aeolus', line 262.
183 30&31 Vict., c.113.
184 First Report of the Royal Commission into the Superior Courts of Law and Courts of Chancery

practice and procedure, and in that way made a significant contribution to the reforming legislation of 1867.[185]

Townsend's position as one of the leading advocates in the court made him a suitable person to replace the discredited Judge Kelly. The very small number of practitioners in the court – some of whom 'had a recreational interest in yachting'[186] – were concerned that, by reason of political patronage, the judgeship might be given to a member of the Bar with no background in admiralty law, and shipping interests made representations as to the necessity for a specialist appointment.[187] The court was not busy, and the transfer of its business to the new High Court was envisaged by the Supreme Court of Judicature (Ireland) Act 1877,[188] but 'the exceptional longevity of Townsend kept dissolution in abeyance until his eventual death in February 1893'.[189] Admiralty proceedings were then assigned to a judge of the High Court, and the court was dissolved.

A sympathetic commentator in 1890 wrote that

> Admiralty suits are so few that the office of judge is almost a sinecure [i.e., without responsibilities]. There are not enough ships sailing into Irish harbours and out of them to come into collision with one another and give rise to Admiralty proceedings. The poverty of Ireland is symbolised in the meanness of her High Court of Admiralty; her pitiful trade in the *dilletante* Admiralty Bar; the paralysis of her industry in the oft-closed door of Judge Townsend's court.[190]

Townsend had family connections with Castletownsend, Co. Cork.[191] He was a prominent member of the Masonic Order, being Deputy Grand Master for Ireland for almost fifteen years.[192] A bust of him in Carrara marble was commissioned in 1867 by some friends and admirers for presentation to the Dublin Grand Lodge for placing in the new Masonic Hall in Molesworth Street.[193] He was appointed as a Commissioner of Charitable Donations and Bequests in 1872.[194]

of England and Ireland, with statements of differences in practice and procedure between England and Ireland (P.P. 1863 (3238) xv.463).

185 *ILT&SJ*, vol. 1, p. 552 (31 August 1867).
186 Kevin Costello, *The court of Admiralty of Ireland, 1575–1893* (Dublin, 2011), p. 225.
187 Costello, op. cit., p. 212.
188 40&41 Vict., c.57, s9.
189 Costello, op. cit., p. 203.
190 Rhadamanthus, op. cit., p. 107.
191 *Journal of the Cork Historical and Archaeological Society*, series 1, vol. 2, p. 56 (1893).
192 *ILT&SJ*, vol. 2, p. 602 (7 November 1868), vol. 27, p. 67 (4 February 1893).
193 *Law Times*, vol. 44, p. 107 (7 December 1867).
194 *ILT&SJ*, vol. 6, p. 110 (2 March 1872).

Stearne Ball Miller

Judge of the court of Bankruptcy 1867–97

Stearne Ball Miller (1812–97) was a judge of the court of Bankruptcy for more than a quarter of a century. On his death in 1897 he was thought to be the oldest sitting judge in the United Kingdom.[195] He had been born in Armagh, the son of the Revd George Miller, DD, was called to the Bar in 1835, and became a QC in 1852. His appointment at the end of 1866 followed heavy canvassing by him and on his behalf for judicial or other legal promotion. He was then the member of Parliament for Armagh City, a constituency that he won as a Conservative in the 1857 general election with a majority of 13 votes (175 to 162), but lost in 1859 (by 201 votes to 137) and regained in 1865 with a majority of 15 (184 to 169).[196]

The vacancy in the court of Bankruptcy which Miller filled arose through the transfer of one of the two existing judges, David Lynch, to the Landed Estates Court. Miller became the senior judge in the court the following year when the other judge, Walter Berwick, died in a major railway accident at Abergele in north Wales. His colleagues thereafter, in succession, were Michael Harrison, who was promoted to the High Court in 1878, Frederick W. Walsh (1811–85), who was appointed in 1879,[197] and Walter Boyd, who replaced Walsh. Miller became a bencher of King's Inns in 1879.[198]

A bankruptcy judgeship was of a lesser standing, in terms of responsibilities, salary and general importance in the overall scheme of things, than a position in the superior courts. Miller's ambition was originally set higher when his party, under Lord Derby, regained office in July 1866, and in the first week of July he put his expectations in writing to Derby, who noted him to Abercorn, the lord lieutenant, in August as an 'eager applicant for professional advancement'.[199] Immediately following the death of the master of the rolls he pressed a claim to be appointed.[200] Derby twice reminded Naas, the chief secretary for Ireland, towards the end of August that Miller was expecting a place ('You will not forget S. Miller if you have an opportunity of providing for him').[201] A week later he said that if Michael Morris succeeded John E. Walsh as attorney general (on Walsh becoming master of the rolls) then 'you would want a strong man, a decided Conservative and Protestant, and able to command a seat in Parliament as solicitor general. I do not know whether, professionally, Stearne Miller stands high enough. In other

195 *ILT&SJ*, vol. 31, p. 216 (8 May 1897).
196 B.M. Walker (ed.), *Parliamentary election results in Ireland, 1801–1922* (Dublin, 1978), p. 249.
197 *ILT&SJ*, vol. 13, p. 41 (18 January 1879); vol. 19, p. 430 (15 August 1885).
198 *ILT&SJ*, vol. 13, p. 211 (19 April 1879).
199 Derby to Miller, 7 July 1866 (acknowledging Miller letter of 6 July) (Derby Papers, 191/1, p. 50); Derby to Abercorn, 10 August 1866 (Derby Papers, 191/2).
200 Abercorn to Naas, 16 August 1866 (Mayo Papers, 11,142 (6)).
201 Derby to Naas, 30 August 1866 (Derby Papers, 190/2, p. 241), also Derby to Naas, 21 August 1866 (Derby Papers, 191/1, p. 174).

respects it would be not only unobjectionable but would be a fair recognition of Parliamentary support, which we cannot afford to disregard'.[202]

Naas replied very frankly that 'Miller is a great difficulty. He is really quite unfit for a law officer and we really could not depend only on such assistance as he and Morris together could give us in Parliament'.[203] He was thinking of Hedges Eyre Chatterton to succeed Morris as solicitor general, and hoping that some other position could be found for Miller. Derby remarked to Abercorn that 'I hope for the sake of the impression to be made in Parliament that you may find the means of doing something for Miller, though I suppose he is hardly equal to the solicitor generalship, especially as we should not have a very strong attorney'.[204]

Whether an appointment could be found for Miller remained an open question for a few weeks more. Naas reported to Derby, at the start of October, that 'with regard to the solicitor general I hope that in a day or two I may be able to tell you that we have found a mode of providing for Miller without making him a law officer, which would relieve us from a very great difficulty as his claims have been very strongly pressed by a great many of our Northern friends'.[205] Four days later as it seemed that he might, despite all, have to be appointed a law officer, Derby remarked that 'I am sorry that you cannot give a more favourable report of the Conservative Bar in Ireland. Miller will be a weak appointment but I do not see how you could do otherwise unless you could have provided for him otherwise, and I agree with you that he would not do for the Landed Estates Court'.[206] The attorney general and the lord chancellor became involved in finding another place, and Miller was told that he could fill a vacancy in the bankruptcy court.[207] Naas told Derby that 'Miller with great difficulty has consented to forego his claim to the solicitor generalship',[208] which was given to Chatterton. Miller's disappointment was evident when he wrote that the dream of his life was to be a law officer with a sure seat in Parliament, 'but my life is in that respect now blighted, and for some reason I have been badly and harshly treated … I could not with any feeling of self-respect press myself further as law officer upon parties who were reluctant to have me'.[209]

However it soon transpired, to Miller's great indignation, that there was not actually a current vacancy in bankruptcy, since the government was awaiting the resignation from the Landed Estates Court of Mountifort Longfield, so that he could be replaced by David Lynch, whom Miller was in turn to replace. Some doubt also existed as to whether Lynch met the formal qualifications for his intended new position. Miller then asked to be given instead the position in the

202 Derby to Naas, 6 September 1866 (Derby Papers, 192/1, p. 2).
203 Naas to Derby, 11 September 1866 (Derby Papers, 155/2).
204 Derby to Abercorn, 14 September 1866 (Derby Papers, 191/2, p. 107).
205 Naas to Derby, 2 October 1866 (Derby Papers, 155/2).
206 Derby to Naas, 6 October 1866 (Derby Papers, 192/1, p. 37).
207 Miller to Naas, 29 October 1866 (Mayo Papers, MS 43,826/3).
208 Naas to Derby, 19 October 1866 (Derby Papers, 155/2).
209 Miller to Naas, 17 October 1866 (Mayo Papers, MS 43,826/2).

LEC 'for which I was much better fitted and which I think should have been offered to me in the first instance'.[210] Naas reassured him that 'the government will do everything in their power to carry out the arrangement which was communicated to you by the chancellor, even though it necessitated introduction of an act of Parliament'.[211] Over the next few weeks, as Longfield and Lynch continued to sit in their respective courts, the unanticipated difficulty was resolved, and by the end of November the Conservatives in Armagh were selecting a candidate for a bye-election (although the writ for this was not moved until the end of January, when Miller's resignation had finally taken place).[212] At Christmas it was reported that the appointments would take effect in the New Year.[213] On 11 January 1867 Lynch was sworn in as a member of the Landed Estates Court and Miller took his seat on the bench soon afterwards.[214]

A plain but unflattering account of Miller in court was given by Ignatius O'Brien (Lord Shandon), who was called to the Bar in 1881, and so would have dealt with him in his later years.

> Judge Miller was an interesting man in his way; he was not a genius or a legal light, but he took his occupation seriously and conscientiously discharged his duties. But he was a soulless old man and only regarded the bi-weekly procession of bankrupts and rogues as the keeper of a menagerie might regard his own wild beasts. He was very deaf too, and only a small portion of the legal arguments which were addressed to him penetrated his brain.[215]

He died in May 1897, and later that summer the court of Bankruptcy was incorporated into the High Court by amending legislation, the remaining bankruptcy judge, Boyd, becoming a justice of the Queen's Bench division.[216] That restructuring had been envisaged in 1895, although an associated prediction that 'Judge Miller will receive a baronetcy and retire from the court of Bankruptcy on a full pension'[217] was not fulfilled. 'The deceased was a man of remarkably fine physique. Although he had reached the advanced age of 85 he may be said to have died in harness, from the effects of a chill caught whilst taking his customary morning ride. Judge Miller, although suffering at the time from the illness which has proved so rapidly fatal, sat in his court on Friday 30th April, having gone there contrary to the advice of his medical attendant. He sank rapidly, however, on Saturday [1 May] and died on Sunday'.[218]

210 Miller to Naas, 29 October 1866 (Mayo Papers, MS 43,826/3).
211 Naas to Miller, 30 October 1866 (Mayo Papers, MS 43,826/3).
212 *Irish Times*, 23 November 1866, 26 January 1867.
213 *Irish Times*, 24 December 1866.
214 *Irish Times*, 12 and 19 January 1867; *Law Times*, vol. 42, p. 282 (9 February 1867).
215 Daire Hogan and Patrick Maume (eds), *The reminiscences of Lord Shandon, lord chancellor of Ireland 1913–18* (Dublin, 2021), pp 197–8.
216 Supreme Court of Judicature (Ireland) (No. 2) Act 1897, 60&61 Vict., c.66, s3.
217 *ILT&SJ*, vol. 29, p. 514 (19 October 1895).
218 *ILT&SJ*, vol. 31, p. 216 (8 May 1897).

Michael Harrison

Judge of the court of Bankruptcy 1868–78, Justice of the Common Pleas division of the High Court 1878–88, of the Queen's Bench division of the High Court 1888–95

Michael Harrison (1823–95) was born in Ballymena, Co. Antrim. He was called to the Bar in 1849, practised on the North East circuit, and became a QC in 1863. 'He was for several years a regular attendant at Quarter Sessions in Belfast, and that aptness in dealing with minute facts which always marked his subsequent career was very much due to this early practice … His connexion with Belfast ensures him the largest experience in mercantile law possible in Ireland'.[219] In August 1867 he was appointed solicitor general, replacing R.R. Warren on his promotion to be attorney general.

At the end of October 1868 he was appointed to fill a vacancy in the court of Bankruptcy. The lord chancellor, Brewster, regarded the bankruptcy judgeship as a very inferior position and, on hearing from Warren in September that neither he nor Harrison would put themselves forward for the vacancy, had noted that that he was 'extremely glad to hear it, for their own sakes and for the credit of the government, to whom it would have been a reproach to have appointed men to their great offices who thought so little of themselves'.[220] There was an expectation that the Conservative government would lose the imminent general election, and arrangements were being made to find a place in the court of Probate for Warren, who told his constituents in Dublin University that he would not stand for re-election.

As solicitor general Harrison would have been at the head of the queue, after the attorney general, for promotion to any available judicial position, and he took the view that the bankruptcy court, although less prestigious and less well paid than the other courts, was the only opportunity for judicial preferment that was likely to come his way in the foreseeable future. It was later said that this was 'one of those junctures that, in the history of the Four Courts, occasionally occur, when, a judgeship falling vacant, there appears to be no eligible person with qualifications so super-eminent as to entitle him to the post as of right'.[221] Ten years later he was promoted to be a judge of the Common Pleas division of the High Court, following the death of Mr Justice Keogh, and when that division was merged into the Queen's Bench division in 1887[222] he became, by length of service, the senior ordinary judge of that division.

A sympathetic profile written in 1890 described him as a 'portly, dignified, comfortable man … without brilliant talents or deep learning [with whom] on the whole the country may be as well satisfied as he is with himself'.[223] It remarked

219 *ILT&SJ*, vol. 2, p. 573 (24 October 1868).
220 Brewster to Mayo, 23 September 1868 (Mayo Papers (NLI), MS 43,875/5).
221 'Rhadamanthus' (W.B. Campbell), *Our judges* (Dublin, 1890), p. 67.
222 Supreme Court of Judicature Ireland (Amendment) Act 1887 (50&51 Vict., c6), s2.
223 Rhadamanthus, op. cit., pp 69, 71.

that 'prosperity shines in his countenance, his person, his gait and his attire'. He lived at Newtown Park House, a substantial country house near Blackrock.

Parnell praised him in the House of Commons in the course of an attack upon other judges, notably Mr Justice Lawson and Mr Justice O'Brien, whose

> conduct in trying political cases, or cases of an agrarian character, has been such as to persuade the Irish people that they are not fit to be entrusted with the trial of such cases. I say there are noble exceptions. For instance, Mr Justice Harrison. He is a fair judge. He tried grave cases the other day and he obtained convictions. He tried murder cases and other important cases and nobody found fault with his conduct on those trials.[224]

He presided over the jury trial of one member of the so-called Tubbercurry conspiracy in 1884, which resulted in an acquittal and the dropping of all other charges.

He was the subject of much less complimentary Parliamentary comments by John Dillon MP in July 1890, arising out of a report of some intemperate remarks that he had made to the grand jury of Co. Galway about the prevalence of lawlessness, and lack of moral courage, in the county. Arthur Balfour, chief secretary for Ireland, asked for details of what he had said, which Harrison supplied in letters that Balfour read out in the House of Commons. He wrote that 'my charge was not committed to writing nor have I any note of it', and he acknowledged that his reference to 'Lynch law' had not been 'felicitously chosen', but said that nobody at the Bar or on the Bench would for a moment imagine that he would in any way have 'advocated the use of illegal methods for the redress of private wrongs, however intolerable those wrongs might be'.[225]

He was respected by the Bar, as

> a very good judge in a jury case. He has a fair impartial mind; and he is one of the most patient men on the Bench. He has a useful faith in counsel's competency to conduct his own case, and so he seldom interrupts him in his examination of witnesses, but allows him to choose his own line of proof. Many judges like to assume the part of an unbriefed counsel, and, by way of 'getting to the point', to run away with the case along what they conceive to be a short cut, but what more frequently turns out to be the long road of endless confusion and perplexity.

As a member of a divisional court he was silent and unobtrusive, and his judgments were 'short, lucid and well expressed'.[226] The lord chief justice, when

224 HC Deb, 3rd series, vol. 276, col. 866 (26 February 1883).

225 HC Deb, 3rd series, vol. 347, col. 374 (21 July 1890); *ILT&SJ*, vol. 34, pp 410–11 (2 August 1890).

226 Rhadamanthus, op. cit., pp 69, 71.

paying tribute after his death, said that 'in relation to the public he was a high-minded and conscientious judge, ever activated by an unfaltering love of justice. In other times other judges sat here whose opinions may perhaps occupy more conspicuous pages in our jurisprudence, but no one ever sat here who was more anxiously desirous to do right'.[227]

He died in October 1895, having been ill for a considerable time and unable to go circuit on assizes in the summer that year.[228] He was buried in his native town.[229]

R.R. Warren

Judge of the court of Probate 1868–77, of the High Court (Probate and Matrimonial Division) 1878–97

Richard Robert Warren (1817–97) was the only son of Henry Warren, who was the youngest son of Sir Robert Warren of Warrenscourt, near Lissarda, Co. Cork.[230] This was a large estate, the house of which was burned in 1921 during the War of Independence, and part of which is now a forest and recreation area owned by Coillte. Warren was educated at Trinity College and was called to the Bar in 1839. He joined the Munster circuit, 'where his family influence as the grandson of Sir Robert Warren Bt, a Cork county magnate, was considerable. After a time, however, Mr Warren, whose disposition rendered nisi prius work somewhat distasteful to him, devoted himself exclusively – an unusual step at that period of the Irish Bar – to equity work, in which he attained a considerable although not an extensive practice'.[231]

Warren became a QC in 1858, and was, briefly, the first chairman of the Incorporated Council of Law Reporting when it was set up in 1866.[232] In the rapid turnover of law officers that took place in 1866 and 1867 he was appointed solicitor general in March 1867 and attorney general in August that year, when he was also elected unopposed as one of the MPs for Dublin University, succeeding Hedges Eyre Chatterton in each of those three positions. He represented himself as being a reluctant law officer and politician, when speaking at a dinner that he gave in October 1868 for 150 of his constituents at which (in the knowledge that he would shortly be appointed the judge of the court of Probate) he announced that he would not stand for re-election at the imminent general election: 'it was true that the high office which he then filled was unsolicited by him. It was also true that the great honour of representing the great University of Dublin in Parliament came to him unsolicited'.[233] He 'marked his grateful sense of the honour conferred

227 *ILT&SJ*, vol. 29, p. 533 (2 November 1895).
228 *ILT&SJ*, vol. 29, p. 506 (12 October 1895).
229 *ILT&SJ*, vol. 29, p. 513 (19 October 1895).
230 *ILT&SJ*, vol. 31, p. 468 (2 October 1897).
231 *Law Times*, vol. 103, p. 482 (2 October 1897).
232 Eamonn G. Hall, *The superior courts of law: 'official' law reporting in Ireland, 1866–2006* (Dublin, 2007), pp 63, 68.
233 *Irish Times*, 21 October 1868; *ILT&SJ*, vol. 2, p. 573 (24 October 1868).

upon him by the University in electing him as one of its members by erecting a handsome glass window in the College Chapel'.[234]

In December 1868 he was appointed judge of the court of Probate, an office he held until his death in September 1897. (The probate jurisdiction, to which matrimonial matters had been added in 1870, and which had become a division of the High Court in 1877, was then folded into the Queen's Bench division of the High Court.[235]) An obituary of his predecessor as probate judge, Richard Keatinge, said that 'in 1868 he retired in favour of the present learned occupant of the office, Judge Warren',[236] a veiled suggestion that he had agreed or been induced to retire on the basis of knowing and approving who his successor would be. There was no expectation that the Conservative government would be returned to office at the general election so – unless a suitable vacancy presented itself – Warren would have been one of the handful of attorney generals in that period not to have been appointed a judge. Writing some sixty years later Serjeant A.M. Sullivan (who had not been born at the time) referred to Warren as 'a bitter pill' who had reportedly 'induced his predecessor to retire by purchasing his library at an enormous price'.[237] At all events, Warren's own library, sold shortly after his death, was described by the auction house as select, valuable and extensive, with fine and complete sets of law reports, 'all in the finest possible condition'.[238]

His quiet demeanour, never raising his voice, was said to give 'a tone and dignity to the proceedings' in his court,[239] although one exception was noted, the case of *Bagot v Bagot*.[240] These proceedings, in a prolonged and complicated probate suit with multiple parties heard in 1878, 'were virtually from beginning to end a duel between Judge Warren and Francis Macdonogh QC, who undoubtedly had the best of the encounter into which it was the general belief that had inveigled the judge to destroy his well-known influence with a jury'.[241] The issue was the good standing of a will made by a testator allegedly under an insane delusion that he was not the father of one of the parties, as to which evidence of personal resemblances between the child and his reputed father had been admitted. The Court of Appeal ordered a new trial, holding that the original hearing, including the judge's charge to the jury, had been unsatisfactory.

He was a committed member of the Church of Ireland, 'of Evangelical instincts',[242] and a member of the General Synod and of the Church Representative Body, from its foundation, and also chancellor of a number of dioceses, including the united dioceses of (1) Cashel and Emly, Waterford and

234 *Irish Ecclesiastical Gazette*, vol. 39, p. 802 (1 October 1897).
235 1897 Act, s5.
236 *ILT&SJ*, vol. 10, p. 113 (19 February 1876).
237 A.M. Sullivan, *Old Ireland: reminiscences of an Irish KC* (London, 1927), p. 70.
238 *Irish Times*, 6 and 16 November 1897.
239 *Law Times*, op. cit., p. 483; *ILT&SJ*, vol. 31, p. 483 (16 October 1897).
240 See LR (I), vol. V (1880–1) 58.
241 *Law Times*, op. cit.; *ILT&SJ*, vol. 31, p. 483 (16 October 1897).
242 *Irish Times*, 25 September 1897.

Lismore and (2) Killaloe and Kilfenora. He wrote a treatise on the law of the Church in 1895, in the preface to which he regretted that 'some eminent ecclesiastical lawyer such as Dr Ball or Dr Longfield' had not undertaken the task, and hoped that his work would 'induce some person with higher qualifications and with more energy and leisure than I can command' to write a comprehensive commentary on the subject.[243] He was a generous benefactor to the church, and published pamphlets on a number of church issues. In 1870 he opposed proposals for early revision of the Prayer Book, warning that changes would 'serve as an excuse for High Church clergymen to sever their allegiance from the Church of Ireland and to set up churches free from her laws and her authority in which without let or hindrance they will have full opportunity to lead captive, by an attractive Ritual, silly women and aesthetic young men'.[244]

He took an active part in a protest against Home Rule made by the church at a special meeting of the General Synod in the spring of 1886. Various resolutions, he said, had been moved by bishops and supported by landed proprietors, and he had been asked as a professional man to propose a resolution of opposition on the basis that Home Rule would 'impoverish … many of those on whose support the maintenance of our church, under God, depends and thereby disable her in the efforts which she is making to supply the spiritual needs of her people'. The income of the church, from its three principal sources of mortgages on Irish land, donations from its members and dividends from investments, would be severely threatened. 'Security of landed property or of industrial liberty cannot and will not co-exist with Irish self-government', which would surely result in civil war or separation.[245] These remarks were addressed to the spiritual and financial implications of Home Rule, but also constituted something of a political commentary by a judge 'from which many in his position would have shrunk'.[246]

Warren was described in 1890 as 'a dignified, elderly gentleman, with a long flowing beard and the usual legal shaven upper lip. He is a serious man, with high notions of the importance of every judicial position, and especially of that particular position which he himself holds. [He] is full of respect for the judges who have gone before him, and has made the most dignified and the most serious among them the models of his own conduct'.[247] The favouritism to relatives, common among Irish judges at the time, was followed by him in the appointment of his son, Henry Charles Warren BL, as chief registrar of the court in 1891.[248] He lived at 12 Fitzwilliam Square and died, while staying for the summer at Dalguise House, at Monkstown, Co. Dublin, in September 1897.[249]

243 R.R. Warren, *The law of the Church of Ireland: an essay* (Dublin/London, 1895).
244 R.R. Warren, *Revision of the liturgy in the Church of Ireland* (Dublin, 1870), p. 7.
245 *The Church of Ireland and the present crisis: report of the special meeting of the General Synod holden at Dublin, 23 March 1886* (Dublin, 1886), pp 52–3.
246 *Irish Ecclesiastical Gazette*, op. cit.
247 Rhadamanthus, op. cit., pp 57–8.
248 *ILT&SJ*, vol. 25, p. 238 (25 April 1891).
249 *Irish Times*, 2 October 1897.

CHAPTER SEVEN

Gladstone's first government, 1868–74

W.E. GLADSTONE BECAME prime minister for the first time in December 1868. In each of his ministries he was to be greatly concerned with affairs in Ireland, and the initial focus of this first period in office was the drafting and passing of legislation for the disestablishment of the Church of Ireland. The new attorney general, Edward Sullivan, was heavily engaged in this project, to an extent that he believed eventually compromised his health and made him very anxious to be appointed to the position of master of the rolls when a vacancy arose in the autumn of 1869. A sitting judge, Thomas O'Hagan, was appointed as the first Catholic lord chancellor for over 150 years, and was made a peer in 1870. Stephen Woulfe Flanagan, a lawyer with a specialised knowledge of land law, was appointed to the Landed Estates Court. Two of the other men appointed, James Lawson in 1868 and Charles Barry in 1872, were former MPs who had lost their seats at the election that brought Gladstone to power. When Richard Dowse, who had won a seat in Parliament in 1868, was appointed to the bench in the autumn of 1872 his successor as attorney general, Christopher Palles, stood unsuccessfully in the resulting bye-election. Palles was appointed as a judge in the last days of the government, in something of a scramble, but then held office for over 40 years, becoming an icon of the Irish judiciary, and as late as 1916 was seen as representing some continuity with the mid-Victorian era.

James Anthony Lawson

Justice of the court of Common Pleas 1868–77, Justice of the High Court 1878–87

James Anthony Lawson (1817–87) was born in Waterford. He was educated at Trinity College and was called to the Bar in 1840. He was the Whately professor of political economy in the university (1841–6), and was the initial secretary (1847–51) and later president (1870–2) of the Statistical and Social Inquiry Society of Ireland. A court official noted that 'I first knew him in 1851 when he was a junior. He had business in all the courts, as he was bold and would undertake anything'.[1] In 1857 he took silk, and also stood unsuccessfully as a Liberal candidate in the Dublin University constituency in the general election. He was appointed solicitor general in 1861 and attorney general in 1865, in each case filling an office vacated by a promotion of O'Hagan.

In the general election held in June 1865, a few months after appointment as attorney general, Lawson was elected to Parliament as member for Portarlington, which was a constituency with one of the smallest electorates in the country,

1 R. Denny Urlin, *Journal and reminiscences* (Letchworth, 1909), p. 136.

polling 46 votes to his Conservative opponent's 35. Reforms of the court of Chancery that were proposed by the Liberal government in successive years in the 1860s, including a Bill that Lawson re-introduced in Parliament in February 1866,[2] were blocked by Conservative opposition until the party came back into office and decided to adopt them. When the legislation was enacted in the summer of 1867 it was thus the Conservative attorney general, Chatterton, who was appointed to the new judicial position of vice-chancellor, which Lawson would have had some expectation of occupying.

As attorney general he prosecuted in some early trials of Fenians. He participated in a macabre scene at the assizes in Tullamore, Co. Offaly, in August 1865 when the aged chief justice of Queen's Bench, Thomas Lefroy, made errors in pronouncing a sentence of death on a man convicted of murder. Lefroy then repeated the sentence more carefully, as dictated by Lawson, who stood beside him for that purpose. In April and May 1866 this incident became the subject of Parliamentary exchanges, when the propriety of Lefroy continuing in office was debated (see p. 135).[3]

He ceased to be attorney general in the summer of 1866 when the Conservatives took office, and he lost his seat (by 69 votes to 51) in the general election of November 1868. In December he was appointed a member of the court of Common Pleas,[4] again succeeding O'Hagan, whose appointment as lord chancellor was a gesture to Catholic opinion. A 'numerous and influential class, especially of the Liberal Protestants, think that an injustice has been done in passing over Mr Lawson'.[5] Lawson's friend Sheridan Le Fanu regarded the 'accomplishing [of] an existing religious triumph' to be a poor reason for passing over Lawson for that office,[6] and believed that he then accepted judicial office out of frustration at a further disappointment of not again being appointed attorney general.[7]

The disestablishment of the Church of Ireland had been a major campaign issue in the general election, and the new government straight away set about implementing this policy, devoting much energy to the preparation and passing of the Irish Church Act. Gladstone had a high opinion of Lawson, and soon after his appointment as a judge noted 'his kindly promised and very valuable aid' in drafting the legislation.[8] Lawson was named in the statute as one of three Commissioners of Church Temporalities,[9] a new body established to address and

2 HC Deb, 3rd series, vol. 181, col. 584 (15 February 1866).
3 HL Deb, 3rd series, vol. 182, cols. 1628–36 (19 April 1866); HC Deb, 3rd series, vol. 183, col. 358 (3 May 1866) and cols. 780–90 (11 May 1866).
4 *ILT&SJ*, vol. 2, p. 702 (19 December 1868).
5 *Law Times*, vol. 46, p. 188 (12 December 1868).
6 Le Fanu to Dufferin, 7 December 1868 (W.J. McCormack, *Sheridan Le Fanu and Victorian Ireland* (Oxford, 1980), p. 219).
7 Ibid., Le Fanu to Dufferin,14 December 1868.
8 Gladstone to Sullivan, 26 December 1868 (Gladstone Papers, Add. MS 44417.261).
9 32&33 Vict., c.42, s3.

resolve many complex administrative and financial issues arising out of the disestablishment of the Church, including management of properties. It settled and paid compensation, ultimately amounting to over £11,500,000, for the disturbance of vested interests, having a dual function as an administrative clearing house for church property and as a court, the dividing line between which was blurred by design.[10] The Act was the first land purchase statute in Ireland, allowing church tenants to buy out the freehold on reasonably attractive terms.

Membership of the Commission, which was eventually dissolved by the Land Law (Ireland) Act 1881,[11] thus involved quite onerous responsibilities, for which a salary of £2,000 was paid. There was some unease at the appointment of a judge to a salaried position, although others overlooked any implications this might have for judicial independence and saw it as a form of recompense to Lawson for not having been appointed lord chancellor.[12] The Judicature Act 1877 subsequently provided that no sitting judge could be appointed to any place of profit under the Crown 'unless otherwise provided by Parliament',[13] a proviso which would have covered Lawson's appointment, since it had been specified in a statute, not simply made pursuant to it. It was later said that 'the incongruity of the two positions was a subject of stricture ... The holding by a judge, the tenure of whose judicial office has been rendered by statute independent of the Crown, of another office of profit at the pleasure of the Crown, would seem inconsistent with the dignity of the judicial position'.[14]

In 1872 Lawson gave a eulogy from the bench to the common law:

> Failing in this chaos of decisions to discover any settled principle which should absolutely govern us, we must have recourse to our common law for rules and analogies to guide our judgment, an alternative to which, for my part, I turn with pleasure, because there we shall find, though often intermixed and obscured by much that is technical, or that perhaps may be deemed narrow, principles of the soundest sense, the truest wisdom, and above all, a power of expansiveness and adaptation, which when properly applied is adequate to the solution of the novel questions that, in the complex relations grown out of an advanced civilisation, are continually coming to the surface.[15]

He was transferred to the Queen's Bench division of the High Court in June 1882, when in the turbulent days of the Land War Gladstone accepted the advice of

10 N.M. Dawson, 'Disendowment under the Irish Church Act 1869' in Kevin Costello and Niamh Howlin (eds), *Law and religion in Ireland, 1700–1970* (Cham, Switzerland, 2021), pp 271–2, 280–1.

11 44&45 Vict., c.49.

12 Urlin, op. cit., p. 136; J.G. Swift MacNeill, *What I have seen and heard* (London, 1925), p. 168.

13 40&41 Vict., c57, s13.

14 *ILT&SJ*, vol. 36, p. 142 (19 April 1902), citing *Law Times*.

15 *Trench v Nolan*, 6 ILTR (1872) 109 at 115.

Spencer, the lord lieutenant, and Law, the lord chancellor, that Lawson was 'probably the strongest judge now on the Irish bench'.[16] The policy and manner of enforcement of the criminal law was then a highly sensitive political issue, and Lawson was among the most heavily criticised of the judges for harshness to persons accused of serious crime connected with protests and disorder. In August 1882 controversy arose when he committed Edmund Dwyer Gray MP to prison for contempt of court, with a fine of £500. This was because the *Freeman's Journal* had published allegations that the jury in a murder trial had behaved in a drunken and disorderly manner in a hotel in which they had been secluded for the night. Gray was not only the publisher of the *Journal* but also the sheriff of the city of Dublin, one of whose functions was to take charge of jurymen in the course of trials. This committal was widely considered to be heavy-handed, and Gladstone remarked to Spencer that, while he understood that there should be no interference with the judges, 'I hope Lawson will interfere with himself. Otherwise I fear that he will have a very disagreeable time when Parliament meets: few to defend his excess of power'.[17] Lawson discharged Gray from prison six weeks later, and the select committee on privileges of the House of Commons later determined that this detention of one of its members did not demand the further attention of the house.[18]

A reference by Parnell in the House of Commons in 1883 to Lawson (and Mr Justice William O'Brien) as 'political judges'[19] was one of many such criticisms. In 1886 Gladstone acknowledged the potentially difficult position under a devolved Irish administration of judges who had 'uneasy relations with popular influences'[20] (see p. 89). The Home Rule Bill he was then introducing would have made provision for early retirement of judges before the required period of pensionable service would otherwise have been completed (although, in Lawson's case, he already had the required 15 years' judicial service). The *Irish Times* noted after Lawson's death in August 1887 that 'in cases where party or political sentiment was aroused on one side or the other [it] has not been possible and it never will be possible in those circumstances that a judge can satisfy popular impressions'.[21]

In November 1882 he was the target of a murder attempt while walking near the Kildare Street Club. All judges had been provided with a police escort since the Phoenix Park murders in May that year,[22] and he was

16 Spencer to Gladstone, 2 June 1882; Gladstone to Spencer, 3 June 1882 (Althorp Papers (BL), Add. MS 76854.46–8).

17 Gladstone to Spencer, 29 August 1882 (Althorp Papers, K5); H.C.G. Mathew (ed.), *The Gladstone diaries: vol. 10 (January 1881–June 1883)* (Oxford, 1990), p. 322.

18 *ILT&SJ*, vol. 16, pp 490–1 (7 October 1882) and p. 576 (25 November 1882).

19 HC Deb, 3rd series, vol. 276, col. 866 (26 February 1883).

20 HC Deb, 3rd series, vol. 304, col. 1070 (8 April 1886).

21 *ILT&SJ*, vol. 21, p. 442 (13 August 1887), citing *Irish Times*.

22 *ILT&SJ*, vol. 16, p. 232 (20 May 1882).

> attended, as usual for some time past, by a guard consisting of two detectives and two army pensioners, [and] was walking along Leinster Street … when the vigilance of one of the pensioners, McDonnell, who was walking on the opposite side of the street, was aroused by the sudden movement of a man who crossed from that side to where the learned judge was walking. Quickly rushing across also McDonnell caught the man as he arrived within a few paces of the judge and, as alleged, was in the act of drawing from his breast pocket what afterwards proved to be a fully-loaded seven-chambered revolver.[23]

A few weeks later there was a report of a plot to assassinate several of the judges as they were being entertained to dinner by Judge Harrison.[24]

Lawson was a sociable man, who engaged in amateur theatricals and was a member of the Hibernian Catch Club.[25] He had homes in Fitzwilliam Street and at Clontra, Shankill, Co. Dublin, where he died in August 1887.

Stephen Woulfe Flanagan

Judge of the Landed Estates Court 1869–77, Justice of the High Court 1878–85

The family of Stephen Woulfe Flanagan (1816[26]–91) came from the west of Ireland, owning land in counties Roscommon and Sligo. He was a nephew of Stephen Woulfe, chief baron of the Exchequer 1838–40. He was educated initially in France and then at Trinity College. His family's connections with the west were shown by his brother John standing (unsuccessfully) as a Liberal candidate in the borough of Sligo in the general election in 1868. Allegations of corrupt practices at that election (and at the previous elections in 1860 and 1865, at which prominent members of the Bar had been candidates (see p. 47) led to an inquiry and to the town constituency being disfranchised and merged in the county Sligo constituency.[27]

Flanagan was called to the Bar in 1838 and joined the Munster circuit. In 1843 he edited a volume of reports of Chancery cases.[28] He was a poor law inspector, and in 1849 had been appointed as secretary, and subsequently master, of the Encumbered Estates Commission (EEC), at a salary of £1,000, a position which he held until that body was superseded by the Landed Estates Court (LEC) in 1858. In the debate in the House of Commons on the setting up of the LEC two MPs in referring to his extensive experience and contribution to the working of the EEC, said that he had in effect been a fourth member of the Commission 'in disguise' or 'in fact' in addition to the statutory three members.[29]

23 *ILT&SJ*, vol. 16, p. 560 (18 November 1882).
24 *ILT&SJ*, vol.16, p. 596 (2 December 1882).
25 *ILT&SJ*, vol. 16, p. 561 (18 November 1882).
26 King's Inns Admission Papers, drawn from original records of the King's Inns, states his date of birth as 4 August 1816 (p. 170). He has been stated elsewhere to have been born in 1817.
27 An Act to disfranchise the boroughs of Sligo and Cashel 1870 (33&34 Vict., c.38).
28 *Reports of cases in Chancery argued and determined in the Rolls court, 1840–42* (Dublin, 1843).
29 HC Deb, 3rd series, vol. 150, cols. 28 (James Whiteside) and 42 (Rickard Deasy) (4 May 1858).

For about a dozen years, until new premises were provided at the Four Courts in 1860, the EEC and then the LEC were based in Henrietta Street, and their workings became something of a closed shop. The original location 'led, as might have been expected, to the formation of a small and exclusive Bar, and the general Bar was naturally discontented'.[30] One of the judges, Mountifort Longfield, gave evidence about this to a select committee of the House of Commons in 1856. Asked whether 'your Bar is too restricted and the locality where you sit in judgment is bad?' he said:

> The Bar is too restricted. The gentlemen who have most of the business are (and it is a very painful circumstance to us) three relations of the commissioners, my brother and the son-in-law and son of Mr Baron Richards. I think that that is an evil, and it cannot be rectified as long as you have the court sitting away from the Four Courts.[31]

In 1858 Flanagan retired with a pension and, returning to the Bar, became a Queen's Counsel in 1859 and, as might have been expected, developed a leading practice in the LEC. He lived at 20 Fitzwilliam Place, and took an active part in the establishment of the Law Reporting Council for Ireland in 1866, serving as its first vice chairman for two years and then as its chairman for 1868–9.[32] Gladstone approved Lord Spencer's proposal to appoint him as one of the two judges of the LEC in May 1869, following the death in April of a sitting judge, William Carey Dobbs.[33] His appointment does not appear to have been connected with any political affiliations that he may have had. When the jurisdiction of the LEC was transferred to the new High Court by the judicature legislation of 1877 he became a Land Judge in that court, from which he retired in November 1885.

The LEC (like the EEC) initially had three judges, and in 1866 the number was reduced to two in 1866 by an amending statute[34] (see p. 181), which recited that a vacancy had arisen owing to the death of one of the judges [Hargreave] 'and it is not expedient, having regard to the state of the judicial business of the court, that such vacancy should be filled up'. On the death of the other LEC judge, David Lynch, in December 1872 Flanagan was asked whether it was necessary to have two judges. He told the chief secretary for Ireland, Lord Hartington, that not appointing a second judge would not in any way interfere with the due despatch of the business of the court, nor impose on him an undue amount of labour. This opinion was subject to him seeing for a trial period of a month whether this would

30 R. Denny Urlin, *Journal and reminiscences* (Letchworth, 1909), p. 36.

31 Report of the Select Committee of the House of Commons on the Court of Chancery (Ireland) Bills, 1856 with minutes of evidence, Q1472 (P.P. 1856 (311), x. 1).

32 Eamonn G. Hall, *The superior courts of law: 'official' law reporting in Ireland* (Dublin, 2007), p. 535.

33 Spencer to O'Hagan, 6 May 1869 (O'Hagan Papers, D2777/8/42).

34 Landed Estates Court (Ireland) Act 1866 (29&30 Vict., c.99); an Act to facilitate the sale and transfer of land in Ireland 1858 (21&22 Vict., c.72).

in fact cause any delay or inconvenience to the public, and a month later he confirmed that 'I see no reason for changing or in any degree modifying the opinion I then expressed'.[35]

Flanagan's view of the matter was not shared or accepted by the legal profession, nor by the judiciary. The Incorporated Law Society of Ireland, representing solicitors, had lost no time in declaring in January 1873 that to have only one judge in the LEC 'will be attended with the most disastrous results to the public', and repeated this in June, while paying tribute to 'the indefatigable energy, zeal and industry of the learned judge of the LEC, by means of which alone there has not been permitted to accrue any arrears in the business of the court'.[36] The *Irish Law Times* supported the call for a second judge.[37]

The government was unpersuaded, and in June 1873 introduced a Bill that repeated the language of the 1866 statute as to it not being expedient to fill up a vacancy. It would have increased the salary of the judge by £500 to £3,500 and raised his status to that of equality with the puisne judges of the other courts. It also provided (section 4) that if the single judge were absent through illness or other cause, or if he or his family had a connection with or interest in any property coming before the court, the lord chancellor could authorise any other judge to act in his place. The master of the rolls, Edward Sullivan, complained to Hartington that the judges had not been consulted about this, and that they found the proposal 'most objectionable [and] highly unreasonable … The practice of that court is of a most peculiar and special character, which the judges are for the most part entirely unused to and which, in the great majority of cases, it would be wellnigh impossible that a judge acting temporarily as a substitute could safely administer'.[38] The *Irish Times* reported this as indicating that the judges 'decline to act as deputies to Judge Flanagan',[39] and the government did not proceed with the Bill, although taking no steps for the time being to appoint a second judge to the LEC.

Agitation for this did not fall away, however, and in August 1875 the government (now of the Conservative party, after the 1874 general election) announced its intention to appoint a second judge,[40] the actual appointment, of the attorney general, Henry Ormsby, being made in November. The total number of Irish judges was then a controversial matter in light of the proposals for judicature legislation that would recast the framework of the courts, and the announcement

35 T.H. Burke, Under Secretary, to Flanagan, 27 December 1872, and Flanagan to Burke, 2 January, 5 January and 3 February 1873 (Correspondence in relation to the Landed Estates Court (P.P. 1873 (247) liv.375)).

36 Resolution of the Council of the Society, 16 January 1873 (P.P. 1873 (247) liv.375); *ILT&SJ*, vol. 7, p. 323 (21 June 1873).

37 *ILT&SJ*, vol. 7, p. 82 (15 February 1873) and p. 335 (28 June 1873).

38 Edward Sullivan MR to Hartington, 21 June 1873 (Correspondence between judges and chief secretary for Ireland in respect of the Landed Estates Court (Ireland) Bill (P.P. 1873 (277) liv.389)).

39 *ILT&SJ*, vol. 7, p. 361 (12 July 1873), quoting *Irish Times*.

40 Statement by Sir Michael Hicks Beach (chief secretary for Ireland), HC Deb, 3rd series, vol. 226, col. 855 (11 August 1875); *ILT&SJ*, vol. 9, p. 410 (14 August 1875).

said that additional related duties would be transferred to the new judge, arising from the intended redundancy of a high legal official (see p. 274).

Flanagan regarded the announcement of this impending appointment, after he had served single-handed in the court for almost three years, as something of a slight or reflection upon him. A few days beforehand he had given a demonstration of his productivity by executing on the last day of the law term 'an unprecedented number of 152 conveyances to purchasers', an increase from the corresponding numbers of 81 in 1872, 108 in 1873 and 120 in 1874.[41] A supportive anonymous solicitor had written a letter to the press earlier in the year contending, with some detailed analysis, that 'the wheels of the court are revolving just as rapidly now as they ever did', and that 'Judge Flanagan has since the death of his late colleague wound up just as many estates in each year as used to be wound up annually by the two judges together'.[42]

He spoke of resignation, but was talked out of this by Lord Cairns, the lord chancellor of Great Britain, who told the prime minister that Flanagan's reaction 'is very foolish, but his resignation would be a great loss and would raise disagreeable remarks. I have no doubt a little civility and flattery would put it all right, and I think an effort should be made in this direction. I don't think a bribe of the Irish Privy Council would be necessary, though McDonnell [an examiner in the LEC] suggests it'.[43] In the event he was soon appointed to be a member of the Irish Privy Council.[44] A few months later he again spoke of resignation in light of provisions in the Judicature Bill,[45] but was again talked out of it. In 1878, having become a member of the new High Court, he was elected a bencher of the King's Inns.

In October 1885 Ormsby retired due to ill health, and in November Flanagan indicated, seemingly at the request of Ashbourne, the lord chancellor, that he was prepared to resign, with a condition that he would be made a member of the Privy Council in England.[46] The prime minister, Lord Salisbury, initially declined to arrange such an appointment, but conceded it later that month, on being told by Lord Carnarvon, the lord lieutenant, that 'a whole chain of legal and judicial appointments depend on it'.[47] Flanagan then resigned, and his appointment to the Judicial Committee of the Privy Council in London, was announced a couple of weeks later.[48] He was succeeded by the solicitor general, John Monroe, who as a single judge discharged what had been the functions of the 'Land Judges', as envisaged by the judicature legislation of 1877,[49] and Monroe's position was taken

41 *ILT&SJ*, vol. 9, p. 387 (31 July 1875).
42 *ILT&SJ*, vol. 9, p. 83 (13 February 1875).
43 Cairns to Disraeli, 14 September 1875 (Disraeli Papers, B/XX/Ca/158).
44 *ILT&SJ*, vol. 9, p. 548 (13 November 1875), vol. 10, p. 61 (29 January 1876).
45 James McDonnell to Lord O'Hagan, 5 April 1876 (Teeling Papers, MS 17874 (10)).
46 Holmes Memoir, *IHS*, vol. 16, no. 62, p. 165, fn62.
47 Holmes Memoir, ibid.; Carnarvon MSS (TNAUK), PRO, 30/6/57/83–100.
48 *ILT&SJ*, vol. 19, p. 596 (21 November 1885) and p. 636 (5 December 1885).
49 1877 Act, s6.

by John George Gibson QC, Ashbourne's brother. Flanagan sat on a few appeals in London. He died in 1891.

His eldest son John (1852–1929) was a journalist with the *Times*, at one time its chief leader writer, and was the author of its series of articles in 1887 on 'Parnellism and Crime' which gave rise to an official inquiry and an intense political drama in 1888–9.[50] A younger son James (1864–1922) was called to the Bar and appointed a resident magistrate, initially in Kerry and later in Newry,[51] where he was shot and fatally wounded as he left Mass at the cathedral in 1922.[52]

Edward Sullivan

Master of the Rolls 1870–83, Lord Chancellor of Ireland 1883–5

Edward Sullivan (1822–85) was born in Mallow, Co. Cork, where his father, one of a numerous family, was a wine and provision merchant. He had a distinguished academic record at Trinity College, and in 1845 was elected auditor of the College Historical Society. He was called to the Bar in 1848, became a QC ten years later and was appointed third serjeant in 1860. It was said that his brother William, as agent for a number of Cork attorneys, 'unquestionably contributed to his rapid rise', creating early opportunities for the display of his natural talents, which included being 'the best man ever known in a bad case, having an utterly unequalled manner of injured innocence and righteous indignation'.[53] He represented the wronged wife, Teresa Yelverton, in a sensational case in the court of Common Pleas in 1861 in which the validity of a marriage was litigated in Ireland and in Scotland, and a passage in his cross-examination of her husband was particularly admired at the time:

> Major Yelverton, did you ever love Teresa Longworth? I did.
> Did you ever love her purely and honourably? (After a considerable pause) Not entirely sir.
> I will repeat my question – did you ever love Teresa Longworth purely and honourably? No.
> Then, your love for her was always founded on dishonour? (After another pause) Yes sir.[54]

The first official legal appointment given to him, by the government of Lord Palmerston, was that of law adviser at Dublin Castle in 1861, in which year he also became a bencher of King's Inns,[55] and he was appointed as solicitor general in 1865. He was appointed attorney general in December 1868 when the Liberal party

50 See, for instance, F.S.L. Lyons, *Charles Stewart Parnell* (London, 1977), chap. 13 (pp 390–423).
51 *ILT&SJ*, vol. 47, p. 92 (29 March 1913).
52 *Irish Times*, 5 June 1922.
53 R.D. Urlin, *Journal and reminiscences* (Letchworth, 1909), p. 135.
54 Report (verbatim) of the trial, *Thelwall v Yelverton* (Dublin, 1861), p. 52.
55 *ILT&SJ*, vol. 15, p. 622 (10 December 1881).

was returned to office. He had become the MP for Mallow at the general election in 1865, and was re-elected in 1868. He was unopposed both times.

The principal government legislative project in 1869, which had been a very prominent election campaign issue, was the disestablishment of the Church of Ireland. The drafting of this measure, the Irish Church Act 1869, and securing its passage through strong opposition in Parliament, transpired to be an exhausting experience for Sullivan, who with Gladstone, the prime minister, bore the weight of preparation and debate,[56] and it affected his health.

That autumn a judicial vacancy arose when John E. Walsh, the master of the rolls, died suddenly on 20 October. The government was taking up the next item on Gladstone's Irish agenda, landlord and tenant legislation to extend more generally the 'Ulster custom' of enhanced tenant rights. Sullivan looked to be appointed to fill the vacancy. He believed that this had been settled with Gladstone early in November,[57] and that he had in any event a clear entitlement as attorney general to be appointed to any judicial vacancy. The prime minster however sought for a number of weeks to persuade him to remain in office as attorney general. 'The government are anxious to get all the assistance possible from him in the preparation of the Land Bill and, consequently, his appointment will be held back as long as possible'.[58] Gladstone's close political associate, Lord Granville, the colonial secretary, told him 'keep Sullivan you must. It was impossible to open the question [of land law reform] the other day in a more acceptable manner to the Cabinet than he did'.[59]

Gladstone had a variety of ideas for retaining Sullivan's services for a time, suggesting that his work and the state of his health might be eased by an understanding that he would not be asked to attend Parliament, and might take six months' rest, while the judicial office would remain unfilled.[60] The chief baron of the Exchequer and the chief justice of Common Pleas, Pigot and Monahan, each of whom had been the head of his court for some 20 years, were said to have been approached by the government inquiring whether, if Sullivan passed up on the position of master of the rolls, either of them would be willing to retire in his favour when his Parliamentary labours had ceased.[61] Sullivan regarded as wholly misconceived a varied scheme that was floated just before Christmas to ask Pigot to exchange his place in the Exchequer for the Rolls, on the basis that he would resign that office when requested to do so to facilitate Sullivan.[62] At an earlier stage Gladstone had explored whether, in the last resort, if there was a difficulty in

56 *ILT&SJ*, vol. 4, p. 31 (15 January 1870).
57 Sullivan to Gladstone, 20 December 1869 (Gladstone Papers, Add. MS 44423.333).
58 *ILT&SJ*, vol. 3, p. 682 (6 November 1869).
59 Granville to Gladstone, 1 November 1869 (Gladstone Papers, Add. MS 44166.203); *Ramm 1868–71*, p. 71.
60 Gladstone to Spencer, 1 November 1869 (Gladstone Papers, Add. MS 44537.123); Gladstone to Granville, 16 December 1869 (Granville Papers, GD 29/57); *Ramm 1868–71*, p. 78.
61 *Irish Times*, 8 November 1869.
62 Sullivan to Gladstone, 20 December 1869 (Gladstone Papers, Add. MS 44424.333).

setting up, or keeping open, for Sullivan an Irish judicial position, he could be told that he would be considered as qualified to take up a judgeship in England.[63]

The position of master of the rolls being left vacant for a time gave rise to complaints that a supposedly unprecedented suspension of the working of the Rolls court was 'a grievous wrong to suitors'.[64] Sullivan was reported as being torn between loyalty to Gladstone and the prospect of judicial office.[65] He 'came to see me [Gladstone] again yesterday to press for a final acceptance of his resignation',[66] and had remained adamant that solemn medical advice on the state of his health made it imperative for him to seek release from Parliamentary work and what he called 'official cares and responsibility'. He assured the prime minister that the judicial work in the Rolls, in which court he had had a leading position for years, would come comparatively easy to him.[67] Gladstone eventually conceded his appointment, just before Christmas, and he was sworn in as master of the rolls at the start of the new law term in January 1870. In a valedictory address to his constituents in Mallow he regretted retiring from political life at such an eventful period of his country's history, but said that the condition of his health, injured by constant work, had left him no alternative.[68]

The landlord and tenant legislation[69] was introduced and enacted after Sullivan had taken up judicial office, but he had been fully engaged in drafting work beforehand. Henry Thring, a parliamentary draftsman, did not mention Sullivan when later giving an account of his work with Gladstone in preparation of the Bill, although the *Irish Times* referred to it as 'the conjoint handiwork of Mr Sullivan and Mr Thring'.[70] In acknowledging to Sullivan that he would be appointed as the master of the rolls Gladstone remarked that he had no doubt but that Thring would be in constant communication with him,[71] and he noted in the middle of January that 'Thring is now in Dublin, having passed a morning with me on his way'.[72]

In 1873 Sullivan publicly and successfully challenged a government proposal in a Bill recently introduced in Parliament[73] for the master of the rolls and other judges to carry out certain functions in the Landed Estates Court (LEC) as an alternative to the appointment of a second judge there (see p. 235). In a letter to the chief secretary he described this as most objectionable and unprecedented, saying that the judges 'altogether object' to any direction to discharge the LEC

63 Gladstone to Granville, 31 October 1869 (Granville Papers, GD 29/57); *Ramm 1868–71*, p. 71.
64 *ILT&SJ*, vol. 3, p. 705 (20 November 1869).
65 *Irish Times*, 8 November 1869.
66 Gladstone to Granville, 16 December 1869 (Granville Papers, GD 29/57); *Ramm 1868–71*, p. 78.
67 Sullivan to Gladstone, 15 December 1869 (Gladstone Papers, Add. MS 44423.314).
68 *Irish Times*, 15 January 1870.
69 Landlord and Tenant (Ireland) Act 1870, 33&34 Vict., c.46.
70 Henry Thring, *Practical legislation: the composition and language of Acts of Parliament and business documents* (2nd ed., London, 1902), pp 5–6; *Irish Times*, 15 January 1870.
71 Gladstone to Sullivan, 28 December 1869 (Gladstone Papers, Add. MS 44423.336).
72 Gladstone to Granville, 15 January 1870 (Granville Papers, GD 29/57); *Ramm 1868–71*, p. 86.
73 Landed Estates Court (Ireland) (Judges) Bill (P.P. 1873 (182) ii.265).

business, and which in any event 'would seriously distract and interfere with their own duties'.[74] He subsequently expressed strong concern at what he believed would be a downgrading of the position of the master of the rolls, including a reduction in salary, in a draft of the Judicature Bill, and the relevant provisions were dropped and did not form part of the final legislation in 1877.[75]

Ball noted that 'after Gladstone's return to office in 1880 Sullivan became far the most notable judicial figure on account of the influence that he exercised in the government of the country'.[76] The office of lord chancellor became vacant in October 1881 when Lord O'Hagan stepped down, and the choice as to who would replace him lay between Sullivan and Hugh Law, the attorney general. Gladstone was initially prepared to accept the recommendation of the lord lieutenant and chief secretary, Cowper and Forster, that Sullivan be appointed, noting that 'I have agreed, not without difficulty, that Sullivan, *not* Law, shall be Chancellor. It is a question of the greater capacity against far the greater service'.[77] However Law was eventually appointed, on the basis of 'more recent and especially strong political claims',[78] his current service for the past 18 months in the tempest of the Land War weighing more heavily than Sullivan's distinguished service some 12 years before. Sullivan received some compensation by being made a baronet,[79] on Forster's suggestion.

A few months later, in the spring of 1882, when Sullivan was considered for nomination as the first Irish Law Lord, Lord Spencer, the lord lieutenant, in advising Gladstone on the appointment, made an unflattering comment on his demeanour as compared to that of the judge that he favoured (and who was appointed), John David Fitzgerald of the Queen's Bench (see p. 445).[80] When Law died unexpectedly in September 1883 consideration was given to the abolition of the office of lord chancellor, with the master of the rolls becoming the head of the Court of Appeal.[81] It was eventually decided that Sullivan would be appointed chancellor. He took office in December,[82] and the attorney general, Andrew Marshall Porter, became master of the rolls.

Sullivan died suddenly in April 1885. He left a very substantial estate, valued for probate at £90,949. He was a noted bibliophile and book collector, and in 1890 an auction of 'the choicer portions of [his] extensive and valuable library of printed

74 Sullivan to Hartington, 21 June 1873 (Correspondence between judges and chief secretary for Ireland in respect of the Landed Estates Court (Ireland) Bill (P.P. 1873 (277) liv.389)); *ILT&SJ*, vol. 7, p. 361 (12 July 1873).

75 Sullivan to O'Hagan, 15 April 1876 (Teeling Papers, MS 17874.10)

76 Ball, p. 312.

77 Gladstone to Granville, 21 October 1881 (Granville Papers, PRO 30/29/124); Agatha Ramm (ed.), *The political correspondence of Mr Gladstone and Lord Granville, 1876–1886, vol. 1 1876–1882* (Oxford, 1962), p. 305.

78 *ILT&SJ*, vol. 19, p. 200 (18 April 1885).

79 *ILT&SJ*, vol. 15, p. 622 (10 December 1881).

80 Spencer to Gladstone, 21 May 1882 (Althorp Papers (BL), Add. MS 76854.22).

81 *ILT&SJ*, vol. 17, p. 543 (20 October 1883). [From *Law Times*.]

82 *Irish Times*, 6 December 1883.

books and manuscripts, engravings and autograph letters' took place at Sotheby's in London.[83]

He and his wife, Elizabeth Bailey (who died in 1898), had five children, four sons and a daughter. He was a member of the Church of Ireland and she was a Catholic. The family lived initially in Eccles Street and from 1863 at 32 Fitzwilliam Place. His eldest son, Edward (1852–1928), the second baronet, stood (unsuccessfully) as the Liberal Unionist candidate in the St Stephen's Green constituency in the 1886 general election. He was a noted bookbinder, and was succeeded in the baronetcy by his brother William (1860–1937). The second son of the marriage, Robert, died in a sailing accident in Killiney Bay in 1877.[84] The youngest son, John (1861–1933), was educated at Trinity College and then lived for a time in England, where he was called to the Bar in 1888, although little is known of any legal work that he may have done. He was received into the Catholic church in 1896, at the Jesuit church in Farm Street, in Mayfair, London, and was ordained at Milltown Park as a member of the Jesuit order in 1907.[85] His edifying and spiritual life as a priest in Ireland gave cause for a process of beatification to be initiated in 1947, which was completed in 2017, and the process of investigation and consideration for canonisation is continuing. A small plaque on the family home marks his connection with the building.

Charles Barry

Justice of the Court of Queen's Bench 1872–83, Lord Justice of Appeal 1883–97

Charles Robert Barry (1823–97) was born in Limerick, the son of a solicitor. He was educated at Trinity College and was called to the Bar in 1845, joining the Munster circuit. His wife Kate was a sister of John David Fitzgerald (later Lord Fitzgerald). In 1862 he was called to the Inner Bar and, having become a bencher of King's Inns the following year, he was the senior bencher at the time of his death in 1897. He owned the state robes of the earl of Clare (John FitzGibbon), who had been lord chancellor of Ireland between 1789 and 1802.[86]

He stood and was elected, as a Liberal candidate, for Dungarvan in the 1865 general election. He had an extensive practice in criminal law, and his defeat at the next election in 1868 was attributed by some to 'the popular prejudice excited against him' on account of having led the prosecutions of James Stephens, Charles Kickham and other Fenian leaders in 1865–6.[87] In initial proceedings before a magistrate in September 1865 Barry had put forward 'a convincing – even hair-raising – *expose* of the Fenian menace', asserting that Fenianism was not simply a

83 Sotheby's, introduction to *Catalogue of sale of library of William O'Brien, property of the Milltown Park Charitable Trust* (London, 7 June 2017).
84 *ILT&SJ*, vol. 11, p. 526 (20 October 1877).
85 See Fergal McGrath SJ, *Fr John Sullivan SJ* (Dublin, 1941), and Thomas J. Morrissey SJ, *Where two traditions meet: John Sullivan SJ, 1861–1933* (Blackrock, 2009).
86 *ILT&SJ*, vol. 34, p. 247 (9 June 1900).
87 *ILT&SJ*, vol. 5, p. 641 (30 December 1871), citing *Saunders's News Letter* (27 December 1871).

political conspiracy for rebellion, separation from Britain and the setting up of an Irish republic, but that its members also had plans for wholesale expropriation of land and private wealth and for a massacre of all the higher and middle ranks of society, not excluding the catholic clergy.[88] There may have been other reasons for his defeat. The victorious candidate in 1868 was Henry Mathews QC (1826–1913), an English barrister, who made large gifts to the clergy in Dungarvan, while Barry complained of how he was 'expected to imbibe large quantities of punch, day and night, with successive batches of electors; and [how] failure in this terrible duty would seriously imperil his popularity'.[89] Mathews was subsequently defeated in the constituency in 1874, 1877 and 1880. In 1886 he became MP for East Birmingham, and was appointed as home secretary. The government considered appointing him in 1889 as a lord of appeal in ordinary, but ultimately nominated Sir Michael Morris.

Gladstone appointed Barry as solicitor general in December 1868, while regretting that he was no longer in Parliament. In that capacity he was nominated, with Serjeant Ballantine, to produce and manage evidence, at the Bar of the House of Commons, for the purpose of a Bill that would have disqualified the mayor of Cork, Daniel O'Sullivan, from office, by reason of the mayor having eulogised a Fenian who had recently shot and wounded a member of the Royal family in Australia. The Parliamentary proceedings were cut short and the Bill withdrawn on the basis that Mr O'Sullivan would resign.[90]

In January 1870 Barry succeeded Edward Sullivan as attorney general. In the New Year of 1872 he was appointed to fill a vacancy in the court of Queen's Bench, and in 1883 to the Court of Appeal to succeed the late Rickard Deasy. Much of his work as a judge was concerned with crime. A contemporary observer thought that 'he made an excellent common law judge [in the Queen's Bench] … There he was more at home than he has ever been in the Court of Appeal … He would have made an excellent and popular chief justice of Ireland, if that more congenial position had fallen to his lot'.[91] A dramatic trial (in fact two successive re-trials) over which he presided early in his judicial career, in 1873, was that of District Inspector Montgomery of the Royal Irish Constabulary. At the second re-trial he was convicted of the murder of a bank cashier, William Glass, at a branch of the Northern Bank in Newtownstewart, Co. Tyrone. The fact that the accused man was a friend of the victim, and had initially been in charge of the investigation into his violent death, generated great public interest in the trial.[92]

88 R.V. Comerford, *Charles J. Kickham; a study in Irish nationalism and literature* (Dublin, 1979), p. 80.

89 K. Theodore Hoppen, *Elections, politics and society in Ireland, 1832–1885* (Oxford, 1984), pp 79 and 81.

90 HC Deb, 3rd series, vol. 196, cols 350–1 (6 May 1869) and cols 575–84 (11 May 1869); *ILT&SJ*, vol. 21, p. 29 (15 January 1887).

91 Rhadamanthus (W.B. Campbell), *Our judges* (Dublin, 1890), p. 42.

92 M. McDonnell Bodkin KC, *Famous Irish trials* (Dublin, 1918), re-issued with an introduction by Eamonn G. Hall (Dublin, 1997), pp 95–103.

In *R v McMahon*[93] (1875) the four judges of the Queen's Bench disagreed on a point raised, by a writ of certiorari, on the conduct of a murder trial which had been moved from Limerick to Cork. Barry and Fitzgerald J held that nothing irregular had occurred and were prepared to affirm the conviction, whereas, as Barry said in his judgment, their more senior colleagues, Whiteside CJ (who cited Magna Carta) and O'Brien J, 'are resolved that judgment shall not be given for the Crown', holding that the trial was flawed. Custom and precedent indicated that in such circumstances he as the junior judge would withdraw 'and thus prevent the unseemly and anomalous state of things which would arise if no judgment at all were pronounced by this court'.[94]

Barry was among those judges who if presiding over a murder trial (for which, upon conviction, there was a mandatory sentence of death, by hanging) 'had the nerve to nudge the jury towards a guilty verdict, and to advise the lord lieutenant, without fussing, whether to commute or execute the sentence'.[95] In the case of Thomas Cuneen, executed after being convicted for murder in 1879, 'I was so convinced of his guilt that if he had protested his entire innocence on the scaffold it would only have shaken my belief in the efficacy of religious ministration and the piety of the attendant ecclesiastics'.[96] He sentenced a total of 18 people to death, of whom 10 were executed. Eight of those sentenced persons, including Myles Joyce, had been convicted of the gruesome murders of other members of the Joyce family in August 1882 in the remote Irish-speaking district of Maamtrasna.[97]

The trials took place in Dublin in November that year, in an atmosphere of great public excitement and alarm. The juries took very little time in reaching verdicts of guilt for the defendants in the first three trials, at which point the remaining five men pleaded guilty. The verdicts were 'warmly welcomed, without exception, in contemporary news reports'.[98] Appeals for clemency were made to the lord lieutenant, and Lord Spencer, as was customary, consulted Barry as the trial judge. Spencer did not intervene to prevent the execution of any of the first three men, Barry having told him that he had no doubt about their guilt and that the juries had likewise had no doubt.[99] Spencer did commute (to penal servitude for life) the sentences of the other five men, and told the Queen that Barry had 'earnestly pleaded' for that mitigation on the basis that the prosecution had 'allowed the idea to prevail both with the counsel for the prisoners and with the judge that the death sentence would not be carried out if they pleaded guilty'.[100]

93 IR 9 CL 309 (1875); W.E. Vaughan, *Murder trials in Ireland, 1836–1914* (Dublin, 2009), pp 156–9.
94 IR 9 CL 309, at 375.
95 W.E. Vaughan, op. cit., p. 258.
96 Barry to Edward Gibson (attorney general), undated [1879] (Ashbourne Papers, B.12/5).
97 The district, which was then in Co. Galway, was transferred to Co. Mayo in 1898.
98 Margaret Kelleher, *The Maamtrasna murders: language, life and death in nineteenth century Ireland* (Dublin, 2018), p. 133.
99 Barry to Spencer, 29 November 1882 (Convict Reference File, 1902, J13, folder 10, National Archives); Kelleher, op. cit., pp 135–6
100 Spencer to the Queen, 11 December 1882 (Peter Gordon (ed.), *The red earl: the papers of the fifth Earl Spencer, 1835–1910* (Northampton, 1981–6), vol. 2, p. 230).

The murders did not have the direct political overtones or resonance of other sensational crimes or 'outrages', but the fact that the early complaints about the case were led by nationalist politicians, principally Timothy Harrington MP, may have had the effect of limiting concern among other sections of society. Barry's contemporary judicial reputation was not affected by the trial, as evidenced by his promotion in 1883. Over time a more general sense of public unease developed about the verdicts, and in particular about the degree to which (if at all) Myles Joyce and other Irish-speaking defendants had properly understood the court proceedings and as to whether, at least in his case, a miscarriage of justice may have taken place.[101] An expert review of his trial by Dr Niamh Howlin in 2017 was unflattering as to the manner in which Barry had presided over it, and concluded that a combination of factors 'meant that his trial was unfair by the standards of late nineteenth century criminal justice'.[102] In April 2018 the president of Ireland granted a posthumous pardon to Mr Joyce.

Barry's expertise in criminal law was acknowledged in 1878 when he was nominated, in company with some of the most prominent English lawyers of the day, to serve on a Royal Commission on the law of indictable offences (i.e., the most serious crimes). A leading law reformer, James Fitzjames Stephen, had drafted a 'Bill of unusual magnitude [425 sections] dealing with the whole subject of indictable offences. The measure would repeal the whole of the present statute law on the subject and substitute a code'.[103] This had been given a second reading in the House of Commons, and a Royal Commission was set up to give detailed consideration to the proposal, since it was impracticable for a Parliamentary committee to do so in the conventional way. Its members were Lord Blackburn,[104] Lord Justice Lush and Fitzjames Stephen, to whom Barry was soon added.[105] The Commission worked intensely for six months, making various amendments to the Bill. Barry's view, shared by Gibson and FitzGbbon, was that there should be a single code of criminal procedure for England and Ireland, with any provisions intended to be applicable only in Ireland being appropriately separately specified.[106] The Commission in its report approved the principle of codification, as 'the reduction of the existing law to an orderly written system freed from the needless technicalities, obscurities and other defects which the experience of its administration has disclosed'.[107] But despite such labour 'this most promising of

101 Professor Kelleher's book (Part III, pp 151–214) refers to the extensive literature on the subject.

102 Niamh Howlin, 'Report on the trial of Myles Joyce, November 1882', prepared for the Irish government (July 2017), p. 31.

103 HL Deb, 3rd series, vol. 241, col. 950 (8 July 1878), remarks of Lord Chancellor (Lord Cairns).

104 Blackburn's criminal law experience included being one of the two judges at the trial in 1867 of five men for the murder of a police officer in Manchester in the course of a rescue of Fenian prisoners. The trial resulted in the conviction and execution of three of defendants, Allen, Larkin and O'Brien (the 'Manchester Martyrs').

105 HL Deb, 3rd series, vol. 241, col. 951 (8 July 1878); *ILT&SJ*, vol. 12, p. 460 (8 September 1878).

106 Barry to Gibson, undated [1879] (Ashbourne Papers, B.12/5).

107 Report of the Royal Commission on the law relating to indictable offences, with appendix containing draft code embodying suggestions, P.P. 1878–9 (c.2345), xx.169, p. 47.

1 Maziere Brady (*The Graphic*, 20 May 1871). Image courtesy of the British Newspaper Archive/Mary Evans Picture Library. See p. 131.

2 The Four Courts, from the west (Lawrence Photograph Collection). Image courtesy of the National Library of Ireland.

3 James Monahan (by A. Lesage). Image courtesy of the Public Record Office of Northern Ireland.

4 Jonathan Christian (by T. Cranfield, *Dublin University Magazine*, vol. 84 [July–December 1874]). MUL MF 14, Licensed under CC BY 4.0 by the Board of Trinity College Dublin.

5 Thomas O'Hagan, 1st Lord O'Hagan (by John Watkins, 1868). © National Portrait Gallery, London.

6 James Whiteside (by James Simonton, 1860s). © National Portrait Gallery, London.

7 'Her Majesty's judges in Ireland 1891' (*The Graphic*, 4 April 1891). Image courtesy of the British Newspaper Archive/Mary Evans Picture Library. Back row (l/r): Christopher Palles, R.R. Warren, John Fitzhenry Townsend, William Moore Johnson, William O'Brien, William Drennan Andrews,

12. Judge Miller (Bankruptcy)
13. Mr. Justice Murphy (Common Pleas)
14. Mr. Justice Gibson (Queen's Bench)
15. Lord Justice Barry (Court of Appeal)
16. Mr. Justice Bewley (Irish Land Commission)
17. The Right Hon. Peter O'Brien (Lord Chief Justice)
18. Lord Ashbourne (Lord Chancellor)
19. The Right Hon. Lord Morris (Lord of Appeal)
20. Lord Justice Fitzgibbon (Court of Appeal)
21. Right Hon. A. M. Porter (Master of the Rolls)

in Ireland, 1891

Michael Harrison, John Monroe, Walter Boyd, Hugh Holmes, Hedges Eyre Chatterton, Stearne Ball Miller, James Murphy, John G. Gibson. Front row (l/r): Charles Barry, Edmund Bewley, Peter O'Brien, Lord Ashbourne, Lord Morris, Gerald FitzGibbon and Andrew Marshall Porter.

8 Lord O'Hagan, statue in Round Hall, Four Courts (by Thomas Farrell, RHA). Image courtesy of the Irish Architectural Archive. See p. 166.

9 James Whiteside, statue in Round Hall, Four Courts (by Thomas Woolner). Image courtesy of the Irish Architectural Archive. See p. 203.

10 David R. Pigot (by T. Cranfield, *Dublin University Magazine*, vol. 83 [January–June 1874]). MUL MF 14, Licensed under CC BY 4.0 by the Board of Trinity College Dublin.

11 Michael Morris (by Lafayette Ltd, from M. McD. Bodkin, *Recollections of an Irish judge* (1914)). Image courtesy of the National Library of Ireland.

12 Edward Sullivan (from M. McD. Bodkin, *Recollections of an Irish judge* (1914)). Image courtesy of the National Library of Ireland.

13 Charles Barry (*The Graphic*, 16 June 1883). Image courtesy of the British Newspaper Archive/Mary Evans Picture Library.

14 Richard Dowse (by Chancellor & Son, from M. McD. Bodkin, *Recollections of an Irish judge* (1914)). Image courtesy of the National Library of Ireland.

15 Christopher Palles (by Chancellor & Son, the *Clongownian*, no. 4, June 1897). Image courtesy of the National Library of Ireland.

16 J.T. Ball (by T. Cranfield, *Dublin University Magazine*, vol. 85 [January–June 1875]). MUL MF 14, Licensed under CC BY 4.0 by the Board of Trinity College Dublin.

17 G.A.C. May, engraving by M. Hanhart, after unknown artist, England, *c.*1877, mezzotint. Image courtesy of the National Gallery of Ireland, NGI.10429.

18 Gerald FitzGibbon, oil on canvas by Walter Frederick Osborne, 1894. Image courtesy of the National Gallery of Ireland, NGI.953.

19 James Murphy (by Chancellor & Son, from M. McD. Bodkin, *Recollections of an Irish judge* (1914)). Image courtesy of the National Library of Ireland.

20 A.M. Porter (relief, by Sophia Rosamond Praeger). Image courtesy of Queen's University Belfast Art Collection.

21 Edward Gibson, 1st Lord Ashbourne (by York & Son, after unknown photographer, 1890s). © National Portrait Gallery, London.

22 'Some well-known Irish judges' (*The Graphic*, 10 June 1899). Image courtesy of the British Newspaper Archive/Mary Evans Picture Library. Back row (l/r): Richard E. Meredith, Gerald FitzGibbon, John Ross, Lord Morris, John G. Gibson, William Kenny. Front row (l/r): Walter Boyd, Hugh Holmes, Samuel Walker, Lord Ashbourne, Andrew Marshall Porter, William Drennan Andrews, Dodgson Hamilton Madden.

23 Hugh Holmes (*Illustrated London News*, 17 July 1897). Image courtesy of the British Newspaper Archive/Mary Evans Picture Library.

24 'Distinguished sons of Clongowes' (Christopher Palles, John Naish and Peter O'Brien, the *Clongownian*, no. 5, Christmas 1897). Image courtesy of the National Library of Ireland.

25 Peter O'Brien (by Chancellor & Son, from M. McD. Bodkin, *Recollections of an Irish judge* (1914)). Image courtesy of the National Library of Ireland.

26 Dunbar Plunket Barton (by Benjamin Stone, 1898). © National Portrait Gallery, London.

27 John Atkinson (by H. Walter Barnett, 1905–20). © National Portrait Gallery, London.

28 Richard Robert Cherry (by Benjamin Stone, 1907). © National Portrait Gallery, London.

29 Arthur Warren Samuels (by Walter Stoneman, 1918). © National Portrait Gallery, London.

all English criminal codification attempts'[108] foundered and was never enacted, although it later provided the foundation for penal codes in some colonies.

Barry was a well-liked and sociable man, and a member of the University Club. He died, suddenly, in May 1897 at his home, 3 Fitzwilliam Square. The *Irish Times* referred to his 'genial and courteous character', and in paying tribute in court to his memory the lord chancellor, Lord Ashbourne, spoke of the 'natural brightness and buoyancy of his disposition … his cheery and sympathetic manner'.[109]

Richard Dowse

Baron of the Exchequer 1872–7, Justice of Exchequer Division 1878–90

Richard Dowse (1824–90) was born in Dungannon, Co. Tyrone, the only son of a merchant. He graduated from Trinity College in 1849 and was called to the Bar in 1852, in which year he married his wife Kate. He practised on the North West circuit, which included his native county, and was called to the Inner Bar in 1863. His practice in criminal law included acting in the defence of some of the Fenians charged with treason in 1865–6 and in the prosecution in 1871 of Robert Kelly for the murder of a policeman, head constable Talbot, in Dublin.

In the general election of 1868 Dowse was elected to Parliament for the City of Londonderry constituency, as a Liberal, defeating the sitting Conservative member, Lord Claude John Hamilton, by 704 votes to 599. His election was unsuccessfully challenged by a petition, in which Christopher Palles acted for him.[110] In January 1870 the solicitor general, Charles Barry, was promoted to be attorney general, replacing Edward Sullivan QC, MP and Dowse was appointed to take the place of Barry. Shortly prior to his appointment Gladstone, the prime minister, had been quite dismissive of the ability of Dowse, saying that to appoint him to be master of the rolls, 'an office of £5,000 a year for life, [would be] little short of ludicrous', and that he was 'impossible' as a potential attorney general.[111]

He became the government's legal spokesman in the House of Commons, since Barry did not have a seat in Parliament. In February 1872, he became attorney general when Barry was appointed to be a judge. He was well respected in Parliament, short as his career there was, for his vigour in debating and his keen wit, as exemplified in a speech in 1869 on the second reading of the Bill to disestablish the Church of Ireland. He spoke 'as an Irish Protestant Episcopalian, sent to Parliament expressly to support the present measure', and taunted Disraeli, the leader of the opposition, with having described the church as an alien church

108 Keith Smith, 'Criminal Law' in Cornish, Anderson, Cocks, Lobban, Polden and Smith (eds), *The Oxford history of the laws of England, vol. XIII, 1820–1914: fields of development* (Oxford, 2010), p. 210.

109 *Irish Times*, 19 May 1897; *ILT&SJ*, vol. 31, p. 243 (22 May 1897).

110 *ILT&SJ*, vol. 3, p. 13 (2 January 1869).

111 Gladstone to Granville, 31 October 1869 and 16 December 1869 (Granville Papers, G.D. 29/57); *Ramm 1868–71*, pp 71 and 78.

> in the days before his voice was silenced by the promptings of ambition ... Hon. Gentlemen opposite were such friends of the Irish Episcopal Church that the moment an Irish Episcopalian came forward to express his opinion they conveyed pretty plainly that they did not want to hear him, inasmuch as they knew more of the subject than he did.[112]

He spoke forcefully shortly afterwards in favour of a resolution for an inquiry into the management of the estates of London companies in the county and city of Londonderry, dating from the Plantation of Ulster in the seventeenth century.[113]

In the autumn of 1872 he was appointed to be a judge (baron) of the court of Exchequer, a vacancy that had arisen in July that year on the death of baron Hughes. It was initially considered that Dowse might pass up the opportunity to take the place, both because his services in Parliament (and for some impending prosecutions) were valued and because of the possibility that a higher judicial position might soon become available through retirement of the head of the court of Exchequer (chief baron Pigot) or the head of the court of Common Pleas (Monahan CJ), both of whom had held office for over twenty years.[114] In October however, after Lord Spencer has expressed concern about keeping a judicial place open or vacant for the political convenience of the government,[115] he accepted the appointment to replace Hughes, and on the death of Pigot fourteen months later that place was filled by Palles. Curiously, at sittings of the court of Exchequer Palles chose not to occupy the centre seat that would ordinarily be taken by the head of the court, and Dowse held centre stage.[116]

Dowse's judicial work in criminal law included murder trials.[117] However his propensity to display levity on the Bench became the core of his contemporary judicial reputation. A report of a hearing at the assizes in Wicklow in 1875 gives a flavour of this.

> During the trial of *Rev R. O'Keeffe v Very Rev Dr McDonald* the plaintiff was cross-examining a witness on matters of canonical law, when one of the jurors intervened and asked Baron Dowse whether his lordship would permit the plaintiff to be putting questions which had no bearing on the case. The learned judge, with pathetic meekness, replied that he was doing his best to keep Fr O'Keeffe within legitimate bounds, but that the plaintiff, being his own counsel, should be allowed considerable latitude. The juror was by no means prepared to approve of this dogma, and retorted that jurors had rights and privileges as well as the parties in the case. 'True', said Baron Dowse,

112 HC Deb, 3rd series, vol. 194, cols. 1955–64 (22 March 1869).
113 HC Deb, 3rd series, vol. 195, cols. 708–13 (13 April 1869).
114 *ILT&SJ*, vol. 6, p. 440 (17 August 1872).
115 Spencer to O'Hagan, 11 August 1872 and 15 September 1872 (O'Hagan Papers, D2777/8/204 and 205).
116 Rhadamanthus, op. cit, p. 61; *Irish Times*, 16 February 1920.
117 Vaughan, *Murder trials in Ireland*, pp 216, 224, 257; Spencer to O'Hagan, 24 August 1873 (O'Hagan Papers, D2777/8/227).

'but one of the privileges of a judge is not to be criticised by a juror'. The duel had now assumed a triangular aspect … But fortunately another juror interposed with a compliment to his lordship on the patience with which he was hearing the case; and the episode concluded by the learned judge stating, *obiter*, that it was the first time he had even been accused of being over patient, and he was really surprised at it himself.[118]

The demeanour in court of Dowse and his jousting with counsel was also noted in 1876 at the assizes in Mullingar. An account of the proceedings there in a complicated action for ejectment (*Purdon v Longford*) was set out in *Famous Irish trials* by M. McDonnell Bodkin who, when this was first published (in 1918), was a county court judge.[119] Decades earlier, as he wrote, 'when studying for the Bar, I had assisted in reporting this remarkable trial for the *Freeman's Journal* … [which] made a vivid impression on my memory'.[120] The verbatim newspaper report referred to laughter in court on many occasions. This was the first in a number of trials between the parties, ultimately hinging on the contents of a will allegedly tainted by lack of capacity on the part of the testator and by undue influence having been exercised over him. Dowse withdrew from the jury the issue of undue influence, and on appeal the full court of Common Pleas held that this was not justified and that the verdict thus obtained could not be upheld, and directed a new trial.[121] A separate jury verdict in the court of Probate was subsequently set aside by Warren J.[122]

In 1889 when referring to the library in the King's Inns Dowse said that the benchers should take another house in Henrietta Street. 'The great thing is that they do not want to spend money. They are keeping it for an Irish parliament to take it from them'.[123] A profile published shortly before his death referred to him as 'a chartered libertine, free to say anything or everything that comes into his head, whether it be *a propos* of the matters before him or not, provided only that it be amusing … Litigants of course are often horrified to see their cases translated into a high class comedy for the diversion of the judge and the junior Bar'. The writer added that 'levity and jesting … trivial jokes and fooling' were particularly out of place in criminal trials.[124] The *Irish Law Times* wondered whether humour

118 *ILT&SJ*, vol. 9, p. 396 (7 August 1875).

119 Bodkin's nomination to the Bench in 1907 had been controversial, with his credentials as a practising barrister, a requirement to be eligible for appointment in the first place, being challenged (unsuccessfully) by the issue of a conditional order for a writ of quo warranto. 'The case, though full of dramatic possibilities, is devoid of legal interest' (*ILT&SJ*, vol. 42, p. 35 (8 February 1908)). See Serjeant A.M. Sullivan, *Old Ireland: reminiscences of an Irish KC* (London, 1927), pp 153–5, and Healy, *OldMC*, pp 186–90.

120 M. McDonnell Bodkin, *Famous Irish trials* (Dublin, 1918, reissued with an introduction by Eamonn G. Hall (Dublin, 1997)), p. 3.

121 *Purdon v Longford*, IR CL, vol. 11 (1877–8), 267.

122 *Longford v Purdon*, LR(I), vol. 1 (1878–9), 75.

123 *Gaffney v Going*, *ILT&SJ*, vol. 23, p. 70 (2 February 1889).

124 Rhadamanthus, op. cit., pp 63–4.

may have been better appreciated in an Irish courtroom than in London.[125] It was said in 1889 of Lord Fitzgerald that 'he had a plentiful supply of Irish humour though he fortunately never posed as a humorist on the Bench'.[126] Decades later James O'Connor advised any judge whose utterances met with applause or laughter in court to 'disinfect yourself without delay in the waters of humility'.[127]

Dowse died suddenly while on circuit in Tralee in February 1890. His jovial personality appears to have been inherited by his only son Richard (1859–1910), 'who was so largely associated with public charities and amusements … he organised charity balls in aid of Mercer's Hospital, the Police-Aided Society, the Children's Hospital Temple Street, Sir Patrick Dun's Hospital and many others'.[128] He had been called to the Bar in 1883 and acted for some time as a registrar to his father, but never practised at the Bar.

Christopher Palles

Chief Baron of the Exchequer 1874–1916 (Queen's [King's] Bench Division of the High Court 1897–1916)

In February 1874 Christopher Palles (1831–1920) was appointed chief baron of the Exchequer, an office (or, more precisely, a title) that he held for the next 42 years. The judges of the court of Exchequer, one of the historic Four Courts, had the title of barons rather than justices, and the president of the court was the chief baron rather than its chief justice. Palles remained chief baron until his retirement in the summer of 1916, 'achieving in the course of his long judicial tenure an extraordinary reputation, not only in Ireland but generally in the common law world. Palles, invariably described as courteous and dignified, shone in an era of great Irish judges'.[129] A comprehensive set of scholarly studies of his judicial legacy in many fields of law, in Ireland and elsewhere in the common law world, was published in 2022.[130] He was called to the Bar in 1852 and became a QC in 1865. 'As a junior he was in very extensive common law practice but on obtaining silk he devoted himself almost exclusively to practice in the courts of equity, only going into common law courts upon special occasions'.[131]

The circumstances in which he took office may not have seemed to be a harbinger of a long and distinguished judicial career. His was the last judicial appointment to be made by Gladstone's first government (1868–74). He had been

125 *ILT&SJ*, vol. 24, p. 162 (22 March 1890) and p. 200 (12 April 1890).
126 Annual Register, 1889.
127 Preface (p. xiv) to *A digest of criminal and quasi-criminal law, 1914–1925* (Dublin, 1925).
128 *ILT&SJ*, vol. 44, p. 81 (2 April 1910).
129 Entry on Palles in *DIB* (by W.N. Osborough).
130 Oonagh B. Breen and Noel McGrath (eds), *Palles: the legal legacy of the last lord chief baron* (Dublin, 2022). Contributors discussed this legacy under headings that included the Judicature Act 1877, company law, the land question, public benefit in charity law, contempt of court, the development of certiorari, compensation for criminal injuries, the doctrine of vicarious liability and tort.
131 *ILT&SJ*, vol. 6, p. 40 (27 January 1872).

appointed solicitor general in January 1872, after some initial hesitation by the prime minister,[132] and then became attorney general in November that year. On each of those appointments he had succeeded Richard Dowse, who had been appointed attorney general in February and a baron of the Exchequer in November. It was an accepted prerogative of the attorney general to be offered any judicial vacancy that might arise, although in November 1873 the future of that practice had been put in doubt in England. The Cabinet then was of the opinion that 'with the passing of the Judicature Act, all claims of either or both law officers to a succession as of right to any particular judicial office (claims which were never adequately established) have naturally dropped; so that their promotion would henceforward rest on qualification and service only, not on the possession of the post of law officer'.[133]

It was also conventional, or at least convenient for the government in terms of handling parliamentary questions and debates, for one or both of the Irish law officers to be a member of Parliament, as Dowse had been for a period (1870–2) when the attorney general, Charles Barry, was not. The appointment of Dowse to the bench necessitated a bye-election for the constituency which he had represented, the City of Londonderry,[134] and Palles stood as the Liberal candidate. At that election, held on 27 November 1872, he received 552 votes, the Conservative candidate[135] 696 and a candidate of the nascent Home Rule movement 89.[136] The Conservative majority over Palles was thus greater than the number of Home Rule votes, contrary to some later commentaries,[137] one of which misstated the Conservative vote as 606. The role of Palles in the decision, which was announced by Dowse in July 1872, to prosecute the bishop of Clonfert and other members of the Catholic clergy for their role in the controversial bye-election in Co. Galway earlier that year, affected his support among Catholic voters, and he lost the support of Presbyterian voters also. Dowse had secured 54% of the vote in his elections in 1868 and 1870 whereas Palles secured 40%. He was 'in reality as unsuited to the circumstances as a candidate could be'.[138] Subsequent suggestions that, if he had been elected, 'his valuable services [in Parliament] to the Liberals in opposition would have prevented his judicial preferment in 1874'[139] are speculative and may not be well grounded.

132 Spencer to O'Hagan, 22 December 1871 (O'Hagan Papers (PRONI), D2777/8/167).
133 Gladstone to the Queen, 12 November 1873 (Letters of Queen Victoria, series 2, vol. 2 (London, 1926), p. 290).
134 Palles represented Dowse in 1868–9 on the petition brought by the losing candidate to set aside the result of the election.
135 Edward Gibson (later Lord Ashbourne) had an interest in being selected as the Conservative candidate, but the nomination had been promised to C.E. Lewis (David Plunket to Gibson, 4 September 1872 (Ashbourne Papers, B119/14).
136 Brian M. Walker (ed.), *Parliamentary election results in Ireland, 1801–1922* (Dublin, 1978), p. 114.
137 E.g., *ILT&SJ*, vol. 50, p. 269 (7 October 1916) (from *Law Times*).
138 Gerald R. Hall, *Ulster Liberalism, 1778–1876* (Dublin, 2011), p. 228.
139 *Law Times* (London), vol. 149, p. 164 (28 February 1920); V.T.H. Delany, *Christopher Palles, his life and times* (Dublin, 1960), p. 74.

The only judicial vacancy to arise while Palles was attorney general was the office of chief baron, when the incumbent, David Pigot (1796–1873), who had held that office since the summer of 1846, died on 22 December 1873. Palles wrote the same day to Lord O'Hagan, the lord chancellor, about the succession to the position, taking the opportunity to discount a rumour that Gladstone had given a promise of 'the first vacant Chiefship' to Mr Justice Lawson, who 'therefore looks upon the present appointment as his just inheritance'. No notice of any such promise had been given subsequently to any prospective law officers, such as himself, before their appointment, and he thus thought it unlikely that it was made.[140] Palles was thus alert to the prerogatives of his office, and any claims by Lawson do not seem to have been entertained.

The lord lieutenant, Lord Spencer, urged Gladstone on Christmas Eve to appoint Palles without delay, before the new law term would begin on 11 January. Gladstone's preference was not to appoint any new judge, with a view to an ultimate restructuring and reduction in the size of the judiciary (as had just been legislated for in England), and he drew Spencer's attention to an editorial in the *Times* (30 December 1873) which had suggested appointing one of the existing barons to be the chief, leaving a puisne judgeship vacant. Spencer's response, supported by the chief secretary, Lord Hartington (later the duke of Devonshire), again urged the appointment of Palles.[141] Gladstone noted of these representations that they 'take for their ground' the report of a Royal Commission on the English and Irish court systems in 1863 which had included a recommendation to the effect that no reduction in judicial numbers in Ireland was appropriate.[142] Gladstone and the lord chancellor of Great Britain, Lord Selborne, whom he consulted, were unimpressed with that argument. (Selborne remarked that although he had been a member of the 1863 Commission he had generally left Irish matters to the Irish members, and should not be seen as supportive of the comments about the report, particularly since it had also acknowledged that the courts might be re-organised.)

Selborne advised however that it would be irregular to leave a vacancy unfilled in the absence of a specific proposal to change the law so as to reduce the number of judicial positions. Any reduction in numbers could be effected only by not filling an existing vacancy or by providing that a vacancy yet to arise would not be filled.

> There is a great and well-founded objection (I think on strictly legal, as well as constitutional grounds) to keeping a vacancy on the judicial bench open, unless a measure for the abolition of the vacant office is at the same time before Parliament. It is also a course sure to be extremely unpopular, even

140 Palles to O'Hagan, 22 December 1873 (Teeling Papers, MS 17872; O'Hagan Papers, D.2777/9/89/10).

141 Spencer to Gladstone, 24 December 1873; Gladstone to Spencer, 30 December 1873; Spencer to Gladstone, 2 January 1873 (Gladstone Papers, Add. MS 44307.182–9).

142 Gladstone to Selborne, 5 January 1874 (Gladstone Papers, Add. MS 44297.1).

> when circumstances may make it justifiable, and that unpopularity may itself become a serious impediment to the success of any proposed legislation with which it may be connected.[143]

Selborne's preference was to reshuffle some of the existing judges, leaving only a puisne judgeship vacant, pending a Cabinet decision on whether a Judicature Bill for Ireland should provide for a general reduction in judicial numbers. The alternatives, as he noted, were to leave the office of chief baron vacant for a time or to make an appointment from the Bar (i.e., most likely Palles).

There was a 'very strong expression of public feeling' against the prospect of no new judge being appointed, led by the Dublin Corporation.[144] Members of the Irish government, Spencer, Hartington and O'Hagan, as well as Palles and Law (the solicitor general), were opposed to any reduction and to leaving any vacancy unfilled, and Selborne commented that in considering their advice and what would be best in the public interest it was difficult to disentangle personal and political considerations.[145] The *Irish Law Times* remarked, when welcoming the eventual appointment of Palles, that 'the profession and public alike rejoice to think that the Bench has been spared the blow with which it was threatened, and the Exchequer Court [has been] restored to its normal condition of high judicial strength'.[146]

Gladstone's disinclination to take any steps that would prejudice a restructuring of the judiciary, as backed up by Selborne, thus left the vacancy unfilled for over a month after the death of Pigot. Any uneasiness that Palles may have been feeling about this can only have been increased by the calling of a snap general election. He told O'Hagan in a letter on 23 January 1874 that the Cabinet had resolved that evening to dissolve Parliament at once, that Gladstone's electoral address to his constituents in Greenwich would be in the papers in London the next morning, and that 'nothing has been settled' about filling the judicial vacancy.[147] The election went badly for the Liberals, and as the constituency results came in during the first week in February it was clear that the Conservatives would form the next government,[148] having won their first general election since 1841.

O'Hagan and Hartington corresponded about the vacancy as the scale of the defeat became clear, O'Hagan pressing for an appointment ('I feel more anxious the more I think about it') and Hartington saying that Gladstone acknowledged that the question of appointment was now quite changed, although it remained one of extreme delicacy, to be settled only by the Cabinet; 'he seems inclined to acquiesce in what may be the general opinion. I shall do my best for the attorney

143 Selborne to Gladstone, 7 January 1874 (Gladstone Papers, Add. MS 44297.7).
144 *ILT&SJ*, vol. 8, p. 30 (17 January 1874).
145 Selborne to Gladstone, 12 January 1874 (Gladstone Papers, Add. MS 44297.11).
146 *ILT&SJ*, vol. 8, p. 98 (28 February 1874).
147 Palles to O'Hagan, 23 January 1874 (Teeling Papers, MS 17872; O'Hagan Papers, D.2777/9/89/11).
148 G.E. Buckle, *The life of Benjamin Disraeli, earl of Beaconsfield*, vol. 5 *(1868–1876)* (London, 1920), p. 283.

general'.[149] Selborne told Gladstone on 14 February that there was no longer any objection to filling the vacancy in the Exchequer:

> I certainly think that the only justification for not filling up the vacant judgeships, in the Irish Court of Exchequer and in the Scotch Court of Session, was in the intention we had of immediately proposing to Parliament a measure for rearranging (more or less) the judicature of those two countries. We have now no prospect of proposing any such measures; nor is there any reasonable ground for supposing that our successors will be purposed to do so during this session of Parliament.[150] Under those circumstances I think you will be fully justified in doing that yourself, which your successor would certainly do if it were left for him; especially in the case of the Irish vacancy; as to which it was not proposed in the plan, recommended by the Irish government and under the consideration of the present Cabinet, to reduce the number of the judges of the Superior Courts in Ireland. But, as it was proposed to us (and we have no right to assume that this might not also be the view of our successors) to merge the Land Court [Landed Estates Court] in the Superior Courts, and obtain power from Parliament not to fill up the vacancy in that court, and as that vacancy has been left open for a very much longer time than the chief baron's place,[151] I should advise that it should be left to our successors to determine, on their responsibility, whether the latter vacancy (that in the Landed Estates Court) should be filled up, or not, and to fill it up with an adherent of their own, if they please. This will, in my opinion, be the most worthy and [illegible] course, and also be defensible in Parliament.[152]

The election defeat thus ensured that Gladstone would delay no longer and would not leave a judicial position open for the Conservatives to fill. Palles was then nominated for the Queen's formal approval, and told O'Hagan on 16 February that he had just received a telegram 'announcing the Queen's pleasure having been given upon my appointment. All secrecy is therefore at an end'.[153] Gladstone went to Windsor Castle the following day to submit his resignation to the Queen. That date and the fact that he travelled there from Waterloo were small qualifications to a quip, later generally attributed to T.M. Healy MP, that Palles had been appointed on the platform of Paddington station.[154] On Saturday 21 February he was sworn

149 O'Hagan to Hartington, 7 February 1874 (O'Hagan Papers, D.2777/8/235); Hartington to O'Hagan, 12 February 1874 (O'Hagan Papers, D.2777/7/B).

150 In fact, a Judicature Bill for Ireland was introduced in Parliament in May 1874 by the new government.

151 One of the two judges in the Landed Estates Court, David Lynch, had died in December 1872.

152 Selborne to Gladstone, 14 February 1874 (Gladstone Papers, Add. MS 44297.19).

153 Palles to O'Hagan, 16 February 1874 (Teeling Papers, MS 17872; O'Hagan Papers, D.2777/9/89/12).

154 See for instance the references to this in Healy, *OldMC*, p. 28, and in Delany, op. cit., p. 84. Healy's remark, although specifically incorrect, might be considered to have been broadly accurate.

in by O'Hagan (one of his last official acts before he stood down later that day as lord chancellor), by which time the Conservative leader, Disraeli, had formed his cabinet and was installed in No. 10 Downing Street, and Gladstone had resigned as leader of the Liberals.[155] Palles could reflect about his appointment, as Wellington is said to have done after the battle of Waterloo, that it had been 'the nearest run thing you ever saw in your life'.

Palles retained his title of chief baron in the course of two court reorganisations, one under the Supreme Court of Judicature (Ireland) Act 1877 by which the Exchequer ceased to be a separate court and became a division (along with the other historic courts) of a unified High Court.[156] The second was in 1897 when it was provided that the Exchequer division 'shall be fused and amalgamated with the Queen's Bench division of the High Court, and the lord chief baron of the Exchequer shall take rank in the Queen's Bench division next after the lord chief justice'.[157]

It has been said that he declined the position of lord chancellor of Ireland more than once, but the reports to that effect were not made contemporaneously and details have not been cited of any such offers to him. His biographer stated that on the successive deaths of two chancellors, Law (who died in 1883) and Sullivan (1885) he declined the appointment.[158] The *Law Times* said in 1912 that he had declined the position 'through a conscientious disapproval of the Home Rule policy of the Liberal government',[159] which could not refer to either year, since a Home Rule policy was not adopted by the Liberal party until 1886, at which point John Naish, who had succeeded Sullivan in May 1885, was re-appointed as chancellor by Gladstone. (That *Law Times* report is the sole source for a separate suggestion that, after completing the 15 years' service on the bench which entitled him to a pension, he 'thought very seriously of retiring from the bench, of being called to the Bar in England, and practising as a stuff gownsman [junior counsel] in the courts of this country'.)[160] Palles also drew the attention of Lord O'Hagan, no longer lord chancellor but still having influence in government, to the fact that 'the circumstances under which a third Law Lord may now be appointed' had arisen,[161] but it does not appear that he was considered then (or at any subsequent time) for appointment. That he was a unionist was well known and, when he was appointed as a member of an official commission of inquiry into Trinity College in 1906, John Redmond told the chief secretary that Palles 'though a Catholic, is not representative in any degree at all of Nationalist views'.[162]

155 G.E. Buckle, op. cit., p. 292.
156 Supreme Court of Judicature (Ireland) Act 1877 (40&41 Vict., c.57), s21.
157 Supreme Court of Judicature (Ireland) (No. 2) Act 1897 (60&61 Vict., c.66), s1.
158 Delany, op. cit., p. 114 (in which the relevant years are mis-stated as 1881 and 1883).
159 *Law Times*, vol. 133, p. 338 (3 August 1912); *ILT&SJ*, vol. 46, p. 203 (10 August 1912).
160 Ibid.; see also *ILT&SJ*, vol. 50, p. 269 (7 October 1916) (from *Law Times*).
161 Palles to O'Hagan, 1 January 1882 (Teeling Papers, MS 17872).
162 Redmond to Bryce, 3 May 1906 (Bryce Papers (NLI), MS 11,013(1)). See also Redmond to Bryce, 12 April 1906 (Bryce Papers, MS 11,012 (4)).

As with the other High Court common law judges Palles would sit, at first instance, with a jury, at the Four Courts or on assize, and might sit as a member of a divisional court of Queen's Bench to hear motions for a new trial and suchlike. As chief baron he was also an ex-officio member of the Court of Appeal,[163] and could be invited to hear appeals. V.T.H. Delany, whose sympathetic biography of Palles[164] was published in 1960, referred to his work as consisting of 'sitting in the Court of Appeal; constituting divisional courts to hear writs of *certiorari*; trying actions at *nisi prius*; and above all, going circuit'.[165]

It was a core function of a judge at first instance to determine whether, as a matter of law, there was admissible evidence on which, as a matter of fact, a jury might find that a defendant had a liability to a plaintiff (or, in a criminal case, was guilty). Whether a judge had correctly determined that point, or had correctly directed the jury on matters of law, and many other aspects of the procedure of a trial, might in turn be the subject of a motion brought before a divisional court asking that court to set aside the verdict and direct that a new trial be held, and the decision of that second court might itself be the subject of an appeal. Where an appeal was taken to the Court of Appeal, or thereafter to the House of Lords, the decision of the higher court, even if adopting or confirming the reasoning of a lower court, would of course have the greater authority.

Contemporary and subsequent commentators on Palles have placed him very high in the pantheon of Irish judges. Ronan Keane, chief justice of Ireland between 2000 and 2004, wrote that 'his reputation as a judge has always been remarkably high. He had ample time to develop the qualities which equipped him to be an outstanding judge: a powerful intellect, a deep and comprehensive knowledge of the law, and a strong and independent personality'.[166] In his lifetime he was referred to by Lord Macnaghten as 'one of the most learned and accurate judges on the Bench'.[167] Obituaries were uniformly complimentary, expressing virtually unqualified admiration. Arthur W. Samuels (1852–1925), a judge of the High Court, who composed the initial entry on Palles for the *Dictionary of national biography*, singled out his 'mastery of law as a science in all its ramifications, his penetrating research, his remarkable "case memory", his grasp of common law, of equity and statute law; his assimilation of every branch of jurisprudence; his methods of historical ratiocination, convincing deduction, and lucid exposition'. Sir John Ross (1853–1935), the last lord chancellor of Ireland, who had been a

163 Supreme Court of Judicature (Ireland) Act 1877 (40&41 Vict., c57), s10.

164 A review (by G.D. Nokes) in the *International and Comparative Law Quarterly* (*ICLQ*, vol. 10, 1961, pp 209–10) referred to the author's 'generous enthusiasm over the attainments of the Chief Baron', while expressing some reservations about his significance in an international context, as did a review (by E.F. Murphy) in the *American Journal of Legal History* (*AJLH*, vol. 6 (1962), pp 216–17).

165 Delany, op. cit., p. 140.

166 Ronan Keane, entry on Palles in *ODNB*.

167 *New South Wales Taxation Commissioners v Palmer (PC)*, [1907] AC 179, at 185.

judicial colleague for 20 years, also writing quite soon after his death, similarly took a very positive but in his case not uncritical view, his opinion being that 'as a lawyer, pure and simple, I think he was the very greatest I have ever met', with an unsurpassed knowledge of equity, criminal law and the common law (which he thought 'was as near perfection as the powers of man could attain to'). 'But he was by no means a man of the world; his conclusions of fact were often hopelessly wrong, and the whole chain of logical reasoning depending on errors of fact would be quite useless'.[168]

Delany referred to Palles as having an 'awesome reverence for precedent', and a taste for a 'voluminous – sometimes, one fears, a laborious – examination of the authorities'.[169] In the same vein Professor Osborough remarked that his discussion of precedent 'seems too laboured or pedantic for modern tastes'.[170] Ronan Keane, while acknowledging this reverence for precedent, maintained that he was also well known for an open-minded approach to novel arguments.[171] Lord Shandon (Ignatius O'Brien, lord chancellor of Ireland, 1913–18) wrote of him that he

> not only had an immense knowledge of case law but his industry was colossal and one might always rely upon Palles's disinterring some forgotten authority which everyone else had failed to discover … His method was always the same, that of piling up analogy on analogy but often he produced a most logical and coherent result. He worshipped technicality as if it were a fetish and even when he was fully conscious that the result at which he arrived was eminently unsatisfactory he was unable to burst the bonds of precedent and technicality. He was ably abetted – indeed, often inspired – by his co-adjutor baron FitzGerald[172] who would subdivide the split hair that his chief had divided.[173]

Henry Hanna who knew Palles well wrote that 'he believed above in the inflexible application of the law. He had no lighter side to his character, having neither wit nor humour'.[174] An obituary of Palles, to the contrary, said that 'although he did not condescend to joke on the bench yet he was a man who possessed a keen sense of humour and was certainly never dull'.[175]

168 Sir John Ross, *Pilgrim Scrip* (London, 1927), pp 15, 17.
169 Delany, op. cit., p. 158.
170 Osborough, *DIB*, op. cit.
171 Keane, *ODNB*, op. cit.
172 Francis FitzGerald was a baron of the Exchequer between 1859 and 1882, and hence a colleague of Palles for eight years, from 1874.
173 Daire Hogan and Patrick Maume (eds), *The reminiscences of Lord Shandon, lord chancellor of Ireland, 1913–1918* (Dublin, 2021), p. 156.
174 Henry Hanna, 'The Bench and Bar of Ireland in the nineteenth century', *American Bar Association Journal*, vol. 22, no 11 (1936), pp 761–7, at 764.
175 *Irish Times*, 16 February 1920.

Palles had studied mathematics at Trinity College, and endowed a prize for proficiency in mathematics at his old school, Clongowes.[176] One observer has referred to his 'tastes for the mathematically exact'[177] as contributing to an unfortunate insistence on technical legal forms. His decision in *Pearson v Dublin Corporation*[178] in withdrawing a substantial negligence claim from the jury and which ultimately led, after a succession of appeals, to the House of Lords ordering a new trial, was seen as 'an instance of how a great lawyer, taking a strong course on technicalities at the trial, may involve the parties in huge expenses'.[179]

Delany's view was that the branch of jurisprudence in which Palles made his most lasting contribution was the law of torts,[180] in particular in the law of negligence.[181] In *Bell v Great Northern Railway*,[182] a case arising out of a major fatal railway accident outside Armagh, Palles in his judgment in the divisional court outlined the concept, of continuing importance to this day, of a defendant having a liability in negligence for psychiatric injury ('nervous shock') to a plaintiff, even if not accompanied by any physical injury. He cited an unreported decision ('and it is a sad commentary upon our system of reporting that a decision so important and so novel has never found its way into our Law Reports'), *Byrne v Great Southern & Western Railway Company*, which had been tried before him in 1882, and been the subject of motions by the defendant company to set aside the verdict that were dismissed by the divisional court in 1883 and by the Court of Appeal in 1884. He said that negligence may give rise to fright and that 'the relation between fright and injury to the nerve and brain structures of the body is a matter which depends entirely upon scientific and medical testimony'.[183] Ross wrote that 'in negligence actions he required an amazing amount of caution on the part of the defendants, particularly when they were railway or shipping companies. In every negligence action the defendant before him always had a nasty time'.[184]

In the field of equity his decision as a member of the Court of Appeal in *O'Hanlon v Logue*[185] confirming that a bequest for the celebration of Masses, whether in public or in private, was charitable in Irish law, and setting aside a

176 *ILT&SJ*, vol. 43, p. 150 (19 June 1909); Delany, op. cit., p. 144.
177 E.F. Murphy, op. cit.
178 [1907] 2 IR 27, 82, 537; [1907] AC 531.
179 *Irish Times*, 16 February 1920; see also Delany, op. cit., p. 159.
180 A tort has classically been defined as a civil wrong. McMahon & Binchy, *Law of torts* (3rd ed., Dublin, 2005), describe the law of torts as being 'no more or no less than a description of those instances of social conduct which the courts consider should be prohibited and should be penalised' (para 1.03).
181 Delany, op. cit., p. 159.
182 26 LR Ir. 428 (1890). See Delany, op. cit., p. 163. The guard of the train was acquitted when prosecuted for his role in the accident (*ILT&SJ*, vol. 24, p. 49 (25 January 1890)). See also, for a modern instance, *Halford v Electricity Supply Board*, [2021] IECA 112 (Court of Appeal, 16 April 2021).
183 At 442.
184 Ross, op. cit., p. 20.
185 [1906] 1 IR 247; Delany pp 170–1; Osborough (*DIB* entry); Keane (*ODNB* entry).

decision of his own some thirty years before,[186] has been seen as an enduring contribution to the law of charitable trusts. It might be said, however, that this case represented not an innovative declaration but a restoration of a line of authority, from decisions in 1823 and 1844, that all legacies for Masses, whether or not said in public, were good charitable legacies. It had been noted soon after an earlier decision of Palles to much the same effect, in 1897,[187] that lawyers (including himself in 1875) had lost sight of those earlier authorities, such an approach having almost dropped out of sight and memory and being treated for a while as a vulgar error.[188] The proper working of the common law in effect rested on an assumption, not borne out by the 1875 case, that the diligence and knowledge and scholarship of its practitioners and of the judiciary would ensure that all relevant prior decisions would be brought forward in legal argument for consideration.

Professor Osborough remarked that Palles 'seems to have particularly relished the challenge of the novel and obscure', citing the remarkable scholarship exhibited in two judgments, over thirty years apart, on the law of fisheries[189] and on marriage law as applicable to a clandestine Catholic ceremony.[190] To Ronan Keane his judgment in that marriage case, *Ussher v Ussher*, was a 'lucid and magisterial survey of the English and Irish law of marriage [which] demonstrated his erudition, his understanding of legal principle and his capacity for closely knit reasoning'.[191] A person who heard the judgment being delivered noted, half a century later in a review of Delany's biography, that Palles 'spouted Latin as if it was his native tongue'.[192]

Palles was seen as being more sympathetic to tenants than other judges. T.M. Healy told the House of Commons that 'the popular party lay their writs in the Exchequer because they believe they get law there; but the landlord party lay their writs in the Common Pleas'.[193] Palles came to be seen in Dublin Castle during the Land War in the 1880s as unduly disposed to find reasons to set aside convictions under the Prevention of Crimes legislation.[194] Ross – acknowledging that his was the perspective of a prosecutor – wrote that

> if a mistake had been made on the Crown side he was quite merciless. We who represented the Crown in the Crimes Act cases had a hectic time. An order for certiorari or habeas corpus would be applied for one day and cause had to be shown by the Crown on the following morning. The cases stated by

186 *Attorney general v Delany*, IR 10 CL 104 (1875).
187 *Attorney general v Hall*, 31 ILTR 49 (1897).
188 *ILT&SJ*, vol. 32, p. 222 (14 May 1898).
189 Osborough, op. cit.; *Duke of Devonshire v Neill*, 2 LR(I), 132 at 144 (1878–9). This extended fishery litigation was ended by a decision of the House of Lords in 1882.
190 *Ussher v Ussher*, [1912] 2 IR 445 (the judgment of Palles is at 492).
191 Keane, *ODNB* entry.
192 Review (by unnamed writer) in *NILQ*, vol. 14 (November 1961), p. 622.
193 HC Deb, 3rd series, vol. 313, col. 986 (14 April 1887).
194 L.P. Curtis, *Coercion and conciliation in Ireland, 1880–1892* (Princeton, 1963), p. 194.

> the resident magistrates were severely analysed by Palles and jeered at by Baron Dowse; if there was the slightest flaw in the proceedings away went your conviction and out went the prisoner, exulting over the failure of the authorities.[195]

To the same effect, a contemporary observer, W.B. Campbell, in a short sketch or profile of Palles published in *Irish Society* magazine, said that 'the Exchequer has of late years been a sort of permanent court of jail delivery.[196] The searching mind of Palles will detect a flaw in proceedings the most regular, and before the tribunal where he presides a clever lawyer, if so minded, with the Habeas Corpus Act in his hand, could empty all the prisons in Ireland'.[197] The unnamed reviewer in the *Northern Ireland Legal Quarterly* remarked that 'the malefactor could hardly believe his ears when he found the great judge directing the jury to acquit him'.[198]

In 1898, on charges arising out of a riot in Belfast when a procession marking the centenary of the 1798 rebellion was attacked by an opposing crowd, Palles gave a direction to the jury to distinguish carefully between an active participant in the riot and a person present merely as a bystander. The *Irish Law Times* commented that an accused person could hardly get a more favourable definition of a riot.[199] Such decisions by Palles derived from his view of a strict adherence to applicable law, not from any sympathy with accused persons as such.

A study of some failures of the government in the course of the nineteenth century to give support in the enforcement of judicial decrees[200] makes reference to a forceful rebuke given by Palles to the government in that connection. This has been generally taken as a classic statement of the doctrine of separation of powers. Scenes of disorder and resistance had been anticipated at evictions in 1886 on the estate of the marquis of Clanricarde at Woodford, Co. Galway, but intervention by the police had initially been deliberately withheld or delayed. Hugh Holmes, then the attorney general, noted in a memoir that the chief secretary, Hicks Beach, 'thought that landlords were too ready to bring ejectments, and with a view to reducing the number he instructed the divisional magistrates to exercise a discretion in giving police protection to the sheriff when executing writs and decrees. This he did notwithstanding my warning that what was proposed could not be legally carried out, and at length this policy was abandoned in consequence of some strong judicial criticism'.[201] That criticism had been made by Palles in January 1887 at the Connaught winter assizes in Sligo when, in passing sentence

195 Ross, op. cit., p. 18.
196 The commission of gaol delivery was an authorisation to the judges of assize to try accused persons and establish whether they should be delivered out of prison.
197 Rhadamanthus (W.B. Campbell), *Our judges* (Dublin, 1890), p. 23; Delany, op. cit., p. 99.
198 *NILQ*, vol. 14, no. 3 (November 1961), p. 621.
199 *ILT&SJ*, vol. 32, p. 499 (5 November 1898).
200 W.N. Osborough, 'Executive failure to enforce judicial decrees' in John McEldowney and Paul O'Higgins (eds), *The common law tradition; essays in Irish legal history* (Dublin, 1990), pp 85–116.
201 Holmes Memoir, *IHS*, vol. 16, no. 63, p. 333.

at the assizes on persons convicted of riot and conspiracy to obstruct at Woodford, he had said, among other things:

> I desire it to be thoroughly understood that the execution of the decrees of the judiciary in this country does not depend – as it does not, I believe, in any civilised country – upon the will of the Executive who, for the moment, may happen to be in office. Into the execution of our writ we cannot allow any question of party politics to enter … Their [the judges'] sworn duty is to give to him who asks it that which he is entitled to by law. It is not competent to them, or to any other person, to go behind the law and ask whether in his own opinion or in the opinion of others, the law is just or unjust. With them the only consideration must be that is the law. They are bound to pronounce the law … When judgment is once given [and after determination of any appeal] it is not competent to anyone in this kingdom, I care not how high he may be, to say that a writ regularly issued on foot of that judgment shall not be executed, or to prevent those who by law are bound to aid in its execution from giving that aid and assistance which the common law and the Constitution requires.[202]

In March 1887 Arthur Balfour was appointed chief secretary for Ireland in succession to Hicks Beach, who retired due to ill health, and in the following four years in which he held that office a much more vigorous policy of police and military support for evictions, including some element of covert financing of landlords, was adopted.[203] This reflected a political decision to resist and challenge the Plan of Campaign for rent abatements for tenants rather than an acknowledgment of judicial strictures. However the remarks of Palles – albeit not part of any judgment – were to be cited in subsequent years as evidence of judicial independence and impartiality, in countering Unionist arguments and apprehensions that the rule of law and more generally law and order would be prejudiced under Home Rule:

> The Unionist complaint is, not so much that an Irish Executive will not be able to enforce the law, but that it will be unwilling to do so in certain cases, and will exercise a dispensing power as to whether the decrees of the courts shall or shall not, in particular cases, be enforced … But it is well settled that a sheriff, or anybody charged with the execution of a writ of a competent court, has the right to require the assistance of constables, and that the Executive has no power to prevent such assistance being given. This was laid

202 *R v Larkin and others* (*ILT&SJ*, vol. 21, p. 18 (8 January 1887)); Thomas F. Molony, 'The judiciary, the police and the maintenance of law and order' in J.H. Morgan (ed.), *The new Irish constitution; an exposition and some argument* (London, 1912), pp 162–3; Delany, pp 102–3.

203 See generally L.P. Curtis, Jr., *Coercion and conciliation in Ireland, 1880–1892* (Princeton, 1963), and L.P. Curtis Jr, *The depiction of eviction in Ireland, 1845–1910* (Dublin, 2011).

> down by the common law judges of England in *Miller v Knox* and still more emphatically by the lord chief baron in the case of the Woodford prisoners.[204]

When the Unionist government was leaving office in 1892 it honoured Palles by nominating him to be a member of the Privy Council in England, and he was sworn in later that year.[205] He had been a member of the Irish Privy Council since 1872. Ridgeway, the undersecretary in Dublin Castle, wrote to Balfour that 'this compliment to his rigid inflexibility in the administration of the Law might induce him to be a thorn in the side of those who may desire to tamper with the Law'[206] [i.e., the incoming Liberal government]. He sat on only one public hearing of the Judicial Committee of the Council, on the hearing of an appeal from a determination by the Supreme Court of Canada on the extent of the right of the Canadian provinces, under the British North America Act 1867, to enact laws regulating marriage. (Delany refers to the hearing as having occupied the best part of a week, although the law report records it as taking place over two days, on 22nd and 23rd July 1912.)[207] He attended also in November 1912 at a conference between a committee of the Council and representatives of the government of Jersey 'in connection with the amendment of their Education Bill to meet the objections of the Catholics ... [which] reached a common conclusion on a topic so fruitful in conflict'.[208]

Senior positions in his court were something of a family business. Henry Vivian Yeo, who had first joined the courts in 1857, retired in 1921 as registrar of the King's Bench division. He had been appointed in the Exchequer division by Palles in 1879, in succession to his father, also named Henry, who had been appointed to the courts as a very young man in 1829, and retired fifty years later,[209] and continued as registrar of King's Bench after the merger of divisions in 1897. 'The older barristers will remember the absolute confidence the Lord Chief Baron had in Mr Yeo's guidance. It was difficult to say which of them was the more accurately versed in rules and procedures'.[210] Palles appointed his elder brother Andrew Palles, an engineer, as his registrar at assizes in 1874, who served up to his death in 1900,[211] after which his nephew Francis Charles Kennedy BL, an official in the King's Bench division, provided that service.[212]

204 Thomas F. Molony, op. cit., p. 162.
205 *ILT&SJ*, vol. 26, p. 636 (3 December 1892).
206 Ridgeway to Balfour, 27 July 1892 (Salisbury Papers); L.P. Curtis Jr., op. cit. (1963), p. 399.
207 In the matter of a reference to the Supreme Court of Canada of certain questions concerning marriage, [1912] AC 880; Delany, op. cit., p. 147.
208 Almeric Fitzroy, *Memoirs* (London, 1925), vol. 2, p. 497.
209 Delany, op. cit., p. 96; *ILT&SJ*, vol. 13, p. 618 (20 December 1879), vol. 31, p. 269 (5 June 1897) and vol. 55, p. 212 (27 August 1921).
210 *ILT&SJ*, vol. 55, p. 157 (25 June 1921). Yeo's successor was C.P. Curran (*ILT&SJ*, vol. 55, p. 218 (3 September 1921)).
211 *ILT&SJ*, vol. 34, p. 55 (27 January 1900); Delany, op. cit., p. 35.
212 *ILT&SJ*, vol. 34, p. 265 (23 June 1900), vol. 55, p. 218 (3 September 1921) and vol. 63, p. 88 (13 April 1929).

Palles was a wealthy man, leaving an estate of £59,000, and he lived in some grandeur. In town his home for about three decades was at 28 Fitzwilliam Place, on the corner with Lower Leeson Street, to which he moved in the late 1870s from Mountjoy Square. It was reported in 1903 that the house was for sale,[213] and in 1910 he assigned it to his niece and companion Elizabeth Mary Palles 'in consideration of the natural love and affection' which he had for her, subject to a lease which he had granted to Charles O'Connor QC.[214] He resided also in a substantial house on Mount Anville Road near Dundrum, Co. Dublin, opposite the well-known convent. The grounds extended to about 25 acres, with glasshouses, one for orchids.[215] The census return for 1911 shows a domestic (indoors) staff of ten, including a valet and a footman. Ms Palles was one of the first group of Irish women, in Co. Dublin, to be appointed as magistrates.[216]

Like many of his judicial colleagues Palles enjoyed travel. Delany noted that through friendship with the Pirrie family in Belfast he developed from 1899 a 'habit of transatlantic voyaging'.[217] William James Pirrie, the first Lord Pirrie (1847–1924), was well placed to facilitate such a habit. He was chief executive (and later chairman) of the Harland & Wolff shipbuilding yard in Belfast, lord mayor of the city for 1896–7 and instrumental in the foundation of the Royal Victoria Hospital, and it was his custom to show hospitality to the judges of assize by giving a dinner in their honour.[218] The dinner in 1899 also marked the conferring of the freedom of the city on Mr T.H. Ismay, managing director of the White Star Line.[219] The shipyard built many ships for that company (of which Pirrie became a director, and which later merged with Cunard). Pirrie believed that a first-class liner should provide the same facilities as a first-class hotel, and this concept 'of the liner as a floating hotel was carried to almost fantastic lengths. Liners came to be fitted not only with deluxe cabins but with ballrooms, "Palm Court" lounges, swimming pools and gymnasia'.[220] Palles was among those invited to travel on the trial voyage in 1899 of the *Oceanic*, the largest and most luxurious passenger ship of its time, and was later reported as 'making speeches in New York in praise of the *Oceanic*.[221] On that journey Pirrie took Palles, not otherwise known (unlike some of his colleagues) to have an interest in sailing, to see a race in Long Island

213 *Law Times*, vol. 115, p. 508 (10 October 1903).
214 Deed of assignment, Palles to Palles, 3 July 1910 (Registry of Deeds).
215 *ILT&SJ*, vol. 32, p. 555 (10 December 1898), quoting from *The World*.
216 *ILT&SJ*, vol. 54, p. 32 (31 January 1920).
217 Delany, op. cit., pp 115–18.
218 Whatever about Pirrie's judicial friendships, his connection with trade and industry proved to be a difficulty after his appointment by the King to the chivalric Order of St Patrick in 1909, since the existing knights declined to take part in his investiture (Peter Galloway, *The most illustrious Order of St Patrick, 1783–1983* (Chichester, 1983), p. 47). The order was the equivalent in Ireland of the Order of the Garter (England) and the Order of the Thistle (Scotland).
219 *ILT&SJ*, vol. 31, p. 362 (7 August 1897); *Law Times*, vol. 107, p. 297 (29 July 1899).
220 R.D.C. Black, 'William James Pirrie' in Conor Cruise O'Brien (ed.), *The shaping of modern Ireland* (London, 1960), pp 177–8.
221 *Law Times*, vol. 107, p. 344 (12 August 1899) and p. 453 (23 September 1899).

Sound for the America's Cup, in which Sir Thomas Lipton, representing the Royal Ulster Yacht Club, was challenging the New York Yacht Club.[222] In 1907, when a passenger on the White Star liner *Adriatic*, he 'won much popularity on the voyage by presiding at the annual concert held for the benefit of the Seamen's Orphanage'.[223] He crossed the Atlantic on the *Laurentic* in 1909 and on the *Celtic* in 1910.[224]

After the sinking of the *Titanic* in April 1912 it was suggested that an illness had prevented him being on board, a report that was soon qualified:

> The report published here that the lord chief baron would, but for the advice of his doctor, have been a passenger on the *Titanic* on her ill-fated voyage is, says the *Law Times*, not quite accurate. It is true that the distinguished judge was invited by the White Star Company to take a trip to New York as their guest, and it is true that his Lordship felt unable to accept the kind offer. But the strongest reason for not accepting was that the voyage would have kept his Lordship away from the opening of the Easter Term at the Four Courts,[225] and from his duties during a portion of the term when it was very doubtful if also two of his colleagues would be able to take their seats owing to illness. The lord chief baron has been on the Bench since 1874, and has never been on any occasion absent at the opening of a term.[226]

Palles retired at the end of June 1916, although his judicial career ended in practice in the summer of 1915. Early in 1915 the *Irish Law Times* commented that although he had attained the age of 83 at Christmas 'nobody suggests or thinks of his retirement; he is so active in mind and so equal to his work that it is almost contempt of court to express such an idea'.[227] However he was unable to sit as a judge in the Michaelmas legal term that autumn. Reports of ill health in November ('his mind and memory are as good as ever they were, but his physical strength does not allow him to move about')[228] continued over Christmas 1915 and into January, when it was reported that 'if he feels unable to go circuit on 1st March he will tender his resignation though, after his long and brilliant service, he might well rest for a year before taking such a step. He loved his work, it was his great and only interest in life, and it will be painful and difficult for him to lay aside the armour which he always so proudly wore'.[229] It was rumoured incorrectly that he

222 *NILQ*, vol. 14, no. 3 (November 1961), p. 622.
223 *ILT&SJ*, vol. 41, p. 231 (7 September 1907).
224 *ILT&SJ*, vol. 43, p. 212 (28 August 1909) and vol. 44, p. 196 (6 August 1910).
225 The Easter term commenced on Monday 15 April 1912. The *Titanic* left Queenstown (Cobh) on 11 April.
226 *ILT&SJ*, vol. 46, p. 136 (25 May 1912), quoting *Law Times*.
227 *ILT&SJ*, vol. 49, p. 9 (9 January 1915).
228 *ILT&SJ*, vol. 49, p. 272 (30 October 1915); *Law Times*, vol. 140, p. 14 (6 November 1915) and p. 75 (27 November 1915).
229 *ILT&SJ*, vol. 49, p. 318 (25 December 1915) and vol. 50, p. 17 (15 January 1916); *Law Times* (London), vol. 140, p. 181 (1 January 1916) and p. 250 (22 January 1916).

had tendered his resignation with effect from 1 April, and it was eventually by letter dated 7 June 1916 that he resigned, this taking effect at the start of July.[230] The government left the resulting vacancy in the High Court open for over a year, not filling it until October 1917, when it appointed William Moore KC, Unionist MP for North Armagh.[231]

Serjeant A.M. Sullivan consulted Palles as to whether he should accept a brief for the defence of Roger Casement at his trial for treason at the Old Bailey in June 1916. Palles told him that he would wish the defence in a great State Trial to be conducted by a representative of the Irish Bar.[232] He donated a portrait of himself to the King's Inns in 1919 (a copy of that by Sir Hubert von Herkomer, completed in 1903, in the collection of Trinity College).[233]

He made a significant contribution to education policy, and its implementation, over many years, including the establishment of the National University of Ireland and University College Dublin.[234] His resignation as a Commissioner of National Education in 1914, a position to which he had been appointed in 1890, was noted as a termination of his connection with public work of every kind outside his judicial functions.[235] After his death in February 1920 his law library (of over 2,000 volumes) was purchased by Archbishop Walsh and presented to UCD.[236]

230 Delany, op. cit., p. 152; *Law Times*, vol. 140, p. 472 (8 April 1916), vol. 141, p. 135 (24 June 1916).
231 *Law Times*, vol. 141, p. 159 (1 July 1916); *ILT&SJ*, vol. 51, p. 264 (3 November 1917).
232 Serjeant A.M. Sullivan, *Old Ireland: reminiscences of an Irish KC* (London, 1927), p. 198; see also R.F.V. Heuston, *Lives of the lord chancellors, 1885–1940* (Oxford, 1964), pp 372–8.
233 Wanda Ryan-Smolin, *King's Inns portraits* (Dublin, 1992), p. 57; Delany, op. cit., p. 120.
234 Delany, op. cit., pp 123–37; *ILT&SJ*, vol. 24, p. 376 (12 July 1890); Donal McCartney, *UCD, a national idea: the history of University College Dublin* (Dublin, 1999), pp 26–8.
235 *ILT&SJ*, vol. 24, p. 376 (12 July 1890) and vol. 48, p. 29 (31 January 1914).
236 *ILT&SJ*, vol. 55, p. 65 (5 March 1921).

CHAPTER EIGHT

Disraeli's government, 1874–80

BENJAMIN DISRAELI returned to office in April 1874, after a general election in which the Conservatives had a significant victory, winning a majority for the first time in three decades, and which in Ireland saw dozens of Home Rule candidates being elected in place of Liberals. Lord Cairns was reappointed as lord chancellor of Great Britain, and his Irish connections and interests played some role in the enactment of the Judicature Act for Ireland in 1877 and in judicial appointments. The intended appointment of J.T. Ball as lord chancellor of Ireland was held over, and the office entrusted temporarily to three lords justices, while Ball served as attorney general and worked on drafting the Judicature Bill. Eventually the clamour of the legal profession for the post to be filled on a permanent basis grew too loud to be ignored, and Ball took office in the New Year 1875. Henry Ormsby was appointed to a vacancy long left open in the Landed Estates Court, which the existing single judge there, Flanagan, saw as a slight upon his work, and he had to be persuaded not to resign in protest. The chief justice of Queen's Bench, Whiteside, died at the end of 1876 and after some other judges had declined the position the attorney general, G.A.C. May, was appointed. Gerald FitzGibbon was appointed to be a lord justice of appeal at the end of 1878, a position that he filled with distinction for the next 30 years. Frederick Walsh was appointed to a vacancy in the bankruptcy court in 1879.

John Thomas Ball

Lord Chancellor of Ireland 1875–80

John Thomas Ball (1815–98) was the son of an army officer, Major Benjamin Marcus Ball. He was educated at Trinity College, and was called to the Bar in 1840, becoming a QC in 1854. He obtained a doctorate of laws (LL.D.) in 1844, and was generally known as Dr Ball, practising largely although not exclusively in civil law, including probate and admiralty law (being named Queen's Advocate in the admiralty court in 1865), and in matrimonial issues. Up to 1870 such matters were within the jurisdiction of separate ecclesiastical courts sitting in Henrietta Street, half a mile north of the Four Courts. He practised also in the Chancery and common law courts and, as a member of the Home circuit, had experience in criminal law as a Crown prosecutor for Co. Westmeath and Queen's County (Laois). He was elected a bencher of King's Inns in 1863. In 1866 he was nominated as a temporary judge for the spring and summer assizes on the Leinster circuit,[1] which (despite its name) included Co. Tipperary, and he presided over a

1 *Irish Times*, 11 August 1866; *Law Times*, vol. 41, p. 652 (21 July 1866).

murder trial at Clonmel.[2] In 1873 he was one of the prosecuting counsel, with the attorney general and solicitor general, for the trial of Dr Duggan, the bishop of Clonfert, for alleged exercise of undue influence over voters in the controversial bye-election in Co. Galway in 1872.[3]

He was a prominent lay member of the Church of Ireland. 'In 1862 I was appointed by Archbishop [Marcus] Beresford (then the primate of the Irish Church) vicar general of the province of Armagh [i.e., a judge of the diocesan court[4]], and was thus brought into relations of confidential communication with him respecting ecclesiastical affairs – relations which were not interrupted by my having filled the office of [lord] chancellor of Ireland from 1875 to 1880, and which continued until his death in 1885'.[5] His activity in the defence of the interests of the church in the disestablishment controversy in the 1860s gave him prominence in his profession and in politics. His position at the Bar up to then 'although distinguished, was not commanding'.[6] He was later appointed as chancellor of the province of Armagh and of the archdiocese of Dublin and assessor in the General Synod.[7]

He stood as a Liberal in the Dublin University constituency in the 1865 general election, when his supporters included legal figures such as Abraham Brewster QC and James Lawson QC.[8] He maintained, with the open support of the archbishop, that the Liberals, then led by Lord Palmerston, were better placed than the Conservatives to defend the church against a growing agitation, in Britain as much as in Ireland, for its status as an established church to be changed and that timely reform would avert potentially more hostile imposed reforms.[9] He was soundly defeated by the two Conservative candidates, James Whiteside QC and Anthony Lefroy, it later being said that 'the moderation of his views was fatal to his hopes'.[10] The subsequent adoption of a policy of disestablishment in Ireland by the Liberals contributed both to their victory in the general election at the end of 1868,[11] and to some party members, including Ball, transferring allegiance to the Conservative party.

He was solicitor general briefly (for seven weeks), and attorney general even more briefly (for eight days), in the final weeks of Disraeli's first government at the end of 1868. He was recommended to Disraeli by Lord Mayo [Lord Naas], who had just stepped down as the chief secretary for Ireland, and who acknowledged that

2 William Ball Wright, *Ball family records: genealogical memoirs of some Ball families of Great Britain, Ireland and America* (2nd ed., York, 1908), p. 143.
3 *Irish Times*, 18 February 1873.
4 R.B. McDowell, *The Irish administration, 1801–1914* (London, 1964), p. 119.
5 J.T. Ball, *The Reformed Church of Ireland, 1537–1889* (London and Dublin, 1890), preface (p. v).
6 *Law Times*, vol. 104, p. 473 (26 March 1898).
7 *Irish Ecclesiastical Gazette*, 25 March 1898.
8 *Irish Times*, 20 June 1865.
9 Andrew Shields, *The Irish Conservative party, 1852–1868* (Dublin, 2007), p. 197.
10 *ILT&SJ*, vol. 9, p. 18 (9 January 1875).
11 John Morley, *The life of William Ewart Gladstone* (London, 1903), vol. 2, pp 245–8; Roy Jenkins, *Gladstone* (London, 1995), pp 280–7.

> some objections may be raised against Ball's appointment in consequence of antecedents, and his having opposed our candidates for the University as a moderate liberal. Still I most strongly advise that he should be offered the solicitorship – feeling sure that you can find no one except himself among the members of the Irish Bar who would be of the least use to you in the coming struggle. I have talked over the matter with the lord lieutenant [Abercorn], Wilson Patten [the new chief secretary] and the lord chancellor [Brewster], and they all agree with me that the offer should be made at once.[12]

The sitting attorney general (R.R. Warren) remained in office until the start of December, and when there was a prospect of him being replaced by Michael Harrison, then the solicitor general, it was reported that Ball would not have accepted appointment as a new solicitor general since he was senior to Harrison at the Bar.[13]

Ball stood as a Conservative in the general election in November 1868 and was easily elected as one of the university's two MPs, overcoming suspicions about the depth or any inconsistency of his convictions. His first speech to the House of Commons was delivered at the start of the second day's debate on the Irish Church Bill[14] providing for disestablishment. Despite his rather solemn speaking style (a 'slow and measured delivery'[15]) this was well received and was subsequently published as a pamphlet. Disraeli, now the leader of the opposition, who had opened the debate, was reported to have said 'Why was he not in Parliament before? This is the best Irish lawyer we have ever had'.[16] Gladstone thought his speech 'elaborate and impressive'.[17] It was subsequently conveyed to the archbishop of Canterbury, in a conciliatory spirit, that the government would be prepared to consider modifications of the Bill, and that 'if his grace would tell Dr Ball that he only wished to propose amendments which it would be possible for the government to accept, that learned gentleman would know better than others how it could be done. The archbishop however seems chiefly to have made use of Dr Ball to supply him with arguments against the government'.[18]

The reputation quickly won by his vigorous opposition to disestablishment was enhanced by contributions to other debates, such as those on the landlord and tenant legislation of 1870. Disraeli commended his work on this, saying that the Bill had been substantially modified at the committee stage of the debate 'much by our friend Ball, who has shown as much resource and knowledge as on the Irish

12 Mayo to Disraeli, 4 October 1868 (Disraeli Papers, B/XX/BD/82).
13 *Law Times*, vol. 45, p. 413 (10 October 1868) and p. 453 (24 October 1868).
14 HC Deb, 3rd series, vol. 194, cols. 1791–1814 (19 March 1869).
15 *ILT&SJ*, vol. 9, p. 18 (9 January 1875).
16 *Law Times*, vol. 104, p. 473 (26 March 1898).
17 Morley, op. cit., p. 264.
18 Granville to Gladstone, 4 August 1869 (*Ramm, 1868–1871*, p. 40); Morley, op. cit., p. 269.

Church Bill and with a happier result'.[19] He spoke also on criminal law enforcement and procedures in 1871 and 1872 and on legislation to limit ritualism and the growing influence of the Oxford Movement within the Church of England[20] in 1874.

His temperament was the subject of frank, although not unfriendly, comment. 'Owing to a delicacy of constitution and an impatience of detail Dr Ball was inclined to procrastination, but in all questions of moment he was unsparing of labour. No document escaped from his pen until the utmost pains had been expended in securing in it lucidity, conciseness and accuracy, and in his published work he carried revision and condensation even to excess'.[21] Brewster told Lord Mayo in October 1868 that 'but for one defect I could say that [Ball] is by far the best man at the Bar. That is a want of *will,* by which I mean tenacity'.[22]

He was returned unopposed, with David Plunket, in the university constituency in the 1874 general election and, on Disraeli's return to office that spring, was again appointed to be attorney general. This was 'understood to be only an interim arrangement',[23] and the plan was that he would remain for a time in the House of Commons where 'his presence was considered indispensable [in] helping to frame, defend and carry through measures',[24] principally the intended judicature reform legislation. The office of lord chancellor was held open for him, with the discharge of its functions entrusted temporarily to three commissioners, including Christian LJ. Criticism of this arrangement grew as it became clear that the reform legislation was going to be significantly delayed,[25] and in the New Year 1875 Ball was appointed lord chancellor. In a farewell address to the university electors he gave his view of disestablishment:

> the alliance which for three centuries continued between the State and the Protestant Episcopal Church has been dissolved. Endowments consecrated from remote antiquity to sacred uses have been seized into the grasp of secular power … the University itself, founded in aid of an established religion, and interpenetrated with its influence, is no longer governed with respect to its tenets, or bound by any obligation to its advancement.[26]

He served as lord chancellor for the next five years. It was said that he did not seek to become lord chancellor again in 1885 when the Conservatives returned to office, and that he declined a peerage,[27] although reappointment may have been unlikely

19 Disraeli to Sir Stafford Northcote, 14 May 1870 (G.E. Buckle, *The life of Benjamin Disraeli, earl of Beaconsfield* (vol. 5, London, 1920), p. 123).
20 Public Worship Regulation Act 1874 (37&38 Vict., c.85).
21 Ball Wright, op. cit., p. 145.
22 Brewster to Naas, 28 October 1868 (Mayo Papers (NLI), MS 43,875/5).
23 *ILT&SJ*, vol. 8, p. 108 (7 March 1874).
24 *ILT&SJ*, vol. 9, p. 17 (9 January 1875).
25 *ILT&SJ*, vol. 8, p. 576 (17 November 1874).
26 *ILT&SJ*, vol. 9, p. 37 (16 January 1875).
27 *Law Times*, vol. 104, p. 474 (26 March 1898).

in any event, in light of the ambitions of a new generation of Conservative lawyers, some 20 years' younger, such as Edward Gibson QC, MP. In his retirement he wrote a history of the reformed Church of Ireland, initially up to 1886 and then in a second edition up to 1889, and also a *Historical review of the legislative systems operative in Ireland from the invasion of Henry II to the Union (1172–1800).*

He married Catherine Elrington, a daughter of Charles Richard Elrington, the Regius professor of divinity in Trinity College. They lived at 71 Merrion Square. Their younger son, Frederick Elrington Ball MRIA (1863–1928), was a historian and antiquarian, whose classic *The judges in Ireland, 1221–1921* was published in 1926. He was active in unionist politics and stood as an independent candidate in the Dublin County South constituency in the 1900 general election, where the resulting split in the unionist vote resulted in the defeat of the sitting MP, Horace Plunkett, and the election of the Nationalist candidate.[28]

Henry Ormsby

Judge of the Landed Estates Court 1875–7, of the Chancery Division of the High Court (Land Judge) 1878–85

Henry Ormsby (1812–87) was a son of the Revd Henry Ormsby, the rector of Kilsheer, Co. Meath.[29] His wife Julia was a daughter of the rector of Powerscourt, Co. Wicklow. After education at Trinity College he was called to the Bar in 1835, joining the North East circuit, and became a QC in 1858.[30] He held office as solicitor general for literally a few days as the Conservative government left office in December 1868, and was re-appointed to that office in 1874. He became attorney general in January 1875, succeeding J.T. Ball. He sought the position of chief justice of the court of Common Pleas, then held by the ailing J.H. Monahan, a few months later and was told briskly by the chief secretary, Sir Michael Hicks Beach, that this was 'out of the question'.[31] In November that year he was appointed as a second judge of the Landed Estates Court ('LEC').

Since the end of 1872 there had been a single judge in the LEC, Stephen Woulfe Flanagan, and whether a second judge was required (as provided for in the underlying statute[32]) had been a matter of continuing controversy. When the Conservatives won the general election in February 1874 the initial sense of Ball, the new attorney general, was that a second judge was not necessary.[33] Lord Cairns, the lord chancellor of Great Britain, told the prime minister in 1874 that this was certainly not required at present, and that consideration of the LEC should be postponed until the pending judicature reform legislation had been

28 Alvin Jackson, 'The failure of unionism in Dublin, 1900', *IHS*, vol. 26, no. 104 (November 1989), pp 377–95.
29 Hugh Montgomery-Massingberd, *Burke's Irish family records* (London, 1976), p. 548.
30 *ILT&SJ*, vol. 8, p. 640 (19 December 1874).
31 Hicks Beach to Abercorn, 13 May 1875 (Abercorn Papers, D623/A/316/16).
32 Landed Estates Court (Ireland) Act 1866 (29&30 Vict., c.99).
33 Law to Spencer, 6 March 1874 (Althorp Papers, Add. MS 76982).

settled.[34] Nevertheless there were frequent rumours of an impending appointment of Ormsby to the court,[35] and solicitors, as represented by the Incorporated Law Society of Ireland, consistently maintained that a second judge was necessary. In 1875 Isaac Butt QC, MP spoke of 'the general opinion of the profession that the work was too much for one judge'.[36] A month later the government announced that it had decided to appoint a second judge,[37] and Ormsby took office about three months later. A.M. Sullivan MP later said that 'it was notorious that Mr Ormsby was appointed not because he was wanted in the LEC but because his position as a law officer of the Crown was wanted for someone else'.[38]

The LEC was incorporated into the Chancery division of the High Court by the judicature legislation of 1877, the judges thereafter being designated as 'land judges', although exercising a wider jurisdiction than the designation might suggest, since, 'if the state of business in connection with their peculiar jurisdiction shall permit, the said judges shall in addition be bound from time to time to assist in the general business of the Chancery division'.[39] Ormsby also sat as a vacation judge[40] and as an assize judge.[41] In October 1885 he retired in consequence of ill health,[42] and this, coupled with the retirement of Flanagan at about the same time, allowed the government to appoint the attorney general, John Monroe, as the sole land judge.

Ormsby was a member of the court of the General Synod of the Church of Ireland.[43] He lived in Fitzwilliam Square and died at Bray in September 1887. Three of his sons became clergymen in the Church of England, one of whom (George Albert Ormsby) was the bishop of British Honduras (Belize) between 1893 and 1908.[44]

George Augustus Chichester May

Chief Justice of Queen's Bench 1877, Lord Chief Justice of Ireland 1878–87

George Augustus Chichester May (1816–92) was born in Belfast, where his father, Edward May (1783–1819), was a clergyman of the Church of Ireland. May's given names were an illustration of the close relationship between his grandfather, Sir Edward May (1751–1814), MP for Belfast 1800–14, and George Augustus Chichester (1769–1844), second marquess of Donegall. The marquess was a

34 Cairns to Disraeli, 13 August 1874 (Disraeli Papers, B/XX/Ca/122).
35 *ILT&SJ*, vol. 8, p. 577 (7 November 1874) and vol. 9, p. 121 (6 March 1875).
36 HC Deb, 3rd series, vol. 225, col. 1314 (9 July 1875).
37 HC Deb, 3rd series, vol. 226, col. 854 (11 August 1875); *ILT&SJ*, vol. 9, p. 410 (14 August 1875).
38 HC Deb, 3rd series, vol. 235, col. 163–4 (22 June 1877). G.A.C. May succeeded Ormsby as attorney general.
39 1877 Act, s7.
40 *Irish Times*, 1 September 1880.
41 *Irish Times*, 30 July 1878, 13 March 1880, 20 July 1882.
42 *ILT&SJ*, vol. 19, p. 550 (24 October 1885).
43 *Irish Ecclesiastical Gazette*, 1 May 1877; *Irish Times*, 2 May 1877.
44 *Burke's Irish family records*, op. cit.

'major Irish landowner and noted spendthrift',[45] and the central role in the history of Belfast of the Chichester (Donegall) family is evidenced by numerous street names. Sir Edward, after whom May Street was named, was an agent and manager of the Donegall estates and engaged in property dealings on his own account. In later life G.A.C. May drew an annual income of about £600 from head rents of properties in a central area of Belfast (Arthur Street and Arthur Square, May Street, Great Edward Street, Cromac Street and Chichester Street), many of them on foot of leases for 91 years granted between 1809 and 1811.[46]

May was educated at Foyle College, Londonderry,[47] a grammar school tracing its origins to 1617, and in England, at Shrewsbury school and at Cambridge University, where he was elected a fellow of Magdalene College. He was called to the Bar in 1844, joining the North East circuit, and became a QC in 1865. His practice lay primarily in equity and property law. In 1867–8 he was the editor of the first official law reports.[48] He stood as a candidate in the 1874 general election in the constituency of Carrickfergus, Co. Antrim, losing to another Conservative, the sitting member, following which he was appointed law adviser at Dublin Castle. In November 1875 he was made attorney general, in succession to Henry Ormsby.[49] The solicitor general at the time, David Plunket, who was something of a reluctant law officer (see p. 87), was not promoted.

Two judicial vacancies arose while May was attorney general, the first following the long-anticipated retirement in January 1876 of James Monahan as chief justice of Common Pleas, and the second on the death of the chief justice of Queen's Bench, James Whiteside, at the end of November 1876. As attorney general (and hence leader of the Bar) May had a prescriptive right or at least expectation of being nominated to fill any judicial vacancy that arose, although in January, having been a law officer for only a few weeks, his claim may not have been strong, and one of the puisne judges in the court, Michael Morris, was appointed. The chief secretary for Ireland, Sir Michael Hicks Beach, took the view that the government would always give an office when vacant according as they saw best; 'if he had not done this, May should have got the chief of Common Pleas, and not Morris, as the old rule was that the attorney general had the right'.[50]

The prospect of May being appointed as head of the Queen's Bench met with resistance, criticism focussing on his inexperience in criminal law and on a sense that, despite his high office, he did not have an appropriate standing among his colleagues. 'At the Bar he had not reached such a position as his talents warranted, and he had practised mainly in equity – on these grounds his appointment was

45 *DIB*, entry on Donegall (by W.A. Maguire). See also Maguire, *Living like a lord: the second marquis of Donegall, 1769–1844* (Belfast, 1984).
46 G.A.C. May, Rental of properties in Belfast, 28 August 1883 (PRONI, D2533/83/1).
47 *Irish Ecclesiastical Gazette*, vol. 28, p. 118 (6 February 1886).
48 Eamonn G. Hall, *The superior courts of law; 'official' law reporting in Ireland, 1866–2006* (Dublin, 2007), p. 66.
49 *ILT&SJ*, vol. 9, p. 579 (27 November 1875).
50 J.J. Hall to Abercorn, 4 March 1876 (Abercorn Papers (PRONI), D623/A/321/17).

vehemently opposed'.[51] The *Irish Times* commented later that 'as a criminal lawyer he has not done much, and for brilliancy at the Bar he was not pre-eminent', a cool enough remark but still warmer than its London correspondent's earlier observation that the vacancy should obviously be filled by a sitting judge 'for the appointment of the attorney general, Mr May, to such an important office is entirely out of the question'.[52] The *Dublin Daily Express*, normally a reliable Tory journal, provoked outrage among a group of Conservative members of the Bar by its disparagement of May's legal ability and a proposal that James Lawson, a sitting judge and former Liberal MP, be appointed.[53] An interval of some ten weeks elapsed after Whiteside's death before it was announced that May would succeed him,[54] during which other candidates (including Hedges Eyre Chatterton[55] and Baron Francis FitzGerald)[56] were canvassed and offers of appointment declined, and it was said that at one point May spoke of resignation if he was not nominated.[57]

When Hicks Beach told May at the end of January 1877 that he had been authorised by the prime minister to offer to appoint him as lord chief justice May responded that he would much rather be an equity judge, and remarked that he had good reason to believe that Chatterton had not really meant to decline the appointment, and would respond favourably if he were to be told that it would suit the arrangements of the government better that he (Chatterton) should accept the chief justiceship. Hicks Beach told him that he would communicate this to Disraeli, but that he did not think that there was a disposition to put any such pressure on Chatterton, at which May said that he would accept the chief justiceship if offered to him while repeating that he did not at all want the place. In the view of Hicks Beach there was logic, from a purely judicial point of view, in what May was proposing, since he thought that Chatterton would make a better chief justice than May, and that May would make a better vice-chancellor than Chatterton. But he believed that May's appointment as chief justice would be the more popular one, both with the judges and with the public, and he told Disraeli that on the whole he could not advise him to raise the subject again with Chatterton.[58]

May served as chief justice for ten years. His conduct in relation to a trial in which he did not participate attracted more attention than any trial over which he did preside. In November 1880, at a turbulent time in the Land War, charges having a mixed legal and political character were brought against Parnell and others for, in essence, 'conspiracy to prevent the payment of rent; conspiracy to resist the process of ejectment; conspiracy to prevent the taking of farms from

51 Ball, p. 311.
52 *Irish Times*, 3 February 1877, 9 December 1876.
53 *Dublin Daily Express*, 9 December 1876; *Irish Times*, 16 December 1876.
54 *ILT&SJ*, vol. 11, p. 64 (10 February 1877).
55 Ball, p. 311.
56 *Irish Times*, 9 December 1876; *ILT&SJ*, vol. 11, p. 16 (13 January 1877); J.G. Swift MacNeill, *What I have seen and heard* (London, 1925), p. 155.
57 Swift MacNeill, op. cit., p. 156.
58 Hicks Beach to Disraeli, 30 January 1877 (Disraeli Papers (Bodleian Library, Oxford), C/V/11c).

which tenants had been evicted and conspiracy to create ill-will among Her Majesty's subjects'.[59] (This was commonly, but perhaps inappropriately, referred to as a State Trial.[60])

An application was made early in December to postpone the trial, which May refused, using language which, as he acknowledged in a statement at the opening of the trial about three weeks later,

> imported that I considered the traversers [i.e., the defendants] guilty of the charges contained in the information laid against them in this case. It occurred to myself that I might have used terms capable of such a construction, and I immediately corrected what I had said, adding – 'I mean that these are the charges and accusations which the traversers will have to answer, and if they can satisfy the jury of their innocence let them be acquitted'. When a speaker delivering an unpremeditated address corrects himself if by inadvertence he has used expressions which did not convey what he intended, and in the same breath explains his real meaning, it is only just, it is certainly usual, to accept his explanation. However this language of mine has occasioned very considerable excitement and has been very bitterly complained of ... Upon the whole, after anxious consideration, and with the concurrence of some whose opinions I highly value, I have come to the conclusion that the due administration of justice will be promoted by not taking part in the case.[61]

Gladstone, the prime minister, was very exercised about what May had said, and thought that he should not sit as a judge in the case.[62] May privately had little doubt about the prosecution, telling Lord O'Hagan, when thanking him for his counsel and support in the incident, that 'Law [the attorney general] is not by any means sanguine as to obtaining a conviction – indeed, seemed to me the other day almost to apprehend an acquittal but I think that is scarcely possible'.[63] At the end of the trial the jury disagreed.

In 1885 and 1886 May repeatedly but unsuccessfully sought a baronetcy (see p. 117). He initially complained about being overlooked and put in an invidious position by the conferring of such an honour on Michael Morris, subsequently letting it be known indirectly that his health was poor and that the granting of such an honour might facilitate or expedite his retirement. A deterioration in May's hearing had been common knowledge among the judiciary at least since the summer of 1885.[64] Hicks Beach, once again holding office as chief secretary, noted in late 1886 when the request for an honour was renewed that the case for this on

59 Margaret O'Callaghan, *British high politics and Nationalist Ireland* (Cork, 1994), p. 62.
60 *ILT&SJ*, vol. 15, p. 98 (19 February 1881).
61 *ILT&SJ*, vol. 15, p. 8 (1 January 1881).
62 O'Callaghan, op. cit., p. 168.
63 May to O'Hagan, 30 December 1880 (Teeling Papers, MS 17,874 (15)).
64 Morris to Gibson, 6 June 1885 (Ashbourne Papers, B.77/2).

objective grounds was not strong, and that May's resignation might shortly be anticipated in any event, so that the granting of an honour would not be necessary to bring it about.[65] A few weeks later, on the first day of the next law term, May's resignation, by reason of ill health, was announced. The *Irish Times*, unfavourably disposed to the last, observed that this had been long anticipated, that 'the date of his resignation was determined by the demand made upon him to fulfil [his duties]', and that 'the public are entitled to get the best service that can be procured, and no personal consideration could be suffered to stand in the way of any necessary step. If anywhere particularly a strong and hale and clear-minded judge is required it is manifestly in the place which is first and most severe on the Irish bench'.[66]

Although May did not receive the honour that he hoped for three of his sons achieved distinction in their respective careers (in the Royal Artillery, in colonial administration and in medicine) and were knighted. Major general Sir Edward May (born 1856) listed his pastimes as hunting, fishing and shooting, interests shared by his brother Sir Francis Henry May (born 1860), who was governor of Fiji (1910–12) and Hong Kong (1912–19), and who engaged also in polo, rifle shooting and yachting.[67] Their brother Sir Chichester Gould May (born 1863) was an eminent physician. In 1853 May had married Olivia Barrington, daughter of Sir Matthew Barrington, a prominent landowner, solicitor and philanthropist, of Glenstal Castle, Murroe, Co. Limerick. She died in 1876. He lived at 13 Fitzwilliam Square, and died in 1892 at his country residence, Lisnavagh, Rathvilly, Co. Carlow. This had been built in 1847 and was later described by Evelyn Waugh, who inspected it (and a number of other country houses in Ireland) when he was contemplating leaving England in the late 1940s, as 'a large prosaic Early Victorian baronial mansion in flat hunting country near Dublin'.[68] May's recreations included riding, and while chief justice he was twice reported as having been thrown by his horse and injured, in the Phoenix Park and at Sandymount.[69] He left a substantial estate, valued at over £54,000 for probate.

Gerald FitzGibbon

Lord Justice of Appeal 1878–1909

Gerald FitzGibbon (1837–1909) was born in Gloucester Street (now Sean McDermott Street) in Dublin. A house in Merrion Square (no. 10) subsequently became the family home, and FitzGibbon lived there for most of his life. In the 1870s he built a house, Kilrock, on the north side of the Hill of Howth. This was

65 Hicks Beach to Londonderry, 19 December 1886 (Papers of 3rd marquess of Salisbury, Hatfield).

66 *Irish Times*, 12 January 1877; *ILT&SJ*, vol. 21, p. 32 (15 January 1887).

67 *Who was who*.

68 Waugh to Nancy Mitford, 29 May 1947 (Mark Amory (ed.), *The letters of Evelyn Waugh* (London, 1980), p. 251); see also Mark Bence-Jones, *Burke's guide to country houses, vol. 1: Ireland* (London, 1978), p. 187.

69 *ILT&SJ*, vol. 11, p. 202 (28 April 1877) and vol. 15, p. 157 (19 March 1881).

referred to as his summer residence, although it became better known for the house party at which, for many years, beginning in 1875,[70] he would extend hospitality to a group of friends in the week after Christmas.[71]

His father, also named Gerald (1793–1882), was born in Co. Limerick and was called to the Bar in 1830, after an earlier commercial career. He took silk in 1841, and in 1860 was appointed a master in Chancery, an important semi-judicial role under the law at the time. When he stepped down from that position in 1878, aged 85, its functions were distributed among other offices and courts, pursuant to the judicature legislation of 1877.[72] He wrote papers on land and education issues between 1868 and 1873, making some reputation as a conservative pamphleteer.[73]

FitzGibbon attended Trinity College, and was part of a generation of undergraduates who subsequently achieved distinction. Men such as W.E.H. Lecky (born 1838), J.P. Mahaffy (1839) and Robert Ball (1840) gave the College a remarkable standing in the academic and wider world at the end of the nineteenth century when, it has been said, 'the reputation of the College was higher than ever before or since'.[74] FitzGibbon was called to the Bar in 1860, and joined the Munster circuit, developing a strong practice quickly, and becoming a Queen's Counsel in 1872. Letters exchanged among his legal friends and contemporaries, David Plunket (later Lord Rathmore) and Edward Gibson (later Lord Ashbourne), give some sense of the timeless challenges of early days at the Bar.[75] The three friends were active in politics as Conservatives, and Plunket was the first to get a start in public office, through his election in 1870 as one of the members of Parliament for Dublin University. In 1875 the appointment of the other member, J.T. Ball, to be lord chancellor gave rise to a bye-election. Ball's promotion was in itself a demonstration (if any was needed) that a seat in Parliament might enhance a career at the Bar and ultimately lead to judicial office. FitzGibbon considered standing in the election but in the event did not, and the seat was won by Gibson.

Also in 1875, a vacancy arose in the office of law adviser at Dublin Castle. This was a part-time office, the primary duties of which involved responding to requests from magistrates for guidance on legal points. The government, having also

70 FitzGibbon to Lord Randolph Churchill, 5 January 1890 (('LRC Papers'), Cambridge University Library, MS Add. 9248/3359).

71 A description of Kilrock was given in *ILT&SJ*, vol. 33, p. 187 (6 May 1898), which also refers to FitzGibbon having met the expense of constructing for public use on the shore a facility that was known at the time as FitzGibbon's Bathing Place.

72 1877 Act, s75: 'After the passing of this Act no successor to the existing Receiver Master shall be appointed.'

73 *ILT&SJ*, vol. 12, p. 199 (20 April 1878), and vol. 15, p. 479 (30 September 1882) and p. 494 (7 October 1882); see also Kenneth Ferguson, *King's Inns barristers, 1868–2004* (Dublin, 2005), pp 40–5, and entry on FitzGibbon in the *DIB* (by C.J. Woods).

74 R.B. McDowell and David Webb, *Trinity College Dublin: an academic history* (Cambridge, 1982), p. 283.

75 See letters to Gibson from FitzGibbon in 1865 (B50/2 and 3, Ashbourne Papers, Parliamentary Archives, London); and from Plunket between 1864 and 1872 (B119/2, 5, 6 and 7, ibid.); Daire Hogan, *The legal profession in Ireland, 1789–1921* (Dublin, 1986), pp 76–7.

considered FitzGibbon, had appointed Frederick Falkiner QC to fill the position. The lord lieutenant, the duke of Abercorn, told Sir Michael Hicks Beach, the chief secretary, that he shared his view about the respective merits of Falkiner and FitzGibbon, which were reportedly also held by Ball (the lord chancellor), Taylor (an MP for Co. Dublin), Plunket and G.A.C. May (the retiring law adviser). They all thought FitzGibbon to be the abler man, but Abercorn apprehended that to appoint him would not be well received in the North nor by many members of the Conservative Bar in consequence of his being widely regarded as only a 'recent and doubtful convert to Conservatism'. Abercorn advised playing for time, so that by appointing Falkiner in the first place, with a clear understanding that he would not seek further promotion to be a law officer, and then 'shunting him into some chairmanship',[76] it would be possible to secure the position of law adviser for FitzGibbon without giving grounds for offence.[77]

In 1876 Falkiner was appointed to be the recorder of Dublin and FitzGibbon succeeded him as law adviser.[78] In addition to his official responsibilities, however, as FitzGibbon told Winston Churchill when, as a young man, he was writing the biography of his father Lord Randolph Churchill (1849–95), 'he had also to give advice and opinions to all and sundry at the [Dublin] Castle', and was a 'legal maid-of all-work'.[79] It was in that context that FitzGibbon first met Churchill, who was the younger son of the viceroy, the duke of Marlborough, and with whom he was to have a warm friendship (see below). When Churchill asked whether he could dismiss a footman without paying his fare back to London 'I told him that, whatever the law was, the lord lieutenant's son couldn't do it'.[80]

FitzGibbon was promoted to be solicitor general early in 1877, succeeding Plunket, as part of a reshuffle in which Gibson was appointed to be attorney general, succeeding May. His judicial career began in December 1878 when he was sworn in to fill a vacancy in the Court of Appeal arising through the resignation in November of Christian LJ as one of the two lords justices of appeal in that court. A vacancy had also arisen just before this in the Common Pleas division of the High Court after the death of William Keogh, which FitzGibbon had no interest in taking. However it was understood then that Christian was on the point of retiring owing to ill health, and FitzGibbon saw the possibility of either being appointed to that impending vacancy or, if Gibson elected to take that position, of succeeding him as one of the MPs for the university. (As it transpired, Gibson was offered the appointment by the prime minister, Beaconsfield, but turned it down, after a strong request to do so from Marlborough.) FitzGibbon told Gibson that he understood that Christopher Palles had previously declined appointment to the

76 This was a reference to being appointed as chairman of the quarter sessions of magistrates in a county, a position made full-time and redesignated as a county court judgeship by the 1877 Act.

77 Abercorn to Hicks Beach, 5 February 1875 (Hicks Beach Papers (Gloucestershire Archives, Gloucester), D2455 – X4–1–1–3(2)and (3)).

78 *ILT&SJ*, vol. 10, p. 424 (22 July 1876).

79 W.S. Churchill, *Lord Randolph Churchill* (London, 1906), vol. 1, p. 77.

80 Ibid.

new Court of Appeal, when it had been established by the 1877 Act, and that Sullivan, the master of the rolls, had likewise declined. He told Gibson that if he [Gibson] were to take the position, FitzGibbon's ability to win the seat in Parliament would depend on the secrecy of the preparations and there being a sudden announcement. He asked Gibson to make up his mind promptly and let him know, and if he preferred to continue as attorney general then FitzGibbon would do his best to become an efficient judge of appeal. He saw that court as one where constant effort and labour would be required, and where he would have real work and an opportunity of making some reputation, neither of which, he thought, would be the case if he were to be a judge in the Common Pleas. He noted that 'above all, personal interest, party interest, public interest, everything urges the immediate settlement of every question of patronage as it arises – all difficulties are trebled by delay'.[81] Following Gibson's acknowledgment that he would not seek the place in the Court of Appeal it was then promptly offered to and accepted by FitzGibbon.[82] Marlborough remarked that the appointment 'is well deserved, and gives general satisfaction even among our enemies'.[83]

The sense expressed by Abercorn in 1875 that FitzGibbon was not a wholly committed Conservative had resurfaced in the course of that exercise of filling the place in the Court of Appeal, and was to be brought up again in very fraught circumstances in 1905 (see p. 455). The lord chancellor, Ball, advised in 1878 that the place should be given to FitzGibbon, not only in light of his merits and eminence at the Bar but also because, if Gibson were to be appointed, and thus leave the House of Commons, it was by no means certain that FitzGibbon would succeed in holding the seat for the Conservatives in the resulting bye-election – 'he was until the other day a Whig and opposed to the Church Establishment'.[84]

FitzGibbon was a pleasant and persuasive speaker, at the Bar and on the Bench, and in his church – he 'stood out among Churchmen as the most impressive and distinguished speaker in the Church of Ireland'.[85] Legal sources agreed:

> the fact that FitzGibbon's judgments are more lucid and understandable as they are *heard* by those present in court than when they are *read* in the Law Reports is accounted for by his great accomplishments as a speaker. By the aid of intonation, emphasis and inflection he is able to make unmistakably

81 FitzGibbon to Gibson, 22 October 1878 (Ashbourne Papers, B50/9); *The Ashbourne Papers: a calendar of the papers of Edward Gibson, 1st Lord Ashbourne*, compiled by A.B. Cooke and A.P.W. Malcomson (Belfast, 1974), p. 111.

82 FitzGibbon to Marlborough, 10 November 1878 (Political Papers of John Winston Spencer Churchill, 7th duke of Marlborough (Cambridge University Library), MS Add. 9271/4/114).

83 Marlborough to Beaconsfield, 14 November 1878 (Disraeli Papers, C/V/20d).

84 Ball to Marlborough, 5 November 1878 (Political Papers of the 7th duke of Marlborough (Cambridge University Library), MS Add. 9271/4/13).

85 *Church of Ireland Gazette*, p. 1049 (22 October 1909). A less sympathetic observation about him in a passage in *Ulysses* might be noted – 'it was the speech of a finished orator, full of courteous haughtiness' ('Aeolus', line 794).

> clear a sentence which, when reduced to writing, may prove ambiguous or difficult of comprehension.[86]

Maurice Healy noted, to the same effect, that

> I never missed an opportunity of hearing him, for never was there a man endowed with so beautiful a speaking voice and so well able to make use of it. He was so tall a man that he had a lean-forward attitude that was almost a stoop.[87] He had an enormous head; and he had one of the most mobile faces that I have ever seen ... An argument in the Court of Appeal when he was a member was an intellectual treat. For FitzGibbon always argued the case with counsel; and whereas nothing is more irritating to counsel than to be interrupted by the judge, this never applied to FitzGibbon's interventions, for the reason that he always listened to the answer to his question.[88]

He took pains however to play down the significance for success at the Bar of debating and oratory, warning in 1898 that 'the fatal gift of fluency would become a deadly one unless it was backed up by sound, solid hard work at unattractive subjects', for which he offered essay prizes. This was said in the course of speaking to the Law Students' Debating Society in King's Inns. He thought it important that students would 'sit down and work hard at certain specified dull and unattractive subjects', and referred to the law relating to the ownership and occupation of land as a subject, above all else, that was 'immediately and directly likely to be useful to a young man when he went to the Bar'.[89]

He had a strong interest in education, and in 1885 was appointed a Commissioner of National Education in succession to the late Mountifort Longfield.[90] The enactment in August that year of the Educational Endowments (Ireland) Act[91] owed much to his exertions, both in persuading Churchill to ensure that a Bill that had been introduced by the previous government would be taken up again, and in redrafting various of its provisions.[92] The Act provided that new judicial commissioners would have power to draft and settle schemes for the modification, on a cy pres basis,[93] of terms and conditions governing charitable

86 Rhadamanthus, op. cit., p. 33.

87 Another report referred to him as a 'medium sized man' (*ILT&SJ*, vol. 28, p. 16 (13 January 1894), quoting from the '*Star*').

88 Healy, *OldMC*, p. 274.

89 *ILT&SJ*, vol. 32, p. 491 (29 October 1898); *Law Times*, vol. 106, p. 38 (12 November 1898).

90 *ILT&SJ*, vol. 19, p. 12 (3 January 1885). He retired from that position on account of ill health in 1896 (*ILT&SJ*, vol.30, p. 280 (27 June 1896)).

91 48&49 Vict., c.78.

92 Holmes Memoir, *IHS*, vol. 16, no. 62 (September 1968), p. 160; W.S. Churchill, op. cit., p. 434.

93 'Cy pres' is an expression, derived from Norman French, meaning 'as near as possible'. A doctrine of jurisprudence so designated may be invoked to permit, under certain conditions, the use of property comprised in a charitable gift for a modified charitable purpose when it has become impossible or impractical to give effect to the original intention of the donor(s).

trusts and property applied or applicable for educational purposes ('educational endowments'), subject to formal approval by the Privy Council of Ireland. It also provided that the first two statutory judicial commissioners would be himself and John Naish, the recently retired lord chancellor of Ireland.[94] They received no payment for their services in addition to their judicial salary (or pension), and the position was by no means a sinecure, requiring the devotion of considerable time to its responsibilities.

The two judicial commissioners generally concurred in their view of applications made under the Act. One exception was a disagreement between FitzGibbon and William O'Brien, a High Court judge who had replaced Naish, on an application relating to a trust established in the seventeenth century by Erasmus Smith, as a result of which no scheme could thus be made for modification of its management and governance. They differed on whether an underlying educational intent of the trust could be severed from a stipulation that the management should be exclusively Protestant, which in FitzGibbon's opinion could not be done.[95] Their separate lengthy judgments were delivered in the court of Chancery, and O'Brien's more rhetorical passages included an observation that his learned colleague 'overlooks time. He stands upon the banks of the Boyne. I stand in the nineteenth century'.[96] A later garbled version of that comment was that FitzGibbon 'in this matter stands on one bank of the river Boyne. I take my stand on the other'.[97] The governance of the schools was a matter of political controversy at the time,[98] and again a generation later. The complexity of the issues raised by the founding documents of the charity (as thus previously considered by the commissioners in the 1890s) was illustrated by the fact that the hearing in the High Court in Dublin in 1931 of an agreed preliminary question about the Trust took 29 days,[99] and that an appeal to the Supreme Court in 1933 was heard over 39 days.[100] The issues were ultimately resolved by agreement, which was incorporated in a private Act of the Oireachtas, the Erasmus Smith Schools Act 1938.[101]

94 48&49 Vict., c.78, ss4, 6 and 24.
95 *ILT&SJ*, vol. 28, p. 528 (27 October 1894).
96 *Irish Times*, 23 October 1894.
97 *Law Times*, vol. 108, p. 139 (9 December 1899).
98 W.J.R. Wallace, *Faithful to our Trust: a history of the Erasmus Smith Trust and the High School, Dublin* (Dublin, 2004), pp 178–88; HC Deb, 4th series, vol. 27, cols. 661–3 (23 July 1894); vol. 29, cols. 15–6 (29 August 1894); vol. 45, cols. 875–6 (29 January 1897) – 'this was another attempt to meddle with Protestant endowments in Ireland' (Mr W. Johnston, Belfast South).
99 *Governors of Erasmus Smith's Schools v Attorney general*, 66 ILTR 57 (1932).
100 *ILT&SJ*, vol. 67, pp 117–19 (22 April 1933).
101 This recited the 'great difficulty and complexity of the questions arising in this action and the heavy further expense which would result from the prosecution of the appeal.' Judgment had been reserved in the Supreme Court, but had not been delivered before the death in December 1936 of the chief justice, Hugh Kennedy. The two surviving judges who had heard the appeal were not in agreement, so if the appeal had been continued a complete re-hearing would have been necessary. The cost of the proceedings in the High Court and Supreme Court were stated to have been upwards of £50,000, and the amount available from the trust annually for educational purposes was said to have been about £9,000 (*ILT&SJ*, vol. 71, pp 101–3 (24 April

Ignatius O'Brien described FitzGibbon's mind as being 'intensely astute [and] very subtle; he saw clearly contingencies that another man would neither see nor trouble about. And he always strived so to limit his utterances that they could be confined to the mere point at issue'.[102] Sir John Ross, a judicial contemporary, wrote that FitzGibbon 'always approached a case from the ethical side – which party had the merits – and thereupon he applied his amazing ingenuity to drag the law to the side of natural justice'.[103] The observations of Peter O'Brien, lord chief justice for the greater part of FitzGibbon's judicial career, were more nuanced and perhaps ultimately not so complimentary:

> his mind was extremely subtle, and he generally formed his judgments through a strange process of reasoning. It was impossible to predict what view of a case he would take, and the ordinary judicial mind often found a difficulty in following his mental windings and twistings. He possessed a wonderful knack, which amounted to a gift, of presenting his own view in the most convincing manner. He had, if I may use the term, an acrobatic mind.[104]

The *Irish Times* in its obituary, having referred to him as 'a sound, if not, perhaps, a profoundly learned lawyer', said that he was also 'a man of the world, and his strong common sense often served to lead him to rapid conclusions, which nevertheless were seldom at fault. His judgments upon all occasions of moment were models of lucidity and completeness, closely reasoned, incisive in diction'.[105]

FitzGibbon was a member of the Court of Appeal for over 30 years, and acquired a very high reputation there. The only positions of greater or corresponding standing in the Irish judicial system were those of lord chancellor, lord chief justice or a Law Lord. Churchill canvassed Salisbury, the prime minister, without success in 1885 and 1886 for FitzGibbon rather than Gibson (Ashbourne) to be appointed as chancellor.[106] In 1897 the *Irish Times* reported speculation that Ashbourne would be appointed as governor general (viceroy) of Canada, making way for FitzGibbon, but nothing came of that.[107] The two appointments to the historic office of lord chief justice[108] that were made while he was a judge, in 1887 (Sir Michael Morris) and 1889 (Peter O'Brien), were given to men with much stronger political connections than he had. There were four occasions in his

1937)). In 1894 the annual income was stated in Parliament to have been much less than £20,000 (HC Deb, 4th series, vol. 27, col. 663 (23 July 1894)).

102 Daire Hogan and Patrick Maume (eds), *The reminiscences of Ignatius O'Brien, lord chancellor of Ireland 1913–1918* (Dublin, 2021), p. 158.

103 John Ross, *The years of my pilgrimage* (London, 1924), p. 201.

104 Georgina O'Brien (ed.), *The reminiscences of Lord O'Brien of Kilfenora* (London, 1916), pp 104–5.

105 *Irish Times*, 15 October 1909.

106 Memorandum (undated [May 1885)], LRC Papers/600; R.F. Foster, op. cit., p. 274.

107 *Irish Times*, 29 September 1897.

108 The lord chief justice was *ex officio* a member of the Court of Appeal, but decisions of his at first instance might themselves be the subject of an appeal to that court.

judicial career when an Irish lawyer was (or might have been) appointed as a Law Lord. He was not considered for appointment in 1882, 1889 or 1900, and although in 1905 his name was put forward the political support for the attorney general, John Atkinson, dashed any chance that he may have had (see p. 455).

The original entry on FitzGibbon in the *Dictionary of national biography* paid a rather convoluted compliment to his 'highly distinguished' standing as judge, in saying that 'in every case [which went to the House of Lords] and where he differed from the colleagues of his own court his opinion was upheld by the House of Lords'. Three such cases were *Royal Exchange Assurance Corporation v Burke*,[109] *Kynoch & Company v Webb*[110] and *McCartney v Londonderry & Lough Swilly Railway Co.*,[111] although cases in which he was in the majority (or a member of an unanimous court) whose judgments were the subject of successful appeals were rather more numerous.[112] In one case, *Aaron's Reef v Twiss*,[113] his judgment was the subject of a handsome tribute from Lord Macnaghten. The defendant shareholder, who lived in Co. Limerick, successfully resisted a demand or call for sums outstanding on partly paid shares issued on foot of a prospectus which Macnaghten described as 'not only a dishonest prospectus but one of the most dishonest documents of that class I have ever seen'. He went on to confirm the judgment of the Court of Appeal in Ireland, saying that FitzGibbon's judgment 'is so complete in all respects and so convincing that I only propose to add a very few words'.[114] In Lord Fitzgerald's speech [judgment] in *Trevor v Whitworth*,[115] a seminal company law case on maintenance of capital in which it was held that a company had no power to purchase its own shares, he referred to a judgment of FitzGibbon[116] as affording 'the ablest criticism which has taken place up to this morning upon the authorities and upon the question which we now have to determine'. Lord Halsbury referred on a subsequent occasion to 'the many appeals upon which I have had to recognise the wisdom and learning which he has ever exhibited upon the bench'.[117]

Members of the Court of Appeal frequently – indeed, as time passed, almost invariably – also sat as judges of first instance on assize, as contemplated by s41 of the 1877 legislation, and hence had direct judicial experience of jury trials, both civil and criminal. In 1896 FitzGibbon heard, with a special jury in Belfast, the

109 33 ILTR 29 (1899); *ILT&SJ*, vol. 33, p. 522 (16 December 1899).
110 *ILT&SJ*, vol. 34, p. 89 (24 February 1900).
111 [1904] AC 301.
112 See, for instance, *Deering v Bank of Ireland*, [1887] AC 20; *Herron v Rathmines & Rathgar Improvement Commissioners*, [1892] AC 498; *White v Bagot*, [1901] 1 IR 529; *French v French*, [1902] 1 IR 172; *Dublin United Tramways Co. v FitzGerald*, [1903] AC 99; *Fullerton v Provincial Bank of Ireland*, [1903] AC 309; *Local Govt. Board for Ireland v McKay*, [1903] AC 402; *Pearson v Dublin Corporation*, [1907] AC 351.
113 [1895] 2 IR 207; [1896] AC 273.
114 [1896] AC 273, at 291.
115 [1887] AC 409, at 431.
116 *In re Balgooley Distillery Company*, LR I, 17 Ch D 239 (1886–7).
117 *Johnston v O'Neill*, [1911] AC 552 at 567.

case which ultimately went to the House of Lords in 1901 as *Quinn v Leatham*.[118] In another case in Belfast, sitting without a jury, he determined various facts, by reference to the custom of the port.[119] He had strong views on expert witnesses, telling a friend that 'architectural, engineering and medical experts will swear black is white and believe it. His opinion was that the tendency of expert evidence is to muddle a jury and defeat the ends of justice by procuring a disagreement'.[120] He queried proposals to establish a court of criminal appeal, on the ground that the existence of such a court might render juries less cautious.[121]

He did not confine his energies to judicial work and to a very industrious participation in church and civil society. His interest in political issues remained strong, and he was widely known to be not only a friend but also something of a political adviser to Lord Randolph Churchill. His steadiness and generally benign character was something of a contrast with the more volatile and flamboyant personality of Churchill, who was described by a biographer as doing his best 'to behave like a character in a classical English political novel, and [whose] career involves all the trappings of romance, opportunism and triviality characteristic of that genre'.[122] FitzGibbon furnished him with advice and commentary and gossip on Irish affairs. He was a loyal friend, and in 1892, when Churchill was a much diminished figure in the wider world, he extended an invitation, which Churchill was unable to accept, to be his guest at a dinner held in the King's Inns to mark the 300th anniversary of the founding of Trinity College.[123] The high opinion that Churchill had of his friend was demonstrated in January 1886 in a comment that he made to the prime minster, Salisbury, as to what he termed the unreliability of the Irish people being evidenced in a concentrated form in the Irish bench. 'I have gone carefully over the list of judges and there is only one in whom the Gov't could confidently rely for law and courage. That is FitzGibbon'.[124] This friendship may not have been to FitzGibbon's advantage in the eyes of Salisbury, whose wary and arm's-length relationship with Churchill disintegrated completely when the latter resigned as chancellor of the Exchequer in December 1886.

In December 1885, a time of great volatility in the two British political parties' relations with Parnell and their approaches to Irish nationalism and the campaign for Home Rule, he advised Churchill (who would shortly become a vehement supporter of Ulster unionism) on the subject, saying 'for heaven's sake don't touch it', adding that no good could come of engaging with Parnell and that Gladstone should be left to do so.[125] In April 1886 he sent Churchill a set of passages from

118 *Leatham v Craig*, [1899] 2 IR 667; *Quinn v Leatham*, [1901] AC 495.
119 *Clydesdale Shipowners Co. Ltd v Gallagher*, [1907] 2 IR 578. See also The SS *Gairloch*, [1899] 2 IR 1.
120 J.F. Fuller, *Omniana: the autobiography of an Irish octogenerian* (London, 1916), p. 204.
121 *ILT&SJ*, vol. 26, p. 358 (9 July 1892).
122 R.F. Foster, *Lord Randolph Churchill: a political life* (Oxford, 1981), p. 7.
123 *Irish Times*, 15 October 1909.
124 Churchill to Salisbury, 13 January 1886 (Papers of the 3rd marquess of Salisbury, Hatfield).
125 FitzGibbon to Churchill, 7 December 1885 (LRC Papers, 1149).

Gladstone's speech introducing the Home Rule bill, marked up with critical annotations.[126] In 1893 he prepared a further commentary, saying that the second bill seemed to be worse than the first and that 'everybody ought to do his best to beat this Bill – my only qualifications are in the legal line – I cannot spout or publish'.[127] Churchill in thanking him said that he would try to make the best use of all that he was sent, and that 'the "lawyer's notes" may develop into orations which may electrify the country'.[128]

FitzGibbon saw himself as a moderniser, and regretted the influence of 'fossilised Toryism'.[129] He made light of the adverse reaction of people he might have so categorised to the promotion of Holmes to succeed him as solicitor general in 1878 (see p. 329). However the suspicion as to the depth of his commitment to the Conservative party which had been a factor in delaying an initial step on to the patronage ladder in 1875 surfaced more dramatically in 1905 (see p. 455). He was a member of the Dublin University Club but not, unlike many of his judicial colleagues, also of the Kildare Street Club,[130] widely regarded as the social headquarters of the landed interest. He noted to Churchill the importance of protecting 'persons, rights and property; not merely land (which nine out of ten people seem to think is the only property in Ireland), but the earnings and investments of industrious men of every class'.[131] He expanded on that theme some months later:

> If prices don't improve the land question will continue to settle itself by the natural disappearance of rents. It is now really impossible to obtain (apart altogether from the League's work[132]) any return from land equal to the judicial rents of four years ago and the landowners are aware of this and consequently are realising that evictions and the like are useless. But in any case the Irish landlords, as you well know, are neither personally nor politically worth the money or the labour which it would require to preserve them from the, I believe, inevitable operation of the economic laws which are crushing them.[133]

The *Law Times* said of FitzGibbon after his death, in October 1909, that

> so far as was permissible for the holder of a high judicial position he took part in public affairs to the manifest benefit of the community [and took] an

126 FitzGibbon to Churchill, 11 April 1886 (LRC Papers, 1469/1470).
127 FitzGibbon to Churchill, 17 February 1893 (LRC Papers, 4090) and 23 March 1893 (ibid., 4157).
128 Churchill to FitzGibbon, 15 March 1893 (Churchill, op. cit., vol. II, p. 469).
129 FitzGibbon to Churchill, 28 October 1886 (LRC Papers, 1932).
130 Records of the Kildare Street & University Club, by kind permission.
131 FitzGibbon to Churchill, 16 January 1886 (LRC Papers, 1354).
132 i.e., apart altogether from, or without taking into account, the activities of the tenant rights organization, the Land League.
133 FitzGibbon to Churchill, 20 July 1886 (LRC Papers, 1558); R.F. Foster, op. cit., p. 280.

> interest of the most active character in many religious and charitable institutions, to which he munificently contributed. [He was] a prominent and attractive personality in legal, literary, artistic, social and political life in Ireland … a great intellectual and moral asset, not only of the judiciary but of the people at large.[134]

The lord chancellor, Samuel Walker, when paying tribute in court said of him that if his great talents had been devoted to some other sphere of labour he would have risen to great eminence in the church, or he might well have become a great political force.[135]

FitzGibbon was a very prominent lay member of the Church of Ireland, acting as the chancellor of the United Diocese of Dublin, Glendalough and Kildare from 1896, in that capacity being, as the archbishop of Dublin said following his death, 'the keeper of my legal conscience'.[136] He was closely involved with the Masonic Order, and in particular its orphan schools, and with the Church of Ireland Training College for teachers (at Kildare Place). The Dublin Diocesan Synod, meeting in the week following his death, noted in a resolution of sympathy to his family that he was 'ever ready to devote time and thought to assist in every good work which came before him', It also resolved to promote a memorial to him,[137] a project taken up at a public meeting of members of the Church of Ireland, chaired by the archbishop of Dublin, held a few weeks later in November 1909 at which James H.M. Campbell KC MP, William Moore KC MP and Arthur W. Samuels KC took a leading part.[138] A memorial statue, by Albert Bruce Joy, in St Patrick's Cathedral in Dublin, was unveiled in 1914.[139]

He was a kindly man, evidenced by his appearing in the police magistrate's court in 1895 seeking clemency for a son of his footman who had taken some articles of silver from his home and had been detained when attempting to pawn them. He said that he did not wish to press charges, and that the father would be able to look after the boy better in the future, after which 'the prisoner was allowed out on his father's bail'.[140] He had previously given evidence in a case about whether a right of way over land existed.[141] He shared the nervousness of his class at the reform of death duties and the introduction of estate duty effected by the Finance Act in 1894, but saw a silver lining in a possible increase or acceleration of demonstrations of parental affection, since 'no man need pay any taxes on anything which he gave to his children while he lived'.[142]

134 *Law Times*, vol. 127, pp 599–600 (23 October 1909).
135 *ILT&SJ*, vol. 43, p. 266 (30 October 1909).
136 *Irish Times*, 19 October 1909.
137 *Irish Times*, 19 October 1909.
138 *ILT&SJ*, vol. 43, p. 290 (27 November 1909).
139 *ILT&SJ*, vol. 48, p. 150 (30 May 1914).
140 *ILT&SJ*, vol. 29, p. 592 (7 December 1895).
141 *Mooney v Lalor*, *Irish Times*, 12 November 1894.
142 *ILT&SJ*, vol. 28, p. 533 (27 October 1894).

He was the subject of portraits in oils by Walter Osborne[143] and Sarah Cecilia Harrison. Osborne's portraits were commissioned by the Masonic Order for itself and for presentation to him, and the second portrait (painted in 1894 and reproduced on the jacket of this volume) was donated to the National Gallery of Ireland in 1932. The Bench and Bar of Ireland subscribed after his death for a full length portrait to be hung in the King's Inns, for which Sir William Orpen was initially given the commission, but the Inn later turned to Harrison.[144] She also painted a portrait (showing him formally dressed but not in his judicial robes) for the University Club.

FitzGibbon's wife Margaret Anne, whom he married in 1864, was a daughter of Francis FitzGerald, a baron of the Exchequer between 1861 and 1882. Their eldest son, also Gerald (1866–1942), was appointed as a member of the Supreme Court in 1924, an office he held up to his retirement in 1938, taking into a third generation a tradition of high judicial office. His daughter Janet married William T. Shone (1850–1938), an army officer (Royal Engineers), later knighted, who had seen service in Afghanistan and Burma.[145] Their son, Sir Terence Shone (1894–1965), had a distinguished diplomatic career in the UK Foreign Service. FitzGibbon and his wife suffered the grief of two young daughters dying, each being described at the time as the youngest member of the family.[146]

Frederick W. Walsh

Judge of the court of Bankruptcy 1879–85

Frederick William Walsh (1811–85) was born in Dublin. After education at Trinity College he was called to the Bar in 1836, and subsequently became a QC. He was elected a bencher of King's Inns in 1871. He was a member of the Representative Church Body and was a trustee of the Adelaide Hospital.[147] In 1878 he received an official appointment as Queen's Advocate in the court of admiralty,[148] and in January 1879 was appointed as the second judge in bankruptcy.[149] The *Irish Law Times* had reported the previous month that 'the vacant judgeship in the court of Bankruptcy has been offered to Serjeant Robinson QC but has been declined by him'.[150]

A member of the Bar eulogising Walsh in court after his death in 1885 remarked that when appointed he had 'set himself to master a practice and law

143 FitzGibbon is thought to have been the original purchaser in 1890 of two paintings of Venetian scenes by Osborne that were donated by a subsequent owner to the University Club in Dublin. See Kathryn Milligan, 'A Venetian mystery: two paintings by Walter Osborne in the Kildare Street & University Club, Dublin', *Journal of the History of Collections* (Oxford, 2018).
144 Wanda Ryan-Smolin, *King's Inns portraits* (Dublin, 1992), p. 28.
145 Obituary, Lieutenant-General Sir William Shone, *The Times*, 13 July 1938.
146 *ILT&SJ*, vol. 12, p. 397 (27 July 1878) and vol. 19, p. 85 (14 February 1885).
147 *Irish Times*, 23 April 1879 and 15 December 1880.
148 *ILT&SJ*, vol. 12, p. 137 (16 March 1878).
149 *Irish Times*, 17 January 1879.
150 *ILT&SJ*, vol. 12, p. 593 (7 December 1878).

which were alike unfamiliar to him', and had done so rapidly and completely.[151] His senior colleague in the bankruptcy court, Judge Miller (see p. 221), on that occasion when noting and regretting Walsh's death, had said perhaps somewhat ungraciously that 'I do not think I am qualified to enlarge upon his judicial qualities, [since] our duties lay rather in parallel lines and, in point of fact, we discharged our duties in separate courts, and had as little united action as could possibly exist where persons were members of the same court.[152]

The bankruptcy courts saw many aspects of human nature, including misconduct, dishonesty, incompetence and bad luck. In 1883 Walsh reduced preferential claims for rent due by the bankrupt lessee of a hotel in Letterfrack, Co. Galway, saying that the lessor, Mitchell Henry MP, who had built Kylemore Abbey in the 1860s, was 'a very rich man, and the bankruptcy was due not to any misconduct of the bankrupt but to occurrences that took place which prevented tourists coming into the country. The bankrupt's misfortunes were brought on by the turbulent times, and he was therefore entitled to some consideration'.[153] In other cases he exercised the court's power to commit a bankrupt or 'contumacious' witnesses to prison for what was described as 'unsatisfactory answering', in effect a contempt of court, when it appeared that a fraud had been committed and prior transactions or asset transfers by the bankrupt had not been disclosed or properly explained.

Walsh, who had been unwell, died in London in August 1885 while visiting his family there.

151 *ILT&SJ*, vol. 19, p. 439 (15 August 1885).
152 Ibid.
153 *Irish Times*, 27 October 1883.

CHAPTER NINE

Gladstone's second government, 1880–5

WHEN GLADSTONE RETURNED to office in April 1880 he re-appointed Lord O'Hagan as lord chancellor of Ireland. It transpired that he would appoint three other men to that position, since Hugh Law, who was appointed when O'Hagan retired in the autumn of 1881, died almost two years later, and Edward Sullivan, nominated to succeed Law, also died in office, in April 1885. John Naish, who succeeded Sullivan, held office for just six weeks before the government resigned at the end of June. O'Hagan's son-in-law, John O'Hagan, was appointed as the first judicial commissioner of the Land Commission, when it was established in 1881, a post which had the status of a High Court judge. Two leading prosecuting counsel, William O'Brien and James Murphy, were appointed to the bench in 1882 and 1883 respectively. W.D. Andrews, a member of a leading family in Comber, Co. Down, was appointed in 1882. William Johnson, MP for Mallow, was appointed at the end of 1882, and Andrew Marshall Porter MP, who had declined a political office in 1882, was appointed the following year to be master of the rolls.

Hugh Law

Lord Chancellor of Ireland 1881–3

Hugh Law (1818–83) was the only son of a land agent, John Law, and was born in Co. Down. He was educated at the Royal School, Dungannon, and at Trinity College, where one of his contemporaries was Hugh Cairns (1819–85), from Belfast, who subsequently had a most distinguished legal and judicial career in England. Law was called to the Bar in 1840, and joined the North East circuit, being called to the Inner Bar in 1860, and came to be a leader of the Bar in both civil and criminal cases. He was elected a bencher of King's Inns in 1870. A careful analysis of his opening speech in a trial for murder at Downpatrick spring assizes in 1871 noted the skill in what he said and how he said it and in what he chose not to say.[1]

One of the functions of the office of law adviser, to which he was appointed in 1868, was to assist in the drafting of legislation, and he was heavily involved in the preparation of the disestablishment statute, the Irish Church Act 1869. This was Gladstone's first great Irish policy measure, and a major controversy in its day, and (whatever views were held on the merits of the scheme) it was accepted that great skill had been shown in the manner by which the Act effected it. Porter MR observed in 1901 that 'there is no statute better drawn than the Church Act. I think

1 W.E. Vaughan, *Murder trials in Ireland, 1836–1914* (Dublin, 2009), pp 170–4.

hardly any so well drawn'.[2] A church journal had said on Law's death that 'he will be remembered chiefly for the consummate manner in which he drafted the Act which pulled down an ancient institution',[3] and it was later said that that Act was 'a masterly exercise in the constitutional dismantling of a great and complicated vested interest'.[4]

He became solicitor general in November 1872, succeeding Christopher Palles. In early 1873 it was reported, 'beyond doubt',[5] that he would be appointed to fill a vacancy in the Landed Estates Court ('LEC'). However the remaining judge, Woulfe Flanagan, maintained that no replacement was needed for his recently deceased colleague, David Lynch, and his view was accepted at the time, not without controversy.

In the 1874 general election Law was elected to represent the constituency of Co. Londonderry, one of a number of Liberal party successes in the north of Ireland which allowed Spencer, the retiring lord lieutenant, to write that 'we have broken into the Orange influences of the North. Derry County, Down County, Dungannon and Coleraine are remarkable places for Liberals to have won. I was at first anxious about the tenant right cry in the North, but Law, who got in, assures me that there is no need of alarm. He and Smyth [the other Liberal candidate in Londonderry] were returned out of gratitude for the Land Act'.[6] The Landlord and Tenant (Ireland) Act 1870[7] had given statutory recognition to the Ulster tenant-right custom, but had 'one fundamental weakness; it did not give Irish tenants the basic security of tenure they sought. They did not want compensation after eviction; they wanted protection from eviction itself'.[8] Tenant right and Home Rule campaigns would soon sweep away much of the Liberal party in Ireland, although Law comfortably retained his seat in the 1880 general election. In Parliament he supported an ambitious and, as it transpired, fruitless, proposal for the codification of the criminal law (indictable offences) for the United Kingdom as a whole.[9]

In 1874 talk of making an appointment to the LEC had been revived, and Cairns, by then lord chancellor of Great Britain in the new Conservative government, told the prime minister that 'the only thing that could justify appointing a second [LEC] judge would be if it were given to Law (undoubtedly the fittest man for it in Ireland) and the seat for Londonderry regained, but I doubt if this latter result could be arrived at'.[10] Cairns returned to this theme the

2 *Bernard v Hungerford*, [1902] 1 IR 89, at 93.
3 *Irish Ecclesiastical Gazette*, vol. 25, p. 750 (15 September 1883).
4 W.E. Vaughan, 'Ireland *c.*1870' in W.E. Vaughan (ed.), '*A new history of Ireland: V. Ireland under the Union; 1, 1801–70* (Oxford, 1989), p. 728.
5 *Irish Times*, 3 and 10 February 1873.
6 Spencer to Dufferin & Ava, 19 March 1874 (Dufferin and Ava Papers (PRONI), D1071/H/B/S/476/33).
7 33&34 Vict., c.46.
8 J.C.W. Wylie, *Irish land law* (4th ed., Dublin, 2010), para. [1.46], p. 34.
9 HC Deb, 3rd series, vol. 245, cols. 324–5 (3 April 1879).
10 Cairns to Disraeli, 13 August 1874 (Disraeli Papers, B/XX/Ca/122).

following year, when a second judge (Henry Ormsby) was appointed, again referring to Law as 'incomparably the fittest man'.[11] In 1876 Law publicly objected to a reference that Disraeli had made to him having supported the appointment of a second judge.[12] One last initiative by Cairns to put him forward for a judicial position was made in October 1878, when a successor to William Keogh was to be appointed. He told Disraeli that lord chancellor Ball and himself thought that the place should be offered to Law,[13] although the lord lieutenant, the duke of Marlborough, counselled against this,[14] and in the event it was given to Harrison, a bankruptcy judge.

Law was appointed attorney general in the government Gladstone formed in May 1880. Much of his work in that office was concerned with addressing a new militancy in campaigns for tenant rights and Home Rule. In January 1881 he led the prosecution in the trial of Parnell and others for conspiracy to induce tenants to withhold their rent, at the end of which the jury were unable to agree on a verdict and were discharged. For a number of months Law was then fully engaged with Gladstone in the House of Commons in advocating and defending the next initiative to address tenant rights, the bill that was enacted as the Land Law (Ireland) Act 1881.[15] This established the Land Commission, and adopted 'the Three Fs', of fair rent, fixity of tenure and free sale of a tenancy. Law had earlier remarked in Parliament, when in opposition, that 'it was difficult to get English members to understand the relations of landlord and tenant in Ireland. They seemed, in fact, to require fresh explanation every year'.[16]

He had been attorney general for some 18 months when Lord O'Hagan stepped down as lord chancellor in November 1881. Law's current service as attorney general favoured his nomination to succeed O'Hagan, and weighed more heavily in the scales than the significant contribution that Edward Sullivan, now the master of the rolls, had made a decade before in the same position in Gladstone's first government. As it transpired, Sullivan did become lord chancellor, after Law's death. In May 1882 Law had cited medical grounds when declining an offer that he would be appointed as a Law Lord (see p. 445). He told Lord Spencer, once again lord lieutenant, that 'he felt he could not possibly undertake the new duty. He says that his health is much impaired, that he can do work such as he has with which he is familiar, but could not bear new work. He spoke as though he could only work for 2 years more and that his doctors order him to take great care of himself'.[17] He died in September 1883 at his country home at Rathmullan, Co. Donegal. His health had been delicate for some time,[18]

11 Cairns to Disraeli, 14 September 1875 (Disraeli Papers, B/XX/Ca/158).
12 HC Deb, 3rd series, vol. 227, col. 2015 (14 March 1876).
13 Cairns to Beaconsfield, 27 October 1878 (Disraeli Papers, B/XX/Ca/238).
14 Marlborough to Beaconsfield, 4 November 1878 (Disraeli Papers, C/V/20c).
15 44&45 Vict., c.49.
16 HC Deb, 3rd series, vol. 247, col. 1235 (2 July 1879).
17 Spencer to Gladstone, 17 May 1882 (Althorp Papers, Add. MS 76854.15).
18 *Irish Times*, 11 September 1883.

but his death was regarded as both very sudden and very sad.[19] His tenure of office as lord chancellor was thus brief. His knowledge of the new law of landlord and tenant was noted in an obituary,[20] which cited his judgments in *Adams v Dunseath*[21] (although Law dissented from material aspects of the majority judgment of the Court of Appeal), *Chaine v Nelson*[22] and *Killeen v Lambert*.[23]

Law lived at 9 Fitzwilliam Square, and was a wealthy man, leaving an estate of just over £70,000. Hugh Law BL (1872–1943), one of his sons, was the Irish Parliamentary Party MP for West Donegal between 1902 and 1918, being elected unopposed each time, and was subsequently a member of the Dáil as a Cumann na nGaedheal TD for Donegal between 1927 and 1932.

John O'Hagan

Judicial Commissioner of the [Irish] Land Commission 1881–9

John O'Hagan (1822–90) was the first Judicial Commissioner of the Land Commission (initially, and formally, the Irish Land Commission), created and established by the Land Law (Ireland) Act 1881.[24] His family were from Newry, and he was educated at Trinity College. He was called to the Bar in 1845, and joined the Munster circuit. At this time he was associated with the Young Ireland movement, contributing to its journal, the *Nation*, and had some contemporary reputation as a poet and translator. Sir Charles Gavan Duffy, who referred to O'Hagan as 'one of the most upright and gifted of Irishmen',[25] was represented by him in a complicated series of trials for sedition and treason-felony in 1848 and 1849: 'my counsel throughout the long contest were Mr Butt [Isaac Butt QC], Sir Colman O'Loghlen and Mr John O'Hagan … Mr Butt had the conduct of the case, and O'Loghlen and O'Hagan anticipated the questions of law that would arise and prepared the line of defence and attack'.[26]

He had a quiet manner, being known more for legal learning than for advocacy, and was called to the Inner Bar in 1865, in which year he married Frances, daughter of Thomas [later Lord] O'Hagan. He was appointed chairman of quarter sessions, in effect a part-time county court judge, successively in Cos. Leitrim, Westmeath and Clare, from which he resigned in 1878.[27] He was elected a bencher of King's Inns later that year,[28] and was appointed third serjeant in May 1881.[29]

19 Palles to Spencer, 'Saturday' [15] September 1883 (Althorp Papers, Add. MS 76982).
20 *ILT&SJ*, vol. 17, p. 490 (15 September 1883).
21 16 ILTR 59 (1882); see Daire Hogan and Patrick Maume (eds), *The reminiscences of Ignatius O'Brien, lord chancellor of Ireland, 1913–18* (Dublin, 2021), p. 159.
22 17 ILTR 49 (1883).
23 17 ILTR 1 (1883).
24 44&45 Vict., c.49.
25 Sir Charles Gavan Duffy, *The revival of Irish literature* (London, 1894), p. 17.
26 Sir Charles Gavan Duffy, *Four years of Irish history, 1845–1849* (London?, 1883), p. 739.
27 *ILT&SJ*, vol. 5, p. 2 (7 January 1871), and vol. 12, p. 33 (19 January 1878).
28 *ILT&SJ*, vol. 12, p. 298 (8 June 1878).
29 *ILT&SJ*, vol. 15, p. 247 (7 May 1881).

After the medieval chalice now known as the Ardagh Chalice was found in Co. Limerick in 1868 a question arose as to whether or not it came within the concept or framework of treasure trove (which was apparently de facto exercised at the time by the Royal Irish Academy on behalf of the State).[30] The law officers said that it did, which was contested by the bishop of Limerick, advised by O'Hagan.[31] Litigation was averted, the chalice was acquired by the Academy and it is now in the National Museum.

He was a Catholic, and in 1879 Lord Cairns, lord chancellor of Great Britain, referred to him as 'an ultramontane of the ultramontanes' when opposing his appointment to the senate of the new Royal University of Ireland, telling Beaconsfield [Disraeli], the prime minister, that this would cause 'alarm and even disgust among Protestants and moderate Roman Catholics'.[32]

The 1881 Act, enacted after marathon debates in Parliament in the summer of 1881, provided for the Land Commission to be a body corporate consisting of three members. These were a judicial commissioner, who would have the standing and tenure and salary of a judge of the High Court, and two others, whose period of office (renewable) would be seven years. Section 41 of the Act specified that the first commissioners would be O'Hagan, Edward Falconer Litton and Mr John E. Vernon, who was the managing agent for, among other estates, the extensive urban land interests of the earl of Pembroke. Consideration was given to appointing an existing judge as the judicial commissioner, and Michael Morris, chief justice of the common pleas division of the High Court, had earlier made an assumption that this would happen.[33]

Gladstone however explained in Parliament that

> it was thought wiser to appoint a gentleman thoroughly qualified to go into the High Court rather than a member of it. The office of a judge is one of great dignity and responsibility, but not on the whole of excessive labour. The work to be performed under the bill will be rather of a novel kind, and it was felt that it would hardly be fair to ask a judge to change his habits and address himself to this novel and constructive work. It was believed that a man having the highest qualifications for being a judge, and at the same time not so far advanced in life as the judges are, would, on the whole, be better able to address himself to this work.

He added that it was important that the members of the Commission 'should be persons entering into the spirit of the bill as between the parties [i.e., as between landlord and tenant]'. He spoke highly of O'Hagan, as did a number of Irish MPs, and his suitability was generally accepted, save for observations from T.M. Healy

30 *Webb v Ireland*, [1988] IR 353, at 382 (per Finlay CJ).
31 Spencer to Lord O'Hagan, 5 October 1873 (O'Hagan Papers, D2777/8/228).
32 Cairns to Beaconsfield, 11 December 1879 (Disraeli Papers, B/XX/Ca/256).
33 Morris to Gibson, 8 May 1881 (Ashbourne Papers, B.77/1).

and John Redmond. There was a novelty in discussing the fitness of a judicial appointment before rather than after it had been made. Healy made a less than gracious comment, that to say of O'Hagan that he 'had managed to go through life without leaving behind sufficient traces of bitterness as to make his appointment to a judgeship not unwelcome was not saying very much', and Redmond thought that he and Litton, while amiable and well disposed, 'were men of considerable weakness of character'.[34] Gladstone acknowledged that he had hoped that the attorney general, Hugh Law, and William Shaw, MP for Co. Cork and then chairman of the Munster Bank (but later to be bankrupted), would have been members of the Commission, but 'the power of government is limited … to command the services of those who, in the free exercise of their own judgment' prefer other public duties.[35] Law would be appointed lord chancellor before the end of the year.

The Act 'was immensely complex and it was said that only Gladstone and a handful of experts thoroughly understood it. Framed in great haste to pass into law the recommendations of the Bessborough Commission, which had reported as recently as January 1881,[36] it was intended to concede to tenants the "three Fs" – fixity of tenure, free sale of the tenancy and fair rents'.[37] The initial function of the Land Commission related to the fixing of fair rents, and from 1885 onwards it became also the main administrator of the process of tenant purchase of landlords' estates. By 1890 the Commission had a staff of over 70 assistant (or sub) commissioners, from whose rulings there was an appeal to the Judicial and other head commissioners. It had the difficult work of administering 'a novel, complicated and far-reaching code, no exposition of which could well be expected to command the entire approval of opposing parties'.[38] In particular its procedures for determining fair rents were inherently unlikely to be satisfactory for either landlords or tenants. J.G. Swift MacNeill remarked that O'Hagan 'was painfully, even morbidly, sensitive lest his activity in Irish national politics in his younger days should militate against his securing the confidence of the public as an upright, impartial judge'.[39] The Commission came over time to be accepted as a part of the legal landscape, as 'landlords and tenants learned (though reluctantly) that courts of justice are competent to *do* justice when authorised by an Act of Parliament to come in and break their mutual private contracts for the public good'.[40]

34 HC Deb, 3rd series, vol. 263, cols. 1392, 1393 and 1391 [Gladstone], 1397 [Healy] and 1416 [Redmond] (20 July 1881).

35 Ibid., col. 1419.

36 Report of the Commission of Inquiry into the working of the Landlord and Tenant (Ireland) Act 1870 and the acts amending the same and whether any and what further amendments of the law are necessary or expedient with a view (firstly) to improve the relation of landlord and tenant in that part of the United Kingdom called Ireland and (secondly) to facilitate the purchase by tenants of their holdings. (P.P. 1881 [c.2779], xviii.1).

37 F.S.L. Lyons, *Charles Stewart Parnell* (London, 1977), p. 157.

38 *ILT&SJ*, vol. 24, p. 578 (15 November 1890).

39 J.G. Swift MacNeill, *What I have seen and heard* (London, 1925), p. 166.

40 Rhadamanthus, *Our judges* (Dublin, 1890), p. 121.

Arthur Balfour, the chief secretary for Ireland, expressed a jaundiced view of O'Hagan in 1887 when writing to the prime minister, Lord Salisbury, after a meeting with the members of the Land Commission: 'they have been working out Tables of Rent Reduction… . it turns out that the reduction in rents will be much less than any of us anticipated… . O'Hagan is so much distressed at this that I believe he has thrown out hints of resigning. He is so incompetent that I should not deeply regret it'.[41]

O'Hagan did resign at the end of 1889, stating that 'my doctors impressed upon me that I ought not and could not with safety continue the course of life which my judicial duties imposed upon me'.[42] He died in November 1890. He had lived in Upper Fitzwilliam Street, before moving to a handsome villa, Glenaveena, on Carrickbrack Road in Howth, overlooking Dublin Bay. A couple of years after his death it was sold to the Sisters of Charity,[43] and became a convent, known as Stella Maris, with generous support from his family.

William O'Brien

Justice of the High Court 1882–99

William O'Brien (1827/8–1899) was born in Midleton, Co. Cork. His birth was noted in obituaries as having taken place in 1832,[44] although the admission records of the King's Inns state his age as 27 on 14 April 1855,[45] which would indicate a birth date some time in 1827 or 1828. He was one of the very few judges not to have attended university, although he came to have a high reputation for scholarship and an interest in books, art and antiques. Nor did he have the common pre-judicial experience of serving as solicitor general or attorney general. He spent some time as a teacher and a journalist with the *Cork Examiner* before taking to the law. After his call to the Bar in 1855 he became a pupil of Edward Sullivan, who had been born in Mallow and had earlier attended the same school in Midleton. Sullivan had become attorney general in 1868, and in 1869, after O'Brien had had 'fourteen years of somewhat thankless obscurity', he was appointed by Sullivan to be junior Crown prosecutor at Green Street, the regular income from which 'liberated [him] from all the anxieties incidental to the changes and chance of a competitive profession'.[46] He was subsequently appointed to be the senior Crown prosecutor in Dublin, and in 1872 became a QC.

An interest in politics led to him being secretary of the Dublin Liberal Association for a time in the 1870s, and he twice stood for election in the constituency of Ennis, losing each time to a Home Rule candidate, by 83 votes to 77 in a bye-election in July 1879 and by 124 votes to 95 in the general election in

41 Balfour to Salisbury, 21 September 1887 (*Salisbury–Balfour correspondence*, p. 209), HH4/50.
42 *ILT&SJ*, vol. 24, p. 36 (18 January 1890).
43 Conveyance dated 27 December 1892 (Registry of Deeds, 1893002243).
44 *Irish Times*, 6 December 1899; *ILT&SJ*, vol. 33, p. 518 (9 December 1899).
45 King's Inns Admission Papers, p. 371.
46 *Law Times*, vol. 108, p. 138 (9 December 1899).

April 1880. In 1879 he had clerical support, and his opponent, who was supported by Parnell, secured the removal from a polling station of a priest who was acting as a personating agent for him, objecting to his presence as potentially improperly exercising a spiritual influence over electors.[47] His support for Home Rule was seen as lightly worn, and he refused calls to demonstrate his commitment by resigning his position as a prosecutor and pledging not to seek or accept any government office until Home Rule had been achieved.[48] An obituary remarked that most likely he would not in any event have enjoyed much success in the political or Parliamentary arena, as 'his speaking style – grandiloquent, somewhat awkward, utterly unconversational – had not the element of freedom and ease and at the same time deference to his audience' that would have been required.[49] It was also said that his command of language compensated for his jerky and spasmodic manner of speech.[50]

In June 1882 when he was appointed a High Court judge the fact that he was a Catholic was a consideration in his nomination. The lord lieutenant, Spencer, remarked to Gladstone that 'I always dislike introducing religion into questions of qualification for offices of importance' before going on to advise that an imbalance between the numbers of Protestant and Catholic judges needed to be addressed. He went on to describe O'Brien as an able man, well fitted, he understood, for the Bench by his ability and courage, although 'rather rough in his manner'. Spencer thought that his election address in 1879 had been foolish and insincere: 'I should not object to him on account of his Home Rule views, did he honestly believe in them, but he is said to have denounced them up to nearly the time of giving his address, and I confess that I think that a man wants strength of character if he adopts a cry which he disbelieves merely to get into Parliament, and these qualities are important for a judge'. Spencer added that two judges he had consulted, Law (the lord chancellor) and Fitzgerald (the new Law Lord), both thought the Ennis episode unfortunate, but did not withhold approval on that account, nor did Sullivan (the master of the rolls).[51]

The judicial robes in which he appeared as a new judge seemed old and well worn, and it transpired that he had purchased them from Fitzgerald, a judge since 1860, whose appointment as a Law Lord in May 1882 had given rise to one of the vacancies which were to be filled at that time.[52] Some of the earliest trials over which he presided were the most controversial of his career. These were the jury trials in the spring of 1883 of the men charged with the Phoenix Park murders of May 1882. In a series of trials over 28 days he pronounced the mandatory sentence of death on six members of the Irish National Invincibles found guilty of involvement in the crime, five of whom were subsequently executed. In the later

47 *Irish Times*, 28 July 1879.
48 *Irish Times*, 24 July 1879.
49 *Law Times*, vol. 108, p. 138 (9 December 1899).
50 *Irish Times*, 6 December 1899.
51 Spencer to Gladstone, 7 June 1882 (Althorp Papers, Add. MS 76854.50–62).
52 Swift MacNeill, op. cit., p. 183.

part of the nineteenth century he was the judge who passed the greatest number (19) of sentences of death.[53] He had a police guard in 1883 and for a number of years thereafter.

He was among the most vocal of the judges who expressed dismay and frustration at the reluctance of juries to find prisoners guilty in what, to the judicial eye at any rate, were clear cases where no reasonable doubt of guilt existed. In 1887, a year in which the subject was particularly controversial, O'Brien addressed the subject at the assizes in both Co. Clare and Co. Kerry. At Ennis he said, following an acquittal, that nothing but a complete failure of justice would ensue if other criminal cases were then to be heard, and he postponed such cases to the next assizes.[54] In Tralee he spoke of a 'tempest of violence and crime sweeping over a considerable portion of this county', and that a jury 'had not done their duty. They had refused to convict persons charged in the clearest and most certain of cases. In all my experience no such example of unfaithfulness to duty on the part of a jury had occurred, and it is as well that it should be understood that so far as the machinery of justice is concerned for the protection of person and property and life in this county law is at an end'.[55]

He dealt heavily with a recalcitrant juror in 1888, when a jury could not agree on whether a poisoning of horses had been accidental or malicious (in which case the owner would have been entitled to compensation). The foreman said that one juror had determined his mind before hearing any evidence, and that juror said that he was being bullied and intimidated. O'Brien gave a direction to the jury that, as matter of law, the incident had been malicious, 'intimating that if they did not agree he would have them locked up for the night', and shortly afterwards a unanimous verdict was announced.[56]

In 1896 he

> found it necessary to make some very severe observations on the county Limerick jurors at the recent assizes. He would request the Crown solicitor to bring under the notice of Her Majesty's attorney general in Ireland the fact that out of four cases alone to be tried before him there was not one conviction, and the vast machinery of an assize town was put in motion, that all the expense to the State was incurred by witnesses and officers of all kinds, and 130 jurors were summoned at great inconvenience to themselves from various parts of the county without one single result conducive in the least degree to the successful vindication of the law or the protection of the community against outrage to property or person ... For a considerable time past this kind of thing was known to have become an intolerable scandal.[57]

53 W.E. Vaughan, *Murder trials in Ireland, 1836–1914* (Dublin, 2009), p. 258.
54 HL Deb, 3rd series, vol. 311, col. 1248 (4 March 1887).
55 *Irish Times*, 19 March and 18 July 1887.
56 *ILT&SJ*, vol. 22, p. 247 (19 May 1888); *Irish Times*, 8 May 1888.
57 *Irish Times*, 12 March 1896; *ILT&SJ*, vol. 30, p. 136 (28 March 1896).

He said that he found no fault with the jurors of the city of Limerick. Richard Adams, a well-known and humorous county court judge, was reputed to have said to a defendant that 'you have been acquitted by a Limerick jury and you may leave the dock without any other stain on your character'.[58]

The jury system was undoubtedly open to abuse. Judges at times expressed frustration at acquittals by juries in criminal trials, without querying that the process of trial by jury for actions at common law and for criminal cases was a central aspect of the common law tradition. It was an accepted feature of trial by jury that on occasion 'juries reacted against laws or punishment of which they disapproved by failing to convict',[59] a historic pattern evident up to early Victorian times when capital punishment was the penalty for numerous offences. However even when some of the rigours of the criminal code had been relaxed there was frequent criticism of juries, not only in Ireland but also in England, for supposed perjury and cowardice.[60] Sir John Newport, MP for Waterford, told the House of Commons in 1811 that he knew of several cases in which verdicts has been given contrary to evidence for the purpose of avoiding the capital parts of the charges, supporting the prior observation of William Wilberforce MP that if laws were too severe 'the sympathies of the people were driven to the side of the criminal'.[61] The great respect that chief baron Palles had for the common law makes even more remarkable his expression in 1900, in a context that was not stated in the news report, of 'the gravest doubt whether a jury ever understood the charge of a judge in a complicated case. Great confusion at times arose from the multiplicity of questions submitted to a jury. The practice of putting voluminous questions to juries did not exist five and twenty years ago. The judge used simply to tell the jury that if they believed this fact and that fact they should find for the plaintiff, and if otherwise they should find for the defendant'.[62] Controversy continued into the twentieth century. In 1913 Cherry LJ was very critical of Belfast juries, saying that religious prejudice had prevented any convictions being recorded for assaults committed in the course of shipyard disturbances the previous July at which 80 people had received hospital treatment.[63] In 1915 he remarked of an acquittal by a Co. Tyrone jury that it was 'the most remarkable and extraordinary verdict I ever heard … no county jury in the south of Ireland would return such a verdict'.[64]

All such comments are indicative of a judicial disposition to fix responsibility for a jury failing to agree upon a verdict, or for a seemingly perverse verdict of acquittal, on the jury supposedly disregarding its duty to find a true verdict rather

58 Healy, *OldMC*, p. 229.
59 A.H. Manchester, *A modern legal history of England and Wales, 1750–1950* (London, 1980), p. 90.
60 Keith Smith, 'Criminal law' in William Cornish, Stuart Anderson, Raymond Cocks, Michael Lobban, Patrick Polden and Keith Smith (eds), *The Oxford history of the laws of England*, vol. 13, *1820–1914: fields of development* (Oxford, 2010), p. 120.
61 HC Deb, 1st series, vol. 19, col. 743 (8 April 1811).
62 *Law Times*, vol. 108, p. 290 (27 January 1900); *ILT&SJ*, vol. 34, p. 75 (10 February 1900).
63 *Law Times*, vol. 134, p. 550 (5 April 1913).
64 *Law Times*, vol. 138, p. 464 (20 March 1915).

than on any shortcomings that there may have been in the prosecution case, or in the evidence brought forward. A jury may well have thought, irrespective of any general political views that its members may have had, that the prosecution had failed to demonstrate the guilt of the defendants for the specific crimes of which they were accused beyond a reasonable doubt. In 1884 the prosecutions for conspiracy to murder and treason felony of a dozen men who had been arrested in Co. Sligo collapsed when the first member of what was called the 'Tubbercurry conspiracy' to be tried was acquitted. The jury added a rider to their verdict of not guilty that they found 'the corroborative evidence [to be] of a most complicated and doubtful nature, and the evidence of the two principal witnesses [to be] unworthy of credence'.[65] All the prisoners were then set free, with no further trials.

O'Brien had an apocalyptic vision of what might transpire if the government did not provide support to sheriffs executing court orders. Resistance would spread to all orders of courts, and 'with that swiftness of intuition with which the lessons of disorder are wont to be applied in this country, leading from evasion to resistance, from resistance to violence and crime, and ending in a state of open confusion in which all law would be at an end'.[66] His presiding over trials that had a political aspect, and his outspoken comments about juries, led to him being 'subjected to the most bitter and envenomed comment by the Nationalist press',[67] and such hostile commentary was to continue decades after his death. A.M. Sullivan, a member of a family deeply involved in Nationalist politics, journalism and law, and who was called to the Bar in 1892, wrote of him (in 1927) that he was 'a disgrace to the Bench. He was a dishonest partisan who brought the administration of justice into disrepute. He hated the people whose political favours he had unsuccessfully sought, and used his position on the bench to wage war upon those whom he disliked'.[68] The first chapter of Maurice Healy's generally genial memoir of the Munster circuit (1939) is largely concerned with a series of unflattering sketches of O'Brien, whose 'attitude to the man in the dock was one of fierce hostility … he regarded the doctrine of fair play for prisoners as mere sentimentality'.[69] That was not the view more generally taken within the profession, and a legal commentator writing in 1890 said that his reputation for being unfair to accused persons was not well founded, and commended him as a courteous, even-tempered, fair-minded and highly intelligent judge, and as a 'broad-minded genial man of the world'.[70]

His judicial career was not confined to criminal trials, and as a judge of the Queen's Bench division, and on assize, he heard cases of a wide variety of subjects, including personal injuries, defamation, breach of contract, and petitions for divorce. When a jury had given a verdict for a husband seeking a divorce O'Brien

65 *Irish Times*, 15 November 1884.
66 *Attorney general v Kissane*, 32 LR Ir (1893) 220, at 244.
67 *Irish Times*, 6 December 1899.
68 A.M. Sullivan, *Old Ireland; reminiscences of an Irish KC* (London, 1927), p. 72.
69 Healy, *OldMC*, p. 16, and more generally pp 12–27.
70 Rhadamanthus, *Our judges* (Dublin, 1890), pp 73–6.

addressed the applicant, saying that his wife appeared to have great affection for him, and was the mother of his children, and that it might conduce to his happiness in the end if he would be willing to be reconciled. The husband's counsel, after a short consultation with his client, indicated that he would be willing to make some reasonable offer to her if she were disposed to start afresh, and the judge wished them well.[71] He heard at the assizes at Armagh the first case in which a claim was made against the Great Northern Railway arising out of a recent major fatal railway accident, and his comments were regarded as helpful in promoting fair and timely settlement of such claims.[72]

He presided over a number of trials for libel or slander, including one in 1884 in which Gustavus Cornwall, secretary to the General Post Office, sued the judge's namesake, William O'Brien MP, editor of *United Ireland*, on foot of sensational allegations of immorality and vice that the journal had made about him. The jury found for the defendant (although the Court of Appeal later ordered a new trial) and Cornwall was arrested.[73] Much of the evidence in the defamation hearing, and in subsequent criminal trials arising out of it, was regarded as unsuitable for publication in daily newspapers. A decade later he was the judge in *Pike v Beamish*, in which a member of the Cork County Club claimed that another member had defamed him by an accusation of cheating at cards in the club. Defences of justification (that what had been said was true) and of privilege (that even if what had been said was untrue the defendant acted under a duty in saying it) were raised. The jury found that the accusation was not true, but that the defendant had not acted with malice.[74]

The last major trial of his career concerned a claim by the Phoenix Brewery company, an amalgamated putative competitor to Guinness in Dublin, against a seller of a business to it for fraudulent misrepresentation of profits. Phoenix claimed that the true value of the business was £100,000, not the £265,000 that it had paid. The case was adjourned while the judge was on assize, and on his return it was announced that the claim had been withdrawn. At a lively annual general meeting of shareholders in the company a few weeks later the chairman said that the judge had encouraged a settlement, and the defendant was elected to the board of directors of the company.[75]

O'Brien was a devout Catholic, attending Mass daily, and was regarded at least by his friends as concealing a kindly, charitable and benevolent disposition behind a stern exterior.[76] He had an ascetic demeanour, and seemed careless, even untidy or shabby, in his dress.[77] He was appointed a member of the board of

71 *Irish Times*, 3 May 1899.
72 *Irish Times*, 22 July 1889.
73 *Irish Times*, 12 and 19 July and 2 August 1884, 16 May 1885.
74 *Irish Times*, 8 May and 28 June 1894; Healy, *OldMC*, pp 25–7.
75 *Phoenix Brewery v Brennan*, *Irish Times*, 30 June, 1 and 22 July and 16 September 1899.
76 J.G. Swift MacNeill, op. cit., p. 182; *ILT&SJ*, vol. 24, p. 518 (9 December 1899).
77 Georgina O'Brien (ed.), *Reminiscences of Lord O'Brien of Kilfenora* (London, 1916), p. 65; J.G. Swift MacNeill, op. cit., p. 182.

Commissioners of Charitable Donations and Bequests in 1884,[78] and subsequently a member of the Educational Endowments Commission, in which capacity he and lord justice FitzGibbon took opposite views on a proposal to restructure the Erasmus Smith Endowment (see p. 278). He assembled a collection of rare books and manuscripts, including some that had been owned by Sullivan and that he purchased on the sale of his late friend's library in 1890. 'O'Brien's library had a similar scope to his friend's, though one suspects that his budget was rather more limited'.[79] (O'Brien left an estate valued at £32,365, that of Sullivan, who died in 1885, was £90,949.) He bequeathed the collection to the Jesuit order.[80] More than a century later, in which period the collection was infrequently made use of by scholars, and in light of concerns about its proper future conservation, the order made a long-term loan of certain items of Irish interest to the National Library of Ireland and put the balance of the collection up for auction, intending to use the proceeds of sale for its charitable purposes.[81] The sale realised an amount of over £2 million.

O'Brien lived at 79 Merrion Square, where he died in December 1899. He did not marry. After his funeral in Westland Row church his remains were interred in its vaults.

William Drennan Andrews

Justice of the High Court 1882–1909

William Drennan Andrews (1832–1924) was a member of a prominent family in Comber, near Newtownards, Co. Down. His maternal grandfather was William Drennan (1754–1820), 'physician, patriot and minor poet',[82] a leading member of the United Irishmen. A family firm in Comber that engaged in linen manufacturing and flour milling gave employment to hundreds of local people.

Andrews was educated at the Royal Belfast Academical Institution, of which Drennan had been one of the founders, and Trinity College. He was called to the Bar in 1855 and to the Inner Bar in 1872. One uncle, Robert Andrews QC, was chairman of quarter sessions in Co. Donegal,[83] and another, John Andrews, was the senior member of the solicitors' profession in Belfast, having worked for over 50 years, on his death in 1875.[84] He was a member of the North East circuit, and a pleasant and helpful colleague at the Bar, with both a good practice in the common law courts and expertise in conveyancing.[85] 'The strain of excessive work and close

78 *ILT&SJ*, vol. 18, p. 128 (8 March 1884).
79 Introduction to catalogue of auction sale of the library of William O'Brien, property of the Milltown Park Charitable Trust, at Sotheby's, London, 7/8 June 2017.
80 *ILT&SJ*, vol. 34, p. 34 (20 January 1900).
81 *Irish Times*, 10 December 2016 and 3 June 2017.
82 Entry on Drennan in the *DIB* (by A.T.Q. Stewart). See J. Larkin (ed.), *The trial of William Drennan* (Blackrock, 1991).
83 *ILT&SJ*, vol. 16, p. 532 (4 November 1882).
84 *ILT&SJ*, vol. 9, p. 600 (11 December 1875).
85 *Irish Times*, 4 December 1924.

application broke down his health and, his eyesight becoming seriously affected about the year 1881, he was obliged temporarily to relinquish his professional efforts'.[86] He was subsequently associated with the Royal Victoria Eye & Ear Hospital in Dublin.[87]

He was an advocate of tenant rights,[88] and stood as a Liberal in a bye-election for the Co. Down constituency in 1878 against the Conservative candidate, Viscount Castlereagh (Charles Stewart Vane-Tempest (1852–1915)), of the great house of Mount Stewart on the Ards peninsula. The father of Andrews 'had been the agent for the Londonderry estate in Co. Down. That his son should oppose Lord Castlereagh, who was the heir to the extensive property, was a proof of honourable independence'.[89] Andrews received 4,701 votes and Castlereagh, whose election expenses, £13,500, were among the highest recorded by any candidate anywhere in Ireland in that era,[90] received 6,076. Castlereagh succeeded his father as marquess of Londonderry in 1884 and was lord lieutenant of Ireland between 1886 and 1889. In 1910, when 'a distinguished gathering of County Down and Belfast gentlemen assembled in the Unitarian Hall, Comber, to entertain Andrews to a banquet upon the occasion of his retirement from the judicial bench',[91] Londonderry, who was then lord lieutenant of county Down, presided and proposed the toast to his erstwhile opponent.

When a number of judicial appointments were being considered in the summer of 1882 G.O. Trevelyan, the chief secretary, was told by an MP that the nomination of Andrews would be very popular with Northern Protestants, and that he had spent a great deal of money for the party on electioneering expenses.[92] A few months later, following baron FitzGerald's resignation, Andrews was appointed a judge of the Exchequer division of the High Court. The division was merged with the Queen's Bench division in 1897, and he became responsible for the probate and matrimonial list of the court.

> Every Friday evening he would cause to be brought home the papers in every motion to be heard on the following Monday. When on the Monday the list was called he would deal out his orders like a pack of cards, except of course in contested cases, which he would hear at length. Under him the business methods of the probate court were the admiration of the Four Courts. I think that he was assisted in these domestic labours. He had as his companion a nephew, not very long called to the Bar when I first appeared in the Library.[93]

86 *Irish Times*, 4 December 1924.
87 *ILT&SJ*, vol. 44, p. 69 (19 March 1910).
88 *ILT&SJ*, vol. 10, p. 11 (1 January 1876).
89 Thomas MacKnight, *Ulster as it is* (London, 1896), vol. 1, p. 347.
90 K. Theodore Hoppen, *Elections, politics and society in Ireland, 1832–1885* (Oxford, 1984), p. 84.
91 *Irish Times*, 31 May 1910.
92 Trevelyan to Spencer, 6 June 1882 (Althorp Papers (BL), Add. MS 76944.43).
93 Healy, *OldMC*, p. 31.

This nephew was James Andrews (1877–1951), who had been called to the Bar in 1900 and later would be appointed successively as a lord justice of appeal (in 1921) and lord chief justice (in 1937) in Northern Ireland. James was one of three nephews of Andrews who achieved distinction, all being sons of his brother Thomas (1843–1916), a prominent Liberal Unionist and local politician. The others were John (J.M., 1871–1956), who was prime minister of Northern Ireland between 1940 and 1943, succeeding Lord Craigavon and being succeeded by Sir Basil Brooke (from 1952, Lord Brookeborough), and Thomas (1873–1912), who was a director of the Harland & Wolff shipbuilding firm and designer of the *Titanic*, and lost his life, with many others, when it sank on its inaugural voyage.[94]

Andrews was 'a gentle and industrious little man ... thin and delicate, with the marks upon his face of study and work and scant repose. His eyes lack the severity that tradition has ascribed to judicial eyes. He is utterly devoid of pompousness ... His voice which is gentle, clear and as a rule unemotional [has] a sharp but inoffensive Northern accent'.[95] That contemporary commentator thought that, if he had faults, it was that the scrupulous care that he exhibited might seem pedantic, and that he was wearisomely slow in taking a note of evidence, unnecessarily prolonging trials.[96] The obituarist in the *Irish Times*, while noting his affable and courteous manner, remarked less positively that Andrews 'did not possess the gift of natural eloquence and he never apparently attempted to acquire it. His delivery was slow and his manner of speech unattractive'.[97]

Andrews married Eliza Galloway in 1857. The couple did not have any children, and she died suddenly in April 1901 when he was away in Belfast at the spring assize.[98] He retired at the end of 1909, aged 77. In 1914 he was one of the three members of the Royal Commission, chaired by Lord Shaw of Dunfermline, which inquired into and reported promptly on the events of Sunday 26 July in which three people were killed when soldiers opened fire on a crowd in the centre of Dublin, at Bachelor's Walk, following the landing of guns at Howth by the Irish Volunteers.[99]

In October 1921 he attended the opening ceremony of the courts of Northern Ireland at the court house on the Crumlin Road, Belfast, and occupied a seat on the bench at the invitation of the lord chief justice and his colleagues (who included his nephew James).[100] Andrews was an elder of the Unitarian (or non-subscribing Presbyterian) church at St Stephen's Green.[101] He lived at 51 Lower

94 Shan F. Bullock, *Thomas Andrews, shipbuilder* (Dublin, Belfast, 1913).

95 Rhadamanthus, *Our judges* (Dublin, 1890), p. 81.

96 Ibid., p. 85.

97 *Irish Times*, 4 December 1924.

98 *Irish Times*, 8 April 1901.

99 Report of the Royal Commission into the circumstances connected with the landing of arms at Howth on 26 July 1914 (P.P. 1914–16 Cd. 7631, xxiv. 805).

100 George Hill Smith, *A sketch of the Supreme Court of Judicature of Northern Ireland* (Belfast, 1926), p. 10.

101 *Irish Times*, 1 April 1910; census return, 1911.

Leeson Street, and in retirement divided his time between Comber and Dublin, where he died in 1924.

William Moore Johnson

Justice of the High Court (Queen's Bench division) 1883–1909

William Moore Johnson (1826[102]–1909) was the son of Revd William Johnson, rector of Knockavilly, Co. Cork, and chancellor of the diocese of Ross and Cloyne. He was educated at Trinity College and called to the Bar in 1853. In 1872 he was called to the Inner Bar, and was subsequently appointed to the office of law adviser at Dublin Castle. He was defeated when he stood as a Liberal in the constituency of Mallow in the general election of 1874, but in 1880, when he benefitted from the absence of a Home Rule candidate, he won a majority of the small electorate (189 votes to 72) and became the town's MP. He was appointed solicitor general in the new government then formed by Gladstone, and was promoted to be attorney general in November 1881.

In the period of just over a year for which he held this office he was very heavily engaged in debate in the House of Commons, defending government proposals (such as the criminal law changes introduced after the Phoenix Park murders in May 1882) and answering questions. He spoke of the difficulty caused by juries defaulting in their duty 'not from any misapprehension, not from any mistake, and not from any inability to weigh the evidence properly, but from a determination not to convict'.[103] When the government was considering filling judicial vacancies at that time Spencer, the lord lieutenant, noted that 'I presume that Mr Johnson, the present attorney general, should be considered as the proper man to fill one of the vacancies after the [Parliamentary] session, and as soon as he can be spared from Parliament. He being a Protestant, the immediate vacancy should be filled by a Roman Catholic'.[104] In the autumn he opened the trial of those charged with the Maamtrasna murders, although other counsel then conducted the prosecution. A comment in an obituary that he had led the prosecution of those charged with the Phoenix Park murders[105] overstated his role, since although much work would have been done in the course of 1882 he had ceased to be attorney general before these trials actually took place, in the spring of 1883.

On 1 December 1882 he was asked in the House of Commons whether he could say when a vacancy in the High Court would be filled, a pointed question in light of him being, as attorney general, the presumptive appointee. He replied that all such appointments were a matter for the government, not for him.[106] Some prosecutions that he then initiated, including one of T.M. Healy MP and Michael

102 That is the year of his birth stated by him to the King's Inns at the time of his admission. It has been variously stated otherwise to be 1825 or 1828.

103 HC Deb, 3rd series, vol. 270, col. 2013 (2 June 1882).

104 Spencer to Gladstone, 7 June 1882 (Althorp Papers, Add. MS 76854.50–62).

105 *ILT&SJ*, vol. 52, p. 305 (14 December 1918).

106 HC Deb, 3rd series, vol. 275, col. 497 (1 December 1882).

Davitt for allegedly seditious speeches, proved to be both controversial and unsuccessful. He sought to have the two men provide sureties (or, as commonly described, to be 'bound over') for future good behaviour. This process was said by him to be part of the inherent and ordinary jurisdiction of a court, but transpired to have its root in a statute enacted in the reign of Edward III (1327–77), as re-enacted in the reign of Charles I (1625–49). Criticism of this invocation of an archaic or 'musty'[107] statute was increased by his action – as he saw it, a simple courtesy to a fellow MP – in greeting Healy in a friendly fashion in court, shaking his hand and conversing with him.[108] Such events led the *Irish Times* to say that the impending resignation of the attorney general, 'the friend of Mr Healy', would be no loss to the government.[109] Johnson's appointment to the vacancy in the High Court was announced on 30 December 1882, and he took his seat on the bench at the start of the new law term in January. He subsequently presented a drinking fountain to Mallow.[110]

On 23 December Johnson had initiated a further prosecution, this time of William O'Brien, editor of *United Ireland*, for seditious libel on foot of an article published that day critical of the administration of justice in recent murder cases. The prosecuting counsel were James Murphy and Peter O'Brien.[111] William O'Brien, who was a native of Mallow, stood in the bye-election resulting from Johnson vacating his seat in Parliament, and easily defeated the government candidate (and new solicitor general), John Naish QC. O'Brien ridiculed Johnson in a speech on the hustings:

> There are two things and only two things in Mr Johnson's political career which will, I believe, result in more benefit to Ireland than to Mr Johnson. One of these is this prosecution, the other is this election, and better than either is the way he has mixed up the two so ingeniously together that he has set you up as a high court of appeal, before whose verdict the verdicts of packed jurors will shrink away like mists before the sun. (Great cheering.)[112]

It was said of Johnson that on the bench he displayed 'a certain mild and polite urbanity of temper, which is suggestive rather of the cleric than of the lawyer', with an appearance that was 'essentially ecclesiastical', that 'of all the Irish judges only he and Warren could, for five minutes, sit and speak in an English court and escape the detection of their nationality', and that he was fair-minded, if long-winded, and 'not a giant among lawyers'.[113] He was the subject of a rebuke in open court

107 *Irish Times*, 27 December 1882.
108 *Irish Times*, 6 December 1882; J.G. Swift MacNeill, *What I have seen and heard* (London, 1925), p. 198.
109 *Irish Times*, 28 December 1882.
110 *ILT&SJ*, vol. 18, p. 283 (31 May 1884).
111 *Irish Times*, 2 January 1883.
112 *Irish Times*, 1 January 1883.
113 Rhadamanthus, *Our judges*, pp 87, 89, 91.

from lord justice Barry in 1892 on foot of a disparaging comment that he was reported to have made a few days previously. A complicated case, *Fulham v Garry*, had been shuttling between the High Court and the Court of Appeal, and on the hearing of a motion for a new trial Johnson was reported to have said that having read the judgment of Barry LJ he was bound to say that either the learned judge had not read the judgment in the High Court or he did not appear to have comprehended it. Barry in due course said that no report of the judgment of Johnson or of his colleagues had been produced to the court. When the case came before them in the Court of Appeal they asked, as always, if there was any report of the judgment in the court below and they were told there was none. The fact that the Court of Appeal had not had sight of the judgment in the High Court was seemingly acknowledged to that court by counsel, but notwithstanding that acknowledgment Johnson did not make any further inquiry or withdraw or qualify language which he had used against a brother judge. Barry concluded by saying that if Johnson would secure that his judgments would on appeal be furnished to the court then he would not only read them but endeavour to do that which Mr Justice Johnson had suggested he was unable to do, namely to 'appear to comprehend them'.[114]

In 1893 the separate court of Admiralty was abolished on the death of judge Townsend,[115] and Johnson (who kept a yacht and had a practical knowledge of seamanship) was assigned the admiralty jurisdiction, when this was transferred to the Queen's Bench division. What was initially a provisional arrangement pending the setting up of a Probate, Matrimonial and Admiralty division of the High Court[116] became permanent when the plan for the establishment of such a division was abandoned in 1897, and he was then confirmed in his position.[117]

In the autumn of 1906, when Porter had indicated his intention to retire as master of the rolls, the government endeavoured to secure Johnson's resignation, to facilitate a wider scheme of other intended judicial promotions. He indicated a general preparedness to step down when lord chancellor Walker wrote and spoke to him a number of times.[118] Bryce, the chief secretary, told the prime minister, Campbell-Bannerman, that it would help very much if the government were able to hold out to him the prospect of an honour such as a baronetcy, noting that Johnson was childless and 75 years of age so that this would not result in a permanent increase in the overall number of baronets. The prime minister was agreeable, hoping that he would have no difficulty in getting the King to agree to conferring a baronetcy on 'my old friend "Pineapple" – he is eminently respectable'. If there transpired to be an objection on the grounds of this being an

114 *Irish Times*, 18 February 1892; *ILT&SJ*, vol. 26, pp 111–12 (20 February 1892).
115 Supreme Court of Judicature (Ireland) Act 1877 (40&41 Vict., c.57), s10.
116 *ILT&SJ*, vol. 27, p. 199 (22 April 1893).
117 *ILT&SJ*, vol. 31, p. 523 (6 November 1897).
118 Walker to Bryce, 17 September 1906 and 20 September 1906 (Bryce Papers (NLI), MS 11,014(1)); Walker to Bryce, 15 October 1906 (Bryce Papers, MS 11,014(2)); Walker to Bryce, 27 December 1906 (Bryce Papers, MS 11,014(4)).

undesirable precedent and so forth he would be willing to have it accounted for on the ground of their old friendship.[119] But, as Walker subsequently reported, Johnson's general expression of willingness to contemplate resignation did not result in him actually being prepared to step down at that time, and although no baronetcy then materialised, one was conferred in November 1909 (see p. 126). He resigned the following month, at the end of the Michaelmas law term. He lived in Lower Leeson Street, and died in December 1918.

James Murphy

Justice of the High Court 1883–1901

James Murphy (1826–1901) came from Limerick. He was educated at Trinity College, and had an interest in classical literature.[120] He was called to the Bar in 1849, joining the Munster circuit, and became a QC in 1866. He had a powerful courtroom presence, notwithstanding that he was 'small and unimpressive in stature and appearance'.[121] He became a bencher of King's Inns in 1871. He had a considerable knowledge and experience of criminal law, and for about a decade was the senior Crown prosecutor in Green Street, an office to which he had first received a junior appointment in 1865.[122] He and William O'Brien QC were considered to be a formidable team, and 'the prisoner and the prisoner's friends had a bad time of it in those days'.[123] 'The two prosecutors revelled in ridiculing an alibi. Mr Murphy usually took the witnesses in hand, and Mr O'Brien made the speech to the jury. They became the terror of the Dublin criminal'.[124]

The major trials in which he appeared for the prosecution, generally with the attorney general, included those of Col. Kelly, the Fenian leader (1867), of Robert Kelly for the killing of constable Talbot (1871), of Parnell and others for conspiracy (1881) and the Maamtrasna murders (1882). In the trial at the end of 1882 of the man accused of the attempted murder of justice Lawson outside the Kildare Street Club Murphy's closing speech included 'with that dramatic instinct which distinguished him at the Bar, holding up the revolver to the jury'.[125] A lesser charge of conspiracy was put to the jury, which needed no more than five minutes to reach a verdict of guilt.[126] A few months later, in April and May 1883, Murphy was one of the prosecutors in the trials of men accused of, or of conspiracy in connection with, the Phoenix Park murders. Again, the juries typically took little time in

119 Bryce to Campbell-Bannerman, 5 October 1906 (Campbell-Bannerman Papers (BL), Add. MS 41211.340–3); Campbell-Bannerman to Bryce, 10 October 1906 (Bryce Papers, MS 11,014(2)).
120 *ILT&SJ*, vol. 35, p. 507 (2 November 1901).
121 *Irish Times*, 6 September 1901.
122 *Law Times*, vol. 40, p. 173 (11 February 1865).
123 Rhadamanthus, *Our judges*, p. 77.
124 *Irish Times*, 6 September 1901.
125 Rhadamanthus, op. cit., p. 78.
126 *Irish Times*, 6 January 1883.

reaching their verdicts – fifteen minutes in respect of Timothy Kelly.[127] Their work was aided at times by strong charges from the judge (William O'Brien) that (as in the case of James Fitzharris) 'it was impossible to reconcile these facts [as brought out in evidence] with the prisoner's innocence and [he] told the jury to do their duty'.[128]

A few weeks later Murphy was appointed to a vacancy in the High Court.[129] He agreed with Edward Gibson QC, MP that 'my appointment – as you say – was entirely unconnected with politics',[130] and while he had no involvement with party politics he plainly had had a very high standing with both of the major government parties over a long period. Almost exactly a year earlier Spencer, the lord lieutenant, had commented to Gladstone on his position at the Bar, saying that he had

> done excellent service. He is considered the leader at the Irish bar in criminal cases. As a lawyer I hear that he is not perhaps quite as good as others, but he would make an excellent judge. His appointment would give great offence to the R. Catholics because he married Judge Keogh's daughter. He is supposed to have taken a part in Keogh's famous Galway judgment which gave such offence to the R.C. bishops.[131] The popular party would attack him also on account of him being Crown prosecutor. I should myself put these objections aside altogether if he is fitted for the judicial bench as I believe him to be, by sound judgment coupled with legal attainments, if the proper opportunity for appointing him occurred.[132]

The filling of a vacancy in June 1882 did not present such an opportunity, since it was William O'Brien who had the benefit of Spencer's strong recommendation that a Catholic be appointed.

In Murphy's judicial capacity, as at the Bar, 'he proved himself a terror to the inveterate and hardened criminal',[133] where 'many a prisoner must have winced at the Bar as he passed sentence, for he had the faculty of harrowing one by his pithy description of the enormity of a crime for which he was about to inflict a penalty. His epigrams … were generally hurled at a prisoner before he disappeared for a lengthened term of penal servitude. He was sometimes inclined to be over-severe in his judgments'.[134] In a eulogy the lord chief justice, Lord O'Brien of Kilfenora, said that in Murphy's 18 years on the bench no verdict obtained in his court was

127 *Irish Times*, 12 May 1883.
128 *Irish Times*, 19 May 1883.
129 *Irish Times*, 6 June 1883.
130 Murphy to Gibson, 9 June 1883 (Ashbourne Papers, B.108/2).
131 6 ILTR 109 at 110–12 (1872).
132 Spencer to Gladstone, 7 June 1882 (Althorp Papers, Add. MS 76854.0050–62).
133 *ILT&SJ*, vol. 35, p. 431 (14 September 1901).
134 *Irish Times*, 6 September 1901. See also Rhadamanthus, op. cit., p. 79.

set aside, a statement described by the *Law Times* as quite mistaken: 'Mr Justice Murphy, though upright, fearless and conscientious, possessed only a moderate share of legal knowledge, and his statements of the law and his judgments were not infrequently reversed in the divisional court and the court of appeal'.[135]

A dramatic murder trial over which he presided was that of Dr Cross of Coachford, Co. Cork, at the Cork winter assizes in 1887, at which the accused was found guilty of poisoning his wife. He had certified her death as due to typhoid, but after her body was exhumed traces of arsenic were found. He had re-married within weeks of his bereavement. A motion by defence counsel for the trial to be moved to Dublin, on account of potential local prejudice among the jury panel against him, was refused.[136]

Murphy's wife Mary was, as mentioned, a daughter of William Keogh. Three of their sons were called to the Irish Bar, one of whom achieved distinction in Northern Ireland and another in England, and two of whom married daughters of lord justice Holmes. Edward Sullivan Murphy KC (1880–1945) was educated at Charterhouse school, was called to the Bar in 1903 and to the Inner Bar in 1918. He was Unionist MP for Londonderry City in the parliament of Northern Ireland for ten years from 1929, and was appointed to be attorney general in 1937, and to be a lord justice of appeal in 1939.[137] Harold Lawson Murphy KC (1882–1942) was also educated at Trinity College, where he was auditor of the College Historical Society and lectured in history. He wrote *A history of Trinity College Dublin from its foundation to 1702*, which was published posthumously in 1951.[138] He was called to the Bar in 1906, and then in 1910 to the Bar in England, where he practised, becoming a KC in 1936. He gave to the library of the Inner Temple his father's brief in respect of the Phoenix Park murders. Their elder brother, William Quinlan Murphy BL, gave various legacies in his will to family and friends, and stated that he left nothing to Harold 'as my estate is so small I could only leave him next to nothing and he is already, thanks to his own ability and skill, a rich man'.[139]

Murphy's home was at Glencairn, Sandyford, Co. Dublin. He died in September 1901, having been unwell for some time and unable to sit as an assize judge for either the spring or the summer circuits that year.[140] After his death his home was bought by Richard 'Boss' Croker (1843–1922), an Irishman who had for a time been a leader of the 'Tammany Hall' Democratic party machine in New York. He owned Orby, which in 1907 was the first winner of the Epsom Derby to be trained in Ireland, and established a stud farm at the property. In 1923 the validity of his will was the subject of an unsuccessful challenge by his eldest son in a jury trial which was heard for 12 days in the High Court, sitting in Dublin

135 *Law Times*, vol. 112, p. 6 (2 November 1901).
136 *Irish Times*, 22 November 1887; Michael Sheridan, *Murder at Shandy Hall: the Coachford Poisoning Case* (Dublin, 2010), p. 142.
137 *ILT&SJ*, vol. 79, p. 297 (8 December 1945).
138 *ILT&SJ*, vol. 76, p. 19 (10 January 1942) and pp 42–3 (7 February 1942).
139 *ILT&SJ*, vol. 67, p. 160 (10 June 1933).
140 *ILT&SJ*, vol. 35, p. 71 (9 February 1901) and p. 253 (8 June 1901).

Castle.[141] Later Glencairn became the official residence of the British ambassador to Ireland.

Andrew Marshall Porter

Master of the Rolls 1883–1906

Andrew Marshall Porter (1837–1919) was born in Belfast, the son of the Revd John Scott Porter and Margaret Marshall. His father (1801–80) was a prominent Non-Subscribing Presbyterian minister, biblical scholar and author, theologian and teacher.[142] Porter later referred to himself variously as a Unitarian[143] or as a Non-Subscribing Presbyterian.[144] An uncle, William Porter (1805–80), was called to the Bar in 1831 and left Ireland in 1839 on his appointment as attorney general of the Cape of Good Hope, an office that he held up to 1865, after which he returned to Belfast and lived with his brother.[145]

Porter was educated at Queen's College Belfast, and, having briefly been manager of an insurance agency,[146] he was called to the Bar in 1860. 'His Belfast connection soon brought him a fair practice in commercial cases, making his junior years very prosperous ones',[147] taxing all his energies to accomplish his work.[148] He became a QC in 1872[149] and a bencher of King's Inns in 1878.[150] At the end of 1881 he was appointed solicitor general and was elected, as a Liberal, to the House of Commons at a bye-election in the Co. Londonderry constituency. The election was hotly contested, and while the defeated Conservatives believed that they had grounds for lodging a petition to nullify the result in the event nothing came of that.[151]

In May 1882 he was offered but declined the position of chief secretary for Ireland, on the resignation of W.E. Forster. Gladstone noted this in his diary, 'I regret Porter, but we are all agreed that Freddy Cavendish stood next'.[152] The man then appointed, Lord Frederick Cavendish MP, was murdered by members of the Irish National Invincibles in the Phoenix Park on the afternoon of his arrival in Dublin. Porter was appointed attorney general in January 1883, and led the

141 *Irish Times*, 1 and 16 June 1923.
142 *Memorial addresses and sermons occasioned by the deaths of the Rev John Scott Porter and the Hon William Porter* (Belfast, 1880), pp 6–26. See also entry on Revd Porter in the *DIB* (by Fionnuala Carson Williams).
143 1901 census return.
144 1911 census return.
145 *Memorial addresses and sermons*, p. 45.
146 King's Inns Admission Papers, p. 406.
147 *ILT&SJ*, vol. 28, p. 3 (6 January 1894).
148 *ILT&SJ*, vol. 53, p. 23 (25 January 1919).
149 *ILT&SJ*, vol. 6, p. 377 (13 July 1872).
150 *ILT&SJ*, vol. 12, p. 298 (8 June 1878).
151 Edward Gibson to Lord Randolph Churchill, 6 December 1881 (LRC, MS Add. 9248.62).
152 H.C.G. Mathew (ed.), *The Gladstone diaries, vol. X (1881–83)* (Oxford, 1990), p. 249, entry for 3 May 1882.

prosecution of the members of the murder conspiracy. In December that year he was appointed as master of the rolls, in the Chancery division of the High Court. Although his practice had largely been in common law business he proved to be a respected Chancery judge, with 'a wide and varied knowledge of many affairs outside the region of pure and simple law', even if, 'for an Irish judge, Porter is preternaturally serious … [at times taking] much too serious a view of life'.[153] It was also said of him at the time that 'he is not much given to moralising; this and an almost total lack of humour aid him in getting through more work than most of his predecessors and any living Irish judge'.[154]

His judgments included one upholding the validity of a provision in a codicil to a will that a daughter of the testator would forfeit a legacy if she married a man 'beneath her in social standing'. A brother of the woman issued a summons seeking a declaration of forfeiture by reason of her having married a former servant of the deceased who, at the time of the marriage, was a clerk at 17*s.* 6*d.* a week and who was then earning £10 a week as an accountant. The judge held that the condition in the codicil was not void on the ground of public policy, nor was it illegal, and nor was it void on the ground of uncertainty, and that consequently the defendant had forfeited her legacy.[155] In 1898 he dismissed an action claiming that the Irish Society and other London companies were trustees of the lands granted to them in the seventeenth century in Co. Londonderry for the public and general objects of the Ulster Plantation and that the rents and profits be ordered to be applied towards such objects, holding that the defendants had purchased their lands and that all their obligations had long ago been discharged.[156]

Porter made inquiries with Ashbourne, the lord chancellor, in 1891 about the granting of an honour (see p. 125), and was made a baronet in 1902, the title having a territorial designation of Merrion Square in the city and county of Dublin, where he and his family had lived (at no. 42). He subsequently resided at Donnycarney House, a handsome building on the Malahide Road in Dublin, which in 1921 was acquired by the Clontarf golf club for use as its clubhouse.[157] Porter retired in October 1906, having indicated some concern about his health, and died in 1919. A memorial tablet or relief subsequently erected in the porch of the entrance hall to what is now known as the Lanyon Building of Queen's University Belfast refers to him as 'distinguished alike for integrity of character and for legal attainments, an eminent advocate and judge whose decisions form one of the most valuable contributions of the Irish bench to judicial learning'. His bearded profile on the sculpture confirms a reputed resemblance to Lord Salisbury, who was prime minister for much of the period for which he served as a judge.

153 Rhadamanthus, *Our judges* (Dublin, 1890), pp 29–30.
154 *ILT&SJ*, vol. 28, p. 3 (6 January 1894).
155 *Greene v Kirkwood*, *ILT&SJ*, vol. 28, p. 94 (24 February 1894).
156 *Attorney general (Johnston) v The Irish Society, the City of London, etc*, *ILT&SJ*, vol. 32, p. 504 (12 November 1898) and p. 540 (3 December 1898).
157 Dermot Gilleece and Johnny Joyce, *Clontarf Golf Club, 1912–1987* (Dublin, 1987), pp 63–5.

In 1869 he married Agnes Horsbrugh, of Horsbrugh, Peeblesshire, in the Scottish borders.[158] The family name became Horsbrugh-Porter when his eldest son, John Scott Porter, who was educated at Charterhouse school in England and Brasenose college, Oxford, succeeded to the baronetcy in 1919. Porter's second son, Alexander, married Frances Maude Gibson, a daughter of Lord Ashbourne, in 1894.[159] His third son, Andrew Marshall Porter, who had been called to the Bar in 1898, died in 1900 of wounds received in active service in the Boer War.[160] A stained glass window was commissioned in his memory and placed in the Graduates Memorial Building in Trinity College in 1902.[161]

John Naish

Lord Chancellor of Ireland 1885 and 1886

John Naish (1842[162]–90) was educated at Clongowes school and Trinity College, where he won prizes in mathematics and experimental science. He was called to the Bar in 1865 and joined the Munster circuit (his father was from Co. Limerick). In 1871 he prepared and published, jointly with Edmund Bewley BL, a lengthy annotated edition of the Common Law Procedure Acts 1853, 1856 and 1870. He took silk in 1880. His success at the Bar was achieved despite him being an

> undemonstrative, unobtrusive, nervous lawyer, whose painful embarrassment and absence of self-possession made it appear that he held the simplest brief with fear and trembling. He was not a great advocate. His capacity as a sound, sagacious and erudite lawyer was indubitable, but its public demonstration was certainly never remarkable.[163]

In 1880 he was appointed law adviser in Dublin Castle by the new Liberal party government under Gladstone. At the start of 1883 he was appointed solicitor general, and at the end of the year attorney general, in each case succeeding Andrew Marshall Porter. Simultaneously with the first of those appointments he was nominated as the Liberal candidate for a bye-election in Mallow arising on the appointment of the sitting member (and attorney general) William Moore Johnson to be a judge. This transpired to be an unsuccessful electoral outing, as had been foreseen some six months previously by Lord Spencer, the lord lieutenant, when considering the prospect of Johnson being advanced to the bench and Naish becoming solicitor general. Spencer had a high opinion of Naish as a legal adviser – 'I cannot speak too highly of him' – and thought that although he would

158 *ILT&SJ*, vol. 3, p. 289 (24 April 1869).
159 *ILT&SJ*, vol. 38, p. 218 (9 July 1904).
160 *ILT&SJ*, vol. 34, p. 245 (9 June 1900) and p. 281 (16 June 1900).
161 *ILT&SJ*, vol. 36, p. 212 (7 June 1902).
162 The year of his birth has usually been referred to as 1841, although the *King's Inns admission papers* (p. 360) show his date of birth as 10 July 1842.
163 *ILT&SJ*, vol. 24, pp 446–7 (23 August 1890).

not get into Parliament he would make an admirable solicitor general, and that the government could cope with only one of its law officers being an MP.[164]

Gladstone's office told Spencer that it understood that the constituency of Mallow, if it were to be vacated by Johnson, would be perfectly safe for a candidate who was both a Liberal and a Roman Catholic, and asked whether Naish might not be 'slipped into it'.[165] Spencer responded by confirming his earlier views:

> I feel strongly that Naish would not get in, and his standing and being defeated would be bad for the government. He is damnified in the Irish mind with the arrest of the suspects (Father Sheehy lives not very far from Mallow) and all Castle government during the last two years. The set against him would be so strong that even if all the Tories voted for him he would not succeed.[166]

Spencer's view transpired to be very accurate. Naish had no local connections, and offered himself as a continuity candidate, saying in his electoral address to the voters that he 'entertain[ed] the same opinions upon public matters as those held by nearly all your representatives in the past'.[167] The Conservatives did not put up a candidate, and his opponent was a nationalist journalist, William O'Brien, a native of the town whom the government had charged at the end of December with publishing a seditious libel (see p. 302). He mounted a much more vigorous campaign than Naish, and won the seat easily, receiving 161 votes to Naish's 89.

In April 1885 the lord chancellor, Sir Edward Sullivan, died suddenly. Whoever was appointed to succeed him had the prospect of a very short period of office, as the government was on the cusp of resignation, its disarray and (lack of) internal cohesion being 'something between a farce and a shambles'.[168] Its troubles included the death of General Gordon in a military debacle in Sudan in February, after which the Queen had sent an excited telegram to Gladstone (which became public, not having been coded) saying that 'These news from Khartoum are frightful and to think that all this might have been prevented and many precious lives saved by earlier action is too fearful'.

Spencer once more spoke up for Naish to fill the vacancy, saying that 'he is a first rate lawyer, is broad-minded and has done us here more service than anyone else since we took office in 1880, [and] though young is highly respected'.[169] When Samuel Walker, the solicitor general, was asked for his view by Henry Campbell-Bannerman, the chief secretary,[170] he also preferred Naish, acknowledging that he had common sense and was a good lawyer, although remarking that he did not have

164 Spencer to Gladstone, 7 June 1882 (Althorp Papers (BL), Add. MS 76854.50–62).
165 Hamilton to Courtenay, 8 June 1882 (Althorp Papers (BL), Add. MS 76854.74–5).
166 Spencer to Gladstone, 10 June 1882 (Althorp Papers (BL), Add. MS 76854.82–6).
167 *Irish Times*, 5 January 1883.
168 Roy Jenkins, *Gladstone* (London, 1995), p. 515.
169 Spencer to Campbell-Bannerman, 14 April 1885 (Althorp Papers (BL), Add. MS 76870.155).
170 He was subsequently prime minister, 1905–8.

any practice or position at the Bar.[171] Walker offered a brisk dismissal of other potential nominees, which Campbell-Bannerman passed on to Spencer: James Lawson of the High Court was unpopular and in poor health, lord justice Barry was superficial and weak, chief baron Palles was 'out of the question', and Porter, the master of the rolls, was unduly rigid. The appointment was not made for a month, however, within which the position was offered to and refused by Lord Fitzgerald, who understandably might have been slow to exchange his permanent office as a Law Lord for the chancellorship in such an uncertain political situation.

Naish was appointed chancellor towards the end of May. To have been a law officer was of course to hold an inherently political position, but this promotion, even apart from his comparative youth, was considered surprising. The seemingly unprepossessing demeanour that marked his work in the Four Courts was noted also in political circles. A contemporary view was that he was 'a man of retiring, studious disposition; constitutionally averse to the noise and excitement of a political career, and at least as constitutionally unfit for it. He had no enthusiasm, no passion, no eloquence, and no delusions. He could address a jury only indifferently well; but to address a political meeting he was as incapable as a shy and nervous schoolboy'.[172] A later assessment was that he was an 'over-conscientious, overworked, over-anxious official without political inclinations, who found himself in a home rule government with which he had little sympathy'.[173]

His term of office lasted six weeks (21 May–1 July), as the government's position rapidly became untenable and it resigned after losing a vote in the House of Commons on 9 June. Edward Gibson QC, MP was quickly reported as his likely Conservative successor,[174] although the best part of a fortnight elapsed before he was sworn in and Naish stood down.[175] His career at the Bar was now at an end, at the age of 42, and his short service as lord chancellor had entitled him to a pension of £4,000. He accepted two judicial appointments, which did not carry any further remuneration, one as an additional member of the Court of Appeal,[176] pursuant to s10 of the 1877 Judicature Act. The other was as a judicial commissioner under the Educational Endowments (Ireland) Act 1885.[177] This was enacted on 14 August, and named him and lord justice FitzGibbon as the first two commissioners. Their work consisted of preparing drafts of 'schemes for the future government and management of educational endowments, which schemes may provide for altering the conditions and provisions of such endowments' (s6), and in considering objections and proposed amendments, at public hearings, to such draft schemes. The Act in effect provided a cy pres mechanism for educational trusts and

171 Campbell-Bannerman to Spencer, 15 April 1885 (Althorp Papers (BL), Add. MS 76870.157).
172 Rhadamanthus, *Our judges* (Dublin, 1890), p. 45.
173 A.B. Cooke and John Vincent, *The governing passion: cabinet government and party politics in Britain 1885–86* (Brighton, 1974), p. 155.
174 *Irish Times*, 18 June 1885.
175 *Irish Times*, 2 July 1885.
176 *ILT&SJ*, vol. 19, p. 440 (15 August 1885).
177 48&49 Vict., c.78.

charities, many of which had been set up under the auspices of the Church of Ireland.[178]

On Gladstone's return as prime minister in February 1886, Naish was re-appointed as lord chancellor. He was uneasy and 'sadly disturbed' by the terms of the first Home Rule bill,[179] and after it was rejected by the House of Commons the Conservatives won the resulting general election, so Naish once more went out of office. His second term as chancellor lasted not quite six months (11 February to 5 August, or 175 days). He subsequently resumed his position in the Court of Appeal,[180] and was a well-respected member of the court, although 'there never came before him any cases with which his name will be associated as a specially learned jurist'.[181] The *Irish Law Times* said of him that 'careless of display, he preferred that even the fruits of his own insight and erudition should be placed wholly at the service of his judicial brethren, who have often had occasion, as in the reported case of *Mandeville v Mandeville*,[182] to avow the aid afforded to them by his industry and intellect'.[183] In that case the Court of Appeal directed its registrar to ask the Chancery registrar in London whether an obscure issue of practice in the administration of an estate had been raised in the courts there, and were told that no previous case was known. FitzGibbon LJ noted that 'Lord Justice Naish discovered a case in 4 Vesey[184] 638' relating to the point.

In 1889 Naish became unwell from a condition then known as Bright's disease, more recently described as nephritis. In August 1890 his 'sudden though not altogether unexpected death'[185] took place at Ems, a spa town or health resort in western Germany, and he is buried there. He had lived at 65 Mountjoy Square, had enjoyed walking in the Dublin and Wicklow mountains,[186] and left a comparatively modest estate, of £7,899.

178 For instance, in August 1886 the commissioners considered a scheme for the reorganisation of the Kildare Place Society's schools and the Church of Ireland Training College (*Irish Times*, 19 August 1886).
179 Holmes Memoir, *IHS* vol. 16, no. 63, p. 325.
180 *Irish Times*, 6 August 1887; *ILT&SJ*, vol. 21, p. 450 (13 August 1887).
181 *Irish Times*, 19 August 1890.
182 23 LR(I) (1889–90) 339.
183 *ILT&SJ*, vol. 24, p. 447 (23 August 1890).
184 The Vesey family, father and son, published Chancery law reports in the eighteenth and early nineteenth centuries.
185 *Irish Times*, 19 August 1890.
186 *ILT&SJ*, vol. 19, p. 265 (23 May 1885).

CHAPTER TEN

The years of Unionist monopoly (1), 1885–92

BETWEEN THE SUMMER OF 1885 and December 1905 the Conservatives (or Unionists, as they were increasingly known) held an effective monopoly on judicial appointments in Ireland. The Liberals were in power for some six months in 1886, when after the general election of December 1885 Gladstone adopted Home Rule as party policy, but lost office when the defeat in the House of Commons of the first Home Rule Bill led to another election. They returned to office for three years after winning the general election of 1892, and were back in opposition after the 1895 election. During those periods in office no judicial vacancy arose, and the only appointment which Gladstone could make was to the office of lord chancellor, the holder of which was in effect a member of the government. In 1886 he re-appointed John Naish, who had held office briefly in May and June 1885, and in 1892 the office was given to Samuel Walker, who had been attorney general in 1886.

Edward Gibson QC, MP was appointed lord chancellor in July 1885 and, as Lord Ashbourne, was to hold that position for all the years up to 1905 in which the Unionist party were in office. Uniquely for a lord chancellor of Ireland, and emphasising the governmental nature of the office, he was also a member of the cabinet in those years. Walter Boyd was appointed a bankruptcy judge in 1885, becoming a High Court judge when the bankruptcy jurisdiction was merged into the court in 1897, and John Monroe was appointed later in 1885. Hugh Holmes, who wrote a memoir with interesting reflections on the interplay between law and politics, was appointed to the High Court in 1887 and to the Court of Appeal in 1897. John George Gibson (Ashbourne's younger brother) and Edmund Bewley (his brother-in-law) were appointed to the High Court and to the Land Commission respectively in 1888 and 1890. Peter O'Brien (who was made a baronet and later ennobled as Lord O'Brien of Kilfenora) was appointed lord chief justice in 1889, holding office until 1913. E. Falkiner Litton was briefly in 1890 the judicial commissioner of the Land Commission. Dodgson Hamilton Madden, the attorney general, was appointed to the High Court in the summer of 1892, as the Unionists were going out of office.

Edward Gibson, Lord Ashbourne

Lord Chancellor of Ireland 1885–6, 1886–92, 1895–1905

Edward Gibson (1837–1913) was a son of a solicitor, William Gibson (1808–72), who in the opinion of judge Hargreave was the most able of the solicitors practising in the Encumbered Estates Commission or its successor, the Landed Estates Court.[1] His father also held office as a taxing master in Chancery.[2] It was said in 1886 that Gibson had inherited 'a handsome fortune, which rendered him quite independent of his profession and enabled him to throw himself unreservedly into the congenial area of political combat',[3] and there is some reference below to this family wealth. 'What an awful lot of money I suppose you will have', Gibson's wife wrote to him, 'it really almost frightens me to think of it'.[4]

Gibson was educated at Trinity College, where in 1858 he was elected auditor of the College Historical Society, developing what were subsequently widely acknowledged to be oratorical and parliamentary debating skills of a high order.[5] Later he succeeded Sir Joseph Napier as the president of the society and took a keen interest in its affairs, chairing many of its meetings. He was called to the Bar in 1860, joining the Leinster circuit, and became a QC in 1872. 'He was early regarded as a great prisoner's counsel largely owing to his self-restraint in cross examination and his skill in the presentation of plausible theories to jurors, who were generally in search of a doubt of which they desired the prisoner to have the benefit'.[6]

He was active in Conservative party politics and stood unsuccessfully in the general election of 1874 in the city of Waterford, where he had some family connections. There existed among Conservatives at this time 'a vein of Irish patriotism as rich as anything to be found among the Fenians or the Home Rulers of the 1870s',[7] and Gibson can be seen as exemplifying this. In 1875 he was elected as one of the MPs for Dublin University at a bye-election that followed the appointment of J.T. Ball QC, MP, the attorney general, to be lord chancellor. He defeated the favoured candidate of the Conservative and university establishment, Alexander Miller QC, a graduate of the college who had made his career at the Bar in England. Gibson's supporters maintained that the seat should be held by a man whose life was spent in Ireland, and not be used as a springboard for the judicial bench in England.[8] Upon election he quickly mended fences and was reconciled with his party, and early in 1877 was appointed attorney general in succession to G.A.C. May.

In November 1878 the prime minister offered Gibson a vacancy in the Court of Appeal[9] which at the urgent request of the lord lieutenant, the duke of

1 R. Denny Urlin, *Journal and reminiscences* (Letchworth, 1909), p. 145.
2 'Taxation' has a meaning in litigation of the computation and determination of legal costs and expenses.
3 *ILT&SJ*, vol. 20, p. 481 (9 October 1886), quoting Pump Court.
4 Cited (undated) in Frances Stonor Saunders, *The woman who shot Mussolini* (London, 2010), p. 28 (from private papers of Violet Gibson, then in possession of the 4th Baron Ashbourne).
5 Patrick Geoghegan, *The College Historical Society; oratory and debate, 1770–2020* (Dublin, 2020), p. 122.
6 *Law Times*, vol. 135, p. 129 (31 May 1913).
7 W.E. Vaughan, 'An element of electoral politics intruded into his life' in Yseult Thornley (ed.), *Unquiet spirit: essays in memory of David Thornley* (Dublin, 2008), p. 47.
8 *Law Times*, vol. 135, p. 129 (31 May 1913).
9 Beaconsfield to Gibson, 4 November 1878 (Ashbourne Papers, B.14/1).

Marlborough, he declined. Marlborough acknowledged that he was fully entitled both to receive the offer and to accept it, but 'from the fact that [your] services are still so needful to the government I am induced on this occasion to request you on public grounds to forego the promotion to which you are entitled and to retain your seat in the House [of Commons]. In doing so you will confer an essential obligation on the government'.[10] Gibson when confirming that he would turn down an 'extremely tempting' offer took the opportunity to remark that he would 'trust that whenever I am desirous of judicial promotion the opportunity may (as now) be available'.[11]

He went out of office when the Conservative party lost the general election of 1880, after which for a short while he became a confidant of Lord Beaconsfield [Disraeli], the party leader.[12] Following his death some twelve months later the party became quite fractured, the authority of Sir Stafford Northcote, its nominal leader in the House of Commons, not being accepted by a so-called 'Fourth Party,' of which Lord Randolph Churchill, the second son of Marlborough, was a leading light. Churchill and Gibson had first met in 1874.[13] Gibson led the Conservative opposition to Gladstone's proposals for land law reform and criminal justice measures in Ireland, subjects on which he had unrivalled specialist knowledge, and spoke frequently on these and other wider political issues. 'He was the ablest Irish Conservative MP of his generation. In eloquence and resourcefulness he easily surpassed most of the English Conservative leaders'.[14] He had a distinguished demeanour, his full head of hair having turned white ('an outward and visible sign of matured experience and dearly bought wisdom'[15]) while he was a young man. Gibson was aware that 'I have a rather loud voice',[16] and one commentator remarked that he 'used to address the House of Commons as if he desired to kill two birds with one stone and was anxious that he might be heard by his constituents on the banks of the Liffey'.[17] His voice was also described as 'sonorous'[18] or 'resonant'.[19] Arthur Balfour noted, less positively, that 'I had rather carry on serious business in the middle of a Manchester cotton mill than within reach of that man's voice!'[20]

10 Marlborough to Gibson, 6 November 1878 (Ashbourne Papers, B.102/2; Political Papers of John Winston Spencer Churchill, 7th duke of Marlborough (Cambridge University Library), MS Add. 9271.114).

11 Gibson to Marlborough, 7 November 1878 (Ashbourne Papers, B.102/3; Marlborough Papers, MS Add. 9271.118).

12 Diary or commonplace-book ('Ashbourne memoir') kept by Edward Gibson 1881–1912 (Ashbourne Papers, A.1/1); *The Ashbourne Papers: a calendar of the papers of Edward Gibson, 1st Lord Ashbourne* (*'Ashbourne Calendar'*), compiled by A.B. Cooke and A.P.W. Malcomson (Belfast, 1974), pp 3–9, 29–30.

13 Ashbourne memoir, p. 31.

14 A.B. Cooke, 'Introduction: Lord Ashbourne's political career' in *Ashbourne Calendar*, p. ix.

15 *ILT&SJ*, vol. 11, p. 104 (3 March 1877).

16 Ashbourne memoir, p. 31.

17 *Irish Times*, 23 May 1913.

18 Rhadamanthus, *Our judges* (Dublin, 1890), p. 9.

19 *Law Times*, vol. 135, p. 129 (31 May 1913).

20 Balfour to Salisbury, 9 March 1887 (Salisbury Papers, Hatfield House); L.P. Curtis, Jr, *Coercion and conciliation in Ireland, 1880–1892: a study in conservative unionism* (Princeton, 1963), p. 337.

When Gladstone's government resigned in June 1885 Lord Salisbury as leader of the Conservatives in the House of Lords took office as prime minister, pending a general election which was held in December. Gibson's very high standing then within the party is indicated by the fact that Salisbury – and others, such as Churchill[21] – envisaged that he might be offered the office of home secretary.[22] This was not a position for which an Irish MP would typically have been considered, although a year later, when Salisbury was forming his second government, it was offered to Sir Edward Macnaghten QC, the MP for North Antrim. Macnaghten declined the offer, and a year later was appointed a lord of appeal in ordinary.[23] In Ashbourne's fragmentary memoir he wrote (in 1890) that at the time

> there was a good deal of anxiety as to what I would be or would aspire to. Having regard to my children, I felt I should look for the Irish chancellorship. I thought that I could readily have been a Secretary of State or some other high cabinet office, but I intimated to Lord S. that on the whole I would like the Irish chancellorship. He wrote me a very civil letter saying that he hoped [I] would let him see me.[24] However I thought that family reasons should prevail, but mentioned that I felt it a wrench separating myself from political life, and that I was reluctant to give up the prospects of cabinet, etc. I really don't know at all how the thing developed. I never was told in terms by Lord Salisbury or by anyone else that I should be a peer or in the cabinet.[25]

His children were all relatively young, the eldest being 16 in 1885, and the office of lord chancellor certainly provided financial security. 'It is not particularly surprising that a relatively wealthy man should have allowed financial considerations to weigh so heavily; those in comfortable circumstances rarely feel comfortable enough'.[26]

The chief secretary, Sir William Hart Dyke, was not a member of the cabinet. Gibson attributed his place in it to Lord Carnarvon, the lord lieutenant, who 'was a delicate man and not equal to much travelling or hardship', and consequently content that Gibson would generally represent the Irish administration at its meetings.[27] Carnarvon thought Gibson to be 'very quick and clear',[28] and remarked to him that 'the attendance there [at cabinet meetings] matters one atom in 99 out

21 Lord Randolph Churchill, rough memorandum of possible appointments, May 1885 (Lord Randolph Churchill Papers (Cambridge University Library), MS Add. 9248.600).

22 Andrew Roberts, *Salisbury: Victorian Titan* (London, 1999), ch. 20, p. 322.

23 Entry on Macnaghten in *ODNB*.

24 Salisbury to Gibson, 15 June 1885 (Ashbourne Papers, B.131/14).

25 Ashbourne memoir, pp 24–5.

26 Cooke, op. cit., p. xvii.

27 Ashbourne memoir, pp 25–6.

28 Peter Gordon (ed.), *The political diaries of the fourth earl of Carnarvon, 1857–1890* (Cambridge, 2000), p. 384 (diary, 18 June 1885).

of 100 cases, and it is a long journey to undertake for so little'.[29] Gibson took the title of his peerage from the village or district of Ashbourne, Co. Meath, where he had an estate of 811 acres,[30] and around which his family had extensive land holdings. Salisbury may have thought that, in light of Gibson's continuing interest in political life, his debating skills should not be lost to his party as he left the House of Commons but should be utilised in the House of Lords. Be that as it may, the general view was that when he ceased to be an MP 'the brilliant period of Lord Ashbourne's career closed. He was no longer the dashing debater and popular orator of the eighties'.[31]

Soon after his appointment Ashbourne introduced the Purchase of Land (Ireland) Bill 1885, which was enacted in August,[32] and was to be long described as the Ashbourne Act. This was the first major step towards a framework for land purchase on a comprehensive scale,[33] and the scheme of the Act, of government funding or assistance for the transfer of farm holdings from landlords to tenants, was to be the basis or principle of all subsequent legislation on the subject. The concept of landlords' entitlement to rent being replaced by payments (bonds or cash) from the government, ultimately to be funded by annuities (of lesser amounts than rents) payable by the tenants over an extended period, was not new, and had been the subject of legislative proposals to the same effect in previous years, most recently earlier that year.[34]

In the second half of 1885 Carnarvon engaged – in a covert and deniable fashion – in an exchange of views with Parnell, exploring the prospect of the Conservatives coming to some understanding with him and the nationalist movement. This initiative had little support among Carnarvon's colleagues, and was abandoned after the December election. The party reverted early in 1886, in the excited atmosphere of Gladstone's adoption of Home Rule, to a more traditional approach of support for the landed interest and the Union and opposition to nationalism. Ashbourne's initial association with Carnarvon, and then a rapid abandonment of him when the political wind changed, damaged his standing with his colleagues as an expert guide on Irish affairs. He suddenly ceased to command the deep respect which he had hitherto enjoyed, and never reclaimed the position he had held earlier in the 1880s. Thereafter party strategy towards Ireland was determined without his input being requested or valued.[35]

29 Carnarvon to Ashbourne, 6 November 1885 (Ashbourne Papers, A25/21); *Carnarvon Diaries*, p. 57.

30 Return of owners of land of one acre and upwards in the several counties in Ireland (Local Government Board, 20 April 1876), P.P. 1876 (422) lxxx.61.

31 *Law Times*, vol. 135, p. 130 (31 May 1913).

32 48&49 Vict., c.73.

33 J.C.W. Wylie, *Irish land law* (4th ed., Dublin, 2010), para 1.52 (p. 37); D.A. Haggar, 'The Land Purchase Acts – a short summary for the use of students', *NILQ*, vol. 11, no. 3 (November 1955), 207 at 211.

34 Annual Register 1885, Part I, pp 97, 124–6; Spencer to Gibson, 1 July 1885 (Ashbourne Papers, B.140/5); Carnarvon to Gibson, 8 July 1885 (Ashbourne Papers, B.25/3); HC Deb, 3rd series, vol. 300, cols. 1072–5 (4 August 1885 – remarks of Samuel Walker MP).

35 Cooke, op. cit., pp ix–x.

In the summer of 1886, when the Conservatives returned to office after the defeat of the first Home Rule bill, Ashbourne had to press Salisbury for reappointment to the cabinet, being reported by the new chief secretary, Sir Michael Hicks Beach, as arguing that nobody could join a government outside the cabinet having sat in it six months before without unendurable loss of position.[36] In contrast to Carnarvon, Hicks Beach (and still less his successor, Balfour) did not press Ashbourne to attend cabinet meetings. In that era (and perhaps any other) he was one of a very small number of members of the cabinet who lived in Ireland, in the sense of having their family home, and not simply an official residence, in this country. At times his gout prevented him from travelling to London for meetings,[37] and at other times he was very conscientious in doing so, once sitting in the Court of Appeal on a Wednesday, attending a cabinet meeting on the Thursday and returning from London to sit again in the Court on Friday.[38] He was cheerfully offered his place again in 1895 by Salisbury, after the general election had once more returned the Conservatives to power after three years in opposition – 'You have fought so steadily in our ranks that it never occurred to me that you could be anywhere else. Suddenly, in the midst of a very distracting existence, I remember that I have never asked you whether you will join our cabinet as chancellor for Ireland. I hope that you will forgive me and consent all the same'.[39]

Despite the evaporation of Ashbourne's political influence after 1885 he thus continued to be appointed to hold office in Conservative governments, both as lord chancellor and in the cabinet, and Balfour did not remove him from office upon becoming prime minister in 1902. 'Somehow it was felt that a Conservative cabinet would be incomplete without his familiar presence and agreeable manner which helped to create a pleasant atmosphere in the cabinet room … Time itself added to his stature'.[40] On his death the *Law Times* referred to his 'genial personality and cheery and amiable disposition'.[41] He transpired to be the exact contemporary in office of Lord Halsbury, lord chancellor of Great Britain, in terms of each man holding office throughout the extended periods (over 17 years in total) for which the Conservatives, in conjunction with the Liberal Unionists, held office between 1885 and 1905. The prospect arose a couple of times that he might step aside, although he declined to become a Law Lord in 1889 (see p. 449) and nothing came of a report in 1897 that he might be appointed governor general of Canada,[42] nor of a suggestion made in 1905 that he might retire from office while remaining a member of the cabinet (see pp 453–4). Salisbury and later Balfour may simply have

36 Hicks Beach to Salisbury, 28 July 1886 (Salisbury Papers); L.P. Curtis, Jr., *Coercion and conciliation in Ireland, 1880–1892*, p. 122.
37 *ILT&SJ*, vol. 26, p. 89 (6 February 1892).
38 *ILT&SJ*, vol. 31, p. 39 (16 January 1897); *Law Times*, vol. 106, p. 173 (24 December 1898).
39 Salisbury to Ashbourne, 22 July 1895 (Ashbourne Papers, B.131/27).
40 Cooke, op. cit., p. x.
41 *Law Times*, vol. 135, p. 130 (31 May 1913).
42 *Irish Times*, 29 September 1897.

found it convenient to have an agreeable, senior and loyal supporter in the cabinet room, and Salisbury was generally known for reluctance to change ministers[43] and certainly to dismiss them. Ashbourne was a prominent contributor to debates in the House of Lords for his party. He had time, amidst his official duties, to write a book on William Pitt the younger (prime minister 1783–1801, 1804–6), *Pitt: some chapters of his life and times*, which was published in 1898.

The *Irish Times* in its obituary following Ashbourne's death in 1913 said that he was 'an accomplished though not (unlike his life-long friend lord justice FitzGibbon) a profound lawyer. He had an eminently judicial mind and alertness of intellect and distinctive faculty of grasping the essential points of a case or train of reasoning more than commonly complex in detail'.[44] It was said of him that in the Court of Appeal 'by good common sense, cleverness and general professional knowledge a man can supply the place of profound erudition in the law', and his readiness to 'take a broad view' of any potential legal complexities and nuances and to pass over or dispose of them briskly was shared by Lord Halsbury.[45] (See pp 470–2 for some commentary on Ashbourne's judicial work in the House of Lords.) He had little interest in adopting in Ireland organisational reforms corresponding to those effected in Britain in the 1890s when the Lord Chancellor's Office, with a permanent secretary or head of department, was established.[46] By reason of his position he had the most influential local voice on legal and judicial appointments in Ireland for the best part of 20 years, although decisions were ultimately made by the prime minister of the day. His more direct responsibility for the appointment – and occasionally the removal – of magistrates was a constant source of bother and requests for patronage.

While Ashbourne held office his brother, John George, was appointed successively to be solicitor general, attorney general and a High Court judge between 1885 and 1888, and he was reported as trying to arrange for his elevation to the Court of Appeal in 1905 (see p. 456). Two members of the Bar, Edmund Bewley and John Henry Mayne Moore, who were married to sisters of Lady Ashbourne, Anna and Ethel respectively, were appointed to the judicial bench, Bewley in 1890 and Moore in 1898. Bewley's appointment was as judicial commissioner of the Land Commission, and a knighthood was arranged for him when he retired from office eight years later (see p. 354). Moore (1852–1933) was appointed to be county court judge of Co. Tipperary, a position that he held until 1921.[47] In 1886 Ashbourne's brother in law, John Mayne Colles (1857–1922), was appointed to be registrar in lunacy, an office (which he held until 1921) under the

43 Roberts, op. cit., chapter 44 (p. 769).

44 *Irish Times*, 23 May 1913.

45 Rhadamanthus, *Our judges* (Dublin, 1890), p. 9; entry on Lord Halsbury (by G.R. Rubin) in *ODNB*.

46 Patrick Polden, *Guide to the records of the Lord Chancellor's Department* (London, 1988), pp 13–17; Richard McBride, 'The failure to modernise the office of the Irish Lord Chancellor (1880–1915): a comparison with the developments in Great Britain' (2023, unpublished paper, The European Society for Comparative Legal History, Seventh Biennial Conference, Augsburg).

47 *ILT&SJ*, vol. 32, p. 594 (31 December 1898), and vol. 67, p. 69 (4 March 1933).

direct jurisdiction of the lord chancellor, the holder of which conducted hearings to determine whether a person was of unsound mind.[48] Colles, who wrote a handbook on the law of lunacy, had been called to the Bar in 1880, had joined the Leinster circuit and had been Ashbourne's private secretary as chancellor for a short time. He was initially appointed by Ashbourne to be one of the executors and trustees of his will (made in 1911) but in a subsequent codicil was replaced by the chief registrar in Chancery, Raoul Couturier de Versan. Ashbourne's third son, Edward Mayne Gibson, who was called to the Bar in 1901, received an appointment as legal examiner in the Lunacy Office in 1903.[49]

Ashbourne thus acquired a reputation for favouring his family in advising upon or making appointments, notwithstanding what might have been the objective merits or grounds for any individual nomination, made from a small pool of prospective candidates at the Bar. This was remarked upon by John Atkinson, the attorney general, in relation to Moore's appointment. He told the lord lieutenant, Lord Cadogan, that for Ashbourne to have suggested that a favourable view would be taken at the Bar of Moore's career or level of practice or political services was absurd, and that he as the leader of the Bar for the time being was better placed than the lord chancellor to offer an authoritative view as to the general opinion at the Bar on such matters.[50]

He was well liked by the Bar and was instrumental in arranging for the King's Inns and the four Inns of Court in London to adopt reciprocal rules for admission in order to facilitate barristers in one country to be called to the Bar in the other. The English Inns had declined to make any such special concessional arrangements in 1877, but agreed to a change in 1899, to waive what had been a requirement that the exams required for ordinary students would have to be passed and a full set of dining terms kept. From that time a call could take place in either country on the basis of a certificate from a law officer in the home country that the barrister was a fit and proper person to be called to the Bar in the recipient country, and only three dining terms had to be kept.[51] Ashbourne also 'took a keen interest in seeing that the Irish Bar got their fair share of Indian and colonial appointments',[52] a constant concern of lord chancellors over the decades.[53]

He had a prominent place in social life, both official and private. As chairman of the benchers he presided over elaborate entertainments of distinguished guests at the King's Inns, such as Lord Halsbury in 1897 and Lord Cadogan (whose judgment, capacity, tact and manner he valued)[54] in 1898.[55] For the tercentenary

48 *ILT&SJ*, vol. 20, p. 22 (9 January 1886); *Irish Times*, 18 December 1922.
49 Law Directory, 1904.
50 Atkinson to Cadogan, 29 December 1898 (Cadogan Papers, CAD/1436/1).
51 *ILT&SJ*, vol. 33, p. 32 (21 January 1899) and p. 131 (25 March 1899); Daire Hogan, *The legal profession in Ireland, 1789–1922* (Dublin, 1986), pp 36–7.
52 *Irish Times*, 3 June 1913.
53 See, for instance, O'Hagan to Spencer, 9 March 1869 (O'Hagan Papers, D2777/8/23).
54 Ashbourne Memoir, p. 29.
55 *ILT&SJ*, vol. 31, p. 117 (13 March 1897); *Law Times*, vol. 102, p. 466 (20 March 1897); *ILT&SJ*, vol. 32, p. 47 (22 January 1898).

celebrations in 1891–2 of the founding of Trinity College in 1592 he took the chair at a London dinner of graduates held in the Middle Temple, where he 'cordially encouraged the new idea of founding and erecting' what was initially named the Graduates Tercentenary Memorial Building (erected early in the twentieth century, and now known as the Graduates Memorial Building or GMB) and also later at a large banquet and reception in the King's Inns.[56] He gave receptions and private balls in his home in Merrion Square, attended by Cadogan.[57] He leased Howth Castle for a time in the 1890s,[58] and received there the duke of York (eldest living son of the prince of Wales, who in 1908 succeeded his father as George V) on a visit to Ireland.[59] He took other houses around Dublin for shorter periods in summer and autumn – Killincarrig House in Greystones in 1901 and Rockfort House, Blackrock in 1904.[60] He transferred his house to Sir John Arnott in 1906, and thereafter made his home in London, at Grosvenor Crescent, Belgravia.[61] The family spent holidays at a villa in Boulogne (Chateau de la Cocherie, Mont Lambert),[62] and travelled extensively in Europe, including frequent visits to St Moritz and other parts of Switzerland.[63] Sir Edward Carson made a waspish comment about Ashbourne's social manner: 'Lord Ashbourne is here [in Bad Homburg] and delights everyone with his knowledge of their pedigree and he has assured most people that he knew at least one of their relatives and "he was a most respectable trustworthy man".'[64]

The view that 'Gibson's success alienated most of his Irish associates',[65] and that politics 'seriously impaired' his closest male friendships, with his contemporaries David Plunket and FitzGibbon,[66] may be over-stated. Plunket was one of the MPs for Dublin University, having first been elected in 1870. He stepped down as solicitor general in 1877 to make way for FitzGibbon, not asserting a claim to become attorney general. Although later holding between 1886 and 1892 a high official post in England as first commissioner of works (comparable to the Office of Public Works in Ireland) he was unambitious. Relations between Gibson and FitzGibbon were civil and business-like – as in a dialogue in 1878 over which of them would fill a vacancy in the Court of Appeal

56 *ILT&SJ*, vol. 25, p. 348 (20 June 1891) and vol. 26, p. 372 (16 July 1892).

57 *ILT&SJ*, vol. 32, p. 91 (18 February 1898), vol. 35, p. 175 (20 April 1901) and vol. 36, p. 56 (8 February 1902).

58 *ILT&SJ*, vol. 29, p. 486 (5 October 1895) and vol. 31, p. 386 (21 August 1897).

59 *ILT&SJ*, vol. 31, p. 386 (21 August 1897).

60 *ILT&SJ*, vol. 35, p. 321 (20 July1901); *Irish Times*, 22 July 1904.

61 Assignment, Ashbourne to Arnott, 23 March 1906; will of Ashbourne, 3 November 1911.

62 *ILT&SJ*, vol. 21, p. 482 (9 October 1886).

63 *ILT&SJ*, vol. 26, p. 264 (21 May 1892), vol. 27, p. 2 (7 January 1893), p. 197 (22 April 1893), p. 638 (23 December 1893). See Ciaran O'Neill, *Power and powerlessness in Union Ireland* (Oxford, 2024), pp 174–5, for observations on travels of members of the Irish elite class in Europe.

64 Carson to Lady Londonderry, undated (Londonderry Papers (PRONI), D2846/1/1/158).

65 R.F. Foster, 'Lord Randolph Churchill and the prelude to the Orange card' in F.S.L. Lyons and Richard Hawkins' (eds), *Ireland under the Union: varieties of tension* (Oxford, 1980), p. 243.

66 Cooke, op. cit., p. xviii.

and the prospect (unrealised) of FitzGibbon succeeding Gibson as MP for the university.[67] They were neighbours in Merrion Square (FitzGibbon at no. 10, Gibson at no. 12), and colleagues in the Law Library and more closely still for almost two years in the Law Room in Dublin Castle and subsequently in the Court of Appeal for over 15 years. Gibson was a constant presence at the annual Christmas residential parties at Howth given by FitzGibbon, who offered him 'cordial but respectful felicitations on your happy restoration' to office as lord chancellor in 1886.[68]

FitzGibbon made comments over time to Churchill about Gibson which tended to be amused and sceptical, and certainly with an element of schadenfreude, but were essentially not unfriendly. Churchill had come to have an intense dislike of Gibson (he thought of him as 'an evil counsellor')[69] and FitzGibbon would have known that he would have been receptive to critical observations or gossip. In July 1886 FitzGibbon thought (correctly), a couple of days before the congratulations mentioned just above, that Ashbourne 'would be sore at not being in the cabinet'[70] (although it quickly transpired that he had been invited to rejoin it). A couple of months later he remarked that the chancellor had been slow to accept a proposal for new bankruptcy procedures for defaulting tenants – 'he does not see it yet, chiefly because he did not discover it for himself',[71] and later remarked that 'the noble Ashbourne is I think a bit down of late'.[72] He expressed alarm on hearing that Churchill had shown one of his letters to Balfour, and hoped that in turn Balfour would not have shown it to Ashbourne.[73]

Ashbourne's wife, Frances, was a daughter of Henry Jonathan Cope Colles, who had been called to the Bar in 1832 and practised on the Leinster circuit. Ashbourne and his wife, who died in 1926, had four sons and four daughters. He was a member of the Church of Ireland and she (and two of their daughters, Frances and Constance) were members of the Church of Christ, Scientist. His eldest son, William (1868–1942), the second Lord Ashbourne, 'has not adopted the profession, the religion or the politics of his father'.[74] He was a prominent figure in the Gaelic League and more generally in the Irish cultural revival at the end of the nineteenth century, and donated the Ashbourne Cup for inter-college camogie. On behalf of the Irish Literary Society he arranged for four Irish yew trees, one from each province, to be planted as a mark of respect at the grave at Epsom of Lord Russell of Killowen, an Irishman who was the lord chief justice of England between 1894 and 1900.[75] Violet Gibson (1876–1956) made an attempt to

67 FitzGibbon to Gibson, 17 October 1878 (Ashbourne Papers, B.50/8) and 22 October 1878 (B.50/9).
68 FitzGibbon to Ashbourne, 30 July 1886 (Ashbourne Papers, B.50/2).
69 Churchill to FitzGibbon, 22 August 1887 (LRC Papers, MS Add. 9248.2633).
70 FitzGibbon to Churchill, 27 July 1886 (LRC Papers, MS Add. 9248.1581).
71 FitzGibbon to Churchill, 24 September 1886 (LRC Papers, MS Add. 9248.1837).
72 FitzGibbon to Churchill, 1 February 1887 (LRC Papers, MS Add. 9248.2384).
73 FitzGibbon to Churchill, 23 February 1890 (LRC Papers, MS Add. 9248.3420).
74 *Law Times*, vol. 135, p. 146 (7 June 1913).
75 *Irish Times*, 6 April 1901.

assassinate Mussolini in Rome in 1926[76] and is commemorated as an 'anti-fascist' on a plaque placed on the family home in Merrion Square by Dublin City Council in 2022. Ashbourne's second son, Henry (born in 1870), who had been 'in indifferent health for a considerable time', died in 1905 at Davos, where he had travelled on medical advice.[77] A great-great-grandson, a descendant of his third son, Edward, established a vineyard near the Cape of Good Hope, South Africa, in 1996 and named the property after Ashbourne. His youngest son, Victor (1875–1922), was called to the Bar, and was instrumental in recruiting a contingent of Irish hunting men and other sportsmen to enlist in the Imperial Yeomanry during the Boer War.[78] He was taken into captivity, along with hundreds of other members of that corps, at Lindley the following summer, and subsequently escaped.[79] His first wife died within a few months of their wedding in 1905, and he was made bankrupt in England in 1915.[80]

Ashbourne died suddenly in London in May 1913, after collapsing when walking in Hyde Park. He was a very wealthy man, the gross value of whose personal estate was £92,325. In his will, made on 3 November 1911, he noted that he had 'already given or settled on my wife and children monies or property of large amount', and that he had given and settled a large sum of money in a marriage settlement for his eldest son in 1896. He also stated that on his own marriage settlement in 1868 and by his father's will certain lands had been settled, of which properties in Co. Meath (at Gaulstown, Creemore, Colmolyn, Robertstown and Collierstown) had been sold for an aggregate amount of over £30,000, and which funds, together with other retained lands in Co. Meath, had been the subject of a further family settlement. A full length portrait by Walter Osborne, which was shown at the annual exhibition of the Royal Academy in London in 1899, was bequeathed by Ashbourne to the King's Inns.[81] A portrait by J. Cyrus Johnson painted in 1881 was left to Trinity College on the death of his son Edward in 1928.[82]

Walter Boyd

Judge of the court of Bankruptcy 1885–97, Justice of the High Court 1897–1916

Walter Boyd (1833–1918) was born in Dublin, and after education at Portora School, Enniskillen, and Trinity College Dublin was called to the Bar in 1856. He practised in criminal law, appearing in murder trials both as a defence counsel[83]

76 See Frances Stonor Saunders, *The woman who shot Mussolini* (London, 2010).
77 *ILT&SJ*, vol. 39, p. 430 (16 December 1905).
78 *Irish Times*, 27 December 1899.
79 *Irish Times*, 25 June 1900 and 29 September 1900.
80 *Irish Times*, 2 September 1915.
81 Wanda Ryan-Smolin, *King's Inns portraits* (Dublin, 1992), p. 31.
82 Anne Crookshank and David Webb, *Paintings and sculptures in Trinity College Dublin* (Dublin, 1990), p. 58.
83 W.E. Vaughan, *Murder trials in Ireland, 1836–1914* (Dublin, 2009), p. 239.

and as senior Crown prosecutor for Armagh, an office to which he was appointed in 1878.[84] His cross-examination of a prosecution witness at such a trial in 1876 was noted as particularly effective – 'three questions had turned the witness into a prevaricator from whom the truth had to be dragged'.[85] This familiarity with criminal law belies the affectionate and entertaining portrait drawn by Maurice Healy of Boyd's conduct in a series of assize sittings in 1910 when he supposedly wreaked havoc with the expectations of counsel and clients as to how a trial would be conducted.[86]

Boyd wrote a treatise on 'The law and practice of the High Court of Admiralty of Ireland' which was published in Dublin in 1868 following the enactment of the Admiralty Court (Ireland) Act 1867,[87] and he was awarded the degree of LL.D. by Trinity College. He was appointed the Queen's Advocate to the High Court of Admiralty in 1879.[88] He lived in Howth, and had a great interest in the sea and all nautical matters, being instrumental in the foundation of the Howth Sailing Club in 1895 and president of the Howth branch of the Lifeboat Institution. He was a master mariner and a Dublin Bay pilot.[89] He was for a time the honorary secretary and a vice-president of the Royal Dublin Society, and a member of the council of the Zoological Society.[90] In the short interlude of Conservative government in the second half of 1885 he was appointed to fill a vacancy in the court of Bankruptcy.[91] He committed Fr Keller, the parish priest of Youghal, Co. Cork, to prison in 1887 for declining to answer questions in the bankruptcy hearing of one of his parishioners.[92]

After four years as one of the two bankruptcy judges he expressed dissatisfaction at his status, noting that it was much inferior in both salary and position to that of a judge of the High Court. He told Arthur Balfour, the chief secretary, that when he accepted his present office, 'which I did not seek or desire', he had been led to believe that he would in a very short time be appointed to the High Court, and asked that he be raised to that dignity and position. He noted that certain duties under the Land Acts had been assigned to him,[93] and that he had in effect thus been acting as a High Court judge.[94] Nothing came of that approach at the time, and he remained a bankruptcy judge until becoming a judge of the High Court (Queen's Bench division) in 1897 when the separate bankruptcy court and

84 *ILT&SJ*, vol. 12, p. 227 (4 May 1878).
85 W.E. Vaughan, op. cit., p. 240.
86 Healy, *OldMC*, pp 108–22.
87 30&31 Vict., c.113.
88 *ILT&SJ*, vol. 13, p. 41 (18 January 1879).
89 *ILT&SJ*, vol. 52, p. 158 (29 June 1918).
90 *ILT&SJ*, vol. 31, p. 376 (14 August 1897); *Irish Times*, 4 November 1905, and 5 February 1912.
91 *ILT&SJ*, vol. 19, p. 478 (5 September 1885).
92 Daire Hogan and Patrick Maume (eds), *The reminiscences of Ignatius O'Brien, lord chancellor of Ireland 1913–1918* (Dublin, 2021), pp 27, 167–70.
93 *ILT&SJ*, vol. 19, p. 607 (21 November 1885).
94 Boyd to Balfour, 25 May 1889 (Balfour Papers, Add. MS 49802.98).

jurisdiction was amalgamated with the High Court. He exercised the admiralty jurisdiction of that court between 1910 and 1916.

Matters coming before him in the High Court included defamation, fatal accidents and personal injuries, probate, divorce and crime, and he sat frequently with other judges as a member of a divisional court hearing motions for new trials, etc. He presided over a trial of James Larkin, the trade union leader, in 1910 at which Larkin was convicted of conspiracy to obtain £147 from dock labourers in Cork supposedly for membership of the National Union of Dock Labourers but which he used for purposes of the new Irish Transport & General Workers' Union. The sentencing of Larkin to imprisonment with hard labour for twelve months was thought to be severe, and following a petition for clemency he was released by the lord lieutenant after serving three months.[95]

A curious incident occurred in *Crofts v Beamish*[96] in which Boyd in effect declined to perform the function of a judge. He was a member of a divisional court hearing a will construction summons, and said that 'I am unable to make up my mind' as to the intention of the testator in using the expression 'next eldest brother'. Since the other two members of the court had come to opposing conclusions the result was that the order of the court recorded that 'it was unable to answer question no. 1 in the summons'. On appeal FitzGibbon LJ, having remarked that Boyd 'did not answer the question at all', said that

> we are of opinion that where plain English words are used in a document, which must have had some meaning to the person who used them, where there is no context to affect their meaning, and there is no latent ambiguity, a court of construction cannot decline the jurisdiction to declare the meaning. If this were not so, the submission of every question of construction to a court would be subject to the risk of a denial of justice, in the form of a declaration that the court, not being sure of the writer's meaning, declined to declare the legal meaning.[97]

Boyd's manner was 'genial and hearty'.[98] Healy said of him that he had shrewd common sense and was 'beloved of all, held in esteem by everyone, but not for his judicial qualities … he had no reputation as a lawyer … he was very obstinate, almost to the degree of stupidity', and became increasingly deaf.[99] Another observer, while acknowledging his decency and hard work, had previously noted that he was 'unduly impressed with the importance of a judge's position … for a judge to be *visibly* and unduly and unseasonably so impressed with his own importance is always ludicrous and never awe-inspiring'.[100]

95 *Irish Times*, 3 October 1910.
96 [1905] 2 IR 345.
97 At 362.
98 *ILT&SJ*, vol. 52, p. 169 (13 July 1918).
99 Healy, *OldMC*, pp 31–3.
100 Rhadamanthus, *Our judges* (Dublin, 1890), pp 114–15.

Boyd's retirement in the spring of 1916 formed part of a series of complicated manoeuvres to placate and find a place for James H.M. Campbell QC, MP (see p. 419). Cherry, the lord chief justice, declined a suggestion made in February that he might consider retiring,[101] at which point Asquith, the prime minister, turned to Boyd, whom he had been told was aged and infirm.[102] Boyd was reluctant to retire but was prepared to facilitate his friend Campbell, although it transpired that Campbell envisaged not that he would replace Boyd but that the attorney general, John Gordon, would do so, and that he in turn would replace Gordon. Boyd's resignation was announced after the end of the spring assizes, together with the conferring on him of a baronetcy.[103] Lord Ashbourne had expressed a lack of enthusiasm for a proposal to confer a knighthood on him some 20 years before, and the suggestion was not pursued.[104]

He and his wife Mary had six children. His eldest son, Walter Herbert Boyd, who was called to the Bar in 1891, was appointed chief registrar in bankruptcy in 1912. He was known for the design of the Howth 17 footer, the oldest one-design keelboat racing class in the world. Boyd's third son, Cecil, a medical doctor, who was the third baronet, played rugby for Ireland a few times at the turn of the century and served in the army during the Great War.[105] The contribution of another son, Henry, to the sporting record of the family consisted of winning the Irish amateur open golf championship in 1905,[106] and the close championship on two occasions. A fourth son served in the Indian police. Boyd died in June 1918. He and his wife described themselves in census returns as Protestants of no denomination, and his funeral service at Mount Jerome cemetery was conducted by Sir William Fry DL, JP, a prominent Dublin solicitor.[107]

John Monroe

Justice of the Chancery Division (Land Judge) 1885–96

John Monroe (1839–89) was from Moira, Co. Down. He was a member of the Church of Ireland, although he took pains to point out when standing for election in Co. Monaghan in 1883 that his maternal grandfather was a Presbyterian minister, also then referring to his father as a tenant farmer. He was educated at Queen's College Galway, and was called to the Bar in 1863. 'For a few years he was briefless, and occupied his time chiefly in noting cases for the Law Reports',[108] but he then developed a good practice, primarily in the common law courts, where he

101 R.F.V. Heuston, *Lives of the lord chancellors, 1885–1940* (Oxford, 1964), p. 272.
102 Asquith to Buckmaster, 17 January 1916 (R.F.V. Heuston, op. cit., p. 273).
103 *ILT&SJ*, vol. 50, p. 96 (15 April 1916).
104 Ashbourne to Cadogan, 14 December 1896 (Cadogan Papers, CAD/850).
105 Edmund Van Esbeck, *The story of Irish rugby* (London, 1986), p. 239; *ILT&SJ*, vol. 49, p. 192 (7 August 1915).
106 *Irish Times*, 7 August 1905; *Belfast Newsletter*, 5 November 1943.
107 *Irish Times*, 1 July 1918.
108 Rhadamanthus, *Our judges* (Dublin, 1890), p. 104.

was noted for his 'skill in cross-examining witnesses, his dexterity in dealing with complex facts and his vigorous addresses to the jury'.[109] His brother Samuel was a solicitor. He represented a man accused of murder in a lurid trial at Downpatrick in 1871, and although the trial resulted in a conviction he and other counsel were commended by the judge for defending the prisoner, John Gregory, 'with an ability that I have rarely seen equalled. Every observation on the evidence that I could possibly make has been anticipated'.[110] He took silk in 1877. He was good natured and good tempered.[111]

In December 1878 he was appointed law adviser at Dublin Castle, a first step of political promotion, and held office until the Conservatives lost the general election of April 1880. In 1883 he stood as the Conservative candidate in a bye-election in Co. Monaghan, when a vigorous Home Rule campaign for T.M. Healy (who resigned his seat in Wexford in order to stand) was characterised as an 'invasion' of the north. A sense of Monroe's gift for rhetoric can be seen from speeches that he made in the campaign, some to audiences of supporters, others to disorderly public meetings. Voters, he said, should repudiate those who would 'sever this little island from the great empire on which the sun never set'. Standing by Conservatism and the Constitution would prevent the county being handed over to the Invincibles. The Land League was the recruiting ground for the Inner Circle of assassins.[112] Monroe lost, receiving 2,011 votes to Healy's 2,376. He remained active in politics in the county, speaking in 1884 at a large loyalist demonstration chaired by a leading (and controversial) Orangeman, Lord Rossmore.[113]

When his party returned to office in July 1885 Monroe was appointed solicitor general. A vacancy arose in the bankruptcy court early in August, which Lord Carnarvon, the lord lieutenant, proposed that he would fill but which the attorney general, Hugh Holmes, discouraged him from taking. Monroe and Holmes were married to sisters, and Holmes soon reflected that, although he thought Monroe should set his sights higher than a bankruptcy appointment, his brother in law and his wife 'fancied that I wanted it for someone else [Walter Boyd, who was appointed] and that I had not been as friendly as I might have been'.[114] Soon afterwards Holmes also then had an involvement, with Ashbourne, FitzGibbon and Lord Randolph Churchill, in persuading Monroe not to compete with Col. Edward James Saunderson for the Conservative nomination for the (re-drawn) constituency of North Armagh in the impending general election. Holmes felt a delicacy in speaking to Monroe about his candidacy in light of the bankruptcy judgeship, and suggested that he consult Churchill, 'who advised immediate withdrawal'.[115] This episode was later characterised as Monroe having been

109 *ILT&SJ*, vol. 33, p. 423 (7 October 1899).
110 W.E. Vaughan, *Murder trials in Ireland, 1836–1914* (Dublin, 2009), pp 170–4, 214.
111 George Hill Smith, *The North East Bar* (Belfast, 1910), p. 74.
112 *Irish Times*, 20 and 22 June 1883.
113 *Irish Times*, 6 September 1884.
114 Holmes Memoir, *IHS*, vol. 16, no. 62, p. 162.
115 Holmes Memoir, p. 162.

'humiliated by the local Orangemen who forced him to stand down in favour of Col Saunderson'.[116]

A couple of months later he was appointed to fill another judicial vacancy that had arisen, this time in the High Court (Chancery division) when Stephen Woulfe Flanagan resigned as Land Judge.[117] Monroe had the announcement of his appointment held back for a couple of days so that he could fulfil a promise to an old friend to speak for him at an election meeting in Mid-Armagh.[118] The fact that he then had no great familiarity with the Land Acts was remarked upon as an instance of barristers being prepared to take up any offered vacancy, irrespective of suitability, on the basis that their party might soon go out of office and that there was no knowing when another opportunity for judicial appointment of any kind might come around. Despite Monroe giving satisfaction in his judicial work he continued to be seen as a square peg in a round hole.[119] In fact his work was not to be confined to the Land Court, and he sat as a vacation judge, and also at times in the Exchequer, Queen's Bench and Probate and Matrimonial divisions, and as an assize judge presiding over criminal trials and common law actions, such as defamation. He was sitting in the courthouse in Cork in March 1891 when fire broke out which destroyed the building.[120] T.M. Healy remarked that as a judge 'Monroe was respected by all for his impartiality and good humour'.[121]

He sat also as a judge in the courts of the Church of Ireland. In 1892 he delivered the judgment of the majority in the court of the General Synod that upheld an objection that had been made, as being contrary to the laws of the church, to the position in which a cross had been placed in St Bartholomew's church, Ballsbridge.[122]

Ill health led to his resignation. He became ill during an outbreak of typhoid fever on Dublin in 1891,[123] and more seriously in February 1895, when he collapsed at a dinner of the North East Bar in the King's Inns. A room at the Inns was converted into a temporary bedroom, and he remained there under medical supervision for a fortnight.[124] He took leave of absence from his duties for two successive periods of six months, and resigned early in 1896 when it became clear, after a time spent in Egypt, that he would be unable to return to work.[125]

116 A.B. Cooke, 'A Conservative party leader in Ulster: Sir Stafford Northcote's diary of a visit to the province, October 1883', *Proceedings of the Royal Irish Academy*, vol. 75.C (1975), p. 76, fn.74.

117 *Irish Times*, 28 November 1885.

118 Hill Smith, op. cit., p. 74.

119 Rhadamanthus, op. cit., p. 103.

120 *Irish Times*, 30 March 1891.

121 T.M. Healy, *Letters and leaders*, p. 226.

122 Kenneth Milne, *St Bartholomew's; a history of the Dublin parish* (Dublin, 2019), pp 19–20; *Irish Times*, 19 November 1892; F.D. How, *Archbishop Plunket: a memoir* (London, 1900), p. 322.

123 *ILT&SJ*, vol. 25, p. 640 (5 December 1891), and vol. 26, p. 67 (30 January 1892).

124 *Irish Times*, 25 and 28 February, 6 and 11 March 1895; *ILT&SJ*, vol. 29, p. 109 (2 March 1895).

125 *ILT&SJ*, vol. 30, p. 2 (4 January 1896) and p. 30 (18 January 1896).

Healy asserted in the House of Commons a few months later that Monroe, having been struck down by an absolutely incapacitating illness, 'went away to Egypt, but he withheld his resignation, knowing that a general election was pending. The moment the party of law and order came into office he handed in his resignation'. Healy was immediately challenged and corrected by R.M. Dane, the Unionist MP for North Fermanagh, who was a member of the Bar. He pointed out that the election had taken place in July 1895, and referred to Monroe's leave of absence, whereupon Healy withdrew his remarks and any personal reflection upon the character of Monroe.[126] However decades later he recycled the allegation in garbled form in his memoirs, writing that 'in 1895 a vacancy in the Irish bench befell, on the death [sic.] of Judge Monroe of the Landed Estates Court [sic.]. He was ill nearly 12 months, but his friends would not allow him to resign until the Tories came back to office, in order to keep out the Liberal attorney general (MacDermot)'.[127]

Monroe was, if not the leader, at least the spokesman of those judges who proposed in 1891 that knighthoods be conferred upon them, as in England. He lived at Bartra, Dalkey, where he died in September 1899. His wife, Lizzie, died ten days later. They were survived by two sons and a daughter, another son having died a few years earlier.[128] One son, Walter Stanley Monroe (1871–1952), was educated at Harrow and after emigrating to Canada as a young man took up a business career and eventually entered politics, being prime minister of Newfoundland between 1924 and 1928.[129]

Hugh Holmes

Justice of the High Court 1887–97, Lord Justice of Appeal 1897–1915

Hugh Holmes (1840–1916) was a native of Dungannon, Co. Tyrone, and was educated there and at Trinity College. He was auditor of the Law Students' Debating Society for 1864–5, and was called to the Bar in 1865, joining the North West circuit. In 1876 he was appointed legal adviser at Dublin Castle, and in 1877 was called to the Inner Bar. He was appointed solicitor general in December 1878, succeeding Gerald FitzGibbon QC, who remarked to Edward Gibson, the attorney general, that this rapid promotion of Holmes 'has, I have reason to know, gone to the very bounds, if not conceivably beyond the limit, of what the very large numbers of middle-aged, old, or senile but nevertheless conscientious and respectable, members of the Bar, University of Dublin, Constitutional, Friendly Brothers and Kildare Street Clubs, and of the Orange Society in Dublin, will stand'.[130]

126 HC Deb, 4th series, vol. 43, cols. 339–42 (21 July 1896).
127 T.M. Healy, op. cit., p. 407.
128 *Irish Times*, 18 November 1893, 3 and 13 October 1899.
129 Entry in *DIB* (by Lawrence William White); Healy, op. cit., p. 226.
130 FitzGibbon to Gibson, 12 December 1878 (Ashbourne Papers, B.50/10).

Holmes went out of office when the Conservatives lost the general election in the spring of 1880, and later remarked that 'if I had felt myself at liberty to follow my own inclination I should probably have kept out of politics when I ceased to hold office ... An ex-law officer, unless he is prepared to break with his party, is not his own master. He is expected, and feels bound, to do something for the cause'.[131] There were two such periods of opposition, after the election defeat in 1880 and in the spring of 1886. After 1880 he became more involved in party political activity, proposing the toast of 'the Conservative members of both houses of Parliament' at a dinner of the Constitutional Club in Dublin in 1883,[132] and advising front bench members of the party at Westminster. He received invitations to stand for election to Parliament in the constituencies of Dungannon and in Enniskillen.

On the Conservatives' return to office in June 1885 the new lord chancellor, Edward Gibson QC (now Lord Ashbourne), invited Holmes both to become attorney general and to stand for election (as it transpired, unopposed) to replace him as one of the Parliamentary representatives for the Dublin University constituency. 'It would have been impossible for me to have obtained a seat in the House of Commons more easily and pleasantly'.[133] The more direct role that he now occupied in government business in the House of Commons exposed him to men who failed to impress him, although they were his own party colleagues.

> Although I did not expect exceptional ability I was surprised that so many occupants of the treasury bench [i.e., the government front bench] were essentially commonplace and far below the intellectual standard required for success in literature and the learned professions. Two things however astonished me still more – first the timidity and want of moral courage which characterised the best of them, and secondly the thoughtless and haphazard way in which important resolutions were arrived at and carried out.[134]

He was re-elected in the general election at the end of 1885 and left office, with the rest of his colleagues, when Gladstone formed his third administration in February 1886. 'I thought it prudent to be prepared for years spent in the cool shade of opposition. We gave up our horses and coachman, and put an end to all unnecessary expenditure'.[135] This second period of opposition transpired to be shorter than Holmes had anticipated, however, as the defeat in the House of Commons of the first Home Rule bill, introduced by Gladstone in April, led to another election in July which the Conservatives won. In this heightened and fraught political atmosphere Holmes engaged himself in the unionist cause, and in March 1886 initiated a debate in the House of Commons with a long speech

131 Holmes Memoir, *IHS*, vol. 16, no. 62, p. 155 and p. 157.
132 *Irish Times*, 29 March 1883.
133 Holmes Memoir, p. 157.
134 Holmes Memoir, p. 159.
135 Holmes Memoir, p. 321.

calling for a statement of what policy the government intended to follow for the restoration and maintenance of social order in Ireland.[136] His friend Lord Randolph Churchill, who had encouraged his initiative, thought this had been a failure, telling Lord Salisbury that Holmes had not spoken well, and indeed that it was unlikely that he would ever be a parliamentary success, as his voice and manner spoiled the substance of what he said.[137] It was said of him, to the same effect, that he did not have, 'nor very likely did he care to have, the power of interesting the House of Commons',[138] and his own view was that 'I had neither sufficient aptitude nor experience to become a figure in Parliament'.[139]

He was re-elected as an MP in July 1886 and re-appointed as attorney general in August. He guided two important pieces of legislation through the House of Commons, the Educational Endowments (Ireland) Act 1885 in his first period of office and subsequently the Prevention of Crime (Ireland) Act 1887. The first of these was heavily amended in the course of its passage through Parliament, much of this prompted behind the scenes by lord justice FitzGibbon.[140] One such amendment, made days before the bill was enacted, provided that schemes of reform of educational charities would be submitted for approval not (as initially proposed) to a Chancery judge but to a panel of two judicial commissioners, the initial appointees being specified in the bill as FitzGibbon and the recently retired lord chancellor, Naish.[141]

The Crimes bill was the subject of vigorous and lengthy debate in the House of Commons, the committee stage eventually being guillotined on 17 June 1887. The purpose of the bill, as Holmes later insisted in a public letter to Arthur Balfour, was to modify the mode of prosecuting offences under common law, not to create any new offences.[142] In his memoir Holmes remarked that it was surprising that the Act had subsequently survived judicial scrutiny since, despite his best efforts, the process of its drafting and passage through Parliament had been quite chaotic. The new chief secretary, Balfour, knew nothing of Ireland, 'his speech introducing [the bill] was ludicrously poor, he gave little promise in any direction of his subsequent success', and sought some 'most fantastic additions' to the draft, including prospective changes of the venue of trials from Ireland to England.[143] Very late in the day, to ensure Liberal Unionist support, the provisions of the bill were confined to 'proclaimed' districts, rendering it necessary to amend almost every section, with all this being rendered still more difficult by the draftsman in the Irish Office having become unwell.

136 HC Deb, 3rd series, vol. 302, cols. 1917–98 (4 March 1886).
137 Churchill to Salisbury, 9 March 1886 (Salisbury Papers, 3M/Churchill/250).
138 Rhadamanthus, *Our judges* (Dublin, 1890), p. 96.
139 Holmes Memoir, p. 321.
140 Holmes Memoir, p. 160; Roy Foster, *Lord Randolph Churchill: a political life* (Oxford, 1981), pp 229–30.
141 HC Deb, 3rd series, vol. 300, cols. 1894–913 (12 August 1885).
142 Holmes to Balfour, 15 September 1887 (*ILT&SJ*, vol. 21, p. 531 (24 September 1887)).
143 Holmes Memoir, p. 337.

There was an outstanding vacancy in the High Court which had arisen earlier in 1887 when Morris had been promoted to be lord chief justice, an office for which (apart from Morris's strong claims in any event) Holmes's service as attorney general may have been considered too short to merit appointment.[144] Holmes had agreed with Balfour that he would be appointed to fill this vacancy when the Crimes bill had been passed, and as soon as the bill had completed the committee stage of its Parliamentary passage, and hence for all practical purposes was in its final form and would not be subject to any further drafting or amendment, he told Ashbourne that he wished to take up the vacancy.[145] He resisted pressure to remain in office, potentially with no definite terminal date, as Balfour 'seemed to think that there would be no difficulty in keeping the place open indefinitely … My difficulty was that both loyalty to the Bar and repeated declarations of the government bound me in honour as I thought – either to accept the judgeship or to allow the vacancy to be filled by another, and I did not see my way to the second branch of the alternative'.[146] His appointment took effect at the start of July, before the bill received its third reading in the House of Commons on 8 July, and it became law on 19 July.

As a judge he was initially considered rather brusque, and as lacking an appropriate judicial demeanour in court.[147] W.E. Wylie thought him to be 'amazingly quick' and as having no time for 'appeal to the jury' oratory from counsel.[148] He was later credited with good insight into human nature. He remarked, for instance, in a case involving the legal consequences of blocking of light to a building in the centre of Belfast by a new neighbouring structure, that 'the evidence, expert and otherwise, given at the trial of this action was, as so often happens in cases of this kind, conflicting, and I fear that witnesses on both sides indulged in considerable exaggeration'.[149] In that case a decision of the Court of Appeal (Walker LC, FitzGibbon and Holmes LJJ), reversing Barton J, was itself reversed by the House of Lords.

In 1897 following the death of lord justice Barry Holmes was appointed to the Court of Appeal and, with the other judges of that court, he also sat regularly at first instance on assize. The period of just over a decade in which he and FitzGibbon sat together on the court has been generally regarded as something of a golden era in Irish jurisprudence.[150] Sir John Ross, having noted that FitzGibbon's approach was based on ethics and natural justice (see p. 279), wrote that

144 Ashbourne to Balfour, 17 June 1887 (Balfour Papers, Add. MS 49815.10), Ashbourne to Balfour, 28 June 1887 (Balfour Papers, Add. MS 49815.18).
145 Ashbourne to Balfour, 17 June 1887 (Balfour Papers, Add. MS 49815.10).
146 Holmes Memoir, p. 337.
147 Rhadamanthus, op. cit., pp 95–6.
148 W.E. Wylie memoir (TNAUK), PRO 30/89/2, p. 8.
149 *Black v Scottish Temperance Assurance Co.* [1908] 1 IR 541, at 573.
150 *ILT&SJ*, vol. 49, p. 23 (23 January 1915).

> Holmes, on the other hand, fought for upholding, rigidly, the settled principles of law; these he thought the Court of Appeal was bound to maintain, no matter how grievously their logical application pressed on individuals in special cases. If these same principles were strained or tampered with, all our law, and with it our civilisation, he thought, would fall into a Serbonian bog.[151]

An example of the disposition described by Ross might be seen in Holmes's dissenting judgment in *Webb v Oldfield, in re Cranston*,[152] when he was not prepared to hold that a testamentary gift to two Vegetarian Societies was charitable. He carefully reviewed the recent authoritative analysis of the four heads of charity given by Lord Macnaghten in *Commissioners of Income Tax v Pemsel*[153] – the relief of poverty, the promotion of education, the advancement of religion and other purposes beneficial to the community – and considered whether such a gift came within the fourth such heading.

> Beyond a few eccentrics no one thinks of connecting [vegetarianism] with public utility, or with the moral or material improvement of mankind. We cannot regard it as we might regard an obscure and novel religious sect, as a doubtful branch of a great and elevating movement. In its most favourable aspect it is a harmless attempt to substitute one kind of food for another. Its promoters no doubt believe in its utility ... But can this belief make a project of this kind a charity in any sense which the law attaches to that term? If it can, it seems to me that every project not actually immoral or illegal must be held a charity.

Holmes noted in *The SS Gairloch*[154] that great weight is to be attached to any finding of fact made by a judge hearing a case on the basis of oral evidence, whose conclusion 'ought not to be reversed by a court that has not the same opportunity of seeing and hearing the witnesses unless it is so clearly against the weight of the testimony as to amount to a manifest defeat of justice'. He observed however that an appellate tribunal would be entitled to prefer its own view of an inference or deduction to be drawn from largely undisputed facts to that drawn by a court of first instance, since such a tribunal was in as good a position to arrive at a correct conclusion as the court of first instance.

In 1989 the United Nations Convention on the Rights of the Child provided that states should secure that the opinion of children is to be ascertained when practical when consideration is being given to their best interests.[155] An observation

151 Sir John Ross, *The years of my pilgrimage* (London, 1924), p. 201.
152 *Webb v Oldfield, In re Cranston deceased*, [1898] 1 IR 431, at 452.
153 [1891] AC 531.
154 *The SS Gairloch, Aberdeen Glenline Steamship Co. v Macken*, [1899] 2 IR 1, at 18.
155 UNCRC, article 12. The Guardianship of Infants Act 1964, s31, as inserted by s63 of the Children and Family Relationships Act 2015, requires a court, when determining the best

made by Holmes in a trial over custody of a child almost a century earlier is reflective of a different social attitude of the time:

> we have not thought it necessary to see the girl; but for my own part I should have done so, had I deemed it necessary for the purpose of ascertaining facts. It would however be contrary to precedent for the court to be guided in a case of this kind by her own wishes. The law has fixed the age of 16 as the period when a female minor can choose her own residence, and little regard ought to be paid to the personal wishes of a child of eleven as against what seems to be for her welfare.[156]

Holmes retired from the bench in the New Year of 1915, and died in April 1916, shortly before Easter. He left a substantial estate, of over £50,000. He had a personal as well as a professional knowledge of the workings of the Land Acts, as owning an estate in Co. Donegal, where he was considered a fair-minded landlord, not raising rents nor carrying out evictions, and on which reasonable terms were agreed for the purchase by the tenants of their holdings in 1904.[157]

He and his wife Olivia Moule, who came from Worcestershire and whose sister Elizabeth married John Monroe, had three sons, all of whom became lawyers, and four daughters, all of whom married lawyers. Of their daughters, Mary married W.C. Gage, a solicitor in Dublin, Elizabeth and Alice married sons of Mr Justice Murphy, Harold Lawson Murphy QC and Edward Sullivan Murphy QC respectively, and Violet married Denis Henry QC, who had lived close to the family home at 3 Fitzwilliam Place. In completing the census return for 1901 Holmes gave a curious collective description of the 'rank, profession or occupation' of his daughters, all then in their 20s and living at home, as being that 'they toil not neither do they spin'.[158] Conolly Gage (1905–84), a grandson of Holmes, was Ulster Unionist MP for Belfast South between 1945 and 1952, and subsequently a county court judge and circuit judge in England. His son Sir William Gage (1938–2023) was appointed a judge of the High Court (Queen's Bench division) in 1993 and a member of the Court of Appeal in 2004.

The eldest son William, born in 1871, was called to the Bar in 1895, and having volunteered for the Boer War was severely wounded in action (losing a leg).[159]

interests of a child, to have regard to the view of the child concerned. The Children (Northern Ireland) Order 1995, article 3, similarly requires a court to have regard to the ascertainable wishes and feelings of a child (considered in the light of his age and understanding).

156 *In re Harriet O'Hara, an infant*, [1900] 2 IR 232, at 258.

157 *New Irish Jurist*, vol. 4 (IV), p. 67 (22 January 1904).

158 'And why take ye thought for raiment? Consider the lilies of the field, how they grow; they toil not neither do they spin. And yet I say unto you, that even Solomon in all his glory was not arrayed like one of these.' (Matthew, 6.28–29).

159 *ILT&SJ*, vol. 34, p. 440 (20 October 1900), p. 495 (1 December 1900), and vol. 35, p. 131 (23 March 1901).

Shortly afterwards he was appointed to be a resident magistrate.[160] Hugh Holmes (1886–1955) was called to the Bar in 1910, having been awarded the Brooke scholarship for first place in his final exams. He served in an artillery regiment during the Great War,[161] and subsequently made his career as a lawyer and judge (KC) in Egypt. He died in Nairobi in 1955, where he was serving as a judge of the supreme court of Kenya.[162]

Valentine Holmes (1888–1956) was educated at Charterhouse school, Surrey, and at Trinity College, where he was auditor of the College Historical Society in 1911–12.[163] He acted as train-bearer and circuit registrar to his father,[164] and then commenced a more substantive legal career in England, where he was called to the Bar in 1913. He also served in an artillery regiment. He had a considerable reputation, particularly in defamation cases,[165] and became a KC in 1945. He was appointed in 1936 as the 'Treasury devil', the name given to the first junior counsel to the Treasury in common law, who undertook all the leading cases for the government in civil matters. When he appeared in that capacity, with the attorney general, in 1941 in the celebrated case of *Liversidge v Anderson*,[166] they became the subject of an unseemly judicial scuffle. The applicant who had been detained under wartime internment regulations sued the Home Secretary, Sir John Anderson, for false imprisonment, and sought to be advised of the basis of his continuing detention. Only Lord Atkin of the five judges who heard Liversidge's appeal in the House of Lords considered – as would now not be disputed – that he was entitled to be given reasons, and in a powerful judgment (speech) he severely criticised, indeed ridiculed, the view that his judicial colleagues had taken. He added that 'I have listened to arguments which might have been addressed acceptably to the court of King's Bench in the time of Charles I'.[167] The presiding judge for the appeal, Lord Maugham (lord chancellor 1938–9), saw fit to write to the *Times* saying that, as counsel were not in a position to reply, 'even to so grave an animadversion as this', he thought it only fair to the attorney general and Mr Holmes to say that in presiding over the hearing he had heard nothing which could justify such a remark.[168] Both Hugh Holmes and Valentine Holmes received knighthoods.

160 *ILT&SJ*, vol. 39, p. 416 (2 December 1905) and vol. 41, p. 134 (18 May 1907).
161 Healy, *OldMC*, p. 277.
162 *ILT&SJ*, vol. 89, p. 252 (22 October 1955).
163 Patrick Geoghegan, *The College Historical Society; oratory and debate, 1770–2020* (Dublin, 2020), p. 196.
164 *ILT&SJ*, vol. 46, p. 98 (20 April 1912) ; *Irish Times*, 8 June 1912, 26 June 1913.
165 *Reavely v Colles* (1936), *Laski v Newark Advertiser Co. Ltd* (1946); Joseph Dean, *Hatred, ridicule or contempt: a book of libel cases* (London, 1953), pp 90 and 228.
166 [1942] AC 206.
167 [1942] AC 206, at 244. See, more generally, Geoffrey Lewis, *Lord Atkin* (Oxford, 1999), chapter 7. The reign of Charles I (1625–49) was the era of the court of Star Chamber.
168 *The Times*, 6 November 1941.

John George Gibson

Justice of the High Court 1888–1921

John George Gibson (1846–1923) was a younger brother of Edward Gibson, the first Lord Ashbourne. He was educated at Portora Royal School, Enniskillen, and Trinity College Dublin, where he was auditor of the College Historical Society. He was called to the Bar in 1870, joining the Leinster circuit, and to the Inner Bar in 1880. He lived in Fitzwilliam Place. This early success at the Bar indicates that Gibson was both well placed and well regarded. An observation by Maurice Healy about him as a judge would have been applicable also in his younger days, that he had good looks, 'dignity and a sense of justice; he was a cultured man, with a charming voice'.[169] The president of the Law Society spoke of his 'splendid physique'.[170] Healy remarked also, however, that Gibson 'loved to rattle off cases by name, leaving his audience to infer that he was well acquainted with their substance, and had discerned in each a bearing on the matter in hand' although such an inference or impression was misleading.[171] Edward Carson, who was called to the Bar in 1877, noted more bluntly to the same effect that he 'suffered from an overdose of undigested case law', and left a very unflattering account of some thoughtless and dismissive conduct of Gibson towards him, as a junior counsel, in a case in which they were working together.[172]

In the general election of November 1885 Gibson was elected to Parliament as member for the Walton constituency in Liverpool, being the first of a number of Irish barristers who stood for election in Liverpool constituencies over the next three decades.[173] (Those other candidates were Charles Hemphill, Cherry and Thomas Molony. George Hill Smith (1833–1926), who was called to the Bar in 1877 and subsequently wrote *The North East Bar* (Belfast, 1910), stood unsuccessfully (as a Conservative) in the Sheffield Attercliffe constituency in the general election in 1892 and in a bye-election in 1894.) His Liberal opponent in 1885, Augustine Birrell, wrote of him that 'he wanted to get in, in order to get on',[174] and after the election he succeeded John Monroe, who had just been appointed a judge, as solicitor general. As Ashbourne's brother he 'could not expect to be seen as an independent politician at all, despite his own native sharpness'.[175] He left office with his party colleagues shortly afterwards when Gladstone again became prime minister, but in the summer of 1886 he was re-elected in his constituency and re-appointed as a law officer when the

169 Healy, *OldMC*, p. 29.
170 *ILT&SJ*, vol. 57, p. 167 (7 July 1923).
171 Healy, op. cit., p. 29.
172 Edward Marjoribanks, *The life of Lord Carson: vol. 1* (London, 1932), pp 32–3.
173 See Daire Hogan, 'R.R. Cherry, lord chief justice of Ireland, 1914–1916' in D.S. Greer and N.M. Dawson (eds), *Mysteries and solutions in Irish legal history* (Dublin, 2001), p. 164.
174 Augustine Birrell, *Things past redress* (London, 1937), pp 101–5.
175 A.B. Cooke and John Vincent, *The governing passion: cabinet government and party politics in Britain, 1885–86* (Brighton, 1974), p. 155.

Conservatives returned to power. A year later he was promoted to be attorney general, in June 1887, and then to be a High Court judge in January 1888. He and his wife had the grief at this time of three of their children dying young, two young sons dying in the same week in April 1887, from diphtheria, and an infant daughter in July 1888.[176]

His work as attorney general rapidly proved to be unsatisfactory to Arthur Balfour, the chief secretary for Ireland, and he was removed from office after little more than six months. The targets of Balfour's frequent criticisms of the perceived inadequacies of Irish advisers (not only legal ones) and judges included not only Gibson but also Ashbourne. Salisbury, the prime minister, sympathised with him in October 1887 for having 'the stupidest set of lawyers in Ireland any government was ever cursed with. There is nothing for it but for you to form your own judgment upon every question of procedure, of law, of drafting, etc'.[177] He complained to Salisbury a couple of weeks later that 'the law officers show much greater ingenuity in picking holes in their own Act [the Criminal Law and Procedure (Ireland) Act 1887[178]] than they ever did in passing it. At every turn I find myself hampered by what may perhaps be good law but is certainly not good sense'.[179] (Both of those criticisms would have extended to Peter O'Brien, then the solicitor general and soon to be the attorney general, but Balfour came to regard him as a great improvement on Gibson.)

A month later on 23 November Balfour asked the principal agent of the Conservative party whether there was any electoral reason why Gibson would not immediately vacate his parliamentary seat,[180] and told Salisbury that he was 'more than ever convinced that Gibson must be promoted, and if so it should be done soon'.[181] He had 'abnormal powers of criticism and his defective power of action [which] form one of the chief reasons for my desiring to promote him. He is an excellent fellow; very able; very loyal and very pleasant to work with in most respects. But if we had allowed ourselves to be guided by him in the matter of the working of the Crimes Act we should have been at a standstill'.[182]

There had then been a vacancy in the High Court for some three months, by reason of the death of James Lawson in August 1887, and Gibson was soon appointed to fill this, in January 1888. A decade later Salisbury was to observe, in the context of difficulties in filling a judicial position in England, that it was more important to have an efficient attorney general than an efficient judge: 'the M.R.

176 Ashbourne to Balfour, 17 April 1887 (Balfour Papers, Add. MS 49815.6); *ILT&SJ*, vol. 21, p. 233 (23 April 1887) and vol. 22, p. 368 (21 July 1888).
177 Salisbury to Balfour, 14 October 1887 (Balfour Papers, Add. MS 49688/151).
178 50&51 Vict., c.20 (1887).
179 Balfour to Salisbury, 27 October 1887 (*Salisbury–Balfour correspondence*, p. 218).
180 There transpired to be no such reason, and at the bye-election in the constituency in February 1888 after Gibson had vacated his seat the new Conservative candidate was elected unopposed.
181 Balfour to Middleton, 23 November 1887 (*Salisbury–Balfour correspondence*, p. 223); Balfour to Salisbury, 23 November 1887 (ibid., p. 224).
182 Balfour to Salisbury, 28 November 1887 (*Salisbury–Balfour correspondence*, p. 226).

[master of the rolls] decides the questions in which individuals are interested, and if he goes wrong he has colleagues and a court of appeal to set him right. But if the attorney general goes wrong in advising the government far greater interests are affected; and there is nobody to set him right except perhaps a remonstrance from his solicitor general which he probably disregards'.[183]

Gibson has been remembered, perhaps slightly unfairly, more for his bearing and good humour than for any contribution to jurisprudence. In 1902 a judgment of his which had been set aside by a divisional court of the High Court, and the decision of which was then affirmed by the Court of Appeal, was restored by the House of Lords.[184] An analysis that he made in 1912 of the relationship between a teacher, the school manager and the national education authorities, what he referred to as 'a kind of triangular pact', was regarded as authoritative, and was cited with approval by the Supreme Court in 1941 and in 2008.[185]

In 1907 he expressed regret 'that there was not a family edition of the morning newspapers, because these papers often contain an amount of prurient matter which, in a French novel, would effectually prohibit its intrusion within the circle of any well-conducted house'. This comment was made in the course of a libel trial, *MacBride v Independent Newspapers Ltd*, over reports of legal proceedings in France between Maud Gonne and Major John MacBride, which were marked by bitter recriminations and accusations by her of cruelty, infidelity and drunkenness.[186] In a murder case in 1917 he referred to the Court for Crown Cases Reserved an issue of whether a jury had sufficient evidence of death where the body of a deceased person had not been found, and that court upheld his decision not to withdraw the case from the jury (see p. 420).[187] W.E. Wylie noted, on an occasion when he appeared before Gibson at the assizes in Derry, that 'he had just finished a rather bad murder case and had had to put his black cap and condemn the man to death. He was nervous, depressed and snappy'.[188]

Having been appointed at the comparatively young age of 41 Gibson served as a judge for a third of a century. He retired in 1921 and died at Colwyn Bay in Wales in 1923.[189] He left a large estate, the personalty being valued for probate at £80,000.[190]

183 Salisbury to Halsbury, 19 September 1897 (R.F.V. Heuston, *Lives of the lord chancellors, 1885–1940* (Oxford, 1964), p. 52).
184 *Macassey v Thompson, Macassey & Huston*, 36 ILTR 162 (1902).
185 *Fox v Higgins*, 46 ILTR 222 (1912); *McEneaney v Minister for Education*, [1941] IR 430; W.N. Osborough, 'Irish law and the rights of the national schoolteacher – I', *Irish Jurist*, vol. 14 (1979), p. 36 at 41; *O'Keeffe v Hickey*, [2009] 2 IR 302, at 313 and 347 (SC).
186 *ILT&SJ*, vol. 50, p. 19 (19 January 1907); entry in *DIB* on MacBride (by Donal P. McCracken).
187 *R v McNicholl* [1917] 2 IR 557; *ILT&SJ*, vol. 51, p. 311 (29 December 1917).
188 W.E. Wylie, memoir (TNAUK), PRO 30/89/2, p. 11.
189 *ILT&SJ*, vol. 57, p. 166 (7 July 1923).
190 *ILT&SJ*, vol. 57, p. 225 (8 September 1923).

Peter O'Brien (Lord O'Brien of Kilfenora)

Lord Chief Justice of Ireland 1889–1913

Peter O'Brien (1842–1914) was the fifth son of John O'Brien, who was elected a member of Parliament for the city of Limerick (as a liberal or Repealer) in 1841 and again in 1847. The family property at Ballynalacken, Co. Clare, was near Kilfenora. He was educated at Clongowes, the Jesuit school in Co. Kildare, and at Trinity College. Some of his contemporaries among the judiciary – such as Morris, Palles and FitzGibbon – distinguished themselves academically, but O'Brien by his own account took a relaxed approach to college life.[191] He was called to the Bar in 1865 and 'read with that great judge and lawyer, chief baron Palles, to whom I always say I am indebted for any knowledge of law I possess. For six months after I was called to the Bar I gave no attention to work; not that I was lazy or an idler, but I was fond of pleasure and energetic in its pursuit'.[192] He credited his wife, Anne (Annie), whom he married in 1867, with 'all my success in life. When I proposed to her she accepted me upon the condition that I should set to work'.[193] They had two daughters, and a son who died in infancy.[194] His uncle James O'Brien was appointed a judge in 1858, and in O'Brien's early years at the Bar he was appointed to act as a registrar on circuit for him, a common small instance of patronage for young relatives of judges at the time.[195]

Early in his career, after joining the Munster circuit, he was successful in having a conviction of a woman charged with infanticide quashed by the Court for Crown Cases Reserved.[196] In 1877 he had a passage of arms with Mr Justice Keogh at the assizes in Cork over the terms of the judge's charge to a jury. A threat by Keogh to have O'Brien removed from court if he did not sit down and stop speaking was protested by him – 'I have been grossly outraged by your lordship, and I say, in the presence of this crowded court, that if this sort of thing goes on, farewell to the independence of the Munster Bar'. Keogh apologised in open court later that day.[197] In 1901 O'Brien was himself to be the subject of similar criticism, to which he did not respond, for his hostile reaction to a request by counsel that he should recuse himself from hearing a case.[198] He successfully defended T.M. Healy at Cork assizes in 1880 on a public disorder charge of making an

191 Georgina O'Brien (ed.), *The reminiscences of Lord O'Brien of Kilfenora* (London, 1916) (hereafter *Reminiscences*), p. 12.

192 *Reminiscences*, p. 14. Christopher Palles was then a member of the Bar, and was not a judge until 1874. He had become a QC in 1865.

193 *Reminiscences*, p. 18.

194 *ILT&SJ*, vol. 62, p. 304 (15 December 1928).

195 O'Brien in turn appointed a nephew, Torlogh O'Brien, as his secretary when he became chief justice. See also, for example, the list of circuit registrars for the spring assizes in 1899 (*ILT&SJ*, vol. 33, p. 80 (18 February 1899)).

196 *Irish Times*, 8 September 1914.

197 *ILT&SJ*, vol. 11, p. 386 (4 August 1877); *Reminiscences*, pp 23–4.

198 *New Irish Jurist*, vol. 1, pp 195–6 (3 May 1901); *Law Times*, vol. 111, pp 28–9 (11 May 1901).

inflammatory speech at Bantry over an eviction.[199] He represented one defendant, T.D. Sullivan, in the trial of Parnell and others for seditious conspiracy in early 1881, in which the jury disagreed and could not reach a verdict, and told the jury that conspiracy could not be established by a coincidence of opinion.[200]

He took silk in 1880, and enjoyed patronage as a criminal prosecutor from the Liberal government in the first half of the 1880s, as junior prosecutor for the city and county of Dublin (at Green Street courthouse) in 1881 and from 1883 as senior Crown prosecutor there. He had a reputation as an able and aggressive counsel, not only in trials with a political aspect. He was one of the prosecuting counsel at the tragic Maamtrasna murder trials in 1882 and at the trial the following year of members of the Irish National Invincibles for the murders in the Phoenix Park in May 1882 of Cavendish and Burke. The judge in the latter trial had police protection, as did O'Brien and other members of the prosecuting team.[201] He declined a brief to represent the *Times* at the Special Commission inquiry that was established in 1887 in London to investigate its articles on 'Parnellism and Crime', and the Parnell movement.[202]

In criminal trials the defence and the prosecution could each challenge prospective members of a jury, although only the Crown had an unlimited power to set them aside or 'stand by'. Judges frequently made public complaints about what they considered to be failures of justice through the intimidation of witnesses and/or of jurors resulting in seemingly perverse acquittals (see comments of William O'Brien (p. 294)). O'Brien's *Reminiscences* (p. 31) cite comments of John David Fitzgerald to that effect in 1880. Defendants and nationalist politicians complained of jury 'packing', when members of the panel of prospective jurors with a presumptive sympathy with the defence would be set aside until a jury composed more or less to the satisfaction of the prosecution had been selected. O'Brien as a leading prosecutor and then attorney general was thus at the heart of jury selection in the 1880s. Reservations have been expressed over whether claims about the extent of jury packing can be verified from available records. Niamh Howlin has noted that 'the cases reported extensively in pamphlets and newspapers [in the 1880s] tended to be exceptional – cases in which the public had a keen interest, often on political grounds – and it is possible that the reports may over-represent the true incidence of jury packing'.[203] W.E. Vaughan has observed that 'it is difficult not to dismiss a great deal of the criticism of the formation of Irish juries as exaggerated'.[204]

199 Dunbar Plunket Barton, *Timothy Healy: memories and anecdotes* (Dublin and Cork, 1933), p. 23.
200 *Reminiscences*, pp 29–30.
201 *Reminiscences*, pp 54 and 62.
202 *Reminiscences*, p. 76.
203 Niamh Howlin, *Juries in Ireland: laypersons and law in the long nineteenth century* (Dublin, 2017), p. 156 (and see more generally chapter 10, 'Challenges and jury packing').
204 W.E. Vaughan, *Murder trials in Ireland, 1836–1914* (Dublin, 2009), p. 164.

Lord Fitzgerald initiated a debate in the House of Lords in 1887 on the administration of the jury laws in Ireland,[205] and spoke of problems having arisen because the jury reforms of 1871 had led to jury panels being largely composed of 'persons wholly unsuited to perform their duties', some ignorant, some illiterate, some subject to intimidation. 'But Roman Catholics were excluded from the jury box, not because they were Roman Catholics, but because they happened to belong to a class whose sympathies were with the accused and who might be subject to intimidation, and for other good reasons'.[206] Lord Ashbourne made a combative contribution to the debate, referring to jury disagreements and acquittals 'in face of the strongest evidence and the most clear judicial guidance and warning'. He had personal experience of having '50, 60, 80 , 90 and 100 persons repeatedly ordered to stand by, not in cases involving political prejudice or passion, but in ordinary cases, in order to get a jury which could be relied upon to do their duty in a fair and decent way'. As an example of 'the great difficulty that was experienced in Ireland in getting an independent jury to fearlessly perform their duty' he cited a Nationalist MP at a demonstration outside the courthouse in Cork in December 1886 as saying that Cork jurors 'will not be made the tools of Mr Peter O'Brien and the Castle'.[207]

O'Brien represented himself in his memoir as ensuring unbiased juries:

> in the South of Ireland at that time juries were intimidated to such an extent that it was impossible to obtain conscientious convictions. I was the first to succeed in getting a jury to convict in that part of the country, and this success won for me the title of 'The Packer'. I certainly eliminated from the jury box, without apology, those who were prejudiced, and I would do it again under similar circumstances. I have always maintained that I ought to have been called 'The Great Unpacker'.[208]

The *Irish Times* thought that his role in exercising 'with a strong hand the right of the Crown to challenge jurors who were more than suspected of being in full sympathy with the persons they were empanelled to try … never forfeited the goodwill of his professional brethren or, indeed, of any well-instructed class of the community'.[209] A cartoon that was published in October 1889, shortly before he became chief justice, had the caption 'Pether the Packer; packing the jury in the court house, Maryborough [now Portlaoise] – "All Catholics stand aside. Papists are perjurers, not to be trusted on their oaths"'.[210] These trials of a number of men accused of complicity in murder and riotous conduct in Donegal had been

205 HL Deb, 3rd series, vol. 311, cols. 1234–52 (4 March 1887).
206 HL Deb, 3rd series, vol. 311, cols. 1236 and 1238 (4 March 1887).
207 HL Deb, 3rd series, vol. 311, cols. 1243, 1247 and 1248 (4 March 1887).
208 *Reminiscences*, pp 43–4.
209 *Irish Times*, 8 September 1914.
210 *United Ireland*, 26 October 1889.

transferred from that county. An RIC inspector had died in the course of trying to arrest a priest who was to be prosecuted for advocating the Plan of Campaign of tenant resistance to rent demands. The 'Packer' name was originally intended by critics as a belittling or derogatory designation of O'Brien but lost its edge over time, and was at times used by some of his colleagues in correspondence when referring to him.

Arthur Balfour was appointed chief secretary for Ireland in March 1887, and later that year greater law enforcement powers were given to the authorities by the enactment of the Criminal Law and Procedure (Ireland) Act,[211] generally known as the 'Crimes Act'. Trials could thereafter be transferred from one county to another, and some charges connected to agrarian violence could be tried as summary offences in a magistrate's court rather than before a jury. A more forceful policy of 'coercion' was adopted,[212] and Balfour's belief that government policy was being hindered and frustrated by inadequate, timid and underpowered advice from the law officers and the lord chancellor led to the replacement of John George Gibson by O'Brien as attorney general in the New Year 1888.[213] O'Brien was attorney general for just under two years, until his appointment as lord chief justice in November 1889.

His professional connection with Balfour marked a political association also. In 1879 he had stood as a Liberal in a bye-election for the Co. Clare constituency, finishing third, well behind both the Home Rule candidate (who won) and the Conservative. In 1880 he took part in an election meeting in Ballsbridge, saying (after the chairman had said that it was the want of Home Rule that had caused pestilence and every misfortune to Ireland) that voters must 'defeat the attempt of the Tory party to wrest from the Liberals a share in the representation of the city of Dublin'.[214] He later wrote that 'when Mr Gladstone became a Home Ruler [in 1886] I was obliged conscientiously to sever my connection with the Liberal party, like so many other Unionists'.[215] In the general election in 1886 'he had some idea of contesting a seat which he finally abandoned'.[216] He regarded himself as a Liberal Unionist, and was acknowledged as such ('not a Conservative party man and never became such')[217] when appointed to be solicitor general at the end of June 1887 and attorney general in January 1888. Both appointments were made by Balfour, who did not accept Lord Ashbourne's recommendation of Madden for the first one.[218] When accepting office as solicitor general he told Lord Londonderry,

211 50&51 Vict., c.20. These statutory special powers were again used by the government decades later during the War of Independence, 1919–21.

212 L. Perry Curtis Jr, *The depiction of eviction in Ireland, 1845–1910* (Dublin, 2011), chapters 5–9.

213 Salisbury to Balfour, 3, 14 October 1887 (Balfour Papers, Add. MS 49688); *Salisbury–Balfour correspondence*, p. 252; L.P. Curtis, *Coercion and conciliation in Ireland, 1880–1892: a study in conservative unionism* (Princeton, 1963), p. 191.

214 *Irish Times*, 1 April 1880.

215 *Reminiscences*, p. 68.

216 *Law Times*, vol. 137, p. 472 (19 September 1914).

217 *ILT&SJ*, vol. 21, p. 362 (2 July 1887) and vol. 22, p. 30 (21 January 1888).

218 Ashbourne to Balfour, 28 June 1887 (Balfour Papers, Add. MS 49815.18).

the lord lieutenant, that his views were in substantial accord with those of the government, that he was certainly a strong Unionist, and that he would heartily co-operate in any measures likely to be introduced by the government.[219]

In October 1889 Lord Fitzgerald, the first Irish lord of appeal in ordinary, died, and O'Brien wrote to Balfour immediately canvassing for appointment to succeed either him or Morris, the lord chief justice. Balfour initially contemplated a reshuffle in which Ashbourne would take the place vacated by Fitzgerald, and O'Brien would take his place as lord chancellor, but when Ashbourne did not co-operate that plan fell apart. Ashbourne did not take at all as high a view of O'Brien's prospects in a reshuffle as O'Brien himself had taken, telling Balfour that a puisne judgeship in the High Court might become available to which in due course O'Brien might be appointed.[220] Morris asked for and was given the place in London, and O'Brien was appointed to his position rather than to that of Ashbourne (see pp 447–9). His subsequent work may have been more enjoyable, and his reputation enhanced, by serving as chief justice rather than lord chancellor. The testing of a chain of evidence and the credibility of witnesses through cross-examination was an aspect of trials in which, both at the Bar and on the Bench, he took a close interest. His daughter was told that 'on the bench he rarely made notes; he was able to pigeon-hole, as it were, the facts of a case in his brain'.[221] By contrast, neither as lord chancellor presiding over the Court of Appeal nor subsequently (having been made a peer) sitting in the House of Lords would he have heard any oral evidence, since appellate courts did not do so and, particularly as a Law Lord, a member of the highest courts in the United Kingdom and in the British Empire, his work would have required detailed analysis of the most complicated legal points.

His background had been at common law and in criminal cases, and an initial comment, noting his limitations, was that 'as a lawyer the lord chief justice does not pretend to deep or varied learning. Of equity he knows about as little as it would be possible for a man of his ability to pick up during a quarter of a century in the courts'.[222] His good humour and easy manner, his demonstrable common sense and his standing at the Bar ensured him respect and popularity as a judge, who 'won the confidence of juries by his rectitude and leniency', according to A.W. Samuels, himself a High Court judge.[223] When he retired Augustine Birrell, the chief secretary for Ireland, wrote to him wondering 'will we get a better Irishman than you to cajole a jury into observing their oaths?'[224] On his death his successor, R.R. Cherry, said, to much the same effect, that 'when he became a judge the chief qualities that distinguished his career were his firmness and his sound common

219 O'Brien to Londonderry, 29 June 1887 (Balfour Papers, Add. MS 49802.13).
220 Ashbourne to Balfour, 17 and 20 October 1889 (Balfour Papers, Add. MS 49815.47 and .49).
221 *Reminiscences*, introduction, p. vi.
222 Rhadamanthus, op. cit., p. 130.
223 Entry on O'Brien by Samuels in *DNB*, 1912–21. He stated that 'the great attorney general proved a great chief justice, enhancing during 24 years the high traditions of that office.'
224 *Reminiscences*, p. 170.

sense. Other judges might have exceeded him in knowledge of case law and statute law but no judge had a firmer grasp of legal principles. Knowing as he did the Irish character most thoroughly he always had great weight with a jury'.[225]

O'Brien wrote in his memoir that he was glad to have pronounced few death sentences, 'and all of them were in cases where the crime was of a terrible and deliberate nature – a fact which, to a slight extent, tends to deaden feelings of pity for the criminal'.[226] One such case was the conviction of Philip King, a labourer of Nolagh, Co. Cavan, who was convicted for the murder of his wife and her mother. O'Brien said, when the jury had given its verdict, that 'I have heard with regret your last protestation of innocence, because no reasonable man who heard your trial would have any doubt of your guilt. It has been my lot in life to be concerned in the trial of many crimes, but in all my harrowing experience I never met aught like yours'.[227] Hanging was the mandatory or automatic sentence of punishment for murder, so for O'Brien not to have passed many sentences of death would have been a consequence of few verdicts of murder having been given by juries in trials over which he presided. A judge would have had an ability to influence a jury, in his summing up and directions, as to the guilt or innocence of an accused person and, if guilty of unlawful killing, as to whether the concept of murder, as compared to manslaughter for instance, would have been applicable. A jury might have been nudged by a judge towards a verdict of murder in a dreadful case more so than in a sad one.

Some 60 years after O'Brien's retirement a writer in the *Irish Jurist* noted that O'Brien 'does not seem to have greatly impressed his contemporaries, yet some of his judgments have a durability which suggests that his critics may have underestimated him'.[228] He cited O'Brien's formulation of the standard of care required from unpaid public representatives,[229] and his exposition of the basis on which a judicial determination might be quashed on grounds of bias (a real likelihood of an operative prejudice), without any disparagement of or imputation of a corrupt motive or conscious bias to the decision maker.[230] The House of Lords adopted, and praised, an analysis made by O'Brien of a point of interpretation of the Dentists Act 1878,[231] in preference to a contrary judgment of the Court of Appeal in England.[232]

He was a member of a divisional court (with Palles CB and Gibson J) which in *Ussher v Ussher*[233] held that a marriage was valid 'according to the law of the realm, according to the common law', although not valid by the law of the Catholic

225 *ILT&SJ*, vol. 48, p. 310 (31 October 1914).
226 *Reminiscences*, p. 100.
227 *Irish Times*, 14 December 1898; *ILT&SJ*, vol. 33, p. 42 (28 January 1899).
228 J.M.G. Sweeney, 'Lord O'Brien's doctrine of bias', *Irish Jurist*, vol. 7, Part 1 (1972), p. 17.
229 *R (Kennedy) v Browne*, 41 ILTR 166, at 169 (1907).
230 *R (de Vesci) v Queen's County Justices*, [1908] 2 IR 285, at 294.
231 *Byrne v Rogers*, [1910] 2 IR 220.
232 *Bellerby v Heyworth and others*, [1910] AC 377.
233 [1912] 2 IR 445.

church since two witnesses, in addition to the priest, had not been present at the ceremony. He told his daughter Georgina that this was 'the most interesting case in which I had to deliver judgment in recent years', and directed her to set out his judgment in full in his *Reminiscences*.[234] The memoir gave no indication that his judgment was one of three delivered by the court.

He had a contemporary reputation as understanding the character of his fellow countrymen and countrywomen, at times polishing his prose for comic effect with a sardonic wit 'seen to best advantage in those passages in his judgments where he makes gratuitous but thoroughly enjoyable reference to the passing social scene'.[235] These include what he said about a claim for expenses of members of the Dublin Corporation for a lunch picnic in the course of an inspection of the reservoir at the Vartry Waterworks.[236] A ratepayer wished to challenge a decision of an auditor to allow lunch expenses for the inspection visit, and the legal point at issue was whether the ratepayer had the standing (locus standi) to do so, but before dealing with that the judge described the outing, and what was charged – champagne, hock, Margaux, whiskey, sherry, cigars, beer, stout, 'minerals in syphons', dessert, sandwiches and 'an allowance for four glasses broken – a very small number under the circumstances'. This was, he said,

> a sumptuous repast for the members of the Corporation on the Wicklow hills. It is certainly not for the benefit of the rate paying citizens of Dublin. I do not say that the members of the Corporation are not to lunch. But I do say that they are not to do so at the expense of the citizens of Dublin. They cannot banquet at their expense in the Mansion House and, in my opinion, they cannot lunch at their expense in Wicklow. I find no legal sanction for lunch of even a moderate character on such an occasion, but certainly the particular luncheon was infected in every part of it with excess.

In *Barrett v Irvine*,[237] a horse dealer sued for the price of a horse sold to a minor on foot of a representation by him that his mother would pay for it. The divisional court set aside the initial jury decision against the mother and held that no agency relationship binding her had been established. O'Brien referred to the family as a fond mother and a spoilt boy, said that the dealer had 'traded *with* him, but *on* her affection for him' and described a pack kept by the son styled as the 'Roscarberry foxhounds … composed of all sorts and conditions of hunting dogs … kept in some out-offices … [as] not quite up to Leicestershire standard'. (Decades earlier he had kept at his brother's house in Clare 'a scratch pack of harriers, the keep of which cost me nothing – they were boarded out among the tenantry'.)[238] He

234 *Reminiscences*, p. 135 and chapter 22 (pp 113–33).
235 W.N. Osborough, 'Peter O'Brien' in A.W.B. Simpson (ed.), *Biographical dictionary of the common law* (London, 1984), p. 391.
236 *R (Bridgeman) v Drury*, [1894] 2 IR 489.
237 [1907] 2 IR 462.
238 *Reminiscences*, p. 15.

concluded that 'no twelve men who fairly considered the evidence could reasonably find a verdict for the plaintiff. This is indeed a curious case, and if Miss Somerville confers further lustre on literature and Roscarberry by bringing out another edition of her charming book perhaps that most interesting writer may be induced to add a new chapter'.

He presided over the trial by jury at Cork of *Wallis v Russell*, as to the application of the implied warranties of fitness for purpose under the Sale of Goods Act 1893 to the (as it transpired, lack of) freshness of two crabs. His scepticism, indeed sarcasm, at the evidence given by the youthful buyer was recorded for posterity by Maurice Healy.[239] The seller's motion to set aside the verdict in favour of the buyer, who (with her grandmother) had become seriously unwell after eating the crabs, was dismissed by a divisional court and also in the Court of Appeal, where FitzGibbon LJ brought out the broader question raised by the case, remarking that the question, 'always a hard one, [was] which of two innocent parties is legally responsible for consequences that neither could avoid … it must be taken that no exercise of skill or judgment by the seller, and no examination by the buyer, could have detected the defect or avoided the consequences. Which party does the law make liable under these circumstances?'[240]

In *FitzGerald v Ryan*,[241] a will construction suit, he sought imaginatively to recreate the state of mind of the testator, a farmer in Co. Limerick. 'Before I advert to the language of the will I shall endeavour to find an armchair in his house that I may sit upon it, and look around upon the conditions of his family and the habits of the social life of his class. I find that this small farmer had no armchair; but the rude seat upon which he sat will suffice. It will enable me to take the necessary survey'. A century later Keane J was to refer to the 'armchair principle'.[242] Contrary to the impression that might be derived from what O'Brien said, interpretation of a will begins with looking first to its language before considering, if any ambiguity or contradiction exists, whether the circumstances in which it was made may assist in clarifying this.[243] Some two decades previously James LJ had said of the possible admission of extrinsic evidence as to a testator's intentions, that 'you may place yourself so as to speak in the testator's armchair and consider the circumstances by which he was surrounded when he made his will to assist you in arriving at his intentions'.[244]

In 1905 O'Brien heard a case about whether displaying the name 'Mac Giolla Bhrighde' in Irish script on a vehicle was in compliance with a requirement that the name of the owner be shown on it in legible characters. A divisional court, on a case stated by magistrates in Co. Donegal, upheld a conviction, and (although

239 Healy, *OldMC*, pp 209–11.
240 [1902] 2 IR 585, at 608–9.
241 [1899] 2 IR 637.
242 *Re Collins, Crowley v Bank of Ireland*, [1998] 2 IR 596, [1998] 2 ILRM 465.
243 See now Succession Act 1965, s90, and Wills and Administration Proceedings (Northern Ireland) Order 1994, article 25.
244 *Boyes v Cook*, 14 Ch D 53 (1880).

'when a boy, [he] had picked up a little Irish from the peasants in Clare')[245] O'Brien remarked that he would not utter the name (otherwise McBride) in the Irish language 'lest my faulty pronunciation might shock the many Irish scholars who take an interest in the case'.[246]

His courtroom sometimes provided excitement over and above the conventional dramas of litigation. In 1891 in Armagh he suspended assize sittings owing to the unsanitary state of the court; 'his Lordship remarked that he and several members of the Bar were ill and that one man had been stricken with typhoid fever. When he accepted the position of chief justice of Ireland it was not on condition that he would have to administer justice in a breeze of sewer gas'.[247] His complaints the following year about the unsanitary condition of the Green Street courthouse – 'today it was impossible to move or breathe in the court. The place was pervaded by a mephitic atmosphere'[248] – led to significant repairs and refurbishment being carried out there.[249] An (undated) incident was recorded at Tullamore, when 'an announcement of not guilty in a murder case was followed by loud cheers. The crier shouted "silence" … and the chief justice (O'Brien) walked quickly to one side of the bench and personally arrested one of those who had joined in the shouting and had him detained in custody'.[250] In Belfast in 1898 a man in the dock who had been convicted of burglary threw a stone 'about the size of a hen's egg' at O'Brien, but at his request received no further punishment or sentence when later charged in another court with that assault.[251] He took a more serious view of the incident in hindsight some fifteen years later in his memoir, saying that 'I once had a narrow escape from death while in the discharge of my duties as a judge …'.[252]

He spoke in favour of votes for women at a meeting of the Conservative and Unionist Women's Franchise Association in Dublin in 1910,[253] at a time when this was a matter of controversy. In 1898 he had said at the Wicklow assizes that he was very much in favour of a proposal before Parliament that would allow accused persons to give evidence on their own behalf; 'he expressed himself in favour of prisoners being cross-examined, and said no judge worth his salt would permit irrelevant cross-examination'.[254] It has always been open to judges to make remarks from the Bench on wider social aspects of legal issues coming before them, and this was particularly so in the days (before the establishment of county councils by legislation in 1898) when they would address the grand jury of each county at the

245 *Reminiscences*, p. 136.
246 McBride, appellant; McGovern, respondent, [1906] 2 IR 181, at 184.
247 *ILT&SJ*, vol. 25, p. 393 (11 July 1891).
248 *ILT&SJ*, vol. 26, p. 112 (20 February 1892).
249 *ILT&SJ*, vol. 28, p. 531 (27 October 1894).
250 Andrew Dunlop, *Fifty years of Irish journalism* (Dublin, 1911), p. 161.
251 *ILT&SJ*, vol. 32, p. 565 (17 December 1898) and vol. 33, p. 141 (1 April 1899).
252 *Reminiscences*, p. 101.
253 *ILT&SJ*, vol. 44, pp 46–8 (19 February 1910); *Reminiscences*, pp 178–90.
254 *ILT&SJ*, vol. 32, p. 365 (13 August 1898).

assizes. Some observations that he made from the bench in Longford in 1903 on the operations of the Land Commission, in implementing the policy of the Land Acts, went rather further than might have been anticipated. He thought that the Commission

> from its intrinsic character, is an elaborate machinery for the injury of the soil and for the demoralisation of the people of Ireland … It had become only too common that prior to the hearing of cases the land was allowed to run down by neglect and improper cultivation, while also claims to the property of landlords, such as that made in the present case, were of not infrequent occurrence. It was with the greatest regret that his Lordship observed the spread of this demoralisation among the peasantry, whom he had known all his life and whose many good qualities he appreciated.[255]

His interest in country pursuits and 'in manly sports of all kinds',[256] including cricket,[257] racing[258] and hunting,[259] and his active promotion of a regatta in Cork in 1902, gave rise to observations such as that the chief justice 'is never seen to greater advantage than in the simple role of a country gentleman'.[260] That seeming simplicity co-existed with a great persistence in seeking honours from the government, resulting in the conferring of a baronetcy (in 1891) and a peerage (in 1900). He neither spoke nor voted in the House of Lords, and having been 'asked by more than one to vote with the Die Hards' in the impassioned debate in the summer of 1911 on the Parliament Bill, limiting the veto powers of the house (see p. 469), declined to do so.[261]

His household was well appointed, with a number of domestic servants.[262] He resided with his family, at different times, at 41 Merrion Square, at Oldtown, Co. Kildare ('where during the recent frost [he] threw open the fine pond at the back of his residence to all skaters who presented themselves'),[263] at Castletown, Celbridge, Co. Kildare (where he gave a ball in honour of the lord lieutenant, and entertained a large party during Punchestown week),[264] at Newlands House, Clondalkin, Co. Dublin and finally at Airfield, a substantial villa on the Bray Road in Donnybrook (across the road from the Montrose estate, now the headquarters of RTÉ). He took a house in Chelsea for the summer social season,[265] and one year

255 *Edgeworth v Maguire*, *ILT&SJ*, vol. 37, p. 103 (7 March 1903).
256 *Irish Times*, 8 September 1914.
257 *ILT&SJ*, vol. 31, p. 393 (21 August 1897).
258 *Reminiscences*, pp 17–18.
259 *Reminiscences*, pp 15–17, 97–99, 159; *ILT&SJ*, vol. 31, p. 521 (6 November 1897) (hosting a hunt meet at Castletown), vol. 32, p. 110 (5 March 1898) (a heavy fall).
260 *ILT&SJ*, vol. 31, p. 521 (6 November 1897).
261 O'Brien to Balfour, 15 November 1911 (Balfour Papers, Add. MS 49814.338).
262 The 1901 census return for the household listed nine domestic servants.
263 *ILT&SJ*, vol. 29, p. 60 (2 February 1895).
264 *ILT&SJ*, vol. 31, p. 87 (20 February 1897) and p. 199 (1 May 1897).
265 *ILT&SJ*, vol. 34, p. 201 (12 May 1900).

when he and his family were being driven by their chauffeur in London his motor car, brought over from Ireland for their holiday, was involved in a minor traffic collision at Hyde Park Corner.[266] He visited spa resorts, including Llandrindod Wells and Tunbridge Wells,[267] and in 1911 travelled with his family to Harrogate, in Yorkshire, 'where they intend to stay for several weeks. In former years Lord O'Brien has been a regular visitor at Carlsbad [in Bohemia],[268] but he is now trying an English cure'.[269]

O'Brien was increasingly troubled by ill health and was absent from court for prolonged periods in 1912 and 1913. In February 1912 he ceased for a time to sit at the Green Street courthouse, suffering from a chill, gout and rheumatism.[270] In November and December that year he could not sit, and after resuming work in January he stepped back in February and went abroad, including a visit to Bath, for a while. Regular reports in the legal press referred to the state of his health and his absence,[271] occasionally in rather unsympathetic terms – 'the lord chief justice is still out of Ireland on what was described, when it commenced fourteen weeks ago, as a short holiday'.[272] He tendered his resignation in the middle of November 1913. His elder daughter Georgina wrote that his resignation took place 'shortly after[wards]' his judgment in *Ussher v Ussher*,[273] although in fact some 18 months had passed. In retirement she acted as his secretary ('amanuensis') in the preparation of a memoir, until it became clear that 'speaking of his early days saddened him'.[274] He died in September 1914 at his home in Donnybrook, leaving an estate of £29,230. The memoir, edited and completed by his daughter, was published a couple of years later. His widow, Lady O'Brien, died in London, in Ovington Gardens, Knightsbridge, in 1928.[275]

Edward Falconer Litton

Judicial Commissioner of the Irish Land Commission 1890

Edward Falconer Litton (1828–90) was a judge for less than a year, although for much of the previous decade his work had involved determining issues of a legal nature. He was a nephew (not, as sometimes stated, a son) of Edward Litton QC

266 *ILT&SJ*, vol. 42, p. 215 (5 September 1908).
267 *Irish Times*, 20 October 1909.
268 *Law Times*, vol. 123, p. 342 (10 August 1907).
269 *ILT&SJ*, vol. 45, p. 216 (2 September 1911).
270 *Law Times*, vol. 132, p. 377 (17 February 1912).
271 *ILT&SJ*, vol. 48, p. 56 (15 February 1913), pp 170 and 172 (21 June 1913) and p. 194 (12 July 1913); *Law Times*, vol. 134, p. 90 (23 November 1912), p. 116 (30 November 1912), p. 165 (14 December 1912), p. 258 (11 January 1913), p. 369 (8 February 1913), p. 550 (5 April 1913); vol. 135, p. 124 (31 May 1913), p. 146 (7 June 1913), p. 191 (21 June 1913), p. 271 (12 July 1913), p. 412 (23 August 1913); vol. 136, p. 18 (1 November 1913).
272 *Law Times*, vol. 135, p. 146 (7 June 1913).
273 *Reminiscences*, p. 135.
274 *Reminiscences*, introduction, p. v.
275 *ILT&SJ*, vol. 62, p. 304 (15 December 1928).

(1789–1870), who was the Conservative member of Parliament for Coleraine between 1837 and 1843, when he was appointed a master in Chancery, and who was later mooted as a potential master of the rolls.[276] A portrait of the elder Litton, by Stephen Catterson Smith the elder, was commissioned for the King's Inns by the benchers following his death.[277]

He was called to the Bar in 1849, joined the Munster circuit, and took silk in 1874.[278] He stood as a Liberal for Co. Tyrone in the 1880 general election and was elected as one of the county's two MPs. He sat for just over a year, and ceased to be an MP upon appointment as a member of the Land Commission in 1881.

The Act which established it, the Land Law (Ireland) Act 1881,[279] was intended to provide for tenants what were known as the 'three Fs' – fair rent, fixity of tenure and free sale of tenancy.[280] In Litton's only significant parliamentary contribution, he had put forward a private member's bill in June 1880 to introduce such reforms, saying that they ought to be the principal feature of any future legislation. His Fixity of Tenure (Ireland) Bill was opposed by the government and by Parnell, who said that some time should be allowed for official government proposals to be developed, and the vote for a second reading in the House of Commons was lost by 45 votes to 187.[281]

Litton was named as one of the first three members of the Land Commission in Section 41 of the 1881 Act. Sir William Findlater MP described Litton as having an excellent temper and great patience and judgment, and William Shaw MP, then the chairman of the Munster Bank, spoke of him as a considerable landowner, who lived on the most pleasant terms with his tenantry.[282] These remarks were intended to establish that Litton would be detached and fair minded in the discharge of his functions, not simply an advocate of tenant interests. An initial period of office of seven years was subsequently extended. Litton was referred to by Gladstone as a 'lay commissioner, who is a gentleman of legal education, but not a legal commissioner in the sense that Mr Justice O'Hagan is'.[283]

Litton was a natural choice to succeed O'Hagan, when he resigned at the end of 1889, and his familiarity with the business of the Commission meant that 'matters go ahead with a speed that is unknown in the other courts, and without which the task of deciding the multitudinous applications, re-hearings and appeals would be all but impossible'.[284]

276 *Law Times*, vol. 41, p. 744 (18 August 1866) and vol. 42, p. 187 (5 January 1867).
277 Wanda Ryan-Smolin, *King's Inns portraits* (Dublin, 1992), p. 43.
278 *ILT&SJ*, vol. 15, p. 520 (8 October 1881) and vol. 24, p. 625 (6 December 1890).
279 44&45 Vict., c.49.
280 F.S.L. Lyons, *Charles Stewart Parnell* (London, 1977), p. 157.
281 HC Deb, 3rd series, vol. 253, cols. 1181–1214 (30 June 1880).
282 HC Deb, 3rd series, vol. 263, cols. 1406 (Findlater) and 1413 (Shaw) (20 July 1881).
283 HC Deb, 3rd series, vol. 271, col. 1617 (6 July 1882).
284 Rhadamanthus, *Our judges* (Dublin, 1890), p. 120.

Litton was 'a gentleman of an amiable disposition and polished manners'.[285] He married four times, and had thirteen children. He lived at 67 Merrion Square, and died in November 1890 at Ardvilling, Cloyne, Co. Cork, an estate that he had inherited from an uncle (in whose memory a fountain was provided in the village).

A similarity of names creates scope for confusion between him and Caesar Litton Falkiner (1863–1908), a son of Sir Frederick Falkiner, who was appointed the recorder of Dublin in 1876.[286] Falkiner was a scholar, a member of the Royal Irish Academy, who was called to the Bar in 1887, and appointed as an assistant legal land commissioner in 1897. He was active in the Irish Unionist Alliance, and stood unsuccessfully as the Unionist candidate in South Armagh in the general election of 1892. He died as a result of an accident while climbing in the Alps, near Chamonix, in 1908.[287]

Edmund Bewley

Judicial Commissioner of the Irish Land Commission 1890–8

The career of Edmund Bewley (1837–1908) at the Bar and as a judge for just over seven years was accompanied to an unusual degree by a scholarly disposition. He was the only son of a doctor in Moate, Co. Westmeath. At Trinity College Dublin he was a gold medallist in Experimental and Natural Science (physics), and held the Regius professorship of Feudal and English Law in the university between 1884 and 1890.[288] He was called to the Bar in 1862, and in his early years, as was common, he prepared some law reports. More substantively, he prepared detailed annotated editions of the Chancery (Ireland) Act 1867 (with Alexander Richie BL)[289] and the Common Law Procedure Acts (with John Naish BL, subsequently to be lord chancellor),[290] and a guide to legal costs.[291] The preface to the first edition, by L.S. Eiffe, of the handbook on the Judicature Act 1877 which later became known by the name of a subsequent editor, J.O. Wylie, acknowledged that in its preparation 'great assistance has been derived from Bewley and Naish's *Common Law Procedure Acts, Ireland*.'

He developed a good practice both in Chancery and common law work, and in 1880 was junior counsel to Francis Macdonogh QC when he was (unsuccessfully) sued by a frustrated client for whom he had not attended in court as agreed.[292] The

285 *Irish Times*, 29 November 1890.
286 *ILT&SJ*, vol. 10, p. 415 (15 July 1876).
287 *ILT&SJ*, vol. 42, p. 197 (15 August 1908); *Irish Times*, 7 and 11 August 1908.
288 *ILT&SJ*, vol. 42, p. 161 (4 July 1908).
289 *The Chancery (Ireland) Act 1867 and general orders and regulations thereunder, copiously annotated, with fees, schedules and forms and precedents* (Dublin, 1867).
290 *The Common Law Procedure Acts 1853, 1856 and 1870, with an appendix containing the general orders of the supreme courts of common law and a collection of statutes relating to the law of evidence and to procedure and general matters* (Dublin, 1871).
291 *The law and practice of taxation of costs in common law business* (Dublin, 1867).
292 *Robertson v Macdonogh*, *Irish Times*, 12 November 1880 and 14 ILTR 108 (1880); *ILT&SJ*, vol. 16, p. 178 (22 April 1882); John Adye Curran, *Reminiscences* (London, 1915), pp 105 and 112–13.

Queen's Bench division confirmed the principle that a barrister's services were not contractual in nature, and that, just as a barrister could not sue for fees due, a client could not sue for counsel's failure to appear or for alleged negligence. In 1881 Bewley was appointed junior Crown prosecutor for Co. Kildare.[293] He was called to the Inner Bar in 1882 and was elected a bencher of King's Inns four years later. It was said of him that 'as an advocate he was able and earnest [and] serenely at home in dry-as-dust legal arguments'.[294] In December 1889 Dodgson Hamilton Madden, the attorney general (and a contemporary in College), described him to Balfour as very well suited to be nominated for the position of Judicial Commissioner of the Land Commission, which had the status of a judge of the High Court. He wrote that Bewley was an excellent lawyer, with relevant experience in that court, that he was a man of the highest character, with probably the best business at the Bar and would command general confidence, and that he was a liberal unionist.[295]

The person then appointed, Edward Falconer Litton, died suddenly within twelve months. Balfour, the chief secretary, recommended Bewley for the fresh vacancy, telling the lord lieutenant: 'I think there should be no delay in appointing the Judicial Land Commissioner. I would strongly advise his Excellency to offer it at once to Bewley. He is a Liberal Unionist and a Protestant, which is necessary in view of the number of Roman Catholics already on the Commission. I understand that there is no man of equal position at the Bar of suitable age. If we delay there will no doubt be pressure from other quarters'.[296] Bewley's appointment was announced a few days later.[297]

The operations of the Land Commission in its dealings with landowners and tenants for the acquisition of estates gave rise to a large volume of legal business and to complex questions of interpretation of the relevant statutes, some of which were hastily or loosely drafted and required amendment from time to time. Its decisions also involved co-operation with the jurisdiction of the 'Land Judge', a member of the Chancery division of the High Court to whom all functions of the Landed Estates Court had been transferred under the Judicature Act 1877, and to which further functions had been assigned under the subsequent Land Acts. There was some contention between the judge and the Commission as to their respective functions and duties, particularly after the appointment of John Ross to be Land Judge in March 1896. Ross, although initially having little background knowledge of land law, was soon critical of some existing practices of the Commission,[298] and made further criticisms of the Commission about eight months later, arising from

293 *ILT&SJ*, vol. 15, p. 618 (3 December 1881).
294 *Irish Times*, 29 June 1908.
295 Madden to Arthur Balfour, 7 December 1889 (Balfour Papers, Add. MS 49815.105).
296 Balfour to the lord chancellor (copy of telegram to the lord lieutenant), 11 December 1890 (Ashbourne Papers, B.9/15).
297 *ILT&SJ*, vol. 24, p. 633 (13 December 1890).
298 *Young v Guinness* (*ILT&SJ*, vol. 30, p. 503 (14 November 1896)).

it declining to comply with a request from him for court valuers to be present at the hearing of some appeals.[299]

In December 1897 Bewley, while defending a settled practice of the Land Commission in considering appeals on the fixing of a fair rent, said that 'in deference to the opinions of the judges of the Queen's Bench division who took part in the hearing of the recent case of *The Queen (Gosford) v The Land Commission*[300] it is right that the Land Commission should take such steps as will make it impossible to contend in the future that anything in the nature of a question of law is involved in the report of the Court valuers'.[301]

All this was a prelude to what, some days later, was described as 'little short of a judicial duel'.[302] On 20 December, in the course of a judgment in the case of Harkness' Estate (No. 2), Ross J expressed himself very bluntly, saying that in its interpretation of section 40 of the Land Law (Ireland) Act 1896[303] the Commission was frustrating the clear meaning and intent of the section and was 'in open defiance of the law'.[304] The point at issue was whether the Commission had discretion as to the amount of government stock (bonds) that it would advance for the purchase of an estate or whether (as Ross maintained) the Land Judge's determination of this was conclusive. Bewley gave his judgment in the case in the court of the Land Commission, vigorously defending the Commission's view, in the first week of January 1898,[305] and vacated his office the following day. The issue was brought before the Court of Appeal (all seven of whose members sat to hear the appeal) which by a majority (consisting of Ashbourne LC, O'Brien LCJ, Palles CB and Walker LJ, with Porter MR, FitzGibbon LJ and Holmes LJ dissenting) upheld Bewley's interpretation, the judgments containing some strong expressions of opinion.[306]

Bewley had shortly before Christmas tendered his resignation, to take effect in the New Year, to the lord lieutenant, who told the prime minster that 'we have known for some time that his deafness would compel him to resign'.[307] Salisbury accepted the lord lieutenant's recommendation, made in conjunction with Ashbourne, that he would receive the honour of a knighthood,[308] which was announced on his stepping down. Bewley's health was thus the ground for his resignation, not any unwillingness to continue to perform his functions in what had become an argumentative and rather unseemly atmosphere. 'It has been

299 *ILT&SJ*, vol. 31, p. 338 (24 July 1897).
300 32 ILTR 26 (1898).
301 *ILT&SJ*, vol. 31, p. 575 (11 December 1897).
302 *Law Times*, vol. 104, p. 384 (26 February 1898). See also vol. 104, p. 313 (5 February 1898).
303 59&60 Vict., c.47. Section 40 was subsequently amended in 1899 (62&63 Vict., c.18, s1) and 1903 (3 Edw. VII, c.37, s58) to ameliorate some of the difficulties to which Ross J had adverted.
304 31 ILTR 176 (1897).
305 32 ILTR 16 (1898); *Irish Times*, 5 and 6 January 1898.
306 [1898] 2 IR 391; 32 ILTR 58 (1898).
307 Cadogan to Salisbury, 22 December 1897 (Salisbury Papers).
308 Ashbourne to Cadogan, 24 December 1897 (Cadogan Papers (Parliamentary Archives), CAD/1273).

obvious for some time past that his Lordship's defect of hearing was not of a temporary character … and it is entirely on account of this increasing physical impediment that, under the advice of the most eminent aurists of the day, his Lordship has placed his resignation in the hands of the lord chancellor'.[309] He was promptly replaced, on 10 January, by R.E. Meredith.[310]

Bewley now, as he acknowledged, with more spare time turned to genealogical research, initially the history of his own family. In 1902 he published *The Bewleys of Cumberland and their Irish and other descendants, with full pedigrees of the family*. He noted that the family name was the Anglicised form of the French name Beaulieu, which in turn had its origins in the Latin bellus locus – a 'fair place', and that the first Irish members had emigrated from Cumberland at the end of the seventeenth century. These were members of the Society of Friends, although Bewley himself was a member of the Church of Ireland, his grandfather having asked in 1801 that he might no longer be considered as a member of the Quaker Society.[311] He published a number of papers on the histories and pedigrees of other families in the *Journal of the Royal Society of Antiquaries of Ireland*, the *Genealogist*, and in the journals of some local history and archaeological societies. He was a committee member of the Parish Register Society of Ireland.[312] The auction notice for the sale of his library after his death referred to a 'small but choice collection of works upon heraldry and genealogy',[313] and some notes and pedigree research papers which he prepared are held in the Genealogical Office in the National Library.

Bewley lived at 40 Fitzwilliam Place. For the visit of Queen Victoria in April 1900, the entrance procession into the city for which passed the front door, the family home had been decorated, like many in the neighbourhood. 'One of the most brilliantly decorated houses in Fitzwilliam Place is that of Sir Edmund Bewley. Over the principal entrance are the Royal arms, flanked with the letter VR and underneath, in a sort of scroll work, are the words "Royal Dublin Fusiliers". Flags and trophies add to the beauty of the design, which we understand was prepared by Lady Bewley'.[314] He and his wife had four children, two sons and two daughters.

In April 1908 he advertised the house as being available 'in perfect order' for lease ('terms very moderate') or sale.[315] He died the following month at Gowran Castle, Co. Kilkenny, which was described as his residence.

309 *ILT&SJ*, vol. 32, p. 15 (8 January 1898).
310 *ILT&SJ*, vol.32, p. 31 (15 January 1898).
311 Edmund Bewley, *The Bewleys of Cumberland and their Irish and other descendants, with full pedigrees of the family* (Dublin, 1902), pp 1, 113, 123.
312 *Irish Times*, 4 January 1907.
313 *Irish Times*, 14 November 1908.
314 *Irish Times*, 2 April 1900.
315 *Irish Times*, 7 April 1908.

Dodgson Hamilton Madden

Justice of the High Court 1892–1919

Dodgson Hamilton Madden (1840–1928) was the only son of the Revd Hugh Hamilton Madden of Templemore, Co. Tipperary, and a member of the well-known Madden family of Hilton Park, Clones, Co. Monaghan. His grandfather and great-grandfather were also ministers, and he was an active lay member of the Church of Ireland, being a member of the General Synod and chancellor successively of the United Dioceses of Ossory, Ferns and Leighlin and the United Dioceses of Cashel, Emly, Waterford and Lismore.[316]

He was educated at Trinity College, and was called to the Bar in 1864, joining the Leinster circuit, although he 'had not been long in practice when he found it more remunerative to remain constantly at the Four Courts, and so gradually ceased to follow the assize'.[317] An early boost to his career was his appointment as a supernumerary Crown prosecutor for Co. Wexford, among a flurry of appointments made as the Conservative party left office in December 1868.[318] He developed an expertise in property law, and a few years after his call to the Bar wrote a book on the registration of deeds[319] and edited one on the Landed Estates Court,[320] a second edition of which was described in 1879 as being 'at once exhaustive and succinct'.[321] In giving evidence to a parliamentary committee in 1878 he refuted some uninformed and disparaging comments from English solicitors as to the workings of the Registry of Deeds.[322] In 1901 a second edition of his book on the registration of deeds was published,[323] and this was regarded for many years as the leading authority on the subject. He became a QC in 1880. He was later described by Gerald FitzGibbon as 'a thoroughly sound Equity lawyer, with a good Chancery practice, a very gentlemanly fellow'.[324]

In July 1887 he was elected a member of Parliament for Dublin University at a bye-election. In February a provisional committee had been formed to support his candidacy for one of the University seats 'at the next vacancy',[325] a coy reference to the expected retirement of one of the sitting members, Hugh Holmes QC, MP. A promotion of Holmes to be a judge was anticipated after a vacancy had arisen early in 1887 in what was then the Common Pleas division of the High

316 *Irish Times*, 8 February 1887; *Irish Ecclesiastical Gazette*, 28 January 1898.
317 *ILT&SJ*, vol. 34, p. 33 (20 January 1900).
318 *ILT&SJ*, vol. 2, p. 673 (5 December 1868).
319 *Registration of deeds and judgment mortgages* (Dublin, 1868).
320 *The Landed Estates Court Act – rules, forms and directions, with notes, schedule of fees and a collection of forms and precedents* (Dublin, 1870).
321 *ILT&SJ*, vol. 14, p. 20 (10 January 1880). A third edition was published in 1889, prepared with the assistance of William M. Jellett BL.
322 *ILT&SJ*, vol. 15, p. 570 (5 November 1881); *Report of the select committee on land titles and transfers* (P.P. 1878 (291) xv.467).
323 *A practical treatise on the registration of deeds, conveyances and judgment mortgages* (Dublin, 1901).
324 FitzGibbon to Lord Randolph Churchill, 20 January 1887 (LRC Papers, MS Add. 9248.2357).
325 *Irish Times*, 12 February 1887.

Court, but this did not take place for a number of months since his continued presence in parliament, as attorney general, was required in connection with criminal law and land legislation. At the end of June, Holmes was appointed, at which point formal nominations for the bye-election could be made. Madden was encouraged to stand in the election by Lord Ashbourne, the lord chancellor, and was also spoken to by J.T. Ball, the former lord chancellor. Ashbourne advised Balfour that Madden would be a stronger candidate than Peter O'Brien, bearing in mind that the latter's Catholicism would undoubtedly alienate some of the electorate.[326] Madden encountered some early difficulty as being considered a Liberal Unionist,[327] whereas his opponent, R.C. Parsons, a brother of the earl of Rosse, was an unequivocal Conservative. Madden sought to quell any doubts about his full support for the government of Lord Salisbury by declaring at the opening of his campaign that 'I have always been a firm supporter of the Conservative party'.[328] The government's backing for Madden was underlined at the end of June by his appointment, on Ashbourne's advice, to the honorific position of third serjeant,[329] where the reshuffle of legal office holders had given rise to a vacancy. He won the election easily, receiving 1,376 votes to 712.

He was disappointed at not being made solicitor general, an office rendered vacant by the promotion of John G. Gibson to replace Holmes, but was appointed to it in the New Year 1888, and then to be attorney general at the end of 1889, in each case succeeding Peter O'Brien QC. Two judicial vacancies arose shortly after the latter appointment, one on the retirement in January 1890 of John O'Hagan as judicial commissioner of the Land Commission and the other on the death of Baron Dowse of the Exchequer division of the High Court in March. Madden's expertise in property and registration law was particularly valuable to the government at this time in connection with the developing policy of encouraging and facilitating transfer of land ownership to tenant farmers. In 1889 he had introduced bills in the House of Commons on the registration of assurances (to reform the Registry of Deeds) and on registration of title (to establish the Land Registry), and although both bills were withdrawn at the end of the parliamentary session[330] the latter was enacted in 1891.[331] The Land Registry system made it possible to create records of what would be the great numbers of new freehold titles of tenants' holdings without prohibitive cost and complexity.

In 1890 the government prevailed on Madden to remain in office as attorney general and not to take up either the Land Commission place or that which was vacant through the death of Dowse. The *Irish Times* remarked that this was no time

326 Ashbourne to Balfour, 17 June 1887 (Balfour Papers, Add. MS 49815.10).
327 Ashbourne to Balfour, 17, 19 and 22 June 1887 (Balfour Papers, Add. MS 49815.10, .12 and .14)
328 *Irish Times*, 1 July 1887.
329 Ashbourne to Balfour, 27 June 1887 (Balfour Papers, Add. MS 49815.16).
330 HC Deb, 3rd Series, vol. 339, col.1740 (19 August 1889).
331 Local Registration of Title (Ireland) Act 1891 (54&55 Vict., c.66).

for Madden's hand to be withdrawn from the plough, and noted that his forbearance from exercising the attorney general's prerogative to take up such a vacancy would create a strong sense of obligation to him for future judicial advancement.[332] A perception existed however that Madden would be made a judge, and in May two candidates announced their interest in standing at the next University election. Col. J.C.J. Lowry, a Co. Tyrone landowner, said that a committee of supporters was being formed 'in view of the probability of a vacancy occurring in the Parliamentary representation of Dublin University at no distant date'.[333] Edward Carson QC more discreetly adopted the expression that had been used by Madden himself three years previously, and said that his committee was being formed for 'the next vacancy'.[334]

The government was anxious to keep Madden in place as attorney general and in that context looked to ensure that, if he did not then take up the existing vacancy, a judicial place would be available to him in the future. An approach was made by Arthur Balfour, chief secretary for Ireland, to Hedges Eyre Chatterton, the vice-chancellor (and a former attorney general), to allow the government to determine when he would resign so that Madden could be appointed to succeed him at a time of its choosing. Balfour wrote that

> my object … is to keep Madden in the H. of Commons for as long as possible, and he is very familiar with all the controversies connected with the legislative projects of the government that concern Ireland. He has assisted at their preparation and his knowledge of the House of Commons is now very great, derived as it is from an experience the want of which no mere ability can supply.[335]

Chatterton declined to co-operate with this scheme (see pp 218–19), remarking cheerfully to Ashbourne that 'there was no hurry' in filling the vacancy, at least up to October that year.[336] The government then actually left open the vacancy in the High Court that had arisen on the death of Dowse, for a much longer period, making no appointment until June 1892, shortly before it went out of office at the general election held in July. At that time Mr Justice Murphy was transferred to the Exchequer division from the Queen's Bench, and Madden was appointed to take his place in the Queen's Bench.

Madden's professional work had initially been concerned primarily in property law, but his service as a law officer to the government for over four years gave him extensive experience in criminal law and related matters. He was highly regarded

332 *Irish Times*, 31 December 1889 and 17 March 1890.
333 *Irish Times*, 15 May 1890.
334 *Irish Times*, 19 May 1890.
335 Balfour to Chatterton, 23 May 1890 (Ashbourne Papers, B.9/11).
336 Ashbourne to Balfour, 29 May 1890 (Balfour Papers, Add. MS 49815.61).

for his work in those offices and his contributions to parliamentary debates, although 'he never posed as an orator'.[337]

Maurice Healy referred to Madden as 'a don that had strayed into the Queen's Bench division', and remarked that although he was good humoured and courteous his judicial reputation was not high.[338] *Boyers v Duke*[339] was a case heard by a divisional court in which he pointed out the distinction between a quotation and an offer to sell, in the context of the fundamental requirement for a valid contract that there should be an offer and an acceptance. The example that he gave indicated a scholarly cast of mind:

> It is a matter of common knowledge that quotations of prices are scattered broadcast among possible customers.[340] Business could not be carried on if each recipient of a priced catalogue offering a desirable article – say a rare book – at an attractive price were in a position to create a contract of sale by writing that he would buy at the price mentioned. The catalogue has probably reached many collectors. The order of only one can be honoured.

In *Powell v McGlynn and Bradlaw*,[341] a High Court jury, a divisional court and the Court of Appeal considered issues of liability for injury caused by a runaway pony and trap. Madden's judgment included a passage[342] in which he commented on what (if any) significance could be attached to an ejaculation 'Humph' that had been uttered by the owner of the pony in conversation shortly after the incident. He presided at the trial of four English suffragettes charged with conspiracy to set fire to the Theatre Royal in Dublin in 1912 prior to a public meeting to be addressed by Asquith, the prime minister. He reminded the jury that 'the question before them was one of the guilt or otherwise of the prisoners [some were acquitted], and not the admission of women to the franchise … but it seemed strange that any rational beings should imagine that their cause would be advanced and recommended to general adoption by a course of crime of this nature'.[343] He sentenced two of the women to five years' penal servitude.

Madden was a scholar of Shakespeare, and wrote two well received commentaries, one on Elizabethan sport in his plays[344] and one of biographical exploration.[345] In the preface to the earlier work (in which he 'brought to his work

337 *Irish Times*, 8 March 1928.
338 Healy, *OldMC*, pp 38–9.
339 [1905] 2 IR 617 (at 625).
340 Although not, as it happened, in this particular case, where a quotation containing an error had been sent to a particular customer.
341 [1902] 2 IR 154.
342 At 176–7.
343 *Irish Times*, 7 August 1912; *ILT&SJ*, vol. 46, p. 202 (10 August 1912).
344 *The diary of Master William Silence: a study of Shakespeare and Elizabethan sport* (London, 1897).
345 *Shakespeare and his fellows: an attempt to decipher the man and his nature* (London, 1916).

the enthusiasm of a sportsman and the judgment of a scholar')[346] he noted that he had been accustomed while at the Bar to spend a portion of each long vacation following the sport of hunting wild deer in the forest of Exmoor, Devon, and had become impressed with the Shakespearian character of such sport. He was elected a member of the Royal Irish Academy in 1901. His antiquarian library collection of works relating to field sports and to horses and horsemanship was sold at Sotheby's in London in 1925.[347]

He was a judge of the Queen's [King's] Bench division of the High Court for over 27 years, retiring in the spring of 1919.[348] This retirement was followed almost immediately by a move to England, the *Irish Times* stating that he and his wife had 'sold their home Nutley, Booterstown, and intend to live near London in future'.[349] The Nutley property was a considerable estate held under lease, comprising 48 acres 'together with the mansion house and offices, gardener's house, coachman's house and gate lodge',[350] where some years later the Elm Park golf club was established and substantial housing development took place. Their new home was at 'The Orchard', East Sheen, Surrey, where he died in March 1928, aged 87.[351]

Madden had a long connection with Trinity College, of which he was a scholar and, as mentioned, one of the members of parliament for the university, and also with Alexandra College. He was vice-chancellor of the university between 1895 and 1919, and had some influence in the appointment of Anthony Traill as provost in 1904.[352] His funeral service took place in the College Chapel.[353] A portrait of him in the robes of a vice-chancellor by A.A. Wolmark was exhibited at the Royal Hibernian Academy annual exhibition in 1908 and is in the College collection.[354]

Samuel Walker

Lord Chancellor of Ireland 1892–5 and 1905–11, Lord Justice of Appeal 1895–1905

Samuel Walker (1830[355]–1911) was a native of Gore Port (otherwise Goreport), Finnea, north Westmeath. He graduated from Trinity College and was called to the Bar in 1855, joining the Home circuit. He became a QC in 1872 and was elected a bencher of King's Inns in 1881. His progress at the Bar was steady and

346 *ILT&SJ*, vol. 41, p. 295 (23 November 1907).
347 *ILT&SJ*, vol. 59, p. 130 (30 May 1925).
348 *Law Times*, vol. 146, p. 463 (26 April 1919).
349 *Irish Times*, 6 May 1919.
350 Memorial of assignment dated 28 April 1919, Madden to Henry C. Backhouse (Registry of Deeds).
351 *ILT&SJ*, vol. 62, p. 60 (10 March 1928).
352 R.B. McDowell and D.A. Webb, *Trinity College Dublin 1592–1952: an academic history* (Cambridge, 1982), p. 358.
353 *Irish Times*, 10 March 1928.
354 Anne Crookshank and David Webb, *Paintings and sculptures in Trinity College Dublin* (Dublin, 1990), p. 93.
355 The memorial to be admitted as a student to King's Inns that was signed by him notes his date of birth as 19 June 1830, although his year of birth has been generally stated as 1832.

'not marked by any rapid acquisition of business'.[356] He developed a reputation for expertise and competence in Chancery matters. Although 'he was never regarded as a great orator'[357] he also had a practice in common law work, with jury trials, and was one of the defence counsel in the trial of Parnell and others in December 1880 and January 1881.

In politics he was a Liberal, and in the early 1880s strongly supported proposals for tenant law reforms. He was appointed solicitor general at the end of 1883, and soon afterwards, in January 1884, was elected unopposed to Parliament for the constituency of Co. Londonderry. The previous MP had been Andrew Marshall Porter QC, the attorney general, who had been promoted to be master of the rolls. Walker had no particular connection with the area, and there was some local controversy over his selection as a candidate.[358] Since the attorney general, John Naish QC, was not an MP Walker was necessarily fairly heavily engaged on government business in the House of Commons, responding to questions on legal and criminal matters. He also participated more generally in debates, since for some time in 1884 the chief secretary for Ireland, G.O. Trevelyan, was affected by exhaustion and ill-health. His official work included advising on draft landlord and tenant legislation, the substance of which, with some variations, was adopted by the Conservative government in the summer of 1885 and became law, being popularly known as the Ashbourne Act.[359] In May 1885 Walker succeeded Naish as attorney general but held office for only a few weeks, since the government resigned at the end of June.

The political situation was fluid towards the end of 1885, when a general election with a greatly expanded electorate was due to be held, and there was talk of the possibility, however unlikely it may have seemed (and which unlikelihood was soon confirmed by events), of a liaison between the Irish Parliamentary Party and the Conservatives. This is brought out by a speech that Walker made on the opening in Belfast of the Ulster Reform Club, saying that 'the Liberals of Ireland will not permit the Union to be tampered with, and any attempt in that direction, no matter by whom, will not be tolerated'.[360] In the election, notwithstanding such sentiments, he was defeated by a Conservative in what was now a redrawn constituency of North Londonderry. He told Lord Spencer, the retiring lord lieutenant, that in his opinion the sole cause of his defeat had been the combination of Orangemen and Parnellites, each having issued a proclamation urging followers to vote against him as the representative of the late government, and remarked that it had been amusing to see priests and parsons working against him together.[361]

356 *ILT&SJ*, vol. 35, p. 37 (19 January 1901).
357 *Irish Times*, 14 August 1911.
358 *Irish Times*, 24 December 1883.
359 Purchase of Land (Ireland) Act 1885 (48&49 Vict., c.73); HC Deb, 3rd series, vol. 300, col. 1072 (4 August 1885).
360 *The Ulster Liberal Unionist Association: a sketch of its history, 1885–1914* (Belfast, 1914), p. 12.
361 Walker to Spencer, 3 December 1885 (Althorp Papers, Add. MS.76988).

A second term of office as attorney general, in the government that Gladstone formed after that election, lasted about six months. Walker did not stand in the 1886 general election resulting from the rejection of the first Home Rule Bill, but stood again and was defeated in the 1892 election, this time in South Londonderry by a Liberal Unionist. When Gladstone then became prime minister for the fourth and last time he appointed Walker as lord chancellor, an office that he held for three years, until the Liberals lost the 1895 general election. He then served (without any remuneration in addition to his annual lord chancellor's pension) as an additional member of the Court of Appeal as was contemplated (if he was so willing to act) by the 1877 Judicature Act, with the title of lord justice of appeal.[362] Initially any such additional judges were not eligible, in the same way as the other appeal court judges were, to serve as assize judges but this restriction was removed in 1897, and thereafter he went on circuit.[363] He was re-appointed as lord chancellor in December 1905 when the Liberals returned to power, receiving the honour of a baronetcy in 1906,[364] and served until his death in August 1911.

Cases coming before the Court of Appeal in which he delivered judgments included *Agnew v Belfast Banking Co.*,[365] in which it was held that a gift made in contemplation of death by suicide would not constitute a valid *donatio mortis causem* (a gift conditional upon and taking effect upon the death of the donor), *Dawson v McClelland (No. 2)*,[366] in which the principle of contemptuous damages (of, say, a farthing, ¼*d.*) was reviewed, and the *Irish Society v Fleming and others*,[367] relating to the law as to the use of drift nets for the capture of salmon in tidal waters.

His family had a military tradition. His father was an army officer and his elder brother Mark (1827–1902) was awarded the Victoria Cross for heroism at the battle of Inkerman in the Crimean War and ended his career as a general. Two of Walker's three sons entered the armed services, one in the Royal Navy (who subsequently served as his father's train-bearer)[368] and one in the Royal Horse Artillery, and his third son was a resident magistrate.

Walker's recreations included country sports. It was reported in 1896 that he had 'taken the shooting of Castle Forbes, Co. Longford, and shot the outlying preserves on Saturday last week'.[369] He lived initially in Rutland Square [now Parnell Square] and subsequently in a handsome house with a pillared entrance at

362 Supreme Court of Judicature Act (Ireland) Act 1877 (40&41 Vict., c.57), s10.
363 Supreme Court of Judicature (Ireland) (No. 2) Act 1897 (60&61 Vict., c.66), s7; *ILT&SJ*, vol. 29, p. 376 (3 August 1895) and vol. 32, p. 100 (26 February 1898).
364 *ILT&SJ*, vol. 40, p. 213 (30 June 1906).
365 [1896] 2 IR 204.
366 [1899] 2 IR 503.
367 [1912] 1 IR 287.
368 *ILT&SJ*, vol. 28, p. 203 (21 April 1894).
369 *ILT&SJ*, vol. 30, p. 522 (28 November 1896).

33 Upper Mount Street, sometimes called Pembroke House, on the corner of Herbert Place, opposite St Stephen's Church. The house and its contents were the subject of detailed description by a London legal magazine in 1901.[370] His household (as recorded in the census of 1911) included a staff of eight, five domestic servants, a butler, a coachman and a groom.

370 *Law Journal*, reproduced in *ILT&SJ*, vol. 35, pp 36–7 (19 January 1901).

CHAPTER ELEVEN

The years of Unionist monopoly (2), 1892–1905

JOHN ROSS, who was to be the last lord chancellor of Ireland (1921–2), was appointed as the Land Judge in 1896, rather to his surprise as he noted in his memoirs. Richard E. Meredith was appointed as the judicial commissioner of the Land Commission in 1898, and a second such commissioner was named in 1903, this being Gerald Fitzgerald, a son of John David Fitzgerald (Lord Fitzgerald of Kilmarnock). William Kenny, a Catholic Liberal Unionist and MP for the Stephen's Green constituency, became a judge in 1898, and another MP, Dunbar Plunket Barton, was nominated in 1900. George Wright, a Cork QC, was appointed in 1901. The long-serving attorney general, John Atkinson MP, was named as a lord of appeal in ordinary in December 1905 on the last day in office of the Conservative government led by Arthur Balfour.

John Ross

Justice of the High Court 1896–1921, Lord Chancellor of Ireland 1921–2

John Ross (1853–1935) was born in Londonderry. Robert Ross, his father, was a Presbyterian minister, and served a term as moderator of the General Assembly of the Presbyterian Church in Ireland. Ross was subsequently involved in the establishment of St Andrew's School in Dublin in 1894.[1] He was educated at Foyle College and at Trinity College Dublin, where he had a distinguished academic record, and was elected auditor of the College Historical Society, of which he became president in 1913 on the death of Lord Ashbourne.

His interest in becoming a barrister was sparked by witnessing, as a schoolboy, some powerful courtroom oratory by Christopher Palles QC when resisting a petition in 1868 to set aside the election of Richard Dowse as MP for the city of Londonderry: 'the tide of battle had been suddenly turned by this wonderful advocate … I was seized with a passion to become a great advocate like Mr Palles'.[2] He was called to the Bar in 1880, practising on the North West circuit, in common law and criminal cases. He noted that one woman was 'the only person defended by me in a criminal trial with whom I ever conversed',[3] but he may have been unusual in that respect. There was no Bar protocol of the time restricting counsel from so engaging with defendants – 'in Ireland this matter has been well settled

1 *Irish Times*, 5 January 1894.
2 Sir John Ross, *The years of my pilgrimage* (London, 1924) (hereafter *Pilgrimage*), p. 28.
3 *Pilgrimage*, p. 62.

for generations. Counsel defending prisoners invariably, if they think it necessary, interview them in person, and very often without a solicitor'.[4] Ross became a QC in 1891, having declined an offer of a silk gown made by Lord Ashbourne, the lord chancellor, in 1889.[5]

In 1882 he married Katherine, the only daughter of Lt.-Col. Deane Mann of Dunmoyle, near Sixmilecross, Co. Tyrone. Ross described the property, since demolished, as having been 'originally a shooting lodge, but many years ago a large mansion house was added, in which there was a big hall. The demesne is well wooded, and surrounded on all sides by grouse moors'.[6] His wife's father initially had some coolness towards the marriage, but a reconciliation took place, and on his death in 1894 his daughter inherited the house and estate. Ross had been a sportsman at university, and enjoyed shooting, cycling and golf, being at one time captain of the Royal Dublin golf club.[7] In 1905 at Dunmoyle

> one of his guests, whose gun went off accidentally, had the misfortune to pepper him with a charge of shot meant for a grouse, the pellets lodging in his face, hand and chest, approaching so perilously near the region of his heart that the learned judge was in good luck to escape as he did without serious hurt. Besides the shock, his lordship had to undergo an operation for the extraction of the pellets … Happily he is now himself again, though bearing the outward and visible signs of the accident.[8]

He declined invitations to stand as the Conservative candidate in his native city at the 1880 election, and later in the decade in the South Tyrone constituency. He did not accept a suggestion from Hugh Law QC, the attorney general 1880–1, that he would join the Liberals, having a suspicion of Gladstone's ultimate attitude to Home Rule. A decade later he was invited to stand in North Antrim, 'and gladly consented, as it was a perfectly safe seat and not likely to be contested'. (This constituency had been represented by Edward Macnaghten[9] before his appointment as a Law Lord in 1887.) However in the general election of 1892 he stood instead, at the request of Arthur Balfour, in Londonderry and after a hard fought contest he won the seat with a majority of 26 votes out of 3,946 cast. When the result became known 'a great peal of bells rang out from the spire of the cathedral, followed by the roar of the cannon all around the ancient walls'.[10] This was a Derry tradition, observed also on the victory of the Conservative candidate in the bye-election in 1872 unsuccessfully contested by Christopher Palles as a

4 *Law Times*, vol. 135, p. 146 (7 June 1913).
5 Ross to Ashbourne, 20 June 1889 (Ashbourne Papers, B125/1); *Pilgrimage*, p. 120.
6 *Pilgrimage*, p. 153.
7 *Pilgrimage*, p. 215.
8 *New Irish Jurist*, vol. 5, p. 331 (15 September 1905).
9 Ross acted, with John Atkinson QC, as counsel for Macnaghten in litigation with his neighbour Anthony Traill, who was provost of Trinity College, 1904–14 (*Pilgrimage*, p. 199).
10 *Pilgrimage*, pp 41, 63–71.

Liberal.[11] Ross was an active constituency MP, for instance asking the Secretary to the Admiralty 'whether it would not be possible on the occasion of the visit of the Fleet to the north of Ireland to send one half of the squadron to Lough Foyle instead of sending the entire Fleet to Lough Swilly',[12] although he was then told that the arrangements could not be changed.

Voting rights at parliamentary elections still depended upon a man meeting complicated property qualifications, and in Londonderry the annual revision of the electoral register was an intensely scrutinised and contested exercise. Ross took an active part in voter registration cases,[13] and it was reported in one case in 1894 that 'the question involved related to the Freeman Roll of Derry and for the purpose of arguing the case the records of the city for the past two centuries would have to be examined'.[14] He was defeated at the general election in 1895 by a margin of 39 votes out of 4,027, and for a time resumed his legal practice, which had been affected by his absences in London on Parliamentary business.

In March 1896 he was notified that the government intended to appoint him as the 'Land Judge' in the Chancery division of the High Court. He owed this, he thought, to Lord Cadogan (the lord lieutenant) and Gerald Balfour (the chief secretary), despite the opposition of Ashbourne.[15] He had connections in politics with the influential Abercorn (Hamilton) family of Baronscourt, near Strabane, and was among those who had accompanied Lord Salisbury, the former (and future) prime minister, throughout his visit to Ulster in 1893 to speak in Belfast and Londonderry against the second Home Rule bill. He had more recently met Salisbury, with Cadogan, on the steps of the Athenaeum club in London.[16]

His lack of familiarity to date with property law did not inhibit him, after his initial surprise, from accepting the position in Chancery, and he proved to be an efficient judge in matters arising under the Land Acts. He drew upon his experience as a pupil of George Price BL, who had a large Chancery and conveyancing practice but who 'when he went into court became tongue tied. He had no power of expression'.[17] He noted later that for the administrative work of the court 'a common law man, accustomed to quick decision, was really more suitable'.[18] An early disagreement with some practices of the Land Commission relating to the administration of land purchases, as articulated by its judicial commissioner, Mr Justice Bewley (see p. 353), was determined in favour of the Commission by the Court of Appeal.[19] Ross was in a position through his increasing expertise to contribute to the drafting of the Irish Land Act 1903[20] (the

11 Thomas MacKnight, *Ulster as it is*, op. cit., vol. 1, p. 272.
12 HC Deb, 4th series, vol. 25, col. 421 (5 June 1894).
13 *McDaid v Chambers*, 29 ILTR 81 (1895).
14 *McDaid v Bruce and others*, *ILT&SJ*, vol. 28, p. 533 (27 October 1894).
15 *Pilgrimage*, pp 133–5.
16 *Pilgrimage*, p. 135.
17 *Pilgrimage*, p. 23.
18 *Pilgrimage*, p. 135.
19 *Re Harkness Estate (No. 2)*, [1898] 2 IR 391; 32 ILTR 58 (1898).
20 3 Edw. 7, c.37.

'Wyndham Act', brought forward by George Wyndham, chief secretary for Ireland), and still more to an amending 1904 Act.[21] The 1903 Act had encouraged sales of estates by providing for a bonus of 12% of the purchase price to be payable to the vendor, and Ross held in an early case that a vendor who was a life tenant of a settled estate would, on ordinary principles of equity, hold the bonus as a constructive trustee within the settlement, and not for his own use and benefit.[22] This treatment of a life tenant was contrary to the undisputed intention of Parliament, as expressed in the debate on the 1903 Bill, and there was much criticism both of the decision and of the apparent failure of the drafting of the section. The 1904 Act re-stated the intended principle more plainly.[23]

Ross heard general Chancery litigation, as assigned to him by the other judges of the Chancery division.[24] In July 1907 the master of the rolls stated that there were some 30 actions, some large, set down for trial in his court, that it would be beyond his physical capacity to attempt to finish all the cases prior to the end of the current law term, and that he had arranged with Mr Justice Ross's consent to transfer six cases to him.[25] 'As the clearances of the Land Judge's Court progressed I had more time for other duty, and became a kind of judicial maid-of-all-work. When illness overtook any of my colleagues I was always glad to sit for them, and I was often required to go circuit'.[26] He was the judge in the trial of a major case relating to rights of netting eels in Lough Neagh, in which his judgment was sustained by the Court of Appeal and later by the House of Lords.[27] T.M. Healy KC, MP, who had represented the defendant fishermen, soon afterwards wrote a book on the subject.[28] When in 1912 Ross sat as an assize judge this was the first time that a Chancery judge had done so for many years,[29] and then and thereafter he dealt in that capacity with a complete variety of matters, not restricted to land law. Maurice Healy paid him a handsome tribute following his death, citing three characteristics, 'his splendid presence; his beautiful use of the English language; and his extraordinary kindness to the young men who had the good fortune to flesh their maiden swords in his court'.[30]

Ross took an interest in Irish troops in the South African [Boer] War, and was instrumental in the erection in 1907 of the commemorative Soldiers' Arch at the

21 *Pilgrimage*, pp 126–7.
22 *In re Ely's Estate*, [1904]1 IR 66.
23 Irish Land Act (3 Edw. 7, c.37), s48; Irish Land Act 1904 (4 Edw. 7, c.34), s3; *Law Times*, vol. 116, p. 191 (2 January 1904), p. 211 (9 January 1904).
24 *ILT&SJ*, vol. 41, p. 276 (2 November 1907).
25 *Irish Times*, 2 July 1907.
26 *Pilgrimage*, p. 162.
27 *O'Neill v Johnston*, [1908] 1 IR 358; [1909] 1 IR 237 (CA); *Johnston v O'Neill*, [1911] AC 552; *Pilgrimage*, pp 149–51.
28 T.M. Healy, *Stolen waters: a page in the conquest of Ulster* (London, 1913).
29 *Law Times*, vol. 132, p. 304 (27 January 1912) (Munster circuit); vol. 136, p. 494 (7 March 1914) (North West circuit).
30 Healy, *OldMC*, pp 278–81, at 278.

Grafton Street corner of St Stephen's Green.[31] During the Great War he spoke on recruiting platforms,[32] and chaired the local committee or selection board of the Inns of Court Officers Training Corps. This met regularly at the Land Judge's Court and sought recruits for training for commissions in the army, its notices stating that 'men of university and public school class, and particularly men of sporting and outdoor experience, or used to handling men, are the most suitable'.[33]

In May 1918 he attended a meeting in Downing Street at which Lloyd George, the prime minister, proposed that three men (Lord French of Ypres, Lord Midleton, a leading southern unionist, and Ross) would act as a commission in place of an appointed lord lieutenant, exercising some substantive permanent administrative powers. The proposal did not fly, and a week later French was appointed as lord lieutenant.[34] In the New Year Honours List in 1919 Ross was made a baronet. In 1921 he was informed by a telephone call from Gerald Horan, the secretary to the lord chancellor and clerk to the Privy Council, that he would be appointed to replace Sir James Campbell as lord chancellor. He had received no prior communication from Lloyd George offering him the position.[35] He had expressed interest to Walter Long MP, a member of the cabinet, a year earlier in being appointed as the first lord chief justice of Northern Ireland.[36] The Government of Ireland Act 1920 had provided that the lord chancellorship would in the future be a purely judicial office, with the same tenure as every other judge, and no longer having any executive government functions,[37] and Ross took office on 27 June 1921, the day on which that provision was brought into effect.[38]

That Act also established a new High Court of Appeal, to which appeals could be taken from the separate courts of appeal of Northern and Southern Ireland respectively.[39] Ross sat as chairman of that court for the first time on 15 December 1921,[40] and thereafter a number of times before its abolition (with the office of lord chancellor) in 1922.[41]

The turmoil and civil unrest connected with the War of Independence after 1919 created great obstacles for the conduct of court business, although 'a functioning court system managed throughout to process an amount of routine litigation which was devoid of political interest and incapable of arousing political

31 *Law Times*, vol. 111, p. 175 (22 June 1901); *Pilgrimage*, pp 217–18.
32 *Law Times*, vol. 139, p. 393 (4 September 1915).
33 *ILT&SJ*, vol. 50, War Supplement, pp 6 and 20 (26 February 1916).
34 *Pilgrimage*, p. 282.
35 *Pilgrimage*, p. 293.
36 Ross to Long, 27 May 1920 (Walter Long Papers (WSHC) 947/336).
37 10&11 Geo. 5, c.67, s44.
38 Government of Ireland (lord chancellor of Ireland) Order 1921 (SR&O 1921, no. 1130, 27 June 1921).
39 10&11 Geo. 5, c.67, s42.
40 *ILT&SJ*, vol. 55, p. 313 (17 December 1921); see also p. 477.
41 Irish Free State (Consequential Provisions) Act 1922 (13 Geo. 5, c.2), s2 and schedule 1, part 6 and schedule 2, part 2.

controversy'.[42] Policies of motor insurance commonly excluded liability for loss due to civil unrest, and the High Court of Appeal heard two appeals brought by insurance companies on the issue of whether they could rely on such exemption clauses as a basis to disclaim any liability to compensate owners of cars which had been taken in 1920 in circumstances suggesting not so much ordinary theft as civil commotion, being commandeered by armed men.[43] The High Court and Court of Appeal in Southern Ireland found for the car owners in each case but, led by Ross, the High Court of Appeal allowed the insurer's appeal in the first case to be heard (*Cooper*), while dismissing the second appeal (*Boggan*). The House of Lords ultimately determined in each case that the insurers had no liability. There was something to be said on each side of the argument, but a dismissive tone and language about the previous judgments that was adopted by Ross in his judgment in *Cooper* allowing the appeal 'was bound to give offence',[44] and duly did so. Ronan LJ and Dodd LJ in their subsequent judgments in the Court of Appeal for Southern Ireland in *Boggan* criticised Ross, indirectly but clearly. Dodd observed that 'it is essential, whatever view a judge should entertain of his own, or may I say, retain [both he and Ronan had sat on the *Cooper* appeal], that all our courts should join together in harmonious administration of the law'. Ross was primarily responsible for having provoked an unseemly and unwonted spectacle of disputation and squabbling among judges.[45]

He sought alternative judicial employment in the House of Lords when the abolition of his office of lord chancellor of Ireland was imminent (see p. 473). When doing so he represented that he had never been differed with by the house: 'when the Irish Court of Appeal reversed me the House of Lords reversed the Court of Appeal and set my order up, and when the Court of Appeal agreed with me the House of Lords agreed with them'.[46] This may have been correct at the time of writing, but in *Boggan* the judgment of the new High Court of Appeal was reversed by the House of Lords, and 'this failure to be consistent spoiled his track record'.[47]

He lived in Fitzwilliam Square, and from 1916 at Oatlands, Stillorgan, Co. Dublin, a substantial house then on the outskirts of Dublin, which later became a school and monastery for the Christian Brothers, and which was demolished in 1968. He led negotiations for the judges with the British government in and after 1921 as to proper compensation for their loss of judicial office upon the

42 W.N. Osborough, 'Law in Ireland, 1916–26', *NILQ*, vol. 23 (1972), p. 48 and in *Studies in Irish legal history* (Dublin, 1999), pp 270–95.

43 *Cooper v General Accident, Fire and Life Assurance Corporation*, [1922] 2 IR 38, 214; *Boggan v Motor Union Insurance Co.*, [1922] 2 IR 184, 222, [1923] 2 IR 136.

44 W.N. Osborough, 'Forcibly commandeered transport and owners' insurance: the deciding of two test cases in the 1920s', *Irish Jurist*, vol. 11 (1976), p. 105, at 121.

45 Ibid., pp 119, 121.

46 Ross to Shortt (home secretary), 22 August 1922 (HO 317/67 (TNAUK)).

47 W.N. Osborough, 'Forcibly commandeered transport', p. 124.

establishment of new courts in the Irish Free State.[48] After 1922 he resided in London (Whitehall Court) and at Dunmoyle. In his retirement he wrote two books of memoirs, which were published in 1924 and 1927.[49] His only son Ronald was educated at Eton and Cambridge University and was called to the Bar in England in 1913 – 'before the War I used to bring my son with me on circuit as registrar, in which capacity he learned a good deal that was subsequently of use to him at the English Bar'.[50] His son served in the Army in the Great War, ending with the rank of major, and was subsequently the Unionist MP at Westminster for Londonderry between 1929 and 1951. He succeeded to the baronetcy.

Richard E. Meredith

Judicial Commissioner of the Land Commission 1898–1906, Master of the Rolls 1906–12

Richard E. Meredith (1855–1916) was the son of a Dublin solicitor, William Rice Meredith, and a member of a wider legal family. His brother Frederick was president of the Incorporated Law Society in 1910–11.[51] He was educated at Queen's College Galway, and called to the Bar in 1879, and to the Inner Bar in 1892. He had been auditor of the Law Students' Debating Society for 1878–9. He was a member of the North East circuit, and over time much of his work lay in Chancery and the Court of Appeal. Following his death it was said that it was 'as the skilful advocate rather than the judge that he would be remembered', and that he had been a 'conscientious and careful – perhaps too careful – judge'.[52] He was made a bencher of King's Inns in 1894. He was counsel in many leading cases on property law, including representing the Giant's Causeway Co. Ltd in an action seeking a declaration of title to the Causeway lands and an injunction restraining entry (except upon payment of a charge for admission).[53] It was eventually determined that there was not – there could not be – any public right to wander or roam over such privately owned land, and the estate was later (in 1962) purchased by the National Trust.[54]

Meredith's judicial career commenced in January 1898 when he was appointed to replace Edmund Bewley as judicial commissioner of the Land Commission. In recommending him to the prime minister for appointment the lord lieutenant had advised that 'there is little doubt that Richard Meredith QC is the man. In fact no

48 *Pilgrimage*, p. 296. See pp 489–90 below.
49 *Pilgrimage*, *Pilgrim Scrip; more random reminiscences* (London, 1927).
50 *Pilgrimage*, p. 291.
51 *ILT&SJ*, vol. 45, p. 119 (13 May 1911).
52 *ILT&SJ*, vol. 50, p. 37 (5 February 1916).
53 *Giant's Causeway Co. Ltd v Attorney general and others*, [1905] NIJR 301; *ILT&SJ*, vol. 32, p. 95 (19 February 1898) and p. 211 (7 May 1898); *Irish Times*, 27 November 1897.
54 Norma Dawson, 'The Giant's Causeway case: property law in Ireland 1845–1995' in Norma Dawson, Desmond Greer, Peter Ingram (eds), *One hundred and fifty years of Irish law* (Belfast & Dublin, 1995), p. 239.

one else could be suggested at all equal to him in ability or general fitness for the post'.[55] Congratulations tendered to him by a senior member of the Bar on the first day that he sat in court included a comment that 'a great reputation has been carried onto the bench untainted by the field of party politics'. A spokesman for the Incorporated Law Society, and the *Irish Law Times* in an editorial, made observations to much the same effect,[56] although it was also said that Meredith had not taken any active or public part in politics, and had not been a law officer nor stood as a parliamentary candidate, but he 'had never concealed his views, which are those of a strong Conservative, on political matters'.[57]

A rumour in the summer of 1906 that he was contemplating resignation was dismissed by the *Irish Law Times* as 'being absolutely without foundation'.[58] In October 1906 he was appointed to replace Andrew Marshall Porter as master of the rolls, notwithstanding advice to James Bryce, the chief secretary, from Sir Antony MacDonnell, the undersecretary at Dublin Castle, that 'he is not of such capacity that we should disregard our own to promote a Tory'.[59] 'It is an open secret that Mr Justice Meredith had little affection for the Land Court business, and his numerous friends rejoice that he has been transferred to a more congenial atmosphere',[60] one where he had previously practised successfully. He appointed his son Edmund (1884–1917), who was called to the Bar in 1907, as his train bearer[61] and subsequently as his secretary. Edmund died in Italy in 1917 of illness contracted when serving with the Red Cross.[62]

Meredith resigned due to continuing ill health, which had impeded his work, in June 1912,[63] and died in February 1916, at a nursing home in Surrey. The family had lived in Fitzwilliam Square.

William Kenny

Justice of the High Court 1898–1921

William Kenny (1846–1921) was the son of a solicitor in Ennis, Co. Clare. After education at Trinity College he was called to the Bar in 1868, and joined the Munster circuit. His practice included probate, divorce and bankruptcy law. He became a QC in 1885, also being elected a bencher of King's Inns the same year. He was a Liberal Unionist and was active in the Irish Loyal and Patriotic Union, the Dublin Unionist Registration Association and the Liberal Union of Ireland.[64]

55 Cadogan to Salisbury, 22 December 1897 (Salisbury Papers).
56 *ILT&SJ*, vol. 32, p. 32 (15 January 1898).
57 *Law Times*, vol. 104, p. 244 (15 January 1898).
58 *ILT&SJ*, vol. 40, p. 194 (16 June 1906).
59 MacDonnell to Bryce, 19 September 1906 (Bryce Papers, MS 11,014(1)).
60 *Irish Times*, 23 October 1906.
61 *Irish Times*, 26 October 1906.
62 Anthony P. Quinn, *Wigs and guns: Irish barristers in the Great War* (Dublin, 2006), pp 105–6.
63 *Irish Times*, 8 June 1912.
64 *Irish Times*, 9 April 1891, 28 July 1891, 12 May 1892.

He spoke at a dinner in the Ulster Hall, Belfast, in honour of the duke of Devonshire, the founder and leader of the Liberal Unionist party at Westminster.[65] In the 1892 general election he stood in the St Stephen's Green constituency and won the seat with a narrow majority of 15 votes out of over 6,000 cast, benefitting from the Nationalist vote (about 55% of the total) being divided between two candidates. A party initiative to increase voter registration[66] led to him having a slightly more comfortable majority in the 1895 election and in a bye-election when, a few weeks later, he was obliged to stand for re-election after being appointed solicitor general by the incoming Unionist government.

Public opposition to Home Rule was not common among Catholics, and Kenny was one of the more prominent of his co-religionists who took that view.[67] A group of Catholics, while deprecating 'certain anti-Catholic utterances to which the excitement of the moment may have given rise', declared that they subscribed to general objections to Home Rule 'so far as [these] rest upon purely secular considerations', and circulated a petition for signature by Catholics declaring it to be 'most prejudicial to our religion and disastrous to the best interests of Ireland'.[68] Kenny told a meeting at Blackheath in London that many Catholics were opposed to Home Rule and, more bluntly, that it would be 'inequitable, unjust, nefarious and monstrous'.[69] 'A Catholic Unionist was never a very popular figure in Ireland; and Kenny was heartily disliked by the Irish Party, who never missed a chance of girding at him in the House'.[70]

He spoke in the House of Commons on the second Home Rule bill in 1893, saying that he represented the intelligence and wealth of the community, 'his constituency was composed of business men, about the largest merchants in Dublin'.[71] When the Nationalist MP for South Donegal queried whether Dublin University should be represented in Parliament he responded in a rather dismissive manner, saying that the university constituency 'was unique in Ireland, inasmuch as it did not contain a single illiterate', unlike the Donegal constituency 'which contained, he believed, a larger percentage of illiterates than any other Irish constituency'.[72]

In 1890 he invoked the lord lieutenant's influence in seeking appointment as a law officer or a judge, complaining that, despite his standing in the profession, it appeared that the 'door to legitimate Bar promotion' in the ordinary course of events had been blocked to him because he was not an MP and did not have a practice in criminal law. If that were the case then he asked to be considered for a

65 *The Ulster Liberal Unionist Association: a sketch of its history, 1885–1914* (Belfast, 1914), p. 108.
66 *Irish Times*, 27 October 1893.
67 John Biggs-Davison and George Chowdaray-Best, *The Cross of St Patrick: the Catholic unionist tradition in Ireland* (Bourne End, 1984), pp 265–70.
68 *Irish Times*, 18 March 1893.
69 *Irish Times*, 24 March 1893.
70 Healy, *OldMC*, p. 37.
71 HC Deb, 4th series, vol. 8, col. 1649 (16 February 1893).
72 HC Deb, 4th series, vol. 14, col. 1414 (12 July 1893).

judicial appointment straight from the Bar.[73] Lord Ashbourne commented (after noting Kenny's political work) that, at least for the time being, his claims were overstated, since a number of his colleagues at the Bar were ahead of him in position and business, and that while he could expect promotion in due course he should be patient.[74] At the end of 1897 his time came and he was appointed to a vacancy in the High Court.

After he had been sworn in and had taken his seat in court it was reported that 'Mr Justice Kenny looked remarkably well in scarlet and ermine and court wig'.[75] Maurice Healy, who was called to the Bar in 1911, initially formed an unfavourable view of Kenny as a judge, 'looking on him as a bitter pill, full of prejudices and fixed ideas', but later thought better of him, both personally and professionally. 'He was a learned and sound lawyer, and never was consciously unjust, although his complete inability to enter into the minds of humble people caused him to err unintentionally'.[76] He was the probate judge for a time,[77] and gave a classic exposition of the doctrine of dependant relative revocation of a will, whereby an apparent revocation may be rendered void and set aside if it was proved to have been done on the basis of a mistake of fact or law on the part of the testator as to the effect of doing so.[78]

He lived in Fitzwilliam Place, and later in Cabinteely, and died in February 1921. His son Edward Kenny (1874–1944) was called to the Bar in 1897, and after serving as an assistant probate registrar was appointed probate registrar in August 1921.[79]

Dunbar Plunket Barton

Justice of the High Court 1900–18

Dunbar Plunket Barton (1853–1937) was the son of Thomas Henry Barton BL, a police or stipendiary magistrate, whose family were connected with the long established Bordeaux wine house of Barton & Guestier.[80] His mother, Charlotte Plunket, was a granddaughter of the first baron Plunket, lord chancellor of Ireland 1830–4 and 1835–41. She was a sister of David Plunket QC, solicitor general 1875–7, and of the 4th baron Plunket, William Conyngham Plunket, archbishop of Dublin 1885–97. Other family legal connections were his uncle Patrick Plunket, a bankruptcy judge who died in 1859, and his cousin Philip Crampton Smyly, who was called to the Bar in 1888 and later appointed chief justice of the colony of

73 Kenny to Londonderry, 13 March 1890 (Balfour Papers, Add. MS 49802.86).
74 Ashbourne to Balfour, 19 March 1890 (Balfour Papers, Add. MS 49815.56).
75 *ILT&SJ*, vol. 32, p. 31 (15 January 1898).
76 Healy, *OldMC*, pp 37–8.
77 *ILT&SJ*, vol. 55, p. 45 (12 February 1921).
78 In the Goods of Irvine, [1919] 2 IR 485, as cited in In the Estate of John Coughlan deceased [2022/PO2985] (Butler J (High Court), 3 November 2022).
79 *Irish Times*, 26 August 1921.
80 Healy, *OldMC*, p. 39.

Sierra Leone.[81] Barton was proud of the Plunket connection, and when called within the Bar as solicitor general he wore a full-bottomed wig that had been worn by his great-grandfather.[82]

He was educated at Harrow school in England and at Oxford University (Corpus Christi college), where in 1877 he was president of the Oxford Union. He was briefly in 1880 private secretary to the duke of Marlborough, the lord lieutenant.[83] After his call to the Bar in 1880 he joined the Leinster circuit. He lectured in the King's Inns, as professor initially of the law of personal property, pleading and evidence[84] and subsequently of the law of personal property, contract and tort.[85] He was appointed as private secretary to the lord chancellor, Lord Ashbourne.[86] In 1889 he was appointed junior Crown prosecutor in Co. Wicklow[87] and became a QC. His practice at the Bar was mixed, primarily in the common law courts, where he had a 'fluency and grace of speech, his utterance clear, cultured and impressive', as was seemingly particularly evidenced in trials for breach of promise of marriage,[88] in which 'some of his appeals to juries were punctuated with felicitously humorous touches'.[89] He was briefed also in murder trials, both as a prosecution counsel and for the defence.[90] He published one legal book, an edited commentary on a land law statute of 1896, written jointly with R.R. Cherry,[91] and contributed statements of the law of perpetuities and of partnership to what was then the new Encyclopaedia of the Laws of England, under the editorship of Lord Halsbury.

He was a strong Conservative, and in the 1880s was active in various party bodies, including the City and County Conservative Club,[92] which had premises at 42 Dawson Street, the City of Dublin Unionist Registration Association[93] and the Primrose League, a women's organisation. He spoke, with Edward Carson QC, at a League event in the Town Hall, Kingstown (now Dun Laoghaire), where the oratory was followed by musical entertainment.[94] He promoted the formation in 1883 of a Conservative Working Men's Club in Dublin, as an organised body of loyalists, saying that 'if capital and wealth and refinement were banished from Dublin there would be no good wages and no market for skilled workmen and

81 *ILT&SJ*, vol. 36, p. 12 (4 January 1902).
82 *Law Times*, vol. 104, p. 219 (8 January 1898).
83 *ILT&SJ*, vol. 34, p. 47 (27 January 1900); *Who was who, 1929–1940*.
84 *ILT&SJ*, vol. 19, p. 298 (6 June 1885).
85 *ILT&SJ*, vol. 22, p. 286 (9 June 1888) and p. 545 (27 October 1888).
86 *ILT&SJ*, vol. 20, p. 22 (9 January 1886) and p. 397 (14 August 1886); *Irish Times*, 7 August 1886.
87 *ILT&SJ*, vol. 23, p. 143 (16 March 1889).
88 *Irish Times*, 25 June 1886, 18 February 1887, 23 February 196, 10 November 1897.
89 *Irish Times*, 27 January 1900.
90 *Irish Times*, 15 July 1889, 25 July 1891.
91 Dunbar P. Barton QC, MP & Richard R. Cherry (eds), *The Land Law (Ireland) Act 1896, with the rules and forms issued thereunder in the Land Commission, Supreme Court and County Courts respectively* (Dublin, 1897).
92 *Irish Times*, 31 March 1883, 31 October 1883.
93 *Irish Times*, 10 June 1889.
94 *Irish Times*, 8 May 1890.

artisans'.[95] He gave an address, later published as a pamphlet, in favour of creating what he called a 'yeoman proprietary' as an element in land law reform, which he distinguished from the more familiar concept of a peasant proprietary.[96] In 1890 he was nominated as Unionist candidate for the East Tyrone constituency,[97] then held by a Nationalist MP, but shortly afterwards moved to the calmer or more promising constituency of Mid Armagh, where he was selected as candidate in May 1891[98] and was elected MP, without opposition, at a bye-election in December caused by the death of the sitting Unionist member. Nor did he have any opposition in the three subsequent elections in which he stood in the constituency, in 1892, 1895 and 1898 (a bye-election). He was well respected as a Parliamentary orator, and was prominent at Unionist demonstrations in England against Home Rule, including addressing meetings at the Royal Opera House, Covent Garden and at Bournemouth.[99]

Barton was appointed solicitor general in January 1898,[100] having been a bencher of King's Inns since 1892. He continued while holding that office to be a director of the Guinness brewery holding company in London.[101] He was appointed to fill a vacancy in the High Court (Queen's Bench division) in January 1900, after some speculation that he might prefer to continue as a member of the House of Commons (as the attorney general, John Atkinson QC, did).[102] He was transferred to the Chancery division in 1904, where he continued until his retirement in 1918. His judgments included one in which his decision was set aside by the Court of Appeal but restored by the House of Lords.[103] The action was for an injunction to compel the defendant to restore the light which the plaintiff had enjoyed at his factory premises, at James's Street South, Belfast, prior to the erection of a new building at the corner of Bedford Street and Donegall Square South. The trial took a fortnight, and before delivering judgment Barton visited Belfast to inspect the premises.[104] He admitted to probate a will made by a testator of admittedly sound mind, memory and understanding but who through paralysis was unable to speak, and who communicated his instructions and approval of his will by closing or keeping open his eyes in response to questions from his solicitor.[105]

He was a companionable man, genial and affable, and a member of numerous clubs, three in or close to Dublin (the Kildare Street Club, the University Club and the Royal St George's Yacht Club in Dun Laoghaire) and five in London (the

95 *Irish Times*, 23 July 1883.
96 Dunbar P. Barton, *A yeoman proprietary in Ireland* (Dublin, 1883); *Irish Times*, 25 June 1883.
97 *Irish Times*, 14 August 1890.
98 *Irish Times*, 20 May 1891.
99 *Irish Times*, 20 April 1893, 21 November 1893.
100 *ILT&SJ*, vol. 32, p. 32 (15 January 1898).
101 *Irish Times*, 15 August 1898, 29 August 1899.
102 *Irish Times*, 13 December 1899.
103 *Black v Scottish Temperance Life Insurance Company Ltd*, [1908] 1 IR 541; 42 ILTR 194 (1908).
104 *ILT&SJ*, vol. 42, p. 76 (28 March 1908).
105 *Ryan v Ryan*, 4 NIJR 164 (1903-04).

Athenaeum, the Beefsteak, the Carlton, the Garrick and the St James's).[106] His main recreation was golf, and he was president of the Golfing Union of Ireland and of three clubs, Royal Dublin, Royal Portrush[107] (where he succeeded Lord Macnaghten in office) and Greenore. During the Great War he chaired a committee of golf clubs that provided entertainment and comforts for wounded soldiers.[108] He presented a cup and a shield bearing his name for eponymous inter-club competitions, which are still contested.[109]

Barton had not distinguished himself academically at Oxford, being awarded a fourth class degree, which was said to be 'by no means a true exposition of his powers as a scholar'.[110] He subsequently wrote a number of books, and was elected a member of the Royal Irish Academy in 1917. His works included a three volume study of Jean Bernadotte (1763–1844), later King Charles XIV of Sweden,[111] and two works on Shakespeare.[112] He also contributed to a book on the Inns of court in London,[113] and published a short book of recollections of T.M. Healy, his old friend and colleague at the Bar and in the House of Commons.[114]

He lived in Clyde Road, Ballsbridge. He had been prepared to retire in 1917, seemingly on the initiative of Sir James Campbell, the lord chief justice, but had been frustrated at a delay in arrangements being made for the appointment of a successor.[115] When he did retire, early in 1918, he was made a baronet. As his only son predeceased him the baronetcy became extinct on Barton's death. Following his retirement he served as an arbitrator in some labour disputes, at the docks in Dublin[116] and at the Harland & Wolff shipyard in Belfast.[117] He was the chairman of the executive council of the Irish National War Memorial at its foundation in 1919. After lengthy negotiations with the government a scheme for this to be located at Islandbridge was adopted in 1931, and it was practically completed early in 1937, prior to his death in September that year.[118]

106 *Debrett's peerage, baronetage, knightage and companionage* (London, 1936).

107 *In Watt v McLaughlin* ([1923] IR 112) Wilson J upheld the validity of a change made in the rules of the club to permit the playing of golf on Sundays, and held that a court of Chancery was not the proper tribunal to determine whether such play was a criminal offence under the Sunday Observance Act 1695 (7 Will. 3 (Ir.), c17, s3).

108 *ILT&SJ*, vol. 50, p. 74 (18 March 1916).

109 William H. Gibson, *Early Irish golf* (Kildare, 1988), p. 84; *The Times*, 13 September 1937.

110 *Irish Times*, 13 August 1892.

111 *Bernadotte: the first phase, 1763–1799* (London, 1914); *Bernadotte and Napoleon, 1799–1810* (London, 1921); *Bernadotte, prince and king, 1810–1844* (London, 1925). Also, *The amazing career of Bernadotte, 1763–1844* (London, 1929).

112 *Links between Shakespeare and Ireland* (London, 1925); *Links between Shakespeare and the Law* (London, 1929).

113 D. Plunket Barton, Charles Benham and Francis Watt, *The story of our inns of court* (London, 1924).

114 *Timothy Healy: memories and anecdotes* (London, 1933).

115 Campbell to Sir Edward Carson, 22 July 1917 (Carson Papers (PRONI), D1507/A/24/12).

116 *ILT&SJ*, vol. 52, p. 169 (13 July 1918).

117 *ILT&SJ*, vol. 54, p. 211 (28 August 1920).

118 *Irish Times*, 17 April 1937.

In retirement he and his wife moved their home to England, taking up residence in Gray's Inn, where he had been called to the English Bar in 1893, and of which he became a bencher in 1898. He wrote a history of the Inn,[119] received the high honour of being elected as treasurer in 1922, and generally fostered its traditions. A portrait in oils by John St Helier Lander was painted in 1932, and he bequeathed this to King's Inns.[120]

George Wright

Justice of the High Court (King's Bench division) 1901–13

George Wright (1847–1913) was the son of a prominent solicitor in Clonakilty, Co. Cork. Three of his brothers also entered the legal profession. He was educated at Portora school in Enniskillen (remarking when he sat as an assize judge in Fermanagh that two of his judicial colleagues had also attended school there)[121] and at Trinity College, where he had an interest in rowing. He was later elected president of the university Boat Club. He was called to the Bar in 1871, joining the Munster circuit, and took silk in 1884. It was said of him that he had 'a blunt cheeriness in all forensic vicissitudes'.[122]

He was one of the counsel for the plaintiff in *Pike v Beamish*, which became known as the Cork Card Case, arising out of an allegation of cheating at cards in the Cork County Club.[123] He made the closing speech to the jury on the 11th day of the trial, telling them that it was 'the most protracted and important case that he had ever been engaged in', and resuming his seat to loud applause in court.[124] The jury found that the plaintiff had been defamed, but without malice.

In 1892, in the final days of an outgoing Conservative government, he was appointed senior Crown prosecutor at Green Street for the city and county of Dublin, having previously held the same position for Co. Kerry and the city of Cork.[125] In 1895 he stood as a Unionist in a bye-election for the Dublin University constituency against W.E.H. Lecky, the distinguished historian, who offered himself as a Liberal Unionist and whose support encompassed 'the college dons and the more strictly scholastic forces among the university alumni'.[126] This outnumbered the largely legal support for Wright, and Lecky was easily elected. In 1900 Wright was appointed as solicitor general, having written to the lord lieutenant setting out his professional position at the Bar,[127] and in 1901 he became a High Court judge (King's Bench division) following the death of Mr Justice

119 D. Plunket Barton, Charles Benham and Francis Watt, op. cit., pp 139–251.
120 Wanda Ryan-Smolin, *King's Inns portraits* (Dublin, 1992), p. 6.
121 *Church of Ireland Gazette*, 17 March 1911.
122 *Irish Times*, 17 May 1913.
123 Healy, *OldMC*, pp 25–6.
124 *Irish Times*, 22 May 1894. See also p. 378.
125 *Irish Times*, 25 July 1892.
126 *ILT&SJ*, vol. 47, pp 143–4 (24 May 1913).
127 Wright to Cadogan, 15 January 1900 (Cadogan Papers, CAD/1720).

Murphy. In hearing criminal trials and all forms of common law litigation he was businesslike, giving 'short shrift to meticulous technicalities' and 'certainly never shrank from putting before the jury the bent of his own generally decided views'.[128]

He died unexpectedly in May 1913 at his residence at Ryecroft, Bray, having been affected by a heart condition for a couple of years, although this had not constrained his work. He lived also with his family at Fitzwilliam Square. He had married Mercy Barrington, of Limerick, with whom he had one son and three daughters. He was a member of the Church of Ireland, and had been elected as a lay member of the court of the General Synod.[129]

Gerald Fitzgerald

Judicial Commissioner of the Land Commission 1903–22

Gerald Fitzgerald (1849–1925) was a son of John David Fitzgerald. He was educated at Trinity College and was called to the Bar in 1871. In 1881 he was appointed an assistant commissioner under the Land Law (Ireland) Act 1881,[130] a position for a year at a time at a salary of £1,000, with jurisdiction to fix fair rents.[131] In 1886 he was appointed a county court judge, initially for Sligo and Roscommon, but within a few months he was transferred to be judge for Meath, Westmeath, Longford and King's County (Offaly).[132] He became a QC in 1892.

In 1890 he was made a (lay) commissioner of the Land Commission, with a salary of £3,000, and the degree of his sympathy with tenants' interests became a subject of comment in the House of Commons later that year. He was the successor to Edward Falconer Litton, who had been nominated in 1881, when the Commission was set up, to be, in effect, a guardian of the interests of tenant farmers. T.M. Healy's supportive remark that Fitzgerald had been a bad appointee in 1881, 'but he has since learned a deal of sense, and he has been behaving very sensibly', led to T.W. Russell, then the MP for South Tyrone, and who for decades led a populist unionist element in Ulster, saying that 'in no way can it be said that [he] was a fit man to put in the place of the tenants' representative on the Commission'.[133] Arthur Balfour, the chief secretary, who had been responsible for this recent appointment, spoke of Fitzgerald's fair-mindedness, saying that he was 'neither a Conservative in politics nor a landlord'.[134]

A provision in the Irish Land Act 1903 named and appointed him to a new position as an additional or second judicial member of the Commission, 'for the purposes of the Land Law Acts and Land Purchase Acts, but not further or

128 *Irish Times*, 17 May 1913.
129 *Church of Ireland Gazette*, 19 April 1907, 25 April 1913.
130 44&45 Vict., c.49, s41.
131 *ILT&SJ*, vol. 15, p. 587 (12 November 1881).
132 *ILT&SJ*, vol. 20, p. 285 (29 May 1886) and p. 464 (25 September 1886). John Adye Curran, *Reminiscences* (London, 1915), p. 237.
133 HC Deb, 3rd series, vol. 349, col. 722 (8 December 1890).
134 HC Deb, 3rd series, vol. 349, col. 736 (8 December 1890).

otherwise'.[135] Although this provision made reference back to the underlying status of a judicial commissioner under section 41 of the 1881 Act, in the opinion of the government Fitzgerald was not a High Court judge nor entitled to rank as such.[136] 'He was thoroughly acquainted with the intricacies of the Land Acts, and his judgments were able and impartial'.[137] By virtue of the Irish Free State (Consequential Provisions) Act 1922 the office of Commissioner of the Land Commission ceased to exist as from the transfer date, the establishment of the Free State.[138] The Land Law (Commission) Act 1923 provided that thereafter the office of Judicial Commissioner would be discharged by a specially assigned judge of the High Court.[139] Fitzgerald lived in Fitzwilliam Square, and on his death in 1925 was buried in the family vault at Glasnevin cemetery.

John Atkinson (Lord Atkinson of Glenwilliam)

Lord of Appeal in Ordinary 1905–28

John Atkinson (1841–1932) was born in Drogheda, where his father Edward (1801–76) was a physician and surgeon. (References in obituaries and biographical dictionaries to 1844 as the year of his birth are not correct, since he stated his date of birth as 13 December 1841 in the papers signed in the King's Inns for his call to the Bar.)[140] The family's origins were in Co. Monaghan, and they were later associated with the Glenwilliam Castle estate at Ballingarry, Co. Limerick, which his father purchased through the Encumbered Estates Commission in the early 1850s. Atkinson took his title from the estate when he became a life peer in 1905, although his connection with it by then was indirect, since his father, who married twice, had bequeathed it to a half-brother's side of the family.

He was educated at the Royal Belfast Academical Institution and Queen's College Galway, and was called to the Bar in 1865, joining the Munster circuit. He was appointed a Crown prosecutor for Co. Kerry in 1879,[141] took silk in 1880, and was elected a bencher of King's Inns in 1885.[142] He was appointed senior Crown counsel for the city and county of Dublin (i.e., prosecutor at Green Street) in 1887,[143] and was one of the counsel for the *Times* at hearings of the Parnell Commission in 1887–8. His representation of the plaintiff in a celebrated defamation suit, *Pike v Beamish*, in 1894, known as the Cork Card Case, was described by Maurice Healy as his greatest triumph at the Bar.[144]

135 3 Edw. VII, c.37, s86(3).
136 HC Deb, 4th series, vol. 129, col. 1328 (10 February 1904).
137 *ILT&SJ*, vol. 59, p. 267 (7 November 1925). See also vol. 60, p. 45 (13 February 1926).
138 12&13 Geo. V, c.2, part III of second schedule.
139 No. 27 of 1923, s3.
140 *King's Inns Admission Papers*, p. 13.
141 *ILT&SJ*, vol. 13, p. 264 (17 May 1879).
142 *ILT&SJ*, vol. 19, p. 298 (6 June 1885).
143 *ILT&SJ*, vol. 21, p. 396 (16 July 1887).
144 Healy, *OldMC*, p. 25.

At the end of 1889 he was appointed solicitor general when Dodgson Hamilton Madden vacated that office on being appointed attorney general. His work included advising on the drafting of statutes, and when a query arose in the course of debate on the Irish Land Bill 1909 about the definition of a 'congested district' contained in the 1891 legislation that established the Congested Districts Board[145] he said in the House of Lords that this had deliberately been made flexible ('the test of a congested district was a somewhat rough one'), avoiding undue precision.[146] Other significant land law legislation was enacted while he served as a law officer, and T.M. Healy noted that his 'silent service in forwarding reforms, both as to land and local government, although a Tory law officer, will never be adequately appreciated by the public'.[147]

When Madden was appointed a High Court judge in the summer of 1892, just before a general election, Atkinson succeeded him again, holding office as attorney general for a few weeks. In 1893 he was put forward as prospective Conservative candidate for the constituency of North Londonderry,[148] and was elected easily at the 1895 general election, when his party was returned to office. He was re-elected unopposed at the 1900 election.

In August 1895 he was re-appointed attorney general and held that office until December 1905. He was thus in prime position for a decade to be appointed a judge, and was well liked by the ministers with whom he worked (except perhaps by Ashbourne, the lord chancellor), but 'steadfastly refused promotion because he had been pressed by the government to continue to serve as a law officer in a time of exceptional difficulty'.[149] He thus did not take up a number of opportunities for judicial appointment that arose, although having some apprehension about the prospect of returning to the Bar. He had a concern that what he referred to as a lucrative private practice (which the law officers could maintain at the time) would be badly affected by his absence from the Four Courts during the Parliamentary sessions when his presence in London was required.[150]

The principal opportunity of appointment that presented itself was for a vacancy in 1897 in the Court of Appeal. The *Irish Times* reported that

> there was excitement in the [parliamentary] Lobby on Monday afternoon when a legal coterie was seen assembled in the very centre of the Hall. There were present the lord chancellor of Ireland, lord chief justice Sir Peter O'Brien, Mr Carson QC, MP and the attorney general for Ireland. They were given respectful distance as it was evident that coercion was being applied to Mr attorney Atkinson. The vacancy caused by the death of lord

145 Purchase of Land (Ireland) Act 1891 (54&55 Vict., c.48).
146 HL Deb, 5th series, vol. 3, col. 1076 (12 October 1909).
147 T.M. Healy, *Letters and leaders*, p. 177.
148 *Irish Times*, 28 November 1893.
149 Viscount Long of Wraxall [Walter Long], *Memories* (London, 1923), p. 168.
150 Atkinson to Gerald Balfour, 4 November 1900 (Gerald Balfour Papers (TNAUK), PRO 30/60/15).

> justice Barry [on 15 May 1897] was evidently under discussion. Mr Atkinson did not look particularly happy, not at all in his usual form.[151]

The government, through the lord lieutenant, Lord Cadogan, asked him not to press his claim, and he asked for an assurance that an effort would be made before the government left office to appoint him to a suitable judicial position. He indicated that if he could be so reassured he would be willing to continue as attorney general, but that if not he would ask to be appointed to the Court of Appeal.[152] Lord Salisbury authorised Cadogan to give the requested assurances in general terms,[153] and the vacant place was filled by the promotion of Holmes from the High Court.[154] Atkinson was then greatly disappointed in 1900 when Lord Lindley was made a lord of appeal in ordinary, in succession to Morris, seeing this as a disregard of the undertaking that he believed had been given to him in 1897. He said then that in conversation with Cadogan at the time he had told him that the offices on which he thought he would have a claim were the places of Ashbourne [lord chancellor] or Morris [lord of appeal in ordinary] as being the only judicial places which were superior to that in the Court of Appeal which he was passing up.[155] A few months earlier he had expressed doubt whether Salisbury was well disposed towards him, and whether he could rely with any confidence upon the assurances that the lord lieutenant had given him in 1897, even though the prime minister had expressly authorised them.[156] He declined offers from the government of appointments to vacancies in the High Court in 1897 and 1900.[157]

Newspaper reports and speculation linked him to other possible vacancies, including replacing FitzGibbon LJ in the Court of Appeal,[158] or Gerald Balfour as chief secretary,[159] or becoming lord chief justice,[160] or a lord of appeal in ordinary in place of Lord Macnaghten.[161] Early in 1905 he declined a proposed appointment to a political office, to succeed George Wyndham as chief secretary.[162] He had played a part in putting pressure on the prime minister, Arthur Balfour (who had succeeded Salisbury in 1902), to ask Wyndham to step down,[163] by reason of a very

151 *Irish Times*, 28 May 1897. See also *ILT&SJ*, vol. 31, p. 275 (12 June 1897).
152 Atkinson to Cadogan, 3 June 1897 (Cadogan Papers, CAD/1113).
153 Salisbury to Cadogan, 7 June 1897 (Cadogan Papers, CAD/1117).
154 *Irish Times*, 16 June 1897.
155 Atkinson to Gerald Balfour, 6 May 1900 (Gerald Balfour Papers, PRO 30/60/15).
156 Atkinson to Cadogan, 12 December 1899 (Cadogan Papers, CAD/1689).
157 Gerald Balfour to Cadogan, 27 October 1897 (Cadogan Papers, CAD/1217/1); Atkinson to Cadogan, 24 October 1897 (Cadogan Papers, CAD/1217/2); Atkinson to Cadogan, 2 January 1900 (Cadogan Papers, CAD/1715); *Law Times*, vol. 108, p. 221 (6 January 1900).
158 *Irish Times*, 29 September 1897.
159 *ILT&SJ*, vol. 34, p. 90 (24 February 1900).
160 *New Irish Jurist*, vol. 1 (I), p. 337 (16 September 1901).
161 *New Irish Jurist*, vol. 2 (II), p. 381 (19 September 1902); *Law Times*, vol. 117, p. 100 (4 June 1904), and vol. 119, p. 489 (14 October 1905).
162 Eunan O'Halpin, *The decline of the Union: British government in Ireland, 1892–1920* (Dublin/Syracuse, 1987), p. 53.
163 Henry W. Lucy, *The Balfour parliament, 1900–1905* (London, 1906), p. 393.

strong Unionist reaction, particularly in Ulster, to a proposed scheme of devolution in which the under-secretary at Dublin Castle, Sir Antony MacDonnell, had a background involvement. He enjoyed good relations with Walter Long, who then became chief secretary, who referred to him as 'the wisest of counsellors. In affairs of state he never failed me and in private life he was the cheeriest of friends'.[164] Long appreciated Atkinson's good humour as a companion on couple of extensive official motoring tours of the country, and another member of the party, Sir Henry Robinson of the Local Government Board, noted Atkinson's poor navigation skills; if the group failed to pass by or locate a view that he had spoken of showing them he would say that he had wished instead to indicate the desolation of the district.[165]

Judges were entitled to retire on full pension after 15 years' service, and in the autumn of 1905, as it became clear that the Conservative government would soon lose office, it was noted in the law journals that 9 of the 15 Irish judges (not counting the lord chancellor) were eligible to retire on that basis.[166] No vacancy in fact did arise at that time, and even if it had Atkinson may not have accepted a position in the High Court having declined a place in the Court of Appeal. Long was reported as denying 'with some vehemence that any member of the Irish judiciary has been approached by the government with a view to his resignation during the existence of the present administration'.[167] Atkinson's refusal of offers of actual appointments, together with none of the mooted possible appointments materialising, led to a scramble to find a place on the bench for him as the Conservative government left office at the end of November 1905.

The drama in November 1905 at the end of which he was appointed a lord of appeal is described in chapter 14. Lord Lindley retired on 29 November 1905, and Atkinson was appointed to succeed him on 4 December,[168] this being announced a few hours after the resignation that afternoon of the prime minister, Arthur Balfour.[169] He advised this by telegram to a leading constituent and also wrote more formally from his home that day to the chairman of the constituency party advising that as 'His Majesty has been graciously pleased to appoint me to the distinguished post of a lord of appeal in ordinary my Parliamentary connection with North Derry is now necessarily severed'.[170] His appointment as a life peer was formally made on 19 December 1905, and the fact that he voted (in a Dublin constituency) in the general election held the following month led to some embarrassment for him, as members of the House of Lords were not entitled to vote in a Parliamentary election. In a letter of explanation and apology to the speaker of the House of Commons he said that 'at the time I voted I did not think

164 Long, op. cit., p. 168.
165 Long, op. cit., p. 370.
166 *Law Times*, vol. 119, p. 461 (30 September 1905); *ILT&SJ*, vol. 39, p. 396 (25 November 1905).
167 *ILT&SJ*, vol. 39, p. 368 (28 October 1905).
168 *Irish Times*, 5 December 1905.
169 R.J.Q. Adams, *Balfour: the last grandee* (London, 2007), p. 225.
170 *Irish Times*, 7 December 1905 (letter dated 4 December 1905).

that any question could be raised as to my right to exercise the franchise, since my patent had not then been delivered to me, nor had I received any summons to the House of Lords'.[171] Atkinson's work in the House of Lords is discussed in chapter 14. He served for over two decades as a Law Lord, retiring somewhat reluctantly in 1928, when aged 86, at the request of the lord chancellor, Lord Cave. He told a friend and former colleague, Lord Buckmaster, that he had had no idea of resigning, as he did not feel unequal to the work (while acknowledging that no man is a good judge in his own cause), and that no reason was given by Cave for dispensing with his services other than that 'I was the oldest of the old fogies and had better resign'.[172]

He had four sons, the eldest of whom, Cecil (1876–1919), was called to the Bar in 1901. He became a KC in 1914 and was appointed the following year as a judge of the High Court in India, where he died in a railway accident in 1919.[173] He had been counsel for the prosecutor in an (unsuccessful) appeal before the High Court against a decision of the magistrates in Dunfanaghy, Co. Donegal, that a law requiring the name of the owner of a cart to be shown on its side in legible characters had not been complied with by painting the name of Niall Mac Giolla Bhrighde in Gaelic script.[174] This was one of the few reported cases in which Patrick Pearse BL appeared in court, representing the defendant. Two other sons, Hector (born 1879) and Hubert (born 1882), served in the army during the Great War.

Atkinson lived in Fitzwilliam Square and later in London, where he died at his home, 39 Hyde Park Gate, in 1932. He is buried, with his wife, in Deansgrange cemetery. He bequeathed to the King's Inns a portrait in oils, painted in 1907 by John St Helier Lander.[175]

171 HC Deb, 4th series, vol. 152, col. 105 (19 February 1906).
172 R.F.V. Heuston, op. cit., p. 304.
173 *ILT&SJ*, vol. 49, p. 309 (11 December 1915) and vol. 53, p. 258 (29 November 1919).
174 McBride appellant, McGovern respondent, [1906] 2 IR 181. This was soon cited and followed in the magistrate's court in Dublin, in Hebron v Cole (New *Irish Jurist*, vol. 5, p. 331 (15 September 1905)).
175 Wanda Ryan-Smolin, *King's Inns portraits* (Dublin, 1992), p. 3.

CHAPTER TWELVE

Appointments between 1906 and 1914

WHEN THE LIBERAL PARTY formed a government in December 1905 Samuel Walker was re-appointed as lord chancellor. He died in office in the summer of 1911 and was succeeded by Redmond Barry, who however soon became seriously unwell and retired early in 1913. His successor was Ignatius O'Brien. James O. Wylie was appointed in 1906 and W.H. Dodd in 1907. On the death of lord justice FitzGibbon in 1909 R.R. Cherry replaced him in the Court of Appeal, and he subsequently replaced Lord O'Brien of Kilfenora as lord chief justice when he retired in 1913 after 24 years' service in that office. The government became increasingly mindful of nationalist concerns when making law officer and judicial appointments. Charles O'Connor was appointed as master of the rolls in 1912, and Thomas Molony to the High Court in 1914 and to the Court of Appeal in 1915. J.F. Moriarty was appointed to the Court of Appeal in 1914 but died within twelve months.

James O. Wylie

Judicial Commissioner of the Land Commission 1906–20

James Owens Wylie (1845–1935) was the son of W.A. Wylie of Rushvale, Ballyclare, Co. Antrim. He was a Presbyterian, and was educated at the Royal Belfast Academical Institution and at what was then known as Queen's College Belfast, later Queen's University. After his call to the Bar in 1872, he joined the North West circuit. In 1881 he was a co-editor of a detailed handbook and guide to the Judicature Act and the rules of practice and procedure made thereunder. He became the sole editor for the second and third editions (in 1895 and 1906)[1] of this monumental work, which was for decades the standard guide and resource for litigation practice and procedure. He was appointed by the lord chancellor as a member of the committee of experts to advise and concur in the making of rules of court.

He was appointed as one of a good number of sub-commissioners under the Land Law (Ireland) Act 1881,[2] whose function (subject to an appeal process) was to determine a fair rent for tenants' holdings. He served in that capacity for some years in Co. Tyrone and in other counties (Carlow, Wicklow, Wexford and Queen's

1 *The Judicature Acts (Ireland) and Orders, Rules and Forms thereunder, copiously annotated* (Dublin, 1895); *The Judicature Acts (Ireland) and Rules of the Supreme Court (Ireland) 1905, copiously annotated* (Dublin, 1906).
2 44&45 Vict., c.49.

County (Laois)),[3] and later served as a legal assistant commissioner.[4] Holding such an appointment could not be combined with practice at the Bar, as was brought out in a parliamentary question about the propriety of him prospectively subsequently returning to the Bar and receiving briefs 'from those solicitors who are now pleading before him in his capacity as a judge'.[5]

He stood as a Liberal candidate in the North Tyrone constituency in the 1886 general election, losing to Lord Ernest William Hamilton, a member of a very prominent local family headed by the duke of Abercorn, half a dozen of the members of which held seats in Tyrone and Londonderry in the course of the nineteenth century. Some years later he was appointed as a revising barrister for the electoral register in the city of Londonderry. The sitting Unionist MP, John Ross, while describing Wylie as 'an advanced Home Ruler', knew him well and had confidence in his impartiality, but at all events he was defeated by a Nationalist in the next general election, in 1895, and his supporters attributed this to the register having been revised to his disadvantage.[6]

Wylie took silk in 1894, and the following year was appointed senior Crown prosecutor for Co. Cavan.[7] In 1906 he was appointed one of the two judicial commissioners of the Land Commission, having the status of a High Court judge, succeeding R.E. Meredith who had been appointed master of the rolls. A tribute was paid to him in 1907 in a debate in the House of Lords on the bill that was enacted as the Evicted Tenants' (Ireland) Act by Lord Lansdowne, a prominent Irish landowner and a Conservative, who said that he would accept him acting in a new appeal capacity under the Act by reason of 'the confidence inspired by Mr Justice Wylie's high character and antecedents and, of course, if they were to substitute some judicial persons as to whom the same feelings were not entertained, a very serious blow would be struck at the Bill'.[8]

Very substantial interests might be subject to determination by a judicial commissioner under the Land Acts. Wylie fixed £238,211[9] as the price of the extensive estates in Co. Galway of the marquis of Clanricarde, whose arguments seeking to restrain the Congested Districts Board from compulsorily acquiring them were ultimately dismissed by the House of Lords.[10] He sat as a High Court judge when all other judges were unavailable, being out on circuit (assizes), hearing 'bankruptcy business and such common law motions as require to be heard promptly',[11] and at least once in an action for construction of a will.[12]

3 *ILT&SJ*, vol. 15, p. 626 (10 December 1881).
4 *ILT&SJ*, vol. 17, p. 215 (21 April 1883).
5 HC Deb, 3rd series, vol. 270, col. 808 (12 June 1882).
6 Sir John Ross, *The years of my pilgrimage* (London, 1924), p. 114.
7 *ILT&SJ*, vol. 29, p. 167 (30 March 1895).
8 *ILT&SJ*, vol. 41, p. 222 (31 August 1907).
9 *ILT&SJ*, vol. 49, p. 184 (31 July 1915).
10 *Marquis of Clanricarde v Congested Districts Board for Ireland*, [1915] IR 422; 49 ILTR 42 (1915).
11 *ILT&SJ*, vol. 48, p. 66 (1 March 1913).
12 In the matter of Randal Kingsmill Moore's Rents, [1917] 1 IR 244.

Wylie was unwell for a time in 1919,[13] and resigned in November 1920, being succeeded by his nephew, William E. Wylie. His second son, Lieut. Arthur Wylie, was killed in action in France in 1915.[14] Wylie and his family lived in Upper Fitzwilliam Street. They moved to England in his retirement, living in Kensington, and he died at Winchester in December 1935.[15]

William Huston Dodd

Justice of the High Court (King's Bench division) 1907–24

William Huston Dodd (1844–1930) was born in Rathfriland, Co. Down, and educated at the Royal Belfast Academical Institution and the Queen's College, Belfast. He taught for some years in schools associated with the Presbyterian church and engaged in some journalism.[16] He entered King's Inns in 1870 and was called to the Bar in 1873. He was said to have enjoyed 'an excellent practice' in the courts of his native county, particularly in matters arising out of the legislation affecting the rights of tenant farmers.[17] He became a QC in 1884 and was a Crown prosecutor for the city and county of Dublin at Green Street.[18] He was appointed third serjeant in 1892, and became a bencher of King's Inns in 1893.[19] He was president of the Statistical and Social Inquiry Society of Ireland for a term between 1894 and 1896, and in his opening address reviewed 'the work of the society and some of the things that have happened since it was founded'.[20]

He was a Gladstonian Liberal, and stood unsuccessfully in the constituencies of North Antrim and South Derry respectively in the general elections of 1892 and 1895. In the election of January 1906 he won the seat of North Tyrone. He had been selected at the end of December 1905 as the Liberal candidate, defeating at a convention a son of the sitting Liberal MP for the constituency, Charles Hemphill QC, who was now retiring at the age of 83. Any existing connection that he may have had with the constituency was not stressed by his proposer, who spoke of his generous support of the fund for voter registration and the fact that he supported Home Rule.[21] North Tyrone was a very marginal constituency, and it was considered that a Liberal rather than a Nationalist candidate would maximise the non-Unionist vote. Hemphill had won the seat in the previous two elections, and the conferring of a peerage on him was announced the day after the selection convention.[22] Dodd won the seat with a majority of nine votes out of almost 6,000

13 *ILT&SJ*, vol. 53, p. 250 (18 October 1919).
14 *ILT&SJ*, vol. 49, p. 70 (20 March 1915).
15 *Irish Times*, 21 December 1935.
16 *Irish Times*, 18 and 22 March 1930.
17 *ILT&SJ*, vol. 41, p. 62 (2 March 1907).
18 *ILT&SJ*, vol. 19, p. 286 (30 May 1885); *Irish Times*, 1 March 1907.
19 A.R. Hart. *A history of the king's serjeants at law in Ireland* (Dublin, 2000), pp 130, 157.
20 W.H. Dodd, *Address at the opening of the 48th session of the Statistical and Social Inquiry Society of Ireland* (Dublin, 1894).
21 *Irish Times*, 28 December 1905.
22 *Irish Times*, 30 December 1905.

cast (2,966 votes to 2,957). He was not appointed a law officer in the new government formed by the Liberal party in December 1905, despite some expectation that, as a prominent Liberal at the Bar, he would become attorney general.[23] In his maiden speech in the House of Commons he called for common purpose for the good of the nation, in a spirit of peace, true friendship and Christian charity, and referred to himself as 'a Protestant of the Protestants, but he stood upon the platform in North Tyrone surrounded by priests of the Church of Rome. He declared that he had never contributed to any ecclesiastical structure connected with the Church of Rome. Yet he was selected as their candidate, and although his opponent was a Catholic [Denis Henry KC] he was elected'.[24]

He sat as an MP for little more than a year, being appointed as a High Court judge in February 1907.[25] There was no immediate cause to appoint an additional judge at the time, and the chief secretary for Ireland, Augustine Birrell, acknowledged, in response to a question from William Moore, Unionist MP for North Armagh, who would himself be appointed a High Court judge in 1917, that a vacancy had existed in the King's Bench division since January 1904.[26] Later that year the law was amended to provide that the next two vacancies in the King's Bench division would not be filled, implementing a proposal made by the previous government in 1904. A judicial re-shuffle in October 1906 had resulted in the promotion of Meredith and Wylie, but hopes of others (Dodd, Charles O'Connor and Cherry) had been raised and then frustrated. The lord chancellor, Walker, advised at the end of December 1906 that the intended appointment of Dodd should proceed, on the basis of there being a reasonable prospect that the solicitor general, Redmond J. Barry, would hold the seat in Tyrone at the bye-election that Dodd's appointment would cause. The object of the promotion was thus to create (and fill) a suitable vacancy in Parliament. Within a few days of Dodd's appointment Barry was nominated to stand at the bye-election,[27] which was held on 8 March, and he held the seat with an even smaller majority than before, of seven votes (3,013 votes to 3,006).

Dodd's judicial work included a wide variety of criminal and common law civil business, and included trials, generally with juries, for personal injuries, contract law, defamation, divorce and actions for breach of promise of marriage. Actions over contested wills and other probate applications included one relating to the will of Martin Carey of Newport, Co. Mayo, who had left £10,000 for the construction of a church in the village.[28] He assisted in the work of the Land Commission court. He was the judge at first instance of a case that ultimately went to the House of Lords, which upheld his judgment, as to whether an old age pension (as introduced in 1909) could be withdrawn if additional information

23 *Irish Times*, 11 December 1905.
24 HC Deb, 4th series, vol. 152, col. 394 (21 February 1906).
25 *Irish Times*, 22 February 1907.
26 HC Deb, 4th series, vol. 169, col. 1270 (25 February 1907).
27 *Irish Times*, 27 February 1907.
28 *Irish Times*, 16 and 23 June 1910. The church was completed and dedicated in 1918.

became available indicating that a person in receipt of a pension had not in fact reached the required age.[29]

Observations that Dodd made from the bench at times savoured more of the tone or atmosphere of the lower courts. The Dublin United Trades Council wrote to him to complain about a remark, which he then sought to explain:

> I asked a convicted prisoner, before I passed sentence on him, what he did for a living. He said 'I am a labourer'. I said, from my experience in prosecutions in Green Street, that that was the answer a corner boy would give. If the prisoner really was a workingman he could tell what trade he followed and where he was employed. So far from making any reflection on the class of labourers my reflections were upon those who pretended to be, when in fact they were not, members of that class. It was certainly in no way my intention to reflect upon the occupation of labourers as a class, and it was very far indeed from my intention to revile the great body of the honest workers of the city of Dublin, in whose reputation for good conduct and good character I take an honest pride as a citizen. I regret much if anything I said could convey such imputations as you justly resent.[30]

He gave offence to rural dwellers also, leading the bishop of Killaloe to protest at what he called the 'sore and bitter feelings aroused in the community', by remarks of the judge (which were self-evidently extraneous to any point arising at a trial) that 'the farmers of Clare looked twice at a halfpenny before they would spend it, and they were slow to give money to a doctor, a lawyer or a priest'.[31]

Other remarks were in the more traditional vein of judges' reactions to criminality and unsatisfactory matters arising in the course of trials. A persistent young offender was told that the judge 'believed in sharp and firm sentences as being the old fashioned form of reform. He had no belief in reformatories, but he had in His Majesty's prisons'.[32] After a jury disagreed, to the evident frustration of the judge, in a trial of a Co. Galway man accused of shooting at a neighbour with intent to kill the foreman said that the jury would like to be excused from further attendance. Dodd refused this request, saying that a murder trial was fixed for the following week and that they all must attend.[33] A man who pleaded guilty at the Cork assizes to perjury at an inquest was told, in rather Biblical terms, to go away and sin no more,[34] and Dodd then said that there had been at least twenty cases of perjury committed before him in the course of the assizes, but if all such cases were to be tried the prisons would be full.[35] During the Great War he made the

29 [1911] 2 IR 88; [1911] AC 401; *Irish Times*, 20 May 1911.
30 *ILT&SJ*, vol. 42, p. 24 (25 January 1908).
31 *Irish Times*, 21 December 1912.
32 *Irish Times*, 8 February 1913.
33 *Irish Times*, 17 June 1914.
34 John, 8:11.
35 *Irish Times*, 3 August 1918.

conventional appeals at the assizes for recruitment. He was appointed in 1918 to inquire into complaints at the treatment of Sinn Fein prisoners in Belfast prison, and his report concluded that the complaints against the prison authorities and certain named officials were unfounded.[36]

His forceful style of addressing and charging a jury is well illustrated by his observations in *Henry v Davey*, a challenge in 1921 to the will of Fr Frank Henry, parish priest of Carrickfergus, Co. Antrim. He had died shortly after making his will in November 1915, leaving much of his estate to charitable causes, and this was contested by members of his family. There was a conflict of evidence as to Fr Henry's state of mind and testamentary capacity, and Dodd expressed a strong opinion to the jury as to the honour and respectability of the persons (a solicitor and a priest) who had witnessed the will, saying that their evidence 'stands out in marvellous clearness (I say so deliberately)'.[37] The jury found that Fr Henry was of sound mind, memory and understanding, and that he did know and approve of the contents of his will. A motion for a new trial was subsequently refused by the Court of Appeal for Southern Ireland.[38]

The judiciary were a symbol of government authority during the War of Independence (1919–21), and Dodd had the common judicial experience of having an armed guard. In the Civil War that followed Dodd, as did other judges, refused habeas corpus applications on the ground that a state of war existed.[39]

His 80th birthday was noted in the probate court in March 1924, shortly before he vacated office on the reconstitution of the courts pursuant to the Courts of Justice Act 1924. He lived in Fitzwilliam Place and subsequently at 32 Leeson Park, where he died in 1930. His recreations included golf.

Richard Robert Cherry

Lord Justice of Appeal 1909–14, Lord Chief Justice of Ireland 1914–16

R.R. Cherry (1859–1923) was born in Waterford, where his father was a solicitor. The Cherry family was of Huguenot origins. He was educated at Trinity College, where he had a distinguished academic record, and was auditor of the College Historical Society.[40] He was called to the Bar in 1881, having been awarded the John Brooke scholarship for first place in the King's Inns examinations,[41] and

36 An Act to constitute a special commission to inquire into certain complaints as to the treatment of prisoners in Belfast prison 1918 (8&9 Geo. 5, c.44); *Irish Times*, 29 March 1919; *Report of inquiry* (P.P. 1919, Cmd. 83, xxvii.881).

37 I am grateful to John G. Gordon DL, who made available to me a copy of the judge's summing up. Mr Gordon's discourse on 'Where there's a will there's a contest: the will of the Very Rev. Frank Henry PP, from Carrickfergus to Rome' was given to the annual general meeting of the Irish Legal History Society in Dublin on 29 November 2024.

38 *Irish Times*, 29 December 1921 and 10 March 1922.

39 *Irish Times*, 30 September 1922 (applications of Beaumont and White).

40 Patrick Geoghegan, *The College Historical Society: oratory and debate, 1770–2020* (Dublin, 2020), p. 164.

41 FitzGibbon LJ to Cherry, 11 February 1882 (Cherry Papers (PRONI), D2166/2/1).

joined the Leinster circuit (of which Co. Waterford formed part). In 1888 he was appointed the first Reid Professor of Penal Legislation, Constitutional and Criminal Law and the Law of Evidence, a chair initially established for a non-renewable five year term on foot of a specific bequest to Trinity College for this purpose.[42] Two series of lectures that he delivered in that capacity were published, one of which included an insistence that a knowledge of the history and purpose and context of a law was essential to a proper understanding of its principles.[43]

Irish land law exemplified that point. In 1888 he published an annotated edition of the Land Acts 1881–7,[44] and this work, known as *Cherry on the Land Acts*, became the most authoritative commentary on landlord and tenant law in Ireland, and in particular the land purchase legislation. It gave him professional prominence at an early stage in his career. When Bewley J, the judicial commissioner of the Land Commission, cast doubt in 1891 on the accuracy of a reference in the volume to one judgment Cherry reacted strongly, writing to the press to set out the care that he had taken with the report – and, by extension, with all the contents of his book – and stating that 'the proposition with which [Bewley J.] does not agree was distinctly laid down by Mr Justice O'Hagan in my hearing in the case of *Walsh v the earl of Bandon*'.[45]

The second edition of his work which was published in 1893 was expanded so as to refer to all relevant statutes since 1860 (the year of Deasy's Act).[46] Cherry became a QC in 1896, and having previously been junior Crown prosecutor for the city of Waterford[47] was made senior Crown prosecutor for Co. Carlow in 1897.[48] He was appointed secretary to the Royal Commission of inquiry into the workings of the Land Acts, chaired by an English judge, Sir Edward Fry, which held public sittings in Dublin, Belfast, Cork and Galway in the autumn of 1897, and the recommendations of which (published in 1898) formed the basis of subsequent legislation, the Irish Land Act of 1903.[49] He and Dunbar Plunket Barton published an edition, with notes and forms, of the Land Law (Ireland) Act 1896.[50] In the

42 D.A. Webb (compiler), J.R. Bartlett (editor), *Trinity College Dublin, Record Volume 1991* (Dublin, 1991), p. 131. In 1975 the arrangements governing the chair were modified.

43 R.R. Cherry, *Lectures on the growth of criminal law in ancient communities* (London, 1890), p. 4. The second published series was *An outline of criminal law as regards offences against individuals* (Dublin, 1892).

44 *The Irish land law and land purchase Acts, 1881, 1885 and 1887, with a complete collection of the rules and forms issued under each Act in the Land Commission, High Court of Justice and County Courts respectively, and an appendix of incorporated statutes, edited, with full notes of the various cases decided under each section and rule* (Dublin, 1888).

45 *ILT&SJ*, vol. 25, p. 401 (18 July 1891).

46 *The Irish land law and land purchase Acts, 1860 to 1891* (Dublin, 1893).

47 *ILT&SJ*, vol. 30, p. 63 (1 February 1896).

48 *ILT&SJ*, vol. 31, p. 278 (12 June 1897).

49 3 Edw. 7, c.37 (1903).

50 59&60 Vict., c.47 (1896). D.P. Barton QC and Richard R. Cherry (eds), *The Land Law (Ireland) Act 1896; with the rules and forms issued thereunder in the Land Commission, Supreme Court and County Courts respectively* (Dublin, 1897).

preface to a third edition of his major book in 1903,[51] he remarked that the bulk of the volume was 'now becoming rather unwieldy for convenient use in court'. (The first edition had 447 pages, the second 769 and the third over 1,000.) That preface also commented that 'it is not alone by legislation that the law has been altered. The decisions of the courts, though professing not to do so, are found insensibly to modify the principles of law in all its branches, and the law of landlord and tenant in Ireland is no exception to this rule'. One of his collaborators, T.H. Maxwell BL, published a supplement in 1910, incorporating the amending Act passed in 1909.[52]

From his College days Cherry had an interest in social, political and economic issues. In its obituary in 1923 the *Irish Times* said of him that 'he was more of the type of an English Radical than an Irish Home Ruler. He was a convinced free trader. His views were very much those of John Stuart Mill on economics and social science'.[53] He read papers in the 1880s to the Statistical and Social Inquiry Society of Ireland and was its president for the term 1908–11, in which capacity he delivered an address on juvenile crime and its prevention.[54] He was a member of the committee of the Society for the Prevention of Cruelty to Children,[55] and supported the Anti-Vivisection Society, and the Society for the Protection of Birds.[56]

An initial political step was his support, while Reid professor, for the candidacy of a colleague at the Bar, Edward Carson QC, then a Liberal Unionist, for the Parliamentary constituency of Dublin University.[57] Cherry's father had been a strong supporter of Edward Gibson (later Lord Ashbourne), who had stood unsuccessfully as a Conservative candidate in the city of Waterford constituency in the 1874 general election.[58] Cherry first stood for Parliament as a Liberal candidate in the Kirkdale division of Liverpool in the 1900 general election. This became known as the 'khaki election', taking place during the war in South Africa, and what were described as his 'pro-Boer' views, which had affected his legal practice in Ireland,[59] contributed to his defeat in an unpromising constituency.

He subsequently inquired with John Redmond MP, the leader of the Irish Parliamentary Party, whether he might stand, without party opposition, as a

51 *The Irish land law and land purchase Acts, 1860 to 1901 (including the Congested Districts Board Acts)* (Dublin, 1903).
52 9 Edw. 7, c.42 (1909).
53 *Irish Times*, 12 February 1923.
54 *Journal of the Statistical and Social Inquiry Society of Ireland*, vol. 12, pp 435–50; *Irish Times*, 25 January 1911.
55 Maud Cherry, *A short memoir of the Right Hon. Richard Robert Cherry, sometime lord chief justice of Ireland* (Dublin, 1924), p. 23; *Irish Times*, 23 June 1896.
56 Cherry, *Memoir*, p. 29.
57 *Irish Times*, 19 May 1890 and 25 June 1892.
58 *Irish Times*, 12 February 1923.
59 W.K. Tarpey BL to Cherry, 23 December 1905 (Cherry Papers (PRONI), D2166/2/2/1/17); Cherry, *Memoir*, pp 15–16.

Liberal candidate in an Irish constituency.[60] Redmond replied that he would welcome Cherry in representing an Irish constituency as a member of an independent party, but could not offer public support to any member of the Irish Bar except on the basis that he would not seek any legal or judicial office.[61] In January 1905 he was nominated as prospective candidate for another Liverpool constituency, the Exchange division, and he was elected there in the Liberal landslide victory in the January 1906 general election.[62] In his campaign he emphasised free trade, old age pensions, education, trade union rights and other social issues. He had been appointed attorney general for Ireland in December 1905 when a Liberal government was formed after the Conservative government resigned before an election was called. His work in government over the next four years included advising on the preparation of the university legislation of 1908[63] and the Irish Land Act of 1909[64] which greatly expanded the functions of the Congested Districts Board. In 1906 he complained to James Bryce, the chief secretary for Ireland, that he had been excluded from consultations on (and not officially informed about) proposals for judicial appointments consequent on the intended retirement of Andrew Marshall Porter. He stressed that he was not then looking for judicial promotion for himself, and accepted that Bryce might not have been aware of how such appointments were customarily handled in Ireland and intended no discourtesy, while still remarking that the lord chancellor, Walker, would have known this.[65]

In 1909 a political crisis developed over the Unionist opposition (particularly the resistance in the House of Lords) to the Finance Bill that would give effect to 'the People's Budget' of Lloyd George. Speculation about an early general election (which eventually was held in January 1910) was fuelled by the unprecedented rejection by the House of Lords of the bill at the end of November, and there was some prospect in the autumn not only of the government losing office but also of Cherry losing his seat in the House of Commons. As attorney general he had first call on being appointed to fill any judicial vacancy, and one had arisen in the Court of Appeal in October through the death of lord justice FitzGibbon.

His wife Mary Wilhelmina Cooper, whom he had married in 1886 (and who died in 1935),[66] expressed her concerns about the toll that the stress and strain of political life had taken on his health, remarking that to be in opposition would be worse than trying to work at his profession. She wondered whether five years more

60 Cherry to Redmond, 17 February 1904 (John Redmond Papers (National Library of Ireland), MS 15,175/7/2).

61 Redmond to Cherry, 22 February 1904 (Cherry Papers (PRONI), D2166/3/2/2, and Redmond Papers, MS 15,175/7/3). Alvin Jackson, *Judging Redmond and Carson* (Dublin, 2018), p. 89.

62 For Cherry's political career in Liverpool see Daire Hogan, 'R.R. Cherry, Lord Chief Justice of Ireland 1914–16' in D.S. Greer & N.M. Dawson (eds), *Mysteries and solutions in Irish legal history* (Dublin, 2005), pp 161–92 at 168–79.

63 8 Edw. 7, c.38.

64 8 Edw. 7, c.42.

65 Cherry to Bryce, 13 and 14 October 1906 (Bryce Papers (NLI), MS 11.014(2)).

66 *ILT&SJ*, vol. 68, p. 186 (6 July 1935).

of politics would be too much for her husband, and asked him to put his health before his career.[67] 'In the interests of his wife and family he considered it would be imprudent to refuse a permanent legal position'.[68] Since the Land Bill had not yet been enacted, however, he continued in office as attorney general and a member of Parliament for a further six weeks, assisting in dealing with numerous amendments to the Bill that had been put forward by the House of Lords, before the formal appointment to the judicial bench was made at the start of December 1909. The honour of the freedom of the city of Waterford was conferred on him in 1910.

He had been an athlete when young, but his health began to fail in later years. His daughter Maud noted that in 1913 he first became aware of the symptoms of a creeping paralysis which 'was to make the rest of his life a constant struggle against increasing weakness'.[69] In February 1914 he became lord chief justice of Ireland, not having sought the office of lord chancellor of Ireland when a vacancy had arisen the year before. Ignatius O'Brien noted that 'he did not feel his own health equal to what would be the more troublesome job [of lord chancellor] and which might at any time terminate on a change of government'.[70] He was among the judges who never had occasion to pronounce the mandatory sentence of death in a murder trial, and it has been said that his views on capital punishment might be inferred from his opposition to vivisection,[71] but he prosecuted in murder trials, at least one of which resulted in the conviction and execution of the accused person.[72] His judgments in his judicial career of seven years were well respected,[73] but his main contribution to Irish law might be considered to be his scholarship in land law and the sharing of his expertise in his books on the subject.[74] Lord Glenavy spoke of a robust direction given to a jury by Cherry, that they were 'faced here with a notorious and peculiar defence – an alibi. I tell you from my long experience that in 99 cases out of 100 that defence is a tissue of falsehoods from beginning to end. I do not think this case is any exception, and I strongly recommend you totally to disregard it'.[75] It may have been different in England: 'now I suppose he [Mr Pickwick] will want to call some witnesses to speak to his character or perhaps to prove a alleybi – I've got some friends as will do either for him, but my advice would be – never mind the character, and stick to the alleybi. Nothing like an alleybi, Sam, nothing'.[76]

67 Minna Cherry to R.R. Cherry, 20 October 1909 (Cherry Papers (PRONI), D2166/1/1/6).
68 Cherry, *Memoir*, p. 22.
69 Cherry, *Memoir*, p. 31.
70 Daire Hogan and Patrick Maume (eds), *The reminiscences of Ignatius O'Brien, lord chancellor of Ireland, 1913–18* (Dublin, 2021), p. 249.
71 W.E. Vaughan, *Murder trials in Ireland, 1836–1914* (Dublin, 2009), p. 259.
72 *ILT&SJ*, vol. 43, p. 318 (4 September 1909).
73 See Hogan, op. cit., pp 183–8, for some commentary on his judgments.
74 *Law Times*, vol. 142, p. 134 (23 December 1916).
75 Seanad Debates, 16 January 1924.
76 Charles Dickens, *The Pickwick Papers* (London, 1837), Chapter 33.

In June 1915 the prime minister, Asquith, who had been given reports of Cherry's ill health and was hoping for his assistance or co-operation in solving and relieving the complications arising from the recent thwarting of James H.M. Campbell's ambition to be lord chancellor, inquired whether he was minded to retire.[77] Cherry declined then to step aside, and refused again in February 1916, when Asquith wrote that he was sorry to hear that his health had not improved and that 'I gather from Birrell [the chief secretary for Ireland] that you have come to the conclusion that it would be right for you to retire'. The prime minster offered to arrange for a suitable 'honorific mark of recognition' – which, although unspecified, might have been a knighthood or a baronetcy – in that connection.[78] A couple of months later Asquith spoke to John Redmond, telling him that 'he had tried his best to get Cherry to resign but had failed up to the present. He said that he would be delighted to put Campbell in Cherry's place tomorrow if Cherry would give way, and asked me did I know of anyone who could bring influence to bear on Cherry to induce him to give way'.[79] Cherry's eventual retirement at the end of the law term in December 1916 took place shortly after the displacement of Asquith as prime minister by Lloyd George, although the arrangements had been made the previous month by Asquith.[80] He continued to sit as a judge for a while longer during an absence of Campbell through illness.[81]

After appointment as a judge he had fulfilled a long-held aspiration of having a country house by taking a lease for ten years of Killincarrig House, near Greystones, Co. Wicklow.[82] He was a prominent lay member of the Church of Ireland, 'a strong Churchman [who] took an active interest in all its affairs'.[83] He was a member of the Representative Church Body and of the board of St Patrick's Cathedral. He had a lifelong interest, from his youth in Waterford,[84] in campanology or change (bell) ringing, and was one of the bell ringers in the cathedral, to which he donated two bells upon his appointment as attorney general in 1905.[85] He lived within earshot of the cathedral for almost 30 years, at his home at 92 St Stephen's Green, until his death in February 1923.

77 Asquith to Cherry, 23 June 1915 (R.F.V. Heuston, *Lives of the lord chancellors, 1885–1940* (Oxford, 1964)), p. 270.
78 Asquith to Cherry, 16 February 1916 (Heuston, op. cit., pp 273–4).
79 Redmond to John Dillon, 3 May 1916 (Denis Gwynn, *The life of Redmond* (London, 1932), p. 482).
80 *ILT&SJ*, vol. 50, p. 317 (2 December 1916); Hogan, op. cit., pp 191–2.
81 Cherry, *Memoir*, p. 31.
82 Cherry, *Memoir*, p. 27.
83 *Irish Times*, 12 February 1923.
84 Report (newspaper not identified), 26 October 1906, in scrapbook of newspaper cuttings, p. 35 (Cherry Papers (PRONI), D2166/4/1/2).
85 Cherry, *Memoir*, p. 8.

Redmond Barry

Lord Chancellor of Ireland 1911–13

Redmond Barry (1866–1913) was born in Cork, where his father was a well-known builder and contractor.[86] He was educated at Blackrock College and at Queen's College Cork. After his call to the Bar in 1888 he made rapid progress in his profession, becoming a QC in 1899. It was said that 'he was especially successful in those jury cases in which forensic eloquence still helps to turn the legal scale', and had a 'suavity of manner'.[87] His practice encompassed criminal law, personal injuries, divorce, probate and defamation, and he was counsel for the plaintiff, Alexis Roche, in a case brought against Sir Timothy O'Brien for slander spoken in the hunting field.[88] The trial drew a fashionable crowd to the courthouse in Cork, but was soon adjourned when it emerged that a connection of Sir Timothy had spoken to a member of the jury about his view of the case, and the prospect of a verdict against O'Brien for nominal damages of a farthing. The jury was dismissed, O'Brien fined and ordered to pay costs, and the trial moved to Dublin.[89]

Barry was appointed solicitor general by the new Liberal government in December 1905, and became more formally identified with the Liberal party in March 1907 when he stood as its candidate and was elected to the House of Commons at a bye-election for the constituency of North Tyrone. Over the next four years he spoke frequently for the government in Parliament. He held his seat, with narrow majorities, in the two general elections in January and December 1910. He was appointed attorney general in December 1909 in succession to R.R. Cherry, who had been appointed to the Court of Appeal.

His criminal law practice had included both defence and prosecution work, although he necessarily ceased to act for defendants when he became a law officer. In response to a suggestion that a good effect – and some financial savings – might be produced if the law officers were to conduct more prosecutions on assizes themselves, not delegating this 'to some counsel in the neighbourhood or someone they send down from Dublin' he said that this would be physically impossible, even if desirable, and outlined the principle on which the law officers would from time to time appear in particular criminal cases. These would be 'selected not for any private reason at all, but because, owing to their great importance and sometimes to their great difficulty, it is felt that it is best the law officers should personally conduct them. Particular cases are selected entirely because of their importance and the public interest taken in them'.[90]

In August 1911 he was appointed lord chancellor following the death of Samuel Walker. His period of office transpired to be short, for no more than a handful of law terms. Serious illness prevented him from sitting in court at all in the first

86 *Irish Times*, 12 July 1913.
87 *Irish Times*, 2 September 1911 and 29 August 1911.
88 *Irish Times*, 23 July 1908.
89 Healy, *OldMC*, pp 247–8. *Law Times*, vol. 126, p. 51 (23 November 1908).
90 HC Deb, 5th series, vol. 22, col. 2601 (17 March 1911).

months of 1913, and he resigned at the end of March. He died at his residence, Corkagh, Clondalkin, Co. Dublin, a few months later, on 12 July.

In 1895 he had married Ethel Pyke of Southport, Lancashire. Their only son, Patrick Barry (1898–1972), was educated at Downside school in Somerset, Sandhurst and Oxford University (Balliol College). He was called to the English Bar in 1923, and was appointed a judge of the High Court in 1950, retiring in 1966.[91]

Charles Andrew O'Connor

Master of the Rolls 1912–24, Justice of the Supreme Court of the Irish Free State 1924–5

Charles Andrew O'Connor (1854–1928) was born in Roscommon, the son of a solicitor, and was educated at Trinity College. In 1877 he became auditor of the College Historical Society, defeating Edward Carson in the election, and invited Lord Randolph Churchill to speak in reply to his inaugural address.[92] He was called to the Bar in 1878, joining the Connaught circuit. He became a QC in 1894 and was elected a bencher of King's Inns in 1896. He had a very good practice in Chancery and probate matters. He drafted a scheme of endowment of the Palestrina Choir at the Pro-Cathedral in Dublin for Edward Martyn,[93] whom he represented in his action in 1907 against the Kildare Street Club. He had previously represented the Stephen's Green Club (of which he was a member) in obtaining an injunction restricting the operation of a veterinary hospital for dogs in premises in a lane off Dawson Street, since the noise of the animals at night was causing annoyance to the members and staff of the club.[94]

When Porter indicated in September 1906 that he would step down as master of rolls O'Connor was put forward by the lord chancellor, Walker, to be his successor.[95] The chief secretary, Bryce, told the prime minister that O'Connor was a leading KC and the only prominent Liberal of mark, except W.H. Dodd, at the Irish Bar.[96] This nomination was queried by the undersecretary MacDonnell, who told Bryce that Walker's view of O'Connor's abilities was not universally shared, and that Dodd was senior to him at the Bar and would vehemently object if he were passed over.[97] As it transpired neither O'Connor nor Dodd was then appointed, although a judicial position for Dodd was found soon afterwards. The possibility

91 *Northern Circuit Directory* (Liverpool, 2005).

92 Patrick Geoghegan, *The College Historical Society: oratory and debate, 1770–2020* (Dublin, 2020), pp 157, 161–2; Charles A. O'Connor, *Philosophy and politics*, inaugural address delivered in the Dining Hall of Trinity College, on 14 November 1877 (Dublin, 1877).

93 Denis Gwynn, *Edward Martyn and the Irish Revival* (London, 1930), p. 198.

94 *Irish Times*, 15 July 1896.

95 Walker to Bryce, 17 September 1906 (two letters) (Bryce Papers, MS 11,014(1)).

96 Bryce to Campbell Bannerman, 4, 10 and 11 October 1906 (Campbell-Bannerman Papers, Add. MS 41211.340, 351 and 356).

97 MacDonnell to Bryce, 19 September 1906 (Bryce Papers, MS 11,014(1)).

was then canvassed by Bryce that O'Connor would be appointed to the place in the Land Commission just vacated by Meredith, who had succeeded Porter, but that idea also had to be dropped when the leading Nationalist MPs, Redmond and Dillon, expressed strong objections.[98]

In May 1907 O'Connor was appointed third serjeant, and he was advanced to being first serjeant in December that year.[99] His political activity at this time included a speech at a public meeting in the Round Room of the Mansion House in March 1907 in support of the Liberal government's proposals for university reform, saying that the objections being raised by Trinity College showed 'the utmost selfishness'.[100] When the Irish Universities Act 1908 came into effect he was appointed a member of the governing body of University College Dublin,[101] and also to be a member of the senate of the new National University of Ireland. When the validity of the appointment as a county court judge of M.M. Bodkin, a prominent nationalist journalist, was challenged he was briefed, with the attorney general and solicitor general, to defend it. The Munster Bar had passed a resolution protesting at the appointment of persons 'having no real business at the Bar',[102] and it was contended that Bodkin had not met the statutory requirement of being a practising member of the Bar for the previous ten years at least.[103] In 1911 he was prominent at a dinner to honour John Redmond, MP,[104] and he presided at a public meeting organised by the Dublin and Counties Liberal Association to promote a proportional representation electoral system.[105] He was spoken of as a potential Liberal candidate for a bye-election in North Tyrone later that year, when Barry vacated the seat.[106]

In 1909 he was appointed solicitor general, and in September 1911 attorney general, an office that he held for some nine months before becoming master of the rolls in June 1912 when Meredith retired. He thus became a judge of first instance in the Chancery division and an ex officio member of the Court of Appeal. 'A more gentlemanly figure never graced the Irish Bar. White-haired, pink-faced, dapper, he might have stepped out of an eighteenth century play'.[107] His judgments comprised determinations of conventional Chancery issues, including a suit on directors' powers to present a petition for the winding-up of a company,[108]

98 Redmond to Bryce, 16 October 1906, Dillon to Bryce, 17 October 1906 (Bryce Papers, MS 11,014(2)).
99 A.R. Hart, *A history of the king's serjeants at law in Ireland* (Dublin, 2000), pp 122–3, 157–8; *Irish Times*, 4 March and 16 December 1907.
100 *Irish Times*, 13 and 18 March 1907.
101 *Irish Times*, 30 December 1908.
102 *Law Times*, vol. 122, p. 524 (6 April 1907). See also vol. 124, pp 286–7 (25 January 1908), pp 309–10 (1 February 1908) and p. 331 (8 February 1908).
103 The King (Markham) v Bodkin, *Irish Times*, 24 January 1908; Healy, *OldMC*, pp 184–90; A.M. Sullivan, *Old Ireland, reminiscences of an Irish KC* (London, 1927), p. 153.
104 *Irish Times*, 19 January 1911.
105 *Irish Times*, 21 April 1911.
106 *Irish Times*, 25 August 1911.
107 Healy, *OldMC* p. 284.
108 *Re Galway and Salthill Tramways Co.*, [1918] 1 IR 62.

and the rule against perpetuities.[109] He heard motions in the King's Bench division when all other judges were out of Dublin on circuit.[110]

Decisions that he made in a number of habeas corpus applications during the War of Independence (1919–21) and the Civil War (1922–3) reviewed the issue of whether, in times of war or armed rebellion, the civil courts had power to restrain the actions of the military authorities. It was generally understood that as a matter of common law the executive arm of government might use force to wage war or repress armed rebellion, and that for this purpose the military arm of the executive might exercise a penal control over the civilian population in affected areas. It was further considered that this control might be exercised by 'courts' of military personnel with no statutory basis, and that the acts of such bodies could not be reviewed or invalidated by the ordinary courts.[111]

In February 1921 the King's Bench division of the High Court adopted or followed that classical view, holding in *R v Allen*[112] that the activity of the military in areas that had been proclaimed to be under martial law could not be controlled by the court. This was despite the applicant prisoner having been sentenced to death for offences for which a lesser penalty was prescribed by a statute (the Restoration of Order in Ireland Act 1920)[113] specifically passed to deal with the state of war or rebellion in Ireland.

O'Connor later that year declined, albeit with some hesitation, to follow *R v Allen*, and in *Egan v Macready*[114] reached a contrary determination. The applicant for an order of habeas corpus, Egan, had been sentenced to death by a military court at Limerick for being 'improperly in possession of ammunition'. At the end of July 1921 O'Connor made absolute a conditional order, and ordered Egan to be set free, on the basis that since a state of war had existed at the date of passing of the Restoration of Order in Ireland Act (9 August 1920) the executive powers of the military authorities (as derived from the prerogative of the Crown) had been limited by Parliament in that Act (which did not prescribe death but only imprisonment for the offence of which Egan had been convicted), and that an offence punishable by death could be tried by no authority other than a court martial under that Act. The military refused to release Egan (and a similarly detained companion) immediately, pending an intended appeal. O'Connor regarded this as a deliberate contempt of court and issued writs of attachment (in effect, arrest), for this contempt, against the military commanders in Ireland, General Macready (who in turn contemplated the arrest of O'Connor),[115] General Strickland and others.[116]

109 *In re Ramadge's Settlement, Hamilton v Ramadge*, [1919] 1 IR 205.
110 *ILT&SJ*, vol. 47, p. 192 (12 July 1913).
111 J.M. Kelly, *Fundamental rights in the Irish law and constitution* (2nd ed., Dublin, 1967), pp 264–5.
112 [1921] 2 IR 241. The court consisted of Molony LCJ and Gibson, Gordon, Moore and Samuels JJ.
113 10&11 Geo. 5, c.31.
114 [1921] 1 IR 265.
115 General Sir F.C.N. Macready, *Annals of an active life* (London, 1924), vol. 2, p. 587.
116 *ILT&SJ*, vol. 55, pp 192–3 (6 August 1921).

A truce had been agreed in the War of Independence earlier that month, and delicate negotiations were taking place between the British government and Sinn Fein about arranging more substantive talks for a settlement. The cabinet decided, on the advice of Sir John Ross, the lord chancellor of Ireland, to override the military view and release the men, since 'the movement for peace in Ireland would be gravely prejudiced if the order of the High Court were flouted'.[117] Austen Chamberlain MP told the House of Commons that this had been done 'solely on the basis of the existing situation in Ireland. The releases were not due to any decision given by a civil court in Ireland. Civil courts have no power to override the decisions of the military courts in the martial law area in Ireland. The decisions of the military officer administering martial law in Ireland will be upheld'.[118] O'Connor put a stay on the writs of attachment.[119] Macready issued a 'special order of the day' to the officers in his command, reciting the government statement,[120] although more privately noting to colleagues that the concept of a military governor being called to account by a judge 'makes the administration of martial law impossible, and if I may be permitted to use the expression, ridiculous'.[121] The point taken by O'Connor was not further resolved, politically or legally, at the time, although his view of the basis of martial law has been generally regarded as mistaken,[122] and the government appeal was not pursued as the peace negotiations proceeded.

The authority of the courts in time of war or armed rebellion was considered again by O'Connor during the Civil War, when in November 1922 he heard an application for habeas corpus on behalf of Erskine Childers,[123] who had been tried and convicted by a military court for being in possession of a gun without proper authority. He said that he approached the case on the basis that, on behalf of Childers, whether a state of war was in existence was disputed (in legal terms, 'traversed'), as to which his own view was that there was overwhelming evidence of such a state. He accepted an affidavit sworn by the adjutant general of the army that a war was raging which necessitated military intervention, and added, in effect as a matter of general knowledge ('I am bound to take judicial notice'), that the Four Courts,

117 Cabinet, 2 August 1921. C.62(21), CAB.23 2 (Records of the Cabinet Office (TNAUK)).
118 HC Deb, 5th Series, vol. 146, col. 437 (10 August 1921).
119 *ILT&SJ*, vol. 55, p. 193 (6 August 1921).
120 W.N. Osborough, 'Law in Ireland, 1916–26', *NILQ*, vol. 23 (1972), pp 48, at 65.
121 Macready, op. cit., p. 590.
122 W.N. Osborough, op. cit.; Ronan Keane, 'Martial law in Ireland 1535–1924' in W.N. Osborough (ed.), *Essays in honour of John M. Kelly* (The *Irish Jurist*, vols 25–27, *Liber Memorialis John M. Kelly*) (Dublin, 1994), p. 150, at 172; Gerard Hogan, 'Hugh Kennedy, the Childers habeas corpus application and return to the Four Courts' in Caroline Costello (ed.), *The Four Courts: 200 years* (Dublin, 1996), p. 177, at 186.
123 *R (Childers) v Adjutant-General of Provisional Forces*, [1923] 1 IR 5.

> one of the noblest buildings in this country [which was] the home of justice for more than a hundred years, is now a mass of crumbling ruins, the work of revolutionaries … I know also that railways have been torn up, railway stations destroyed, the noblest mansions burned down, roadways made impassable, bridges blown up, and life and property attacked in almost every county in southern Ireland. If this is not a state of war, I would like to know what is.[124]

The government had the duty of re-establishing peace and order and saving the country from utter destruction. He dismissed the application, not regarding his own judgment in *Egan v Macready* as an applicable precedent, on the ground that there was in force no statute (such as the 1920 Act which had governed his decision in that case) which could operate to inhibit acts of the Irish Army. Childers was executed the following morning, despite a pending appeal.

A few months later as hostilities in the civil war ceased in stages in April and May 1923 a question arose as to whether persons detained without trial under the inherent powers of the military could still lawfully be interned. O'Connor did not accept that the war was over when a habeas corpus application was determined by him on 15 June 1923. A few weeks later a fresh such application by Mrs Nora Connolly O'Brien, a daughter of James Connolly, was initially refused by O'Connor, but was granted, on 31 July, by the Court of Appeal (Molony LCJ and Ronan LJ), which on the following day ordered her release, on the grounds that a state of war no longer existed.[125] The Public Safety (Emergency Powers) (No. 2) Act 1923 was enacted within a matter of days to provide a lawful basis for continued internment.

O'Connor was a member of the judiciary advisory committee established in January 1923 under the chairmanship of Lord Glenavy, the report of which led to the judiciary being restructured by the Courts of Justice Act 1924. This abolished the position of master of the rolls, and O'Connor, according to Hugh Kennedy, the chief justice, was the first person asked to accept judicial office in the Irish Free State.[126] He served for a year as a member of the supreme court (preferring that to the position of president of the High Court, which had also been offered to him), before retiring, in light of his wife's ill health.[127] He moved to London, where he died in 1928 at his home in Thurloe Square in south Kensington. He had previously lived in Upper Mount Street, Fitzwilliam Square, and at 28 Fitzwilliam Place, the former home of Christopher Palles, from whom he had taken a lease for 21 years in 1910.[128]

124 [1923] IR 5, at 13.
125 *R (O'Brien) v Military Governor of the Military Internment Camp*, [1924] 1 IR 32.
126 *ILT&SJ*, vol. 62, p. 246 (13 October 1928).
127 Charles Lysaght, review of *The Four Courts: 200 years* in *Irish Jurist*, 32 (1997), p. 465.
128 Memorial of lease dated 9 June 1910 made between Palles and O'Connor (Registry of Deeds).

Ignatius O'Brien (Lord Shandon)

Lord Chancellor of Ireland 1913–18

Ignatius O'Brien (1857–1930) was born in Cork. He was called to the Bar in 1881 and to the Inner Bar in 1899 and became a bencher of King's Inns in 1907. He was popular with his colleagues and was elected as a member of the Bar Council in 1910. He was associated with the Liberal party and with the mainstream Irish Parliamentary Party, incurring the hostility of other factions within the broader nationalist camp, including that of T.M. Healy MP. He was appointed as third serjeant in June 1910, as second serjeant in June 1911, as solicitor general in December 1911, as attorney general in June 1912 and as lord chancellor in March 1913,[129] leaving office in June 1918. He was created a baronet in the New Year's Honours List in 1916 and a peer in 1918, taking the name Lord Shandon, from his native city.

O'Brien's wrote a memoir in retirement,[130] giving an affectionate account of his upbringing, but with a sombre view of the working life and culture of the Bar and of the economics of legal practice. A young barrister's education at the King's Inns would have been quite inadequate, and on the day of his call to the Bar O'Brien did not have the price of his dinner and had to do without. He remarked that a new entrant to the Law Library could have a long wait for an opportunity to build a practice and might dissipate his funds and his talents in traditional and improvident high living, and that although he did not personally enjoy life on circuit (the Munster circuit), and eventually gave it up, it made people tolerant of each other – 'each Assize Bar very much resembled a family, if not always a happy family, still bound together by ties of friendliness'.

In a high-profile case in May 1887 he succeeded in obtaining the release of a priest, Canon Keller, who had been imprisoned for contempt of court in refusing to answer questions in bankruptcy procedures taken against certain tenants withholding rent on the Ponsonby Estate near Youghal, Co. Cork, during the Plan of Campaign in the Land War. Bankruptcy and banking and commercial law cases of one kind or another constituted the principal part of his practice in the decade after he had become a Queen's Counsel, and in a number of these cases he was instructed by John L. Scallan, a prominent solicitor whose sister Annie he had married in 1886. His income doubled in the first year after he had taken silk (by no means a universal experience). In 1910 it was reported that he 'has a very large practice in all the courts',[131] and in 1913 that he had an extensive

129 These five appointments were reported in *ILT&SJ*, vol. 44, p. 21 (22 June 1910), vol. 45, p. 137 (3 June 1911) and p. 300 (9 December 1911), vol. 46, p. 164 (29 June 1912) and vol. 47, p. 93 (29 March 1913).

130 Two bound typescript copies of this memoir were made, one of which is in the library of King's Inns, and the other is in the possession of the Horan family, to a member of which it was bequeathed by O'Brien. An edition of the memoir, *The reminiscences of Ignatius O'Brien, lord chancellor of Ireland 1913–1918* (Four Courts Press, Dublin), was published in 2021.

131 *ILT&SJ*, vol. 44, p. 21 (22 January 1910).

practice in Chancery and bankruptcy and was leading counsel to the Dublin Corporation.[132]

Maurice Healy in describing O'Brien as garrulous in his judicial role said that as between him and Lord Justice Ronan 'it was hard to say which talked more, or more irrelevantly'.[133] Slightly more generously, he also said that O'Brien

> was by no means the least creditable appointment made by the Liberals. He had enjoyed a fairly good practice, most of it in bankruptcy; he had been standing counsel to the *Freeman's Journal*, but this was his only connection with politics. His appearance was most truculent and earned him the sobriquet 'Pugnacious O'Brien'.[134] His real nature was kindly, and he spent his considerable means with unostentatious generosity. But when he became lord chancellor the fable of the inflated frog became true. Never was a judge so pompous or, for that reason, so inefficient … O'Brien insisted upon informing counsel of the way his mind was operating … Usually … both he and Ronan were insuppressible and counsel were unable to make the simplest statement without interruption.[135]

O'Brien said of his appointment to be lord chancellor in March 1913 that he had requested an interview with the prime minister, Asquith, at which he asked for the position, although, contrary to what he wrote, there were not vacancies in the offices of both lord chancellor and lord chief justice at that time. As a member of the Privy Council in Ireland he had an involvement in governmental or official business from time to time, the nature of which would vary depending on the personality and interests of the holder of the office, the requirements of the government and his standing with it. The casual nature of how a lord chancellor's advice might be sought on official business of a non-judicial character was demonstrated on the afternoon of Sunday 26 July 1914 in relation to the gun-running by the Irish Volunteers at Howth. The events of the day, including the shooting dead of three people at Bachelor's Walk, beside the Liffey, were soon made the subject of inquiry by a Royal Commission.[136] The under-secretary at Dublin Castle, Sir James Dougherty, being unable to communicate with either the attorney general or the solicitor general, consulted the lord chancellor, and the

132 *ILT&SJ*, vol. 47, p.93 (29 March 1913). O'Brien was briefed for the Corporation in two reported cases, Rice v White [1904] 2 IR 8, and the extended case involving the exact specification of the waste water treatment works at the Pigeon House, *Pearson v Dublin Corporation* [1907] 2 IR 27 and 537, [1907] AC 351. See also W.N. Osborough, *Law and the emergence of modern Dublin* (Dublin, 1996), pp 117–19.

133 Healy, *OldMC*, p. 136.

134 O'Brien was aware of this name, 'but he himself considered that a more pertinent nickname would have been "Pertinacious O'Brien". His strength lay in sticking to his point.' (*The Times*, obituary, 12 September 1930).

135 Healy, op. cit., pp 198–9.

136 *Report of the Royal Commission into the circumstances connected with the landing of arms at Howth on July 26, 1914* (P.P. 1914–16 (Cd. 7631) xxiv. 805).

Commission noted that the 'learned judge after giving through the telephone his views, which were adverse to any attempt to seize arms or to interfere with the men on the march to Dublin, was good enough to proceed personally from his residence at Dundrum by motor car to the Castle'.[137]

In May and June 1915, and for three years after that, his holding of office was under threat from the ambition of James H.M. Campbell to displace him, and he wrote in his memoir of 'the petty annoyances and worry that every day brings, the constant intrigues to oust one, the bitterness and jealousy hardly concealed as much from those whose only incentive is envy as from those who are openly enemies', and that 'intrigues never ceased to induce the Premier to get rid of me', primarily by Unionists but also by a section of nationalist opinion. The formation of the coalition government in May 1915 marked the end of whatever level of informal involvement in governmental affairs that O'Brien may previously have had. He said this to Asquith, prior to a debate in the House of Commons on the Easter Rising,[138] in which he was criticised (or perhaps simply abused) by Healy.[139]

Two judgments of the Court of Appeal of some public interest were reversed by the House of Lords. *Hollinshead v Hazleton*[140] concerned the disposition in bankruptcy of the salary of an Irish member of Parliament who had been elected after having been made bankrupt. The law of Ireland and that of England and Scotland provided in the same way that an MP would forfeit his seat upon becoming bankrupt but differed in respect of whether a bankrupt could become an MP in the first place. O'Brien, with chief baron Palles, had taken the view that there was some ground of public policy which should entitle an MP to retain his parliamentary salary, irrespective of bankruptcy, and which should prevent the application of the ordinary rule of distributing a bankrupt's income among his creditors. *McEllistrim v Ballymacelligot Co-operative Agricultural and Dairy Society Limited*[141] became a leading case, for some decades, on the law of restraint of trade in contract, in the United Kingdom as well as in Ireland. The plaintiff objected to a new rule introduced by the defendant society, prohibiting him from selling milk to any other creamery for so long as he was a member, as being an unlawful or unreasonable restraint of trade, and in 1917 Barton J upheld his complaint. The Court of Appeal took a different view, regarding itself as bound by its recent decision in the case of *Coolmoyne and Fethard Co-operative Creamery Limited v Bulfin*[142] as to the validity of an identical rule. In the event the House of Lords held in the course of the Ballymacelligott appeal that the Coolmoyne case had been wrongly decided.[143]

137 *Report of the Commission*, paragraphs 19 and 20.
138 O'Brien to Asquith, 8 May 1916, Asquith Papers (Bodleian Library, Oxford), 38:160
139 HC Deb 5th series, vol. 82, cols. 964–5 (11 May 1916).
140 50 ILTR (1916) 29, [1916] AC 428.
141 [1918] 1 IR 313, 53 ILTR (1919) 121, [1919] AC 548.
142 [1917] 2 IR 107.
143 53 ILTR (1919) 121, [1919] AC 548.

O'Brien's judgment in the Coolmoyne case is of interest as containing some reflections by him of an almost political nature:

> It is quite conceivable that the agreement which the plaintiffs [the society] have entered into in this case, so far from its producing a mere local monopoly, may really operate as a weapon against monopoly, because it enables a number of small and financially weak men, by banding themselves together, to resist successfully the competition of large and possible wealthy corporations, whose object may be to control not only the local but the general market …
>
> The whole of this question of huge trade combinations, and how far the law will interfere with them, is practically a question more for the Legislature than for our Courts. Our law has been built up upon a condition of things in which a vast number of people are engaged, to use a popular expression, 'in a small way of business', and the rules regulating the relation of traders so engaged, applied to large trade organizations, may or may not be what the legislature may consider wise to permit; but it is for the legislature to interfere. Trade combinations on a huge scale are taking place all over the world, England and Ireland not excepted. In many respects they are to the public advantage. In others – I do not suggest this is one – possibly they cannot be so, as leading to the aggrandisement of individuals. But illegality cannot be presumed; it must be proved as a fact.[144]

His dismissal and replacement by Campbell finally took place in the early summer of 1918 at a time when Nationalist goodwill towards the government had in effect become irrelevant, in the light of the conscription crisis and the rise of Sinn Fein. The prime minister, Lloyd George, wrote to O'Brien at the end of May – O'Brien noted that this was delivered to his home on Sunday 2 June – saying that arising from important readjustments in the government of Ireland he considered that the time had come to relieve O'Brien of 'the heavy charge which you have been called upon to carry as lord chancellor of Ireland', and (in a postscript) offering him a peerage.[145] In his memoir he wrote that he welcomed an end to a very unpleasant situation, and a retirement with some dignity.

This removal from office as lord chancellor ended O'Brien's judicial career. His remark in the memoir that he was 'technically entitled to sit as a Law Lord', requires qualification. Section 5 (read with section 25) of the Appellate Jurisdiction Act 1876 provided that a former lord chancellor of Ireland would be eligible – rather than entitled – to be present at the hearing and determination of any appeal by the House of Lords, but this was subject to being requested to do so by the lord chancellor of Great Britain for the time being, and there was no prospect of

144 [1917] 2 IR 107, at 125 and 126.
145 Lloyd George to O'Brien, 30 May 1918 (Lloyd George Papers (Parliamentary Archives), LG/F/45/5/1).

O'Brien being so requested. Joining the House of Lords gave him a new legal position as a member of the legislature, and over the next few years he contributed to debates, initially primarily on Irish matters but later speaking more broadly. He attended the house to vote in favour of the Treaty in December 1921. In 1926–7 he composed his memoir, and he died in September 1930. He and his wife had moved to England in 1920, and they are buried in London.

Thomas Molony

Justice of the High Court 1913–15, Lord Justice of Appeal 1915–18, Lord Chief Justice of Ireland 1918–24

Thomas Molony (1865–1949) was born in Dublin, and was the youngest son of a hotel proprietor. He was educated by the Christian Brothers at O'Connell's School, North Richmond Street, Dublin, and at Trinity College, where he had a brilliant academic record. He was called to the Bar in 1886 and to the Inner Bar in 1899. He was appointed Crown counsel for county Carlow in 1906, and for the county and city of Dublin in 1907. He was appointed successively as second and then third serjeant in 1911.

'In terms of Irish politics he was a Home Ruler of the old stamp'[146] but, like a number of other barristers who did not subscribe to the self-denying ordinance against seeking office that was required of members of the Irish Parliamentary Party, he adopted the designation of a Liberal. In the December 1910 general election he stood unsuccessfully as the Liberal candidate in the West Toxteth constituency, in Liverpool. Official appointments flowed in quick succession after 1912, first as solicitor general and then as attorney general the following year. He was made a judge of the High Court in 1914 and a lord justice of appeal in 1915. The government nominated him as a member of two inquiries into killings of civilians by soldiers, the shooting of three men at Bachelor's Walk in Dublin in July 1914 after the landing of arms at Howth by the Irish Volunteers and the killing of Francis Sheehy Skeffington in the course of the 1916 Rising.[147] In June 1918 he succeeded Sir James Campbell as lord chief justice of Ireland. He persuaded the government subsequently that the Government of Ireland Act 1920 should provide for him to 'be entitled to retain the rank and title of lord chief justice of Ireland' rather than the proposed description of lord chief justice of Southern Ireland (which would have been applicable to his successors, if the Act had continued in force in the Irish Free State).[148] The lord chief justice became the titular head of

146 Nial Osborough, 'The title of the last lord chief justice of Ireland', *Irish Jurist*, vol. 9 (1974), pp 87–98, at 88, and in *Studies in Irish legal history* (Dublin, 1999), pp 315–26, at 316.

147 *Report of the Royal Commission into the circumstances connected with the landing of arms at Howth on 26 July 1914* (P.P. 1914–16, Cmnd. 7631, xxiv. 805); *Report of the Royal Commission on the arrest and subsequent treatment of Mr Francis Sheehy Skeffington, Mr Thomas Dickson and Mr Patrick James McIntyre* (P.P. 1916, Cd. 8376, xi. 311).

148 Osborough, op. cit., pp 87–98 and 315–26; 10&11 Geo. 5, c.67, s39 and schedule 7, part III, para. 1(c).

the judiciary upon the abolition of the office of lord chancellor of Ireland at the end of 1922.

The administration of justice by the established courts during the War of Independence between 1919 and 1921, and then in the Civil War that followed in 1922–3 presented many challenges and difficulties, practical and political. Military protection was required for the judges, who rebuffed attempts by the government to engage them in the establishment of special courts, sitting without a jury, which would dispense summary justice, including the death penalty for crimes of disorder (see pp 69–70). After the occupation of the Four Courts in April 1922 by members of the IRA opposed to the Anglo-Irish Treaty the courts sat at the King's Inns, and eventually, pending the rebuilding of the Four Courts, at Dublin Castle.

The civil courts were required at the time to consider the nature of martial law and its relation to the common law when determining applications that were made to them seeking to prevent the carrying out of executions under sentences of death passed by military courts. In *R v Allen*[149] Molony stated that 'it is the sacred duty of this court to protect the lives and liberties of all of His Majesty's subjects, and to see that no one suffers loss of life or liberty save under the laws of the country; but when subjects of the King rise in armed insurrection and the conflict is raging, it is no less our duty not to interfere with the officers of the Crown in taking such steps as they deem necessary to quell the insurrection and to restore peace and order and the authority of the law'. In *R v Strickland*[150] he stressed that the judiciary had the power and the duty to decide whether a state of war existed which justified the application of martial law, and rejected an implication by counsel that the functioning of the assizes in Cork had required the consent of the military, saying that he did not sit in Cork by permission of any general. 'I sat in Cork by virtue of His Majesty's command, which no general could dispute'.

Other issues considered by Molony in judgments at this time included whether a local authority was obliged to pay compensation under the malicious injuries code for theft resulting from damage to property caused by riotous soldiers,[151] and two actions arising from the first incident in the War of Independence, the killing of two members of the Royal Irish Constabulary at Soloheadbeg in Co. Tipperary on 21 January 1919, the day on which the First Dáil met. One such action was for false imprisonment arising from the arrest and detention of a young boy, a possible witness to the incident, for the expressed purpose of protecting him from potential malefactors,[152] and the other concerned the assessment and distribution of compensation payable upon the murder of one of the RIC men, who was unmarried.[153]

149 [1921] 2 IR 241.
150 [1921] 2 IR 317.
151 *Tyler v Cork County Council*, [1921] 2 IR 8.
152 *Connors v Pearson*, [1921] 2 IR 51.
153 *O'Connell and others v County Council of Tipperary (South Riding)*, [1921] 2 IR 103.

After the existing judicial establishment was replaced in 1924 by the new judiciary of the Irish Free State Molony moved to England. He was created a baronet of the United Kingdom in the New Year Honours List in 1925. He had many connections and interests outside his legal and judicial career, including a long association with Trinity College, of which he was (as lord chief justice) ex officio a visitor, and was appointed vice-chancellor in 1931. He succeeded Lord Carson as president of the College's Dining Club in London in 1935. Between 1920 and 1924 he was president of the Statistical and Social Inquiry Society of Ireland, to which he read some papers on legal subjects. He became a director of the National Bank after his retirement. He was a member of the committee for the Irish National War Memorial, in due course established at Islandbridge, and subsequently of a committee to raise funds for the Royal Air Force from Irishmen in Britain during the Second World War. He was made an honorary bencher of the Inn of Court of Northern Ireland in 1926 and of the Middle Temple in 1933.

He was married to Pauline Mary Rispin, daughter of a livestock salesman, and they had three sons, one of whom was killed in action during the Second World War, and three daughters. The family lived at Fitzwilliam Place before the move to England, where they lived in Wimbledon, and where he died in 1949. A portrait by Sir William Orpen, showing him robed as lord chief justice, was presented to him by the solicitors of Ireland in 1925. It has been loaned by the Molony family to the King's Inns, where it is 'the most striking example of early twentieth century painting. The tense pose of the hands, together with the solemnity of the chief justice's expression, combine to make this a powerful composition'.[154]

John Francis Moriarty

Lord Justice of Appeal 1914–15

The judicial career of John Francis Moriarty (1854–1915) was short, lasting less than a year. He was the son of a prominent citizen in Mallow, a solicitor, who died in 1889.[155] After his education at the Jesuit college of Stonyhurst, in Lancashire, and at Trinity College, he was called to the Bar in 1877, joining the Munster circuit. He was appointed a circuit Crown prosecutor for Co. Cork and Co. Clare in 1882,[156] and from 1891 until he became a law officer in 1913 he was a prosecutor for the county and city of Cork. When a bye-election was taking place in Mallow in January 1883 (see p. 302) Moriarty indicated that he would stand as an independent Liberal supporter of the government, although he withdrew at the last moment without having been formally nominated.[157] He canvassed voters as 'their townsman and personal friend',[158] and he and his family were reported as

154 Wanda Ryan-Smolin, *King's Inns portraits* (Dublin, 1992), p. 48.
155 *ILT&SJ*, vol. 23, p. 527 (12 October 1889).
156 *ILT&SJ*, vol. 16, p. 328 (8 July 1882).
157 *Irish Times*, 23 January 1883, farewell address to electors.
158 *Irish Times*, 6 January 1883.

being 'very popular, having given at all times a good deal of employment and been kind to their tenants, many of whom reside in the town'.[159] The successful candidate, William O'Brien, referred to him as a clever ambitious young barrister, 'a Crown prosecutor of local manufacture'.[160]

He was 'tall and powerfully built',[161] with an imposing presence (at times wearing a monocle), 'a generous cheerful fellow of enormous ability'.[162] All that, coupled with his family legal connection, might have augured well for his career at the Bar, but this did not progress smoothly. The complimentary remarks as to his demeanour cited above were made in the memoirs of what were at the time two younger members of the Bar, Maurice Healy and A.M. Sullivan, part of the so-called 'Bantry Band' of inter-related political families from West Cork. However neither of them was particularly well disposed towards Moriarty, and each also had reservations about what they saw as his lack of character, conduct going beyond being a lovable rogue in the fellowship of the Bar – he was 'entirely unscrupulous in his conduct of a case', and (contrariwise) 'he would rather play tricks and lose than play fair and win'.[163]

His obituary in the *Irish Law Times* referred cryptically to 'some ups and downs' in his career, and the attorney general when paying tribute in court to him said that he 'had a hard fight in this life – a curious fight – [and that] out of his weakness he had made himself strong'.[164] His career was said to have been interrupted by some period of absence from the Four Courts, although there was no break in his listing as a subscriber to the Law Library nor in his appointment as a Crown prosecutor. The obituary in the *Irish Times* stated that 'for some years interests other than his profession engaged his attention, and for a time he resided in the United States'.[165] J.G. Swift MacNeill (a contemporary, called to the Bar in 1876) said that 'he abandoned his practice at the Bar and, drifting, became a constant attendant at turf meetings and a heavy better. A considerable period of his life suffered almost total eclipse'.[166] More precisely, both Sullivan and Maurice Healy said that Moriarty became bankrupt,[167] and T.M. Healy, uncle of Maurice and another member of the Bantry Band, also referred to it as a fact (see below). However no petition for his bankruptcy was recorded at the time as having been filed or heard in Ireland, between 1874 and 1903,[168] and it is unlikely that a bankruptcy would not have affected his subsequent prominence in the profession nor been the subject of adverse comment. Maurice Healy provided an unflattering

159 *Irish Times*, 3 January 1883.
160 *Irish Times*, 13 January 1883.
161 Healy, *OldMC*, p. 90.
162 A.M. Sullivan, *Old Ireland: reminiscences of an Irish KC* (London, 1927), p. 95.
163 Healy, op. cit., p. 90; Sullivan, op. cit., p. 93.
164 *ILT&SJ*, vol. 49, pp 114–15 (8 May 1915).
165 *Irish Times*, 8 May 1915.
166 J.G. Swift MacNeill, *What I have seen and heard* (London, 1925), p. 193.
167 Sullivan, op. cit., p. 94; Healy, op. cit., pp 88 and 195.
168 Indexes to petitions in bankruptcy listings in those years, as published in the *Irish Law Times*.

account of Moriarty's supposed demeanour at a bankruptcy hearing, and remarked that many records of bankruptcy were said to have perished in the destruction by fire of the courthouse in Cork in 1891.[169]

Whatever his financial position from time to time may have been, a decision of the Court of Appeal in England in 1891[170] did not reflect well on his character. The case related to a technical point of banking law, and was in substance concerned with which of two parties should bear a loss resulting from his dishonesty and/or financial default. In April 1889 he had sent to his bank in Dublin, National Bank, a cheque for £450 drawn in his favour by a Mr Silke, who shortly afterwards instructed his bank (in London) to stop payment of the cheque, 'on the ground that it had been obtained from him by false representations'. (T.M. Healy wrote that the cheque represented winnings from a bookmaker from a race at Doncaster.)[171] The bank in Dublin had provisionally credited Moriarty's account with the payment, pending receipt of funds from the London bank, and he had drawn cheques against that credit, leaving a balance of £47. Since he 'failed to provide' funds to the bank to make good the shortfall arising on his account (when the credit entry had been reversed after the incoming payment was stopped) the bank sued Silke, on foot of his cheque, and won its case. Moriarty's dealings with Silke and with the bank had given each of them cause for complaint, and indeed he may have previously tried the patience of any creditors who were paid sums out of this temporary credit with the bank.

At all events Moriarty continued in practice, appearing at least once for a client before the bankruptcy judge,[172] and took silk in 1904. Any money troubles seemed to be behind him, and he lived at 92 Lower Leeson Street and later at 47 St Stephen's Green. Within a few years he had become one of the leaders of the common law Bar. He represented the plaintiff in the celebrated west Cork case of the spoiled son, *Barrett v Irvine*, which O'Brien LCJ remarked might serve as inspiration for fiction.[173] In 1911–12 he represented the wronged wife in the celebrated case of *Ussher v Ussher*.[174] The breadth of his practice was illustrated in February 1913, when he was successively engaged in an action for breach of promise of marriage, in a divorce suit, in an action for personal injuries and in a case over custody and guardianship of infant children.[175] Later in 1913, as attorney general, he prosecuted Jim Larkin in the course of the Dublin Lockout for having used seditious language, and incitement to riot and to steal, and Larkin, although acquitted on the incitement charge, was sentenced to imprisonment for seven

169 Healy, *OldMC*, p. 88.
170 *National Bank v Silke*, [1891] 1 QB 435. Two phrases from the report (at pp 436 and 438) are quoted later in the paragraph.
171 T.M. Healy, *Letters and leaders*, vol. 2, p. 526.
172 *Irish Times*, 14 November 1900.
173 [1907] 2 IR 462.
174 *Ussher v Ussher*, [1912] 2 IR 445.
175 *Irish Times*, 12, 13, 15 and 20 February 1913.

months.[176] The prosecution, and the tone in which it was conducted, was considered by the cabinet to have been unwise and unnecessary, and as the sentence was seen as excessive Larkin was released early.[177]

Early in his career Moriarty had associated himself with Parnell, representing Mrs Katherine O'Shea in proceedings against her husband, Captain O'Shea, to have the trusts of her marriage settlement carried out,[178] and after the split in the Parliamentary Party he gave a legal opinion favourable to the claim of Parnell's supporters to take over the office of the *United Ireland* publication.[179] Two decades later he was well placed in Liberal and nationalist circles, and in 1908 began to receive official appointments indicative of good and high standing at the Bar, beginning with appointment as third serjeant in June 1908. In 1909 he became a bencher of King's Inns and was appointed senior Crown prosecutor for the city of Cork, a position in which he succeeded the late Sir Francis Brady (1824–1909), who had held it for almost half a century. In 1910 he became First Serjeant, in which capacity he sat as a temporary High Court judge of assize in Tipperary in 1912.[180]

T.M. Healy noted on 9 April 1913 that 'Birrell [the chief secretary] said to me today he was disposed to appoint Moriarty solicitor general. He began by saying he was tired of duffers, which I sympathised with. I thought the strongest point which the Opposition could raise was the bankruptcy, and he said that he would inquire into that, yet with such an air that I knew he would gloss it over. [He said] that he wanted help, and not the mere advancement of Moriarty'.[181] Birrell also told Healy that chief baron Palles favoured the appointment, and that John Ross had written to him unasked in support of Moriarty. A few days later the appointment was made,[182] following which the Munster Bar entertained him at a dinner in the King's Inns. Within a couple of months, arising out of the promotion of Molony, the attorney general, to the bench Moriarty was promoted to take his place.[183]

In November 1913 the lord chief justice, Lord O'Brien of Kilfenora, retired, and during an extended period of three months in which the position was not filled there was speculation that Moriarty as attorney general might succeed him, following recent precedent (May in 1876 and O'Brien himself in 1889) – 'it usually happens that the choice falls upon the attorney general'.[184] The credentials of lord justice Cherry, legal and political, and indeed his recent length of service as

176 *Irish Times*, 28 October 1913.
177 CAB 41/34, 12 November 1913 (TNAUK); Leon O Broin, *The chief secretary: Augustine Birrell in Ireland* (London, 1969), pp 77–8.
178 *Irish Times*, 17 May 1890.
179 Sullivan, op. cit., p. 53.
180 *ILT&SJ*, vol. 46, p. 69 (16 March 1912).
181 T.M. Healy, *Letters and leaders*, p. 526.
182 *Irish Times*, 26 April 1913.
183 *Irish Times*, 28 June 1913.
184 *Law Times*, vol. 136, p. 121 (29 November 1913).

attorney general, weighed more strongly than those of Moriarty, and the appointment was given to him. In June 1914 Moriarty was appointed to fill the vacancy thus created in the Court of Appeal.

He was a judge for less than twelve months, taking his seat for the first time on 26 June 1914 and, having become unwell while on holiday in Wales in April 1915, he died in Birmingham in early May.[185]

185 *ILT&SJ*, vol. 49, p. 94 (17 April 1915) and p. 114 (8 May 1915).

CHAPTER THIRTEEN

Appointments between 1915 and 1921

STEPHEN RONAN WAS MADE a member of the Court of Appeal early in 1915. Subsequently the complex politics of the coalition government that was formed in May that year shaped most appointments. The appointment of Jonathan Pim to the bench in June 1915 was a direct result of the formation of the coalition, and (as in Pim's case) the promotion of John Gordon in 1916 arose from the desire to create a vacancy in the office of attorney general. James Campbell's successive appointments as lord chief justice (in the New Year 1917) and lord chancellor (17 months later) reflected his constant pressure on his Unionist party colleagues to resolve the very untidy situation that remained after he had been denied the latter office in May 1915. William Moore MP was appointed to the bench in 1917, and two other Unionist QCs, John Blake Powell and Arthur Samuels, in the next two years. James O'Connor, a representative of traditional nationalist opinion, was made a High Court judge in April 1918 and then almost immediately was promoted to the Court of Appeal. In 1920 William E. Wylie succeeded his uncle as judicial commissioner of the Land Commission.

Stephen Ronan

Lord Justice of Appeal 1915–24

Stephen Ronan (1848–1925) was born in Cork, the son of a solicitor, Walter Ronan. Another son bore his father's name, also becoming a solicitor, and was appointed to act as assize registrar to his brother when he was appointed a judge.[1] Ronan was educated at the Queen's College Cork. After his call to the Bar in 1870 he joined the Munster circuit, of which he became in due course the senior member or 'father'. He is the subject of a chapter (VIII) in Maurice Healy's classic account, as 'a book of memories and traditions', of that circuit.[2] As a junior counsel he was one of the representatives of the *Times* at the special commission in London in 1888–9 arising out of the articles it had published on 'Parnellism and Crime' in 1887. He was a Crown prosecutor in Munster, and his cases included the dramatic trial of Dr Philip Cross for the murder by poisoning of his wife, Mary Laura, at their home at Dripsey, near Coachford, Co. Cork, in 1887.[3]

He became a QC in 1889, and for decades was acknowledged as one of the leaders of the Bar. 'His frail form – he looks as though a puff of wind would blow

1 *Irish Times*, 11 February 1915.
2 Healy, *OldMC*.
3 Michael Sheridan, *Murder at Shandy Hall: the Coachford Poisoning Case* (Dublin, 2010); T.M. Healy, *Letters and leaders*, vol. 1, pp 220–2.

him away – belies his fiery and indomitable spirit'.[4] Healy said of him that 'he was cranky and irritable; he broke out into quarrels in court upon the least provocation; he was afraid of nobody'.[5] W.E, Wylie acknowledged that when at the Bar Ronan had a reputation for lacking in humanity and being 'a dry old fossil', but said that in his own dealings with him Ronan was a 'big hearted generous man'.[6] In 1899, when considering with Lord Cadogan, the lord lieutenant, who might be appointed as the successor on the bench of the late William O'Brien, Lord Ashbourne noted Ronan's position in the front rank of the Bar and that he was both a Liberal Unionist and a Catholic (which, if correct then, was no longer the case in 1911, as in the census return that year he stated that he had 'no denomination').[7] Ashbourne also remarked that he would probably be a better law officer than a judge, an observation borne out by the opinions of others after his eventual appointment to the bench in 1915. Cadogan observed that Ronan 'was a very able lawyer in good practice, but personally not popular and especially distasteful to the attorney general [John Atkinson] who would I believe resign if he were appointed'.[8] The appointment was given to George Wright.

His appointment to the Court of Appeal in January 1915, at the age of 66, was seen as a belated tribute to his pre-eminent position, not as a political exercise. If anything, it may have represented a setting aside of political opposition and, as Healy speculated, of episcopal disfavour of his atheism.[9] Augustine Birrell, the chief secretary for Ireland, hoped 'that Ronan will prove a good judge … He has ploughed a lonely furrow, reached the top of his tree, and to boycott him at the bidding of the poorest elements in the Irish Parliamentary Party would have been humiliation'.[10]

Healy wrote of him, with some anecdotal instances, that once appointed 'he promptly distinguished himself by becoming the most impossible judge we had ever known'.[11] T.C. Kingsmill Moore, later (1951–65) a member of the Supreme Court, also gave a cool assessment of his work as a judge when writing the initial entry on him in the *Dictionary of national biography*:[12]

> Everyone expected great things of him. But the appointment came too late. He had been overlong an advocate easily to forsake the active for the passive role. As an assize judge he was prone to take the case out of the hands of counsel and even in the Court of Appeal his impatient intellect led him

4 *ILT&SJ*, vol. 49, p. 23 (23 January 1915), citing *Dublin Evening Mail*.
5 Healy, op. cit., p. 123.
6 W.E. Wylie, Memoir, p. 13 (TNAUK, PRO 30/89/2).
7 Ashbourne to Cadogan, 10 December 1899 (Cadogan Papers, CAD 1685/1).
8 Cadogan to Salisbury, 18 January 1900 (Salisbury Papers).
9 Healy, op. cit., p. 132.
10 Birrell to Nathan, 21 January 1915 (Nathan MS (Bodleian Library, Oxford) 449); Leon Ó Broin, *The chief secretary: Augustine Birrell in Ireland* (London, 1969), p. 155.
11 Healy, op. cit., p. 124. See also p. 199.
12 *DNB, 1922–30* (London/Oxford, 1937). See also the subsequent entry on Ronan in the *ODNB*.

> continually to interrupt the course of the argument with questions on points which eventually proved to be unimportant. His judgments, clear, erudite and lengthy, smacked too much of special pleading, and laboured under the tyranny of multitudinous decisions. He lacked the temper of a great judge, the capacity to ground himself on broad principles, rather than on their exposition in decided cases and to adapt the essence of those principles to the changing needs of the times.

Ronan lived in Fitzwilliam Square. He left office with almost all of his brother judges when the new court system was established in the Irish Free State in June 1924, being then in any event over the new statutory age of retirement. He died in 1925.

Jonathan Pim

Justice of the High Court (King's Bench) 1915–24

Jonathan Ernest Pim (1858–1949) was the only Irish judge to be a member of the Society of Friends. Members of the wider Pim family were very prominent in many fields of Dublin business.[13] The firm of Pim Brothers, of which each of his father, brother and nephew were subsequently the managing director and/or chairman, opened what became a substantial retail store in South Great George's Street in the 1840s, and his father was instrumental in the development further up the street in the 1870s of the South City Markets building.[14] Pim's uncle, also named Jonathan (1806–85), was twice elected a Liberal MP for the city of Dublin, in 1865 and 1868, but lost his seat in the general election of 1874.

Pim was educated at Trinity College and was called to the Bar in 1886. His advancement in the profession came rapidly in the space of a couple of years, between the summers of 1913 and 1915, when he was successively appointed solicitor general (June 1913), attorney general (July 1914) and a judge (June 1915). He had become a QC in 1909. When at the Bar he had a general practice, which included representing a number of businesses, such as the Dublin, Wicklow and Wexford Railway, Pim Brothers and the Alliance Gas company.[15] He was appointed a revising barrister for the electoral lists in the counties of Waterford (1895) and Tyrone (1901 and 1905). As a law officer he conducted prosecutions for murder at assizes.

He was active in politics before his appointment as a judge. In 1911 there was a vacancy in the office of recorder of Belfast, and (although, in the event, Pim was not appointed) J.B. Armour noted that 'the rumour is that Jonathan Pim will be

13 Richard S. Harrison, 'Pim Brothers – merchants, manufacturers and entrepreneurs of nineteenth century Dublin', *Journal of the Friends Historical Society*, 59 (3) (2002), pp 236–56.

14 Obituary of Thomas Pim in *Irish Times*, 20 January 1896; Christine Casey, *The buildings of Ireland: Dublin* (London, 2005), p. 492.

15 *Irish Times*, 23 April 1900, 14 November 1900 and 19 January 1904.

the man. Jonathan began lately to see that the Liberals were likely to have to divide the loaves and the fishes for some time to come and therefore set his sails accordingly'.[16] In April 1913 at a meeting of the Young Ireland branch of the United Irish League he seconded a vote of thanks (which had been proposed by T.M. Kettle) to a speaker on economic aspects of Home Rule.[17] In November that year he took the chair at a meeting of the Dublin and Counties Liberal Association.[18] His appointment as a judge of the High Court filled a vacancy that had existed for some time, and was made as a part of a reshuffle of legal positions that followed the failure of the attempt to replace Ignatius O'Brien with James Campbell as lord chancellor of Ireland in May and June 1915 on the formation of a coalition government, as it was accepted that then some other place had to be found in the Irish administration for a unionist lawyer. In order to make the office of attorney general available for John Gordon KC, the MP for South Londonderry, Pim was appointed a judge. The *Freeman's Journal* reported this on 11 June under the headline 'The Attorney General raised to the Bench to make room for Mr Gordon'.

Maurice Healy gave a dismissive account of Pim's appointment and competence, writing that he

> brought a nice bouquet of an old-world garden on to the Bench, but, alas! very little else. It was not his fault; he had modestly inquired whether his name might not be considered for a county court judgeship, and was asked whether he had gone mad, when a Liberal administration were in despair for the lack of law officers. So Jonathan found himself solicitor general, and subsequently attorney general; he continued urbane and charming, and in due course ascended the Bench. He probably had more general culture than any of his contemporaries, but he was not of the timber from which judges are carved, and I fancy that his retirement, which I trust he still enjoys, came as a relief to him.[19]

As a judge he heard a wide variety of cases, not only in criminal law but also in defamation, contract, probate, landlord and tenant, trespass, personal injuries and bankruptcy, together with a number of cases of a character that no longer arises – actions for seduction, breach of promise and criminal conversation. He sat at times in the Chancery division of the court and on the Court of Appeal. The operation of the existing judicial system was severely affected and circumscribed by the war of independence and the civil war, but continued until the Courts of Justice Act 1924[20] came into force. In April 1924 it was reported that 'the opinion is

16 J.B. Armour to W.S. Armour, undated [September 1911] (J.B. Armour Papers, D 1792/A/3/2/3).
17 *Irish Times*, 5 April 1913.
18 *Irish Times*, 25 November 1913.
19 Healy, *OldMC*, p. 282.
20 No. 10 of 1924.

entertained in well-informed legal circles that the master of the rolls [Charles O'Connor], Mr Justice Pim and Mr Justice Wylie will be asked to remain in office'[21] but, although that speculation transpired to be correct in the case of O'Connor and Wylie, Pim's judicial carer ended then. He died some 25 years later in April 1949 at his home, 4 Burlington Road. He was not married.

John Gordon

Justice of the High Court 1916–22

John Gordon (1849–1922) was born in Shankill, Co. Down, and educated at the Royal Belfast Academical Institution and Queen's College Belfast. He was called to the Bar in 1877, joining the North East circuit, and to the Inner Bar in 1892, and became a bencher of King's Inns in 1898. He 'was not a forensic orator but made anything he wanted to say quite clear, avoiding rhetoric and using as few words as possible'.[22]

He was a Presbyterian, whose wife, Dorothy Mary, a member of the Church of Ireland, was a daughter of Robert Keating Clay, a prominent solicitor who was president of the Incorporated Law Society of Ireland in 1903, and is mentioned in *Ulysses*. A character in the Circe ('Nighttown') sequence who remarks that 'I see Keating Clay is elected chairman of the Richmond Asylum' was slightly misinformed. On 16 June 1904 he had been re-elected as deputy chairman of the committee of management of the Richmond District Asylum (at Grangegorman), after the committee had argued about the position of the chairman (a Mr Jones) and himself.[23] He died three weeks later, on 4 July.

Gordon stood at a bye-election in Mid Armagh in 1900 as a Unionist, but was defeated by another party member, as the local supporters were, at least temporarily, disunited.[24] In the campaign he had accepted that he was not a local man, although maintaining that in his professional work he had gone frequently to Armagh, 'and been brought into contact with the feelings and habits of the people of the district'.[25] He was elected for the party in the constituency of South Londonderry at the general election later that year, and held his seat at successive general elections in 1906 and 1910. He was appointed senior Crown prosecutor in Belfast in 1905, and as attorney general in June 1915 when the coalition government was formed, in place of the sitting holder of that office, Jonathan Pim. In April 1916 he was appointed to the High Court in succession to Walter Boyd, whose resignation had been arranged by James H.M. Campbell, who wished to hold Gordon's office.

21 *Irish Times*, 12 April 1924.
22 *Irish Times*, 30 September 1922.
23 *Irish Times*, 17 June 1904.
24 *Irish Times*, 30 January 1900.
25 *Irish Times*, 5 February 1900.

In 1917 the government considered whether it might become necessary to assume control of the alcoholic drinks industry during the war and the period of demobilisation, and thereafter to acquire compulsorily businesses engaged in the manufacture and supply of intoxicating liquors. Committees were established in England, Ireland and Scotland to inquire into the terms and financial arrangements for any such acquisition and any earlier period of control, and Gordon was appointed by the government as chairman of the Irish committee.[26] It met frequently, issuing its report in May 1918,[27] setting out possible terms of compulsory acquisition of breweries, distilleries and wholesalers, and recommending that if the retail trade was not purchased a scheme should be adopted for reduction of at least half of existing licences. No such plan of control and acquisition was subsequently adopted.

The family lived in Fitzwilliam Place and later at Llanmaur, a country house at Shankill, near Bray. Gordon died suddenly on a tram in College Green in the autumn of 1922.

James H.M. Campbell (Lord Glenavy)

Lord Chief Justice of Ireland 1917–18, Lord Chancellor of Ireland 1918–21

James Henry Mussen Campbell (1851–1931), the first baron Glenavy, was born in Dublin. He was educated at Trinity College, with which he had a long connection. He was auditor of the College Historical Society, was a Unionist MP for Dublin University (1903–16) and was appointed as its vice-chancellor (1919–31). He was called to the Bar in 1878 and joined the North East circuit, becoming a QC in 1892, and a bencher of King's Inns in 1894. His imposing and confident presence and force of personality (tipping over at times, in the opinion of John Ross, to a bullying of witnesses)[28] brought him to the front rank of both the Bar and politics. He was a very able man with 'an unattractively sure sense of his personal merit'.[29] Maurice Healy wrote of Campbell's prosecuting address to the jury in a murder trial in Cork in or about 1905: 'I learned afterwards that he had left the House of Commons at 8 o'clock the night before, not having opened the brief; he read and mastered it before his trip across on the night mail, which reached Cork at 10.35 next morning; and at 11 o'clock he began a masterly statement of the case to the jury. Admittedly it was an easy case; but few counsel would today treat a prosecution for murder so cavalierly'.[30]

His ability and political connections led to legal patronage appointments, as Crown prosecutor for the winter assizes in Belfast in 1898 and 1899,[31] as senior

26 *ILT&SJ*, vol. 51, p. 164 (7 July 1917).

27 *Irish Times*, 11 May 1918; *Report into the manufacture and sale of intoxicating liquors* (P.P. 1918, Cmd. 9042 xi.145).

28 Ross to Walter Long, 27 May 1920 (Walter Long Papers (WSHC), 947/336).

29 Alvin Jackson, *The Ulster Party: Irish Unionists in the House of Commons, 1884–1911* (Oxford, 1989), p. 110.

30 Healy, *OldMC*, p. 218.

31 *ILT&SJ*, vol. 32, p. 516 (12 November 1898) and vol. 33, p. 483 (18 November 1899).

Crown prosecutor at Green Street in Dublin in 1900,[32] and then as solicitor general in October 1901.[33] He was briefly (for about a fortnight) attorney general in December 1905, as the Conservative party went out of office. On 28 November he had sought appointment to a prospective vacancy (which in the event did not arise) in the Court of Appeal, shortly switching his request for promotion to the newly vacated office of attorney general, saying that to be attorney general even for a day or two would greatly enhance his position as an MP, imminently to be in opposition, as well as at the Bar.[34]

He was called to the Bar in England in 1899,[35] at Gray's Inn, of which he became a bencher in 1901, and after 1905 'Campbell for some time essayed to follow in the footsteps of, and indeed under the patronage of, Carson at the English Bar. In this country [England], however, he was not a success at the Bar. The vigour of his methods of cross-examination and of his speeches to juries, which were in contrast with the conversational style characteristic of forensic addresses in this country failed to gain him the ear of the judges or of the juries'.[36] Healy noted that members of the Irish Bar rated Campbell much above Carson, acknowledging that 'Carson was quiet, sarcastic and imperturbable, Campbell was flamboyant, hectoring and excitable … [and] well known as about as tough-skinned a man as ever wore wig and gown'.[37]

He was elected to the House of Commons as a Unionist MP at a bye-election in 1898 for the St Stephen's Green division in Dublin. It was a marginal constituency, and Campbell won a narrow victory over the Nationalist candidate, Count Plunkett (3,525 votes to 3,387, a 51/49% division). The expectation that the Unionists would not hold the seat at a bye-election was one reason why at the end of 1899 Campbell was not appointed to fill a vacancy in the High Court arising on the death of William O'Brien.[38] Campbell arranged for friends and supporters to lobby on his behalf, and personally made a forceful plea for appointment to the vacancy, referring to his political services. He expressed no doubt but that the seat was safe and indeed, to the contrary, asserted that not appointing him would lead to unionist voters being disheartened and abstaining at the polls resulting in the loss to the party in due course not only of the Stephen's Green constituency but also the neighbouring South County Dublin seat.[39]

32 *Law Times*, vol. 108, p. 315 (3 February 1900).
33 *Law Times*, vol. 111, p. 577 (26 October 1901).
34 Campbell to Long, 28 November 1905, enclosing letter of that date to J.S. Sandars (secretary to the prime minister) (Walter Long Papers (BL), Add. MS 62409); Campbell to Long, 3 December 1905 (Walter Long Papers (WSHC), 947/59).
35 *Law Times*, vol. 107, p. 3 (6 May 1899).
36 *The Times*, 23 March 1931.
37 Healy, op. cit., pp 95 and 253.
38 Ashbourne to Cadogan, 10 December 1899 (CAD 1685/1); R.W.E. Middleton (principal agent, Conservative Central Office) to Ashbourne, 11 December 1899 (CAD 1688/1).
39 Cadogan to Ashbourne, 7 December 1899, Campbell to Ashbourne, 7 December 1899 (Cadogan Papers, CAD 1685/2).

The appointment was given to the solicitor general, Dunbar Plunket Barton QC, the MP for Mid Armagh. Nor was Campbell then appointed to succeed Barton as a law officer, since this would have been required him to step down as an MP and seek re-election. Cadogan believed that, even if his seat were safe, 'the pro-Boer agitators would make the most of the opportunity' of a bye-election, and it might appear that 'the disloyal feeling in Ireland is worse than it really is'.[40] In the general election later that year he duly lost his seat, his small majority of 138 votes being changed by a lower unionist turnout into a nationalist majority of 556 (2,873 votes to 3,429).[41] In March 1903 he won a hard fought bye-election for the Dublin University constituency, receiving 1,492 votes to 1,421 for his opponent, Arthur W. Samuels QC. That was the last contested election that he fought and, with Sir Edward Carson QC, he was returned unopposed for the university at the next general election in 1906, and at the two general elections in 1910. Between 1903 and 1905 both of the university MPs held office as solicitor general, Campbell in Ireland and Carson in England. Campbell was a diligent constituency MP, alert to protecting the status of the university throughout his parliamentary career,[42] and took a leading part in organising resistance to Home Rule.

In May 1915 growing criticism of the war effort, in light of recent military setbacks such as the failure of the landing at Gallipoli in April, led to consensus on a reconstruction of the government on a broader basis, with the Unionists joining the Liberals in a coalition government. Campbell showed great anxiety for promotion, writing to his party leader, Andrew Bonar Law, that 'If there is going to be a "reshuffle" I want the Irish Chancellorship. *You* can get it for me and I think that I have earned it by much longer and harder service than others whose names I see mentioned'.[43] Nationalist opposition frustrated his ambition then, and three anxious years of persistent petitioning and solicitation would pass before he succeeded in being appointed.

When the new Cabinet was announced on 25 May there was widespread Liberal and Nationalist dismay at the inclusion of Carson, the leader of the Ulster Unionist resistance to Home Rule, as attorney general for England,[44] and at reports that Campbell would replace the sitting lord chancellor, Ignatius O'Brien. The prospect of not one but two of such men having responsibility for the rule of law and the administration of justice, in England or Ireland, provoked 'a feeling in Ireland of the most intense character'.[45] Nationalist opinion rallied to the defence

40 Cadogan to Salisbury, 18 January 1900 (Salisbury Papers).

41 Alvin Jackson, 'The failure of unionism in Dublin, 1900', *IHS*, vol. 26, no. 104 (November 1989), pp 377–95.

42 See for instance HC Deb, 5th series, vol. 42, cols. 1763–70 (21 October 1912).

43 Campbell to Bonar Law, 19 May 1915 (R.F.V. Heuston, 'Legal history and the author: some practical problems of authorship' in W.N. Osborough (ed.), *The Irish Legal History Society: inaugural addresses* (Dublin, 1989), p. 29).

44 An office which, as it transpired, he held for a few months only, resigning in October 1915.

45 Redmond to Asquith, 7 June 1915 (Gwynn, op. cit., p. 430).

of O'Brien not so much for his own merits but because he was not (and was an obstacle to) Campbell.[46]

What had initially seemed to be a question of local judicial patronage escalated at Westminster into a more fundamental issue of inter-party goodwill and understanding. Bonar Law told Lloyd George, a prominent Liberal, on 4 June that 'I am really greatly alarmed about the Campbell business. Of course if it comes to the breaking point we may have to give way but I think the pressure of our party will be so strong that some of those in the Cabinet would resign and at the best even if we feel and I think that this may be the case that we cannot resign we shall start with very little prospect of doing useful work together'.[47] A few days later the wider crisis was defused, but on a basis that was to leave Campbell complaining for the next three years that he had been let down. Asquith, the prime minister, told Redmond, the leader of the Irish Parliamentary Party, that 'the whole Campbell business has given me an infinity of trouble … The claim of the Chancellorship for Campbell has now been withdrawn, subject to suitable provision (which I have undertaken) being made for him, and to a place of minor importance being found for a Unionist in the Irish Administration'.[48] Difficulties arose in finding an appointment for Campbell either in Ireland or in England. The initial plan was that he would be appointed as lord chief justice of Ireland, to replace R.R. Cherry, or as a lord of appeal in ordinary, but both Cherry and one sitting Law Lord (Atkinson) who it was thought might have been prepared to retire were unwilling to do so.[49] There was no shortage of peers eligible to sit on appeals to the House of Lords. Talk of Campbell being appointed to a judicial position in England was strongly resisted by the lord chancellor of Great Britain. In April 1916, a few days before Easter, Campbell arranged to be appointed as attorney general.

The arguments that he used in extensive correspondence with Bonar Law and with Asquith to advance his claims are an indication of how articulate he could be – perhaps especially in his own behalf – as an advocate, changing tack and re-ordering his arguments to meet changing circumstances. One theme was his sense of financial insecurity, and Bonar Law was reportedly 'pained, and indeed shocked, by the avidity of his old friend'.[50]

In the first week of November 1916 Cherry indicated his intention to retire and Asquith offered his position to Campbell, although it transpired that the

46 Daire Hogan, *Ignatius O'Brien and the law* in Daire Hogan and Patrick Maume (eds), *The reminiscences of Ignatius O'Brien, lord chancellor of Ireland, 1913–18* (Dublin, 2021), pp 44–5; Daire Hogan, 'James Henry Mussen Campbell QC, MP: a life in law and unionist politics' in Niamh Howlin and Felix M. Larkin (eds), *Confluences of law and history: Irish Legal History Society discourses and other papers, 2011–21* (Dublin, 2025), pp 218–31, at 222–5.

47 Bonar Law to Lloyd George, 4 June 1915 (Bonar Law Papers, 53/6/22).

48 Gwynn, op. cit., p. 432. The letter is misdated as 9 May in the authorised biography of Asquith (Spender & Asquith, op. cit., vol. 2, p. 169).

49 R.F.V. Heuston, *Lives of the lord chancellors, 1885–1940* (Oxford, 1964), p. 273.

50 Robert Blake, *The unknown prime minister: the life and times of Andrew Bonar Law, 1858–1923* (London, 1955), p. 254.

arrangements for Cherry's retirement were delayed for some weeks. Campbell was greatly affected by the death in action in France at this time of his third son, Philip.[51] Asquith was replaced by Lloyd George as prime minister early in December, and Campbell's appointment was announced on 21 December, the last day of the Michaelmas law term, coupled with the honour of a baronetcy.[52] He was formally sworn in as lord chief justice on 11 January 1917, and in a change from recent practice took his oath of office in open court, in 'a public function of a really impressive character'.[53] At Campbell's request Bonar Law arranged for Lloyd George to confirm Asquith's pledge that the first vacancy of lord of appeal in the House of Lords would be offered to him.[54]

He was a judge for four and a half years, for some 17 months (to June 1918) as lord chief justice and the balance (to June 1921) as lord chancellor, thus sitting successively as a common law judge as the head of the King's Bench division of the High Court and in Chancery and as head of the Court of Appeal. He appointed his brother William Mussen Campbell, a retired colonel in the Indian Field Artillery, to be his circuit registrar and subsequently his private secretary.[55] His appeal judgments included careful reviews of whether compensation payable for the felling for military purposes of trees on an estate (as contrasted with trees felled by accident or wind) was the property of the tenant for life or of the trustees of a settlement,[56] and of the nature of an easement of a right of way by necessity.[57]

He presided over the Court for Crown Cases Reserved in a case as to whether a jury had sufficient evidence of death, on foot of a confession of the defendant, where the body of a deceased person had not been found, in which the court upheld the decision of the trial judge at assizes not to withdraw the case from the jury and affirmed a conviction.[58] Campbell's judgment rejected forcefully arguments put forward by defence counsel that were based upon some previous observations by Palles CB limiting the reliance that could be placed upon of a confession in a case of murder.[59]

> I confess to the greatest difficulty in following the reasoning of Palles CB … I have asked in vain and searched in vain for any decision which supports, much less establishes, the proposition that, in the absence of the finding of the body, the confession of the accused cannot supply proof that the act was done … I therefore express in the clearest and strongest way the unqualified dissent of every member of this court from the proposition that the case of

51 *Irish Times*, 11 November 1916.
52 *Irish Times*, 22 December 1916.
53 *Law Times*, vol. 142, p. 203 (20 January 1917); *Irish Times*, 12 January 1917.
54 Bonar Law to Campbell, 6 January 1917 (Bonar Law Papers, 84/6/37).
55 *Irish Times*, 26 October 1929.
56 *Gage and Roper v Pigott and de Jenner*, [1919] 1 IR 23.
57 *Maguire v Browne*, [1921] 1 IR 148.
58 *R v McNicholl*, [1917] 2 IR 557; *ILT&SJ*, vol. 51, p. 311 (29 December 1917).
59 *The Queen v Sullivan*, 20 LR Ir. (1887) 550, at 570.

> murder is an exception to the general and accepted principle of our common law that the confession of the accused may be the highest and most satisfactory proof of guilt, and our refusal to give any countenance to the proposition that in a charge of murder, in which the accused has made a full and free confession of the commission of the crime … the case can never go to the jury unless there is proof of the finding of the dead body.[60]

The *Irish Times* had remarked in 1917 that on his appointment Campbell 'now leaves the exciting arena of politics for the cooler atmosphere of the judicial bench',[61] but his new status as a judge did not end his participation in political life. His involvement in various informal discussions aimed at securing a compromise settlement over Home Rule 'led more hard-line unionists to regard him as an opportunistic lawyer who had used them to secure office for himself, while nationalists continued to cite his 1912–14 Ulster speeches as setting precedents for the Easter rising and as treasonable utterances which should have disqualified him from public office'.[62] He and Carson attended a meeting in Downing Street in April 1918 and advised the war cabinet against the possible extension of conscription to Ireland.

After Lloyd George decided at the end of April on a new political initiative in Ireland, perhaps combining the introduction of Home Rule with conscription, Campbell was asked if he would take a political office, as one of a triumvirate of persons who, as lords justices, would replace the lord lieutenant of Ireland.[63] He declined and the plan did not proceed, and when he took this opportunity to bring up again the prospect of being appointed lord chancellor Bonar Law told him that 'if there is a vacancy I feel sure that L.G. will offer it to you and I shall certainly do my best to make sure of that'.[64] Campbell's apprehensions that, as had happened three years before, a promised appointment might be blocked proved groundless, and in the first week of June O'Brien was dismissed and Campbell appointed. He was unable to take his seat in court for some three weeks, having trouble with his sight.[65]

His relations with the government transpired afterwards not to be as warm as might have been expected. He expressed frustration at a lack of consultation on the appointment in August 1918 of James O'Connor as a member of the Court of Appeal in succession to Thomas F. Molony, who had replaced him as lord chief justice. (John Ross had a low opinion of Campbell's abilities and thought that he should not have been made a judge, but shared his reservations about the

60 *R v McNicholl*, at 588, 589, and 592.
61 *Irish Times*, 11 January 1917.
62 Entry on Campbell in *DIB* (by Patrick Maume).
63 Diary of Field Marshal Sir John French (Lord French of Ypres), 29 and 30 April 1918 (Imperial War Museum, London, PP/MCR/C32, JDF 1, volume R).
64 Bonar Law to Campbell, 8 May 1918 (Bonar Law Papers, 84/7/29).
65 *Law Times*, vol. 145, p. 170 (29 June 1918).

appointment of O'Connor and Molony.)[66] He then referred publicly to conscription as a 'danger and disaster', adding that he was 'not responsible for government policy'.[67] Some two years later, in August 1920, a few days after the passing of the Restoration of Order in Ireland Act had introduced martial law and courts martial, T.M. Healy noted that 'James Campbell is sick of this regime'.[68] In September he stated that he had not been for many months associated with the executive.[69] His influence within the government had evaporated, as recorded at the end of September 1920 in excited terms by Mark Sturgis, one of the most senior British officials in Dublin Castle: Campbell, he wrote, was 'a poltroon of the most contemptible dye – does nothing and apparently things of nothing but the best way to show SF [Sinn Fein] that he is neutral and passive, and by God a thief since he continues to draw his salary'.[70] The government did not accept a recommendation that he made (in October 1920) of clemency and commutation of a sentence of death passed by a court martial on Kevin Barry, a young Republican student, who had participated in a fatal ambush of an army unit in Church Street, near the Four Courts.[71] He took an active part in encouraging the erection of war memorials, for the Bar,[72] as a national memorial,[73] and for Trinity College.[74]

He was raised to the peerage in 1921 after his retirement on 27 June as lord chancellor, that being the day on which, pursuant to the Government of Ireland Act 1920, the office of lord chancellor ceased to have any executive governmental functions and became a purely judicial office.[75] His grandson, Patrick Campbell, the third baron Glenavy, wrote that 'when he became the first baron he took his title from Glenavy more because he liked the sound of it than because of landed estates in the area. I doubt, in fact, if he'd ever been in the village in his life'.[76] Although any family connection with the village of Glenavy in Co. Antrim may thus have been tenuous he had given its name to his house in Milltown in the Dublin suburbs. The benchers of Gray's Inn in London commissioned a portrait, by Sir William Orpen RA, for the hall of the Inn, which was exhibited at the Royal Academy summer exhibition in 1923.[77] The portrait bears out his grandson's

66 Ross to Edward Shortt, chief secretary for Ireland, undated [autumn 1918], as forwarded by Ross to Austen Chamberlain, 21 January 1919 (Austen Chamberlain Papers (Cadbury Research Library, University of Birmingham), AC 24/1/39).
67 *Irish Times*, 24 August 1918; *Law Times*, vol. 145, p. 327 (24 August 1918), p. 343 (31 August 1918).
68 T.M. Healy, *Letters and leaders*, vol. 2, p. 627.
69 *Law Times*, vol. 150, p. 149 (4 September 1920).
70 Michael Hopkinson (ed.), *The last days of Dublin Castle: the Mark Sturgis diaries* (Dublin, 1999), p. 48 (29 September 1920).
71 Hopkinson, ibid., p. 63 (31 October 1920).
72 *ILT&SJ*, vol. 53, p. 132 (31 May 1919).
73 *ILT&SJ*, vol. 53, p. 209 (30 August 1919).
74 *ILT&SJ*, vol. 53, p. 268 (8 November 1919), vol. 62, p. 264 (3 November 1928) and p. 277 (17 November 1928).
75 Government of Ireland Act 1920 (10&11 Geo. 5, c.67), s44; Government of Ireland (lord chancellor of Ireland) Order 1921 (SR&O 1921, no. 1130 (27 June 1921)).
76 Patrick Campbell, *My life and easy times* (London, 1967, paperback edition 1968, p. 67).
77 *Irish Times*, 23 July 1921; *ILT&SJ*, vol. 57, p. 124 (19 May 1923).

comment that 'he was extremely good-looking, in a most distinguished and autocratic way, with silvery white hair and an elegantly drooping white moustache'.[78]

In the early years of the Irish Free State Campbell became a prominent symbol of unionist acceptance and co-operation with its government, not only as a member and the first chairman of the Senate (1922–8) but also as head of an official committee that was appointed and sat very urgently in 1923, the recommendations of which formed the basis of the restructuring of the judicature that was effected by the Courts of Justice Act 1924.[79] Before this engagement in the governance of an independent Ireland, however, he had inquired whether, as a member of the House of Lords, he might sit on the hearing of appeals from lower courts in the United Kingdom, since he was eligible for such a function.[80] The lord chancellor, Lord Birkenhead (his former colleague, F.E. Smith), rebuffed these inquiries, as did Bonar Law, who 'sent a thunderous rebuke'.[81] He had been formally introduced into the House of Lords in November 1921,[82] and contributed (as his only speeches in the house) to the debates in December 1922 on the statutes that gave effect under the law of the United Kingdom to the Treaty that had been signed twelve months before.[83]

He was a prominent lay member of the Church of Ireland, being variously and at different times a member of the Representative Church Body and of the General Synod, Chancellor of the United Dioceses of Dublin, Glendalough and Kildare and an advocate and subsequently a lay judge in the court of the General Synod, and was remembered in the church as 'a commanding figure' with strong opinions.[84] Campbell left a very substantial estate on his death in 1931, which was valued for probate purposes in England at over £90,000, somewhat belying his earlier expressions of financial concerns.

William Moore

Justice of the High Court (King's Bench) 1917–21, Lord Justice of Appeal, Northern Ireland 1921–5, Lord Chief Justice of Northern Ireland 1925–37

William Moore (1864–1944) was a member of a family 'connected with county Antrim since the Plantation of Ulster',[85] and that was long established at Moore Lodge, Finvoy, Ballymoney.[86] His father was an eminent physician. He was

78 Campbell, op. cit., p. 76.
79 See Niamh Howlin (ed.), *A century of courts; the Courts of Justice Act 1924* (Dublin, 2024).
80 Appellate Jurisdiction Act 1876 (39&40 Vict., c.59, ss5 and 25).
81 Heuston, 'Legal history, etc', op. cit., p. 3c.
82 HL Deb, 5th series, vol. 47, col. 217 (9 November 1921).
83 HL Deb, 5th series, vol. 52, cols. 192 and 197–8 (1 December 1922).
84 *Church of Ireland Gazette*, 28 March 1931. See also Robert Marshall, 'The constitution of the Church of Ireland in action: ritualist litigation in a Disestablished Church, 1871–1937' in Kevin Costello and Niamh Howlin (eds), *Law and religion in Ireland, 1700–1970* (Cham, Switzerland, 2021), pp 289–326, at pp 298 and 315.
85 *Irish Times*, 13 December 1924.
86 C.E.B. Brett, *Buildings of County Antrim* (Belfast, 1996), p. 154.

educated at Marlborough school in England and at Trinity College. He was called to the Bar in 1887 and became a QC in 1899. He was a member of the North East circuit, and had a good practice at quarter sessions in Co. Antrim and at sittings of the High Court in Belfast. He became a bencher of King's Inns in 1910.

He was elected to Parliament as a Unionist at a bye-election in North Antrim in 1899, retaining his seat at the general election in 1900, being unopposed each time. In May 1900 he joined in the protests from Irish MPs when on the retirement of Lord Morris as a Law Lord an English judge was appointed to replace him.[87] In September 1902 he was appointed parliamentary private secretary to George Wyndham, the chief secretary for Ireland.[88] 'Mr Moore has a thorough knowledge of the working of the Land Law Acts and the Land Purchase Acts, and he has considerable experience in his practice as a lawyer of the administration of the Local Government Act 1898. It is with respect to these Acts that the great mass of Irish questions asked in Parliament arise, and it is with reference to such topics that a layman such as Mr Wyndham requires professional guidance'.[89]

In 1904 a plan of devolution of powers to an Irish government was worked up by Lord Dunraven, a Unionist peer, with the co-operation behind the scenes of Sir Antony MacDonnell, the under-secretary and head of the civil service in Dublin Castle. A great controversy arose following the disclosure of this scheme and of MacDonnell's apparent (if deniable) part in it, which led to Moore resigning his position in protest, and eventually to Wyndham losing office in March 1905. The Unionist members of Parliament in Ulster declared their collective repudiation of the plan as 'a step, however disguised, towards Home Rule',[90] and Moore joined in a hostile questioning of Wyndham in the House of Commons about the whole affair.[91] He was instrumental in the establishment of the Ulster Unionist Council as a co-ordinating or umbrella body in 1904–5.[92] He lost his seat to an independent more populist unionist at the general election in 1906, but was returned at a bye-election in 1907 as the member for North Armagh, and retained that seat (unopposed) at the two general elections in 1910. Up to the time of his appointment as a judge in 1917 he was prominent in the campaign in Ulster against Home Rule. He was one of the first unionists to speak of a right of armed resistance,[93] and to emphasise a British identity of unionists over any wider Irish national identity.[94]

His daughter's view, although not doubting his commitment to the (increasingly Ulster-centric) unionist cause, was that he was always ambitious for

87 HC Deb, 4th series, vol. 83, col. 617 (18 May 1900).

88 *ILT&SJ*, vol. 36, p. 380 (27 September 1902).

89 *New Irish Jurist*, vol. 2, p. 398 (3 October 1902).

90 *Irish Times*, 24 October 1904.

91 HC Deb, 4th series, vol. 141, col. 326 (16 February 1905) and col. 610 (20 February 1905).

92 *Irish Times*, 24 October 1904; Andrew Gailey, *Ireland and the death of kindness; the experience of constructive unionism, 1890–1905* (Cork, 1987), pp 229–31; Alvin Jackson, *The Ulster Party: Irish Unionists in the House of Commons, 1884–1911* (Oxford, 1989), pp 236–7.

93 Alvin Jackson, op. cit., p. 318.

94 Brian Walker, *Dancing to history's tune* (Belfast, 1996), p. 115.

legal promotion and had seen a seat in Parliament as a means to achieve this.[95] In June 1915 he was appointed senior Crown prosecutor for the city of Belfast, in place of (and by) John Gordon QC, MP, who had been appointed attorney general. The Revd J.B. Armour was a neighbour in Ballymoney, a Presbyterian minister there for over 50 years from 1869 and a supporter of Home Rule. He wished Moore well in seeking appointment as a law officer in 1917, while privately thinking him quite unsuitable, for two reasons, as 'he is not well up in the law, his reputation at the Bar being low, and further because he has been so violent as a politician, irritating the Nationalists whenever he got on his legs'.[96] James Campbell twice proposed that Moore be appointed solicitor general, once in December 1905 as the Unionist government was imploding (and Campbell had been promoted from that office to be attorney general) and again early in 1917.[97] In November 1917 he was appointed a judge, a promotion which Campbell, by then the lord chief justice, had been trying to arrange since the spring of that year.[98] The vacancy on the bench which he filled had existed for almost 18 months, since the retirement of Palles.

His appointment subsequently drew adverse comment from opposite ends of the political spectrum, Sir John Ross, one of his judicial colleagues, later privately remarked that his appointment had been made 'to the astonishment of everybody', and indicated a 'degradation of the Irish bench'.[99] Hugh Kennedy, the attorney general of the Irish Free State, was equally unflattering in 1923, telling W.T. Cosgrave, the president of the Executive Council [government], that 'William Moore, whom I saw but once in twenty years hold a brief, was forced on the High Court bench by the Whips of the English Tory party who said he never failed when called to speak at a Tory meeting in remote parts of Britain, though even decent Tories regarded his poison gas with dislike and contempt'.[100]

He was the only High Court judge in 1921 who exercised an election (as provided for in the Government of Ireland Act 1920) to serve as a member of the judiciary of Northern Ireland. He was initially appointed as a member of the Court of Appeal and on the death of Denis Henry in the autumn of 1925 he was appointed lord chief justice, a position he held up to his resignation in 1937. He was made a baronet in 1932.[101] His interests included breeding Hereford cattle. He was chancellor of the united diocese of Down and Connor and Dromore,[102] and a

95 Alvin Jackson, op. cit., p. 59.
96 J.B. Armour to W.S. Armour, 13 June 1917 (Papers of J.B. Armour (PRONI), D1792/A/3/8/22).
97 Alvin Jackson, op. cit., p. 279; J.B. Dougherty (MP for Londonderry, 1914–18) to Armour, 15 December 1916 (Armour Papers, D1729/A/1/1/18); Walter Long to Bonar Law, 5 January 1917 (Bonar Law Papers, 81/2/9).
98 Campbell to Sir Edward Carson, 22 July 1917 (Carson Papers (PRONI), D1507/A/24/12).
99 Ross to Austen Chamberlain, 21 January 1919 (Austen Chamberlain Papers (University of Birmingham, Cadbury Research Library, special collections), AC24/1/38); Sir Declan Morgan, 'Centenary lecture on the lord chief justices of Northern Ireland' (Belfast, 8 December 2021), para. 31.
100 Kennedy to Cosgrave, 13 August 1923 (Hugh Kennedy Papers (UCDA), P. 4/1390(3)).
101 *Irish Times*, 3 June 1932; *ILT&SJ*, vol. 66, p. 143 (11 June 1932).
102 *Church of Ireland Gazette*, 5 July 1929, 8 December 1944.

member of the court of the General Synod of the Church of Ireland. A protracted case before the court about liturgical practices at St John's church, Sandymount, Dublin, was determined at a sitting of the court in Belfast.[103] His son Joseph, after service in the army during the Great War, became an inspector in the Royal Ulster Constabulary.[104] Moore died in 1944.

James O'Connor

Justice of the High Court 1918, Lord Justice of Appeal 1918–24

James O'Connor (1872–1931) had a varied career in the legal profession, beginning (and ending) as a solicitor and being, at different times, a member of the Bar in Ireland and in England, a law officer, a judge of the High Court and of the Court of Appeal, and ultimately a litigant. He was born in Wexford, and after qualifying as a solicitor in 1894 he worked for some years in practice with his brother Michael (M.J.), who had qualified in 1888 and established a well-known local firm. In 1900 he was called to the Bar and his progress there was rapid, leading to him taking silk in 1908.

He was a prolific author, first publishing in 1894 a compilation of examination papers of the Law Society.[105] In 1903 he wrote a short guide to the laws relating to motor cars, setting out the Locomotives Act 1896 and the Motor Car Act 1903, with relevant regulations.[106] The following year he prepared a much more substantial guide (of over 600 pages) to alcohol licensing laws, as most recently set out in the Licensing (Ireland) Act 1902.[107] This expertise helped him in developing a practice in licensing law.[108] In 1911 he published the first edition of his *Irish justice of the peace*, a guide or digest of the criminal offences that could be tried summarily before magistrates.[109] For the second edition in 1915, which had over 2,000 pages (an increase of over 600 pages on the first edition), he 'has arranged very advantageous terms for purchasers who already possess the first edition. Upon a return of the old copy a substantial allowance will be made'.[110] In 1925 George Gavan Duffy (1882–1951), later to be a justice and then president of the High Court, published an updated *Digest of the criminal and quasi-criminal law 1914–1925* as a supplement for the District Court of the 1915 edition. This contained a preface by O'Connor now containing 'advice to district justices' in place of advice to magistrates, in which he observed that 'silence has its uses. On the bench its

103 *Church of Ireland Gazette*, 16 October 1936.
104 *Irish Times*, 31 August 1931; *Burke's peerage and baronetage*.
105 *The Examination Papers of first examinations for solicitors' apprentices; a compilation of all the papers from 1878 to 1894* (*ILT&SJ*, vol. 28, p. 247 (12 May 1894)).
106 *Handbook to the Motor Car Acts* (Dublin, 1903).
107 *The Licensing Laws of Ireland, and the practice and procedure connected therewith* (Dublin, 1904).
108 *The King (Powell) v Mahony, The King (McCormack) v Mahony* (*Irish Times*, 8 May 1908).
109 *The Irish Justice of the Peace; a treatise on the powers and duties of justices of the peace in Ireland* (Dublin, 1911).
110 *ILT&SJ*, vol. 49, p. 23 (23 January 1915).

energy paralyses the bore. Sit still, look wooden and say nothing is the best method for dealing with the long-winded advocate'.[111] Also in 1925 O'Connor published a history of Ireland since 1798, written from a constitutional Nationalist perspective, and containing reflections on the turmoil of recent years.[112]

He was a strong supporter of Home Rule, and consulted and liaised with John Redmond MP, the Irish parliamentary party leader from 1900. That year he inquired of Redmond (another Wexford man, although he represented the city of Waterford in Parliament) whether he might be supported as a candidate for the party in the general election that autumn in any one of a number of possible constituencies, in Wexford, Wicklow or Dublin,[113] although nothing came of that. These political sympathies contributed to his appointment by the Liberal government as solicitor general at the end of June 1914, although he acknowledged to Redmond that if he had been a member of the parliamentary party he could not have accepted any form of official patronage or appointment and that 'I know you could not actively interfere for me'.[114] At a very early stage of the crisis in May 1915 over the formation of a coalition government and James H.M. Campbell's ambition to become lord chancellor he was told that he might be removed from office to make way for a unionist lawyer, at a time when chief baron Palles was thought to be on the point of resignation – 'if they were to treat me fairly they would give me that judgeship'.[115] As it transpired it was Pim, the attorney general, who was moved, and O'Connor remained in his position. When in June 1916 Palles finally did resign O'Connor wrote to the prime minister asking to be appointed to fill that vacancy, although saying to Redmond that 'while I have done so, and intend to press my claim, yet at the same time this is subject to any expression from you of your wishes – which I am always, in the interest of the country, prepared to conform to'.[116] The government decided not to fill the vacancy at that time.

On two occasions, in light of the wartime necessity of the Unionist party having a senior representative in the government of Ireland, the convention of the solicitor general filling a vacancy in the office of attorney general was set aside. In 1915 Pim's promotion had been for the explicit purpose of enabling John Gordon QC, MP to succeed him, and in 1916 similarly a judicial vacancy was created for Gordon in order to make his position available to Campbell. O'Connor continued in office as solicitor general until February 1917 when he succeeded Campbell (who had been appointed lord chief justice) as attorney general. In April 1918 he was appointed a judge of the High Court, thus leaving what had become an office

111 Preface to *A digest of criminal and quasi-criminal law 1914–1925*, p. xii; see also G.M. Golding, *George Gavan Duffy 1882–1951: a legal biography* (Dublin, 1982), pp 30–1.

112 *A history of Ireland 1798–1924* (2 vols, London, 1925).

113 O'Connor to Redmond, 13 and 27 September 1900 (John Redmond Papers (National Library of Ireland), MS 15,214/2/1 and 2).

114 O'Connor to Redmond, 3 July 1914 (Redmond Papers, MS 15,214/2/6(2)).

115 O'Connor to Redmond, 16 May 1915 (Redmond Papers, MS 15,214/2/7).

116 O'Connor to Asquith, 9 June 1916 (Asquith Papers, 45:3); O'Connor to Redmond, 12 June 1916 (Redmond Papers, MS 15,214/2/8).

of increasing responsibility and worry, and from which he might have felt obliged to resign if very controversial proposals to introduce military conscription in Ireland had been implemented by the government.[117] A few months later he was promoted to the Court of Appeal to fill a vacancy arising when Thomas Molony was appointed to be chief justice in succession to Campbell, who had become lord chancellor. Molony was a Catholic, as was O'Connor, and their respective appointments within a few weeks of each other were intended by the government to denote some respect for mainstream Catholic or nationalist opinion. Campbell did not have a good opinion of O'Connor's position at the Bar and his general abilities, and had objected to his appointment to the Court of Appeal, complaining to Bonar Law, his erstwhile party leader, that it would impede the proper functioning of the court.[118] He was placated by assurances of greater consultation with him on future judicial appointments and the two men, with Stephen Ronan (of whom Campbell had an equally poor opinion),[119] constituted the Court of Appeal for the next three years, until Campbell's resignation in July 1921. The court was briefly designated as the Court of Appeal for Southern Ireland under the Government of Ireland Act 1920.[120] In the confusing political situation in 1921 O'Connor played some role as an intermediary for Sinn Fein in preliminary contacts with the government.[121]

He was not appointed to any judicial office in June 1924 when the courts of the Irish Free State were reconstituted. Any prospect of this that may have existed was not helped by him expressing his opinion in the autumn of 1923 that the Courts of Justice Bill, which the government had recently introduced in the Oireachtas, would tend to degrade the administration of justice.[122] This was said to be the first public criticism of the reform proposals from within the legal profession.[123] Somewhat ironically, in a previous letter to a newspaper in 1920 O'Connor had criticised a judicial colleague, Arthur W. Samuels, for having praised and advocated an Education Bill then before Parliament when addressing a meeting of the Protestant Orphan Society.[124] Samuels, he said, had deliberately and lamentably breached a judicial tradition of not becoming involved in political controversy, and he could not let this pass by in silence for fear of encouraging a repetition, which would be disastrous for the judiciary.[125]

117 O'Connor to Laurence O'Neill (Lord Mayor of Dublin), 12 April 1918 (Laurence O'Neill Papers (National Library of Ireland), MS 35,294/2/14).
118 Campbell to Bonar Law, 3 July 1918 (Bonar Law Papers, 83/5/2). See also letter Campbell to Bonar Law (undated, Bonar Law Papers, 84/5/4) and Campbell to Bonar Law, 8 July 1918 (Bonar Law Papers, 85/5/7).
119 Campbell to Bonar Law, 3 July 1918 (Bonar Law Papers, 83/5/2).
120 10&11 Geo. 5, c.67, s39(1).
121 Michael Hopkinson (ed.), *The last days of Dublin Castle: the Mark Sturgis diar*ies (Dublin, 1999), p. 103; Thomas Jones, *Whitehall diary: vol. 3, Ireland 1918–25* (London, 1971), p. 52.
122 *Irish Independent* and *Irish Times*, 8 October 1923.
123 *Irish Times*, 8 October 1923.
124 *Irish Times*, 1 May 1920.
125 *Irish Times*, 3 May 1920.

O'Connor became something of a philosopher of judicial life. In a submission in the spring of 1923 to the Judiciary Committee chaired by Glenavy he said that one of the 'well-defined principles for a judicial system' was that a judge 'must be independent of pecuniary temptation; he must be a personage in the land, able to surround himself with the things that make for repose, dignity and culture; therefore he must be well paid'.[126] He expanded on that theme some six months later in a letter to the newspapers, saying that the proposed new judicial salaries were too low and that the argument that the bench was too highly paid was a fallacy (see pp 58–9). The following year he said that in the termination of his office as a judge he had lost 'a position of considerable influence, and even of intellectual pleasure'.[127]

That statement was made in the course of his application to the committee established by the British government pursuant to the Irish Free State (Consequential Provisions) Act 1922 to assess compensation for the judges on their loss of office in 1924 (1922, in the case of Sir John Ross). The committee's determination required the UK Treasury to provide O'Connor with an annual allowance which, with his pension, would put him in receipt of an income equivalent to his full salary for 11 years. He moved to England and was called to the Bar by the Middle Temple in May 1925 and to the Inner Bar, becoming a KC, a few weeks later.[128] However his intended practice at the Bar in England was affected by ill health, and he returned to Ireland with the intention of practising as a solicitor, in the family firm in Wexford, and at his request was disbarred both in Ireland and in England.[129]

When he made an application to the High Court to be re-admitted as a solicitor the chief justice, Hugh Kennedy, took the view that this was not simply a formality, and directed that notice of this be given to the attorney general so that the public interest would be considered.[130] The court set out some considerations which, in the ordinary course of events, would suggest that the practice of law would have been abandoned forever by any person holding judicial office:

> it is beyond doubt that if a man should step down from the privileged position of the bench and throw off what is a sacred office to engage in the rough-and-tumble of litigious contest, and compete with the practitioners for the feed business of the courts, perhaps challenge the decisions which he pronounced, or even fail to support them in argument, he will shake the authority of the judicial limb of government, and mar the prestige and

126 Submission to Judiciary Committee, undated [April] 1923 (Hugh Kennedy Papers, P. 4/1092(84)).

127 Claim of Rt. Hon. James O'Connor for compensation for loss of office, 25 June 1924 (T 164/105/9 (TNAUK)).

128 *ILT&SJ*, vol. 59, p. 110 (9 May 1925) and p. 129 (30 May 1925).

129 *ILT&SJ*, vol. 63, p. 281 (23 November 1929).

130 *In Re the Solicitors' Acts and Sir James O'Connor*, [1930] IR 623; *ILT&SJ*, vol. 63, p. 299 (14 December 1929) and p. 305 (21 December 1929). See also G.W. Hogan, 'Chief Justice Kennedy and Sir James O'Connor's application', *Irish Jurist*, vol. 23 (1988), pp 144–59.

> dignity of the courts of justice upon which the whole structure of the State must always lean.[131]

O'Connor's special circumstances, however, were held to permit approval of his re-admission, subject to him undertaking not to exercise any right of personal audience in the courts.

A knighthood was conferred on O'Connor in the New Year Honours List in 1925.[132] He died in London at the end of December 1931.

John Blake Powell

Justice of the High Court 1918–23

John Blake Powell (1861–1923) was a native of Sligo, where his family, who were Catholics, had a retail business in the town centre. He qualified as a solicitor in 1884, and (unlike almost all other judges appointed at that time) does not appears to have attended university.[133] As a young man he was an active horseman, hunting and playing polo.[134] In 1894 he switched to the other side of the legal profession and was called to the Bar. His professional progress was steady on the Connaught circuit, where he was appointed as a junior (and subsequently senior) Crown prosecutor for Co. Leitrim in 1903 and senior Crown prosecutor for Co. Sligo in 1914.[135] He became a QC in 1905, represented his circuit on the Bar Council, and was elected a bencher of King's Inns in 1909.

His career, much of it in the field of criminal law, was largely spent in the west of Ireland, and included trials for murder and for lesser offences such as sheep stealing, affray, a case of arson on the Aran islands (1908), and civil cases for defamation and probate issues. Clients included the bishop of Galway and the Galway Harbour Commissioners. He represented T.M. Healy KC in his (successful) petition against the validity of the election of his opponent, Richard Hazelton, in the North Louth constituency in the December 1910 general election.[136] He represented the Dublin Metropolitan Police at public hearings of a commission of inquiry into allegations of the use of excessive force by the DMP in the course of labour disturbances in the city in August and September 1913.[137]

John F. Larkin, later to be attorney general for Northern Ireland (2010–20), has remarked on the nature of Powell's conservatism, combining courage and a regard for moderation, and an enduring attachment to the common law and the values of

131 [1930] IR 623, at 631.
132 *ILT&SJ*, vol. 59, p. 5 (3 January 1925).
133 He was a solicitor's apprentice for five years, a period which could generally be shortened to three for university graduates.
134 *Irish Times*, 22 September 1923.
135 *ILT&SJ*, vol. 37, p. 22 (10 January 1903) and vol. 48, p. 120 (25 April 1914).
136 *Irish Times*, 24 February 1911.
137 *Irish Times*, 24 January 1914.

social order.[138] He was an active member of the Irish Unionist Alliance, the 'effective and recognised medium for southern unionist opinion and propaganda',[139] which became more active in and after 1910 as the prospect of Home Rule loomed larger. He spoke at a public meeting in Dublin that gathered representatives of the provinces of Leinster, Connaught and Munster.[140] In 1917 he was one of the five nominees of the Alliance in the Irish Convention, a representative assembly convened by the government that summer in order to seek (ultimately without success) a consensual approach on devolution that might bridge the deep divisions between nationalist and unionist opinion.[141] Powell took an active part in the Convention during the nine months or so for which it sat,[142] working closely with Lord Midleton, the leader of southern unionism,[143] and remaining in contact with him after appointment as a judge.[144]

He was appointed solicitor general in April 1918, in the last days of the Convention, despite being unwell at the time. 'Mr Powell has suffered from a breakdown in health owing to overwork, and has been ordered complete rest by his doctor, but we are pleased to learn that he is making good progress towards recovery'.[145] The ill health which prevented him from taking up his duties initially had cleared by the autumn.[146] At the end of the Trinity law term in early August that year James O'Connor, who had only a few months before been appointed as a judge in the Chancery division of the High Court, was promoted to the Court of Appeal. An interval then occurred during which various names were canvassed as his successor in the High Court,[147] and eventually at the end of November 1918 Powell was appointed.[148] His lack of significant experience in Chancery matters transpired not to be a difficulty. Larkin's careful review of Powell's short judicial career referred to his 'painstaking and meticulous judgments' as being 'characterised by an extensive discussion of authorities, lucid arrangement of the arguments and a tightly confined decision'.[149]

The war of independence and the civil war placed great pressure on the judiciary, as an organ of the contested state. Powell was the judge to whom in May 1921 an application was made for a writ of prohibition directed to the military

138 John Francis Larkin, 'Aspects of the career of John Blake Powell', *Irish Jurist*, vol. 20 (1985), p. 403, at pp 423–4.
139 Patrick Buckland, *Irish Unionism 1: the Anglo-Irish and the new Ireland, 1885–1922* (Dublin/New York, 1972), p. 19 (and see, more generally, pp 15–28).
140 *Irish Times*, 14 October 1911.
141 R.B. McDowell, *The Irish Convention, 1917–18* (London, 1970).
142 Larkin, op. cit., pp 411–17.
143 Buckland, op. cit., pp 100–2.
144 R.B. McDowell, *Crisis and decline: the fate of the Southern Unionists* (Dublin, 1997), p. 107.
145 *ILT&SJ*, vol. 52, p. 106 (4 May 1918).
146 Larkin, op. cit., p. 417; A.W. Samuels to Bonar Law, 2 May 1918 (Bonar Law Papers, 83/3/6); *ILT&SJ*, vol. 52, p. 267 (2 November 1918).
147 Lawrence W. McBride, *The greening of Dublin Castle* (Washington, DC, 1991), p. 251.
148 *ILT&SJ*, vol. 52, p. 290 (30 November 1918).
149 Larkin, op. cit., p. 419.

authorities against taking any steps to give effect to sentences of death which had been passed by a military court on two men, Clifford and O'Sullivan.[150] He held, following recent authority,[151] that where a state of war existed the civil courts had no jurisdiction to interfere with proceedings of the military authorities, a decision affirmed on appeal in the Court of Appeal and the House of Lords. The sentences were not carried out, however, as a truce was soon declared, and executions were suspended.[152]

The state of Powell's health led to absences from court between April and June 1922 and again early in 1923, when he was absent on the opening of the courts in Dublin Castle in April.[153] A case in the Irish Reports for 1923 is reported as having been heard by Samuels J ('sitting in for Powell J').[154] After spending some time in recuperation in the south of France, and having returned briefly to court in June, he died in September at his home, 41 Fitzwilliam Place.

Arthur W. Samuels

Justice of the High Court 1919–24

Arthur Warren Samuels (1852–1925) was the son of a proctor, one of an order of lawyers (equivalent to solicitors) which practised in the ecclesiastical and admiralty courts prior to their jurisdiction being joined with the ordinary courts in the 1870s. The family lived at Langara, Glenageary Road, Kingstown (now Dun Laoghaire). Samuels was educated at the Royal School Dungannon, Co. Tyrone, and at Trinity College Dublin, and was called to the Bar in 1877, joining the Leinster circuit. In 1891 he was appointed professor of personal property, contract and tort in the King's Inns,[155] of which he became a bencher in 1900. He took silk in 1894, and held appointments as junior Crown prosecutor in the city and county of Kilkenny and the North Riding of Co. Tipperary,[156] and senior Crown prosecutor in Co. Kildare.[157] His subjects of legal expertise included probate and matrimonial law, including divorce.[158] 'He excelled more as a chamber lawyer than in court practice. He had a profound knowledge of law but was not an attractive or brilliant speaker, his manner being somewhat slow and methodical'.[159]

150 (1921) 55 ILTR 153.
151 *R v Allen*, [1921] 2 IR 241.
152 David Foxton, *Revolutionary lawyers: Sinn Fein and Crown courts in Ireland and Britain, 1916–1923* (Dublin, 2008), pp 279–85.
153 *ILT&SJ*, vol. 56, pp 103 (22 April 1922), 108 (29 April), 119 (13 May), 142 (10 June), 259 (28 October); *Irish Times*, 12 April 1923.
154 *Hughes v Dundalk Harbour Commissioners*, [1923] 1 IR 88.
155 *ILT&SJ*, vol. 25, p. 321 (6 June 1891).
156 *IT&SJ*, vol. 29, p. 516 (19 October 1895).
157 *IT&SJ*, vol. 31, p. 269 (5 June 1897).
158 A.W. Samuels, 'The law of divorce in Ireland', *Journal of the Statistical and Social Inquiry Society of Ireland*, vol. 9, part 66 (1886–7), pp 186–92; *ILT&SJ*, vol. 45, p. 6 (7 January 1911).
159 *Irish Times*, 13 May 1925.

He was an active member of the Statistical and Social Inquiry Society of Ireland, of which he was president between 1906 and 1908. His expertise and interest in economic, financial and taxation issues is evident from a number of papers that he delivered to meetings of the society. In 1895 he published a letter in the *Irish Times* criticising and opposing any suggestion that the number of judges should be reduced, while acknowledging that the 'reductionist theory' had some plausibility because 'there has been for the last few years at some portions of the sittings some falling away of legal business ... a natural consequence of the disturbed condition of the country for several years [having] had an extraordinary effect in checking litigation'.[160] This was followed a few months later by the delivery to a meeting of the society of a more elaborate paper on the same subject (later published as a pamphlet), in which he outlined the reductions already made in judicial numbers since 1877, and concluded by writing 'let there be for the future no judicial reductions without remission of suitors' fees. If there is to be a cheap administration let there also be a cheap law'.[161]

He stood for election to Parliament in 1903 as a Unionist at a bye-election in Dublin University following the retirement of W.E.H. Lecky, for whom he had previously acted as election agent. He lost to James H.M. Campbell QC, but was elected at another bye-election in 1917 after Campbell was appointed as lord chief justice. On that second election he was nominated by the Lord Primate, the archbishop of Armagh, an indication of his standing in the Church of Ireland, in which he was a member of the Representative Church Body and the chancellor of a number of dioceses, including latterly that of Armagh.[162] In June 1917 he was appointed solicitor general, and in April 1918 as attorney general. He held his seat in the general election of 1918. In July 1919, after some hesitation as to whether he would accept the position,[163] he was appointed to be a High Court judge.

His only son, Capt. Arthur P.I. Samuels, a member of the Bar and a captain in the Royal Irish Rifles, part of the 36th Ulster Division, was killed in action at Messines in Belgium in September 1916. He was then aged 28. He had been elected auditor of the College Historical Society in Trinity College in 1910,[164] following which he engaged in research into the early history of the society and Edmund Burke's connection with it. The manuscript of this work was nearing completion when war was declared, and following his son's death Samuels regarded himself as under a trust to continue his research and finish and publish it, which was achieved in 1923.[165] The introduction that he wrote in September

160 As reprinted in *ILT&SJ*, vol. 29, p. 541 (9 November 1895).

161 *A suggestion for the removal of taxes on litigation in Ireland as a condition of the reduction of the judicial establishment* (Dublin, 1896); *ILT&SJ*, vol. 30, pp 77–80 (at 80) (15 February 1896).

162 *Church of Ireland Gazette*, 12 June 1925.

163 *Irish Times*, 7 June and 3 July 1919.

164 He thus went one step further than his father, who had been defeated in an election for auditor some 40 years before by John Ross, later a judicial colleague (John Ross, *The years of my pilgrimage* (London, 1924), p. 18).

165 The late Arthur P.I. Samuels, *The early life, correspondence and writings of the Rt. Hon. Edmund*

1922, in the early months of the Civil War, is redolent of the alarm and uncertainty and fragility of those days. He queried whether there would be left any longer a place for men such as his son's generation in their native land, and noted that the published work set out at greater length than his son had envisaged the text of a number of documents, from the Public Record Office, in light of 'the execrable destruction of that magnificent and irreplaceable collection' and also others 'as a similar fate may now be awaiting other libraries and depositories of documents'.[166]

He lived in Merrion Square and later at Cloghereen, Baily, Howth. He was a founding member of Howth Sailing Club, and 'a fearless man in a boat, and it never blew too hard for him to carry a topsail'.[167] He ceased to be a member of the High Court in 1924, when it was reconstituted under the Courts of Justice Act of that year. He died while on a holiday in France in May 1925.

William E. Wylie

Judicial Commissioner of the Irish Land Commission 1920–4, Justice of the High Court 1924–36

William Evelyn Wylie (1881–1964) was brought up in Coleraine, where his father was a Presbyterian minister, and was educated there and at Trinity College. He was awarded the Brooke scholarship at the King's Inns and was called to the Bar in 1905, joining the North West circuit. He became a KC in 1914, at what was a relatively early stage in his career.[168] He had a wide practice, in civil and criminal law, including acting for parties in actions for breach of promise of marriage.[169] His criminal law practice was enhanced when he represented a father and stepmother in a difficult and troubling case in 1912 in which they were charged with the murder of a young member of their family through neglect, and a jury in Londonderry returned a verdict of manslaughter.[170]

On 26 July 1914 three people were killed by soldiers at Bachelor's Walk, in the centre of Dublin, following a gun running at Howth by the Irish Volunteers. Wylie represented W.V. Harrel, the assistant commissioner of the Dublin Metropolitan Police, a central figure in the events of the day, at hearings of the subsequent Royal Commission of inquiry.[171] In 1915 he joined the Territorial Army, and served with the Trinity College Officers' Training Corps during the Easter Rising the following year. On the nomination of James Campbell, the attorney general, he was

Burke LL.D., with a transcript of the minute book of the Debating 'Club' founded by him in Trinity College Dublin (Cambridge, 1923).

166 Arthur W. Samuels, introduction to his son's work on Burke, pp x and xi.

167 *Irish Times*, 13 May 1925.

168 *ILT&SJ*, vol. 48, p. 186 (4 July 1914).

169 *Irish Times*, 12 December 1907, 15 February 1908, 19 November 1913.

170 *Irish Times*, 19 December 1912; A.R. Hart, *A history of the Bar and Inn of Court of Northern Ireland* (Belfast, 2013), p. 49.

171 *Irish Times*, 8 August 1914. *Report of the Royal Commission into the circumstances connected with the landing of arms at Howth on 26 July 1914* (P.P. 1914–16, Cd.7631 xxiv. 805).

appointed as a prosecutor at the courts martial that followed very quickly upon the suppression of the Rising. Those he prosecuted included Patrick Pearse, Thomas MacDonagh, Thomas Clarke, John MacBride and W.T. Cosgrave.[172] In 1917 he was appointed senior Crown prosecutor for the city and county of Londonderry.[173]

In February 1919 he was a member of the initial committee of an Irish Centre Party, a short-lived initiative of Stephen Gwynn (1864–1950), which proposed self-government for Ireland within the British empire, with a central parliament and provincial assemblies.[174] A few months later he sought to be appointed to a vacancy in the office of solicitor general, and asked General Sir John Maxwell, the commander in chief during the Rising, to put in a word for him.[175] Maxwell did so, to good effect, as did Campbell, by then the lord chancellor, who described Wylie as a 'trained and courageous lawyer'.[176] The government thought it important that the person holding the office of solicitor general would be a member of the House of Commons (D.M. Wilson KC, the MP for Down West, was appointed), but Wylie was offered a related position at Dublin Castle, with the title of law adviser. This was an office, or least a title, which had been in abeyance – in effect, thought to have been abolished – since the 1880s, and was re-established for him.[177] The offices of attorney general and solicitor general had become even more politicised than usual at that time, and Wylie through being in effect a supplemental law officer for, and advising and representing, the government came to be publicly associated with it. His salary was £2,000 and, although he had a right to continue in private practice, his official business became very time consuming.

'My job at first was to prosecute at all important criminal cases and appear for the Crown in all their civil actions, to represent the Crown at inquests on murdered policemen, soldiers and civilians, and try to get coroners' juries to find a proper verdict of murder or add riders condemning the crime'.[178] He thus represented the authorities – variously described as the Crown, the attorney general and the military authorities – at inquests, such as that into the killing of Tomas MacCurtain, lord mayor of Cork, in 1920,[179] at which named government officials and policemen were accused of wilful murder. He conducted prosecutions of persons charged with murders of members of the Royal Irish Constabulary.[180] At

172 W.E. Wylie, Memoir (Wylie Papers (TNAUK) PRO 30/89/2, pp 23–32), and Leon Ó Broin, *W.E. Wylie and the Irish Revolution 1916–1921* (Dublin, 1989), pp 21–9. Wylie wrote, although did not complete, a memoir, which in 1984 was given to the National Archives (UK), and this was drawn upon by Mr Ó Broin in his writing. References are given herein both to pages in the memoir and (if applicable) in the book.
173 *ILT&SJ*, vol. 51, p. 176 (31 July 1917).
174 *Irish Times*, 1 February 1919.
175 Wylie Memoir (PRO 30/89/2), p. 38; Ó Broin, op. cit., p. 55.
176 Campbell to Bonar Law, undated [July] 1919 (Bonar Law Papers, 87/3/4).
177 *ILT&SJ*, vol. 53, p. 167 (12 July 1919).
178 Wylie Memoir (PRO 30/89/2), p. 39; Ó Broin, op. cit., p. 56.
179 *Irish Times*, 25 March 1920; PRO 30/82/2, pp 43–5.
180 *Irish Times*, 23 April 1920, 28 October 1964.

the same period he also prosecuted what might be called ordinary crime, including a man accused at the Antrim assizes of the murder of a woman with whom he had been keeping company, what Wylie described as 'a tragic story, full of human passion'.[181]

His legal functions naturally led to him becoming more generally involved with his official colleagues in Dublin Castle as an adviser on the political situation, and at high level meetings in London he expressed his view – on occasion directly to Lloyd George, Bonar Law, Sir Edward Carson and Winston Churchill – that a policy of attempting to achieve a military defeat of militant Republicanism was bound to fail, and urging contact with Sinn Fein.[182] In August 1920, as the Restoration of Order in Ireland Act[183] was passed, he felt increasingly out of sympathy with government policy, and in particular what would have been a requirement to assist in the enforcement of martial law. T.M. Healy noted in a letter to his brother on 16 August that 'Wylie KC has behaved pluckily over the new Coercion Act and resigned. Yet the government desires to keep him'. Three days later Healy wrote that 'Wylie's resignation may appear at any moment, as he kicks at giving further assistance at courts martial'.[184] His resignation letter[185] appears to have been neither pressed nor accepted at this time, and was reportedly withdrawn, at the request of Bonar Law[186] by early September.[187] He expressed his concern at the failure of the government to prevent reprisals by the military on civilians and their property, and at its seeming to 'wink at crime', saying that murder was all the more aggravated if done by members of a uniformed and disciplined force and that such a state of affairs could not co-exist with civil government.[188]

In his memoir he gave an account of how, mindful of what would have seemed his uncertain future prospects at the Bar, he then asked Sir Hamar Greenwood, the chief secretary, for a judicial appointment. He wrote that Greenwood said, and at Wylie's request confirmed in writing, that he would be appointed to the first vacancy, whereupon Wylie took an immediate step to create such a vacancy, travelling to Belfast on the evening of his conversation with Greenwood in order to meet his uncle, James O. Wylie, the judicial commissioner of the Irish Land Commission. His uncle was in poor health and, on being shown Greenwood's letter, he 'just smiled, walked over to a writing table in the corner, wrote out his resignation, asked me to keep his crier,[189] and said "good luck"'.[190] He presented

181 *Irish Times*, 19 July 1920.
182 Wylie Memoir (PRO 30/89/2), p. 52; Ó Broin, op. cit., pp 78–82.
183 10&11 Geo. 5, c.31.
184 T.M. Healy, *Letters and leaders*, vol. 2, p. 624 and p. 627.
185 Wylie to Greenwood, [date not stated] August 1920 (Wylie Papers, PRO 30/89/3/2).
186 Michael Hopkinson (ed.), *The last days of Dublin Castle: the Mark Sturgis diaries* (Dublin, 1999), p. 34 (2 September 1920).
187 Wylie Memoir (PRO 30/89/3/3); Ó Broin, op. cit., pp 117–19.
188 Wylie, memorandum, date not stated [September] 1920 (Wylie Papers, PRO 30/89/3/4).
189 Court official, personally attending on a judge.
190 Wylie Memoir (PRO 30/89/2); p. 60; Ó Broin, p. 123.

this resignation letter to a surprised Greenwood the next morning and, after consultation with Lloyd George,[191] a few weeks later, early in November 1920, his appointment was announced, the fact that a nephew was succeeding his uncle being duly noted in the press.[192] In that dramatic account of his appointment he made no reference to a letter than he had received from Greenwood a few months ago earlier, promising him a High Court appointment when the present difficult period had ended or after two years, whichever period might be shorter.[193]

He took his seat in court on 11 November. In 1921 he travelled, with lord chief justice Molony, as an assize judge on the Munster circuit,[194] and was rostered for the Connaught circuit,[195] but otherwise (and for the rest of his judicial career) his work as a judge remained in the channel of the Land Acts, including the Land Act 1923. This was one of the first statutes enacted in the Irish Free State and provided for the compulsory (rather than voluntary) and automatic transfer of ownership to tenants of agricultural land and for acquisition of land by the Land Commission to relieve congestion and secure economic holdings. He had been assigned the duties of the land judge in succession to Sir John Ross following the latter's appointment as lord chancellor in 1921. The Government of Ireland Act 1920, having set out the intended judicial establishment of the separate courts of Southern Ireland and Northern Ireland, had provided that the judicial commissioner would be an additional judge in each jurisdiction 'for the purposes of his powers and duties in relation to land purchase'.[196] In 1924 Wylie was appointed a judge of the new High Court, on the basis of an understanding he set out that his judicial duties would be referable to the functions under the Land Acts which he then discharged. He was the youngest of the judges under the existing court system, and hence the person most affected by the outcome of the statutory arrangements (see pp 492–3) for the British government to pay compensation for loss of office, in addition to acceleration of pension rights. He made a robust, even excited, presentation to the committee of judges in London that was established to determine such compensation and was awarded an allowance for life of £700.[197] For so long as he held judicial office his salary of £2,500 paid by the Irish Free State was topped up to the amount of his former salary by the British government. He resigned his office in 1936, and began to receive his full pension and allowance from that government, not having accrued any pension rights from the Irish government.

He had a long-standing and influential involvement in the affairs of the Royal Dublin Society. On its behalf he had negotiated both with the British government

191 Hopkinson (ed.), op. cit., p. 52 (6 October 1920).
192 *Irish Times*, 5 November 1920 ('Appointment of new Irish judge: nephew succeeds uncle.').
193 Greenwood to Wylie, 25 May 1920 (Wylie Papers, PRO 30/89/3/1).
194 *ILT&SJ*, vol. 55, p. 40 (12 February 1921) and p. 53 (19 February 1921).
195 *ILT&SJ*, vol. 55, p. 159 (23 June 1921).
196 10&11 Geo. 5, c.67, s39 and Seventh Schedule, parts I (1(2)) and II (1(2)).
197 Memorandum by M.C. Trickett of hearing of claims, 25 July 1924 (T 164/49/9 (TNAUK)); memorandum of determination of allowances by committee, 21 October 1924 (T 164/153/11 (TNAUK)).

(in 1922) for compensation for use by the army of its grounds at Ballsbridge during the Great War and with the Irish government (in 1924) for compensation for the acquisition from the society of Leinster House.[198] 'For over 40 years [he] was pre-eminent among those directing the society's affairs. The "judge", as he was generally known, was a master of the terse and pointed remark which closured any discussion which appeared to him aimless or unpractical'.[199] It was said in similar fashion of his position in the Stephen's Green club (where he took up residence in 1953, following the death of his wife in 1950)[200] that 'he possessed grip where grip was called for'.[201] He died in 1964.

Wylie had a particular interest in equestrian sport, but more generally was a sportsman in college and all his life. When presenting prizes to students at Wesley College in 1920 he used an extended sporting metaphor – playing the game – as a rule or guide to life:

> Remember that there are referee and touch-line critics in the game of life, and you may get away on the blind side of the scrum, but it will soon be spotted, and you will be marked down accordingly. Wherever the ball goes, try and be there, but keep playing the game. If you keep pushing you will get through the scrum. There is a second rule, and it applies to another sport that I am fond of, and that rule is – always ride straight at your fences. Go straight at them, and you will find that they are not as bad as they look when you get there. Never think about falling, but if you do fall try and land on the other side of the hedge. Then get up and go on. Keep your temper and never be discouraged. Stick at it and you will eventually win. The three great assets in life are honesty, pluck and fortitude. Keep these in view, and if it comes to a tight corner you will find that those who are on your side are those who follow such rules and not those who are known as brilliant fellows.[202]

He noted in this memoir, and in the same way drew a wider lesson from, the cheerful spirit of his friend Anthony Babington[203] in an important golf match. With his ball in a difficult position Babington, an excellent golfer, 'gave himself the chance of winning with a superbly played shot out of the rough born of sheer courage – "give me the niblick, boy, a game is never lost till it is won".'[204]

198 *Irish Times*, 14 October 1964.
199 *Irish Times*, 31 October 1964.
200 Change of address card (Wylie Papers (PRO/30/89/21/7)).
201 Niall O'Kelly, 'Plus ca change: 1922–1945' in Cornelius F. Smith and Bernard Share (eds), *Whigs on the Green: the Stephen's Green Club, 1840–1990* (Dublin, 1990), pp 80, 101.
202 *Irish Times*, 15 December 1920; *ILT&SJ*, vol. 54, pp 306–7 (18 December 1920).
203 Anthony Brutus Babington (1877–1972), called to the Bar 1900, KC 1918, attorney general of Northern Ireland 1925–37, lord justice of appeal 1937–49.
204 Wylie Memoir (PRO 30/89/2), p. 7. In the period of which Wylie was writing golf clubs were known by names rather than numbers. A niblick was a lofted iron club. 'Boy' was a manner of addressing a youthful caddy.

CHAPTER FOURTEEN

The first Irish Lords of Appeal in Ordinary

BETWEEN 1870 AND 1921 five Irish judges sat as members of the highest court of appeal of the United Kingdom, the House of Lords. The composition and functioning of the house in its judicial capacity had been reformed by the Appellate Jurisdiction Act 1876. This specified that any appeal to the house was to be heard by 'not less than three of the following persons, in this Act designated Lords of Appeal; that is to say (1) the lord chancellor of Great Britain for the time being, (2) the lords of appeal in ordinary to be appointed as in this Act mentioned [generally referred to as 'Law Lords'], who were to be appointed (in effect, and in law from 1887) as life peers[1] and (3) such peers of Parliament [i.e., hereditary peers] as are for the time being holding or have held any of the offices in this Act described as high judicial offices'.[2] Three of the five Irishmen (Lords Fitzgerald, Morris and Atkinson) came within the second of those categories, having been appointed as lords of appeal in ordinary and the other two (Lords O'Hagan and Ashbourne) were current or former lord chancellors of Ireland, one of the specified high judicial offices in the third category.

There were three other Irish holders of such offices – a lord chief justice and two former lord chancellors – who also came within the third category but did not sit as judicial members of the house. Their circumstances are noted below, and also those of a number of Irishmen who had made their careers at the Bar in England and were appointed as Law Lords. The lord chancellor of Great Britain who introduced the Appellate Jurisdiction Act, Lord Cairns, had been born and brought up in Belfast and educated at Trinity College.

Senior members of the judiciary had been created peers and thus sat as members of the House of Lords since medieval times. By the 1870s any overlap of judicial and legislative functions consisted only of such judges having a parliamentary function, not in legislators exercising any general judicial functions. An archaic procedure existed whereby a member of the House of Lords might be

1 Appellate Jurisdiction Act 1876, 39 & 40 Vict, c.59, s6. The words 'in ordinary' denoted that holders of this office, unlike other peers, were to be paid a salary (David Hope (Lord Hope of Craighead), 'Law Lords in Parliament' in Louis Blom-Cooper, Brice Dickson and Gavin Drewry (eds), *The judicial House of Lords, 1876–2009* (Oxford, 2009), p. 165). Receipt of a salary implied 'regular attendance – a proper job' (Stephen Sedley LJ, *London Review of Books*, 28 April 2011).

2 Appellate Jurisdiction Act 1876, s5. High judicial offices were defined in section 25 of that Act as the office of lord chancellor of Great Britain or Ireland, or of paid judge of the Judicial Committee of the Privy Council or of judge of one of Her Majesty's superior courts of Great Britain or Ireland.

tried by his peers, which was invoked in 1901 for the trial of Earl Russell for bigamy, after he had been divorced by his wife on the (uncontested) ground of his bigamous adultery.[3] With that exception, peers without legal knowledge had effectively been excluded from judicial functions since 1844, when it was established that lay peers should abstain from voting on legal appeals.[4] This was settled in an appeal brought by Daniel O'Connell and others against convictions for conspiracy to commit various seditious acts in the course of the campaign for Repeal of the Act of Union, including 'excit[ing] the liege subjects of our Lady the Queen to discontent with, and hatred of, and disaffection to the government, laws and constitution of this realm by law established'.

The hearing of that appeal, as with the original trial itself, was a major political event, and the possibility of some of the lay peers attempting to vote when the appeal was being determined had been anticipated by the prime minister, Sir Robert Peel. He told the home secretary months earlier that 'the decision ought to be left to the law lords and on no account [should] a political vote [be] taken'.[5] When the decision was announced Peel noted that 'lamentable as are the results of the judgment of the lords, [t]he permanent evil of the overruling [of] the majority of the law lords by the votes of unprofessional peers would have been, I think, greater than the reversal of the sentence'.[6]

The House of Lords thus acknowledged, in substance if not in form, the concept of the independence and separation of the powers of government – executive, legislative and judicial. That was reflected formally in the constitution of the Irish Free State adopted in 1922, which provided (in article 69) that 'a judge shall not be eligible to sit in the Oireachtas', a provision carried forward in article 35.3 of the 1937 constitution.[7] In the United Kingdom, over time and in stages, the discharge of the judicial functions of the House of Lords was – and was seen to be – separated from its legislative functions, culminating in the establishment of the Supreme Court in 2009, pursuant to the Constitutional Reform Act 2005. That Act provides (s137(3)) that any peer who is a member of the Supreme Court (and it has been customary to confer life peerages on the members) is, for their period of office, disqualified from sitting or voting in the House of Lords.

In the 1870s however, as for centuries past, the House of Lords in its judicial capacity was considered to be the High Court of Parliament, the ultimate repository of royal justice.[8] The termination of its appellate jurisdiction for

3 The trial of Earl Russell, [1901] AC 446.

4 Ian Holloway, '*O'Connell v The Queen*: a sesquicentennial remembrance', *NILQ*, vol. 46(1) (1995), pp 63–71; Hope, op. cit., p. 165.

5 Peel to Sir James Graham, 7 April 1844 (C.S. Parker (ed.), *Sir Robert Peel, from his private papers*, vol. 3 (London, 1899), p. 67); Holloway, op. cit., p. 69.

6 Peel to Lord Brougham, 21 September 1844 (Parker, op. cit., n8, p. 125); Holloway, op. cit., p. 70.

7 See the House of Commons Disqualification Act 1975 (c.24, s1) for a similar provision applicable in the United Kingdom.

8 Louis Blom-Cooper, 'Style of Judgments' in Blom-Cooper, Dickson and Drewry (eds), op. cit., p. 155.

England that was legislated for in 1873 never took effect and was reversed by the 1876 Act. The conduct of that appellate judicial function was regarded as a part of the ordinary business of the house. Before 1876 the house had not heard appeals when Parliament was not sitting,[9] and until the 1940s appeals were heard in the chamber of the house itself, as the first order of business on any day, and only after these had been concluded was other business taken up.[10]

The Lords of Appeal also sat on, indeed were the mainstay of the judicial panels for, appeals to the Judicial Committee of the Privy Council. An Act introduced by Lord Brougham, the lord chancellor, in 1833[11] had reformed the conduct of the judicial business of the Council, which served in effect as a court of appeal for all parts of the British Empire. It had certain vestigial domestic appellate functions, as amended from time to time, including patent law and ecclesiastical law. Its decisions (in the form of a single judgment or speech, without notice of any dissent) formally or technically constituted advice to the monarch as to the disposition of an appeal, which advice had to be given the effect of a judgment by the full Council ('The Queen in Council'). Members of the House of Lords who exercised judicial functions were invariably sworn as members of the Privy Council in England (if not already members), which was separate from the Privy Council in Ireland, the quasi-judicial functions of which are referred to on pp 70–2.

A commentary on the Judicial Committee published in 1912 noted that

> the system of parceling out enormous tracts of country in Africa, Eastern Asia and Polynesia into Protectorates of the Great Powers was one of the features of European diplomacy in the latter part of the nineteenth century, and one of the functions of the protecting state was to exercise jurisdiction and to set up courts. Thus, having started as an appellate tribunal (in the fourteenth century) for cases originating in the Channel Islands, the Privy Council has come through its Judicial Committee to acquire jurisdiction in appeals brought from British courts in every quarter of the globe and to be called upon to administer every possible system of law. It has a wider jurisdiction than any court known to history, and it is unique in the variety of its suitors.[12]

An earlier edition of that commentary had said that 'its jurisdiction is undoubtedly more extensive, whether measured by area, population, variety of nations, creeds, languages, laws or customs than that hitherto enjoyed by any court known to civilization'.[13] Fitzgerald in the 1880s, Morris in the 1890s and Atkinson in the first

9 Selborne to Gladstone, 2 October 1881 (Gladstone Papers, Add. MS 44297.191).
10 Hope, op. cit., pp 165–8.
11 The Judicial Committee of the Privy Council Act 1833 (3&4 Will. IV, c.41).
12 Norman Bentwich, *The practice of the Privy Council in judicial matters* (London, 1912), pp 13, 15.
13 F. Safford and G. Wheeler, *The practice of the Privy Council in judicial matters* (London, 1901), preface; *ILT&SJ*, vol. 36, p. 3 (4 January 1902).

decades of the twentieth century sat as members of the Judicial Committee of the Privy Council on the hearing of appeals from courts in every continent, including appeals from Gibraltar, Malta, Cyprus, Canada and Australia and their states and provinces, including New South Wales, Western Australia, Victoria, Queensland and Tasmania, Ontario, Quebec, Nova Scotia, New Brunswick, Alberta, British Columbia, Newfoundland, New Zealand, Fiji, the Cape of Good Hope, Transvaal, Natal, Bechuanaland, Nigeria, Eastern Africa, Trinidad and Tobago, the Turks and Caicos Islands, Jamaica, the Windward Islands, Mauritius, Ceylon, Penang, Singapore, Hong Kong, Rangoon, the Seychelles, Bengal, His Majesty's Supreme Court for China and Korea at Shanghai and His Majesty's Supreme Court for the Ottoman Dominions.[14]

The Judicial Committee was potentially of much greater legal significance for Ireland than that imperial overview might suggest. It was envisaged in each of the three Home Rule bills that were introduced in 1886, 1893 and 1912 that it would have some jurisdiction in Irish legal matters. The Government of Ireland Bill in 1886, which was defeated in the House of Commons by 341 votes to 311, provided that any question as to the extent of the powers conferred on the new legislature in Ireland would be determined by the Committee, and that on any relevant sitting of the Committee there would be added to its number 'such members of Her Majesty's Privy Council, being or having been Irish judges, as to Her Majesty [i.e., to the government] may seem meet'.[15]

The 1893 Bill, passed by the House of Commons but defeated in the House of Lords by 419 votes to 41, modified this proposal by terminating any appeal from Ireland to the House of Lords, substituting the Committee for appellate purposes, and providing that on a sitting for any such appeal 'there shall be present not less than four Lords of Appeal ... and at least one member who is or has been a judge of the Supreme Court in Ireland'.[16] That approach was adopted also in the 1912 Bill, which was enacted in September 1914 and simultaneously suspended for the duration of the war which had just started.[17] In the Government of Ireland Act 1920, which regulated the judicial system in Northern Ireland for decades to come, the procedure for ultimate appeal to the House of Lords was preserved, and the jurisdiction of the Judicial Committee was limited to determining constitutional questions, as to whether any act of the devolved parliaments, north or south, was within the powers of such parliament.[18] It was uncommon for any issue to arise in that context as to the validity and good order of a statute of the parliament of Northern Ireland, but two such cases were determined in London in the 1930s.[19]

14 'There is no court that seems to have so wide a jurisdiction, or that gives you so comprehensive an idea of the geographical extent and imperial grandeur of the British Empire' (*ILT&SJ*, vol. 28, p. 208 (21 April 1894), quoting from *The World*).

15 Government of Ireland Bill 1886, s25.

16 Government of Ireland Bill 1893, s22.

17 Government of Ireland Bill 1912, s28; Suspensory Act, 1914 (4&5 Geo. V, c.88).

18 Government of Ireland Act 1920 (10&11 Geo. V, c.67), s49.

19 *In re a reference under the Government of Ireland Act 1920*, [1936] AC 357; *Gallagher v Lynn*, [1937] AC 863.

In the 1920s and 1930s the Judicial Committee had a contested function as a court of appeal from the Irish Free State in the evolving relationship between the new state and the United Kingdom.[20]

As a matter of constitutional practice the appointment of a lord of appeal in ordinary was made by the monarch on the advice of the prime minister, who by convention consulted and acted upon the advice of the lord chancellor.[21] (The last such appointment prior to the establishment of the Supreme Court was that in 2009 of Sir Brian Kerr (Lord Kerr of Tonaghmore, 1948–2020), who was then lord chief justice of Northern Ireland.) Before 1921 three such appointments were made from the Irish judiciary or Bar, and one appointment was made for which an absence of connection with Ireland gave rise to controversy. These appointments were made in 1882 (Lord Fitzgerald), 1889 (Lord Morris), 1900 (Lord Lindley) and 1905 (Lord Atkinson). The first two persons so appointed already held office as judges in Ireland, the third appointee was a distinguished English judge and the fourth was the attorney general for Ireland.

The circumstances of those four appointments will first be reviewed, following which there will be some commentary on the contribution that each of the three Irishmen made to the judicial work of the House of Lords and to the Judicial Committee of the Privy Council and on their respective contributions to parliamentary business. The contribution to that judicial work of the two other members of the Irish judiciary, Lord O'Hagan (between 1870 and 1883) and Lord Ashbourne (between 1886 and 1913) will be reviewed. Lastly there will be reference to the appointment of other Irish judges to the Judicial Committee of the Privy Council, namely Sir Joseph Napier, Stephen Woulfe Flanagan, Christopher Palles and Gerald FitzGibbon, and on four other appointments as a Law Lord of Irishmen who had been in practice at the English Bar, namely Lords Macnaghten, Russell, Collins and Carson.

APPOINTMENTS OF LORDS OF APPEAL IN ORDINARY

The first Irishman to be appointed as a Law Lord, in May 1882, was John David Fitzgerald, who had been a judge of the Queen's Bench since 1860. Fitzgerald was the fourth Lord of Appeal to be appointed, the first two, Lords Blackburn and Gordon in 1876 having been drawn from the English judiciary and the Bar of Scotland respectively. Lord Watson who was appointed in 1880 following the death of Lord Gordon was also Scottish. The 1876 Act had provided (in section 14) for the appointment of additional Law Lords as and when the existing membership of the Judicial Committee of the Privy Council was reduced, which condition was satisfied early in December 1881 when one of its members, Montague Edward Smith, retired.

20 Thomas Mohr, *Guardian of the Treaty: the Privy Council Appeal and Irish sovereignty* (Dublin, 2016).

21 Hope, op cit., p. 165.

In making an appointment of a new Law Lord the prime minister would have been advised by the lord chancellor of Great Britain, Lord Selborne, as to the suitability of candidates. It was by no means clear when an appointment would be made, nor that an Irish judge or lawyer would be appointed. Selborne's initial suggestion to Gladstone was that he should consider the claims of the English law officers, 'either of whom I should think well qualified to be useful in the house [of lords], both politically and in debate'.[22] He was unenthusiastic about appointing an Irish judge. He then conceded the force of a point made to him by Gladstone that each part of the United Kingdom ought to be represented in its highest court, while observing that Lord O'Hagan, who only a few weeks previously had stepped down as lord chancellor of Ireland, was in effect a representative of Ireland for that purpose. He noted that O'Hagan 'likes the judicial work of the H. of Lds and will be sure to be a pretty regular attendant while Parliament is sitting', noting for good measure that the number of Irish appeals was in any event 'extremely few'.[23] A couple of days later he referred again to this rarity of Irish appeals and, in effect counting O'Hagan as equivalent to a lord of appeal in ordinary, wrote that 'in the abstract there is less reason for a second Irish law lord than for a second Scotch'.[24] W.N. Osborough has observed that, certainly before 1877, little difficulty may have arisen by reason of any lack of special knowledge of Irish law on the hearing of appeals from Ireland in the House of Lords. With the exception of land law, key areas of Irish private law were identical with English, and a judicious detachment and frame of mind may have been promoted by remoteness from Irish conditions.[25]

The prospective Irish nominees at the time were Hugh Law, who had succeeded O'Hagan as lord chancellor, and Edward Sullivan, the master of the rolls, each of whom was a former attorney general. Selborne commented on Law that

> from the judicial point of view – of the political you [Gladstone] are the best judge – I doubt the expediency of conferring the appointment upon one who is not only a second Irishman but who has only just been placed upon the bench and had not yet had an opportunity of acquiring any judicial reputation. It would, I think, suggest to most men that it had been prompted by political rather than judicial reasons, which in the case of this particular office I should hardly think desirable. In that respect the appointment of Sullivan would (I think) be preferable to Law's.[26]

22 Selborne to Gladstone, 13 December 1881 (Gladstone Papers, Add. MS 44297.221).
23 Selborne to Gladstone, 23 December 1881 (Gladstone Papers, Add. MS 44297.223).
24 Selborne to Gladstone, 25 December 1881 (Gladstone Papers, Add. MS 44297.227).
25 W.N. Osborough, 'The Irish legal system, 1796–1877' in (i) Caroline Costello (ed.), *The Four Courts: 200 years* (Dublin, 1996), pp 33–79 at 46 and (ii) W.N. Osborough, *Studies in Irish legal history* (Dublin, 1999) pp 239–69, at 247.
26 Selborne to Gladstone, 25 December 1881 (Gladstone Papers, Add. MS 44297.227).

He modified his position a couple of days later on being informed that the government saw some advantage in promoting Law and putting Sullivan into his place as lord chancellor, saying that if 'complete and satisfactory assurances of Law's equality with Sullivan (in point both of reputation and actual attainments)' could be given than he would not oppose 'an arrangement which on balance of all the material considerations might then seem for the public benefit. I must submit that (after all) the judicial considerations ought to be the most weighty in settling this question. There would be no serious inconvenience in a little delay'.[27] He noted that the law newspapers were speculating that an Irish appointment might be made.[28] On New Year's Day 1882 Christopher Palles drew O'Hagan's attention to the fact that it had now become possible to appoint a third Law Lord,[29] perhaps an indication of his own interest in the position.

After that flurry of correspondence over Christmas 1881 four months elapsed without a decision being made on who should be appointed. Selborne told Gladstone in April that while an appointment might be desirable it was not literally necessary,[30] and this hesitation had set the tone. Early in May Lord Cairns queried the delay and contended that the 1876 Act had not contemplated that such an interval of time would elapse without the position being filled, to which Selborne replied that 'the deliberations necessary as to the proper person being appointed' were in hand.[31] Gladstone was prepared to appoint Law who, however, told Spencer, freshly re-appointed as the lord lieutenant, that his health was uncertain and declined the position. He recommended two judges, Sullivan and Fitzgerald, to Spencer, whose view was that 'as a matter of policy it seems to me that it would be as well to appoint an Irish judge if his legal position is good enough',[32] and who subsequently gave his assessment of the two men to Gladstone:

> Fitzgerald is less impulsive than Sullivan and is of course a considerably older man[33] but I always considered him the calmest and wisest adviser on difficult questions of policy that I could find in Dublin when I was last here [as lord lieutenant 1868–74]. I think he would be a very useful peer and would carry great weight with him. I have no reason to think that his powers are failing. To my mind he is more presentable than Sullivan, his Irish accent and diction are less peculiar and he is not so diminutive in height.[34]

27 Selborne to Gladstone, 27 December 1881 (Gladstone Papers, Add. MS 44297.229).
28 Selborne to Gladstone, 29 December 1881 (Gladstone Papers, Add. MS 44297.235).
29 Palles to O'Hagan, 1 January 1882 (Teeling Papers (NLI), MS 17872).
30 Selborne to Gladstone, 13 April 1882 (Gladstone Papers, Add. MS 44297.251). See also Selborne to Gladstone, 14 January 1882 (Gladstone Papers, Add. MS 44297.244).
31 HL Deb, 3rd series, vol. 269, cols. 448–54 (11 May 1882).
32 Spencer to Gladstone, 17 May 1882 (Althorp Papers, Add. MS 76854.15–6; Gladstone Papers, Add. MS 44308.265).
33 Something of an overstatement, as Fitzgerald had been born in 1816 and Sullivan in 1822.
34 Spencer to Gladstone, 21 May 1882 (Althorp Papers, Add. MS 76854.20).

Selborne had been told by Sir William Harcourt, the home secretary, that Law would not take the position and that nor would Sullivan, on foot of which he told Gladstone that if – as the prime minister intended – the post was to be offered to an Irishman 'the only other Irish judge who would, as far as I am able to form an opinion, be thoroughly well qualified for the appointment is J.D. Fitzgerald. I know that some think him not at all inferior to Sullivan and his general judicial character stands extremely high'.[35] Gladstone's instinct had been that Fitzgerald would be 'far less presentable and efficient than Sullivan' as a Lord of Appeal,[36] but he took Spencer's comments as showing a slight preference for him[37] and, on hearing that Harcourt agreed with Selborne in approving Fitzgerald's nomination,[38] advised the Queen to appoint him.[39] The title of Lord Fitzgerald of Kilmarnock that he adopted was taken from the name of his house in Killiney, Co. Dublin, itself drawn from the town of that name in Ayrshire and giving his title a Scottish air. The house stood on grounds of about 10 acres on the southern slope of Killiney Hill, on Military Road. It had stables for six horses, and was close to a railway station.[40]

In April 1885 Sullivan, who had succeeded Law as lord chancellor of Ireland in 1883, died suddenly. In the following month Lord Fitzgerald paid a handsome tribute to him in a judgment in the House of Lords on an appeal from a decision of the Court of Appeal in Ireland, remarking that 'no one who knows, as I do, the minute and conscientious care with which Sir Edward Sullivan examined all the cases which came before him could adopt the suggestion [made by an appellant in person] that an important point affecting the rights of the parties escaped his attention'.[41] Fitzgerald was invited to succeed him as lord chancellor, but declined to do so, following which John Naish QC was appointed. The entry on Fitzgerald in the *Oxford dictionary of national biography*, originally written by one of his sons, states that 'in 1885 he was offered the lord chancellorship of Ireland with a hereditary peerage which he at first accepted but, on further consideration, he later declined'. It was later said that he had declined the hereditary peerage that he was offered on the ground of lack of means to support its dignity.[42] Ashbourne, then the lord chancellor, remarked to Arthur Balfour, the chief secretary for Ireland, in 1889 that although Fitzgerald had first consented to the change he had subsequently had second thoughts, and abandoned the idea on account of his age[43] (he was then aged 69).

35 Selborne to Gladstone, 19 May 1882 (Gladstone Papers, Add. MS 44297.255).
36 Gladstone to Spencer, 20 May 1882 (Althorp MSS K5) (*Gladstone diaries*, vol. 10 (January 1881–June 1883), edited by H.C.G. Matthew (Oxford, 1990), p. 267).
37 Gladstone to Spencer, 22 May 1882 (Althorp Papers, Add. MS 76854.33).
38 Gladstone to Spencer, 21 May 1882 (Althorp Papers, Add. MS 76854.41).
39 Gladstone to the Queen, 24 May 1882 (Royal Archives RA Vic/Hqin/A/55/88).
40 Fitzgerald to Spencer, 30 May 1883 (Althorp Papers, Add. MS 77077).
41 Wakefield v Maffet (1884–85) 10 App. Cas., 432 at 434.
42 *Law Times*, vol. 107, p. 449 (23 September 1899).
43 Ashbourne to Balfour, 15 November 1889 (Balfour Papers, Add. MS 49815/51).

An incomplete account of this episode was given in a memoir published in 1925 by J.G. Swift MacNeill, a professor of constitutional law at the King's Inns between 1882 and 1888 and then (1887–1918) the MP for South Donegal. He wrote that Fitzgerald refused the position 'on the ground that his acceptance of the post would deprive him of a seat in the House of Lords, which at the time was held only during the tenure of the office of Lord of Appeal'.[44] MacNeill made no reference either to an offer of a hereditary peerage nor to any initial intention of accepting the position, since if Fitzgerald had become a hereditary peer he would have continued to be a member of the House of Lords, and to have been eligible – as coming within the third category of eligibility set out in section 5 of the 1876 Act – to sit in a judicial capacity there, as had been demonstrated by Lord O'Hagan (to Fitzgerald's personal knowledge). The 1876 Act was amended in 1887 to provide that a retiring lord of appeal in ordinary would continue to be entitled to sit and vote in the House of Lords during his lifetime, by repealing the original provision that each such lord shall 'during the time that he continues in office as a lord of appeal in ordinary, and no longer', be entitled to a writ of summons to attend, and to sit and vote in the House of Lords.[45] This was an initiative to reflect the circumstances, and retain the services, of Lord Blackburn (1813–96), who had retired in December 1886, and it was known as the 'Blackburn clause'.[46] A linkage of the amendment to Fitzgerald's circumstances that was made by MacNeill does not seem well-founded.

Fitzgerald died on 16 October 1889, and Ashbourne promptly told Balfour, the chief secretary, that Lord Salisbury, the prime minister, should consider the Irish aspect of the succession question before any appointment was made, adding his first thoughts on the situation. These were that the lord chief justice, Sir Michael Morris, might take the position, failing which the lord chief baron, Palles, would do so, and that if Morris wished to transfer to London then Palles would succeed him, which would facilitate a merger of the Exchequer division of the High Court with the Queen's Bench.[47] On the following day Morris wrote to Ashbourne expressing a double assumption that Fitzgerald's successor would be taken from the Irish Bench and that Ashbourne would not be interested in the position, and saying that for some (unstated) reasons, 'personal and public', he would wish to be appointed.[48] A couple of days later Peter O'Brien, the attorney general, wrote in quite direct terms to Balfour to say that an Irish lawyer should be appointed to the vacancy, that this should be himself if Morris was not nominated, and that if Morris were to be nominated then he would in turn expect to succeed him as chief

44 J.G. Swift MacNeill, *What I have seen and heard* (London, 1925), p. 153. See also *ILT&SJ*, vol. 46, p. 214 (24 August 1912), and vol. 49, p. 212 (28 August 1915),

45 Appellate Jurisdiction Act 1887, 50 & 51 Vict., c.70, s2.

46 Patrick Polden, 'The early years of the House of Lords, 1876–1914' in Blom-Cooper, Dickson and Drewry (eds), op. cit., p. 185.

47 Ashbourne to Balfour, 17 October 1889 (Balfour Papers, Add. MS 49815.47).

48 Morris to Ashbourne, 17 October 1889 (Ashbourne Papers, B77/9).

justice.[49] Ashbourne told Balfour in a further letter the same day, rather more elegantly, that it would be important to appoint an Irish successor to Fitzgerald, noting that he himself was now the only Irish Lord eligible to hear appeals, nine of the others being English and two Scottish and that in practice his duties in Ireland gave rise to great difficulty in him doing so.[50] He also remarked that the Irish land and registration laws required special knowledge, that there would be no difficulty in providing a suitable successor, and that he would be ready at any time to discuss this.[51] He similarly told Lord Salisbury at the same time that there were strong reasons why the successor should be drawn from the Irish legal profession, out of whom a selection could be made from several suitable and able men.[52]

Salisbury did not share the general assumption thus made in Ireland about the nationality of the new Law Lord to be appointed in succession to Fitzgerald. His initial intention was that the Home Secretary, Henry Matthews QC, MP, a member of the English Bar, would be appointed to fill the vacancy. Queen Victoria and Salisbury shared a strongly held opinion that Matthews was incompetent,[53] as referred to a number of times in correspondence between them and in notes over a period of more than two years, most definitively in letters from him of 7 December 1890 and 11 January 1891.[54] Salisbury was always slow to dismiss ministers, and some of his observations to the Queen in relation to Matthews had referred to the possibility of arranging for his appointment as a judge, either as a member of the Court of Appeal or as a Law Lord. That last letter of January 1891 spelled out, as had been foreshadowed by the December letter, that a conclusive reason for not appointing Matthews to be a judge was the prospect that the Conservative party would not retain his seat in parliament at the resulting bye-election in his constituency in Birmingham. In 1889 the weak political situation in that constituency had been directly relevant also to the selection of the successor to Fitzgerald. Salisbury told Balfour on 1 November that 'Middleton has been to see Joe and it is quite clear I think that a seat in Bm must not be vacated[55] … Under those circumstances Ireland will carry off the booty … . I suppose Morris is your candidate'.[56]

49 O'Brien to Balfour, 20 October 1889 (Balfour Papers, Add. MS 49814/300).
50 Ashbourne's work in Dublin already frequently presented a difficulty for him in attending meetings of the Cabinet, never mind serving in a judicial capacity in the House of Lords.
51 Ashbourne to Balfour, 20 October 1889 (Balfour Papers, Add. MS 49815/49).
52 Ashbourne to Salisbury, 20 October 1889 (Salisbury Papers).
53 Andrew Roberts, *Salisbury, Victorian Titan* (London, 1999), chap. 30, p. 506.
54 See also a letter from Salisbury (31 October 1888), the Queen's Journal (17 November 1888), a letter from the Queen (27 June 1890), her Journal (7 August 1890), a letter from Salisbury (5 October 1890), and a reply from the Queen (7 October 1890), in *Letters and Journals of Queen Victoria* [3rd Series, 1886–91], vol. 1 (London, 1930), pp 445, 450, 618, 626, 646, 647, 660–661, and vol. 2 (London, 1931), pp 6–7.
55 Richard W.E. Middleton (1846–1905) was the principal agent at Central Office of the Conservative party between 1885 and 1903. 'Joe' was Joseph Chamberlain MP, the Liberal Unionist leader and the central figure in Birmingham ('Bm') politics. In 1889 Matthews was the MP for East Birmingham, the only Parliamentary constituency in the city that was held by the Conservatives.

Balfour in fact initially favoured Ashbourne for the position, noting later that 'if we were to consider the judicial position of the candidates at all there really was no alternative but to take [Morris] or Ashbourne'.[57] He thus did not necessarily think him better fitted than Morris to be a Law Lord but had a wider patronage scheme in mind of replacing him as lord chancellor with Peter O'Brien. He told Salisbury that 'I have no reason to think he [Ashbourne] wants it; but many why he should be made to take it'.[58] Ashbourne declined the post, unwilling to give up his position as lord chancellor of Ireland, with a seat in the cabinet, although indicating – to Balfour's private derision – that, to avoid any implication of having been demoted, he would look more favourably on the suggestion if he could be given a step up in the peerage, which would have been from a barony to a viscountcy, perhaps an earldom.[59]

Morris was offered the appointment by Lord Salisbury on 22 November.[60] He took the title of Lord Morris of Spiddal, in the county of Galway, and O'Brien was appointed to succeed him as lord chief justice. Morris retired in May 1900, although subsequently sitting occasionally in the House of Lords in a judicial capacity,[61] including for the appeal in *Quinn v Leatham*[62] in the summer of 1901. He participated in the hearing over five days in May and June, but after becoming ill he took no further part.[63] The decision of the house in the appeal was given on 5 August and he died on 8 September.

Morris did not give his friends among the Irish judiciary and government any indication of his intention to retire. This surprise about his sudden stepping down contrasted with some speculation four years previously when it was 'believed in legal circles that Lord Morris will, in the near future, resign his position of lord of appeal in ordinary'.[64] An offer of a hereditary peerage was reported to have influenced the retirement. A well-informed Parliamentary correspondent and diarist, Henry Lucy, after referring to Morris as 'a man of constitutionally jovial temperament', noted that

> when remark was accidentally dropped in his hearing that at threescore years and ten a man who had spent his days in the service of the state might reasonably think of exchanging a life peerage for one of hereditary rank, Lord

56 Salisbury to Balfour, 1 November 1889 (Balfour Papers, Add. MS 49689/79); *Salisbury–Balfour correspondence*, p. 299.
57 Balfour to Salisbury, 26 February 1890 (Balfour Papers, Add. MS 49688/82); *Salisbury–Balfour correspondence*, p. 307.
58 Balfour to Salisbury, 2 November 1889 (*Salisbury–Balfour correspondence*, p. 299).
59 Ashbourne to Balfour, 15 November 1889 (Balfour Papers, Add. MS 49813.31); Balfour to Salisbury, 16 November 1889 (Salisbury Papers 3/71); *Salisbury–Balfour correspondence*, p. 300.
60 Maud Wynne, *An Irishman and his family* (London, 1937), p. 149.
61 *Duke of Bedford v Ellis and others*, [1901] AC 1, *Hoddinott v Newton Chambers & Co.*, [1901] AC 49 and *C.I.R. v Priestley*, [1901] AC 208.
62 [1901] AC 495.
63 *ILT&SJ*, vol. 35, p. 233 (8 June 1901) and p. 320 (30 July 1901).
64 *ILT&SJ*, vol. 30, p. 182 (25 April 1896), citing *Law Times*.

> Morris thought no evil. Himself simple-minded as a child, he could not conceive duplicity in another, especially that other a colleague highly placed in the service of the Crown. To his ingenuous mind there was naturally presented the prospect of his office passing on in just heritage to another Irish jurist, who would bring to the discharge of its onerous duties the full vigour of early manhood.[65]

Morris then, by Lucy's account, supposedly learned 'when he opened his morning paper' that the government had appointed as his successor Sir Nathaniel Lindley, the master of the rolls in England, who was one year younger than himself. There are elements of sarcasm in Lucy's references to Morris being an innocent and unduly trusting bystander to duplicitous conduct on the part of the government since, whatever about the quality of his contribution to the judicial work of the House of Lords, there was no doubt whatever about his shrewdness and native intelligence.

The decision not to appoint an Irish successor to Morris was predicted to be, and was, controversial. The appointment in 1889 of one Irish judge to succeed another was seen as an applicable precedent, a point of view that was strongly articulated when that expectation was not fulfilled upon the retirement of Morris. The most senior members of the government of Ireland – Lord Cadogan (the lord lieutenant), Gerald Balfour (the chief secretary) and Lord Ashbourne (again the lord chancellor) – were frustrated, and exchanged remorseful correspondence, at the fact that Lord Salisbury had not consulted them about the appointment.[66] It transpired almost immediately, as Cadogan reported to Ashbourne, that Salisbury 'had deliberately *not* appointed a successor to Lord Morris from Ireland, in order to 'break through a custom' which he thinks gives an undue share in the Appeal Court to Ireland'.[67] John Atkinson QC, MP, the attorney general, was particularly exercised at the appointment (see p. 380). Ashbourne told him that neither he nor Lord Cadogan knew anything of the arrangements until they were completed, and that Salisbury had wished to assert the principle that the House of Lords was an imperial court, which led Atkinson to observe that he had always thought of Ireland as itself being a part of the Empire and that it should be an object of the Unionist party to keep it so.[68]

When it became known that Morris was retiring and that his successor would not be drawn from the Irish Bench or Bar a general meeting of the Bar was held in the Law Library on 11 May 1900. The meeting unanimously adopted a resolution protesting that the appointment of a 'member of the English Bench, however distinguished, to fill the vacancy created among the Lords of Appeal in Ordinary by the retirement of Lord Morris was a distinct violation of the understanding hitherto observed that Ireland should be represented in the Court

65 Henry W. Lucy, *A diary of the unionist parliament, 1895–1900* (Bristol/London, 1901), p. 368.
66 Cadogan to Ashbourne, 7 May 1900 (Ashbourne Papers, B.22/17).
67 Cadogan to Ashbourne, 8 May 1900 (Ashbourne Papers, B.22/18).
68 Atkinson to Gerald Balfour, 6 May 1900 (Gerald Balfour Papers (TNAUK), PRO 30/60/15).

of Ultimate Appeal by the selection from the Irish Bench or Bar of at least one of the four lords of appeal in ordinary'.[69] Unionist and Nationalist barristers were united in their outrage and dismay. The principal legal professional journal, the *Irish Law Times*, published an editorial welcoming this 'manly remonstrance' of the Bar and describing the lack of an Irish Law Lord as an 'insult to the Irish Bench and Bar'.[70]

The subject was raised in the House of Commons on 18 May.[71] T.M. Healy QC, MP moved a resolution for the adjournment of the House (which was defeated, by 144 votes to 99) for the purpose of discussing 'the refusal of Her Majesty's present advisers to recognize the just claims of Ireland to representation in the final court of appeal for the three kingdoms, and the breach of constitutional usage involved in the appointment of an English judge to the vacancy created by the resignation of the Irish Law Lord'. The arguments that had been articulated at the Bar meeting seven days before were recycled and given a fresh airing. Contributors to the debate included Charles Hemphill QC, MP (the attorney general between 1892 and 1895, who had also spoken at the Bar meeting), and William Moore QC, a Unionist MP who was subsequently to be appointed a High Court judge (in 1917). The fact that Lord Ashbourne was eligible to sit in the House of Lords in a judicial capacity[72] was discounted, on the grounds that he would be too busy to do so and/or might be unable to do by virtue of having participated in a decision of the Court of Appeal in Ireland from which an appeal was being taken.

Arthur Balfour, who was then the leader of the House of Commons, replied to the debate for the government and, in denying that any unwritten protocol or understanding as to Irish representation had been broken, said that very few appeals from Ireland, an average of one a year, had been heard in the House of Lords for the previous five years. That was also the average level of Irish appeals over a longer time frame, both for the 1880s and for the 1890s as a whole. In that latter decade ten cases from the Court of Appeal in Ireland were taken to the House of Lords, two each being heard in 1892, 1893 and 1896, one in 1895, 1898, 1899 and 1900 and none in 1890, 1891, 1894 and 1897 (taking the law reports for those years as an indication of appeals heard in each such year respectively). Morris was not a member of the court in four of those ten appeals (Ashbourne was for one), he simply concurred in five of them and he dissented in one of them.[73] (By way of comparison, Morris sat as a member of the Judicial Committee of the Privy Council on the hearing of over 30 appeals from the supreme court of New South Wales and of 10 appeals from that of the state of Victoria.) No very strong argument for the necessity of a member of the Irish bench or Bar being appointed

69 It might be noted that section 27 of the Constitutional Reform Act 2005 provides that in the selection of judges for the Supreme Court it must be ensured 'that between them the judges will have knowledge of, and experience of practice in, the law of each part of the United Kingdom.'

70 *ILT&SJ*, vol. 34, pp 209–13 (19 May 1900); *Irish Times*, 12 May 1900.

71 HC Deb, 4th series, vol. 83, cols. 593–629 (18 May 1900).

72 By virtue of para (3) of s5 of the Appellate Jurisdiction Act 1876.

73 *Herron v Rathmines and Rathgar Improvement Commissioners*, [1892] A.C. 498.

to succeed Morris, primarily in connection with the discharge of appellate judicial functions for Irish law, could have been based solely upon the level of Irish business or upon the contribution that Morris had made to such business.

Balfour did not speak, and perhaps in an official capacity could not openly speak, of a consideration that the *Irish Law Times* was to acknowledge in its editorial on the subject. This was that Morris's work as a Law Lord had been undistinguished and had not promoted confidence in the quality of the Irish judiciary. On taking leave of the bench in Ireland in 1889 Morris had said that 'I follow Lord Fitzgerald, of whom the lord chancellor of England, but the other day, said "it would be most difficult to replace him". I cannot expect that any future lord chancellor would be entitled so to speak of me; but I do hope that the reputation of the Irish bench is safe in my hands'.[74] That hope had not been realized, and it was now said that his appointment in 1889 had been 'a singularly unfortunate one. Lord Morris cannot be considered an erudite lawyer, and we are afraid that on the principle *ab uno disce omnes* [from one you may speak of all] the English authorities may have taken him as a standard whereby to judge of the fitness of other Irish candidates'.[75] Salisbury in any event had reasons, for management of judicial patronage in England, not to appoint an Irish lawyer to the vacancy, and this preference would have been facilitated by such contemporary views on Lord Morris (which were to be amply confirmed by obituaries the following year). These English considerations, taken with the small number of Irish appeals, fortified his intention not to appoint another Irishman.

The promotion of Lindley was a central part of a reshuffle of judicial and official legal positions in England that was facilitated by the retirement of Morris. This had been in train for some time, at least a week before it was made public, as Balfour told Salisbury on 1 May that Carson was prepared to accept gratefully appointment as solicitor general in England.[76] The promotion of Carson and the honouring (announced later that month) of certain other Irish judicial figures – O'Brien, as well as Morris, to become a hereditary peer, and lord justice FitzGibbon to be a member of the Privy Council in England – were not seen as any form of solace or balm for the slight to the standing of the Irish bench and Bar that was represented by Morris's successor not being an Irishman. James H.M. Campbell QC, MP had said at the Bar meeting on 11 May 1900 that

> while they all regarded the selection of Mr Carson with very great pleasure and satisfaction, it was a foolish, absurd and grotesque argument to use to say that his selection was in any way, so far as the Irish Bar was concerned, a compensation for their being deprived of the right to which the Irish Bench and Bar were entitled. So far from being a compensation, it only accentuated the grievance.[77]

74 Address in court by Morris on 2 December 1889 (*ILT&SJ*, vol. 23, p. 636 (7 December 1889)).
75 *ILT&SJ*, vol. 34, p. 210 (19 May 1900).
76 Balfour to Salisbury, 1 May 1900 (Salisbury Papers).
77 *ILT&SJ*, vol. 34, p. 212 (19 May 1900).

Balfour had predicted as much to Salisbury: 'I understand that making Peter the Packer a peer of the United Kingdom will by no means reconcile the Irish Bar to losing a piece of patronage worth £5,000 a year'.[78]

Lord Lindley held office for five and a half years until November 1905. No vacancy occurred among the Law Lords, and hence no opportunity to press Irish claims to a seat there, until his retirement. Atkinson was appointed to replace him after backstage drama in which, notwithstanding what had then become more than ten years' continuous service (since July 1895) as attorney general, it seemed possible that he would leave office without promotion to any judicial office. His prospects in the autumn of 1905 were quite precarious. His expectations of becoming either a Law Lord or lord chancellor of Ireland had been made known in 1897 but nothing had yet come to pass. At different times that autumn, although it seemed likely that Lindley would resign, nobody knew (i) when he might do so, or (ii) whether, if and when this happened (and if the Conservative government was still in office), the place would be offered first to Atkinson's English counterpart, or (iii) whether, if and when it was offered to an Irish judge or lawyer, Atkinson would be the nominee. When Kipling's poem 'If' (written in 1895) was published in 1910 Atkinson would have had cause to reflect upon the hypothesis of one of its couplets, 'If you can meet with Triumph and Disaster, and treat those two impostors just the same'.

In January 1905, as Lindley wrote in a memoir,[79] he had a 'bad fall' in the street (at the duke of York's Steps, at the foot of Lower Regent Street) in which 'my head fell heavily on the pavement. I was not stunned but was a good deal cut and I bled freely'. He soon was advised to leave off all work on account of concussion. In April he broached with the lord chancellor, Lord Halsbury, the possibility of retirement, but was encouraged to take a long rest. Over the summer this rest included a visit to the Antrim coast to stay with his colleague Lord Macnaghten at his home, Runkerry, near Portballantrae. (Later visitors to Macnaghten that year, on September 22, included Atkinson and Walter Long, the chief secretary, companions on a motoring tour.)[80]

Atkinson's prospects of a high judicial position depended on whether Lindley – or the prime minister, Arthur Balfour[81] or, indeed, potentially Ashbourne or Macnaghten – would resign. In August Balfour told Long that 'Atkinson's future has long caused me great anxiety. It may perhaps be useful for you to know that if Ashbourne thought fit, having regard to all the circumstances of the case, to resign the chancellorship, I have the best reason to know that the King would be willing to make him a viscount when the Ministry came to an end; and I should of course

78 Balfour to Salisbury, 7 May 1900 (Salisbury Papers). The salary of a Law Lord was actually £6,000.

79 This paragraph is drawn from a manuscript autobiography of Lord Lindley held in the Library of King's College, London (Laws/Folio KV5. L64, p. 133). See also Victoria Barnes, 'Interrogating the self-told narrative: Lord Lindley's autobiography, his life and legal biography', *The Journal of Legal History*, vol. 41(2) (2020), pp 143–63, at 147.

80 Walter Long, first viscount Long of Wraxall, *Memories* (London, 1923), p. 379.

81 Balfour had succeeded his uncle, Lord Salisbury, as prime minister in July 1902.

be delighted that he should in the meanwhile retain his seat in the cabinet'.[82] Ashbourne had been prepared to exchange the office of lord chancellor for that of Law Lord in 1889 if he were to receive a step up in the peerage from a barony, but he was not willing to retire and thus make his position available to Atkinson when such a step up was now indicated as available to him. It was not unknown for a lord chancellor to be put under pressure to resign, and thus in effect to be dismissed (see pp 8 and 403), but in practical terms Balfour could only look to induce Ashbourne to retire and was not in a position to compel him to make room for Atkinson.

Ashbourne wrote a rather bland letter to Balfour a few days later, with reference not to the possibility of his own retirement but instead to a general expectation that Lindley would not sit again and would probably retire before November and (not naming Atkinson or any other person) pressed the claims of the Irish bench and bar to provide his successor. He reminded Balfour of his reply to the debate in the House of Commons in May 1900 on the subject of such Irish claims, and then said that at no time had the standing and ability of the Irish judges and law officers been higher, and that there would be no difficulty in finding a person well qualified for appointment.[83] Balfour passed on this letter to Long, remarking that it did not augur well 'for your negotiations with him in reference to Atkinson', and adding a further complication in saying that when Lindley did resign (and he had little doubt but that he would) he would feel obliged to offer the place to Sir Robert Finlay, the English attorney general.[84] He might not accept it, 'but if he did, and if you fail in your negotiations with Ashbourne, the only chance for Atkinson is that Macnaghten should be induced to resign also. Do you see any means of arriving at so desirable a conclusion?'[85]

At this time, the autumn of 1905, there was a febrile political atmosphere. The Conservative (Unionist) party had won convincing victories at the general elections in 1895 and 1900, but its political position in 1904 and 1905, marked by deep internal divisions, had become very weak. Electoral law at the time (and until 1911)[86] provided that seven years might elapse between one general election and another, but there was no expectation of the government surviving in office until October 1907 when an election could no longer be postponed. (The general election, when it was held in January 1906, resulted in a crushing defeat for the Conservatives, comparable to the landslide reverses that took place in 1945, 1997 and 2024.) Roy Jenkins noted that beforehand 'there hardly seemed to be a safe Conservative seat left in the country', and that by November 1905 'although no one knew whether Balfour would resign or dissolve [Parliament] or exactly when he would act he clearly could not much longer avoid doing one thing or another'.[87]

82 Balfour to Long, 10 August 1905 (Walter Long Papers, 947/59 (WSHC)).
83 Ashbourne to Balfour, 18 August 1905 (Walter Long Papers (WSHC), 947/59).
84 Finlay was appointed lord chancellor of Great Britain in December 1916 when Lloyd George became prime minister.
85 Balfour to Long, 1 September 1905 (Walter Long Papers (WSHC), 947/59).
86 Septennial Act 1715 (1 Geo. I, s2, c.38); Parliament Act 1911 (1&2 Geo. 5), c.13, s7.
87 Roy Jenkins, *Asquith* (London, 1964), pp 157 and 165. See also John Kendle, *Walter Long, Ireland, and the Union, 1905–1920* (Dun Laoghaire, 1992), pp 33–5.

The choice for Balfour lay between calling the general election himself or resigning (in anticipation of, rather than after, an election defeat) in the hope that Conservative fortunes would be boosted by a new focus on divisions within the opposition Liberal party that might be exacerbated by the process of forming a government (which would call an immediate election). The House of Commons was in recess and not sitting at the time so for the moment the fact that the Liberals were a minority in Parliament was of no significance. Irish unionists reacted with consternation and despair at the prospect of the government resigning earlier than might be unavoidable or absolutely necessary, and Long conveyed to Balfour his own view that an early resignation would mean disaster to Ireland and ruin to the Unionist cause.[88] At all events, towards the end of November there was increasing speculation that Balfour would imminently resign, and Atkinson noted to Long on 23 November that newspaper reports about this seemed well sourced and authoritative.[89] By 30 November Long had prepared a list of persons the conferring of honours on whom would be recommended to the King by the outgoing prime minister.[90]

This prospect of the government resigning in turn increased the attention in legal circles as to whether Lindley, who had resumed work in the autumn, would step down. J.S. Sandars, the principal private secretary to the prime minister, told Long on 24 November that, at Balfour's request, he had seen Halsbury, the lord chancellor, at the House of Lords and was writing to inform Long how matters stood. Halsbury had said that Lindley might be persuaded by him to go, and that if lord justice FitzGibbon (but not Atkinson) were to be put forward as his replacement then he would be prepared to offer some assistance to bring about this resignation, and in turn FitzGibbon's existing place on the Court of Appeal could be offered to Atkinson.[91] Atkinson reacted strongly on learning that FitzGibbon might be nominated to fill the prospective vacancy and (while not for the moment reminding Long of his own claims) told him that FitzGibbon would be entirely undesirable and unsuitable on political grounds. (His judicial suitability would never have been in issue.) He suggested that, going back to the 1870s, FitzGibbon had never wholeheartedly been a supporter of the unionist cause, and that he was friendly with and had had some relationship as an adviser to John Morley (the chief secretary for Ireland 1892–5, and whose authorised biography of Gladstone, in three volumes, had been published in 1903). He thought that FitzGibbon would be an unreliable supporter and potentially a formidable opponent if he were to join in debates on Irish political issues in the House of Lords. In all the circumstances it would be better even to appoint an English lawyer rather than FitzGibbon.[92]

88 F.E. Ball to Long, 23 November 1905 (Walter Long Papers (WSHC), 947–59); Long to Balfour, 30 November 1905 (Balfour Papers, Add. MS 49776.153–4).
89 Atkinson to Long, 23 November 1905 (Walter Long Papers (WSHC), 947–116.
90 Atkinson to Long, 30 November 1905 (Walter Long Papers (WSHC), 947/60).
91 Sandars to Long, 24 November 1905 (Walter Long Papers (WSHC), 947/59).
92 Atkinson to Long, 25 November 1905 (Walter Long Papers (BL), Add. MS 62409.70).

The possibility of FitzGibbon being appointed disappeared almost as soon as it was raised although it had become public when *Irish Times* reported on 27 November that 'the elevation of lord justice FitzGibbon to the appellate tribunal of the House of Lords would be warmly welcomed in the Temple [the legal quarter in London] as he is an erudite lawyer', adding that there would be 'widespread and hearty congratulations to Mr Atkinson on his elevation to the Bench' (as FitzGibbon's presumed successor in the Court of Appeal).[93] The name was then put forward of FitzGibbon's colleague lord justice Holmes, who had taken the place in the Court of Appeal in 1897 that had been declined by Atkinson, and an offer of which was now made to him again, and promptly turned down. (Learning of the possibility of FitzGibbon or Holmes being appointed, the indefatigable Campbell made a claim to Sandars, with Atkinson's blessing, for any vacancy that might thus arise in the Court of Appeal, and a few days later transferred his claim to that of the actual vacancy, in the office of attorney general, that had been created by Atkinson's promotion.[94])

Atkinson unburdened himself to Long on 28 November as to the injustice of now being overlooked, and complained of how Ashbourne was conducting himself. He again recited the 1897 assurances and expressed indignation and astonishment at seemingly being abandoned by colleagues. He asserted that Ashbourne had systematically been prejudicing him in the eyes of Lord Halsbury, whom he was leading to look for qualifications never mentioned in a recent comparable promotion in Scotland. Andrew Murray (the first Lord Dunedin) had been the senior law officer in Scotland (the Lord Advocate) between 1896 and 1905, thus holding a position corresponding to Atkinson's office of attorney general. He was appointed in March 1905 to be the head of the judiciary in Scotland, as Lord President of the Court of Session and Lord Justice General. Atkinson regarded it as mean and defamatory for any doubt to be cast on his legal ability and work ethic and passed on a rumour that Ashbourne's underlying object was to promote his brother John George Gibson, a judge of the High Court, to a vacancy in the Court of Appeal that would arise if any of its members was made a Law Lord.[95]

Long warmly recommended Atkinson to Balfour, saying that informed legal circles, including Sir Patrick Coll, lately retired as chief Crown solicitor, held a high opinion of him and relaying Atkinson's comments about the unsuitability of FitzGibbon. He remarked that to offer FitzGibbon's place to Atkinson would be to add insult to injury, that – whatever else might be done – the place in the House of Lords should not be offered to FitzGibbon, and that for Ashbourne to have fostered any antipathy to Atkinson was mean and contemptible conduct.[96]

93 *Irish Times*, 27 November 1905.
94 Campbell to Sandars, 28 November 1905 (Walter Long Papers (BL), Add. MS 62409.78); Campbell to Sandars, 3 December 1905 (Walter Long Papers (WSHC), 947/59).
95 Atkinson to Long, 28 November 1905 (Walter Long Papers (BL), Add. MS 62409.72).
96 Notes for letter, Long to Balfour, undated [late November] 1905 (Walter Long Papers (WSHC), 947/59).

Lindley wrote in his memoir that in the autumn of 1905 'I soon found that I could not do my work properly: my power of attention and power of getting a clear view of what I was attending to failed me and I felt all in a muddle. With great reluctance therefore and on my 77th birthday, 29 November 1905, I resigned my judicial post'.[97] His resignation was amply justified by the state of his health but was ultimately prompted by a direct request from Halsbury to retire.[98] Sandars had asked Halsbury on 29 November 'whether you have negotiated Lord Lindley's resignation … as soon as he [Balfour] hears from you he will acquaint you with his views of dealing with the vacancy'.[99] Balfour seemingly remained concerned about Finlay's position,[100] but on Sunday 3 December Atkinson received a telegram confirming his appointment to the vacancy.[101] Balfour went to Buckingham Palace the following afternoon to tender his resignation to the King, and some hours later (shortly before 9.00 p.m.) it was announced from Downing Street that the King had been pleased to approve the appointments of Atkinson as a lord of appeal in ordinary and of Campbell to be his successor as attorney general.[102] Atkinson's nomination to judicial office by an outgoing government was thus a very close-run thing, even more so than that of Palles in broadly comparable circumstances some thirty years before. Long's reference to Atkinson's nomination in a memoir published in 1923, that 'by a rare piece of good fortune a vacancy occurred among the lords of appeal and the prime minister was good enough to confer the appointment upon him', was extremely economical with the truth.[103]

An intended appointment as a lord of appeal in ordinary that never took place was that of Campbell in 1915. In June that year he was prevented by vehement Nationalist opposition from taking up the position of lord chancellor of Ireland, and was then told by the prime minister, Asquith, that he proposed to arrange for his appointment as a Law Lord, although this would have to await enabling legislation.[104] It soon became clear however that there was no appetite, in an atmosphere of wartime economy and austerity, for creating an additional judicial position (and, indeed, a superfluous one, since there was an ample supply of legal peers eligible to sit on appeals). Atkinson was approached with a view to him retiring so as to create a vacancy to which Campbell might be appointed but declined to co-operate in such an arrangement.[105] When Campbell was appointed as lord chief justice of Ireland in December 1916 he asked for confirmation that

97 Lindley memoir, p. 134.

98 R.F.V. Heuston, entry on Lindley in A.W.B. Simpson (ed.), *Biographical dictionary of the common law* (London, 1984), p. 314; see also Robert Stevens, *Law and politics: the House of Lords as a judicial body, 1800–1976* (London, 1977), p. 112.

99 R.F.V. Heuston, *Lives of the lord chancellors, 1885–1940* (Oxford, 1964), p. 62.

100 R.F.V. Heuston, *Lord chancellors*, p. 326.

101 Campbell to Long, 3 December 1905 (Walter Long Papers (WSHC), 947/59).

102 *Irish Times*, 5 December 1905.

103 Long, *Memories*, op. cit., p. 168. It has been said, more generally of the memoir, that it concealed more than it revealed about Long and his involvement with Ireland (Kendle, op. cit., p. 238).

104 Asquith to Campbell, 11 June 1915 (Bonar Law Papers, BL 50/4/29).

105 Asquith to Campbell, 13 July 1915 (Asquith Papers, 28:5).

the offer of appointment as a Law Lord was still binding and Lloyd George, the new prime minister, authorized Bonar Law to confirm this.[106]

JUDICIAL AND PARLIAMENTARY WORK OF THE IRISH LORDS OF APPEAL IN ORDINARY

Those were the circumstances of the appointments of Lords Fitzgerald, Morris and Atkinson respectively. As to what they did once appointed, an important preliminary point to be noted is that, while their work ranged far outside the scope of the matters that would have occupied them on the bench in Ireland, it included comparatively few appeals in criminal law. Appeals in criminal cases to the House of Lords had been 'all but impossible' prior to the passing of the Court of Criminal Appeal Act 1907, as 'in theory a writ of error had lain, but that was obsolete'.[107] Section 1(6) of the Act established, for England, a procedure for a further appeal from the new court to the House of Lords if the attorney general gave leave for this on the basis that the case raised a point of law of exceptional public importance and that it was in the public interest that a further appeal should be brought. When Roger Casement sought leave for such a further appeal in July 1916, after his conviction for treason at the Old Bailey and the dismissal of his initial appeal, this was refused by the attorney general, F.E. Smith, who had conducted the prosecution. Between 1907 and 1916 such leave to appeal had been granted in only two cases.[108]

The domestic appeals in the House of Lords in the 1880s and 1890s thus simply did not draw upon what had been a major part of the experience of both Lord Fitzgerald and Lord Morris. In the debate in the house on the Law of Evidence (Amendment) Bill 1886, which would have removed the prohibition on a criminal defendant giving evidence on his own behalf, Fitzgerald said that he believed that there was no noble and learned lord present who had a larger experience of criminal law than he had.[109] Morris made a similar statement when the subject was debated again in 1891 – 'few persons have had longer experience than I have had in criminal trials'.[110] Matters of criminal law did however arise in some appeals heard by the Judicial Committee of the Privy Council. Fitzgerald sat as a member of the Committee in 1887 on an appeal from British Honduras which became a leading case in establishing the basis of criminal appeal from territories in the British Empire. As stated in the headnote of the law report, 'Her Majesty

106 Campbell to Bonar Law, 10 December 1916 (Bonar Law Papers, 81/1/44); Bonar Law to Lloyd George, 22 December 1916 (Bonar Law Papers, 84/6/20); Bonar Law to Campbell, 6 January 1917 (Bonar Law Papers, 84/6/37).

107 Patrick Polden, 'The courts of law' in *Oxford history of laws*, vol. 11, pp 804 and 541.

108 R.F.V. Heuston, op. cit., p. 377.

109 HL Deb, 3rd series, vol. 303, col. 227 (9 March 1886).

110 HL Deb, 3rd series, vol. 353, col. 1068 (26 May 1891).

will not review criminal proceedings unless it be shown that by a disregard of the forms of legal process, or by some violation of the principles of natural justice, or otherwise, substantial and grave injustice has been done'.[111]

For the first couple of years after Fitzgerald's appointment Lord O'Hagan, as a former lord chancellor of Ireland, continued to sit on appeals, and they were members of the same court on a number of occasions. These included (as one of O'Hagan's last appeals) the final hearing of what had become extraordinarily extended litigation over fishery rights on the river Blackwater in Co. Waterford, *Neill v Duke of Devonshire*.[112] Lord Selborne LC said (at 138) that 'in this case there have been two actions and seven trials, three trials in which the jury did not agree, two in which the verdict was against and two (including the last) in which it was in favour of the respondent. Unless your Lordships should have been persuaded that, at the last trial, the jury were misdirected as to any material question of evidence or other matter of law you will probably be of opinion that this prolonged litigation ought at last to have an end'. The hearing in the House of Lords was itself interrupted and delayed by one of the counsel, Francis Macdonogh QC, being taken ill there. The complexities of the case included reference back to a document of title of 1215, and the litigation had commenced with a trial over 17 days in 1869.[113]

A brief commentary by Lord Lowry on Fitzgerald was expressed in approving if unspecific terms, without reference to any case, to the effect that his judgments 'were undemonstrative but are notable for their clarity and their relevance to the main point in the case. Their author also had the happy knack of being right. His deep learning ranged widely, and his statutory interpretation is impossible to fault. In short, he was a very good judge'.[114] Fitzgerald's contributions to the decisions of the Lords of Appeal were at times rather tentative. In *Bowen v Lewis*[115] the four judgments (formally styled 'speeches' to the house) which came before his were evenly divided so he had the decisive voice on the appeal, a circumstance which did not arise very often. He said that 'when such great authorities as the noble and learned Lords who have preceded me [Lords Cairns, Blackburn, Selborne and Bramwell] differ in opinion I need not say that I express mine with diffidence and hesitation'. (He agreed with Cairns and Blackburn.) That diffidence had been foreshadowed in a remark that he made in a letter to Lord Spencer at the time of accepting appointment, that he now felt that 'I am not of sufficient capacity for so high and important an office and that I have been vain and rash in accepting it. I'll do my best'.[116] (This might be contrasted with the cheery self-confidence of Lord

111 *In re Dillet* (1887) 12 App. Cas. 459. Kenneth Keith, 'The interplay with the Judicial Committee of the Privy Council' in Blom-Cooper, Dickson and Drewry (eds), op. cit., p. 335.

112 (1882–3) 8 App. Cas. 135.

113 *ILT&SJ*, vol. 16, p. 227 (20 May 1882).

114 Lowry, op. cit., p. 195.

115 (1883–4) 9 App. Cas. 890. Fitzgerald's speech is at 923. See also *ILT&SJ*, vol. 18, p. 427 (16 August 1884) about a case concerning an ejectment from land worth £14 a year.

116 Fitzgerald to Spencer, 'Whit Monday' [29 May] 1882 (Althorp Papers, Add. MS 77077).

Campbell, a member of the English Bar, who held office as lord chancellor of Ireland for a few weeks in 1841: 'short as my experience was, I saw enough to persuade me that I should have been complete master of the court, and that I should have given general satisfaction'.)[117] Fitzgerald spoke to the same effect as in the Bowen case shortly afterwards when he remarked, in *Great Eastern Railway Co. v Goldsmid*,[118] that

> I took some objection to the form of the injunction. I thought that it was rather too extensive and might cover acts – and I am still rather inclined to think that it might cover acts – which otherwise would be legal and right. But I have had no experience in courts of equity now during a period of over twenty years, and I yield my judgment entirely on that point to the life-long experience and sounder judgment of the lord chancellor.

A certain amount of language of that sort would of course represent no more than the ordinary respect and courtesies that members of a collegiate court would have expressed and extended to each other. For instance, Lord Atkinson remarked in 1911 that 'I share the regret expressed by Lord Halsbury that I am unable to concur in the judgment of the lord chancellor and have, of course, by reason of that circumstance all the less confidence in my own opinion'.[119] Fitzgerald's diffidence, however, whenever it arose, was expressed in rather more self-deprecating terms than other judges seemed to find necessary. In an appeal in 1887 concerning a copyright matter (whether a delivery of lectures by a university professor was a communication to the world, such as to entitle anyone to (re)publish them without permission) he dissented from the majority view, saying that he had 'struggled against this conclusion, as I am conscious how superior my noble and learned friends [Lord Halsbury and Watson] are to me in knowledge and judgment, but I have been unable to agree with them'.[120]

He expressed a more conventional acknowledgment of superior analysis by his brother judges in the seminal company law case of *Trevor v Whitworth*[121] in 1887, in which it was determined that a company had no general power to purchase its own shares, this being an unlawful reduction of capital. Fitzgerald concurred, and said that 'upon carefully reading the two very elaborate opinions which have already been delivered upon this subject, and the very weighty opinion which has yet to be delivered by my noble and learned friend who sits near me [Lord Macnaghten] and deliberately considering them, I have laid aside what I intended to be my own judgment and I need only state my entire concurrence in those opinions'. He delivered concurring judgments in two other cases that raised novel

117 Quoted in J.B. Atlay, *The Victorian chancellors* (London, 1906), vol. 2, p. 147.
118 (1883–84) 9 App. Cas., 927 at 964.
119 *Smith v Lion Brewery Company Limited*, [1911] AC 150, at 158.
120 *Caird v Sime* (1887) App. Cas. 326, at 353.
121 (1887) 11 App. Cas. 409. Fitzgerald's speech is at 431.

questions of law in the new financial economy of the 1880s, *Derry v Peek*[122] and *Colquhoun v Brooks*.[123]

Fitzgerald was more confident when forming judgments on subjects such as agricultural practice in Ireland – 'I am aware from my own judicial experience how much lettings of dairy farms vary'[124] – while on another occasion professing 'inacquaintance with colliery operations', and hence 'difficulty in reaching a conclusion satisfactory to myself on this appeal'.[125] More significantly perhaps, in 1889 he remarked that 'I have to confess that I am ignorant on the subject of navigation',[126] a curious admission from a member of a court where very many appeals concerned shipping or marine insurance cases.

He tried the patience of his brother judges in 1888 in a case concerned with bills of sale and an assignment of future book debts,[127] in saying that 'I hope your Lordships will excuse me if, for the present, I hesitate, and for the reasons I have given, decline to express either assent to or dissent from the conclusions of my noble and learned friends'. Lords Watson and Herschell both remarked (at 553) that the matters referred to in Fitzgerald's judgment were not germane to the appeal and had not been referred to in the arguments of counsel.

Fitzgerald sat as a member of the House of Lords on 180 appeals, occasionally delivering the leading judgment, and sat as a member of the Judicial Committee of the Privy Council, a few hundred yards away in Downing Street, another 40 times, delivering its (single) judgment 9 times. His successor, Lord Morris, heard 191 appeals, rarely delivering a leading judgment, and sat as a member of the Judicial Committee 122 times, delivering its judgment 13 times.

Obituaries of Morris commonly referred, as the *Law Times* did, to his high intelligence and quick wit ('pungent though kindly'), before conceding that he 'was not either a great or a profound jurist. He had however sterling common sense and a desire to do right. His decisions will not be perused by those in search for treasures of legal wisdom and learning'.[128] In the same vein the *Irish Law Times* said that 'if he cannot be described as a great lawyer it can truly be asserted that his vast logical ability always enabled him to seize on the drift of even the most subtle arguments, and generally to arrive at a sound conclusion'.[129] One of the best known, if rather laboured, examples of his wit arose in the course of argument in the important and politically sensitive trade union case of *Allen v Flood*,[130] as to

122 (1889) 14 App. Cas. 337. The determination in this case of the nature of directors' liability for errors in a prospectus was widely thought to be unsatisfactory as unduly favourable to them and was soon modified by Parliament in the Director's Liability Act 1890.

123 (1889) 14 App. Cas. 493. It was held that a partner's profits from a trade carried on exclusively abroad and not received in the United Kingdom were not liable to income tax.

124 *Westropp v Elligott* (1883–84) 9 App. Cas. 815, at 842.

125 *Netherseed Colliery Company v Bourne* (1888) 13 App. Cas. 228 at 238.

126 The Ceto (1889) 14 App. Cas. 670, at 693.

127 *Trilby v Official Receiver* (1888) 13 App. Cas. 523. FitzGerald's speech is at 536–40.

128 *ILT&SJ*, vol. 35, p. 550 (30 November 1901), quoting from the *Law Times*.

129 *ILT&SJ*, vol. 35, p. 432 (14 September 1901).

130 [1898] AC 1.

whether it was lawful to injure a man in his trade by refusing to work with him. Lord Herschell, a former lord chancellor, was prone to interrupt counsel, or 'as it is delicately put by Lord Davey, 'his rapidity of mind led him to anticipate the argument and take it out of the hands of counsel,' a foible which gained in him in his last years. During the argument in *Allen v Flood* his interruptions were so persistent that Lord Morris was heard to ejaculate 'I understand now what molesting a man in his business means'.[131]

Professor Robert Stevens has remarked that 'technical lawyers have regarded Morris as one of the least – if not the least – distinguished members of the house in these years [1876–1912]. He did not profess to be a great lawyer but simply made an honest attempt to judge a case on the merits as he saw them. He cared little for precedent, though he was a party to Halsbury's decision in *London Street Tramways v London County Council,* [1898 AC 375]'.[132] That quite short judgment in which Morris and all the other members of the court concurred was to be taken for the next seventy years or so in English law as the basis for an approach of the House of Lords, as a self-binding precedent, of not being prepared to overrule its own previous decisions. The wider significance of that doctrine of *stare decisis* [to stand by decided matters] is now seen as an avowal that the Law Lords did not make law and were simply engaged in ascertaining it.[133]

A 'concern for the spirit rather than the letter of the law resulted in his often being in a dissenting minority'.[134] He dissented from the majority view 16 times, rather more than the handful of times that Fitzgerald had done or that Atkinson was to do. In one case he said that he had some doubt about the decision of the majority (in fact, of all the other members of the house who heard the appeal) but 'I do not intend to dissent formally from the judgment which has been proposed, especially as my dissent would be of no practical value'.[135]

Morris was a member of the court for some of the most significant or leading decisions of the 1890s. These included Pemsel's case[136] (1891) on the headings or categories of charity, in which he concurred with Lord Macnaghten's luminous (although seemingly inaudible)[137] exposition (1891), *Aaron's Reefs Ltd. v Twiss*[138] (1896), in relation to a fraudulent prospectus, *Salomon v Salomon*[139] (1897), confirming the independent corporate existence and personality of a company, separate from that of its owners and not being any form of agent or trustee for

131 J.B. Atlay, *The Victorian chancellors* (London, 1906), vol. 2, p. 461. See also R.F.V. Heuston, *Lives of the lord chancellors, 1885–1940* (Oxford, 1964), p. 110, and Maud Wynne, *An Irishman and his family* (London, 1937), p. 148.

132 Stevens, op. cit., p. 109.

133 Polden, op. cit., p. 544.

134 Stevens, op. cit., p. 109. The entry on Morris in the *ODNB* also makes reference to the spirit of the law.

135 *Comber v Leyland*, [1898] AC 524 at 533.

136 [1891] AC 531.

137 *ILT&SJ*, vol.25, p. 434 (8 August 1891).

138 [1896] AC 273.

139 [1897] AC 22.

them, *Russell v Russell*[140] (also in 1897), a scandalous divorce case that preceded the trial of Lord Russell in 1901 above referred to, and, as mentioned, *Allen v Flood* and *London Tramways Company v London County Council* (1898). The decision of the house in *Mogul Steamship v McGregor & Co*[141] (1892) has been taken as a high point of a narrow judicial approach to the tort of conspiracy, at least where business interests were concerned. 'The house refused to offer any remedy to a shipping company that had been driven out of business by a competing ring of shipping companies that had carried goods below cost with the express purpose of driving the first company out of business'.[142] Morris remarked in the course of his brief judgment that he 'was not aware of any stage of competition called "fair", intermediate between lawful and unlawful'.

Morris had little to say (either at all, or in the length at which he spoke, if he did speak) on any of these cases. One contributing factor for this reticence may have been that he was typically among the last of the members of the house sitting on any case to give his judgment. He ranked in precedence not only behind hereditary peers (such as Lord Ashbourne, when also sitting on an appeal), but also behind two Lords of Appeal in Ordinary who had been appointed before him, Lords Watson and Macnaghten, both highly distinguished judges. They held office for almost all of his term in the case of Watson (up to 1899) and for all of it in the case of Macnaghten. Over the years he may have thought that others more senior or more learned in the law than him would have already expressed anything that he might have wished to say.

His judgments when given, if they went beyond an expression of concurrence, were short, their brevity offering comparatively little engagement with the legal issues arising on an appeal or opportunity for subsequent analysis. In his observations on Lord Morris Lord Lowry referred to three cases in 1900 in which he gave judgment.[143] In *Seaton v Burnand*[144] Morris considered in a very practical fashion the nature of a judge's summing up and what questions were properly to be left to a civil jury, drawing on his own experience as a common law judge at first instance. *Cartwright v Sculcoates Union*[145] was a case on the rateable valuation of premises, and he took a commonsense view, observing in passing that the premises in question as a public house was 'at a corner – they generally are so as to capture two streets'. In the third case, *Powell v Mains Colliery Co. Ltd*,[146] he dissented on a point under the Workmen's Compensation legislation, convincingly in Lord Lowry's view, although it might be noted that none of the other judges had agreed with him. These judgments were very short, his Seaton judgment ran to three pages in the printed law reports, the Cartwright judgment to two, and the Powell

140 [1897] AC 535.
141 [1892] AC 25 (Morris at 49).
142 Stevens, op. cit., p. 158.
143 Lowry, op. cit., p. 197.
144 [1900] AC 135.
145 [1900] AC 150.
146 [1900] AC 366.

judgment again being two. In the significant competition law case (concerning the validity of a restrictive covenant on the sale of a business) of *Nordenfelt v Maxim Nordenfelt Guns and Ammunition Company*[147] his judgment was a single page. (He remarked in that case that 'we have now reached a period when it may be said that science and invention have almost annihilated both time and space' echoing an earlier observation in *Mogul Steamship v McGregor & Co.*[148] that they were living in 'days of almost instant communication with almost all parts of the world'.)

The judgment in *McLeod v St Aubyn*,[149] concerning contempt of court, has been taken in the entry on Morris in the *Oxford dictionary of national biography* to be his best-known contribution as a member of the House of Lords, although it is of little if any legal importance. The island of St Vincent, in the Caribbean Sea, had a population at the time of about 40,000 people, and the appeal to the Judicial Committee of the Privy Council was taken from a fairly plainly erroneous decision of its supreme court, the name of which suggested or denoted rather more grandeur than its actual circumstances. The judicial establishment of the island consisted of the (acting) chief justice and a single magistrate. Morris's judgment occupies 11 pages in the Law Reports, eight of which are taken up by a recitation of the (interesting) facts.

Morris's daughter noted in her biography of him that he 'hated the sight of a writing table, and notwithstanding the classical scholarship of his youth he was a poor writer and always disliked it. It is customary to write out judgments delivered in the House of Lords law cases, but otherwise [he] never wrote out a speech delivered there or elsewhere'.[150] In that light an observation by Stevens that 'his judgments are written in a prose style that frequently animates the subject under discussion'[151] may seem surprising but is a rare example of Homer nodding. The two judgments cited to illustrate that comment, *Chadwich v Manning*[152] (accurately described by Stevens as 'reads like a novel') and *Reddaway v Banham*[153] (a subtle description of varieties of fraud), came in fact from the pen of Macnaghten, not Morris.

Lord Atkinson's judicial career between the end of 1905 and his retirement in 1928, at the age of 86, was one of the longest of any of the Law Lords (that of Lord Reid, between 1948 and 1975, was the longest of all). The *Times* in its obituary observed that 'his weakness lay in a deficiency in the sense of style which rendered his judgments diffuse and even somewhat obscure'.[154] Lord Lowry took a much more positive view, writing that 'his judicial performance lacked nothing in competence and impartiality', and admiring his 'clarity of reasoning, grasp of

147 [1894] AC 535 at 574.
148 [1892] AC 25.
149 [1899] AC 549.
150 Wynne, op. cit., p. 210.
151 Stevens, op. cit., p. 109.
152 [1896] AC 231 at 238.
153 [1896] AC 199 at 221.
154 *The Times*, 14 March 1932.

principle and felicity of language',[155] and set out carefully to rebut a more critical, indeed distinctly less flattering, view that had been expressed a few years earlier by Professor Stevens. He had referred to Atkinson as 'not a distinguished judge. Not only was he not a first-rate lawyer, but he showed little interest in the appellate process. Insofar as he had a judicial style, it was a formalistic one. Yet under the guise of restating the law he was able to inject his own extremely Conservative brand of politics'.[156]

Atkinson delivered a number of leading judgments, some on issues arising under the law of Scotland, and his concurring judgments were generally substantive, not formal. He frequently joined in decisions to reverse judgments of the Court of Appeal in Ireland,[157] at times in acerbic language, most notably when saying in his judgment in *Considine v McInerney*, that the lower court's conclusion was 'as illogical as it is unjust and oppressive to the employer ... the unsoundness of the contention is shown by the absurd result to which it leads'.[158] He found absurdity also in an English appeal, saying that 'the suit out of which this appeal has arisen was wrongly framed, was unsatisfactorily conducted and has led to illegal if not indeed absurd results'.[159]

A unanimous decision of the House of Lords in 1910 that a trade union had no power to levy a political contribution from unwilling members for the purpose of securing parliamentary representation for working men[160] generated a major political controversy. In Atkinson's concurring judgment he observed that it had not been disputed that 'members of trade unions were not on joining required to subscribe to any political creed, or submit to any political test, no more than are persons who become shareholders in a railway company'. Funding from trade unions was crucial to the development of the Labour Party, and the law was soon changed by a provision in the Trade Union Act 1913[161] that expressly permitted a portion of union subscriptions to be paid into a political fund, with members having a right to opt out of contributing.

Many cases arose under the Workmen's Compensation Acts 1897 and 1906[162] as to whether or not fatal injuries had been incurred by a deceased worker 'out of and in the course of his employment' (thus entitling his dependant(s) to

155 Lowry, op. cit., pp 199 and 201.
156 Robert Stevens, entry on Lord Atkinson in A.W.B. Simpson (ed.), *Biographical dictionary of the common law* (London, 1984), p. 20.
157 *Pearson v Dublin Corporation*, [1907] AC 351; *Cooke v Midland Great Western Railway*, [1909] AC 229; *Mackey v Woods*, [1918] AC 59; *Yourell v Hibernian Bank*, [1918] AC 372; *McEllistrim v Ballymacelligott Co-operative Agricultural and Dairy Society Ltd*, [1919] AC 548, and cases cited in following footnote.
158 [1916] 2 AC 162, at 174. See also his remarks in his leading judgment in *Hollinshead v Hazelton*, [1916] 1 AC 428, at 450.
159 *London Association for Protection of Trade v Greenlands Ltd.*, [1916] 2 A.C. 15.
160 *Osborne v Amalgamated Society of Railway Servants*, [1910] AC 87; R.F.V. Heuston, *Lives of the lord chancellors, 1885–1940* (Oxford, 1964), pp 163–5.
161 2&3 Geo. 5, c.30.
162 60&61 Vict., c.37 (1897); 6 Edw. 7, c.58 (1906).

compensation). Atkinson was generally thought (including by one of his colleagues, Lord Dunedin, a Law Lord between 1913 and 1932[163]) to have a disposition to take the employer's side in such disputes. He was the sole dissenter in *Innes v Kynoch*,[164] holding that since it was uncertain how a fatal infection had occurred the employer should not be fixed with liability. He was however frequently in agreement with his colleagues as to whether compensation was payable.[165]

The opening passage of his concurring judgment in the wartime case of *Rex v Halliday (ex parte Zadig)*,[166] in which the lawfulness of internment under emergency powers (the Defence of the Realm Regulations) was upheld, is a good illustration of the judicial view of the exigencies of war and of the mood and temper of the times:

> Several of the topics to which learned counsel for the appellant addressed themselves in the course of their arguments, however interesting historically, had, in my view, little if any relevancy to the question to be decided in this case, such, for instance, as the scope and nature of the legislation passed by the Parliament of England on the several occasions in her history when she was at war. The question for decision in this case is what the legislature has done by this statute of November 1914, not what it did by legislation passed centuries before that date. It may be that so dear to the legislature of those days was the personal liberty of the subject that it sacrificed, or endangered, the interest of the State and hampered the nation in its struggle for victory in order to preserve that liberty. For myself I do not at all think it was so. Or it may have been that the circumstances at the time did not need such drastic remedies as do those of the present time. However precious the personal liberty of the subject may be, there is something for which it may well be, to some extent, sacrificed by legal enactment, namely national success in the war, or escape from national plunder or enslavement.

In addition to their judicial work the Law Lords as members of the legislature were entitled to participate in the other work of the House of Lords to the extent that they might choose to do so, irrespective of its subject matter. When Lord Morris was appointed to succeed Lord Fitzgerald the *Times* expressed the hope that he 'will not consider it necessary to limit himself too strictly to his judicial duties, but that he will take his share in general debate, especially on Irish questions, as Lord Fitzgerald frequently did to great public advantage'.[167] Each of these three Irish Law Lords had sat in the House of Commons, Fitzgerald between 1852 and 1860, Morris more briefly between 1865 and 1867, and Atkinson for ten years

163 *Simpson v London, Midland and Scottish Railway*, [1931] AC 351, at 357.
164 [1919] AC 765.
165 For instance, in *Bourton v Beauchamp*, [1920] AC 100; *A.G. Markey v Barkey*, [1923] AC 790.
166 [1917] AC 260, at 271.
167 *ILT&SJ*, vol. 23, p. 636 (7 December 1889), quoting from the *Times*.

(1895–1905), and had served as attorney general. The business of the House of Lords was conducted in a more genteel and respectful atmosphere than that of the House of Commons, members referring to each other as 'noble lords' and to the Law Lords, as 'noble and learned lords'.

Fitzgerald's contributions to debates in the house largely related to legal reforms. In 1884 he introduced private legislation to reform the constitution of the Cork Butter Market. This gave effect to the outcome of a consultation process among the various interested parties (the Cork Corporation, butter merchants and butter brokers) for the reform of its governance, which he had chaired at the request of the lord lieutenant.[168] He introduced the Barristers' Admission (Ireland) Bill in 1885,[169] after it had been passed in the House of Commons, which removed the obligation for students of the Irish Bar to keep terms at one of the inns of court in London. He also spoke on contempt of court legislation,[170] on the intended abolition of the position of law adviser at Dublin Castle,[171] on the Land Purchase Bill 1885 (the 'Ashbourne Act'),[172] the workings of the Landed Estates Court[173] and firearms legislation.[174] Two legal reform proposals that Fitzgerald strongly advocated were to permit an accused person to give evidence on his own behalf[175] and the establishment of a court of criminal appeal. Those reforms, long sought, were eventually enacted for England, but not Ireland, in 1898 and in 1907 respectively.[176] (Lord Ashbourne said in one of the many debates on reform of the law of evidence that 'he ventured to think that there was not a single judge or any other person interested in the administration of the law in Ireland who would not deplore the omission' to legislate for Ireland also.[177]) He last spoke in Parliament in August 1889 when he introduced a debate, in the form of a question to the prime minister, to press for the establishment of such a court of appeal.[178] Public opinion had been much exercised that summer by the sensational trial of Florence Maybrick, who had been convicted of the murder of her husband by arsenic poisoning. Fitzgerald said, perhaps rather naively, that he raised the subject in

168 HL Deb, 3rd series, vol. 289, col. 775 (19 June 1884); FitzGerald to Spencer, 11 February 1884 (Althorp Papers, Add. MS 77077); Colin Ryan, *At the sign of the cow: the Cork butter market, 1770–1924* (Cork, 1998), p. 97. Fitzgerald was made a freeman of the city of Cork for his services in connection with this market reform (*ILT&SJ*, vol. 18, p. 428 (16 August 1884)).

169 HL Deb, 3rd series, vol. 298, col. 2 (8 May 1885).

170 HL Deb, 3rd series, vol. 277, col. 1609 (6 April 1883).

171 HL Deb, 3rd series, vol. 279, col. 378 (10 May 1883).

172 HL Deb, 3rd series, vol. 299, col. 1776 (24 July 1885).

173 HL Deb, 3rd series, vol. 319, col. 225 (12 August 1887).

174 HL Deb, 3rd series, vol. 334, cols. 1365–7 (2 April 1889).

175 HL Deb, 3rd series, vol. 303, col. 228 (9 March 1886). See, more generally, Claire Jackson, 'Irish political opposition to the passage of criminal evidence reform at Westminster, 1883–98' in John McEldowney and Paul O'Higgins (eds), *The common law tradition: essays in Irish legal history* (Dublin, 1990).

176 Criminal Evidence Act 1898 (61&62 Vict., c.36); Criminal Appeal Act 1907 (7 Edw. VII, c.3).

177 HL Deb, 4th series, vol. 32, col. 6 (25 March 1895); see also remarks of Ashbourne at HL Deb, 4th series, vol. 10, col. 188 (16 March 1893).

178 HL Deb, 3rd series, vol. 339, col. 1297 (15 August 1889).

principle, without reference to recent events, but received sharp criticism anyway from the lord chancellor for potentially inflaming public opinion – 'I cannot forbear to point out to him that all people are not invested with the same judicial temper, and that when he proceeds to point out the defects of the present mode of administering justice his comments will have a wider operation then he intended. There is no doubt that such questions as these are not appropriately discussed at time of public excitement about them'.[179] Both of these reforms had become law in Northern Ireland and the Irish Free State respectively by 1930. A person charged with an offence (and his or her spouse) was declared to be a competent witness for the defence in 1923 (NI) and 1924 (IFS), and courts of criminal appeal were established in 1930 (NI) and 1924 (IFS).[180]

Lord Morris observed in 1895 that he did not often intervene in debates in the House, especially debates in party matters.[181] When speaking in 1891 and 1895 on the proposals in those years to permit accused persons to give evidence,[182] he deplored that the law in Ireland on the subject was not to be changed. He spoke also on the financial relations between Great Britain and Ireland (in essence, as to whether Ireland was overtaxed),[183] and on the withdrawal of a military guard from the judges of assize in Cork in 1897.[184] A remark in 1896 that the over-taxation of his country 'largely arose from the successful exertions to impose taxation upon Ireland by that great financial enemy of Ireland, Mr Gladstone'[185] is probably best understood not as a serious political point but as a mischievous reference to Gladstone having extended income tax to Ireland and raised the tax on whiskey and other spirits when chancellor of the Exchequer decades earlier. He raised two matters of local interest, being the retirement – or, as many believed, in effect the dismissal – of the president of the Queen's College, Galway in 1895[186] and whether Galway should be a county borough under the provisions of the Local Government (Ireland) Bill 1898, which created county councils. The Bill provided for six other cities to be county boroughs (and hence, under section 21, 'an administrative county of itself'), and Morris proposed an amendment to add Galway to that list. The House of Lords adopted the amendment to the relevant schedule of the Bill, over Lord Ashbourne's opposition, but this was not accepted by the House of Commons and it did not form part of the final statute.[187]

179 HL Deb, 3rd series, vol. 339, col. 1304 (15 August 1889).
180 Criminal Evidence Act (Northern Ireland) 1923 and Criminal Justice (Evidence) Act 1924; Criminal Appeal (Northern Ireland) Act 1930 and Courts of Justice Act 1924, s8.
181 HL Deb, 4th series, vol. 30, col. 434 (11 February 1895).
182 HL Deb, 3rd series, vol. 353, cols. 1068–9 (26 May 1891) and 4th series, vol. 32, cols. 7–8 (25 March 1895).
183 HL Deb, 3rd series, vol. 34, col. 335 (27 May 1895) and vol. 38, col. 1582 (23 March 1896).
184 HL Deb, 4th series, vol. 47, col. 1286 (25 March 1897).
185 HL Deb, 4th series, vol. 38, col. 1582 (23 March 1896).
186 HL Deb, 4th series, vol. 30, col. 434 (11 February 1895).
187 HL Deb, 4th series, vol. 62, col. 992 (25 July 1898). Local Government (Ireland) Act 1898 (61&62 Vict., c.37).

Lord Atkinson did not avoid partisan subjects when making contributions to parliamentary debates, contrary to T.M. Healy's assertion that 'in his twenty years as a Law Lord he never trespassed on the political domain'.[188] He gave a detailed critique of the Evicted Tenants (Ireland) Bill 1907 and the Land Bill of 1909, saying of the former that 'it has been my good or evil fortune through a long official career in Ireland to have taken part in shaping the agrarian legislation that has been passed for that country from 1889 to 1905, and I do not like the last and fairest member of this legislative progeny to be mutilated before my eyes in silence'.[189] He had strong views on the constitutional position of the House of Lords, an issue of bitter political controversy in the first decade of the century. The ability of the house to refuse to pass legislation that had already been approved by the House of Commons, while seen in Ireland primarily in the context of Home Rule, had a wider context in British politics. After 1905 the Unionist majority in the House of Lords engaged more generally in obstruction of the legislative programme of the Liberal government, leading Lloyd George, then the chancellor of the Exchequer, to say that the House of Lords 'is not the watchdog of the constitution, it is Mr Balfour's poodle'[190] (Arthur Balfour, the former prime minister, then being the leader of the opposition). As a constitutional crisis developed in those years Atkinson voted as part of the large majority in the House of Lords (75 to 350) that rejected the budget (the Finance Bill) in November 1909, precipitating a general election in January 1910 (and resulting in the curious title of the Finance (1909–10) Act 1910). More significantly, because the vote was expected to be very close, much more so than the 1909 vote, he was one of a number of 'ditchers' or die-hard Unionists (including Lord Halsbury) who voted against the Parliament Bill in August 1911. This Bill provided that the House of Lords thereafter could delay but no longer block legislation that had been approved by the House of Commons, and was passed in the House of Lords by 131 votes to 114.[191] Lords Collins and Macnaghten also voted against the budget in 1909 and in 1911 Macnaghten voted for a Unionist resolution (passed by 281 votes to 68) declaring that a government plan to create a sufficient number of new peers, if necessary, in order to secure the passing of the Bill was 'a gross violation of constitutional liberty'.[192] In 1922 when Lord Carson was under criticism for expressing strong political opinions while a Law Lord (see p. 482) he asserted that in 1912 Macnaghten had felt it 'his duty when he thought danger and calamities were threatening his native land to come forward as a lord of appeal in ordinary and sign the Covenant for resistance to Home Rule if any attempt was made to put it into force against that portion of his country from which he came'[193]

188 T.M. Healy, *Letters and leaders*, p. 177.

189 HL Deb, 4th series, vol. 179, col. 1718 (6 August 1907). Atkinson is recorded in Hansard as making 135 speeches or interventions on the 1909 Bill in October and November 1909.

190 See generally Roy Jenkins, *Mr Balfour's poodle* (London, 1954).

191 HL Deb, 5th series, vol. 9, col. 1073 (10 August 1911).

192 HL Deb, 5th series, vol. 9, col. 878 (8 August 1911).

193 HL Deb, 5th series, vol. 49, col. 932 (29 March 1922).

OTHER APPOINTMENTS

Lords O'Hagan and Ashbourne made contributions to the judicial business of the house primarily but not only in the periods in which they were not holding office as lord chancellor of Ireland. Attention to the functions of that office, even if the holder were not also (as Ashbourne, exceptionally, was) a member of the Cabinet, would have precluded any close degree of attention to judicial business in London, as Ashbourne had acknowledged in 1889 (see p. 449). O'Hagan had been made a peer in 1870 and sat as a judge in the House of Lords on over 100 appeals between 1872 and 1883, principally in the years 1874–80. These appeals included two leading cases from Ireland, *Doherty v Allman*[194] (on ameliorating waste) and *O'Rorke v Bolingbroke*[195] (on unconscionable transactions). He concurred in the decision in *Ashbury Railway Carriage & Iron Company v Riche*[196] that a company had no capacity to ratify a transaction that was outside its powers. He gave a frank description of some judicial appellate work when telling Lord Spencer, the lord lieutenant, in 1872 that 'I have been working at the appeals in the House of Lords, [not legible, perhaps 'heavy and stupid enough'?] and the dullness of the labour has been unrelieved by political excitement'.[197]

Ashbourne's position, like that of O'Hagan but over a more extended period of time, was more political than that of the lords of appeal in ordinary. He had been a member of the House of Commons (for Dublin University), and a leading debater for the Conservative party, before being made a peer. For over 25 years after 1885, for 17 of which he was lord chancellor, he was a front bench member in the House of Lords, speaking on many party political subjects, including major speeches against the Home Rule bills of 1893 and 1912.[198] He was responsible for the management in the house of the Bill that was enacted as the Local Government (Ireland) Act 1898.[199]

He sat in 137 appeals in the House of Lords and 20 in the Privy Council, of which 124 in the House of Lords and 18 in the Privy Council, or over 90% of the total, took place in the years (1886, 1892–5, and after 1905) when the Unionists were in opposition and he was out of office. The only appeal in which he sat in 1897/8 was an important one, *Allen v Flood*,[200] which raised issues of boycotting in the context of a trade union dispute. It occupies 181 pages in the law reports, reflecting its significance in the law of torts and its political sensitivity. The lord chancellor, Lord Halsbury, revived a historic procedure, widely regarded as defunct and not used since, of asking a panel of eight judges of the High Court in England to give advisory opinions to the lords, having first established an unusually

194 (1877–78) 3 App. Cas. 709.
195 (1876–77) 2 App. Cas. 714.
196 (1875) LR 7 HL 653.
197 O'Hagan to Spencer, 10 March 1872 (O'Hagan Papers, D 2777/8/191).
198 HL Deb, 4th series, vol. 17, cols. 239–54 (6 September 1893), and 5th series, vol. 13, col. 721 (30 January 1913).
199 Cadogan to Ashbourne, 10 May 1898 (Ashbourne Papers, B.22/7).
200 [1898] AC 1.

large panel of nine members of the house to hear the appeal. It was held by a majority of 6–3 (with Halsbury, Ashbourne and Morris constituting the minority) that a trade union official who, arising out of what used to be called a demarcation dispute, induced an employer to dismiss two workers belonging to a rival trade union by threatening strike action had not committed an actionable wrong. Macnaghten showed Ashbourne a draft of his judgment.[201]

A related issue came before the house a few years later in *Quinn v Leathem*,[202] the headnote to the official report of which includes the statement '*Allen v Flood* explained, and its real effect stated'. The house upheld a decision of the Court of Appeal in Ireland (on which appeal Ashbourne had sat) that where the trial court found that a combination of people, as distinct from an individual, using such methods had caused damage to a business the tort of conspiracy would then have been committed. The former chief justice of Ireland, Ronan Keane, has remarked that 'of the Irish appeals *Quinn v Leathem* is perhaps the one that left the most enduring impression on the common law'.[203]

Ashbourne's judicial work in the House of Lords was deprecated in a remark made about him in 1908 by Lord Loreburn (lord chancellor between 1905 and 1912) that 'I have to keep him away … useless or worse'.[204] (Three quarters of a century later Loreburn was himself to be the subject of a crisp dismissal by Professor Heuston, that 'he was not interested in law, and his perfunctory judgments are of no interest to the jurist'.)[205] The lord chancellor was responsible for nominating the panel of judges to hear any appeal, and the comment was made to the prime minister, Asquith, in the course of an exposition of Loreburn's apprehension of an increasing difficulty in maintaining a strong final court. The impression thus given by him of reluctance to make use of Ashbourne's services was not however borne out by the facts. In the cases reported in the official law reports (Appeal Cases) between 1907 and 1912, which broadly correspond to appeals heard in those years, Ashbourne sat 71 times, an average of a dozen a year, including particularly active years as reported in 1908 and 1909, when he sat 18 and 25 times respectively. The appeals on which he sat over the years included the Nordenfelt restrictive covenant case in 1894, *Russell v Russell* in 1897 (in which he dissented), *Pearson v Dublin Corporation* in 1907,[206] an important stamp duty case, *C.I.R. v Maple & Co. (Paris)*[207] and the long running Lough Neagh eel fishery

201 Macnaghten to Ashbourne, 9 December 1897 (Ashbourne Papers, B.98/2).

202 [1901] AC 495. The manner in which this case and *Allen v Flood* were considered by the House of Lords was the subject of a detailed review by Prof. Heuston in 'Judicial prosopography', *Law Quarterly Review* (1986), pp 90–113.

203 Ronan Keane, 'The role of the Law Lords in relation to Ireland until 1922' in Blom-Cooper, Drewry and Dickson (eds), op. cit., p. 298.

204 Loreburn to Asquith, 27 December 1908 (Asquith Papers), 11.247; R.F.V. Heuston, *Lives of the lord chancellors, 1885–1940* (Oxford, 1964), p. 148.

205 Entry on Loreburn in A.W.B. Simpson (ed.), *Biographical dictionary of the common law* (London, 1984), p. 445).

206 [1907] AC 351.

207 [1908] AC 22.

case.[208] At first sight 'useless' would seem an unjustified and harsh remark on his judicial contribution and reputation.

Three Irish judges who were eligible to participate in the judicial business of the House of Lords, but did not do so, were Lord O'Brien of Kilfenora, Lord Shandon and Lord Glenavy. O'Brien was lord chief justice of Ireland between 1889 and 1913, being made a peer in 1900. Salisbury told Cadogan at the time that Balfour had proposed O'Brien's peerage 'in order to strengthen the H. of Lords Appeal Court in its Irish element'.[209] Although O'Brien was not regarded as overworked in his discharge of the duties of lord chief justice there would have been obvious practical difficulties in his sitting on appeals in the House of Lords, much as Ashbourne saw in 1889 for a lord chancellor, and the question of him doing so may not have arisen. He would have sat at first instance or been a member of a divisional court, or of the Court of Appeal, on a number of Irish cases that were the subject of appeals to the Lords so could not have provided Irish law expertise for any appeal on such cases. It thus seems unlikely that Balfour's comment was meant seriously, and since O'Brien was an inveterate seeker of position and honours his elevation to the peerage in May 1900 most likely reflected non-legal considerations. Notes taken by Salisbury's private secretary, Sir Schomberg McDonnell, about proposals for the conferring of honours record limpidly, in the case of O'Brien, that the proposers (in 1898) had been Cadogan and 'self'.[210] In 1904 he attended, with some other legally qualified peers, a meeting of the committee of privileges of the House of Lords on a claim to an Irish peerage, the barony of Le Power and Coroghmore.[211] The long-standing claim, going back centuries, was not concluded until 1922.

Shandon was the title taken by Ignatius O'Brien (lord chancellor of Ireland, 1913–18) on being removed from office and simultaneously offered a peerage in the summer of 1918, and Glenavy was the title taken by James H.M. Campbell (his successor, 1918–21). Lord Birkenhead was the lord chancellor of Great Britain in those years, and both Shandon and Glenavy were told by him that they would not be called to sit as members considering any appeal.[212]

Two appointments to the House of Lords that did not take place were those of Denis Henry and Sir John Ross. Edward Jones, a lord justice of appeal in Northern Ireland, stated in his autobiography, published in 1987, that Denis Henry had been offered a position as a lord of appeal at about the time that he accepted office as lord chief justice of Northern Ireland (in August 1921).[213] The maximum

208 *Johnston v O'Neill*, [1911] AC 552.

209 Cadogan to Ashbourne, 7 May 1900 (Ashbourne Papers, B.22/17).

210 Honours nomination book (Schomberg McDonnell Papers (PRONI), D4091/A/3/4/1).

211 *ILT&SJ*, vol. 38, p. 97 (27 February 1904); Sir John William Rivallan De La Poer, *Proceedings and minutes of evidence taken before the committee for privileges* (London, 1922).

212 R.F.V. Heuston, 'Legal history and the author; some practical problems of authorship' in W.N. Osborough (ed.), *The Irish Legal History Society: inaugural addresses* (Dublin, 1989), p. 30.

213 Edward Jones, *Jones LJ, his life and times; the autobiography of the Right Honorable Sir Edward Jones* (Enniskillen, 1987); A.D. McDonnell, *The life of Sir Denis Henry: Catholic unionist* (Belfast, 2000), p. 92.

permitted number of Law Lords at the time, under the Appellate Jurisdiction Act 1913, was six. Any such offer would thus have related to the only vacancy among them that existed in 1921 (indeed, between 1918 and 1923), namely that arising on the death of Lord Moulton in March 1921, which was filled by the appointment of Carson in May. In August 1922 Sir John Ross, faced with the imminent abolition of the office of lord chancellor of Ireland, and willing to continue in judicial work if possible, proposed to the home secretary that he would be appointed as an additional lord of appeal in ordinary, and that the statute of 1913 just referred to would be appropriately amended. He wrote that if he survived Lord Atkinson [Ross was a decade younger] it would then not be necessary to appoint another Irish lawyer in Atkinson's place upon his retirement, and that the government might find it useful to 'have me on hand in London to consult as to facts, when any Irish difficulty presented itself, as many are likely to do'. The government did not consider it practical to introduce any such statutory amendment.[214]

Some Irish judges, sitting or retired, in addition to the Lords of Appeal in Ordinary, were appointed as members of the Judicial Committee of the Privy Council. These included Sir Joseph Napier (lord chancellor of Ireland in 1858–9), Stephen Woulfe Flanagan (judge of the Landed Estates Court 1869–77, and of the Chancery division, 1878–85), Christopher Palles (chief baron of the Exchequer, 1874–1916) and Gerald FitzGibbon (lord justice of appeal, 1878–1909). Napier sat on over 50 reported appeals between 1869 and 1873, Woulfe Flanagan on four in 1888 and 1889, and Palles on a single appeal in 1912. The hearing of this appeal, about the marriage laws of Quebec, was arranged to suit his convenience, the Committee sitting on a Monday and Tuesday to facilitate his return to Belfast later in the week to take up his place at the assizes.[215]

FitzGibbon did not sit on the hearing of any appeal, and indeed at the time of his appointment in May 1900 was not expected to do so. Ashbourne told Salisbury in May 1900 that 'it would be well received by the legal profession in Ireland if you offered FitzGibbon a seat on the English Privy Council', this comment being made at the time of the controversy over the successor to Morris not having been an Irish lawyer. He wrote again a week later to emphasise that being eligible to be summoned to sit as a member of the Judicial Committee would be a mark of respect to FitzGibbon 'but of course his judicial duties over here fully occupy his time'.[216] The vice-chancellor, Hedges Eyre Chatterton, declined an invitation from Balfour in 1890 to accept a place on the Council.

Lastly, for completeness, it might be noted that four other appointments of Irishmen as lords of appeal in ordinary were made in this period, each of whom

214 Ross to Shortt, 27 August 1922 (TNAUK, HO 317/67); Shortt to Ross, 18 October 1922 (TNAUK, CO 739/16).

215 *ILT&SJ*, vol. 46, pp 190 and 203 (23 July and 10 August 1912). See also V.T.H. Delany, *Christopher Palles: his life and times* (Dublin, 1960), p. 147.

216 Ashbourne to Salisbury, 7 and 14 May 1900 (Salisbury Papers).

had been in practice at the English Bar. The first of these was Sir Edward Macnaghten (Lord Macnaghten of Runkerry), an MP for constituencies in Co. Antrim from 1880 up to his appointment in 1887, and who in the next quarter of a century, up to his death in 1913, was to become one of the most distinguished of all Law Lords. His father, Sir Edmund Charles Workman Macnaghten, had been called to the Bar in 1813, held a judicial office in Calcutta, and was MP for Co. Antrim 1846–52. The second Irishman was Sir Charles Russell (Lord Russell of Killowen), MP for Dundalk 1880–5, who was appointed in 1894 but within a matter of weeks was appointed lord chief justice of England and did not sit thereafter in the House of Lords in a judicial capacity. (His fourth son, Francis Xavier Joseph Russell, was appointed a lord of appeal, with his father's title, in 1929 and served up to his death in 1946, and his son, Charles Ritchie Russell, was in turn appointed as a lord of appeal with the same title in 1975 and served up to 1982.) The others were Sir Richard Henn Collins (Lord Collins of Kensington) who was appointed in 1907 and Sir Edward Carson (Lord Carson of Duncairn) in 1921.

Macnaghten and Russell spent their careers at the Bar entirely in England, and the former had a substantial home on the coast of Co. Antrim, and maintained strong links there, where he sat as a magistrate. Russell had practised as a solicitor in Belfast for a couple of years in the 1850s before being called to the Bar in England.[217] Collins was born and educated in Ireland, at Dungannon and Trinity College, before finishing his education at Cambridge University and being called to the English Bar. He was master of the rolls for six years before appointment as a Law Lord in 1907 but being already quite unwell he made little contribution in that office before he retired in 1910.

Carson was called to the Irish Bar in 1877 and became a QC in 1889. He practised in Ireland for about 15 years and then spent the latter and more significant part of his legal career at the English Bar, to which he was called in 1893. A few months later it was noted that he had 'come back to his old haunts at the Four Courts specially' for a case.[218] He was appointed solicitor general in England (and knighted, as was customary for law officers there) in 1900 and held office as attorney general for a few months in 1915. He was MP for Dublin University 1892–1918 and for the Duncairn division of Belfast 1918–21. His standing in 1921 derived not so much from his leading position in law and at the Bar as from politics and his leadership for the previous decade (up to February 1921) of the Ulster Unionists. His appointment as a Law Lord in May 1921 was made possible, as mentioned above, by the death in March of Lord Moulton, a Law Lord since 1912, and was not seen as reflecting a position at the Irish Bar. He retired in 1929 and died in 1935.

217 R. Barry O'Brien, *The life of Lord Russell of Killowen* (London, 1901), pp 29–55.
218 *ILT&SJ*, vol. 28, p. 75 (10 February 1894).

CHAPTER FIFTEEN

Change and continuity in the early 1920s

IN THE EARLY 1920s significant changes took place in the court system and judiciary of Ireland, in parallel with the great political changes on the island. Between 1920 and 1922 political settlements were made by the British government both with the unionist community in Ulster, which for decades had resisted any form of devolved government for Ireland ('Home Rule'), and with the wider nationalist community which, after decades fruitlessly seeking such Home Rule, had become radicalised and now sought independence. The latter settlement was rejected by a section of the Republican movement in the south, leading to a destructive but 'futile and half-hearted'[1] civil war in 1922–23. Between 1919 and 1923 there was a widespread breakdown in civic order by reason of the guerrilla insurgency of the Irish Republican Army, the actions of official military forces (including reprisals and much other undisciplined and unlawful, indeed lawless, conduct that was approved or tolerated by the British government), the collapse of ordinary policing, sectarian violence, and lastly in consequence of the civil war.

The courts and judiciary were a branch of (and hence in any event publicly associated with) a widely contested structure of government, and one element in that contest was a challenge to the official courts, both by disrupting their workings, particularly at local level, and by the operations of a system of alternative courts. Dáil Éireann was a national assembly or parliament proclaimed in January 1919 and composed of the Sinn Fein MPs elected at the general election in December 1918 who had not taken their seats at Westminster. It set about creating an alternative system of government (what has sometimes been described as a 'counter-state') with ministries, new laws in the form of decrees, etc. In June 1920 this shadow government took steps to establish courts of law and equity, in due course comprising Parish, District and Circuit Courts and a Supreme Court.[2] These existed for a couple of years until they were suspended by the new independent government. A handful of members of the Bar served interchangeably as judges of the Circuit and Supreme Courts.

'Dáil Court' was defined in a statute passed in 1923 as 'any court which was constituted under a decree made in the year 1920 by the Minister for Home Affairs purporting to act under the authority of Dáil Éireann' etc.,[3] as to which Johnston J observed in the High Court in 1934 that 'it is evident that the legislature was not

1 Tom Garvin, *1922: the birth of Irish democracy* (Dublin, 1996), p. 45.

2 Dáil Decree no. 18 (29 June 1920, 5/1920); Brian Farrell, 'The legislation of a 'revolutionary' assembly: Dáil decrees, 1919–1922', *Irish Jurist*, vol. 10 (1975), pp 112–27; Mary Kotsonouris, *Retreat from Revolution: the Dáil courts, 1920–24* (Dublin, 1994), pp 23 and 29.

3 Dáil Éireann Courts (Winding-up) Act 1923, s1.

very clear as to what exactly had happened in that year'.[4] Many courthouses used by the established lower courts were closed by county councils or deliberately destroyed and rendered unusable. This prevention, disruption and associated boycotting of sittings of those courts, and diversion of disputes to the Dáil courts, was of significance in political terms as a local assertion or manifestation of national spirit and sovereignty,[5] and in legal terms these courts provided a pressure valve for the resolution of local disputes.

The Government of Ireland Act, which was enacted in December 1920,[6] made provision for separate parliamentary, governmental and judicial systems north and south of the border that it defined. Northern Ireland was constituted by s1 of the Act as six of the nine counties of Ulster (Antrim, Armagh, Down, Fermanagh, Londonderry and Tyrone) and Southern Ireland as all the other counties (26) on the island. The Act had different political and governmental effects north and south of that border when its principal (non-judicial) provisions were brought into operation in May 1921, after the government had made 'such regulations as seem necessary or proper for setting in motion the parliaments and governments of Northern Ireland and Southern Ireland'.[7] General elections were then called for the two parliaments. The Northern Ireland parliament, which had a large Unionist majority, met in June and nominated ministers for the government, with Sir James Craig MP becoming prime minister. In the corresponding election in the South, which the Dáil had resolved in May would 'be regarded as elections to Dáil Éireann',[8] no constituency was contested and every candidate was returned unopposed. Sinn Féin held every seat except the four in the Dublin University constituency. The parliament of Southern Ireland met formally on 28 June 1921, attended only by those university members (one of whom was Gerald FitzGibbon KC, a son of lord justice FitzGibbon and later (1924–38) a judge of the Supreme Court of the Irish Free State) and 15 nominated senators,[9] and was opened by the lord chief justice of Ireland, Thomas F. Molony. Since the great majority of its members had abstained from attendance and did not take the required oath of membership within 14 days of the parliament being summoned it was not properly constituted, no government could be formed under the 1920 Act and the parliament was defunct.[10] The existing structure of government, headed by the chief secretary for Ireland as a member of the cabinet, accordingly continued in place. In August the newly elected Dáil met, thus constituting the second Dáil, in succession to the first Dáil proclaimed in January 1919.

4 *O'Crowley v Minister for Justice and Minister for Finance*, [1935] IR 536 at 544.
5 See W.N. Osborough, 'Law in Ireland, 1916–26' in (1) *NILQ*, vol. 23 (1972) p. 48 and (2) W.N. Osborough, *Studies in Irish legal history* (Dublin, 1999), p. 270, at p. 50 and pp 271–2.
6 10&11 Geo. 5, c.7.
7 Government of Ireland Act 1920, ss69 and 73; Statutory Rules & Orders (SR&O) 1921, no. 533 (24 March 1921). See generally Arthur S. Quekett, *The constitution of Northern Ireland* (2 vols, Belfast, 1928).
8 Dáil Éireann debates, vol. F, no. 21 (10 May 1921).
9 *Irish Times*, 29 June 1921.
10 Government of Ireland Act 1920, s72(1).

The Act did have a uniform effect north and south, however, with respect to the judicial system, and on the appointed day for that purpose, 1 October 1921,[11] the structure of the Irish superior courts, as established by statute in 1877, was changed by the constitution of separate courts in each part of Ireland. This reformation of the court system endured and established firm roots in Northern Ireland, but was short-lived in what became the independent south, as the Irish Free State, where it was replaced in 1924 by new courts.[12] The two court systems were briefly linked by the cross-border element of a common High Court of Appeal for Ireland, presided over by the lord chancellor of Ireland.[13] This existed for some 15 months, sitting about 20 times between 15 December 1921[14] and 5 December 1922, the day before it was abolished,[15] and a number of its judgments are reported in the 1922 and 1923 Irish Reports. It sat in Dublin and in Belfast, as occasion required, depending upon whether the appeal it was hearing arose from the Court of Appeal in either city.[16] The northern judge who most commonly sat in the court was Andrews LJ, although Henry LCJ travelled to Dublin on five separate occasions in 1922 to sit as a member of the Court.[17]

The new superior courts in the North had a total complement of five judges,[18] which remained their number for decades, perhaps reflecting a modest workload,[19] largely 'run of the mill stuff',[20] until provision was made for two additional High Court judges to be appointed in 1968.[21] Four of the five men first appointed had not previously held judicial office. The first lord chief justice was Denis Henry, who in August was appointed before the court itself had formally been established

11 SR&O 1921, no. 1527 (27 September 1921).

12 Courts of Justice Act 1924.

13 Government of Ireland Act 1920, s42. See Richard McBride, 'Sir John Ross: the last lord chancellor of Ireland, 1921–1922' in David Capper, Conor McCormick and Norma Dawson (eds), *Law and constitutional change* (Cambridge, 2025), pp 181–97.

14 *ILT&SJ*, vol. 55, p. 313 (17 December 1921).

15 Memorandum in 1922 Irish Reports; Irish Free State (Consequential Provisions) Act 1922 (13 Geo. 5 (session 2), c2), s6(1).

16 Government of Ireland Act 1920, s42(3).

17 Memorandum on the setting up of the Supreme Court of Judicature of Northern Ireland and other matters incidental thereto, 1 October 1921–31 July 1922, p. 25, para. 40 (T311/CAB 6/57 (PRONI)). This memorandum, dated 31 August 1922, was written by Moore LJ (A.R. Hart, *A history of the Bar and Inn of Court of Northern Ireland* (Belfast, 2013), p. 104), although it is stated to be signed by A. Newton Anderson, permanent secretary to the Supreme Court of Judicature. Moore LJ had intended that this would be published as a record or narrative of this setting up but the lord chief justice and the prime minister, Sir James Craig, decided against publication; *ILT&SJ*, vol. 56, p. 48 (25 February 1922), p. 124 (20 May 1922), p. 170 (15 & 22 July 1922), p. 264 (4 November 1922) and p. 289 (2 December 1922).

18 See Lord Carswell, 'Founding a legal system: the early justices of Northern Ireland' in Felix M. Larkin and N.M. Dawson (eds), *Lawyers, the law and history: Irish Legal History Society discourses and other papers, 2005–2011* (Dublin, 2013), pp 15–28, for some account of the first (and some subsequent) judges.

19 Sir Declan Morgan, *Centenary lecture on the lord chief justices of Northern Ireland* (Belfast, 8 December 2021), paras 34 and 38.

20 Lord Carswell, op. cit., p. 23.

21 Administration of Justice Act 1968, s1(1)(d).

(as required by law)[22] and was duly sworn in, at the Town Hall in Portrush, Co. Antrim, by the lord chancellor, Sir John Ross. Henry subsequently received a baronetcy.[23] The two lords justices of appeal were William Moore, the only existing judge who exercised a statutory option to sit in Northern Ireland,[24] and James Andrews, and the first two High Court judges were Daniel Martin Wilson and Thomas Watters Brown, both of whom had been MPs for constituencies in Co. Down, and law officers. Mr Brown was appointed a few months later than the other judges, in February 1922,[25] and the official photograph of the new Supreme Court of Judicature taken at the opening of the court in October 1921 thus shows four judges.[26]

The judges of the superior courts were generally understood to be nominated by the Northern Ireland cabinet. However this was a matter not of law but of advice or recommendation and custom and practice, since the law relating to the superior courts and their judges was not within the competence of that cabinet, as being one of the matters reserved to the British government under the 1920 Act. Judicial appointments (in the form of advice to the monarch) were thus a responsibility of that government,[27] initially through the home secretary. The ordinary working of the recommendation procedure was demonstrated in 1925 when Craig, the prime minister, thanked William Joynson-Hicks, the home secretary, 'for the promptitude with which you met my wishes regarding the appointment [of William Moore] to the vacant lord chief justiceship'.[28] The announcement in Belfast at that time of another appointment, to the High Court, drew a protocol reproof – too late, as it transpired – from the Home Office, which observed 'that the official announcement of appointment in reserved matters should really come from Whitehall and that any announcement made here [i.e., in Belfast] should take the form of a statement that an appointment was being announced in London'.[29] A much more substantive controversy arose in 1946 when the home secretary declined to approve the recommendation from Belfast for the appointment of the attorney general, William Lowry, to fill a vacancy in the Court of Appeal and instead appointed Samuel Clarke Porter, the father of the Bar. (Lowry was appointed to the High Court the following year.)

Porter, who was then aged 71, had bypassed the government at Stormont when seeking appointment,[30] using his links with the Labour party then in office in London. He had stood as a Labour candidate in the Belfast Pottinger constituency in the 1918 general election, and in his practice had specialised in trade union and workmen's compensation law. Sir Basil Brooke, the prime minister, argued strongly

22 Government of Ireland Act 1920, schedule 7, part 3, 1(d).
23 *ILT&SJ*, vol. 56, p. 295 (9 December 1922).
24 Government of Ireland Act 1920, schedule 7, part 3, 1(a).
25 *ILT&SJ*, vol. 56, p. 21 (28 January 1922).
26 A.R. Hart, op. cit., p. 90.
27 Government of Ireland Act 1920, ss 4(1) and 47(1).
28 Craig to Joynson-Hicks, 21 October 1925 (CAB 9/I/10/1 (PRONI)).
29 Tallents to Blackmore, 22 October 1925 (CAB 9/I/10/1 (PRONI).
30 *Irish Times*, 12 July 1956; Sir Declan Morgan, op. cit., para [40].

but unsuccessfully that for a recommendation to be rejected was unprecedented, saying that 'as the constitutional position is not understood by the general public' it will look as if the government at Stormont 'has been rebuffed by the Imperial government'.[31] In 1949 responsibility for the appointment of judges in the superior courts was transferred from the home secretary to the lord chancellor of Great Britain. On the retirement of Sir James Andrews as lord chief justice in 1951 the chancellor required some persuasion before accepting that Lord MacDermott, who had been appointed a lord of appeal in ordinary in 1947, could be spared from the judicial work of the House of Lords to return to Belfast to take office in succession to Sir James.

The sittings in Belfast of the new courts took place initially in the courthouse of the Antrim County Council on the Crumlin Road, where the new court was inaugurated with some ceremony on 25 October 1921,[32] the first day of the Michaelmas law term. The accommodation there for the courts and their administrative offices and the Bar was inadequate in many respects but had to suffice for a decade pending the construction and opening in 1933 of the Royal Courts of Justice building in Chichester Street. Other potential locations, including a part of the grounds of the Royal Belfast Academical Institution at College Square,[33] were considered. Sir Charles Brett, a distinguished solicitor and architectural historian, has described the building as 'an interesting study in the Recessional-Imperial style of British architecture'. He observed that it was 'much more satisfactory internally than externally', that its central hall was 'in many ways, the best room in the city', and that the courtrooms were 'both impressive and practical – even comfortable'.[34] The internal layout and design was widely considered to be more satisfactory for the profession, judiciary and public than the courts in Dublin and London, and credit for insistence on this was given to the attorney general (1925–37), Anthony Brutus Babington.[35]

In this new court system there was an emphasis upon the continuity with the former judicial regime. Under s41 of the 1920 Act all enactments and rules relating to the court established in 1877 were to be applicable to the new courts to be constituted, north and south, save as specifically provided in the Act or as might be subsequently modified or adapted. The machinery of the new superior courts in the North 'almost inevitably followed the machinery of the Dublin courts with such modifications and excisions as were then thought expedient'.[36] Henry LCJ acknowledged the constant help and advice in the establishment of the new superior courts in the North that was given by Molony LCJ, who also made available all the experience and services of the staff in the Four Courts.[37] The

31 Brooke to Chuter Ede, 26 February 1946 (CAB 9/I/10/3 (PRONI)).
32 *Irish Times*, 26 October 1921; George Hill Smith, *A sketch of the Supreme Court of Judicature of Northern Ireland* (Belfast, 1926), p. 10.
33 *ILT&SJ*, vol. 58, p. 32 (2 February 1924).
34 C.E.B. Brett, *Court and market houses of the province of Ulster* (Belfast, 1973), p. 50.
35 A.R. Hart, op. cit., pp 129–34; Lord Carswell, op. cit., p. 26.
36 Lord MacDermott, 'Law and practice in Northern Ireland', *NILQ*, vol. 10 (1953), p. 47, at 71.
37 SCJNI 1922 memorandum, p. 28, para. 46.

salaries of the judges, as modified (reduced for future appointments in 1926, and raised in 1952[38]), continued to be expressed as those payable by virtue of s18 of the 1877 Act. Assizes continued to be held, and that system 'was still in fairly flourishing condition'[39] in 1957 when Robert Carswell, later Lord Carswell, was called to the Bar, although it was discontinued in 1979.[40] On the new circuit of Northern Ireland 'many of the venerable traditions and customs of the old assize circuits of Ireland are maintained with scrupulous care'.[41] The grand jury, as a historic element in the criminal jurisdiction of the assizes, remained a part of the judicial system in the North.[42] It was discontinued in the South.[43]

The legal profession in the North re-structured itself. The Northern Law Society was converted into the Incorporated Law Society of Northern Ireland as a new representative and regulatory body for solicitors.[44] In January 1922 the Bar, which in October 1921 had appointed a committee to prepare rules, established a Bar Council (to which the Northern Ireland Parliament made a grant of £4,000 to fund an initial stock of law books and reports)[45] and a circuit of Northern Ireland, which was formally acknowledged by regulation with effect from 1 February.[46] The Council soon declined an invitation to nominate members to the Bar Council in Dublin on the basis that the latter Council had no role or function in relation to that circuit.[47] Regulations were made in January 1922 to re-arrange the circuits to reflect the existence of two separate jurisdictions, and the North East and North West circuits, both of which had included counties on each side of the new border, ceased to exist. A new Midland circuit was set up, consisting of counties Meath, Westmeath, Longford, Cavan, Donegal, Monaghan and Louth. County Offaly was joined to the Connaught circuit, the Munster circuit comprised counties Cork, Clare, Kerry and Limerick, and the Leinster circuit comprised counties Wicklow, Wexford, Waterford, Tipperary, Laois, Kilkenny, Carlow and Kildare.[48]

In October 1921 the benchers of King's Inns established a separate Northern committee for all matters of education and discipline in the North.[49] However it soon became evident that the preservation within the framework of that Inn of a

38 Supreme Court of Judicature (Northern Ireland) Act 1926; Judicial Offices (Salaries, etc.) Act 1952.
39 Robert Carswell, 'Eheu fugaces: fifty years in the Northern Ireland courts' in Daire Hogan and Colum Kenny (eds), *Changes in law and practice* (Dublin, 2013), p. 3 at 5.
40 Judicature (Northern Ireland) Act 1978, s46(4); Hart, op. cit., p. 261.
41 Editorial on 'A review of the Supreme Court of Northern Ireland', *NILQ*, vol. 7 (1946), pp 3–19, at 7.
42 Editorial, op. cit., p. 6.
43 Courts of Justice Act 1924, s27.
44 SCJNI 1922 memorandum, p. 25, para. 39; Alan Hewitt, *The Law Society of Northern Ireland* (Belfast, 2010).
45 *ILT&SJ*, vol. 57, p. 268 (27 October 1923).
46 Hart, op. cit., p. 183; SCJNI 1922 memorandum, p. 23, para. 36; Order in Council, 31 January 1922 (*ILT&SJ*, vol. 56. p. 38 (11 February 1922)).
47 Hart, op. cit., p. 99.
48 Order in Council, 5 January 1922 (*ILT&SJ*, vol. 56 p. 7 (statutes/orders, 1922)).
49 SCJNI 1922 memorandum, p. 20, para. 31(6).

single governing body for the Bars of what had become two distinct and politically hostile entities was not sustainable. In the course of 1925 the strains and tensions arising from 'inexorable and irreconcilable changes in the political, constitutional and legal frameworks within which the Bar had to exist in each jurisdiction'[50] had transpired to be no longer capable of containment, let alone management. At the end of July 1925, after some acrimonious correspondence, the Northern committee dissociated itself from the King's Inns, and in January 1926 the establishment of a separate Inn of Court of Northern Ireland was resolved upon at a meeting of the Bench and Bar, chaired by the lord chief justice. For decades thereafter, until a rapprochement took place in the 1970s,[51] there was to be little formal contact or co-operation between the judicial and Bar establishments in the two jurisdictions, although a level of amity and historic goodwill was symbolised in 1938 by the joint conferring of honorary degrees by Dublin University on the two chief justices, James Andrews and Timothy Sullivan.[52]

The new Inn took steps to develop an association with the inns of court in London, as had been envisaged a few years earlier,[53] and in 1928 it made arrangements to restore an old requirement (made optional in 1885) that students for the Bar would attend three terms of commons – would 'dine', as commonly understood – at one of those inns of court. The Inn also required students to pass one of the Bar Final exams in London, and permitted them to attend law lectures in London for one year as an alternative to then attending a course of legal education at Queen's University Belfast.[54]

The constitution of the superior courts in the North as an integral element in the governance of Northern Ireland, within the United Kingdom, was thus firmly established from the autumn of 1921, whatever about the numerous and varied practical problems that had been presented and many of which remained to be addressed or at least coped with.[55] Events in the South took a different course. The superior courts in Dublin were similarly formally re-constituted on 1 October 1921 as the Supreme Court of Southern Ireland, with divisions as before of the High Court and the Court of Appeal. They had a greater seeming continuity with the old court regime than in Belfast, not least in their location at the Four Courts, in the fact that 'an established administrative machine was on hand to oversee the innovations',[56] and in complete continuity of their membership (with the exception of Moore J), extending even to the title of the lord chief justice of Ireland, since

50 Hart, op. cit., p. 109, and see more generally chapter 4, 'King's Inns and the foundation of the Inn of Court of Northern Ireland' (pp 93–109), and A.R. Hart, 'King's Inns and the foundation of the Inn of Court of Northern Ireland: the northern perspective' in Felix M. Larkin and N.M. Dawson (eds), *Lawyers, the law and history* (Dublin, 2013), pp 194–208.

51 Hart, op. cit., pp 317–20.

52 *ILT&SJ*, vol. 72, p. 205 (9 July 1938).

53 Hart, op. cit., p. 98.

54 Editorial, op. cit., pp 16–17; Lord MacDermott, op. cit., p. 75; Hart, op. cit., pp 137–42.

55 SCJNI 1922 memorandum, pp 2–13, paras. 3–20 and pp 28–9, paras. 47–8.

56 W.N. Osborough, 'Law in Ireland, 1916–26', (1) op. cit., p. 52; (2) op. cit., p. 274.

Thomas F. Molony had successfully resisted, for himself, a proposed title of lord chief justice of Southern Ireland. The political situation in Dublin at the time, however, was extremely fluid and uncertain. A truce or ceasefire in the war of independence had been agreed in July 1921, following which negotiations between the government and representatives of Dáil Éireann commenced in London on 11 October. The public awaited the outcome of these talks with 'hope, impatience and apprehension',[57] and (as appears below) the judges expressed concerns about their prospects and security for their pensions. The talks eventually resulted in the signature of articles of agreement for a treaty between Great Britain and Ireland (generally known as the Treaty) on 6 December 1921 in Downing Street. This was approved by the parliament in London on 16 December and by the Dáil on 7 January 1922.[58] Those voting against the Treaty in London included (in the House of Commons) T.W. Brown, shortly to be appointed a judge of the High Court in Belfast, and (in the House of Lords) the two Irish lords of appeal, Lord Atkinson and Lord Carson, who spoke for the first time in the house.[59] This was the first in what became a series of highly critical speeches by him in the debates over the next twelve months, up to December 1922, on the legislation later required to give effect to the Treaty, in which he made many accusations of betrayal, treason and treachery against the government and his former Unionist colleagues. The lord chancellor, his old associate Lord Birkenhead, challenged the propriety of a lord of appeal participating in political controversy in this way, leading in turn to a heated debate in the House of Lords on that subject in March 1922.[60]

The Treaty provided (in article 17) for the establishment of a provisional government 'by way of provisional arrangement for the administration of Southern Ireland during the interval which must elapse between the date hereof and the constitution of a parliament and government of the Irish Free State[61] in accordance therewith'. This government was set up on 16 January 1922, following which it took possession of Dublin Castle, the historic centre of government and administration 'which for centuries had been the symbol as well as the citadel of British rule in Ireland',[62] and a withdrawal of British military forces commenced. In a proclamation on the date of appointment the new government directed that 'all Law Courts, Corporations, Councils, Departments of State, Boards, Judges, Civil Servants [etc.] hitherto acting under the authority of the British government shall continue to carry out their functions unless and until otherwise ordered by

57 Michael Laffan, *The resurrection of Ireland: the Sinn Fein party 1916–23* (Cambridge, 1999), p. 346.

58 HC Deb, 5th series, vol. 149, col. 363 (16 December 1921) and HL Deb, 5th series, vol. 48, col. 217 (also 16 December 1921); Dáil Debates, vol. T, no. 15 (7 January 1922).

59 HL Deb, 5th series, vol. 48, cols. 37–53 (14 December 1921) – 'What a fool I was. I was only a puppet, and so was Ulster, and so was Ireland, in the political game that was to get the Conservative party into power' (at col. 44).

60 HL Deb, 5th series, vol. 49, cols. 931–73 (29 March 1922).

61 The Irish language translation of which was Saorstát Éireann.

62 Annual Register 1922, p. 10.

us, pending the constitution of the parliament and government of Saorstát Éireann [etc.]'.[63] On 1 April, following enactment of the Irish Free State (Agreement) Act[64] the previous day, the British government formally transferred to the provisional government, in its various ministries and departments (Finance, Home Affairs, Agriculture, Education, etc), responsibility for the functions, powers and machinery of government.[65]

A couple of weeks later, on Good Friday, the Four Courts was occupied and then fortified by units of the IRA opposed to the Treaty, evicting the courts and enormously disrupting their work and that of all their associated offices and departments.[66] Rory O'Connor, a leader of that occupation, said that courts functioning with the authority of the provisional government, including the High Court, were being stopped by the IRA.[67] The building was destroyed some weeks later at the end of June in the commencement of hostilities in the civil war. The courts initially accommodated themselves for the rest of the year and the early months of 1923, as best they could, in the King's Inns, where it was noted that the judges and the Bar necessarily worked without 'their usual forensic costumes'.[68] They then moved to other quarters that had been prepared in Dublin Castle, remaining there until the autumn of 1931, when reconstruction of the Four Courts had been completed. In November 1922 an application for a writ of habeas corpus was made to Charles O'Connor, the master of the rolls, on behalf of Erskine Childers, a leading Republican who had been sentenced to death. O'Connor refused the application (see pp 398–9) and, in his judgment, after referring to himself as 'sitting in this temporary makeshift for a court of justice', said that the courts were functioning

> only under difficulties which, were it not for the courage and devotion to duty of its officers, would have been insurmountable. Can the court be said to be freely functioning when it requires the protection of a military guard, when the circuits of the judges are interfered with and when some of the County Court judges dare not enter their districts? I would like to know what would be the display of military force which would be required if Erskine Childers or any other prominent member of the IRA was brought to trial in Green Street? The truth is that the courts are just struggling for continued existence in the state of war which is now prevailing. They are not functioning as in times of peace.[69]

63 *ILT&SJ*, vol. 56, p. 15 (21 January 1922).
64 12 Geo. 5, c.4.
65 Provisional Government (Council of Ireland) Order, 1922 (1 April 1922).
66 *ILT&SJ*, vol. 56, p. 100 (22 April 1922).
67 *Irish Times*, 15 April 1922; Kotsonouris, op. cit., p. 74.
68 *ILT&SJ*, vol. 56, p. 144 (10 June 1922).
69 *R (Childers) v Adjutant-General of the Forces of the Irish Provisional Government*, [1923] 1 IR 5, at 15.

On 13 July 1922 the provisional government decreed that sittings of the Dáil Supreme Court would be suspended,[70] this winding-up being effected 'in a brusque and bureaucratic manner; once Irish nationalists had begun to control the apparatus of the state they could dispense with their earlier revolutionary measures'.[71] The 1920 decree 'purporting to establish courts of law and equity and criminal jurisdiction as part of the government of the Irish republic' was 'rescinded and declared to be of no effect' in more general terms by the Minister of Home Affairs a few days later, on 25 July.[72] Hugh Kennedy, then the law officer to the provisional government, told a solicitor who inquired in August 1922 about the status of some existing business before a Dáil court that 'no consideration will be given to purported hearings after the date of the decree. The courts have ceased to exist and the persons who sit in the name of such courts have no authority'.[73] The abrupt revocation of the authority of the Dáil courts led to a period of legal confusion, which was addressed the following year by the enactment of the Dáil Éireann Courts (Winding-up) Act 1923, recited as being 'an Act for the appointment of Commissioners to dispose of cases which were pending in courts established under the authority of Dáil Éireann, to establish a register of decrees of such courts and to make other provisions for the purposes of winding-up the courts aforesaid, and relieving certain hardships and anomalies which have arisen in connection with those courts'.[74] The Act provided for good order that the authority of all Dáil courts (except parish and district courts outside Dublin, for which a revocation date of 30 October 1922 was applicable) 'shall be deemed to have been withdrawn on 25 July 1922'.[75]

The 13 July decree stated that

> the courts which were instituted as a war measure by the Dáil were devised to supply tribunals acceptable to the Irish people whilst other courts were functioning under the British government. These former British courts are now in Irish hands under the terms of the Treaty. They are now Irish courts, and the necessity for duplication no longer exists … The government elected by the Irish people has a complete judicial system in its hand for which it is paying. There is no reason, therefore, why the government should not get the value of the public money which is being expended on the staff and personnel of these courts.[76]

70 Irish government: official statement re suspension of sittings of courts, 13 July 1922 (Hugh Kennedy Papers, UCDA, P. 4/1067).
71 Laffan, op. cit., p. 318.
72 Iris Oifigiuil, 1 August 1922; *O'Crowley v Minister for Justice and Minister for Finance*, [1935] IR 536, at 540; Kotsonouris, op. cit., p. 83.
73 Kennedy to Reddin & Reddin (Hugh Kennedy Papers, UCDA P. 4/1067).
74 See generally Mary Kotsonouris, *The winding up of the Dáil courts, 1922–1925* (Dublin, 2004).
75 Dáil Éireann Courts (Winding-up) Act 1923, s1(2).
76 *ILT&SJ*, vol. 56, p. 172 (15 & 22 July 1922); Osborough, 'Law in Ireland 1916–26', (1) op. cit., pp 50–1, and (2) op. cit., p. 272.

The government's concerns about the Dáil courts went beyond such funding issues, however, since its opponents in the civil war fundamentally denied that it was a lawfully constituted government at all (as was later brought out in the affidavit filed on behalf of Mr Childers in his application – 'Captain Childers does not recognise the legality of the Provisional Government ... he recognises the authority only of the Irish Republican Government and army').[77] Republican sympathisers made applications to the Dáil Supreme Court to challenge the legitimacy of the third Dáil (elected in June 1922) and for a writ of habeas corpus in respect of prisoners taken at the surrender of the Four Courts garrison, which the provisional government ignored.[78]

In January 1923 the government appointed a committee to advise on the establishment in accordance with the Constitution[79] (now in force) of courts for the exercise of the judicial power and the administration of justice in the state. This Judiciary Committee, as it was known, was chaired by the former lord chief justice and lord chancellor James Campbell (now Lord Glenavy), and its members included Charles O'Connor and Hugh Kennedy (1878–1936), who was the law adviser to the government and would soon be chief justice. Its terms of reference were expressed in suitably formal language, but were coupled with an introductory letter in more stirring terms addressed by the head of government, W.T. Cosgrave, to its members. This was written a few weeks after the independence of the Irish Free State had been recognised, and expressed a spirit or aspiration of national self-sufficiency in discounting or challenging the existing basis of jurisprudence in Ireland:

> In the long struggle for the right to rule in our own country, there has been no sphere of the administration lately ended which impressed itself on the minds of our people as a standing monument of an alien government more than the system, the machinery, and the administration of law and justice which supplanted in comparatively modern times the laws and institutions till then a living part of the living national organism. The body of laws and the system of judicature so imposed upon this nation were English (not even British) in their seed, English in their growth, English in their vitality. Their ritual, their nomenclature, were only to be understood by the student of the history of the people of Southern Britain. A remarkable and characteristic product of the genius of that people the manner of their administration prevented them from striking root in the fertile soil of this nation.
>
> Thus it comes that there is nothing more prized among our newly won liberties than the liberty to construct a system of judiciary and an administration of law and justice according to the dictates of our own needs and after a pattern of our own designing. This liberty is established and the

77 [1923] IR 5, at 8–9.
78 Garvin, op. cit., pp 170, 176.
79 Articles in the Constitution dealing with the judicial branch of government were 64–72 and 75.

headline is set in the Constitution drawn up and passed by the elected representatives of our people.[80]

Cosgrave also requested the Committee to approach its work 'untrammelled by any regard to any of the existing systems of judicature in this country', and when thanking them later for their work he acknowledged 'with gratitude that the work of the Committee has been directed in the spirit of my letter of 29 January last by which it was convened'.[81] The report of the Committee was delivered to the government in May 1923, and formed the basis of the Courts of Justice Act 1924 by which in June that year new courts – Supreme, High, Circuit and District – were established.[82] Any recommendations in a transformative spirit related not so much to the superior courts but to the lower courts, the design of which was drawn from the model of the Dáil courts. The jurisdiction of the existing High Court and Court of Appeal was transferred to the new High Court and Supreme Court respectively.[83] The provisional government as late as June 1922 had envisaged assizes being held[84] and the Committee had recommended (at p. 20 of the report) that commissioners of assize should be sent outside Dublin to such centres as the government might determine. However under the new Act that historic system of regular sittings of the High Court in towns on each circuit ceased to exist, and all appeals or other applications to a judge of assize that were pending in 1924 would be heard by a judge to be nominated for the purpose.[85] Provision was initially made for the possibility of High Court judges, under the title of Commissioners of the High Court Circuit, being sent outside Dublin with power to exercise any civil or criminal jurisdiction of the High Court, but this provision was never put into effect and was repealed only a couple of years later.[86] A court of criminal appeal, long resisted by nationalist opinion in previous decades, was created by the Act, and such a court was also created in Northern Ireland in 1930.[87]

There were nine judges in the superior courts, the Supreme Court having three members, presided over by the chief justice, and the High Court having a maximum of six, being a president and not more than five ordinary members.[88] This composition of the superior courts was little altered over the next fifty years. The membership of the Supreme Court was increased to five judges in 1936[89]

80 Cosgrave to members of the Judiciary Committee, 29 January 1923 (Report of Judiciary Committee, p. 4, and Hugh Kennedy Papers UCDA, P. 4/1090).
81 Ibid., p. 5; Cosgrave to Lord Glenavy, 11 June 1923 (Report of Judiciary Committee, p. 8).
82 See generally Niamh Howlin (ed.), *A century of courts: the Courts of Justice Act 1924* (Dublin, 2024).
83 Courts of Justice Act 1924, ss17 and 18.
84 Draft commissions of assize, undated [June 1922] (Hugh Kennedy Papers, UCDA, P. 4/1067); minutes of the provisional government, vol. 2 (5 June 1922) – summer assizes (NAI); Kotsonouris, op. cit., pp 78 and 147.
85 Courts of Justice Act 1924, s103.
86 Courts of Justice Act, ss3 and 36(v); Courts of Justice Act 1926, s2.
87 Courts of Justice Act 1924, s8; Criminal Appeal (Northern Ireland) Act 1930.
88 Courts of Justice Act 1924, s4 (High Court) and s5 (Supreme Court).
89 Courts of Justice Act 1936, s4(1).

(a step long sought by Kennedy CJ although he died before the increase actually took effect), and in 1953 and again in 1973 provision was made for one additional ordinary member to be appointed to the High Court.[90] A retirement age (of 72) was introduced for judges of the superior courts, with lower ages applicable to the other courts. (No retirement age was applicable to judges of the superior courts in Northern Ireland until provision was made across the United Kingdom in 1959 for judges of all such courts to vacate office upon reaching the age of 75.)[91]

Kennedy was appointed chief justice, and Timothy Sullivan, a member of a well-connected extended West Cork legal family, became president of the High Court. Three men who had been judges in the former court system were appointed to new places – Charles O'Connor as a member of the Supreme Court, and W.E. Wylie and Thomas Lopdell O'Shaughnessy (who since 1905 had been recorder of Dublin, having the status of a judge of the county court) as members of the High Court. All other existing judges of the superior courts lost their positions on the abolition of their courts. (O'Connor and O'Shaughnessy both retired in 1925, and Wylie in 1936.) The other judges appointed were Gerald FitzGibbon to be the third member of the Supreme Court and, for the High Court, James Creed Meredith (who had been a member of the Dáil Supreme Court), William Johnston (who had been a county court judge) and James A. Murnaghan.

The prospect of fostering or restoring a native or domestic Irish jurisprudence was very much on Kennedy's mind in these seminal years for the court system. He made an inquiry to Eoin MacNeill TD, the professor of early (including medieval) Irish history at UCD, about any information from the 'ancient law tracts of Ireland' that might be helpful for the Judiciary Committee, saying that 'insofar as the existing system is based upon English history we hope to cut it out and start afresh'.[92] He provided Cosgrave with a draft of the letter that was sent to the Judiciary Committee.[93] He told the *Irish Times* in an interview in October 1923 that the government's approach to the creation of a new judiciary was to have the ground cleared of existing institutions.[94] On the inauguration of the new courts on 11 June 1924 he acknowledged the emotion of the moment in speaking of it as a time 'when the silence of the Gael in courts of law is broken and that within what was once the Pale – the moment when, after a week of centuries (sic), Irish courts, fashioned in freedom by an Oireachtas again assembled, are thrown open to administer justice according to laws made in Ireland by free Irish citizens for the well-being of our dearly beloved land and its people'.[95] In 1925 when rules of court were being adopted for the costume or robes to be worn by Bench and Bar he was

90 Courts of Justice Act 1953, s11; Courts Act 1973, s1(1).

91 Courts of Justice Act 1924, s12; Judicial Pensions Act 1959, s2. See Daire Hogan, 'The introduction of a retirement age for judges' in Niamh Howlin (ed.), op. cit., pp 84–91.

92 Kennedy to Mac Neill, 22 August 1922 (Hugh Kennedy Papers UCDA, P. 4/1067).

93 Kennedy to Cosgrave, [undated] (Hugh Kennedy Papers, UCDA, P. 4/1083).

94 *Irish Times*, 10 October 1923.

95 *Irish Times*, 12 June 1924; *ILT&SJ*, vol. 58, pp 151–2 (14 June 1924). The 'week of centuries' phrase appears in these newspaper reports, although some other expression such as 'a lapse of centuries' or 'a week of ceremonies' may have been intended.

unable to persuade his judicial colleagues to approve new robes drawn from what was known of the costumes worn by the brehons or judges of the old Gaelic Ireland, and wrote to Cosgrave in frustration:

> I am disappointed. I had thought that the new courts of the Saorstát were to be distinguished as the national courts, set up in the hour of freedom. Now however, after a brief spell it seems that they are to have symbols of the old servitude imposed upon them, for that is what it comes to ... Neither the Bar nor the judges have the right to stamp a character on the courts contrary to the spirit of the Constitution and of the state as lawfully determined by the people.[96]

The processes of establishing new court systems on each side of the border had obvious parallels with each other. They were an element in the quite solemn creation of a new machinery of governance and of new institutions of state, in each case reflecting local political aspirations, realities, dynamics and culture. The language used by Cosgrave in January 1923 and by Kennedy was of course far removed from anything that would have been recognised, and from the ethos being fostered, at the same time in the courts in Belfast. The 1924 Act contemplated that rules of court might make provision for the use of the national language in court, reflecting a wider national policy of promoting this use, and Kennedy attached importance to this.[97] He proposed to the benchers of King's Inns in 1925 that a knowledge of the Irish language should be introduced as a condition for admission of students for the Bar to the Inn.[98] Although this was not accepted at the time some four years later a new statutory requirement was adopted (for both branches of the legal profession) that prior to admission to practice aspiring barristers and solicitors would have demonstrated (in an exam) a competent knowledge of the Irish language.[99]

The reconstruction of the Four Courts was completed in 1931, although the government was not prepared to approve of any formal ceremony being arranged for the new law term in October that year to mark the re-opening and transfer back of the courts from Dublin Castle. The Minister for Justice had in mind both the avoidance of any unnecessary expenditure at a time of stringent austerity and, more confidentially, the possibility that such a ceremony might give rise to an attempt by what he termed 'the forces making for anarchy' to destroy the building.[100] The

96 Kennedy to Cosgrave, 3 July 1925 (Hugh Kennedy Papers, UCDA, P. 4 1167/8–9).

97 Courts of Justice Act 1924, s36(v); *ILT&SJ*, vol. 60, p. 48 (20 February 1926) and p. 301 (4 December 1926).

98 *ILT&SJ*, vol. 59, p. 262 (31 October 1925); Minutes of meeting of benchers, 26 October 1925.

99 Legal Practitioners (Qualification) Act 1929, ss3 and 4(2). This was introduced as a private member's bill (*ILT&SJ*, vol. 62, p. 252 (17 October 1928) and p. 271 (10 November 1928)).

100 Gerard Hogan, 'Hugh Kennedy, the Childers habeas corpus application and the return to the Four Courts' in Caroline Costello (ed.), *The Four Courts: 200 years* (Dublin, 1996), pp 177–219, at pp 207–17. See Hugh Kennedy Papers (UCDA), P. 4/1058.

rebuilding, noted in the *Irish Law Times* in August,[101] was not received as well as the contemporary new court building in Belfast. A writer in the *Irish Times* some seven years later remarked that

> the Four Courts have been frigidly rebuilt. Aggressively heraldic rubber flooring in the vast entrance hall under the dome 'cocks a snoot' at the dignified walls; the various court rooms have a starkness reminiscent of mission halls; the corridors are depressingly institution-like, and it is difficult to imagine conviviality in the up-to-date but austere restaurant. Possibly the exuberance of the Irish spirit will survive the deadening effect of architectural 'improvements', but imagination boggles at the thought of raconteurs around a radiator.[102]

As the new courts and judiciary in the South took shape the existing judges faced the prospect of their services being dispensed with. Their number fell in any event in the course of 1921 through the death of William Kenny in February, the retirement of John George Gibson in April and the vacancy arising when Sir John Ross was promoted to replace Campbell at the end of June. None of these vacancies were filled, in light of the impending court re-structuring provided for by the 1920 Act (as was made explicit in the House of Commons in the case of Ross[103]). That Act had made provision for the potential early retirement of individual judges, in much the same manner as the earlier Home Rule bills had done, acknowledging the possibility of payment of an accelerated full pension notwithstanding that the statutory qualification of 15 years' judicial service had not been met.[104] A rather different prospect, that there might be a compulsory termination of the services of all judges rather than simply a facilitation of individual early retirements, arose in the autumn of 1921, as the Treaty negotiations progressed. Ross as head of the judiciary wrote, at the request of the judges, to the lord lieutenant with copies to the prime minster, the lord chancellor and the other ministers who were engaged in the negotiations, expressing their concerns about their position and their pensions. In particular he emphasised the importance to them of the pension obligation remaining a charge upon the Consolidated Fund of the United Kingdom (in other words, a liability of the British government), and not being transferred to a new Irish government.[105]

Article 10 of the Treaty signed in December provided that the government of the Irish Free State would pay 'fair compensation on terms not less favourable that those accorded by the Act of 1920 to judges, officials, members of police forces,

101 *ILT&SJ*, vol. 65, p. 202 (22 August 1931). See also Christine Casey, *The buildings of Ireland: Dublin* (New Haven and London, 2005), pp 92–9.

102 *Irish Times*, 3 April 1939. The comments were made in a review (anonymous) of Healy's *OldMC*.

103 HC Deb, 5th series, vol. 143, col. 2313 (30 June 1921).

104 Government of Ireland Act 1920, schedule 7, part 3, 1(b).

105 Ross to Lord Fitzalan, 28 October 1921 (CAB 27/163(32) (TNAUK)); Government of Ireland Act 1920, s47(2).

and other public servants who are discharged by it or who retire in consequence of the change of government effected in pursuance hereof'.

The judges' initial representations to government resulted, Ross later said in a further memorandum, in 'assurances of the most positive character',[106] but their concerns were heightened by continuing disorder and sectarian violence in Ireland in the first six months of 1922, and by the development of bitter divisions within the Republican movement over the Treaty settlement and governance of the South. They became increasingly alarmed, and sent delegations to London to emphasise their apprehension, that what Ross in a letter to Birkenhead, the lord chancellor of Great Britain, in March 1922 referred to as 'all the solemn guarantees binding on the honour of the King and people will be swept away'.[107] In that letter Ross made a proposal that 'in this state of things there is only one thing to be done and that is to have an Act at once providing that in case a judge is removed or obliged to retire he shall be entitled to his full pension notwithstanding short service and further to compensation for loss of office to be assessed by an independent tribunal, such pension and compensation to be charged on the Consolidated Fund, less such amounts as may be paid by the Irish Free State'. The ongoing and indeed worsening turmoil and instability in the Irish Free State may have had a silver lining for the judges as helping to emphasise or reinforce the responsibility of the British government both for their existing prospective pensions and for the loss that would arise from termination of their appointments on the abolition of their courts. What Ross had proposed formed the basis of the compensation arrangements adopted nine months later.

The Constitution of the Irish Free State, adopted in December 1922[108] and to which the Treaty was scheduled, provided for the continuation in operation of the existing courts and judiciary then holding office pending the establishment of a new court system – the courts 'shall for the time being continue to exercise the same jurisdiction as heretofore and any judge or justice, being a member of any such court, holding office when this Constitution comes into operation, shall for the time being continue to be a member thereof and hold office by the like tenure and upon the same terms of service as heretofore' etc.[109] It also provided that if any judge 'is not with his consent appointed to be a judge of [the new courts] he shall, for the purpose of article 10 of the scheduled treaty, be treated as if he had retired in consequence of the change of government effected in pursuance of the said

106 Memorandum by lord chancellor Ross on the position of judges affected by the establishment of the Free State, submitted to the Cabinet sub-committee to consider the position of judges of the High Court and other persons holding office on judicial tenure, 22 June 1922 (CAB 27/163(32–3) (TNAUK)); Ross to Churchill (secretary of state for the colonies), 28 June 1922, enclosing copy memorandum (CO 739/16 (TNAUK)).

107 Ross to Birkenhead, 17 March 1922 (CO 739/16 (TNAUK)). Ross later similarly referred to guarantees 'binding upon His Majesty, upon both houses of Parliament and upon the nation' (Ross to Churchill, 28 June 1922 (CO, 739/16 (TNAUK)).

108 The Constitution of the Irish Free State (Saorstat Éireann) Act 1922 (no. 1 of 1922); The Irish Free State Constitution Act 1922 (13 Geo. 5 (session 2), c.1).

109 Constitution, article 75.

treaty, but the rights so conferred shall be without prejudice to any rights or claims that he may have against the British government'.[110]

Such claims would have arisen under the Irish Free State (Consequential Provisions) Act 1922, passed on the same day in December as Parliament had approved (as a matter of UK law) the Constitution. This made provision for payment of compensation to any judge whose services were not continued upon the dissolution or abolition of the Supreme Court of Southern Ireland, and for 'any pensions and allowances payable thereunder [to] be charged on and payable out of the Consolidated Fund'.[111] (Glenavy was taunted by Carson over the fact that his (existing) judicial pension was so charged and payable, in the debate in the House of Lords on that final legislation required to give effect to the Treaty. Glenavy had earlier spoken of his confidence in the new government in the South and Carson said that 'the eulogiums he pronounced upon them led me to the conclusion that he would wind up saying that he himself intended to transfer his pension as an ex-lord chancellor of Ireland from the Consolidated Fund to the Irish Fund administered by the provisional government'.)[112] Although the British government thus accepted a liability to compensate any former judges it had an expectation, by reference to the undertakings as to such liabilities that were set out in the Treaty and the Constitution, that any sums paid out in that way would be recouped by it from the Irish government.

The compensation circumstances and procedures were as follows:

> When a new court is established by the parliament of the Irish Free State in the place of any existing court or courts, every existing judge then holding office as a judge of any such existing court shall, on such abolition of office, be entitled to receive by way of compensation for loss of office a pension equivalent to two-thirds of his salary and, in addition, an annual allowance payable for such period and of such amount, not exceeding (when added to the amount of his pension) his full salary, as may be determined to be reasonable and just, regard being had to the tenure and character of his existing office, the probability of his further continuation therein but for the establishment of the parliament and government of the Irish Free State and all the circumstances of the case. The amount of the annual allowance shall, subject as aforesaid, be determined by a committee consisting of the lord chief justice of England,[113] the master of the rolls in England and a judge of the Supreme Court of England nominated by the lord chancellor of Great Britain.[114]

110 Constitution, article 76.
111 Irish Free State (Consequential Provisions) Act 1922 (13 Geo. 5 (session 2), c.2, s2).
112 HL Deb, 5th series, vol. 52, col. 197 (1 December 1922).
113 This was Gordon (now Lord) Hewart, who was attorney general between 1919 and March 1922, and then lord chief justice up to 1940, and who had been one of the signatories to the Treaty in 1921.
114 Irish Free State (Consequential Provisions) Act 1922, schedule 2, part 1 (2).

This committee sat in 1923 and heard the claim of Sir John Ross, whose office as lord chancellor of Ireland had been abolished,[115] and in the summer of 1924 when it determined the claims of the other existing judges who had subsequently been deprived of office. The claimants, who included the three men who in June 1924 had accepted appointment to one of the new courts, put forward actuarial evidence of their respective life expectancies (and hence, by extension, of their presumed future judicial service). They were awarded annual payments which varied between £1,000 (Molony LCJ) and £550 (Pim J), such awards being generally but not invariably made for the lifetime of the claimant, and the payment to Dodd J was awarded for a period of three years, in light of his age (80) at the time of abolition of his office.[116] Ross received £750 p.a. The Act provided that if a compensated judge accepted a new judicial office in Great Britain or Ireland then the pension and any allowance would be suspended or abated so that, taking into account the salary of his new office, his aggregate income from all such sources for past or present judicial service would not exceed the salary of his abolished office.[117] W.E. Wylie, to his great displeasure, was affected by this restriction, since he was continuing to receive a judicial salary under the 1924 Act (although of a lesser amount than before, £2,500 rather than £3,500), and up to his retirement in 1936 abatements were applied by the British government to his pension and to the allowance of £700 which he had been awarded.[118]

By the end of 1925 almost all of the men who had been sitting in the existing superior courts in 1921 no longer held prominent positions in judicial, public or civic life, the exceptions being William Moore, now the lord chief justice of Northern Ireland, W.E. Wylie and Lord Glenavy, president of the Senate of the Irish Free State. Two judges had died in office (in addition to Kenny in 1921), namely John Gordon in 1922 and John Blake Powell in 1923. John George Gibson died in 1923 in Wales, having retired in April 1921. After 1924 Thomas Molony and, for a time, James O'Connor took up residence in England, as did Charles O'Connor (and Thomas Lopdell O'Shaughnessy) on their retirements in 1925. A number of their colleagues who had left office prior to 1921 had moved to London, namely Ignatius O'Brien (now Lord Shandon) and Dunbar Plunket Barton (both of whom had retired in 1918), and Dodgson Hamilton Madden (1919). Sir John Ross had homes in London and Co. Tyrone. It was noted in 1927 that six former Irish judges who had received honours, of a peerage, baronetcy or knighthood, were living in England.[119] Glenavy, Dodd, Pim, Ronan and Samuels (both of whom died in 1925) continued to live in Ireland.

115 Note of committee determination, 7 March 1923 (T 164/32/8 (TNAUK)).
116 Note of committee determination, 21 October 1924 (T164/153/11 (TNAUK)).
117 Irish Free State (Consequential Provisions) Act 1922, schedule 2, part 1 (3).
118 Memorandum by J.M. Trickett (Treasury official), 25 July 1924 (T164/49/9 (TNAUK)); note of committee determination, 21 October 1924 (T164/153/11 (TNAUK); PRO 30/89/6 (TNAUK)).
119 *ILT&SJ*, vol. 61, p. 8 (8 January 1927).

Bibliography

PRIMARY SOURCES

A. Manuscripts and archives

Abercorn Papers (D623, Public Record Office of Northern Ireland, Belfast)
Althorp Papers (British Library, London)
J.B. Armour Papers (D1792, PRONI)
Ashbourne Papers (Parliamentary Archives, London)
Asquith Papers (Bodleian Library, Oxford)
Arthur Balfour Papers (British Library)
Gerald Balfour Papers (The National Archives, London)
Bonar Law Papers (Parliamentary Archives)
Bryce Papers (National Library of Ireland, Dublin)
Charles Kendal Bushe Papers (IE MS.4002, Library of Trinity College Dublin)
Cabinet Papers (PRONI)
Cadogan Papers (Parliamentary Archives)
Cairns Papers (TNAUK)
Campbell-Bannerman Papers (British Library)
Carnarvon Papers (TNAUK)
Carson Papers (D1507, PRONI))
Austen Chamberlain Papers (Cadbury Research Library: special collections – University of Birmingham)
Chatterton Papers (IE MS.6401/1, Library of Trinity College Dublin).
Cherry Papers (D2166, PRONI)
Lord Randolph Churchill Papers (Cambridge University Library)
Papers of the 14th earl of Derby (Liverpool Record Office)
Disraeli Papers (Bodleian Library)
Dublin Diocesan Archives
Dufferin & Ava Papers (D1071, PRONI)
Eglinton Papers (National Archives of Scotland, Edinburgh)
Membership registers, Grand Lodge of Freemasons of Ireland 1733–1923
Gladstone Papers (British Library)
Granville Papers (TNAUK)
Halsbury Papers (British Library)
Harcourt Papers (Bodleian Library)
Hicks Beach Papers (Gloucestershire Archives, Gloucester)
Holmes Papers [manuscript autobiography] (MIC 197, PRONI)
Hugh Kennedy Papers (University College Dublin Archives)
Admission Papers, Library of the Honorable Society of King's Inns, Dublin
Lindley Papers [manuscript autobiography] (Library of King's College, London)
Lloyd George Papers (Parliamentary Archives)
Londonderry Papers (D2846, PRONI)
Walter Long Papers ((1) British Library (2) WSHC)

Schomberg McDonnell honours nomination book (D4091, PRONI)
Political Papers of the 7th duke of Marlborough (Cambridge University Library)
Mayo Papers (NLI)
Nathan Papers (Bodleian Library)
O'Hagan Papers (D2777, PRONI)
Laurence O'Neill Papers (NLI)
John Redmond Papers (NLI)
Records of the Cabinet Office (CAB) (TNAUK)
Records of the Colonial Office (CO) (TNAUK)
Records of the Home Office (HO) (TNAUK)
Records of the Treasury (T) (TNAUK)
Registry of Deeds, Dublin
Papers of the 3rd marquess of Salisbury (Hatfield House, Hertfordshire)
Teeling Papers (NLI)
Whiteside Papers (NLI)
Wylie Papers (TNAUK)

B. Newspaper and periodicals

Belvederian
Church of Ireland Gazette
Clongownian
Daily Express
Dublin University Magazine
Freeman's Journal
Irish Ecclesiastical Gazette
Irish Independent
Irish Jurist
Irish Law Times & Solicitors' Journal
Irish Times
Law Quarterly Review
Law Times
New Irish Jurist and Local Government Review
Northern Ireland Legal Quarterly
Spectator
Times

C. Parliamentary papers

Report of select committee on legal education in Ireland and England, P.P. 1846 H.C. (686) x.1.
Report of select committee on official salaries, P.P. 1850 H.C. (611) xv.179.
Report relating to an investigation held at Castlewellan into the occurrence at Dolly's Brae on 12 July 1849, P.P. 1850 (1143) li.331.
Report of Royal Commission into Encumbered Estates Court, P.P. 1854–5 xix.527.
Report of the select committee on the Court of Chancery (Ireland) Bills, P.P. 1856 H.C. (311) x.1.
Correspondence between the lord chancellor of Ireland and Mr Baron Richards on removal of latter from office as chief commissioner of the Encumbered Estates Court, P.P. (1857) (sess. 2) (90) xlii.421.
Final report of Her Majesty's commissioners appointed to inquire into the superior courts of common law and the courts of Chancery in England and Ireland, P.P. 1863 (3238) xv.1.
Court of Admiralty (Ireland) Bill, P.P. 1866 (133) i.7.

First report of the Royal Commission on the Judicature of England, P.P. 1868–9 (4130) xxv.1.
Landed Estates Court (Ireland) Bill, P.P. 1873 (182) ii.265.
Correspondence between judges and chief secretary for Ireland in respect of Landed Estates Court (Ireland) Bill, P.P. 1873 (227) liv.389.
Correspondence relative to vacancy caused in the Landed Estates Court by the death of the Hon. Judge Lynch, P.P. 1873 (247) liv.375.
Resolutions of Irish judges in reference to the Supreme Court of Judicature Bill, P.P. 1873 (273) liv.335.
Report of select committee on working of jury system in Ireland, P.P. 1873 H.C. (283) xv.389.
Report of the commissioners on the local government board and general register office, P.P. 1873 (789) lxvii.379.
Paper on Supreme Court of Judicature (Ireland) Bill, signed by the common law judges of Ireland P.P. 1876 (278) lxi.357.
Copy of all correspondence between the Treasury and the lord chief justice of Ireland with respect to the appointment of Mr Blackham to an office in the court of Queen's Bench in Ireland, P.P. 1876 (332) lxi.351.
History of the Court of Judicature (Ireland) Bill 1874 and of the Supreme Court of Judicature (Ireland) Bill 1876, P.P. 1877 (181) lxviii.145.
Copies of the Charge addressed by Mr Justice Keogh to the Grand Jury of Londonderry on 18 March 1878 and of certain letters from Mr Justice Keogh to the lord lieutenant and attorney general for Ireland relating thereto, P.P. 1878 (112) lxiii.463.
Return of civil cases in Ireland for each year 1873–82, P.P. 1884 (288) lxiii.327.
Supreme Court of Judicature (Ireland) Bill 1885, P.P. 1884–5 (55) v.531.
Government of Ireland Bill 1886, P.P. 1886 ii.461.
Correspondence between the Treasury and the Irish government as to the remuneration of the attorney general and solicitor general for Ireland, P.P. 1887 lxvii.379.
Return of number of persons specially protected by Royal Irish Constabulary, July 1887 and January 1888, P.P. 1888 (5809) lxxxiii.305.
Government of Ireland Bill 1893, P.P. 1893–4 ii.251.
Government of Ireland Bill 1912, P.P. 1912–13 (136) ii.505.
Report of the Royal Commission into the circumstances connected with the landing of arms at Howth on 26 July 1914, P.P. 1914–16, Cmnd. 7631 xxiv.805.
Report of the Royal Commission on the arrest and subsequent treatment of Mr Francis Sheehy Skeffington, Mr Thomas Dickson and Mr Patrick James McIntyre, P.P. 1916, Cd. 8376, xi.311.
Report of proceedings of Irish Convention, P.P. 1918, Cd. 9019 x.697.

SECONDARY SOURCES

Brian Abel-Smith and Robert Stevens, *Lawyers and the courts: a sociological study of the English legal system, 1750–1965* (London, 1969).
R.J.Q. Adams, *Bonar Law* (London, 1999).
R.J.Q. Adams, *Balfour: the last grandee* (London, 2007).

Mark Amory (ed.), *The letters of Evelyn Waugh* (London, 1980).
Annual Register.
Anonymous [Jonathan Christian], *The court of Chancery under the Chancery (Ireland) Act 1867* (Dublin, 1872).
Anonymous, *The Ulster Liberal Unionist Association: a sketch of its history, 1885–1914* (Belfast, 1914).
J.B. Atlay, *The Victorian chancellors* (London, 1906).
F.E. Ball, *The judges in Ireland, 1221–1921* (London, 1926).
J.T. Ball, *The Reformed Church of Ireland, 1537–1889* (Dublin, 1886).
Dunbar Plunket Barton, *A yeoman proprietary in Ireland* (Dublin, 1883).
Dunbar Plunket Barton, *Timothy Healy: memories and anecdotes* (Dublin and Cork, 1933).
Dunbar Plunket Barton QC, MP and Richard R. Cherry (eds), *The Land Law (Ireland) Act 1896, with the rules and forms issued thereunder in the Land Commission, Supreme Court and County Courts respectively* (Dublin, 1897).
Sir Dunbar Plunket Barton, Charles Benham and Francis Watt, *The story of the Inns of Court* (Boston, 1924).
Mark Bence-Jones, *Burke's guide to country houses, vol. 1: Ireland* (London, 1978).
Norman Bentwich, *The practice of the Privy Council in judicial matters* (London, 1912).
Edmund Bewley, *The law and practice of taxation of costs in common law business* (Dublin, 1867).
Edmund Bewley, *The Bewleys of Cumberland and their Irish and other descendants, with full pedigrees of the family* (Dublin, 1902).
Edmund Bewley and Alexander Richie BL, *The Chancery (Ireland) Act 1867 and general orders and regulations thereunder, copiously annotated, with fees, schedules and forms and precedents* (Dublin, 1867).
Edmund Bewley and John Naish, *The Common Law Procedure Acts, 1853, 1856 and 1870, etc.* (Dublin, 1871).
John Biggs-Davison and George Chowdaray-Best, *The Cross of St Patrick: the Catholic Unionist tradition in Ireland* (Bourne End, 1984).
R.D.C. Black, *Economic thought and the Irish question, 1817–1870* (London, 1960).
R.D.C. Black, 'William James Pirrie' in Conor Cruise O'Brien (ed.), *The shaping of modern Ireland* (London, 1960).
Edward Blackburne, *Life of the Right Hon. Francis Blackburne* (London, 1874).
Robert Blake, *The unknown prime minister: the life and times of Andrew Bonar Law, 1858–1923* (London, 1955).
Louis Blom-Cooper, 'Style of judgments' in Louis Blom-Cooper, Brice Dickson and Gavin Drewry (eds), *The judicial House of Lords, 1876–2009* (Oxford, 2009), pp 145–63.
M. McDonnell Bodkin, *Famous Irish trials* (Dublin, 1918, edited, with an introduction, by Eamonn G. Hall (Dublin, 1997)).
Simon Bradley and Nikolaus Pevsner, *The buildings of England, London 6: Westminster* (London, 2003).
J.C. Brady, 'Legal developments, 1801–79' in W.E. Vaughan (ed.), *A new history of Ireland: V. Ireland Under the Union: I, 1801–70* (Oxford, 1989), pp 451–81.
Oonagh Breen and Noel McGrath (eds), *Palles: the legal legacy of the last lord chief baron* (Dublin, 2022).
C.E. B. Brett, *Court houses and market houses of the province of Ulster* (Belfast, 1973).
C.E.B. Brett, *Buildings of County Antrim* (Belfast, 1996).

Raymond F. Brooke, *The brimming river* (Dublin, 1961).
Patrick Buckland, *Irish Unionism 1: the Anglo-Irish and the New Ireland, 1885–1922* (Dublin/New York, 1972).
G.E. Buckle, *The life of Benjamin Disraeli, earl of Beaconsfield*, vol. 5, *1868–1876* (London, 1920).
Shan F. Bullock, *Thomas Andrews, shipbuilder* (Belfast, 1913).
O.J. Burke, *History of the lord chancellors of Ireland from 1186 to 1874* (Dublin, 1879).
O.J. Burke, *Anecdotes of the Connaught circuit* (Dublin, 1885).
Burke's Irish family records, ed. Hugh Montgomery-Massingberd (London, 1976).
Michael Byrne, *Legal Offaly* (Tullamore, 2008).
Fergus Campbell, *The Irish establishment, 1879–1914* (Oxford, 2009).
Patrick Campbell, *My life and easy times* (London, 1967).
William Bennett Campion, *Memoir* (Dublin, 1911).
Lord Carswell, '*Eheu fugaces*: fifty years in the Northern Ireland courts', in Daire Hogan and Colum Kenny (eds), *Changes in practice and law* (Dublin, 2013), pp 3–22.
Lord Carswell, 'Founding a legal system: the early judiciary of Northern Ireland' in Felix M. Larkin and N.M. Dawson (eds), *Lawyers, the law and history: Irish Legal History Society discourses and other papers, 2005–2011* (Dublin, 2013), pp 15–28.
R.P. Carton QC, 'The Irish Bar as profession' in *Clongownian*, vol. 1, no. 2 (June 1896), p. 12.
Christine Casey, *The buildings of Ireland: Dublin* (New Haven and London, 2005).
Christine Casey and Alastair Rowan, *The buildings of Ireland: north Leinster* (London, 1993).
J.P. Casey, *The office of attorney general in Ireland* (Dublin, 1980).
J.P. Casey, *The Irish law officers: roles and responsibilities of the attorney general and the director of public prosecutions* (Dublin, 1996).
Catholic Truth Society, *The value of scholastic philosophy* (Dublin, 1909).
Maud Cherry, *A short memoir of the Right Hon. Richard Robert Cherry, sometime lord chief justice of Ireland* (Dublin, 1924).
R.R. Cherry, *The Irish Land Law and Land Purchase Acts, 1881, 1885 and 1887 etc* (Dublin, 1888).
R.R. Cherry, *Lectures on the growth of criminal law in ancient communities* (London, 1890).
R.R. Cherry, *The Irish Land Law and Land Purchase Acts, 1860 to 1901 (including the Congested Districts Board Acts)* (Dublin, 1903).
Jonathan Christian, *The coming Court of Final Appeal for Ireland* (Dublin, 1874).
The Church of Ireland and the present crisis: report of a special meeting of the General Synod holden at Dublin, 23 March 1886 (Dublin, 1886).
W.S. Churchill, *Lord Randolph Churchill* (London, 1906).
Tomas Clancy, 'The Four Courts building and the development of an independent Bar of Ireland' in Caroline Costello (ed.), *The Four Courts: 200 years* (Dublin, 1996), pp 80–104.
Raymond Cock, 'Victorian barristers, judges and taxation; a study in the expansion of legal work' in G.R. Rubin and David Sugarman (eds), *Law, economy and society: essays in the history of English law, 1750–1914* (Abingdon, 1984), pp 445–69.
R.V. Comerford, *Charles J. Kickham: a study in Irish nationalism and literature* (Dublin, 1979).
R.V. Comerford, *The Fenians in context: Irish politics and society, 1848–82* (Dublin, 1985).

R.V. Comerford, 'Churchmen, tenants and independent opposition, 1850–56' in W.E. Vaughan (ed.), *A new history of Ireland, V. Ireland under the Union: I, 1801–70* (Oxford, 1989), pp 396–414.

A.B. Cooke, 'A Conservative party leader in Ulster: Sir Stafford Northcote's diary of a visit to the province, October 1883', *Proceedings of the Royal Irish Academy*, vol. 75C (1975), pp 61–84.

A.B. Cooke and A.P.W. Malcomson (eds), *The Ashbourne Papers: a calendar of the papers of Edward Gibson, 1st Lord Ashbourne* (Belfast, 1974).

A.B. Cooke and John Vincent, 'Ireland and party politics 1885–87, an unpublished Conservative memoir', *Irish Historical Studies*, vol. 16, no. 62, (1968–9), pp 154–72; no. 63, pp 321–38; no. 64, pp 446–71.

A.B. Cooke and John Vincent, *The governing passion: cabinet government and party politics in Britain, 1885–86* (Brighton, 1974).

Kevin Costello, *The court of Admiralty of Ireland, 1575–1893* (Dublin, 2011).

Philip Cecil Crampton, *Addresses and replies on Judge Crampton's retirement from the bench, with some of his charges to grand juries* (Dublin, 1859).

Virginia Crossman, *Politics, law and order in nineteenth-century Ireland* (Dublin, 1996).

Anne Crookshank and David Webb, *Paintings and sculptures in Trinity College Dublin* (Dublin, 1990).

C.P. Curran, 'Figures in the Hall' in *Record of the centenary of the charter of the Incorporated Law Society of Ireland, 1852–1952* (Dublin, 1953), pp 75–82 (reprinted in Caroline Costello (ed.), *The Four Courts: 200 years* (Dublin, 1996), pp 169–76).

John Adye Curran, *Reminiscences* (London, 1915).

L.P. Curtis jr, *Coercion and conciliation in Ireland, 1880–1892* (Princeton, 1963).

L.P. Curtis jr, *The depiction of evictions in Ireland, 1845–1910* (Dublin, 2011).

Mary E. Daly, *Dublin, the deposed capital: a social and economic history, 1860–1914* (Cork, 1984).

N.M. Dawson, 'The Giant's Causeway case: property law in Ireland 1845–1995' in N.M. Dawson, Desmond Greer, Peter Ingram (eds), *One hundred and fifty years of Irish law* (Belfast and Dublin, 1995), pp 239–57.

N.M. Dawson, 'Disendowment under the Irish Church Act 1869' in Kevin Costello and Niamh Howlin (eds), *Law and religion in Ireland, 1700–1970* (Cham, Switzerland, 2021).

Joseph Dean, *Hatred, ridicule or contempt: a book of libel cases* (London, 1953).

V.T.H. Delany, 'Lord Justice Christian and law reporting', *NILQ*, vol. 12 (1956–8), pp 46–52.

V.T.H. Delany, *Christopher Palles: his life and times* (Dublin, 1960).

Sir John William Rivallan de La Poer, *Proceedings and minutes of evidence taken before the committee for privileges* (London, 1922).

Charles Dickens, *The Pickwick papers* (London, 1837).

W.H. Dodd, *Address at the opening of the 48th session of the Statistical and Social Inquiry Society of Ireland* (Dublin, 1894).

A.G. Donaldson, *Some comparative aspects of Irish law* (Durham, NC and London, 1957).

James S. Donnelly Jr, *The land and the people of nineteenth century Cork: the rural economy and the land question* (London, 1975).

James S. Donnelly Jr, 'Landlords and tenants' in W.E. Vaughan (ed.), *A new history of Ireland: V. Ireland under the Union: I, 1801–70* (Oxford,1989), pp 332–49.

Alan Dowling, 'The genesis of Deasy's Act', *NILQ*, vol. 40 (1989), 53.
Sir Charles Gavan Duffy, *Four years of Irish history, 1845–1849* (London, 1883).
Sir Charles Gavan Duffy, *The revival of Irish literature* (London, 1894).
Andrew Dunlop, *Fifty years of Irish journalism* (Dublin, 1911).
L.S. Eiffe (assisted by A. Houston and J.O. Wylie), *The Judicature Acts (Ireland) 1877 and 1878 and orders, rules and forms thereunder, copiously annotated* (Dublin and London, 1881).
A.C. Ewald, *The life and letters of the Rt. Hon. Sir Joseph Napier, Bt.* (London, 1892).
Tony Farmar, *Ordinary lives* (Dublin, 1991).
Brian Farrell, 'The legislation of a "revolutionary" assembly: Dáil decrees, 1919–1922', *Irish Jurist*, vol. 10 (1975), pp 112–27.
Kenneth Ferguson, *King's Inns barristers, 1868–2004* (Dublin, 2005).
William Dwyer Ferguson LL.D and Geo. Napier Ferguson BL, *A treatise on the Supreme Court of Judicature Act (Ireland) 1877, with schedule of rules, orders of court and forms of procedure and notes of cases* (Dublin, 1878).
Almeric Fitzroy, *Memoirs* (London, 1925).
D.A. Fleming and A.P.W. Malcomson, *'A volley of execrations': the letters and papers of John FitzGibbon, earl of Clare, 1772–1802* (Dublin, 2005).
R.F. Foster, 'To the Northern Counties Station: Lord Randolph Churchill and the prelude to the Orange card' in F.S.L. Lyons and Richard Hawkins (eds), *Ireland under the Union: varieties of tension* (Oxford, 1980), pp 237–88.
R.F. Foster, *Lord Randolph Churchill: a political life* (Oxford, 1981).
Charles Ffrench Blake Forster, *The Irish chieftains, or a struggle for the crown* (Dublin, 1872).
David Foxton, *Revolutionary lawyers: Sinn Fein and Crown courts in Ireland and Britain, 1916–1923* (Dublin, 2008).
J.F. Fuller, *Omniana: the autobiography of an Irish octogenerian* (London, 1916).
Andrew Gailey, *Ireland and the death of kindness: the experience of constructive unionism, 1890–1905* (Cork, 1987).
Peter Galloway, *The Most Illustrious Order of St Patrick, 1783–1983* (Chichester, 1983).
Tom Garvin, *1922: the birth of Irish democracy* (Dublin, 1996).
Patrick Geoghegan, *The College Historical Society: oratory and debate, 1770–2020* (Dublin, 2020).
William H. Gibson, *Early Irish golf* (Kildare, 1988).
Peter Gordon (ed.), *The red earl, the papers of the fifth earl Spencer (1835–1910)* (Northampton, 1981–6).
Peter Gordon (ed.), *The political diaries of the fourth earl of Carnarvon, 1857–1890* (Cambridge, 2000).
Desmond Greer, 'A security against illegality? The reservation of Crown cases in nineteenth-century Ireland' in N.M. Dawson (ed.), *Reflections on law and history* (Dublin, 2006), pp 163–202.
'Guilty or not guilty': speeches from the dock or protests of Irish patriotism, containing, with introductory sketches and biographical notices, speeches delivered after conviction (Dublin, 1867).
Denis Gwynn, *Edward Martyn and the Irish Revival* (London, 1930).
Denis Gwynn, *The life of John Redmond* (London, 1932)
D.A. Haggar, 'The Land Purchase Acts – a short summary for the use of students', *NILQ*, vol. 11, no. 3 (1955), p. 207.

Eamonn G. Hall, *The superior courts of law: 'official' law reporting in Ireland, 1866–2006* (Dublin, 2007).
F.G. Hall, *The Bank of Ireland, 1783–1946* (Dublin, 1949).
Gerard R. Hall, *Ulster Liberalism, 1778–1876* (Dublin, 2011).
Henry Hanna, 'The Bench and Bar of Ireland in the nineteenth century', *American Bar Association Journal*, vol. 22, no. 11 (1936), pp 761–7.
Robin Harcourt Williams (ed.), *Salisbury-Balfour Correspondence: letters exchanged between the Third Marquess of Salisbury and his nephew Arthur James Balfour, 1869–1892* (Hertfordshire Record Society, 1988).
Charles Harpum, 'The vice chancellors – an Irish postscript', *Law Quarterly Review*, vol. 99 (1983), p. 32.
Richard S. Harrison, 'Pim Brothers – merchants, manufacturers and entrepreneurs of nineteenth century Dublin', *Journal of the Friends Historical Society*, vol. 59 (3) (2002), pp 236–56.
A.R. Hart, 'Fighting FitzGerald: mad, bad and dangerous to know – an eighteenth-century murder trial', *NILQ*, vol. 49 (1998), p. 221.
A.R. Hart, *A history of the King's serjeants at law in Ireland* (Dublin, 2000).
A.R. Hart, *A history of the Bar and Inn of Court of Northern Ireland* (Belfast, 2013).
A.R. Hart, 'King's Inns and the foundation of the Inn of Court of Northern Ireland: the northern perspective' in Felix M. Larkin and N.M. Dawson (eds), *Lawyers, the law and history: Irish Legal History Society discourses and other papers, 2005–2011*, pp 195–208.
Angus Hawkins, *The forgotten prime minister; the 14th earl of Derby: vol. II, Achievement: 1851–1869* (Oxford, 2008).
Edmund Hayes, *Reports of cases argued and determined in the court of Exchequer [1830–32] (Dublin, 1837) and [1832–34]* (Dublin, 1843).
Edmund Hayes, *Crimes and punishments or a digest of the criminal statute law of Ireland* (2nd ed., Dublin, 1842).
Maurice Headlam, *Irish reminiscences* (London, 1947).
Maurice Healy, *The old Munster circuit* (Dublin, 1939).
T.M. Healy, *Stolen waters: a page in the conquest of Ulster* (London, 1913).
T.M. Healy, *Letters and leaders of my day* (London, 1928).
R.F.V. Heuston, *Lives of the lord chancellors, 1885–1940* (Oxford, 1964).
R.F.V. Heuston, entries on Lord Lindley and Lord Loreburn in A.W.B. Simpson (ed.), *Biographical dictionary of the common law* (London, 1984).
R.F.V. Heuston, 'Judicial prosopography', *Law Quarterly Review*, vol. 102 (1986), pp 90–113.
R.F.V. Heuston, 'Legal history and the author: some practical problems of authorship' in W.N. Osborough (ed.), *The Irish Legal History Society: inaugural addresses* (Dublin, 1989).
Alan Hewitt, *The Law Society of Northern Ireland* (Belfast, 2010).
Daire Hogan, *The legal profession in Ireland, 1789–1922* (Dublin, 1986).
Daire Hogan, '"Arrows too sharply pointed": the relations of lord justice Christian and Lord O'Hagan, 1868–1874' in John F. McEldowney and Paul O'Higgins (eds), *The common law tradition: essays in Irish legal history* (Dublin, 1990), pp 61–84.
Daire Hogan, '"Vacancies for their friends": judicial appointments in Ireland, 1866–67' in Daire Hogan and W.N. Osborough (eds), *Brehons, serjeants and attorneys; studies in the history of the Irish legal profession* (Dublin, 1990), pp 211–30.

Daire Hogan, 'R.R. Cherry, lord chief justice of Ireland, 1914–1916' in D.S. Greer and N.M. Dawson (eds), *Mysteries and solutions in Irish legal history* (Dublin, 2001), pp 161–92.

Daire Hogan and Patrick Maume (eds), *The reminiscences of Ignatius O'Brien, lord chancellor of Ireland, 1913–18* (Dublin, 2021).

Daire Hogan, 'Ignatius O'Brien and the law' in Daire Hogan and Patrick Maume (eds), *The reminiscences of Ignatius O'Brien, lord chancellor of Ireland, 1913–18* (Dublin, 2021), pp 25–50.

Daire Hogan, 'The introduction of a retirement age for judges' in Niamh Howlin (ed.), *A century of courts: the Courts of Justice Act 1924* (Dublin, 2024), pp 84–91.

Daire Hogan, 'James Henry Mussen Campbell QC, MP: a life in law and unionist politics' in Niamh Howlin and Felix M. Larkin (eds), *Confluences of law and history: Irish Legal History Society discourses and other papers, 2011–21* (Dublin, 2025), pp 218–31, at 222–5.

Gerard Hogan, 'Chief Justice Kennedy and Sir James O'Connor's application', *Irish Jurist*, vol. 23 (1988), pp 144–59.

Gerard Hogan, 'Hugh Kennedy, the Childers habeas corpus application and return to the Four Courts' in Caroline Costello (ed.), *The Four Courts: 200 years* (Dublin, 1996), pp 177–219.

W. Holdsworth, *A history of English law*, vol. 1 (London, 1903), pp 177–219.

Ian Holloway, '*O'Connell v The Queen*: a sesquicentennial remembrance', *NILQ*, vol. 46 (1) (1995), pp 63–71.

David Hope (Lord Hope of Craighead), 'Law Lords in Parliament' in Louis Blom-Cooper, Brice Dickson and Gavin Drewry (eds), *The judicial House of Lords, 1876–2009* (Oxford, 2009), pp 164–77.

Michael Hopkinson (ed.), *The last days of Dublin Castle: the Mark Sturgis diaries* (Dublin, 1999).

K. Theodore Hoppen, *Elections, politics and society in Ireland 1832–1885* (Oxford, 1984).

K. Theodore Hoppen, *Governing Hibernia* (Oxford, 2016).

F.D. How, *Archbishop Plunket, a memoir* (London, 1900).

Niamh Howlin, *Juries in Ireland: laypersons and the law in the long nineteenth century* (Dublin, 2017).

Niamh Howlin, *Report on the trial of Myles Joyce, November 1882* (Dublin, 2017).

Niamh Howlin, 'The prehistory of the Offences against the State Act' in Mark Coen (ed.), *The Offences against the State Act 1939 at 80: a model counter-terrorism Act?* (Oxford and Dublin, 2020).

Niamh Howlin (ed.), *A century of courts: the Courts of Justice Act 1924* (Dublin, 2024).

H. Montgomery Hyde (ed.), *A Victorian historian: private letters of W.E.H. Lecky, 1859–1878* (London, 1947).

Alvin Jackson, 'The failure of unionism in Dublin, 1900', *Irish Historical Studies*, vol. 26, no. 104 (November 1989), pp 377–95.

Alvin Jackson, *Judging Redmond and Carson* (Dublin, 2018).

Claire Jackson, 'Irish political opposition to the passage of criminal evidence reform at Westminster, 1883–98' in John McEldowney and Paul O'Higgins (eds), *The common law tradition: essays in Irish legal history* (Dublin, 1990), pp 185–201.

Roy Jenkins, *Asquith* (London, 1964).

Roy Jenkins, *Gladstone* (London, 1995).

Thomas Jones, *Whitehall diary (vol. 3, Ireland 1918–1925)* (London, 1971).
James Joyce, *Ulysses* (Paris, 1922).
Edward Keane, P. Beryl Phair, Thomas U. Sadleir (eds), *King's Inns admission papers, 1607–1867* (Dublin, 1982).
Ronan Keane, *The law of local government in the Republic of Ireland* (Dublin, 1982).
Ronan Keane, *Equity and the law of trusts in Ireland* (London, 1988).
Ronan Keane, 'Martial law in Ireland, 1535–1924' in W.N. Osborough (ed.), *Essays in honour of John M. Kelly* (*The Irish Jurist*, vols 25–7, *Liber memorialis John M. Kelly*) (Dublin, 1994), p. 150.
Ronan Keane, 'The role of the Law Lords in relation to Ireland until 1922' in Louis Blom-Cooper, Brice Dickson and Gavin Drewry (eds), *The judicial House of Lords, 1876–2009* (Oxford, 2009), pp 295–303.
Kenneth Keith, 'The interplay with the Judicial Committee of the Privy Council' in Louis Blom-Cooper, Brice Dickson and Gavin Drewry (eds), *The judicial House of Lords, 1876–2009* (Oxford, 2009), pp 315–38.
Margaret Kelleher, *The Maamtrasna murders: language, life and death in nineteenth-century Ireland* (Dublin, 2018).
J.M. Kelly, *Fundamental rights in the Irish law and constitution*, 2nd ed. (Dublin, 1967).
Peter Kelly, introduction to H. Delany and D. McGrath, *Civil procedure in the superior courts* (third edition, Dublin, 2012).
C.S. Kenny, *Outlines of criminal law* (11th ed., Cambridge, 1922).
Mary Kotsonouris, *Retreat from revolution: the Dáil courts, 1920–24* (Dublin, 1994).
Mary Kotsonouris, *The winding-up of the Dáil courts, 1922–1925* (Dublin, 2004).
Michael Laffan, *The resurrection of Ireland: the Sinn Fein Party, 1916–23* (Cambridge, 1999).
John Larkin, 'Aspects of the career of John Blake Powell', *Irish Jurist*, vol. 20 (1985), pp 403–24.
John Larkin (ed.), *The trial of William Drennan* (Blackrock, 1991).
H.B. Leech, *Registration of title v registration of assurances* (London and Dublin, 1891).
Thomas Lefroy, *Memoir of Chief Justice Lefroy* (Dublin, 1871).
Geoffrey Lewis, *Lord Atkin* (Oxford, 1999).
Viscount Long of Wraxall [Walter Long], *Memories* (London, 1923).
Mountifort Longfield, *A proposal for an act to authorise the issue of land debentures in connection with sales made by the Landed Estates Court, with a copy of the proposed act* (Dublin, 1861).
Mountifort Longfield, *Plan of 'Parliamentary tenant right', applicable equally to all parts of Ireland* (Dublin, 1870).
Mountifort Longfield, 'Chapter 1 – Ireland' in Cobden Club, *Systems of land tenure in various countries* (London, 1870).
Lord Lowry, 'The Irish Lords of Appeal in Ordinary' in D.S. Greer and N.M. Dawson (eds), *Mysteries and solutions in Irish legal history* (Dublin, 2001), pp 193–216.
Henry W. Lucy, *A diary of the Unionist parliament, 1895–1900* (Bristol and London, 1901).
Henry W. Lucy, *The Balfour parliament, 1900–1905* (London, 1906).
F.S.L. Lyons, *Charles Stewart Parnell* (London, 1977).
Charles Lysaght, review of *The Four Courts: 200 years*, *Irish Jurist*, vol. 32 (1997), 465.
Lawrence W. McBride, *The greening of Dublin Castle* (Washington, DC, 1991).

Richard McBride, 'The failure to modernise the office of the Irish lord chancellor (1880–1915): a comparison with the developments in Great Britain' (2023, unpublished paper, The European Society for Comparative Legal History, Seventh Biennial Conference, Augsburg).

Richard McBride, 'Sir John Ross Bt: the last lord chancellor of Ireland, 1921–1922' in David Capper, Conor McCormick and Norma Dawson (eds), *Law and constitutional change* (Cambridge, 2025), pp 181–97.

Donal McCartney, *W.E.H. Lecky: historian and politician, 1838–1903* (Dublin, 1994).

Donal McCartney, *UCD, a national idea: the history of University College Dublin* (Dublin, 1999).

W.J. McCormack, *Sheridan Le Fanu and Victorian Ireland* (Oxford, 1980).

Donal P. McCracken, *You will dye at midnight: threatening letters in Victorian Ireland* (Dublin, 2021).

Lord MacDermott, 'Law and practice in Northern Ireland', *NILQ*, vol. 10, no. 2 (1953), pp 47–77.

A.D. McDonnell, *The life of Sir Denis Henry: Catholic Unionist* (Belfast, 2000).

R.B. McDowell, *The Irish administration, 1801–1914* (London, 1964).

R.B. McDowell, *The Irish Convention, 1917–18* (London, 1970).

R.B. McDowell, *Land and learning: two Irish clubs* (Dublin, 1993).

R.B. McDowell, *Crisis and decline: the fate of the Southern Unionists* (Dublin, 1997).

R.B. McDowell and D.A. Webb, *Trinity College Dublin 1592–1952: an academic history* (Cambridge, 1982).

John F. McEldowney, 'The case of *The Queen v McKenna* (1869) and jury packing in Ireland', *Irish Jurist*, vol. 12 (1977), pp 339–54.

John F. McEldowney, 'Lord O'Hagan (1812–85): a study of his life and period as lord chancellor of Ireland (1868–74)', *Irish Jurist*, vol. 14 (1979), pp 360–77.

John F. McEldowney, 'William Neilson Hancock', *Irish Jurist*, vol. 20 (1985), pp 378–402.

Fergal McGrath SJ, *Fr John Sullivan SJ* (Dublin, 1941).

Thomas MacKnight, *Ulster as it is* (London, 1896).

J.A.L. McLean, 'The Supreme Court of Judicature of Northern Ireland', *NILQ*, vol. 23 (1972), pp 82–90.

General Sir F.C.N. Macready, *Annals of an active life* (London, 1924).

B. McMahon and W. Binchy, *Law of torts*, 3rd ed. (Haywards Heath, 2005).

J.G. Swift MacNeill, *What I have seen and heard* (London, 1925).

Dodgson Hamilton Madden, *Registration of deeds and judgment mortgages* (Dublin, 1868).

Dodgson Hamilton Madden, *The Landed Estates Court – rules, forms and directions, with notes, schedule of fees and a collection of forms and precedents* (Dublin, 1870).

Dodgson Hamilton Madden, *A practical treatise on the registration of deeds, conveyances and judgment mortgages* (Dublin, 1901).

A.H. Manchester, *A modern legal history of England and Wales, 1750–1950* (London, 1980).

Edward Marjoribanks, *The life of Lord Carson*, vol. 1 (London, 1932).

Robert Marshall, 'The constitution of the Church of Ireland in action: ritualist litigation in a Disestablished Church, 1871–1937' in Kevin Costello and Niamh Howlin (eds), *Law and religion in Ireland, 1700–1970* (Cham, Switzerland, 2021), pp 289–326.

H.C.G. Mathew (ed.), *The Gladstone diaries: vol. 10 (January 1881–June 1883)* (Oxford, 1990).

Kathryn Milligan, 'A Venetian mystery: two paintings by Walter Osborne in the Kildare Street & University Club, Dublin', *Journal of the History of Collections* (Oxford, 2018).
Kenneth Milne, *St Bartholomew's: a history of the Dublin parish* (Dublin, 1963).
E.B. Mitford, *Life of Lord Redesdale* (London, 1939).
Thomas Mohr, *Guardian of the treaty: the Privy Council appeal and Irish sovereignty* (Dublin, 2016).
Thomas F. Molony, 'The judiciary, the police and the maintenance of law and order' in J.H. Morgan (ed.), *The new Irish Constitution; an exposition and some argument* (London, 1912).
Sir Declan Morgan, *Centenary lecture on the lord chief justices of Northern Ireland* (Belfast, 2021).
John Morley, *The life of William Ewart Gladstone* (London, 1903).
W. O'Connor Morris, *Memories and thoughts of life* (London, 1895).
Thomas J. Morrissey SJ, *Where two traditions meet: John Sullivan SJ, 1861–1933* (Blackrock, 2009).
Lawrence S. Moss, *Mountifort Longfield: Ireland's first professor of political economy* (Ottawa, IL, 1976).
Antoin E. Murphy, 'Mountifort Longfield's appointment to the chair of political economy in Trinity College, Dublin, 1832', *Hermathena*, no. 135 (winter 1983), pp 13–24.
James H. Murphy, *Ireland's Czar: Gladstonian government and the lord lieutenancies of the Red Earl Spencer, 1868–86* (Dublin, 2014).
H.R.N. [John Joseph Dunne], *Here and there memories* (London, 1896).
F.H. Newark, *Notes on Irish legal history* (Belfast, 1960).
Conor Cruise O'Brien, *Parnell and his party* (Oxford, 1957).
Georgiana O'Brien, *Reminiscences of Lord O'Brien of Kilfenora* (London, 1916).
R. Barry O'Brien, *The life of Lord Russell of Killowen* (London, 1901).
R. Barry O'Brien, *Dublin Castle and the Irish people* (London, 1909).
Leon Ó Broin, *The chief secretary: Augustine Birrell in Ireland* (London, 1969).
Leon Ó Broin, *W.E. Wylie and the Irish Revolution, 1916–1921* (Dublin, 1989).
Margaret O'Callaghan, *British high politics and nationalist Ireland* (Cork, 1994).
James O'Connor, *A history of Ireland, 1798–1924* (London, 1925).
Ulick O'Connor, *The Fitzwilliam story, 1877–1977* (Dublin, 1977).
J.R. O'Flanagan, *The Irish Bar* (London, 1879).
J. O'Hagan BL and S.A. Jackson BL, *An inquiry into taxes on law proceedings in Ireland* (Dublin, 1852).
Thomas O'Hagan, *Occasional papers and addresses* (London, 1884).
Eunan O'Halpin, *The decline of the Union: British government in Ireland, 1892–1920* (Dublin/Syracuse, 1987).
Nial O'Kelly, 'Plus ca change: 1922–1945' in Cornelius F. Smith and Bernard Share (eds), *Whigs on the Green: the Stephen's Green Club, 1840–1990* (Dublin, 1990).
Ciaran O'Neill, *Catholics of consequence: transnational education, social mobility and the Irish Catholic elite* (Oxford, 2014).
Ciaran O'Neill, *Power and powerlessness in Union Ireland: life in a palliative state* (Oxford, 2024).
W.N. Osborough, 'Law in Ireland, 1916–26' in (1) *NILQ*, vol. 23 (1972), pp 48–81 and (2) W.N. Osborough, *Studies in Irish legal history* (Dublin, 1999), pp 270–95.

W.N. Osborough, 'The title of the last lord chief justice of Ireland' in (1) *Irish Jurist*, vol. 9 (1974), pp 87–98 and (2) W.N. Osborough, *Studies in Irish legal history* (Dublin, 1999), pp 315–26.

W.N. Osborough, 'Forcibly commandeered transport and owners' insurance: the deciding of two test cases in the 1920s' in (1) *Irish Jurist*, vol. 11 (1976), pp 105–25 and (2) W.N. Osborough, *Studies in Irish legal history* (Dublin, 1999), p. 296.

W.N. Osborough, 'Irish law and the rights of the national schoolteacher – I', *Irish Jurist*, vol. 14 (1979), p. 36.

W.N. Osborough, 'Peter O'Brien' in A.W.B. Simpson (ed.), *Biographical dictionary of the common law* (London, 1984).

W.N. Osborough, 'Executive failure to enforce judicial decrees' in John F. McEldowney and Paul O'Higgins (eds), *The common law tradition; essays in Irish legal history* (Dublin, 1990), pp 85–116.

W.N. Osborough, *Law and the emergence of modern Dublin* (Dublin, 1996).

W.N. Osborough, 'The Irish legal system, 1796–1877' in (1) Caroline Costello (ed.), *The Four Courts: 200 years*, pp 33–79 and (2) W.N. Osborough, *Studies in Irish legal history* (Dublin, 1999), pp 239–69.

C.S. Parker (ed.), *Sir Robert Peel, from his private papers*, vol. 3 (London, 1899).

Susan M. Parkes, 'Higher education, 1793–1908' in W.E. Vaughan (ed.), *A new history of Ireland: VI. Ireland under the Union: II, 1870–1921* (Oxford, 1989), pp 539–70.

Henry E. Patton, *Fifty years of Disestablishment: a sketch* (Dublin, 1922).

L. Paul-Dubois, *Contemporary Ireland* (Dublin, 1908).

David Plunket, *The life, letters and speeches of Lord Plunket* (London, 1867).

Patrick Polden, 'The early years of the House of Lords, 1876–1914' in Louis Blom-Cooper, Brice Dickson and Gavin Drewry (eds), *The judicial House of Lords, 1876–2009* (Oxford, 2009), pp 181–97.

Patrick Polden, The superior courts of common law' in *The Oxford history of the laws of England, vol. XI: 1820–1914: English legal system* (Oxford, 2010), pp 569–645.

Memorial addresses and sermons occasioned by the deaths of the Rev. John Scott Porter and the Hon. William Porter (Belfast, 1880).

Arthur S. Quekett, *The constitution of Northern Ireland* (2 vols, Belfast, 1928).

Anthony P. Quinn, *Wigs and guns: Irish barristers in the Great War* (Dublin, 2006).

Agatha Ramm (ed.), *The political correspondence of Mr Gladstone and Lord Granville, 1868–1876* (London, 1952).

Agatha Ramm (ed.), *The political correspondence of Mr Gladstone and Lord Granville, 1876–1886* (Oxford, 1962).

Report of the proceedings in the case of Fitzgerald v Northcote and another (London, 1866).

Report (verbatim) of the trial, Thelwall v Yelverton (Dublin, 1861).

Rhadamanthus [W.B. Campbell], *Our judges* (Dublin, 1890).

Andrew Roberts, *Salisbury: Victorian Titan* (London, 1999).

Tim Robinson, *Connemara: listening to the wind* (Dublin, 2006).

John Ross, *The years of my pilgrimage* (London, 1924).

John Ross, *Pilgrim Scrip: more random reminiscences* (London, 1927).

Bláthna Ruane, 'Regime change: the fate of the senior Crown judiciary following the Anglo-Irish treaty 1921', *Irish Jurist*, vol. 54 (2015), p. 105.

Colin Ryan, *At the sign of the cow: the Cork butter market, 1770–1924* (Cork, 1998).

Wanda Ryan-Smolin, *King's Inns portraits* (Dublin, 1992).

F. Safford and G. Wheeler, *The practice of the Privy Council in judicial matters* (London, 1912).

Arthur P.I. Samuels, *The early life, correspondence and writings of the Rt. Hon. Edmund Burke LL.D., with a transcript of the minute book of the Debating 'Club' founded by him in Trinity College Dublin* (Cambridge, 1923).

Arthur W. Samuels, 'The law of divorce in Ireland', *Journal of the Statistical and Social Inquiry Society of Ireland*, vol. 9, part 66 (1886–7), pp 186–92.

Arthur W. Samuels, *A suggestion for the removal of taxes on litigation as a condition of the reduction of the judicial establishment* (Dublin, 1896).

Frances Stonor Saunders, *The woman who shot Mussolini* (London, 2010).

Lord Selborne, *Memorials: Part 2 – personal and political, 1865–1895* (London, 1898).

Michael Sheridan, *Murder at Shandy Hall: the Coachford Poisoning Case* (Dublin, 2010).

Andrew Shields, *The Irish Conservative Party, 1852–1868* (Dublin, 2007).

A.W.B. Simpson (ed.), *Biographical dictionary of the common law* (London, 1984).

Cornelius F. Smith and Bernard Share (eds), *Whigs on the Green: the Stephen's Green Club, 1840–1990* (Dublin, 1990).

George Hill Smith, *The North East Bar* (Belfast, 1910).

George Hill Smith, *A sketch of the Supreme Court of Judicature of Northern Ireland* (Belfast, 1926).

Keith Smith, 'Criminal Law' in Cornish, Anderson, Cocks, Lobban, Polden and Smith (eds), *The Oxford history of the laws of England, vol. XIII, 1820–1914: fields of development* (Oxford, 2010), pp 3–409.

E. OE. Somerville and Martin Ross, *An incorruptible Irishman: the life and times of Charles Kendal Bushe, 1767–1843* (London, 1932).

Sotheby's, *Catalogue of sale of the library of William O'Brien, property of the Milltown Park Charitable Trust* (London, 2017).

J.A. Spender and Cyril Asquith, *The life of H.H. Asquith, Lord Oxford and Asquith* (London, 1932).

David Steele, ''The judicial House of Lords: abolition and restoration 1873–6' in Louis Blom-Cooper, Brice Dickson and Gavin Drewry (eds), *The judicial House of Lords 1876–2009* (Oxford, 2009), pp 13–29.

Robert Stevens, *Law and politics; the House of Lords as a judicial body 1800–1976* (London, 1979).

Robert Stevens, entry on Lord Atkinson in A.W.B. Simpson, *Biographical dictionary of the common law* (London, 1984).

A.M. Sullivan, *New Ireland* (London, 1877).

A.M. Sullivan KC, *Old Ireland: reminiscences of an Irish KC* (London, 1927).

J.M.G. Sweeney, 'Lord O'Brien's doctrine of bias', *Irish Jurist*, vol. 7, part 1 (1972), p. 17.

George Teeling (ed.), *Selected speeches and arguments of the Right Hon Thomas, Baron O'Hagan* (London, 1885).

Henry Thring, *Practical legislation: the composition and language of Acts of Parliament and business documents*, 2nd ed. (London, 1902).

Thomas Towey, 'Hugh Kennedy and the constitutional development of the Irish Free State', *Irish Jurist*, vol. 12, no. 2 (1977), pp 355–70.

Charles Townsend, *The British campaign in Ireland, 1919–1921* (Oxford, 1975).

R. Denny Urlin, 'The Landed Estates Court (Ireland) as it affects the profession and the public', *Law Times*, vol. 38, p. 193 (7 February 1863).

R. Denny Urlin, *Journal and reminiscences* (Letchworth, 1909).

Edmund Van Esbeck, *The story of Irish rugby* (London, 1986).

W.E. Vaughan, 'Ireland *c.*1870' in W.E. Vaughan (ed.), *A new history of Ireland: V. Ireland under the Union: I, 1801–70* (Oxford, 1989), pp 726–800.

W.E. Vaughan, 'Paying for the Christmas dinner: the college's income and expenditure' in Charles H. Holland (ed.), *Trinity College and the idea of a university* (Dublin, 1991), pp 55–88.

W.E. Vaughan, 'An element of electoral politics intruded into his life' in Yseult Thornley (ed.), *Unquiet spirit: essays in memory of David Thornley* (Dublin, 2008), pp 44–7.

W.E. Vaughan, *Murder trials in Ireland, 1836–1914* (Dublin, 2009).

Letters of Queen Victoria, Second Series 1862–78 (London, 1926).

Letters and journals of Queen Victoria, third series 1886–1891 (vol. 1, London 1930; vol. 2, London 1931).

B.M. Walker (ed.), *Parliamentary election results in Ireland, 1801–1922* (Dublin, 1978).

B.M. Walker, *Dancing to history's tune* (Belfast, 1996).

W.J.R. Wallace, *Faithful to our trust: a history of the Erasmus Smith Trust and the High School, Dublin* (Dublin, 2004).

John Edward Walsh, *Sketches of Ireland sixty years ago* (Dublin, 1847).

John Edward Walsh, *The life and times of George Robert FitzGerald* (Dublin, 1852).

R.R. Warren, *Revision of the liturgy in the Church of Ireland* (Dublin, 1870).

R.R. Warren, *The law of the Church of Ireland: an essay* (Dublin and London, 1895).

D.A. Webb (compiler) and J.R. Bartlett (editor), *Trinity College Dublin, Record Volume 1991* (Dublin, 1991).

James Whiteside, *The city of Rome and its vicissitudes: a lecture* (Dublin, 1861).

William Ball Wright, *Ball family records: genealogical memoirs of some Ball families of Great Britain, Ireland and America*, 2nd ed. (York, 1908).

J.C.W. Wylie, *Landlord and tenant law*, 4th ed. (Dublin, 2022).

J.C.W. Wylie, *Irish land law*, 4th ed. (Dublin, 2010).

J.O. Wylie, *The Judicature Acts (Ireland) and orders, rules, and forms thereunder, copiously annotated* (Dublin, 1895).

J.O. Wylie, *The Judicature Acts (Ireland) and the Rules of the Supreme Court (Ireland) 1905, copiously annotated* (Dublin, 1906).

Maud Wynne, *An Irishman and his family: Lord Morris and Killanin* (London, 1937).

Index

The principal entry (or entries, in a few cases) for each judge holding office between 1866 and 1921 is/are shown in **bold** *print*

Abercorn, Duke of, 28, 52, 106, 140, 365, 384
on F. Falkiner and G. FitzGibbon, 275
Andrews, James, 300, 477–9, 481
Andrews, W.D., **298–301**, 41, 44, 45, 70(n)
Anglicisation, 149, 204–5
Ardagh Chalice, 290
Armour, Revd J.B., 413–14, 425
Armstrong, Richard, 15, 47
Ashbourne, 1st Lord, *see* Gibson, Edward
Ashbourne, 2nd Lord, *see* Gibson, William
Asquith, H.H., 83, 457
and R.R. Cherry, 393
and I. O'Brien, 401–2, 419
assizes, 42, 45, 47, 186, 188, 212, 254, 264, 280–1
Atkinson, John (Lord Atkinson), **378–82, 453–7, 464–6, 469**, 78, 81, 120, 450, 482
income, 82–3,
on retirement, 104,
on Chatterton, 215
on Lord Ashbourne, 320, 456
on Lord Salisbury, 380

Babington, Anthony Brutus, 438, 479
Balfour, Arthur, 57, 85, 88, 123, 469
on honours, 88, 123, 124, 218–19
on E. Bewley, 352
on H.E. Chatterton, 218–19, 357
on E. Gibson, 315
on J.G. Gibson, 337
on J. O'Hagan, 292
on appointment of a Law Lord, (1889) 447–9, (1900) 449–53, (1905) 453–7
Balfour, Gerald, 365, 379(n), 450
Ball, Frederick Elrington, 268
Ball, John Thomas, **264–8**, 54, 76, 276
on J. Christian, 157
on G. FitzGibbon, 276
on Judicature Bill, 7, 15, 16, 30
on salary of lord chancellor, 92
Bar Council, 64, 480–1
Bar of Ireland, 34
judicial reforms, opposition to, 15, 23–5, 46, 51
Barrington, Jonah, 20, 188
Barry, Charles, **241–5**
and W. Johnson, 305
Barry, Kevin, 422
Barry, Redmond, **394–5**, 8, 81, 83, 386
Barton, Dunbar Plunket, **372–6**, 114, 115, 126, 389, 492
Berwick, Walter, **186–7**
Bewley, Edmund, **351–4**, 42, 309, 319, 365, 389
Biggar, Joseph, MP, 150
Birkenhead, Lord, *see* Smith, Frederick Edwin
Birrell, Augustus, 83, 386
on J.G. Gibson, 336
on J. Moriarty, 409
on S. Ronan, 412
Blackburn, Lord, 159, 244
Blackburne, Francis, **133–4**, 13, 75, 90, 194–8
Bodkin, Matthew McDonnell, 247, 396
Boyd, Walter, **323–6**, 41, 56, 62, 94, 102, 126
Brady, Maziere, **129–31**
Brett, Sir Charles, 479
Brewster, Abraham, **191–8**, 13, 94, 224, 206
on J.T. Ball, 267
on R. Keatinge, 177–8
and Lord Derby, 105
Brooke, Sir Basil (Lord Brookeborough), 300, 478–9
Brooks, Raymond F., 50

Brown, Thomas Watters, 478
Bryce, James, 115, 370, 391
on W. Johnson, 303
on C. O'Connor, 395
Bushe, Charles Kendal, 87, 119
Butt, Isaac, 76, 95, 147–8, 177, 269, 289

Cadogan, Lord
and P. O'Brien, 125–6
and J. Atkinson, 380, 450
Cairns, Hugh (Lord Cairns), 18, 24, 106, 121
and Judicature Bill, 6, 7, 14, 15
and S. Woulfe Flanagan, 236
and H. Law, 286–8
and J. O'Hagan, 290
Campbell, James Henry Mussen (Lord Glenavy), **416–23**, 48, 69, 78, 80, 81, 82, 83, 96, 99, 393, 456, 491, 492
and honours, 119, 126
and Judiciary Committee (1923), 485–6
and I. O'Brien, 402, 452, 457, 472
Campbell, John (Lord Campbell), 8, 92, 119, 459–60
Campbell-Bannerman, Sir Henry, 303
Campion, William Bennett, 62–3
Carnarvon, Lord, 236, 316–17, 327
Carson, Edward (Lord Carson of Duncairn), 64, 78, 80, 95–6, 357, 373, 417, 452, 469, 474, 482, 491
on J.G. Gibson, 336
Casement, Roger, 263, 458
Cave, Lord, on J. Atkinson, 382
Chamberlain, Austen, 65, 398
Chatterton, Hedges Eyre, **213–19**, 72, 79, 108, 271, 357, 473
Chelmsford, Lord, 119, 189, 193
Cherry, Richard Robert, **388–93**, 47, 77, 85, 295, 344, 373, 391
Childers, Erskine, 398–9, 483, 485
Christian, Jonathan, **151–60**, 17, 35, 91, 188, 268
on H.E. Chatterton, 216–17
on law reports, 152, 188
on J. Whiteside, 152
Church of Ireland, 139, 182, 227, 228
and J.T. Ball, 265–6
and G. FitzGibbon, 283
judicial membership, 109, 111–12
law, 11, 171, 177, 264
disestablishment, 230–1, 245–6, 265–8, 286–7
Churchill, Lord Randolph, 327–8
and G. FitzGibbon, 86, 275, 277, 281–2
and E. Gibson, 315–6, 322
on H. Holmes, 331
Churchill, Winston, 69, 275
circuits, 44–5, 399, 400, 480
Civil War, 166, 213, 398–9, 405, 434, 475, 482
Clanricarde, Marquis of, 384
Clonfert, Bishop of, 249, 265
Clongowes Wood school, 116, 256, 309, 339
Cockburn, Lord, 39, 139
Coleridge, Lord, 39
Colles, John Mayne, 319–20
Collins, Sir Richard Henn, 474
Commissioners of Charitable Donations and Bequests, 113, 220, 298
common law, 157, 231
Cork Butter Market, 467
Cork County Club (*Pike v Beamish*), 297, 376, 378
Cosgrave, W.T., 435, 485–7
County Courts, 36, 61, 79, 123–4
court of Admiralty, 20, 188–9, 219–20
Court of Appeal, 45–6, 311–12
court of Bankruptcy, 9, 37, 186, 222–4, 324
status of judges in, 94, 136
Court of Criminal Appeal, 467–8, 486
Court of Crown Cases Reserved, 9, 162, 167–8, 338, 420
Court of Exchequer Chamber, 11
Courts of Justice Bill 1923, 428
Courts of Justice Act 1924, 486, 488
Craig, James (Lord Craigavon), 300, 476, 478
Crampton, Philip, 103
Crimes Act 1887, 331–2
criminal trials, 9, 147, 167–9, 212, 242–4, 281, 296, 305–6, 467–8
appeals in Ireland, 467, 486
of Fenians, 140, 161, 214, 230, 241, 245
Cullen, Cardinal Paul, 164, 203
Curran, John Adye, 211

Dáil courts, 475–6, 484–5, 487
Dáil Éireann, 475–6, 484–6
Deasy, Rickard, **173–6**, 76, 109
Derby, Earl of, *see* Stanley, Edward
De Versan, Raoul Couturier, 320
Dillon, John, MP, 94, 396
Disraeli, Benjamin (Earl of Beaconsfield), 14, 18, 200, 251, 253, 271, 274
 on J.T. Ball, 266–7
 on F. Blackburne, 134
 on J. Christian, 156
 and E. Gibson, 315
Dobbs, William Carey, **185**
Dodd, William Huston, **385–8**, 88, 368, 492
Donegall, Marquess of, 269–70
Dowse, Richard, **245–8**, 13, 30, 34, 35, 53, 61, 148, 257, 363
Dublin Corporation, 33, 56, 345, 401

Easter Rising, 434–5
Ecclesiastical Titles Act 1850, 144, 161
educational endowments, 277–8, 311, 331
Eiffe, L.S., 31
Encumbered Estates, 12, 146, 179, 180–1, 183, 199, 133, 234
Epsom Derby, 306

Falkiner, Caesar Litton, 351
Falkiner, Frederick, 125, 275, 351
Famine, Great, 180.
FitzGerald, Francis A., **170–3**, 68, 255, 271, 280, 284
Fitzgerald, Gerald, **377–8**, 42
Fitzgerald, John D., **139–41**, **443–7**, **458–61**, **466–8**, 66, 68, 147, 235, 248, 293, 311, 340–1
FitzGibbon, Gerald, **273–84**, 45, 46, 56, 70(n), 79, 85, 86, 90, 149, 311, 325, 329, 331
 and E. Gibson, 275–6, 321–2
 and J. Atkinson (1905), 455–6
FitzGibbon, John (Earl of Clare), 91, 241
Flanagan, Stephen Woulfe, **233–7**, 70, 102, 109, 156, 473
Four Courts,
 construction and enhancements, surroundings, 32–3
 destruction (1922), 398, 483
 reconstruction, 488–9
French, Lord, of Ypres, 69, 367, 421(n)

Galgorm Castle, 183
George, John, **208–9**
Giant's Causeway, 369
Gibson, Edward (Lord Ashbourne), **313–23**, **447–50**, **453–6**, 29, 36, 46, 53, 57, 71, 72, 91, 124, 274, 327, 341, 373
 declines judicial appointment (1877), 85
 estate on death, 99
 on H.E. Chatterton, 218
 on W. Kenny, 372
 on W. Keogh, 149
 on P. O'Brien, 343
 on S. Ronan, 412
Gibson, John George, **336–8**, 56, 77, 89, 342, 456, 489, 492
Gibson, Violet, 323
Gibson, William, 322
Gladstone, William Ewart, 67, 74, 83, 154
 on R. Dowse, 245
 on Home Rule, 89
 on judicial establishment, workload, 54, 97, 290
 on W. Keogh, 128
 on Land War, Land Commission, 286, 288–91
 on appointment of Law Lord (1882), 445–6
 on G.A.C. May, 272
 and T. O'Hagan, 121, 160, 164
 and C. Palles, 250–2
Glenavy, Lord, *see* Campbell, J.H.M.
Gonne, Maud, 338
Gordon, John, **415–16**, 81, 492
Government of Ireland Act 1920, 422, 425, 437, 476–81
Grantham, Justice, 62
Granville, Lord, 121, 238
Gray, Edmund Dwyer, MP, 232
Greenwood, Hamar, 69, 436–7

habeas corpus, 397–9
Halsbury, Lord, 90, 280, 318–19, 462
 and J. Atkinson, 453–7
Hancock, W. Neilson, 13

Harcourt, Sir William, 66, 67, 68
Hargreave, Charles, **182–4**, 8, 313
Harrison, Michael, **224–6**, 53, 94, 233, 266
Hartington, Lord (Duke of Devonshire), 234, 235, 250, 371
Hayes, Edmund, **138–9**, 208–9
Healy, Maurice
  on incomes at the Bar, 96
  on W.D. Andrews, 299
  on G. FitzGibbon, 277
  on W. O'Brien, 296
Healy, Timothy (T.M.), 83, 252, 257, 291, 302, 340, 366, 375, 377, 430, 451
  on law officers being appointed judges, 89
  on J. Atkinson, 379
  on J. Monroe, 329
  on I. O'Brien, 400–2
Hemphill, Charles, 336, 385, 451
Henry, Denis, 69, 81, 84, 386, 472–3, 477–9
Hicks Beach, Sir Michael, 258
  on H.E. Chatterton, 271
  on E. Gibson, 318
  on G.A.C. May, 117, 271–3
  on H. Ormsby, 268
High Court of Appeal (1921–2), 367, 477
Holmes, Hugh, **329–35**, 36, 46, 47, 56, 79, 82, 89, 97(n), 258,
  and A. Balfour, 331–2
  and J. Monroe, 327–8
Holmes, Valentine, 335
Home circuit, 44
Home Rule, 253, 259, 293, 424
  opinion of G. FitzGibbon, 281
  opinion of R.R. Warren, 112
  Unionist opposition, 371, 424–5, 474
  and Judicial Committee of Privy Council, 442–3
House of Lords, 155, 159, 253
  judicial functions of, 16–19
  Daniel O'Connell appeal, 163
Howlin, Niamh, 244
Howth, gun-running, 300, 401–2, 404, 434
Hughes, Henry, **173**, 13, 46, 53, 213

Inns of Court, London, 144, 320, 375, 376, 422, 467
  keeping terms at, 8, 200, 467, 480–1
Inn of Court of Northern Ireland, 151, 480–1
Irish National War Memorial, 375

Jellett, Hewitt Poole, 152–3
Jesuit Order, 241, 298
Johnson, William Moore, **301–4**, 41, 56, 79, 126
Joyce, James (*Ulysses*), 219, 276(n), 415
Joynson-Hicks, William, 478
Judicature Bills 1874–7, 7, 15, 19, 21–9
Judicature Acts, 1887, 1897, 1907, 40–1
Judicial Committee of the Privy Council (Dublin), 70–3
Judicial Committee of the Privy Council (London), 114, 119, 120, 125, 196, 218, 236, 260, 441–3
judiciary
  ages, length of service, 102–4
  clubs, 114–15
  divisional courts, 'en banc', 36–9, 54–6, 60
  education, 100
  estates on death, 98–9
  experience upon appointment, 106, 137
  family relationships, 101–2
  honours, 116, 123–5
  independence, 20, 231, 232, 259
  Judicature Bill 1876, 26
  and juries, 294–6, 301, 305, 340–2, 377
  length of judicial vacancies, 246, 250–1, 263
  and non-jury courts, 65–70,
  numbers, 99–100
  pensions/compensation (1921–4), 427, 429, 482, 489–92
  promotions of judges, 99
  and public schools, 116
  registrars, train-bearers, 50, 178, 215, 228, 260, 339, 361, 369, 370
  religion, 108–10, 162, 211, 293, 301
  remuneration, 93–4
  residences, 98, 165, 260–1
  workloads, 22, 51, 53, 57–65, 143, 182, 477, 486–7
Judiciary Committee (1923), 423, 429, 485–7
juries, 35, 146, 148, 155, 163, 169, 176, 177, 225, 232, 246, 254, 258, 281, 293, 314, 387, 394

juries (*continued*)
  and alibis, 392
  judicial criticism of, 294–6, 301
  directions to, 294, 305, 344, 377, 388
  Juries (Ireland) Act 1871, 155, 163
  'packing', 340–2

Keane, Ronan, 253–4, 257, 471
Keatinge, Richard, **176–8**, 196
Kelly, Thomas, **188–90**, 20
Kennedy, Frank, 260
Hugh Kennedy, 484
  chief justice, 487–8
  on W. Moore, 425
  and J. O'Connor, 429–30
Kennedy, Thomas, BL, 63
Kenny, John, 216
Kenny, William, **370–2**, 56, 81, 104, 489
Keogh, William Nicholas, **144–51**, 30, 140, 156, 305, 339, 305, 339
Kildare Street Club, 114–15, 232, 304
King's Inns
  and Northern Ireland, 480–1
  and relocation of courts (1922–3), 483
  and Irish language, 488
Knighthoods for judges, 123–5, 329

Land Commission, 42, 348, 350–3, 437
  establishment of, 288, 290–1
Landed Estates Court, 12, 37, 51, 153, 179, 183, 185, 222–3, 252, 268
landlord and tenant law, 469
  Deasy's Act (1860), 174–5
  Irish Church Act 1869, 231
  Landlord and Tenant (Ireland) Act 1870, 153–5, 238, 287
  Land Law (Ireland) Act 1881, 185, 288–91, 350
  Purchase of Land (Ireland) Act 1885, 317,
  Local Registration of Title (Ireland) Act, 1891, 356
  Land Law (Ireland) Act 1896, 353, 365
  Irish Land Act, 1903, 365–6, 377
  Irish Land Act, 1909, 392
  Land Act 1923, 437.
Law, Andrew Bonar, 47
  and J.H.M. Campbell, 418–21, 423
law adviser, 78, 237, 274, 286, 436, 467
Law, Hugh, **286–9**, 26–7, 29, 66–7, 81, 364
  on J. Christian, 159
  on trial of Parnell (1881), 272
Law Life Assurance Co., 145
law officers, 83–7
  salaries, 96–7
law reporters, 138, 174, 204, 233, 234, 256, 270
  J. Christian comments on, 152, 157–9
law terms (sittings), 9, 43, 49
Lawson, James, **229–33**, 66, 113, 131, 250, 271, 304
Lecky, W.E.H., 81, 274, 376
  on qualities of lawyers, 79
Le Fanu, Sheridan, 230
Lefroy, Thomas, **135–7**, 193, 230
Liberal Unionism, 342, 352, 356, 361, 370, 376, 412
Liffey, condition of, 33
Lindley, Nathaniel (Lord Lindley), 381, 450, 452–7
Litton, Edward Falconer, **349–51**, 290–1
Liverpool, Irish MPs, 336
Lloyd George, David, 367
  and Budget (1909), 391
  and I. O'Brien, 403
  and J.H.M. Campbell, 420
Londonderry, Lord, 299
Long, Walter, 367, 379–81, 453–7
Longfield, Mountifort, **179–82**, 70(n), 234
lord chancellor,
  great seal, 90
  head of judiciary, 130
  histories, 166
  salary and pension, 91–2
Lowry, J.C.J., 81
Lowry, Sir Robert (Lord Lowry), 4, 150–1, 459, 463, 464–5
Lowry, William, 478
Lynch, David, **187**

Maamtrasna murders, 43, 243–4, 301, 304, 340
MacDermott, Lord, 34, 50, 479
MacDonnell, Sir Antony, 115, 381, 424
  on W.H. Dodd and C. O'Connor, 395
  on R.E. Meredith, 370
McDonnell, Sir Schomberg, 472

Macdonogh, Francis, QC, 25, 47, 77, 82, 105–6, 227, 352, 459
Macnaghten, Lord, 254, 280, 316, 333, 364, 375, 453, 462–3, 469, 474
MacNeill, Eoin, 487
McQuaid, Archbishop John Charles, 185
Macready, General F.C.N., 397–8
Madden, Dodgson Hamilton, **355–9**, 218, 343, 352, 492
Marlborough, Duke of, 105, 275, 288, 315, 373
martial law, 397–8
Martyn, Edward, 114, 395
Masonic Order, 113, 220, 283, 284
Matheson, Charles L., 47
Mathews, Henry, QC, MP, 242, 448
May, George Augustus Chichester, **269–73**, 39, 53, 57, 67, 79, 83, 95, 117
Mayo, Earl of, *see* Naas, Lord
Meredith, Richard E., **369–70**, 42, 50, 58, 114
Middleton, Richard W.E., 337, 448
Miller, Stearne Ball, **221–3**, 105, 120
Molony, Thomas F., **404–6**, 77, 83, 127, 421, 476, 479, 481–2, 492
Monahan, James, **141–4**, 13, 53, 193, 238
Monroe, John, **326–9**, 53, 123
Moore, William, QC, MP, **423–6**, 46, 65, 88, 263, 386, 451, 477–8, 492
Moriarty, John F., **406–10**, 47, 77, 111
Morley, John, 87, 455
Morris, Michael (Lord Morris and Killanin), **210–13**, **447–52**, **461–4**, **468**, 39, 40, 49, 53, 57, 72–3, 99, 117, 119, 120, 123, 125, 212
  and Judicature Bill 1877, 30,
  and Lord Derby, 104
Murphy, Edward Sullivan, 306
Murphy, James, **304–7**, 70(n), 149, 305

Naas, Lord, 194, 196, 208
  on J.T. Ball, 265–6
  on A. Brewster, 194–7
  on F. FitzGerald, 96, 209
  on J. George, 209
  on E. Hayes, 138
  on R. Keatinge, 178,
  on T. Kelly, 189
  on S.B. Miller, 221–2
  on M. Morris, 210–11
  on P. Plunket, 187
Naish, John, **309–12**, 42, 57, 79, 93, 278, 351
Napier, Joseph, **192–6**, 13, 79, 82, 104, 138, 174–5
  on J.D. Fitzgerald, 133
  and T. O'Hagan, 107
Newport, Sir John, 295
Nisi Prius, 10, 34–5, 107, 152, 167, 226

O'Brien, Ignatius, **400–4**, 79, 83, 90, 119, 126, 492
  on G. FitzGibbon, 279
  on S.B. Miller, 223
  on C. Palles, 255
  on D.R. Pigot, 176
O'Brien, James, **137**
O'Brien, Peter (Lord O'Brien of Kilfenora), **339–49**, 33, 46, 53, 56, 61, 83, 88, 89, 98, 119, 123, 125–6, 279, 472
  on M. Morris, 212
O'Brien, William (judge), **292–8**, 70(n), 109, 111, 278, 304
O'Brien, William (MP, journalist), 297, 302, 310
O'Connell, Daniel, 9, 163, 176
  trial/appeal (1843–4), 131–2, 440
  and T. O'Hagan, 160, 162
O'Connor, Charles Andrew, **395–9**, 70, 261, 483, 485, 492
O'Connor, James, **426–30**, 51, 127, 421, 492
  on judicial mentality, 58–9, 65, 97
  on humour in court, 248
  and J.H.M. Campbell, 421
O'Hagan, John, **289–92**, 113–14
O'Hagan, Thomas (Lord O'Hagan), **160–6**, 13, 76, 106–7, 109, 121–2, 200, 470
  and appointment of C. Palles, 250–2
  and Lord Selborne, 444
O'Loghlen, Michael, 109
Ormsby, Henry, **268–9**, 156, 235
O'Shaughnessy, Thomas Lopdell, 35, 127, 487, 492

Palles, Christopher, **248–63**, 19, 39–41, 44, 53, 56, 62, 67, 81, 83, 163, 363, 399, 420, 427, 445, 447, 473

Palles, Christopher (*continued*)
on assizes procedure, 49
Court of Appeal (declines nomination), 276
Galway election, 148
on juries, 295
knighthood (declines), 124
length of service, 102
religion, 111
Parliamentary Elections Act 1868, 79, 147
Parliamentary constituencies
Co. Antrim North, 364, 385, 424
Armagh City, 221
Co. Armagh North, 424; South, 351; Mid Armagh, 374, 415
Athlone, 144
Carrickfergus, 185, 270
Co. Clare, 342
Coleraine, 350
Co. Cork, 174, 179
Co. Donegal South, 371
Co. Down, 299
Dublin, St Stephen's Green, 81, 371, 417–18
Dublin University, 80–1, 101, 201, 205, 226, 265–6, 274–6, 314, 330, 355–7, 376, 433
Co. Dublin South, 268, 417
Dungarvan, 241
Ennis, 139, 292
Enniskillen, 199
Galway, 101, 141, 210–11
Co. Galway, 147, 249
Liverpool: Exchange, 391; Kirkdale, 390; Walton, 336; West Toxteth, 404
Londonderry City , 81, 245, 249, 364, 384
Co. Londonderry, 81, 287, 307, 360; North, 360; South, 301, 379, 385, 415
Mallow, 179, 238–9, 301–2, 309–10, 406
Portarlington, 229–30
Sligo, 233
Co. Tyrone, 350; North, 81, 384–5, 394
Waterford, 314
Wexford, 209
Parnell, Charles Stewart, 271–2, 281, 288, 317, 350, 409
on judges' salaries, 94
on M. Harrison, 225
on W. Keogh, 145
Pearse, Patrick, 382, 435
Peel, Sir Robert, 119, 132, 192
and Daniel O'Connell appeal, 440
Pennefather, Edward, 132, 168
Pennefather, Richard, 130, 168, 208
Perrin, Louis, 139
Phoenix Park murders (1882), 66, 98, 144, 293, 301, 307, 340
Pigeon House drainage works, 33, 56
Pigot, David R., **167–70**, 193, 238
Pim, Jonathan, **413–15**, 79, 492
Plantation of Ulster, 62, 160, 246, 308, 425
Plunket, David, 78, 81, 274, 321, 372
lack of ambition, 87
Plunket, Patrick, 187, 372
Plunket, William (Lord Plunket), 8, 87, 90, 119, 121–2, 372–3
Porter, Andrew Marshall, **307–9**, 81, 108, 114, 125, 286
Porter, Samuel Clarke, 478
Portora Royal School, 323, 336, 376
Powell, John Blake, **430–2**, 108, 492
Privy Council of Ireland, 70–3, 236
Public schools in England, 116, 139, 406, 424

Queen's College Belfast, 207, 307, 383, 385
Queen's College Cork, 207, 394, 411
Queen's College Galway, 207, 411, 468
Queen's University Belfast, 71

Redesdale, Lord, 91, 92, 119
Redmond, John, MP
and R.R. Cherry, 77, 390, 393
on M. Morris, 212
on C. O'Connor, 396
on J. O'Connor, 427
on C. Palles, 253
resident magistrates, 8
Restoration of Order in Ireland Act, 1920, 69, 397, 422, 436
Richards, Baron, 168, 183
Romilly, Sir John, 12
Ronan, Stephen, **411–13**, 88, 111, 368, 492

Ross, John, **363–9**, 41, 42, 45, 48, 62, 65, 81, 82, 88, 108, 126, 213, 255–6, 384, 398, 492
- and E. Bewley, 353
- on J.H.M. Campbell, 422,
- on G. FitzGibbon, 279,
- on W. Moore, 425
- on C. Palles, 257
- and judicial pensions and compensation (1921–3), 473, 489–92

Ross, Ronald, MP, 369
Royal Belfast Academical Institution, 116, 192, 298, 378, 383, 385, 479
Royal Commission on law of indictable offences, 244–5
Royal Commission on Judicature, 14
Royal Commission on courts in England and Ireland, 13, 28, 51, 250
Royal Courts of Justice, Belfast, 479
Royal Courts of Justice, Strand, London, 32
Royal Irish Academy, 114, 165, 184, 185, 359, 375
Royal Dublin Society, 165, 437–8

Sadleir, James, 132–3
Sadleir, John, MP, 132, 145, 146
St Bartholomew's Church, Ballsbridge, 112, 328
Salisbury, Marquess of, 74, 279, 380
- on appointment of Law Lords, 447–52
- on politics in judicial appointments, 75–6
- and R. Churchill, 281
- and E. Gibson, 316–19
- on knighthoods, and honour for P. O'Brien, 123
- on law officers, 337–8
- and J. Ross, 365

Samuels, Arthur Warren, **432–4**, 24, 59, 78, 80, 256, 343, 428, 492
Saunderson, Edward James, 327–8
Scotland, judicial system, 52
Selborne, Lord, 17, 19, 459
- on appointment of C. Palles, 250–2
- on appointment of Law Lord (1882), 443–6

select committee on official salaries, 92, 95
Smith, Erasmus, Trust, 278
Smith, Frederick Edwin (Lord Birkenhead), 69, 423, 458, 482, 490
Smith, Thomas Berry Cusack, **131–3**
Special Commission, 'Parnellism and Crime' (1888), 43, 237
Spencer, Earl
- and C. Barry and Maamtrasna trial, 243
- on F. FitzGerald, 172
- on S.W. Flanagan, 234
- on W.M. Johnson, 301
- on judicial vacancies, 246, 250–2
- on appointment of Law Lord (1882), 445–6
- on non-jury courts, 66–8
- on J. Lawson, 231–2
- on J. Naish, 309–10
- on W. O'Brien,301

Stanley, Edward (Lord Derby), 75, 110
- and Ireland, 74
- and F. Blackburne, 121, 194–7
- and A. Brewster, 191–7
- and S.B. Miller, 221–2
- and M. Morris, 210–1, 222
- and J. Napier, 120–1, 195–6
- and J.E. Walsh, 206–7, 210
- and J. Whiteside, 200–2

Statistical and Social Inquiry Society of Ireland, 113–14, 165, 180, 185, 229, 385, 390, 406, 433
Stephen, James Fitzjames, 244–5
Stephen's Green Club, 115, 395
Stokes, Sir William, 169
Sugden, Edward (Lord Sugden), 8, 92, 119, 154
Sullivan, Serjeant A.M., 263, 296
Sullivan, Edward, **237–41**, **444–6**, 20, 35–6, 52(n), 57, 78, 122, 292, 298
- asserts right to judicial appointment, 84
- objects to Landed Estates Court work, 235

Sullivan, John, SJ, 241
Sullivan, Timothy, 481, 487
superior courts of Northern Ireland, 477–81
superior courts of Southern Ireland, 477, 481, 483
superior courts of the Irish Free State, 486–8
Swifte, Ernest G., 157–8

Taylor, T.E., MP, 194, 210
Thring, Henry, 239
Townsend, John Fitzhenry, **219–20**
Treasury, attitude to judicial expenditure, 25, 28–9, 50, 57
Treaty (1921), 482, 489–2
Trevelyan, G.O., 67, 299
Trinity College, Dublin, 179, 182, 229, 274, 309, 359, 389, 406, 481
  College Historical Society, 149, 314, 363, 388, 395, 416, 433–4
  judicial alumni, 100–1
  tercentenary (1892), 320

Ulster Unionism, 327, 360, 364–5, 386, 415, 424, 469
University Club, 114, 245, 282, 284
University College Cork, 71
University College Dublin, 263
University College London, 182
university education, 164, 165, 207, 263, 290, 389
Urlin, R. Denny, 82, 150(n), 184, 193(n)

vice-chancellor (*see also* Chatterton, Hedges Eyre), 10, 213, 216, 230
Victoria, Queen, 252, 448

Walker, Samuel, **359–62**, 36, 56, 81, 91, 93, 386, 395
  on C. Barry, W.M. Johnson, J. Lawson, C. Palles and A.M. Porter, 303
Walsh, John Edward **203–8**, 209
War of Independence, 68–70, 397–8, 405, 422, 432, 435–6
Warren, Robert Richard, **226–8**, 41, 302, 124
  on Home Rule, 112
  and resignation of R. Keatinge, 178
Whiteside, James, **198–203**, 40, 105, 133, 140, 147, 169, 174, 183, 193, 199
  on A. Brewster, 194
  and J. Christian, 152
  and Judicature Bill, 7, 27–9
Wilberforce, William, 295
Wilson, Daniel Martin, 435, 478
Wright, George, **376–7**, 45, 56, 78
Wylie, James O., **383–5**, 31, 55(n), 81, 436
Wylie, William E., **434–8**, 78, 385, 492
  on J.G. Gibson, 338
  on S. Ronan, 412
Wyndham, George, 96, 365–6, 380, 424

Yelverton case, 142, 237
Yeo, Henry, 260

Zetland, Lord, on knighthoods, 124–5

IRISH LEGAL HISTORY SOCIETY SERIES*

1 Daire Hogan and W.N. Osborough (eds), *Brehons, serjeants and attorneys: studies in the history of the Irish legal profession* (1990)
2 Colum Kenny, *King's Inns and the kingdom of Ireland: the Irish 'inn of court', 1541–1800* (1992)
3 Jon G. Crawford, *Anglicizing the government of Ireland: the Irish Privy Council and the expansion of Tudor rule, 1556–1578* (1993)
4 W.N. Osborough (ed.), *Explorations in law and history: Irish Legal History Society discourses, 1988–1994* (1995)
5 W.N. Osborough, *Law and the emergence of modern Dublin: a litigation topography for a capital city* (1996)
6 Colum Kenny, *Tristram Kennedy and the revival of Irish legal training, 1835–1885* (1996)
7 Brian Griffin, *The Bulkies: police and crime in Belfast, 1800–1865* (1997)
8 Éanna Hickey, *Irish law and lawyers in modern folk tradition* (1999)
9 A.R. Hart, *A history of the king's serjeants at law in Ireland: honour rather than advantage?* (2000)
10 D.S. Greer and N.M. Dawson (eds), *Mysteries and solutions in Irish legal history: Irish Legal History Society discourses and other papers, 1996–1999* (2000)
11 Colum Kenny, *King's Inns and the battle of the books, 1972: cultural controversy at a Dublin library* (2002)
12 Desmond Greer and James W. Nicolson, *The factory acts in Ireland, 1802–1914* (2003)
13 Mary Kotsonouris, *The winding-up of the Dáil courts, 1922–1925: an obvious duty* (2004)
14 Paul Brand, Kevin Costello and W.N. Osborough (eds), *Adventures of the law: proceedings of the 16th British Legal History Conference, Dublin 2003* (2005)
15 Jon G. Crawford, *A Star Chamber court in Ireland: the Court of Castle Chamber, 1571–1641* (2005)
16 A.P. Quinn, *Wigs and guns: Irish barristers and the Great War* (2006)
17 N.M. Dawson (ed.), *Reflections on law and history: Irish Legal History Society discourses and other papers, 2000–2005* (2006)
18 James Kelly, *Poynings' Law and the making of law in Ireland, 1660–1800* (2007)
19 W.E. Vaughan, *Murder trials in Ireland, 1836–1914* (2009)
20 Kevin Costello, *The Court of Admiralty of Ireland, 1575–1893* (2011)
21 W.N. Osborough, *An island's law: a bibliographical guide to Ireland's legal past* (2013)
22 Felix M. Larkin and N.M. Dawson (eds), *Lawyers, the law and history: Irish Legal History Society discourses and other papers, 2005–2011* (2013)
23 Daire Hogan and Colum Kenny (eds), *Changes in practice and law: a selection of essays by members of the legal profession to mark twenty-five years of the Irish Legal History Society* (2013)
24 W.N. Osborough, *The Irish stage: a legal history* (2015)
25 Thomas Mohr, *Guardian of the Treaty: the Privy Council appeal and Irish sovereignty* (2016)
26 Joseph C. Sweeney, *The life and times of Arthur Browne in Ireland and America, 1756–1805* (2017)
27 Niamh Howlin, *Juries in Ireland: laypersons and law in the long nineteenth century* (2017)
28 Patrick Hyde Kelly (ed.), *The case of Ireland's being bound by acts of parliament in England, stated, Dublin 1698* (2018)
29 Mary Phelan, *Irish speakers, interpreters and the courts, 1754–1921* (2019)

30 Coleman A. Dennehy (ed.), *Law and revolution in seventeenth-century Ireland* (2020)
31 Daire Hogan and Patrick Maume (eds), *The reminiscences of Ignatius O'Brien, lord chancellor of Ireland 1913–18: a life in Cork, Dublin and Westminster* (2021)
32 Peter Crooks and Thomas Mohr (eds), *Law and the idea of liberty in Ireland: from Magna Carta to the present* (2023)
33 Bríd McGrath, *The operations of the Irish House of Commons, 1613–48* (2023)
34 Niamh Howlin (ed.), *A century of courts: the Courts of Justice Act 1924* (2024)
35 Niamh Howlin and Felix M. Larkin (eds), *Confluences of law and history: Irish Legal History Society discourses and other papers, 2011–21* (2025)
36 Sparky Booker and Kevin Costello (eds), *A sense of place: studies in Irish and British legal history in memory of W.N. Osborough* (2025)
37 Daire Hogan, *The judges of Ireland, 1866–1921* (2026)

ALSO AVAILABLE

The Irish Legal History Society (1989)

*Volumes 1–7 are published by Irish Academic Press

Irish Legal History Society

Established in 1988 to encourage the study and advance the knowledge of the history of Irish law, especially by the publication of original documents and of works relating to the history of Irish law, including its institutions, doctrines and personalities, and reprinting or editing of works of sufficient rarity or importance.